Engaging the Doctrine of

THE CHURCH

Engaging the Doctrine of THE CHURCH

Matthew Levering

Published by Word on Fire Academic, an imprint of
Word on Fire, Elk Grove Village, IL 60007

Printed in the United States of America

Cover design, typesetting, and interior art direction by David Shankin,
Clark Kenyon, and Nicolas Frederickson.

ISBN: 978-1-685782-22-1

Library of Congress Control Number: 2025936359

To Roger Nutt

Contents

Acknowledgments

Parts of these chapters have been delivered as conference papers and/or have been published. A portion of chapter 1 was delivered at a conference entitled "Descent of the Dove: Knowing and Loving in Spirit and Truth" at Pusey House in Oxford in July 2022, and it will appear in *The Dove Descending: Knowing and Loving in Spirit and Truth*, ed. George Westhaver and Jonathan Price (James Clarke, 2025). I thank George Westhaver for the invitation and those who attended the conference for their insights, as well as Richard Conrad, OP, and the Blackfriars Dominicans with whom I stayed. An earlier version of chapter 2 appeared as "The Church as the Family of God: Benedict XVI's *Africae Munus* and Joseph Ratzinger's *The Meaning of Christian Brotherhood*," in *Africae Munus: Ten Years Later*, ed. Maurice A. Agbaw-Ebai and Matthew Levering (St. Augustine's, 2022), 168–205. Although I did not deliver the paper at the *Africae Munus* conference that Fr. Maurice and I co-organized at Mundelein Seminary, I was aided by listening to the other conference papers that later became part of the edited volume.

An earlier version of chapter 3 appeared as "The Cross at the Center of the Mystical Body: A Thomistic Approach," *New Blackfriars* 104, no. 1114 (2023): 689–714. It was written for a special issue of *New Blackfriars* at the kind invitation of Brian Davies, OP, for which I am grateful. A portion of chapter 4 took shape through the auspices of Joe Mangina and David Ney, who did me the honor of inviting me to contribute to Ephraim Radner's Festschrift. It has appeared as "People of the New Exodus: Radner and Catholic Ecclesiology," in *Figural Reading and the Fleshly God: The Theology of Ephraim Radner*, ed. Joseph L. Mangina and David Ney (Baylor University Press, 2025). An earlier version of chapter 5 appeared as "Mother Church: Can Receptivity Be Squared with Resistance?," *The New Ressourcement* 1, no. 2 (2024): 395–445. Lastly, an earlier version of chapter 7 has been published as "Catholicity and the Catholic Church: Protestant Concerns and (Roman) Catholic Perspectives," *Pro Ecclesia* 32, no. 3–4 (2023): 219–46; my thanks to Phillip Cary, the former editor of the journal, for accepting it.

Many of the chapters were also test-run in public lectures. Some of these lectures are available on YouTube and demonstrate, I hope, how much the paper was improved by the experience of delivering it and discovering its weaknesses. I presented "Mother Church: Can Receptivity Be Squared with Resistance?" to the inaugural New Ressourcement conference sponsored by Word on Fire, in Rochester, Minnesota, early in November 2023. I thank Bishop Robert Barron, Jason Paone, and David Augustine for their exemplary hospitality. I presented parts of two chapters—"Catholic" and "The Family of God"—to the Annual Intellectual Retreat of the Religious Sisters of Mercy, in Alma, Michigan, in late June 2023. I thank Mother Mary Christa Nutt, RSM, and many other Sisters for encouragement, improvements, and prayers. I presented "The Cross at the Center of the Mystical Body: A Thomistic Approach" as the Aquinas Lecture at the Dominican School of Philosophy and Theology in Oakland, California, in early March 2023. I thank Bryan Kromholtz, OP, and Dennis Klein, OP, for the invitation and the whole Dominican community for its warm hospitality. I presented "Catholicity and the Catholic Church: Protestant Concerns and (Roman) Catholic Perspectives" to the faculty of Concordia Theological Seminary in Fort Wayne, Indiana, in early December 2022. I thank Benjamin Mayes for the invitation and the faculty and students for the benefit of their wisdom.

Two anonymous peer reviewers for Word on Fire Academic significantly improved the manuscript, as did my longtime friend and former student Dr. David Augustine in his role as associate editor of Word on Fire Academic. It is a great privilege for me to publish this volume, and (God willing) future volumes of my Engaging the Doctrine series, with Word on Fire, aided by their superb staff. Let me thank Baker Academic and Cascade for publishing three volumes each of the previous six volumes in this series.

Jim and Molly Perry, who endowed the chair that I hold at Mundelein Seminary, have been extraordinary in every way for the eleven years I have been here; may God bless them. My colleagues here have also been wonderfully gracious. I thank Mary Bertram, John Lehocky, Trish Kristan, Jessica Boettcher, and many others for their help with the conferences I host here and for much else. My wife, Joy, has been so generous. Beloved Joy, "I give thanks to God always for you because of the grace of God which was given you in Christ Jesus" (1 Cor 1:4). My brother Brooks continually astounds me by reading my books, and his love of the Lord Jesus Christ is an inspiration.

This book is dedicated to Roger Nutt, my friend for over twenty years and a master of Aquinas's thought and Charles Journet's ecclesiology. Roger is Provost and Vice President of Academic Affairs at Ave Maria University, where I taught for nine years in the 2000s and where I had the privilege of being Roger's colleague. His scholarly acumen is matched by his gift for leadership, but both are grounded in his deep faith. Roger has devoted his life to testifying in word and deed to the truth of Jesus's saying, "I have come as light into the world, that whoever believes in me may not remain in darkness" (John 12:46).

Introduction

1. SETTING THE SCENE

This book is the seventh in my "Engaging the Doctrine" quasi-dogmatics, after volumes on revelation, the Holy Spirit, creation, marriage, Israel, and Jesus Christ (and Mary). In taking up the doctrine of the Church, I am amazed by how beautiful the Church is and what a joy it is to be Catholic. Intra-Catholic controversies and ecumenical debates necessarily receive significant attention in this book. But the core of the book is not the controversies but the perennial truths about the Church in relation to Christ and the Spirit drawing us to the Father. If we anchor our gaze elsewhere, we lose touch with the sap of the Gospel, and everything becomes mere intramural squabbles about power. Had it not been for fear of misunderstanding, I would have subtitled the book "reflections upon a Church in eschatological crisis" because sharing in Christ's tribulation (the path of the cross) is what the Church always is: the eschatological community or inaugurated messianic kingdom undergoing the crisis of the "labor pains" of the new creation (Rom 8:22), "bearing abuse for him [Christ]" and seeking the glory of the "city which is to come" (Heb 13:13–14), nourished by Christ's "altar" and "by the blood of the eternal covenant" (Heb 13:10, 20), and guided by "the great shepherd of the sheep" who pours forth his Spirit (Heb 13:20).

What I love about the Church as Christ's eschatological community are the realities of faith to which the New Testament everywhere testifies, and through which believers "encourage one another and build one another up" (1 Thess 5:11). In the chapters that follow, therefore, I will focus attention on the images of the Church that emphasize intimate communion with Christ and the Spirit—namely, the Church as the Bride of Christ, the Family of

God, the Body of Christ, the People of God, and our Mother, whose members rejoice in "put[ting] on the breastplate of faith and love, and for a helmet the hope of salvation" (1 Thess 5:8). I recognize, however, that as the Protestant theologian Stanley Hauerwas warns (echoing Paul, who urges "let us not sleep, as others do, but let us keep [spiritually] awake and be sober" [1 Thess 5:6]), the Church faces a constant pull toward worldliness as part of awaiting the fullness of the "day of the Lord" (1 Thess 5:2). Hauerwas states, "Christians . . . are tempted to become invisible, justifying their identification with the surrounding culture in the name of serving their neighbor. One of the names given such invisibility is Constantinianism, a term that describes the strategy of Christians when they become an ally of Caesar."[1]

Whatever one thinks of the historical Constantine or of proper church-state relations, there is no doubt that one of the temptations of the Church in every age is to become a Church drained of the vibrancy of divine revelation, sacramental mystery, and transformative holiness, and thereby to become a worldly and lifeless Church. This reductive path can even be taken in the name of renewing the Church, as happens in Tomáš Halík's *The Afternoon of Christianity: The Courage to Change*.[2] The Reformed

1. Stanley Hauerwas, *Matthew* (Brazos, 2006), 62.

2. See Tomáš Halík, *The Afternoon of Christianity: The Courage to Change*, trans. Gerald Turner (University of Notre Dame Press, 2024). Halík dismisses alternatives to his plan of renewal through classical religious liberalism by arguing that the alternatives are mere "ideologies that declare a certain form of the Church and its knowledge (a certain state and form of theology) to be perfect, thus preventing the possibility of development and reform" (22); see also his rhetorical question, "How can we resist the temptation to turn the Church and religion into a ghetto, a locked and fortified bunker, a mausoleum of yesterday's certitudes or a private garden for consumers of soothing and soporific drugs?" (30; cf. 61 for the denial that religiously liberal Christianity is itself "a mausoleum of yesterday's certitudes"). As he goes on to say (misinterpreting the first Christians' relation to Judaism), "Faith must be brought into a new space, as when Paul brought Christianity out of the confines of the Judaism of his day. . . . I believe that the Christianity of tomorrow will be above all a community of a new hermeneutic, a new reading, a new and deeper interpretation of the two sources of divine revelation, scripture and tradition, and especially of God's utterance in the signs of the times" (58). In his view, all who question this "new hermeneutic" are "traditionalists," and "traditionalism is either a temporary 'infantile disorder' of immature converts or a cover for psychologically unbalanced people who will create serious problems for Church structures" (63). He lumps Pope Saint John Paul II and Joseph Ratzinger / Pope Benedict XVI into this category. Halík calls for the ordination of women and "a completely new model of pastoral ministry," "a new understanding of the priest's

theologian Michael Allen rightly exhorts, "The dependence of the church upon God's Word, spoken unto her from the outside, finds fruition in the stature of faith and the stance of trust. We attend to it. We are alert to it."[3] But in fact, we all too readily allow "the cross of Christ [to] be emptied of its power" (1 Cor 1:17). A worldly Church attends more to what the world judges necessary than to what Jesus Christ accomplished for us and requires of us, as revealed by the prophets and apostles and as anchored in cruciform love. As the theologian José Arangüena says, "The Church can be said to have been born principally in the Cross."[4] Or as Paul remarks when confronted by the cultured Corinthians and their slide into worldliness, "I decided to know nothing among you except Jesus Christ and him crucified" (1 Cor 2:2).

The distorted image of a worldly Church devoted to power and prestige and far distant from the life of the cross appears throughout William Langland's *Piers Plowman* in the late fourteenth century. In a representative scene from the poem, a vicar comments, "I never knew a cardinal who didn't come from the pope / And when they come we clerics pick up the tab for their stay, / For their furs and feed for their palfreys and plundering followers. / . . . 'The country is the more cursed that cardinals come into / And where they hang out lechery reigns longest.'"[5] Such a Church also meets us when Bernard of Clairvaux writes to Archbishop Henry of Sens in the mid-twelfth century. Bernard remarks that the faithful work of a bishop will be achieved "not by *recherché*

mission in the Church and in society," "even greater scope for the involvement of the laity," "the decentralization of the Church," the end of priestly celibacy, recognition that Jesus did not institute a cultic or hierarchical priesthood, substitution of orthopraxy for orthodoxy, "the courage to experiment," the welcoming of "a new reformation," moral approval of committed sexual relationships between members of the same sex, and "the shift from Catholicism to catholicity" (63–70, 199, 207).

3. Michael Allen, *The Fear of the Lord: Essays on Theological Method* (T&T Clark, 2022), 46. I concur with Allen's affirmation, "Jesus was, is, and shall be; therefore, his Word and the church's witness to that Word can be trusted" (46).

4. José Ramón Pérez Arangüena, *La Iglesia: Iniciación a la Eclesiología*, 4th ed. (Rialp, 2001), 29. All translations are my own unless otherwise credited.

5. William Langland, *Piers Plowman: The C Version*, trans. George Economou (University of Pennsylvania Press, 1996), 207.

clothes, grand buildings and a parade of horseflesh, but by moral elegance, spiritual zeal, and good works. Yet how many act otherwise! One may observe in certain prelates a positive cult of clothing, but no, or next to no, cult of the virtues."[6] Such a worldly Church appears more recently when Hans Küng, addressing the newly elected Pope Francis in 2013, urged him to "[carry] out the long-overdue, radical structural reforms and the urgently needed revision of the obsolete and unfounded theology behind the many problematical dogmatic and ethical positions that his predecessors have attempted to impose upon the Church."[7] With unconscious irony, Küng places his hope in the power of Pope Francis to bring about the end of "the monarchical-absolutist papacy" and its domination of the Church.[8] Küng advocates doctrinal rupture that can

6. Bernard of Clairvaux, "On the Conduct and Office of Bishops," in *On Baptism and the Office of Bishops*, trans. Pauline Matarasso (Cistercian, 2004), 37–82, at 42. See also Bernard of Clairvaux, *Five Books on Consideration: Advice to a Pope*, trans. John D. Anderson and Elizabeth T. Kennan (Cistercian, 1976).

7. Hans Küng, *Can We Save the Catholic Church?* (William Collins, 2013), xvii.

8. Küng, 6. For background, see Hans Küng, *Infallible? An Unresolved Enquiry*, new expanded edition, trans. Eric Mosbacher, Edward Quinn, and John Bowden (Continuum, 1994)—much of which was originally published in German in 1970. See also Hans Küng, *The Church—Maintained in Truth: A Theological Meditation*, trans. Edward Quinn (Seabury, 1980), where Küng defends an account of the "indefectibility" of the Church that allows for plentiful errors and reversals of prior definitive teaching, even while in every epoch God continues to renew the Church in truth. He argues, "The Church's persistence in truth cannot be given expression in infallible propositions. A genuinely concrete form of persistence in truth must be conceived differently. It is not a question of the permanence of certain propositions, but again of the permanence of the Church itself in truth. . . . In the concrete, the Church is maintained in truth whenever *Jesus himself* and not some other secular, political, or clerical figure *remains the truth* for the individual or community"—and whenever this truth (Jesus) is "imitated and given living expression" in true discipleship (*The Church—Maintained in Truth*, 19–20). If so, however, it follows that "the Church's persistence in truth" cannot itself be an infallible or definitive proposition. Küng contends, "In the Church there will always be a sufficient number of people who so live according to the gospel that the message can be perceived and that to speak of the ecclesial community remaining in the truth makes sense, a permanence in the truth which cannot be nullified by individual erroneous propositions even if these have an official character. . . . Even a possibly false dogma (and how many a dogma has been forgotten today or touches the Christian's sense of faith marginally at best) cannot destroy the Church's being and truth. The totality of faith consists in the integrity of commitment, not in completely correct propositions" (36). Küng assumes that "the gospel" is clear enough and so people will live by "Jesus himself" even when the Church's definitive teachings include numerous false teachings about "the gospel." He gives a fuller explanation in chapter 4 of *The Church—Maintained in Truth*, where he appeals to community and tradition, which he sharply distinguishes from "the ecclesiastical system" and which the theologian interprets "in a critically scientific spirit" (42). Again, he claims to employ "the gospel" or faith in Jesus as his measure for determining what is true in the Church's dogma, but it is unclear how he is so sure about knowing what "the gospel"

only be a corruption of dogma, not a development of it, for the sake of refitting the Church to accord with the norms of our day.

Ecclesiastical worldliness deeply troubled Joseph Ratzinger/Pope Benedict XVI. In a 2011 address given to Church employees in his native country of Germany, Pope Benedict described Christ's Church as a participation in the eternal processions of the Son and Holy Spirit, a participation opened up for us "by virtue of the fact that Christ, the Son of God, as it were stepped outside the framework of his divinity, took flesh and became man, not merely to confirm the world in its worldliness and to be its companion, leaving it to carry on just as it is, but in order to change it."[9] He suggests that everything about the Church should be measured by Christ's mission. Ecclesial worldliness can be diagnosed whenever "the Church becomes self-satisfied, settles down in this world, becomes self-sufficient and adapts herself to the standards of the world."[10] One sign that this is happening is when the Church "gives greater weight to organization and institutionalization than to her vocation to openness towards God, her vocation to opening up the world towards the other."[11] A Church drawn toward

is. See also Hans Küng, *On Being a Christian*, trans. Edward Quinn (Doubleday, 1976), where he indicates that "the gospel" or "Jesus" is what present-day historical-critical scholarship can reveal with respect to Jesus's kingdom preaching. For a critique of Küng on this point, see Robert Barron, *The Priority of Christ: Toward a Postliberal Catholicism* (Brazos, 2007).

9. Pope Benedict XVI, "Address to Catholics Engaged in the Life of the Church and Society," September 25, 2011, vatican.va. See also Gerhard Ludwig Müller, "Das trinitarische Grundverständnis der Kirche in der Kirchenkonstitution 'Lumen Gentium,'" *Münchener Theologische Zeitschrift* 45, no. 4 (1994): 451–65.

10. Pope Benedict XVI, "Address to Catholics Engaged in the Life of the Church and Society." See also, for background, Santiago Madrigal, SJ's *Karl Rahner y Joseph Ratzinger: Tras las huellas del Concilio* (Sal Terrae, 2006), 167–68.

11. Pope Benedict XVI, "Address to Catholics Engaged in the Life of the Church and Society." See also Martin Onuoha's astute summary in his *Actio Divina: The Marian Mystery of the Church in the Theology of Joseph Ratzinger (Benedict XVI)* (Peter Lang, 2021), 60: "[Ratzinger/Benedict] fought tooth and nail against a view of the Church as a bureaucratic structure administering social welfare services and programs for political action." Onuoha's remark is quoted by Tracey Rowland, "Joseph Ratzinger on Democracy within the Church," *Communio* 50, no. 4 (2023): 635–56, at 636. Rowland aptly describes the view of the Church against which Ratzinger fought as "Catholic Inc." Instructively, Rowland goes on to contrast Ratzinger's (and Hans Maier's) *Demokratie in der Kirche: Möglichkeiten und Grenzen* (Lahn, 2000) with Karl Rahner, SJ's *Freiheit und Manipulation in Gesellschaft und Kirche* (Kösel, 1970), in which Rahner supports individual national churches (within the Catholic Church) being governed by a synodal structure comprised of bishops, priests, and laity. See also Oliver Putz, "'I Did Not Change;

worldliness will focus not on opening up *the world* to God by proclaiming and sacramentally mediating the redemption won by Christ, but rather on securing its own life *in this world* by conforming its message to the tendencies of fallen humanity.[12]

A Constantinian Church, in short, attempts to serve the world on the world's terms as an instrument for this-worldly ends.[13] Not surprisingly, then, the Church's dogmatic and moral teaching becomes negotiable. In *Unity of the Churches: An Actual Possibility* (1983), Karl Rahner and Heinrich Fries proposed that the mainline Christian churches, including the Catholic Church, should band together under a new umbrella structure, allowing each church to keep its distinctive doctrines while embracing full intercommunion and recognition of one another's ministry, and with the pope as a figurehead no longer able to enunciate binding doctrine. The ultimate surviving doctrines in this new Church would be determined later.[14] Rahner's 1972 *The Shape of the*

They Did!': Joseph Ratzinger, Karl Rahner and the Second Vatican Council," *New Wineskins* 2, no. 1 (2007): 11–31.

12. See, for example, Eberhard Schockenhoff, "Der Glaubenssinn des Volkes Gottes als ethisches Erkenntniskriterium? Zur Nicht-Rezeption der kirchlichen Sexualmoral durch die Gläubigen," in *Der Spürsinn des Gottesvolkes: Eine Diskussion mit der Internationalen Theologischen Kommission*, ed. Thomas Söding (Herder, 2016), 305–30.

13. What I mean by "Constantinian" can also be expressed by the term "Erastian," even if the Church has not become directly controlled by the government. For John Henry Newman's critique of Erastianism, see chapter 1 of my *Newman on Doctrinal Corruption* (Word on Fire Academic, 2022).

14. See Heinrich Fries and Karl Rahner, *Unity of the Churches: An Actual Possibility*, trans. Ruth C. L. Gritsch and Eric W. Gritsch (Paulist, 1985). For background, see Ulrich L. Lehner, "The Ecumenical Vision of Beda Mayr, OSB (1742–1794)," in *A Defense of the Catholic Religion: The Necessity, Existence, and Limits of an Infallible Church*, by Beda Mayr, OSB, trans. Ulrich L. Lehner (The Catholic University of America Press, 2023), 1–20, drawing upon Franz Xaver Bantle, *Unfehlbarkeit der Kirche in Aufklärung und Romantik: Eine dogmengeschichtliche Untersuchung für die Zeit der Wende vom 18. zum 19. Jahrhundert* (Herder, 1976). Discussing the sixth section of Mayr's *A Defense of the Catholic Religion*, Lehner notes that "it is in this section that he introduces the concept of *limited ecclesiastical infallibility*. For him, such a humbler understanding of infallibility could bring about a reunification with the Protestant churches. This, however, would come at a price. It meant that the Catholic Church not only had to become aware of the limits of infallible doctrinal decisions, but also acknowledge that many of the doctrines that divided Protestants and Catholics were *not directly revealed*, as the Church claimed. . . . This theory silently presupposed that there were doctrines that could be proven neither from Scripture nor tradition, and which had been erroneously transmitted as *truths of faith*" (Lehner, "The Ecumenical Vision of Beda Mayr," 12). Lehner rightly continues, "Mayr *reverses* what *indirect revelation* meant. For him it is no longer revealed by God, not even by conclusion, and thus not a necessary part of the faith. Indirectly revealed teachings are supererogatory to him. They are pious and useful, but

Church to Come denies that Catholics today should be expected to adhere to a shared orthodoxy; argues that "human nature" is so historically mutable that the moral norms of the past no longer hold because human nature (whatever it is) has evolved; leaves open the question of whether a lay person can consecrate the Eucharist; advocates for women priests within a sharply changed understanding of priesthood; and calls for democratic participation of laypeople in the Church's deliberative bodies.[15]

With an eye to implementing such changes, a 1977 meeting of the international editorial board of *Concilium*, toward the end of Pope Paul VI's life, produced a book ambitiously titled *Toward Vatican III: The Work That Needs to Be Done*.[16] Although they were much in the minority, some of the more keen-eyed contributors to this volume warned against the danger of ecclesiastical worldliness. David Burrell raised the fundamental question: "Has *aggiornamento* too easily played into our Constantinian tendencies?"[17] The answer was all too clearly yes.

not necessary for salvation. Likewise, he conflates *dogmata ecclesiae* and *doctrinae Catholicae* in order to make settled doctrine appear to be open to abandonment and reinterpretation. Had the Catholic Church followed it, it would have had to acknowledge that it taught errors for hundreds of years: namely, that certain truths were *dogmata fide divina credenda* [but were in fact false]. The Church would have appeared to have inflated God's word and thus commit theological suicide" (16). Lehner observes that Mayr's ideas echo those of the Catholic thinker François Véron in his *Méthodes de traiter des controverses de religion* (A. Taupinart, 1638) and his *Règle générale de la foy catholique, separée de toutes autres doctrines inférieures en authorité* (A. Taupinart, 1645). Lehner also directs attention to Walter Kasper's *Dogma unter dem Wort Gottes* (M. Grünewald, 1965).

15. See Karl Rahner, SJ, *The Shape of the Church to Come*, trans. Edward Quinn (Seabury, 1974), which was written to inform the German Synod of Würzburg (1971–75). For background about that synod and for the argument that the Würzburg Synod is today continuing (this time not only in Germany but also in the worldwide Church), see Stephan Knops, "Die Würzburger Synode: Krisenindiz—Zeitdiagnose—Zukunftsplan," in *Synodalität in der katholischen Kirche: Die Studie der Internationalen Theologischen Kommission im Diskurs*, ed. Markus Graulich and Johanna Rahner (Herder, 2020), 136–52. For a brief discussion of Rahner's book in the context of the Würzburg Synod and of efforts to give the laity a greater voice, see (in the same volume) Johanna Rahner, "Klerus und Laien: Genese und Transformation eines typisch katholischen Paradigmas," 170–95, at 190–91. María García-Nieto Barón points out that Pope Francis "is working to open up processes that allow for the presence of women inside the government of the Church," without accepting that the sacrament of holy orders is open to women. Barón, *La presencia de la mujer en el gobierno de la Iglesia: Perspectiva jurídica* (EUNSA, 2023), 77.

16. See *Toward Vatican III: The Work That Needs to Be Done*, ed. David Tracy with Hans Küng and Johann B. Metz (Seabury, 1978).

17. David B. Burrell, CSC, "The Church and Individual Life," in *Toward Vatican III*, 124–33, at 133. Burrell's solution—exploring Catholic forms of "sectarian" communities—is unsatisfying but understandable.

II. THE CHURCH AND ACCOMMODATION TO THE WORLD

Over the centuries, Catholic reflection on the Church has often proceeded in relation to this Constantinian temptation, either giving in to it or resisting it by means of a renewed attention to the mysteries of faith that preserve the Church in vitality and joy.[18] Ratzinger comments, "The Roman state was false and anti-Christian precisely because it wanted to be the totality of human capacity and hope. . . . But when Christian faith, faith in man's greater hope, decays and falls away, then the myth of the divine state rises up once again."[19] Often this happens unconsciously. To cite a recent example, John McGreevy's *Catholicism: A Global History from the French Revolution to Pope Francis* contains the following final sentence, expressing his hopes for Catholicism: "Let's hope that these young Catholics will be better positioned, in the words of [Pope] Francis, to be 'citizens of our respective nations and of the entire world, builders of a new social bond.'"[20] For McGreevy, there is nothing controversial in this claim: in his view, the Church's history and core meaning revolve around its contributions to local and global citizenship, as this citizenship is understood today by secular governments that consider themselves to be avatars of the arc of history.

Claiming the mantle of Pope Francis, McGreevy makes clear that his dream is for a new Catholicism focused on building up global civilization (the kingdom of God) while discarding outdated doctrines.[21] A similar note is sounded by the theologian

18. See Gonzalo Barbed Martín, *Una anciana muy joven: Historia de la Iglesia* (Ediciones Palabra, 2022), 10.

19. Joseph Ratzinger, "Biblical Aspects of the Question of Faith and Politics," in *Church, Ecumenism and Politics: New Essays in Ecclesiology*, trans. Robert Nowell (Crossroad, 1988), 147–52, at 148.

20. John T. McGreevy, *Catholicism: A Global History from the French Revolution to Pope Francis* (Norton, 2022), 422.

21. See also Robert Blair Kaiser, *Inside the Jesuits: How Pope Francis Is Changing the Church and the World* (Rowman & Littlefield, 2014), filled with observations such as the following: "Before the council, we'd thought we were miserable sinners when, really, we were being noth-

Massimo Faggioli. His *Joe Biden and Catholicism in the United States*, published to coincide with Biden's inauguration in 2020, functions as a laudation to America's second Catholic president, who is portrayed as leading the way toward a renewed Catholicism that fits both with American ideals and with the vision of Pope Francis. Faggioli places the Constantinian onus on the Republican Party and neo-conservatism, which he deems to be the archenemy of Catholic and American progress. The Democratic Party is here the bearer of Catholicism's future insofar as it is assisting the Church in updating itself and discarding outmoded ways and doctrines while remaining recognizably Catholic.[22]

Faggioli's book on Biden recalls Eusebius of Caesarea's celebratory tome on Constantine, in which, having lived through a period of intense persecution of Catholics by the Roman Empire, Eusebius rejoices that the Church no longer needs to be countercultural because it now aligns with the governing regime. As Eusebius says, "They danced and sang in city and country alike, giving honour first of all to God our Sovereign Lord, as they had been instructed, and then to the pious emperor with his sons, so dear to God. Old troubles were forgotten, and all irreligion passed into oblivion. . . . Thus all tyranny had been

ing but human. After the council, we had a new view of ourselves. We learned to put a greater importance on finding and following Jesus as 'the way' (as opposed to what we said in the Creed, simply giving voice to a set of doctrines we may or may not have understood). What mattered was what we *did*: helping to feed the hungry, clothe the naked, and find shelter for the homeless. That's what made us followers of Jesus. . . . Before the council, we identified *salvation* as 'getting to heaven.' After the council, we knew we had a duty to bring justice and peace to the world in our own contemporary society" (80–81).

22. See Massimo Faggioli, *Joe Biden and Catholicism in the United States* (Bayard, 2021). See also, more recently, Faggioli's suggestion that Robert Barron's evangelizing efforts (in the quest for a "new ressourcement") are Trumpist. Faggioli published this viewpoint in his online article "Will Trumpism Spare Catholicism? Emerging Alignments Are Cause for Concern," *Commonweal*, April 22, 2024, but when Word on Fire protested the connection with Donald Trump, *Commonweal* first adjusted the passage and then removed it from the article, whose current version can be found at https://www.commonwealmagazine.org/will-trumpism-spare-catholicism. I should add that Faggioli's more recent writings have sounded a somewhat less positive note with respect to the Biden presidency, as he (Faggioli) seeks to reset the boundaries of "centrism" in American Catholicism, with Barron supposedly in the "right wing."

purged away."[23] If by Constantinianism one means that the state generally supports Catholic moral principles and, in certain ways, assists the Church in carrying out the prophetic and sacramental mission Christ gave to his apostles, then this is surely good. In practice, however, Constantinianism entails more than this, as the near-disastrous ecclesiastical meddling of the fourth-century descendants of Constantine already showed. For Constantinians across the centuries, appeal to the Holy Spirit has the role of seconding the arc of history sanctioned by the state while instrumentalizing the doctrine of Christ—the very doctrine sanctioned, in point of fact, by the (real) Holy Spirit in and through Scripture and Tradition.[24]

Consider the experiences of the fourteenth-century Doctor of the Church, Catherine of Siena.[25] Influenced as a young girl in Siena by the Dominican church and cloister of San Domenico, Catherine lived during a time when some Italian cities formed an anti-papal league to fight the army of the Papal States. Intent on averting such war, she came out in favor of a crusade against the Muslims in the Holy Land in 1375, seven years after making her "mystical espousal" to Christ (she remained living in her parental home). In 1376, she worked to help the city of Florence gain release from the interdict that Pope Gregory XI had placed on the city. To do this, she had to travel to Avignon, because the popes had been living for decades in the luxury of Avignon, fully under the sway of the French court. She helped to convince Pope Gregory XI to move back to Rome, but not long after her death, the

23. Eusebius, *The History of the Church from Christ to Constantine*, trans. G. A. Williamson, rev. and ed. Andrew Louth (Penguin, 1989), 332–33.

24. On the work of the Holy Spirit, consider Archbishop Anthony Fisher, OP's remark about Pope Francis's understanding of synodality: "Unlike politicized, bureaucratic, or corporate conceptions of the church, Pope Francis insists that the Holy Spirit is the great protagonist in the church's life. Without the Spirit, the pope says, we can hold an ecclesial UN meeting or diocesan parliament . . . but it will not be a true synod." Fisher, *Unity in Christ: Bishops, Synodality, and Communion* (The Catholic University of America Press, 2023), 51. The key is how one conceives of the continuity of the work of the "Spirit of truth" (John 14:17).

25. For background to Catherine's teachings and life, see Paul Murray, OP, *Saint Catherine of Siena: Mystic of Fire, Preacher of Freedom*, 2nd ed. (Word on Fire, 2020).

Church endured the Great Schism in which three popes, allied with different powerful rulers, vied for recognition.

Moving back in time closer to Constantine, Maximus the Confessor in the seventh century had his tongue and right hand cut off for stubbornly rejecting Monothelite and Monenergist understandings of Jesus Christ.[26] The Byzantine emperor Heraclius, crowned in 610, sought to foster the unity of his empire, which had been weakened by a lengthy war with the Persians, Avars, and Slavs and by the Monophysites' rejection of the Council of Chalcedon. Various efforts in the late fifth and sixth centuries had been made to achieve ecclesiastical reunion, but the hoped-for reunion had proven elusive. Emperor Justinian in the sixth century launched a campaign of persecution against the Monophysites, but this persecution had the result of rendering them even firmer in their beliefs.[27] Around 630, Emperor Heraclius and Patriarch Sergius of Constantinople developed a compromise: they affirmed that, although Christ had two natures, Christ had a single "energy." This compromise seemed to be working until a monk named Sophronius, soon to be elected Patriarch of Jerusalem, declared Monenergism to be heretical.

In this situation, Patriarch Sergius drafted an imperial edict, signed by Emperor Heraclius in 638, that was intended to resolve the divisions once and for all. This imperial edict affirmed Monothelitism. Its purpose was to assist the emperor in unifying the empire, a task that had become even more urgent due to the rise of Islam and its conquering armies. In 653, Pope Martin I, who had supported Maximus by convening a council against Monothelitism and Monenergism, was arrested and condemned by the emperor. Given the fraught political situation, his successors did not dare to speak out. Maximus, however, remained resistant. He

26. For the spiritual significance of Maximus's doctrine, see Luke Steven, *Imitation, Knowledge, and the Task of Christology in Maximus the Confessor* (Cascade, 2020).

27. For severe ecclesiastical corruption under Emperor Justinian and Empress Theodora, see the work by their contemporary Procopius, *The Secret History*, trans. G.A. Williamson and Peter Sarris (Penguin, 2007).

denied that the emperor had any right to define dogma, as Emperor Heraclius's imperial edict had tried to do. As a result, Maximus was first exiled, and then, when he still would not recant, was tortured and endured the trial in Constantinople that led to his mutilation and death.[28]

Constantinianism reduces the Church to being above all an ally of those who exercise temporal power. The Gospel of John provides some sharp warnings in this regard. Jesus instructs his disciples, "If the world hates you, know that it has hated me before it hated you. If you were of the world, the world would love its own. . . . Remember the word that I said to you, 'A servant is not greater than his master.' If they persecuted me, they will persecute you; if they kept my word, they will keep yours also" (John 15:18–20). Although Peter in the Gospel of Matthew tries to convince Jesus that he (Jesus) will not be crucified, Jesus insists upon his cruciform path (see Matt 16:24–25).

When the Church accommodates itself to the world—generally by arguing that necessity and common sense require abandoning some of the Gospel's 'saltiness' (see Matt 5:13), as distinct from reforms that make Jesus's words and deeds more present—the Church wounds itself. A portrait of just such accommodation to the world comes from the pen of the religiously liberal Catholic biblical scholar Alfred Loisy. According to Loisy, over

28. For background, see Paul M. Blowers, *Maximus the Confessor: Jesus Christ and the Transfiguration of the World* (Oxford University Press, 2016); and see also, for the role allotted to the emperor in the Byzantine Church, Francis Dvornik, *Byzantium and the Roman Primacy*, trans. Edwin A. Quain, SJ (Fordham University Press, 1966). On the one hand, Dvornik warns against trying "to reconstitute an ecclesiological system which we suppose to have existed in the Byzantine Church. We must understand that Byzantine theologians [like their Western contemporaries in the first millennium] never did develop an ecclesiological system in the modern sense" (16). On the other hand, he makes clear that "in Byzantium, the problem of the Roman Primacy was intimately connected with that of the imperial power": "Christian Hellenism . . . saw in the Emperor a representative of God upon earth, almost the viceregent of Christ. According to this political conception, the Christian Emperor not only had the right but also the duty to watch over the Church, to defend the Orthodox faith, and to lead his subjects to God. . . . While in the Byzantine Church, the Emperor continued to be the lawmaker, using the right which Christian Hellenism had granted to him, in the West it was the Sovereign Pontiff who, increasingly, became the sole lawgiver in the Church" (18–20). Dvornik adds, "To explain these differences, the theologian might be tempted to seek for reasons in the order of ecclesiology, but in that path, the historian will be reluctant to follow him" (19).

the centuries the Church has always done whatever needed at the time to spread the original impulse of eschatological hope and charity, rooted in Jesus's mistaken belief that the kingdom of God was imminent.[29] On this view, the measure of doctrinal development is vitality (or life): Do the doctrines still function successfully to spread the original impulse of hope and charity? If not, then the doctrines must change, as (Loisy thinks) they have done frequently in the past. He argues that in the original Jewish context, the disciples preached Jesus as the Messiah of the one God, whereas in the Hellenistic context, believers preached Jesus as the divine Logos or Word.[30] Loisy approves of such falsification, and he advocates squaring Christianity with the modern world by whatever means necessary. Similarly, Loisy's fellow early twentieth-century modernist George Tyrrell mocked Pope Pius X and all others who embrace "a body of divinely guaranteed terms and definitions and statements, final and valid for all ages and nations."[31] Tyrrell rejects such a notion of dogma, and he affirms

29. See Alfred Loisy, *The Gospel and the Church*, trans. Christopher Home (Isbister, 1903), 177–78. For background, see Tomáš Petráček, *The Bible and the Crisis of Modernism: Catholic Criticism in the Twentieth Century*, trans. David Livingstone and Addison Hart (University of Notre Dame Press, 2022), 29–34, 203–13; Emil Goichet, *Alfred Loisy et ses amis* (Cerf, 2002); Jeffrey L. Morrow, *Alfred Loisy and Modern Biblical Studies* (The Catholic University of America Press, 2018); and the essays in *Catholic Modernism: Tyrrell, Loisy, and the Ongoing Challenge to Dogmatic Christianity*, ed. Matthew Levering and Jeffrey L. Morrow (Emmaus Academic, forthcoming). While sympathetic to Loisy, Petráček observes that "from 1875 to 1908 [Loisy] suffered a crisis of faith in the traditional understanding of the church" and "he had for some time before [his excommunication in 1908] questioned the divinity of Jesus Christ" (*The Bible and the Crisis of Modernism*, 211). Petráček underplays the real radicalism of Loisy when he (Petráček) writes that for *The Gospel and the Church* (just as for religiously liberal Catholics today), "the permanent communion of the church . . . requires a balance of tradition—by which the body of doctrine is preserved—and the unending work of human reason to adapt the formulations of old dogmas to reflect current scientific and philosophical realities. Dogmas and other formulations are imperfect; they cannot provide complete expressions of absolute truth; yet they are the least imperfect expressions of absolute truth available to humanity. But they too must serve the faith, not dictate it. Dogma is not poured out of the sky by God; it is formed along the historical continuum of theological inquiry. Divine in origin and content, dogma is nonetheless human in structure and composition" (33). The question is what is required for "tradition" to preserve "the body of doctrine," granted that dogmas, while not perfect, are "divine" in "content."

30. See Loisy, *The Gospel and the Church*, 195.

31. George Tyrrell, *Medievalism: A Reply to Cardinal Mercier* (Longmans, Green, 1908), 123. Tyrrell observes somewhat earlier, "It is the historical and not the philosophical difficulty that inspires the reconstructive effort of the Modernist pure and simple. It is the irresistible facts concerning the origin and composition of the Old and New Testaments; concerning the

that radical accommodation to the world is necessary for the ongoing life of the Church. As Tyrrell says, a modernist's "faith in the world is more fundamental than his faith in the Church," because the world is God's creation, and God guides its progress, ensuring that the Church will adapt with it.[32]

By contrast, the Catholic Church's true reality displays what John Henry Newman calls the dogmatic principle. The Church is the bearer of ontological truth about divine and historical realities. God really is the Trinity, and the incarnate Son really was and is the Messiah. With regard to doctrinal development, the dogmatic

origin of the Christian Church, of its hierarchy, its institutions, its dogmas; concerning the gradual development of the Papacy; concerning the history of religion in general—that create a difficulty against which the synthesis of scholastic theology must be and is already shattered to pieces" (108).

32. Tyrrell, 147. For Tyrrell's understanding of revelation and dogma (and his view that dogma has a symbolic and practical value but not an enduring truth-value), see also Tyrrell, "Semper Eadem II" and "'Theologism'—a Reply," in his *Through Scylla and Charybdis: Or, the Old Theology and the New* (Longmans, Green, 1907), 133–54 and 308–54. For an early and insightful critique of Tyrrell's position (using writings published prior to the above-named texts), see Eugène Franon, "The Religious Philosophy of Fr. Tyrrell" (originally published in French in 1906), in *Defending the Faith: An Anti-Modernist Anthology*, ed. and trans. William H. Marshner (The Catholic University of America Press, 2017), 197–210, at 201. See also, for a postconciliar adaptation of Tyrrell's perspective (without citing Tyrrell), Edward Schillebeeckx, OP's *Church: The Human Story of God*, trans. John Bowden (Crossroad, 1990). Schillebeeckx deems Jesus to be (or to have been experienced as) the pinnacle of "revelation," whose content is fundamentally inexpressible: see *Church*, 26–27. He remarks, "Of no single period in the tradition of faith, not even that of the Bible, may the cultural forms and historical context be absolutized. But this certainly does not mean that these historical and socio-cultural mediations are worthless for faith or to be neglected. On the contrary, they have a very positive function, for all their relativity, since they are the only possible vehicles for the meaning of the offer of revelation to which the answer is given in faith, precisely because the gospel, which is not bound to one culture, can nevertheless be seen and found *in* the special features of particular, culturally limited structures of understanding" (37). He goes on to claim that "the offer of revelation is not an empty cipher: it has meaningful content, though this can never be grasped or objectified" (38); and he sides with Tyrrell, though in denser language, when he states, "Therefore the question of Christian identity through the changing centuries can be answered only by a comparison of differing cultural forms of the Christian experience of faith, interpretation of faith, and praxis of faith, as an answer to God's offer of revelation in Jesus. The only difference between the past Christian tradition and the new Christian traditions that we shall have to hand down and make lies in the fact that we can make comparisons with the past after the event. . . . The identity in the meaning of the gospel cannot primarily lie at the level of the Bible and the past tradition of faith, at least as such, and therefore cannot be found in a material repetition of that past. . . . The identity of meaning can only be found in the fluctuating 'middle field,' in a swinging to and fro between tradition and situation, and thus at the level of the corresponding relationship between the original message (tradition, which also includes the situation of the time) and the situation, then and now, which is different each time. The fundamental identity of meaning between the successive periods of Christian understanding of the offer of revelation is not to be found in corresponding terms . . . but on corresponding relationships between all the terms involved" (39, 41; see 43 and 224–25 for the consequences for dogma).

principle entails that theologians, using the tools of logic, can reasonably defend a dogma's "continuity of principles and logical sequence" vis-à-vis prior teaching, so as to show that there has been no rupture or corruption in the handing on of the saving truth of divine revelation.[33] At the same time, logical continuity is not by any means all there is. As Guy Mansini says, "The Church as a whole is mysterious in her being and agency. She possesses, as it were, a personality, sometimes figured as Christic (the Body of Christ), sometimes as Marian (the Bride of the Lamb), sometimes as Pneumatic (the Temple of the Holy Spirit)."[34]

As should be expected from these three images of the Church (Body, Bride, Temple of the Spirit), the power of grace can be seen in the Church's members. Of course, if one looks only for sins, there are plenty of sins to be found. Robert Jenson comments, "Description of the virtues definitive of the church's life may well have a sour ring in many ears; the life of the church manifests them all too incompletely."[35] Erasmus of Rotterdam aptly portrays early sixteenth-century Christendom as devoted to the folly of worldliness in his *The Praise of Folly*, whose purported author is "Folly."

Nevertheless, if one looks upon the Church with the eyes of faith, one perceives extraordinary grace. Erasmus has his narrator, Folly, say the following (the opposite of Erasmus's own view): "No fools seem more senseless than those people who have been completely taken up, once and for all, with a burning devotion to Christian piety: they throw away their possessions, ignore

33. Guy Mansini, OSB, *The Development of Dogma: A Systematic Account* (The Catholic University of America Press, 2023), 109, citing John Henry Newman, *An Essay on the Development of Christian Doctrine*, 6th ed. (University of Notre Dame Press, 1989), 169. The dogma's "power of assimilation" or "conservative action on past adumbrations of the dogma" (Mansini, 110) is also capable of logical defense. In the same vein, see Reinhard Hütter, "Progress, Not Alteration of the Faith: Beyond Antiquarianism and Presentism: John Henry Newman, Vincent of Lérins, and the Criterion of Identity of the Development of Doctrine," *Nova et Vetera* 19, no. 2 (2021): 333–91.

34. Mansini, *Development of Dogma*, 108.

35. Robert W. Jenson, *Systematic Theology*, vol. 2, *The Works of God* (Oxford University Press, 1999), 210.

injuries, allow themselves to be deceived, make no distinction between friend and foe, . . . find satisfaction in fasts, vigils, tears, and labors."[36] Such Christians exist; they are the heart of Catholic parishes, religious communities, schools, and hospitals.

Thus, for example, a profound sense of divine mercy—and therefore a profound mercy toward others—characterizes Catherine of Siena's outlook. In her book *The Dialogue*, which is framed as God's instruction to her about the mysteries that most trouble her, God tells her about Jesus: "The fiery chariot of my only-begotten Son came bringing the fire of my charity to your humanity with such overflowing mercy that the penalty for sins people commit was taken away."[37] She imagines Christ as a Bridge; he bridges earth and heaven in a manner that infinitely exceeds what any mere creature could accomplish. We cross this Bridge when we are united to him by faith and Baptism; we are empowered to walk along the Bridge by charity and all the virtues (especially humility); we are strengthened on the Bridge by the Eucharist and holy obedience. God tells Catherine that the "lack of charity for me and for your neighbors is the source of all evils," and God continues by bemoaning the cruelty of worldly "greed, which not only refuses to share what is one's own but takes what belongs to others, robbing the poor, playing the overlord, cheating, defrauding, putting up one's neighbors' goods—and often their very persons—for ransom."[38]

Catherine describes worldly logic, straining for control rather than embracing divine revelation, as "selfish love."[39] A person in thrall to selfish love cannot love and cannot sacrifice for anyone else's good. Nor can such a person love God. The logic of the world cannot go beyond worldly goods to an "infinitely desirous

36. Desiderius Erasmus, *The Praise of Folly*, trans. Clarence H. Miller (Yale University Press, 1979), 132.

37. Catherine of Siena, *The Dialogue*, trans. Suzanne Noffke, OP (Paulist, 1980), 112. She means the everlasting penalty.

38. Catherine of Siena, 35.

39. Catherine of Siena, 35.

love," seeking God (Love) above all else, and thereby truly being able to love one's self and neighbor.[40]

Catherine does not adopt false mercy in the sense of pretending that sin is not sin or in the sense of pretending that the world is not deeply ill due to pride and vice, but instead she exhibits real mercy by expressing at every step the greatest love for sinners. She combines this with a deep humility, well aware that she, too, has "sinned so much" and has been "the cause and instrument of every evil."[41] She knows how much she relies upon the mercy and infinite goodness of "divine eternal Love" personally loving her, a sinner.[42]

Equally importantly, in the midst of the pastoral and doctrinal chaos of her day, Catherine shows respect for the Church and its hierarchical priesthood as part of her love of Christ and God. In *The Dialogue*, Catherine has God say the following about those who attack the Church "under the pretext of correcting the faults of my ministers": "O dearest daughter, grieve without measure at the sight of such wretched blindness in those who, like you, have been washed in the blood, have nursed and been nourished with this blood at the breast of holy Church!"[43] Catherine highlights the transformative power of the sacraments, which mediate the power of Christ's cross to believers. Catherine also points to the holy priests and bishops who have, over the centuries, "[given] off within the mystic body of holy Church the brightness of supernatural learning, the color of a holy and honorable life in following the teaching of my Truth, and the warmth of blazing charity."[44]

Her confessor Raymond of Capua's *Life of St. Catherine of Siena* contains numerous stories about how Catherine lived her faith. Reading this contemporaneous biography of Catherine,

40. Catherine of Siena, 42.
41. Catherine of Siena, 49.
42. Catherine of Siena, 49.
43. Catherine of Siena, 220.
44. Catherine of Siena, 222.

one sees that although there was much corruption in the Church, there were also many great souls who were being nourished by the Church's teaching and sacraments. Raymond describes Catherine giving alms to the poor and caring for the sick as though caring for Christ himself. Raymond also tells about a woman, a member of the Sisters of Penance of St. Dominic, who became bitterly envious of Catherine, an envy that developed into hatred and detraction. In response, Catherine tried "to placate her with acts of humility and kindness," as well as by praying for her and visiting her, including when the woman became seriously ill.[45] According to Raymond, Catherine implored Christ for "a special grace, the ability to perceive the beauty of all the souls she came into contact with, so that she would be the more prompted to work for their salvation."[46] The point for my purposes is that in the midst of this terribly corrupt period in the Church's life, Christ nevertheless brought to be—through the instrumentality of the Church—a great saint who built up the Church rather than tearing it down.

Like Catherine, Bernard of Clairvaux was a man who could recognize his own sinfulness.[47] Indeed, for Bernard, the humble and merciful person always treats the sinner as a fellow sinner, a brother or sister. From this perspective, Bernard was able to help the Church of his day to fight against its own worldliness. Bernard's ability to name and condemn ecclesiastical sins in a constructive way is on display in his *On the Conduct and Office of Bishops*. He describes the risks of ecclesiastical promotion: "Blinded to danger by their own ambition, they have their appetites further whetted by these signs of success which they observe with envy. Limitless ambition and insatiable greed! . . .

45. Raymond of Capua, *The Life of St. Catherine of Siena*, trans. George Lamb (TAN, 2003), 134.

46. Raymond of Capua, 137.

47. For background, including with respect to Bernard's struggle with nervous illness and overzealous mortification leading to digestive problems (also experienced by Catherine), see Brian Patrick McGuire, *Bernard of Clairvaux: An Inner Life* (Cornell University Press, 2020).

Made a bishop, he wants to be an archbishop."[48] Bernard goes on to deplore how a bishop always seeks to increase the size of the territory he governs. He writes all this to an actual archbishop, Henry of Sens, whom he desires to lift up to the higher things of Christ. Hardly without error himself, Bernard's greatness consists in his willingness to call himself and others to be what a Christian should be—and can be by the Spirit's power.

To give a final example, Gertrude the Great in the thirteenth century recalls a dark time in which she had "largely lost the delight of the presence of God."[49] Gertrude's account of what happens next is extraordinary. She interiorly sees a blossoming garden with a stream of honey, and she hears God ask her whether she would prefer dwelling in this garden, with its pleasures, over communion with God. God then shows her a seemingly inferior garden. Lastly, God interprets these two visions. The blossoming garden watered by honey symbolizes "an easy, honorable life, without any trouble, finding favor in human eyes and a reputation for every kind of holiness."[50] Gertrude has rejected this garden; she wants instead the greatest possible communion with Christ, which, as God explains, is symbolized by the thornier garden of the second vision. Overjoyed by hearing this explanation of her time of dark trial (in configuration to Christ), Gertrude then describes herself as follows: she "leant on the bosom of her beloved with such great pressure and constant adherence that it seemed to her that the force of all creation would not be strong enough to shift her even a little."[51]

48. Bernard of Clairvaux, "Letter 42: To Henry, Archbishop of Sens," in *On Baptism and the Office of Bishops*, trans. Pauline Matarasso (Cistercian Publications, 2004), 37–82, at 70. For further background to Bernard's theology and life, see Adriaan H. Bredero, *Bernard of Clairvaux: Between Cult and History* (Eerdmans, 1996); and G.R. Evans, *Bernard of Clairvaux* (Oxford University Press, 2000).

49. Gertrud the Great of Helfta, *The Herald of God's Loving-Kindness: Book Three*, trans. Alexandra Barratt (Cistercian, 1999), 33.

50. Gertrud the Great of Helfta, 34.

51. Gertrud the Great of Helfta, 34. For further background to Gertrude's theology, see Ella Johnson, *This Is My Body: Eucharistic Theology and Anthropology in the Writings of Gertrude the Great of Helfta* (Liturgical, 2020).

When addressing contemporary conflicts and debates, we must emulate the courage, charity, and patient trust of these saints, and we must also remember that these saints are still with us in the Church, united in prayer with the will of the Lord Jesus.[52] The constant presence of the saints and the blessed angels, under Christ's Headship, does not imply any cheap triumphalism, as though the Church today (or Catholics today) could avoid sharing in "the great tribulation" (Rev 7:14). Far from it. In the midst of internal and external trials, believers must implore Jesus for help and rely on his power while actively seeking to do his will and (as Michael Allen emphasizes) praying to possess "his joy to the fullest, the very joy that carried him in his darkest hours (Heb 12:2)."[53] Again, joyful trust in the Lord does not mean passivity on the part of believers, as though nothing could destabilize Christ's Church. After all, Jesus warns in a manner that crushes complacency, "When the Son of man comes, will he find faith on earth?" (Luke 18:8). Our task when faced with worldliness in the Church is to "[speak] the truth in love" while letting "no evil talk come out of [our] mouths, but only such as is good for edifying . . . that it may impart grace to all who hear" (Eph 4:15, 29).

III. ECCLESIOLOGICAL REFLECTIONS FOR A CONFLICTED CHURCH

There already exist numerous comprehensive systematic studies of, or introductions to, the Catholic Church. I think especially of such works as Benoît-Dominique de La Soujeole's *Introduction to the Mystery of the Church* and Charles Journet's multi-volume *The Church of the Word Incarnate*. Journet brilliantly provides an integrated theology of the Trinitarian missions, the Church (inclusive

52. For the importance of the Church Triumphant, see E. L. Mascall, *Corpus Christi: Essays on the Church and the Eucharist*, 2nd ed. (Longmans, Green, 1965), 21. See also Mascall, *Christ, the Christian and the Church: A Study of the Incarnation and Its Consequences* (Longmans, Green, 1946).

53. Allen, *Fear of the Lord*, 47.

of its hierarchy and jurisdiction), and the history of salvation.[54] Among the great *ressourcement* theologians, Yves Congar, Louis Bouyer, and Joseph Ratzinger particularly stand out for the careful attention that they give to the Church; and Hans Urs von Balthasar is not far behind. *Lumen Gentium* and the *Catechism of the Catholic Church* offer profound and doctrinally weighty ecclesiologies.[55] Guy Mansini's recent textbook *Ecclesiology* is noteworthy for its insight and erudition.[56] Readers seeking comprehensive theological accounts of the Church should consult these writings, which have informed my book.

What I seek to offer instead is a set of reflections on the reality of the Church, filled with the Spirit of truth and united to Christ on the path of his cross, in light of the ongoing problems of sin, conflict, error, and division. The theological reality of the Church is not its ideal reality but rather is its revealed (in Scripture and Tradition) reality.[57] My first five chapters focus upon biblically

54. See Benoît-Dominique de La Soujeole, OP, *Introduction to the Mystery of the Church*, trans. Michael J. Miller (The Catholic University of America Press, 2014); and see the multi-volume English translation of Charles Journet, *The Church of the Word Incarnate* (Emmaus Academic Press, 2025). See also John F. O'Neill, *Trinitarian Ecclesiology: Charles Journet, the Divine Missions, and the Mystery of the Church* (The Catholic University of America Press, 2024). For Journet, as O'Neill says, the Church is "a visible communion in fully Christic charity. Each individual who possesses charity is related properly to the Holy Spirit. . . . The assumed humanity of Christ that is related to the person of the Holy Spirit is the conjoined instrument of the Word for distributing habitual grace and charity to others by which they are indwelt by and related to the Holy Spirit" (*Trinitarian Ecclesiology*, 339–40).

55. For discussion, see Joseph Ratzinger, "The Ecclesiology of the Second Vatican Council," in *Church, Ecumenism and Politics*, 3–28, including its "Appendix: Modern Variations of the Concept of the People of God." Indebted to Endre von Ivánka's *Rhomäerreich und Gottesvolk: Das Glaubens-, Staats- und Volksbewußtsein der Byzantiner und seine Auswirkung auf die ostkirchlich-osteuropäische Geisteshaltung* (Karl Alber, 1968), Ratzinger addresses distortions of the notion of the "people of God": "The oldest roots of the transformation of the concept of the people of God into something political are visible in Eusebius of Caesarea: in his idea of Christians as the 'third nation' to which the 'two others,' the pagans and the Jews, lead up. If Clement of Alexandria presented the providential role of the Greeks, what we get with Eusebius is the evaluation of the Roman Empire in terms of salvation history and its classification within God's plan of salvation. . . . From this point of view Constantine's empire appears not just as the summit of Roman civilization but as the fulfilment and completion of that line of tradition whose prototype is to be found in Abraham. This nation of people is now at work absorbing the other nations into itself and creating from all of them the 'new people of God' promised by the prophets" (Ratzinger, "The Ecclesiology of the Second Vatican Council," 23).

56. See Guy Mansini, OSB, *Ecclesiology* (The Catholic University of America Press, 2021).

57. Ratzinger points out that theologians can themselves act as though theology is irrelevant: "Theology can quite simply, instead of seeking truth itself in its authoritative texts, explain

revealed images of the Church: Bride of Christ, Family of God, Body of Christ, People of God, and Mother. To these chapters, I add two further ones, on the Church's marks of apostolicity and catholicity, respectively. An earlier book, *Engaging the Doctrine of the Holy Spirit*, already took up ecclesiological themes, including the kingdom of God, the Church and the Holy Spirit, and the marks of unity and holiness; and I discussed the Church in relation to the people of Israel in my *Engaging the Doctrine of Israel*.[58] This explains why I do not treat either Israel or the kingdom of God in the present book, as well as why the present book only treats two marks of the Church and does not explore the image of the "Temple of the Spirit." Mariological reflections, with intrinsic reference to the Church, shape my *Engaging the Doctrine of Jesus (and Mary)*, and so I have not repeated that material in this book.[59]

While affirming that the Church is constituted by the Holy Spirit's action, the ecclesiologist Nicholas M. Healy states, "Conflict, error and sin are inherent aspects of the concrete church."[60] Although I do not agree with all that he means by this (since the "concrete church" includes its divine dimension), I attend to

the historical conditions in which these texts arose, try to reconstruct their original significance by using historical methods, and compare them critically with the interpretations which have come into being during the course of their history" (Ratzinger, "Theology and the Church's Political Stance," in *Church, Ecumenism and Politics*, 152–64, at 157). As Ratzinger indicates, such positivism makes attractive (by comparison) critical theory's turn to praxis.

58. See my *Engaging the Doctrine of the Holy Spirit: Love and Gift in the Trinity and the Church* (Baker Academic, 2016); and my *Engaging the Doctrine of Israel: A Christian Israelology in Dialogue with Ongoing Judaism* (Cascade, 2021).

59. See my *Engaging the Doctrine of Jesus (and Mary): A Traditional, Historical-Critical, and Mariological Christology* (Cascade, 2025). For an extensive discussion, covering every angle, see Pierre Kocian, OSB, *Marie et l'Église: Compénétration des deux mystères* (Parole et Silence, 2018). See also John L. Nepil, *A Bride Adorned: Mary-Church Perichoresis in Modern Catholic Theology* (Emmaus Academic, 2023), 29: "Mary and the Church are first and foremost Christological realities. Without a doubt, the greatest concern in the history of the Mary-Church parallel has been preserving their right relationship to Jesus Christ. . . . Just as without him Mary and the Church would not exist, so too Mary and the Church are unintelligible apart from Christ." See also the work of the Protestant art historian Matthew J. Milliner, *Mother of the Lamb: The Story of a Global Icon* (Fortress, 2022); and Carrie Frederick Frost, *Maternal Body: A Theology of Incarnation from the Christian East* (Paulist, 2019).

60. Nicholas M. Healy, *Church, World and the Christian Life: Practical-Prophetic Ecclesiology* (Cambridge University Press, 2000), 175.

both the divine and the human dimensions of the Church, a task that includes reflecting upon error and conflict. I take inspiration from Hans Urs von Balthasar's essay "Casta Meretrix" ("Chaste Harlot"), which sets forth the mystery of the Church in striking terms, drawn from the New Testament and the Church Fathers. As Balthasar states, "The New Testament speaks of the safeguards granted Christ's Church, but at the same time, in harsh juxtaposition, there is the threat of abuse, the possibility of defection. Nowhere is the immaculateness of the bride an established fact for the bride just to accept and not to worry about any further."[61] For Balthasar, and I agree with him, the solution is to face up to sin and to reach out for the cross, for Christ our Savior. The crucified Christ alone, not the Church's resources as such, is our "salvation and security."[62] The Church must follow the Savior always by "follow[ing] the way of the Cross in penance and conversion."[63]

In Mary, of course, the Church is fully holy; and the Church's sacraments and teachings are holy, as are the Church's offices or "structures she is given and guaranteed from above."[64] The issue is how to balance appreciating the beauty and truth of the Spirit-filled Church with the necessity of addressing the Church's present woundedness and conflict; and the resolution must be

61. Hans Urs von Balthasar, "Casta Meretrix," trans. John Saward, in *Explorations in Theology*, vol. 2, *Spouse of the Word* (Ignatius, 1991), 193–288, at 208. I should note that Balthasar draws insight regarding the sinfulness of the members of the Church from Emile Mersch, SJ, *The Theology of the Mystical Body*, trans. Cyril Vollert, SJ (Herder, 1951), 303. Mersch distinguishes between actions of the Church in which it is Christ who is acting (as in the sacraments and in solemn doctrinal and moral teaching), and actions of the Church in which it is humans who are acting (and who therefore inevitably act to some degree as sinners). See also Jacques Maritain, *On the Church of Christ: The Person of the Church and Her Personnel*, trans. Joseph W. Evans (University of Notre Dame Press, 1973), 40: "The Church is the Beloved of Christ, she is His plenitude. And yet this same Church is penitent. She accuses herself, often in very harsh terms, she weeps for her failures, she begs to be purified, she pleads unceasingly for forgiveness (she does so every day in the Lord's Prayer), she sometimes cries out to God from the depths of the abyss, as from the depths of his anguish one who fears damnation. . . . The penitence of the Church shows us that if, in the image of Christ immaculate, the Church also is immaculate, she is not so however in the same manner as He is. In other words the mystical Body of Christ is not in the same relationship with its members as the physical body of Christ is with its."

62. Balthasar, "Casta Meretrix," 210.

63. Balthasar, 210.

64. Balthasar, 210; cf. 193.

cross-centered. Without this emphasis on the cross, ecclesiology would not be recognizable as the fruit of divine revelation within our sinful history. Indeed, without this emphasis, ecclesiology risks becoming an illusory sociology of immanent human progress.

The Catholic Church really is God's Bride, Family, Body, and People. Yet, the Catholic Church regularly endures turmoil and disillusionment, in which the face of the Church can be obscured. This fact can be deeply distressing. At times, Catholics have responded by falling into hasty solutions that do not address the spiritual root of the problem.[65] To take a contemporary example, in a nation that contains over sixty million non-Catholics, the Catholic Church in Germany in 2022 received only 1,447 converts—while over 500,000 Germans disaffiliated from the Catholic Church in that same year. Evangelization has nearly disappeared in German Catholicism, as has faith in the triune God,

65. See Adam A. J. DeVille's *Everything Hidden Shall Be Revealed: Ridding the Church of Abuses of Sex and Power* (Angelico, 2019). DeVille argues that the Church's structures of authority must be changed, now that we know the extent of the "sinister agenda" that pope and bishops have foisted upon the Church in their desperate cleaving to power (12). He recognizes, of course, that "no structures are fail-safe; no systems or processes are perfect; none can perfectly guarantee there will be no future problems" (14). But the will-to-power of the pope and bishops must be opposed, given that "for those who know a modicum of church history, it has always been this way—a powerful clergy descending into corruption until the much larger body of lay faithful in various ways rises up to push for change" (15). I disagree with this reading of Church history; it has just as often been holy clergy rising up to push deeply corrupt laity to change. To solve the problems in the Church of today, DeVille proposes the creation of "full and standing synods so that the task of governing a diocese now involves the laics and clergy having both voice and vote in matters of policy (not doctrine) and election, including the election of bishops. The national conferences of bishops, in turn, would be reconstituted so that . . . these conferences would become real, full, and properly functioning synods, again having legislative and electoral powers" (18–19). My concern is that this would further bog down the Church's members in party-politics, neglecting the real heart of the Church's life. It would end up privileging Church bureaucrats and turning the bishops (even more than already is the case) into bureaucrats and politicians. On the other hand, I agree with DeVille that the Church should resist an "unhealthy fixation of papal father-figures" (24), as though popes never err in any way. See also Antonio Rosmini's romantic view of the early Church, forgetting that politics generally involves bitter struggle and the early Church was often riven by doctrinal and moral disagreements: "In those days the people may be said to have been a faithful counsellor to the Church's rulers. An account was rendered by the Bishop to the people of all that he did in the government of the diocese. . . . Hence also arose the intimate union of Bishops with their presbyters, whose advice they sought in every matter concerning the government of the Church." Rosmini, *Of the Five Wounds of the Holy Church*, ed. H. P. Liddon (Rivingtons, 1883), 88–90; and see 246–54 on the election of bishops by clergy and laity.

the Paschal Mystery of Christ, and the Eucharist. Among the 20 million German Catholics in 2022, only about 1 million attended Mass on any given Sunday—and the German Church actually *employs* 800,000 people, likely constituting a significant portion of the weekly Mass attendance.[66]

The co-president of the German "Synodal Way," Irme Stetter-Karp, had this to say in light of the 2022 data cited above: "The Church has squandered trust, particularly badly as a result of the abuse scandal. But it is also currently not showing enough determination to implement visions for a future of being a Christian in the Church."[67] In her view, the solution to revitalizing Catholic faith in Germany is to insist that the Church's understanding of the priesthood, the Eucharist, marriage, and human sexuality have all been wrong since nearly the beginning, and to institute democratic procedures like those enjoyed by German Protestants (whose churches are equally empty). Why this solution would reignite Catholic life and practice is unclear. Common sense suggests that it would bury the German Catholic Church once and for all, but Stetter-Karp imagines that a new liberative Church is already taking shape, one that will finally serve the world's progress. She sides with the theologians who, in Ratzinger's words, see "two Churches as existing today: one which is an instrument of liberation and which . . . seeks to bring the society of the future into being—the kingdom of God . . . ; the other that maintains society as it has existed up till now and is in reaction against this new Church."[68]

66. See Luke Coppen and Brendan Hodge, "German Catholics Left Church in Record Numbers Last Year," *The Pillar*, June 28, 2023, https://pillarcatholic.com/p/german-catholics-left-church-in-record. See Tracey Rowland's discussion of the German Catholic Church's "Febronianism" (what I have called "Constantinianism") in her *Unconformed to the Age: Essays in Catholic Ecclesiology* (Emmaus Academic, 2024), 116.

67. See Coppen and Hodge, "German Catholics Left Church."

68. Ratzinger, "Theology and the Church's Political Stance," 159. Ratzinger cites the work of Ernesto Cardenal; see for example Cardenal's *The Gospel in Solentiname*, trans. Donald D. Walsh (Orbis Books, 2010). Ratzinger goes on to say, with respect to attempts in the two decades after the Council to democratize the Church: "The concept of grassroots democracy . . . seems especially suitable for transfer to the Church because it appears to correspond in its inner nature with the idea of the congregation and thus of the structure of the people of God

From the very opposite end of the theological spectrum, the British Catholic thinker John Rist proposes six reforms to address Catholicism's contemporary difficulties: (1) ending the pope's ability to appoint bishops; (2) returning the election of the pope to the Roman clergy and restructuring the College of Cardinals so as to enable the college to dismiss a pope for heterodoxy; (3) encouraging local bishops to represent local interests while embracing unity in doctrine and morality; (4) restricting the term "infallibility" to mean only "that the Church and the pope must always cling to basic Catholic dogma" (limited to doctrines warranted explicitly by the Church Fathers); (5) recognizing a hierarchy of non-dogmatic truths; and (6) suppressing the Jesuits.[69] Rist also suggests that "the pope's title of 'Patriarch of the West' should be

that is based on the local Church. Satiety with the anonymity of large-scale societies makes its contribution to let the idea of the self-determining small community seem the solution and on this basis to present the Church an oasis of freedom. The universal Church and its sacramental structure now become the official Church which belongs, along with all other political, social and economic large-scale structures, to the powers that block freedom, while Christianity in the sense of Jesus is only to be found in the congregation and the congregation forms the clear and understandable framework in which everyone can share in everything and so freedom is realized" (Ratzinger, "Theology and the Church's Political Stance," 194). Ratzinger responds critically, "When the element of the congregation is isolated and separated off from the broad stream of the sacramental community of the entire Church the freedom of the congregation evaporates into play-acting and becomes void. . . . Because the unreality of this kind of retreat can never remain hidden for long, there is in the Church too the shift to the radical idea of freedom," namely, "the freedom of the kingdom of God"—which entails "levelling the Church down to the sphere of the political" (194–95).

69. John M. Rist, *Infallibility, Integrity and Obedience: The Papacy and the Roman Catholic Church, 1848–2023* (James Clarke, 2023), 213–14. Rist makes clear that he holds to a different view of papal infallibility than that taught dogmatically by Vatican I. Along lines explicitly influenced by Ignaz von Döllinger, he states, "Infallibility . . . should be understood to mean that the Church, through its official magisterium—its bishops, popes and councils—will be infallibly led to all truth—eventually. . . . At any particular time present teachings should be accepted as truth as far as we know it, but subject to correction if shown to be based on unavoidable ignorance or theological contradiction. To engage in the search for such correction is part of the task of the theologian, the other part being to teach accurately what has come to be known over time and until the present, without intruding as certain truths possible corrections which every theologian has a duty to discuss with his colleagues, indeed with any member of the Church who shows himself or herself equipped to engage in theological debate, it being understood that such people do not constitute a rival 'magisterium.' Indeed, the term 'magisterium' itself, as we have implied, has been a source of unnecessary confusion and excessive clericalism. It needs to be viewed in line with our revised account of an *eventually* complete inerrancy guaranteed by the Holy Spirit. We should recall that among the Orthodox the infallibility even of councils, let alone of individuals, has never been insisted on. . . . What is certain is that the Church can do without further double-think about infallibility and inerrancy. God, we are taught, will lead us to all truth, yet—and leaving aside the *depositum fidei*—we do not know what degree of truth we have thus far obtained" (216). The content of the *depositum fidei*, however, is precisely what

restored"—as indeed Pope Francis did in April 2024—and that the pope should, at his installation as pope, be required to take "an oath to act in accordance with scripture and tradition."[70]

Rist and Stetter-Karp are far apart in many of their beliefs, but they nevertheless have a fundamental similarity. They both offer largely political and managerial solutions to the difficulties facing the Catholic Church. Ecclesiologically, the real solutions must go deeper. Origen is correct that "he who is called to the office of the bishop is not called to rulership but to service to the whole Church. . . . In the Church he who leads is the servant to all [see Mark 9:35]."[71] But while servant-leadership is necessary, Protestant and Orthodox history shows that reducing the power of the pope does not result (to say the least) in any guarantee of greater truth and love. The quest for a managerial solution to the Church's problems—as distinct from spiritual repentance and recommitment to Jesus Christ crucified and to the life of faith and the sacraments—is bound to fail. It should not surprise us that the quest to fix the Church managerially unites Catholics from otherwise opposite doctrinal perspectives.

What is needed instead is further personal and communal immersion in what Balthasar calls "the sacrificial fire of the Cross,"[72] which, as a Spirit-filled fire in Jesus himself, is the heart of the Church as God's Bride, Family, Body, and People. In this sense, the present book's third chapter, on the cross at the center of the Body of Christ, is the main theme of this book. It is the

is at issue—although Rist indicates (like Döllinger) that this content is known by the end of the patristic period and that anything else belongs to the realm of probability at best.

70. Rist, 215.

71. Origen, *Homilies on Isaiah*, trans. Elizabeth Ann Dively Lauro (The Catholic University of America Press, 2021), 89.

72. Hans Urs von Balthasar, "Who Is the Church?," trans. A. V. Littledale with Alexander Dru, in *Explorations in Theology*, 2:143–91, at 2:180. See also Matthias Joseph Scheeben's reflections on the altar fire, which I discuss in chapter 5 of my *Engaging the Doctrine of Jesus (and Mary)*. For the Passion of Christ as revealing the deifying love of God and as establishing justice by freely paying Adam's penalty (death) so as to overcome our just bondage to death, see St. Peter Chrysologus, "Sermon 72B," in his *Selected Sermons*, vol. 3 trans. William B. Palardy (The Catholic University of America Press, 2005), 6–11.

cross to which the Spirit unites us as Christ's Bride, Family, and Body in the Eucharistic liturgy, glorifying the Father.[73]

IV. THE PLAN OF THE WORK

Let me now describe the seven chapters in more detail. Chapter 1 analyzes the Church as the Bride of Christ. I place this chapter first because it is for me the most wondrous image of the Church, due to the fact that the purpose of creation is the unfathomably intimate marriage of God and creation through Jesus Christ who is the "bridegroom" (John 3:29).[74] The Letter to the Ephesians portrays human marriage as "a great mystery" insofar as it signifies Christ and the Church (Eph 5:32). With the cross at the very center, Ephesians 5:25–27 urges that husbands should love their wives "as Christ loved the Church and gave himself up for her, that he might sanctify her, having cleansed her by the washing of water with the word, that he might present the Church to himself in splendor." Already in the Scriptures of Israel, God repeatedly promised to marry his people: "For your Maker is your husband,

73. Tracey Rowland states aptly, "Without the theology of the Cross and, in particular, the understanding of Christ as the Paschal lamb, there can be no proper understanding of the Eucharist; and without a proper understanding of the Eucharist, there can be no proper understanding of the priesthood, or the Church. . . . Christ has become detached from the Cross as a prime cause of the contemporary crisis within Western Christianity" (*Unconformed to the Age*, 144). For the view that the theology of the cross has been profoundly abused in a manner that has ecclesiological implications, so that "the condemned figures outside of the church" such as "Gnostics, Jews, heretics, radicals, Black Americans" are the ones who "absorb divine punishment and wrath, and by doing so highlight the divine preservation of the elect body"—and for a sharp critique of the theology of martyrdom as "a transactional logic of debt and surplus, dependent . . . on surrogate holy bodies and excrescent reprobate ones"—see Travis E. Ables, *The Body of the Cross: Holy Victims and the Invention of the Atonement* (Fordham University Press, 2022). While I disagree with his critique of the theology of martyrdom and merit, I agree with him that the cross must never be conceived as God taking out his wrath upon an innocent victim who placates God's wrath by standing in for sinners, and I agree with him that the history of Christian violence against Jews and heretics (et al.) is shameful. For my understanding of Christ's cross, see chapter 5 of *Engaging the Doctrine of Jesus (and Mary).*

74. See chapter 1 of my *Engaging the Doctrine of Marriage: Human Marriage as the Sign and Sacrament of the Marriage of God and Creation* (Cascade, 2020). In addition to the critical feminist work that I address therein, see Susan A. Ross, "The Bride of Christ and the Body Politic: Body and Gender in Pre–Vatican II Marriage Theology," *Journal of Religion* 71, no. 3 (1991): 345–61.

the Lord of hosts is his name" (Isa 54:5). By his saving cross, the New Adam has united the Church, the New Eve, to himself.

Chapter 1 introduces this image of the Church as Christ's Bride through two medieval commentators on the Song of Songs: Bernard of Clairvaux and Gregory of Narek. The Church as Bride is holy, filled with the gifts of Christ the Bridegroom. The Bride yearns to join her ascended Lord. But the Bride is not yet what she will fully be at the consummation of all things; indeed, the Bride remains far from this perfection. I explore how Bernard and Gregory, in their respective commentaries, understand the Church as Christ's Bride in the economy of sanctification. I then turn to Yves Congar and Anscar Vonier, who both made significant contributions to twentieth-century Catholic ecclesiology. Congar held that the neo-scholastic theology of his day was too unwilling to admit the sins that mar the Church. By contrast, Vonier held that theologians were overemphasizing the Church's wounds and underestimating the sacramental power by which Christ, through the Church, ministers to the woundedness of the Church's members. Vonier emphasizes that Christ's Ascension makes possible the sacramental radiation of his cruciform glory in his Bride the Church, through the power of the Spirit. Both Vonier and Congar see this as Christ's sharing of his catholicity with his Bride. I seek to offer a balanced perspective, praising God for the grace of the Holy Spirit that continues to perfect his bridal members who take seriously (in Origen's words) "what it means to share communion with the Church."[75]

The second chapter explores the Church as the Family of God. The apostle Paul states, "When we cry, 'Abba! Father!' it is the Spirit himself bearing witness with our spirit that we are children of God, and if children, then heirs, heirs of God and fellow heirs with Christ, provided we suffer with him in order that we may also be glorified with him" (Rom 8:15–17; see also Gal 4:7).

75. Origen, *Homilies on Psalms 36–38*, trans. Michael Heintz (The Catholic University of America Press, 2023), Homily 2, Psalm 37 [38], p. 200.

As children of God and heirs of God, we belong to God's Family. Indeed, through faith in Christ and baptism into his death and Resurrection, we "are all sons of God" (Gal 3:26)—sons in the Son, sons of the Father by the Spirit. The establishment of the Family of God began with his people Israel. God tells Moses, "You shall say to Pharaoh, 'Thus says the Lord, Israel is my first-born son'" (Exod 4:22). Yearning for redemption, Isaiah reminds God, "You, O Lord, are our Father" (Isa 63:16). The Pentecostal theologian Ivan Hartsfield comments, "Christ is elevated to be the head of a new humanity. In response to the familial relationship established between Christ and his brothers and sisters, Christ proclaims God's holy character to his family and sings praises with them in the midst of his church."[76] The eschatological Family of God comes about through our filial adoption in Christ.

Chapter 2 explores the Church as the Family of God in light of the urgent need for human political and economic development, given that (as Ramiro Pellitero says) "the relations between Christians are characterized by a familial spirit" and a family cares for and shares with each other.[77] Focusing on African Catholic theology—which gives a very significant role to image of the Church as a Family and sometimes leans in a liberationist direction—my chapter begins by examining the New Testament background to the image of the Church as God's Family. I then investigate how recent African theologians have treated the Church as God's Family, with an eye to both the contributions and the pitfalls of this image. Third, I set forth the place of the Family of God in Pope Benedict XVI's post-synodal apostolic exhortation *Africae Munus* (2011). My final section treats Joseph Ratzinger's *The Meaning of Christian Brotherhood*. The writings of Ratzinger/Benedict clarify the ways in which emphasizing the Church as God's Family need

76. Ivan L. Hartsfield, *Sanctified Imagination: Christian Holiness in Afro-Pentecostal Tradition* (Pickwick, 2023), 108. Hartsfield is here drawing upon C. H. Mason, "God's Oath," in *The History and Life Work of Bishop C. H. Mason, Chief Apostle, and His Co-Laborers*, by Mary Mason (Church of God in Christ, 1987), 53–54.

77. Ramiro Pellitero, *Eclesiología*, 2nd ed. (EUNSA, 2019), 89.

not lead to kinship-based exclusion or utopian politics but rather should lead to witnessing to God's Family and inspiring others to come to share in Christ's inheritance, won on the cross.

My third chapter investigates the Church as the Body of Christ. The image of the Church as Christ's Body comes from the apostle Paul. Describing the differentiated unity of the Church—in light of some believers' refusal to be subject to ecclesiastical authority—Paul instructs the Romans, "For as in one body we have many members, and all the members do not have the same function, so we, though many, are one body in Christ, and individually members one of another" (Rom 12:4–5). In 1 Corinthians he makes the same point, noting that "you are the body of Christ and individually members of it" and emphasizing that "God has so composed the body, giving the greater honor to the inferior part, that there may be no discord in the body, but that the members may have the same care for one another. If one member suffers, all suffer together; if one member is honored, all rejoice together" (1 Cor 12:24–27). In the Old Testament, the people of Israel similarly comprise a differentiated unity in the sight of God. The cross of Christ, bearing our sins, reconciles the whole human race. Christ calls all people to become members of his reconciled and Spirit-filled Body.

Since Christ came to "reconcile us both [Jews and Gentiles] to God in one body through the cross" (Eph 2:16), I argue in this chapter that the cross must have a central place in our understanding of the Body of Christ. In the first half of the twentieth century, the central place of the cross was recognized by theologians such as Emile Mersch, Fulton Sheen, Charles Journet, and Pius Parsch. Pope Pius XII's 1943 encyclical *Mystici Corporis* also fully integrates the cross. By contrast, as I show, from around 1960 onward, Thomistic theologians emphasized communion ecclesiology and the Spirit's work in a manner that (perhaps because they felt that the cross had been overemphasized) largely left out the cross from the theology of the Body of Christ. I discuss such theologians as Jérôme Hamer, Marie-Joseph Le Guillou, George Sabra, Jean-Pierre Torrell, and Herwi Rikhof. Fortunately, this neglect of the cross is not determinative of *Lumen Gentium*'s theology of the Body of Christ. As a final step, I retrieve Aquinas's theology of the Mystical Body and show that Aquinas attends to the cross. I conclude that the cross must be central to our theology of the Church as the Mystical Body, because the Body of Christ is the Body of the crucified (and risen) Lord, and it is by the power of the cross that he saves us and configures us to his cruciform love as his Body.

My fourth chapter examines the Church as the People of God. In Romans 9:25, Paul quotes Hosea 2:23 while discussing the inclusion of the Gentiles in the Church: "As indeed he [God] says in Hosea, 'Those who were not my people I will call 'my people,' and her who was not beloved I will call 'my beloved.'" The First Letter of Peter describes the Church as "a holy nation, God's own people" (1 Pet 2:9). Peter continues along the same lines as found in Hosea and Paul: "Once you were no people but now you are God's people; once you had not received mercy but now you have received mercy" (1 Pet 2:10). In preparing for the exodus from Egypt to the promised land, God assures Israel, "I will take you for my people, and I will be your God; and you shall know that I am the Lord your God" (Exod 6:6–7). Likewise, God identifies Israel as a holy people in Deuteronomy 7:6, where Moses tells the Israelites, "For you are a people holy to the Lord your God; the Lord your God has chosen you to be a people for his own possession." Despite Israel's sins and exile, God promises in Isaiah 62:11–12, "Say to the daughter of Zion, 'Behold, your salvation comes; behold, his reward is with him, and his recompense before him.' And they shall be called The holy people, The redeemed of the Lord." This promise is fulfilled in Christ. On behalf of the whole Church, Paul praises God the Father who "chose us in him [Christ] before the foundation of the world, that we should be holy and blameless before him" (Eph 1:3–4).

Chapter 4 begins with some background regarding the People of God and synodality as conceived by contemporary theologians such as Rafael Luciani and Massimo Faggioli, in light of the work of Yves Congar and Avery Dulles.[78] As a second step, I turn to Vatican II's Dogmatic Constitution on the Church, *Lumen Gentium*, which contains a portrait of the Church as the People of God that underscores the spiritual greatness of this people in its journey in the world. The third section of the chapter explores the reception of Vatican II's image of the People of God by *Concilium* theologians in the late 1960s and early 1970s, including Richard McBrien, Léon-Joseph Cardinal Suenens, and Gregory Baum. I suggest that these theologians moved from preconciliar "hierarchology," in which ecclesiology was sometimes reduced to the pope and his powers, to a vision of the People of God that repeated the same mistake of giving power (in this case, democratic power) the lead role in ecclesiology.[79] Today, the notion that the Church—through a "synodal conversion" described by

78. For reflection on the meaning and practice of synodality, see the International Theological Commission, *Synodality in the Life and Mission of the Church*, March 2, 2018, available at vatican.va; and the essays, comprising diverse German perspectives, in *Synodalität in der katholischen Kirche: Die Studie der Internationalen Theologischen Kommission im Diskurs*, ed. Markus Graulich and Johanna Rahner (Herder, 2020)—most helpfully perhaps Karl-Heinz Menke, "Hans Küngs Definition der Kirche als Synode und das ITC-Dokument 'Synodalität in Leben und Sendung der Kirche,'" 196–219, which focuses critically on Küng's *Structures of the Church*, trans. Salvator Attanasio (Thomas Nelson & Sons, 1964). For further background, appreciatively explicating Pope Francis's broader theological vision, see Juan Carlos Scannone, SJ, *Theology of the People: The Pastoral and Theological Roots of Pope Francis*, trans. Kris Fankhouser and Carmen Fernandez-Aguinaco (Paulist, 2021); Stella Morra, *Dio non si stanca: La misericordia come forma ecclesiale* (EDB, 2015); Severino Dianich, *Magistero in movimento: Il caso papa Francesco* (EDB, 2016); Massimo Borghesi, *The Mind of Pope Francis: Jorge Mario Bergoglio's Intellectual Journey*, trans. Barry Hudock (Liturgical, 2018); and Austen Ivereigh, *The Great Reformer: Francis and the Making of a Radical Pope* (Henry Holt, 2014).

79. The use of the term "hierarchology" can be misleading, not least due to the overly negative approach to Pseudo-Dionysius that characterizes the work of Yves Congar (who coined the term). See Ephrem Reese, OP, "Congar's Imperfect Critique of 'Hierarchiology'," *Nova et Vetera* 20, no. 2 (2022): 545–73; and my appreciative analysis of Pseudo-Dionysius's ecclesiology in *Christ and the Catholic Priesthood: Ecclesial Hierarchy and the Pattern of the Trinity* (Hillenbrand Books, 2010). Defending oft-maligned Jesuit theologians against the charge of hierarchology, see Bernhard Knorn, SJ, "The Church and the Churches: Ecclesiology and the View of Non-Catholic Christians in the Roman School," in *The Roman School: Nineteenth-Century Jesuit Theology and Its Achievements*, ed. Aaron Pidel, SJ, Matthew Levering, and Justin M. Anderson (Brill, 2024), 55–77; and Eric J. Demeuse, *Unity and Catholicity in Christ: The Ecclesiology of Francisco Suárez, S.J.* (Oxford University Press, 2022). It seems to me that, in some ways at least, "hierarchology" existed and deserves critique.

Austen Ivereigh as "one vast act of self-transcendence, opening the Church as an institution to the Spirit and the people, and to the Spirit in the people"—is at long last becoming the Church that Jesus intended, the Church of the book of Acts, overestimates the transformative power of democratic leadership-sharing, as centuries of Protestant experience will confirm.[80] The focus on power puts the ecclesiological emphasis in the wrong place.

With this danger in view, the last section of chapter 4 examines the theological reflections on the Church as the People of God offered by the Anglican theologian Ephraim Radner. Radner is best known for his erudite insistence upon the Church's sinfulness, beginning with the division of the Church and Israel, and continuing onward in a history that is filled with the presence of deeply humbling Christian abuse of the Gospel. Radner's attention to sin, death, and brokenness rightly grounds ecclesiology in our need for a Savior. Radner also emphasizes the importance of the diversity of nations in the Church, as well as the importance of recognizing the Church as a concrete "people" in order to avoid turning the Church into something otherworldly and apolitical. Here again the cross takes center stage: the People of God is such a people when following Jesus's cruciform path.[81]

80. See Austen Ivereigh, "Foreword: Embracing Synodal Conversion," in *Witnesses of Synodality: Good Practices and Experiences*, ed. Jos Moons, SJ (Paulist, 2024), ix–xiii, at xi. Much better is Pope Francis's *Walking Together: The Way of Synodality* (Orbis Books, 2023). Francis warns against living "a 'gaseous,' vague Christianity . . . without the necessary 'bite' of the Gospel," and he emphasizes, "We are asked to adopt an attitude aimed at living the Gospel and making it transparent. . . . Evangelization lived in this way is not a tactic of ecclesial repositioning in today's world, or an act of conquest, domination, or territorial expansion; it is not a 'retouching' that adapts the Church to the spirit of the times but makes her lose her originality and prophetic mission. Nor does evangelization mean an attempt to recover habits and practices that made sense in other cultural contexts. No, evangelization is a path of discipleship in response to love for the One who first loved us (cf. 1 John 4:19); a path, then, that makes possible a faith that is lived, experienced, celebrated, and witnessed with joy" (88, 90–91).

81. Tomáš Halík offers the kind of historicist reading of the "people of God" that I seek to challenge in this chapter. He states, "Let us go back to the definition of the Church as God's people journeying through history. This image represents the Church in motion and in a process of constant change. God shapes the form of the Church in history, is revealed in it, and teaches it through the events of history. God happens in history. This dynamic conception of God in the perspective of process theology is the impetus for a dynamic understanding of the Church. Both the institutional form of the Church and its theological knowledge evolve in the course of history. . . . If our theology, our constant reflection on faith, were to lose its open

Chapter 5 explores the Church as our Mother. In Galatians 4, Paul provides an allegorical reading of Genesis's story of Sarah and Hagar and argues that the Church stands in the place of Sarah and of the heavenly Jerusalem. He states, "The Jerusalem above is free, and she is our mother" (Gal 4:26). Paul goes on to apply the prophecy of Isaiah 54:1 to the Church. Isaiah 54:1 reads, "Sing, O barren one, who did not bear; break forth into singing and cry aloud, you who have not had labor pains! For the children of the desolate one will be more than the children of her that is married." In symbolism that biblical scholars have connected to Israel, Mary, and the Church, Revelation 12 likewise supports the identification of the Church as our Mother (as Jerome says, "The Apocalypse of John contains as many mysteries as words").[82] After describing "a woman clothed with the sun, with the moon

and pilgrim character, it would become an ideology, a false consciousness" (*The Afternoon of Christianity*, 186–87). Of course there is change (providentially guided by God), but there are constants as well. See also, for another example of the well-meaning historicism about which I am concerned, Tobias Nicklas, "All Must Interpret for All, and All Can Err: A Roman Catholic Perspective," in Stefan Alkier, Christos Karakolis, and Tobias Nicklas, *The Promise of Ecumenical Interpretation: Protestant, Catholic, Orthodox*, trans. Jacob N. Cerone and David M. Moffitt (Fortress, 2024), 33–52, at 33, 38–39: "Even if God's word is given to us in the Bible, we can never possess it immediately, directly, and for all times with complete certainty. . . . As much as we might sometimes wish it were otherwise, it would be neither in keeping with the greatness of God nor the diversity of human life (i.e., profoundly inhuman!) to view the goal of appropriate biblical interpretation simply as the distillation of biblical truth as if it were an eternally fixed entity (to be cast almost in a kind of catechism) in order to carry it unabridged and forever secured to the next generations. This would mean keeping the word of God, but not preserving it. The truth given by God cannot be brought under control and ultimately tamed in this way. . . . The diversity of voices in which the word of God expresses itself in human words in no way contradicts the idea of the living, *singular* truth of the *one* God, which for us humans can never be fully grasped or defined, that is, limited or brought under control." Although of course the Word of God cannot be exhaustively apprehended and is not transmitted in a merely static mode, Nicklas does not leave sufficient room for enduringly true dogma, which can indeed be defined and which succeeds in articulating realities of faith. Nicklas goes on to undermine dogma (and thus our ability to know ontological truth about the "Word" and the "Spirit") through further exaggerated language, though he contends that he is not "contradict[ing] the doctrine of infallibility": "As the Word of God in the Spirit this word always breaks through anew today and in the future. No one—be it an apostle, a bishop, or even the pope—can be sure of possessing the spirit of God in a particular decision" (46). Although for Nicklas magisterial statements can be given respect but can never be "entirely certain" (49), he wants also to affirm that "the Church as a temple of the *Spirit of God* (and only as such!) is in a position 'to *elucidate* in a binding manner the written and transmitted word of God)' (and thus *serve* it)" (50)—but I note that such elucidation (if binding and enduring) distills "biblical truth" as "eternally fixed" and "defined."

82. Jerome, "Epistle 53 to Paulinus," in *Exegetical Epistles*, vol. 1, trans. Thomas P. Scheck (The Catholic University of America Press, 2023), 196–216, at 215.

under her feet, and on her head a crown of twelve stars," the seer observes that "she was with child and she cried out in her pangs of birth, in anguish for delivery" (Rev 12:1–2). When she gives birth to the Messiah, she flees "into the wilderness, where she has a place prepared by God, in which to be nourished for one thousand two hundred and sixty days" (Rev 12:6). This Mother is the Church.

My chapter begins with a discussion of Galatians 4. Drawing on the work of David L. Schindler, I then suggest that for the Church to function as our Mother—nourishing and strengthening us in faith—we must constantly maintain a stance of receptivity toward the Church, from which we receive the Gospel and the sacraments. Indebted to Hugo Rahner and Max Thurian, among others, I show that Mary is the model of Mother Church and the model of all believers in receiving the fullness of Christ's gifting.[83] The question, however, is whether a stance of Marian receptivity toward Mother Church can be squared with *any* resistance—not "opposition" but "tension"—vis-à-vis the Church's Magisterium. In considering this question, I note that Henri de Lubac wrote frequently about Mother Church and about the need for receptivity toward the Church, while also locking horns with the Magisterium of Pope Pius XII. De Lubac's writings and example make clear that a Catholic theologian must reverence the Church

83. See also the recent observation by the Protestant theologian Brad East: "Mary is a figure of the Church. How so? The Church is chosen by God to bear His Son to the world. She contains within herself the good news—the marvelous fact—that God has drawn near to us, has become one of us, and she lives to share this news with others. In this role she is the handmaid, which is to say the servant, of the Lord God's mission to the world. Mary, by the grace of the Father through the power of the Spirit, bore within herself and gave birth to God's only-begotten Son. Likewise the Church, by faith in the Lord through the work of the Spirit in baptism, bears within herself and gives birth to sons and daughters of God. . . . The union of love between a man and a woman in marriage is a sign of the union of love between Christ and the Church [cf. Eph 5:32]. The one points to the other. This is why Mary, like the Church—or rather why the Church, like Mary—is the bride of Christ, and thus the new Eve to His new Adam. No human being ever knew Christ with greater intimacy than Mary. He is her own flesh and blood ('I am my beloved's and my beloved is mine,' Song 6:3); the *carne* of the incarnation is all Mary's. His human nature comes entirely from hers. So the Church, once again, finds herself reflected in Mary: the daughter and mother of God, the bridge of the King, the ark of the Lord, the root of the Messiah, the arch-prophet of the gospel of Jesus Christ." East, *The Church: A Guide to the People of God* (Lexham, 2024), 10, 13.

as Mother and must model Marian receptivity, but need not agree with all that the Magisterium says or renounce all activities that cut against the grain of the current Magisterium.

De Lubac remained obedient to Pope Pius XII, and this is an important lesson against strident opposition. Proper obedience does not mean actively consenting to what is false or doing what is sinful, but it does entail patience and humility, rather than stridency, in response to what one perceives as an error on the part of the Magisterium, whose authority the Holy Spirit bestows for the good of the whole Church. As John Henry Newman said, in words that came to have personal meaning for him in his own struggles with the Magisterium of Pope Pius IX, "Obedience to our ecclesiastical superior may subserve our growth in illumination and sanctity, even though he should command what is extreme or inexpedient, or teach what is external to his legitimate province."[84]

The book's final two chapters examine two marks of the Church—apostolicity and catholicity, respectively—in light of divisions among Christians.[85] Chapter 6 investigates the mark of apostolicity. In Ephesians 2:20, we read that the Church is "built upon the foundation of the apostles and prophets, Christ Jesus himself being the cornerstone." Paul instructs his appointed successor, Timothy, to guard the truth handed on to him by Paul

84. Newman, *An Essay on the Development of Christian Doctrine*, 87. This passage is present in the 1845 edition: see Newman, *An Essay on the Development of Christian Doctrine* [1845], ed. Stanley L. Jaki (Real View Books, 2003), 118.

85. Veli-Matti Kärkkäinen, an eminent Lutheran theologian, comments, "It is useful to consider the marks as both gifts and tasks. . . . On the one hand, they are gifts from God. We do not make the church one, holy, catholic, and apostolic; only God can. On the other hand, we see only too clearly that any church in the world, including our own, is far from those markers. Hence, each description [i.e., each mark] is also a matter of hope, which leads to action to more closely attain their realization." Kärkkäinen, *An Introduction to Ecclesiology: Historical, Global, and Interreligious Perspectives*, 2nd ed. (IVP Academic, 2021), 14. Although I recognize this element of hope and striving, I believe that the Catholic Church actually possesses these four marks rather than simply being "far from" them. Kärkkäinen's second chapter is "The Church as the People of God: Roman Catholic Ecclesiology," and he highlights (mistakenly in my view) the ecclesiology of Hans Küng as representative of Catholic ecclesiology. For Kärkkäinen's perspective—grounded in an extraordinary range of contemporary sources—see also the second part of his *Hope and Community*, vol. 5 of his *A Constructive Christian Theology for the Pluralistic World* (Eerdmans, 2017).

(in communion with the other apostles): "Follow the pattern of the sound words which you have heard from me, in the faith and love which are in Christ Jesus; guard the truth that has been entrusted to you by the Holy Spirit who dwells within us" (2 Tim 1:13–14). For its part, the book of Acts emphasizes the Church's apostolicity by remarking that the early Church "held steadfastly to the apostles' teaching and fellowship" (Acts 2:42). Lest there be any doubt about ongoing apostolicity (after the deaths of the apostles), the book of Revelation depicts the Church as the New Jerusalem whose "walls . . . had twelve foundations, and on them the twelve names of the twelve apostles of the Lamb" (Rev 21:14). As Didymus the Blind remarks in his commentary on Zechariah 7, "Jerusalem prosperous and inhabited along with its surrounding cities represents in a spiritual sense the Church and the orthodox beliefs."[86]

To explore the meaning of apostolicity, chapter 6 begins with the perspective of the Presbyterian theologian John Flett, who argues that Karl Barth is correct to define apostolicity as the apostles' stance of turning toward Christ and depending utterly upon Christ. Barth emphasizes that Christ must always be free to determine the Church's structure and dogma afresh, by speaking new words to the Church through the scriptural Word. By contrast, the *Catechism of the Catholic Church* understands apostolicity as involving apostolic succession and an enduringly true apostolic deposit of faith. In evaluating this claim, I first survey the perspectives of Barth and of the Orthodox theologian John D. Zizioulas. For Zizioulas—and I agree with him—the Church has both a historical connection to the apostles and a direct connection to the apostles arising from the fact that the Church even now participates in the kingdom-life of Christ. I then take up the perspective of Irenaeus of Lyons, in light of the work of biblical scholars such as Markus Bockmuehl and Richard Bauckham on

86. Didymus the Blind, *Commentary on Zechariah*, trans. Robert C. Hill (The Catholic University of America Press, 2006), 135.

the significance of the early Church's memory. In my view, Irenaeus's appreciation for the actual historical link to the apostles—through apostolic succession and apostolic tradition— remains requisite for the Church's understanding of apostolicity today. Yet, although some Christians lack apostolic succession, this hardly means that they entirely lack apostolicity. On the contrary, insofar as they ground themselves in the apostolic Scriptures and seek to live in accordance with the cruciform pattern of life manifested by Christ and the apostles, they have a real and effective participation in apostolicity.

The seventh and final chapter treats the Church's catholicity. Christ intends for the Church to be universal. In Mark 16:15, Jesus commands his disciples, "Go into all the world and preach the gospel to the whole creation." The Church is to be universal because Jesus is universal, and God's lordship is universal. In Matthew 28:18, Jesus lays claim to the fullness of all authority or power. Ephesians 1:10 proclaims that God has willed "to unite all things in him [Christ], things in heaven and things on earth." According to Ephesians 1:23, the Church is Christ's "body, the fulness of him who fills all in all." In Isaiah 49:6, God promises to accomplish a work through his chosen "servant" that will fill the whole earth: "It is too light a thing that you should be my servant to raise up the tribes of Jacob and to restore the preserved of Israel; I will give you as a light to the nations, that my salvation may reach to the end of the earth." Christ fulfills this prophecy.

Protestant theologians have raised the concern that the Catholic understanding of catholicity is merely an extension of the ancient Roman imperial mentality. In addition, some Protestant theologians have argued that the Catholic Church has been narrow and uncatholic by insisting that only churches united to the Church of Rome can be fully "catholic." Moreover, if the Catholic Church is already catholic or universal, then ecumenical dialogue hardly seems to be necessary for Catholics: as Rabanus Maurus commented in the year 819, the Catholic Church "is called 'catholic' [or 'universal'], because there is one Church of Christ in the whole world, which is both His spouse and His body."[87] In setting forth these ecumenical concerns in chapter 7, I draw upon the writings of Kenneth Collins and Jerry Walls, Kevin Vanhoozer (and Daniel Treier), and Hans Boersma. In response to these concerns, I draw attention to the portraits of catholicity articulated by Aidan Nichols, Avery Dulles, and Hans Urs von Balthasar, among others. These theologians emphasize Christ and the Trinity as the universal fullness toward which the Church strives, a fullness that Christ manifests on the cross.

***

Wondrously, the Church is Christ's Bride, Family, Body, and People; the Church is our Mother; the Church is apostolic and catholic. It is therefore possible and necessary to say joyfully with the theologian Paulinus Odozor, CSSp., that, in actual fact and not merely as a distant ideal, "the Christian life is a life centered on love."[88] If this were not true in the concrete life of believers, then there would be no Bride, Family, Body, or People—all of which are held together by Christ's cruciform love flowing through and uniting his members in love by the grace of the Holy Spirit. But at the same time, the Church is in certain serious ways weak, marred by sins, and susceptible to errors.

For this reason, the Church cries out for the consummation that Christ has promised. On the one hand, believers can say now with Odozor, "God is with me," since the Lord is intimately with each member of his Bride, Family, Body, and People. On the other hand, the difficulties constantly faced by the Church show

87. Bl. Hrabanus Maurus, *On the Formation of Clergy*, trans. Owen M. Phelan (The Catholic University of America Press, 2023), 28.

88. James Nkemngong, *Odozor: The Man, the Priest and the Scholar: Interview with Rev. Fr. Paulinus I. Odozor* (privately printed, 2024), 69. This interview-book was published in celebration of Odozor's fortieth anniversary of his priestly ordination, and it radiates living faith and real community in Christ.

that believers are still "*preparing* for a future with God."[89] The Church has already "come to Mount Zion and to the city of the living God, the heavenly Jerusalem" (Heb 12:22). The eschaton is already breaking in through the Church. It is already the case that the Church is "the temple of the living God" (2 Cor 6:16) and "a holy temple in the Lord; in whom [believers] are built into it for a dwelling place of God in the Spirit" (Eph 2:21–22). Yet, the Church suffers from "drooping hands," "weak knees," and "what is lame"; and the Church experiences tribulation and needs healing especially from the temptation of worldliness (Heb 12:12–13).

May the day come soon when Christ Jesus everlastingly "presents the Church to himself in splendor, without spot or wrinkle or any such thing" (Eph 5:27), and may we all be together with him, sharing in his glorification of the Father by the Spirit. And may believers here and now pray for and forgive one another, and "strive for peace with all men, and for the holiness without which no one will see the Lord" (Heb 12:14).

89. Nkemngong, 71 (italics mine).

1

Bride of Christ

I. INTRODUCTION

That the Church is the Bride of Christ is a biblical datum. In the prophecy of Hosea, God promises an eschatological day in which Israel will be fully his faithful Bride: "And in that day, says the Lord, you will call me, 'My husband,' and no longer will you call me, 'My Ba'al'" (Hos 2:16).[1] In the Gospel of John, John the Baptist presents Christ as the Bridegroom who comes to inaugurate the marriage of God with his people, the Bride.[2] John the Baptist explains his own relationship to Christ in terms of this nuptial imagery. He states, "He who has the bride is the bridegroom; the friend of the bridegroom, who stands and hears him, rejoices greatly at the bridegroom's voice; therefore this joy of mine is now full" (John 3:29). Similarly, in the book of Revelation, the seer has a vision of the final consummation of things, in which he sees (among other things) "the holy city, new Jerusalem, coming down out of heaven from God, prepared as a bride adorned for her husband" (Rev 21:2).[3] This glorious Bride is the fulfillment of God's promise to marry his people Israel. The Bride is

1. For discussion of prophetic texts regarding the marriage of God and Israel, in dialogue with the concerns of feminist biblical scholars, see my *Engaging the Doctrine of Marriage: Human Marriage as the Image and Sacrament of the Marriage of God and Creation* (Cascade, 2020), chapter 1.

2. See Jocelyn McWhirter, *The Bridegroom Messiah and the People of God: Marriage in the Fourth Gospel* (Cambridge University Press, 2006). Admittedly, as McWhirter says, "although John [the Baptist] asserts that Jesus 'has the bride,' she is never described and her role is never delineated" (142). Yet McWhirter recognizes that John's Gospel uses "marriage as a metaphor for the relationship between Jesus and believers," with believers constituting the Church (141).

3. For a theological commentary, see Peter J. Leithart, *Revelation 12–22* (Bloomsbury, 2018), 343–46.

specifically the Bride of Christ, according to the angel's remark to the seer: "Come, I will show you the Bride, the wife of the Lamb" (Rev 21:9). When in Ephesians 5 Paul seeks to explain how husbands should relate to their wives (and vice versa), he depicts the Church as the Bride of Christ.

I agree with Ephraim Radner, therefore, that the image of the Church as Christ's Bride "is not just one among many possible ways that the Church has been described. It is in fact arguably a foundational concept."[4] But the image of the Church as the Bride of Christ has not been central to recent Catholic ecclesiology. It receives little attention, for instance, in either *Lumen Gentium* or the *Catechism of the Catholic Church*. In these Magisterial texts, the image of the Church as Bride is not absent; thus, the *Catechism* observes at an important juncture, "It is in the Church that Christ fulfills and reveals his own mystery as the purpose of God's plan: 'to unite all things in him.' St. Paul calls the nuptial union of Christ and the Church 'a great mystery.' Because she is united to Christ as to her bridegroom, she becomes a mystery in her turn."[5] Nevertheless, not the nuptial image but the images of People of God and Body of Christ are by far the governing ones in recent Catholic ecclesiology.

Although there are good reasons for the centrality of the images of the People of God and Body of Christ, I maintain that the nuptial image merits special prominence. As the Episcopalian theologian Mark McIntosh says, the Church's nature is to be a

4. Ephraim Radner, *Church* (Cascade, 2017), 6–7.

5. *Catechism of the Catholic Church*, 2nd ed. (Libreria Editrice Vaticana, 1997), §772. Since I am citing the *Catechism* as an authority, see Avery Dulles, SJ, "The Challenge of the Catechism," in his *Church and Society: The Laurence J. McGinley Lectures, 1988–2007* (Fordham University Press, 2008), 157–74. Dulles describes the perspective of the religiously liberal Catholic theologians who opposed the publication of a universal catechism: "According to a widely prevalent view, religious truth consists in an ineffable encounter with the transcendent. This encounter may be expressed in symbols and metaphors, but it cannot be communicated by propositional language, since it utterly surpasses the reach of human concepts. All statements about revelation, moreover, are said to be so culturally conditioned that they cannot be transferred from one age or one cultural region to another. Every theological affirmation that comes to us from the past must be examined with suspicion because it was formulated in a situation differing markedly from our own. Each constituency must experience the revelation of God anew and find language and other symbolic forms appropriate to itself" (157).

sign of communion with God in the world and to point us toward the beatitude of perfect communion.[6] Arguably, there is no image for this interpersonal communion that is as sublime as the image of God's Bride, although Body of Christ comes close.[7] No mode of human interpersonal communion is deeper and more intimate than the one-flesh union of marriage. Even now, Christ has bestowed his gifts upon his bridal Church, and he is fashioning the Church into a perfect Bride that will fully commune with him in his divine life. The Orthodox theologian Paul Evdokimov comments that "the *essential nature of the Church* . . . is *communion between God and humankind*; it is prefigured in Eden, anticipated prophetically in the Old Covenant, accomplished in the Incarnation, and fully revealed in the Heavenly City (Rev 21:22), the living temple of the marriage of the Lamb," whose intimacy is expressed by the Song of Songs.[8] Similarly, in her vision of the Lord and the Servant, Julian of Norwich emphasizes that "the spouse, God's son, is at peace with his beloved wife, who is the

6. See Mark A. McIntosh, *Divine Teaching: An Introduction to Christian Theology* (Blackwell, 2008), 199.

7. Although in his *Introduction to the Mystery of the Church* Benoît-Dominique de La Soujeole, OP, focuses on the Church as the Body of Christ, the Temple of the Spirit, and the People of God, he also remarks: "Some biblical scholars think that the theme of the Church as the Bride of Christ is what led St. Paul to the theme of the Church as the Body of Christ. The account of the creation of woman from the side of sleeping Adam (Gen 2:21) is said to supply the immediate precedent for the theme of the Body of Christ. The bond between husband and wife is indeed a very close tie. . . . In the theology of the Old Testament, a man who marries incorporates his wife into himself. Moreover, the theme of Christ the Bridegroom is quite evident in the New Testament." De La Soujeole, *Introduction to the Mystery of the Church*, trans. Michael J. Miller (The Catholic University of America Press, 2014), 76. With both appreciation and caution, de La Soujeole adds, "This comparison of husband and wife to Christ and the Church is enlightening, but it is to be handled with care. It is enlightening because the Church is the Body of Christ inasmuch as she is Bride. . . . Moreover, this parallelism allows us to underscore the nature of Christ's dominion over the Church: a dominion of love. The limitation, however, is that the union between husband and wife is moral; it leaves intact the distinction of persons. But for the union of Christ and the Church this is insufficient. There is a relation in terms of which it is correct to say that Christ and the Church are 'all one thing' because one and the same life animates Christ and the Church, and become some of the most decisive acts for salvation (the preaching of the Gospel and the celebration of the sacraments) truly are conjoined acts of Christ and the Church" (76–77). In my view, however, de La Soujeole has minimized the one-flesh union (Gen 2:24) of husband and wife in a perfect marriage, as the marriage of Christ and his Bride is.

8. Paul Evdokimov, *Orthodoxy*, trans. Jeremy Hummerstone, updated by Callan Slipper (New City, 2011), 132.

fair maiden of endless joy."[9] Frances Young relates that Origen, in commenting on the Song of Songs, "focuses on the wisdom and understanding that comes to the church through Christ, her bridegroom."[10]

The present chapter will focus on the Church as Christ's Bride. Given the sins that often mar the face of the Church, it is important not to forget that Christ has truly "adorned" his Bride (Rev 21:2) with his gifts and that Christ's purpose is to "present the Church to himself in splendor" (Eph 5:27) in a union so intimate as to be "one flesh." Admittedly, Christian divisions can be exacerbated by contemplating the Church as Bride, since the controversies of the Reformation "drove all Christians to a desperate but divergently pursued search for the authentic Bride," grounded in a shared desire to be "identified . . . with the ecclesial woman embraced by her divine Bridegroom."[11] This fact should discourage ecclesiastical triumphalism, but it should not discourage love for the Bride.

My approach in this chapter is fairly simple. I will begin with Bernard of Clairvaux's and Gregory of Narek's respective testimonies to the Church as Christ's Bride in their commentaries on the Song of Songs. These commentaries depict the human yearning for God, to whom Christ draws us in his ascent to the right hand of the Father. Our yearning for God shines a light on the nuptial purpose of the Church, the community of persons who seek "to meet the bridegroom" and who make ready for the fullness of "the marriage feast" (Matt 25:1, 10). This is the healthy "otherworldly" aspect of the Church: its yearning for eschatological consummation, for the coming of Christ and the consummation of the Church as Bride. I wish to place strong emphasis on this

9. Julian of Norwich, *Showings*, trans. Edmund Colledge, OSA, and James Walsh, SJ (Paulist, 1978), 278.

10. Frances M. Young, *Brokenness and Blessing: Towards a Biblical Spirituality* (Baker Academic, 2007), 107.

11. Radner, *Church*, 6. Radner reminds us that "when there are disagreements, jealousies, betrayals, the Church that is bound to every Christian's love can, and has, become the object of deep bitterness and conflict, sometimes reaching a deadly pitch" (6).

new-exodus ascent in my ecclesiology: we must desire to be fully with the Lord.

Second, I turn to reflections by Yves Congar on the Church as Bride, followed by some insights of Anscar Vonier. Congar emphasizes the Bride's ongoing purification; Vonier emphasizes the sacramental graces and holiness that enliven the Bride. The fruit of the Spirit's work—the consummation of the new exodus and true liberation—will be the fullness of the "marriage of the Lamb" when "the Bride, the wife of the Lamb" will come in the splendor of perfect holiness or charity "out of heaven from God" (Rev 19:7; 21:2, 9). Ecclesiology must express this eschatological ordering to the marriage of God and his people—Bridegroom-Messiah and Bride, joined as one flesh.

II. BERNARD OF CLAIRVAUX AND GREGORY OF NAREK

Bernard of Clairvaux

Not surprisingly, in his commentary on the Song of Songs, Bernard depicts the Bride as the Church and the Bridegroom as Christ. The Song of Songs, of course, is marked by the absence of the Bridegroom and by the Bride's yearning for him. Even if Christ is present constantly to and in the Church, believers may experience Christ as absent when they are undergoing physical or spiritual suffering. Bernard explains such instances: "He [the Bridegroom] wishes to increase her desire, test her affection, and exercise her faculty of love."[12] He adds that the Bridegroom is Christ as known in the Spirit; thus, Christ is already present even in our Spirit-inspired yearning for him.

12. Bernard of Clairvaux, *On the Song of Songs*, vol. 4, *Sermons 67–86*, trans. Irene Edmonds (Cistercian, 1980), Sermon 75.1, p. 97.

Commenting on Song of Songs 1:4, "Draw me after you,"[13] Bernard notes that the Bride wants to go with the Bridegroom but is unable to do so of her own resources. He explains, "She who asks to be drawn wills to be drawn; she would not have asked if she possessed the power to follow her loved one of her own free will."[14] Since the Bride is the Church, the meaning of Song of Songs 1:4 is that the Church begs to be drawn after Christ "as her eyes followed the ascent of her Bridegroom into heaven."[15] The members of the Church have to deal not only with the difficulty of attaining virtue or holiness, but also with the burden of mortality and of the flesh's hunger, tiredness, passions, and disease. Here the Church and the individual soul are equally the Bride. The whole Church on earth is caught up in the human condition. Believers yearn for the perfection of life with Christ in God, by comparison to the trials of this life.

Christ's drawing the Church (and the soul) in an upward ascent takes place through the grace of the Holy Spirit, since without grace it is not possible to share Christ's life. Grace is needed not least because, although all people want the joys of divine life, few want the hardships involved in following Christ. Many people, says Bernard (speaking to Christ), want to "reign with you but not to suffer with you."[16] Often it is only on a person's deathbed, when there is no other option, that a person wishes to convert; but by then it may be too late to have the holiness that would interiorly fuel a good death.[17]

13. Song of Songs 1:3 in the Vulgate.

14. Bernard of Clairvaux, *On the Song of Songs*, vol. 2, *Sermons 21–46*, trans. Kilian Walsh, OCSO (Cistercian, 1983), Sermon 21.2, p. 5.

15. Bernard of Clairvaux, Sermon 21.1, p. 23.

16. Bernard of Clairvaux, Sermon 21.1, p. 23.

17. For a contemporary discussion of the good death, see David Deane, *The Tyranny of the Banal: On the Renewal of Catholic Moral Theology* (Lexington Books, 2023), chapter 4: "Dying and the Tyranny of Despair." Deane remarks, "Within premodern Christianity there is a clear understanding of the end or goal of life. This clear understanding makes possible an understanding of actions that are coherent with this end as rational and good. Within the secular, such notions of the good are less explicit. Therefore, a good death is increasingly seen as an easy death, a death that is quick or painless. It is because of this that 'physician assisted dying' represents the closest the secular can come to an account of a good death. In a context in which our panicked

Moreover, even if grace enables us to run after Christ, we must in this life never stop begging for grace, since there will be periods of dryness and apathy. Bernard concludes by observing that he hopes that his sermon will have filled his hearers' "desires with the memory of the generous kindness of him who is the Church's bridegroom, our Lord Jesus Christ."[18]

In an earlier sermon on the Song of Songs, Bernard recalls that even after his conversion, he still found himself feeling cold toward God. This coldness was reversed only by remembering or encountering a holy person. He notes that love for a human person affected him more than love for God, even though it was love for the human person that renewed his love *for God*. On this basis, Bernard comments that "the bride is the Church. She it is to whom much has been forgiven because she loves much."[19] The reference here is to Luke 7:47, in which Jesus forgives the woman who came to the house where Jesus was staying and anointed his feet with ointment. When we love and serve others, we stimulate our yearning for God in Christ. The sinner who is cold toward God will find that by loving others, the heart moves once more toward the Bridegroom. The Church is the "bride" who, though a sinner (or prostitute), has been forgiven because of her other-centered love—a love called forth by Christ.[20]

Commenting on another passage from the Song of Songs—"The king has brought me into his chambers" (1:4)—Bernard describes the Bride either as a soul who has converted many others, or else more likely as the Church. The Bride has been brought into Christ's "chambers" inasmuch as she is constantly

necrophobia is expressed as necrophilia, it is fitting that we imagine a good death as one in which we are actively killed. In contrast, the premodern approach . . . sees dying as a part of life. Life is a space in which virtues are practiced, shaping us as virtuous things. Dying, as a core part of this life, is also understood as a space for practicing the virtues" (150–51).

18. Bernard of Clairvaux, *On the Song of Songs*, Sermon 21.11, 2:13.

19. Bernard of Clairvaux, *On the Song of Songs*, vol. 1, *Sermons 1–20*, trans. Kilian Walsh, OCSO. (Cistercian, 1971), Sermon 14.7, p. 103.

20. Unfortunately, Bernard casts aspersions on "the Jew" in this sermon.

concerned for "those whom she has begotten through the Gospel."[21] The Bride is the "mother" of her people, who trust in her promise that "they will not at all be excluded by the favors bestowed" on the Bride.[22] Although the Bride dwells in the bedroom of the King (Christ), receiving great graces, the Bride still needs to be fully "conformed to her Bridegroom, who ascended into heaven and yet promised to be with his followers on earth until the end of the world."[23]

In a later sermon, Bernard reflects upon the temptations and trials that have troubled the Constantinian Church, after the era of Roman persecution of Christians ended. As Bernard depicts these centuries, heresies began to plague the Church because ambitious, worldly people came into the Church. Worldly people do not yearn for Christ or seek his grace, let alone strive to serve others rather than themselves. Bernard considers heresies to be the fruit of worldly ambition on the part of the heresiarch. Seeking to advance their own fame, the originators of the heresies "abandoned the Church, their mother, and for long afflicted her with diverse and perverse doctrines."[24] Bernard then bemoans the fact that the Church in his own day is befouled by something almost even worse, namely, hypocrisy. This "foul corruption permeates the whole body of the Church."[25] People are no longer public heretics, but they are interiorly enemies of Christ, despite their outward show of allegiance. What they seek from the Church is not Christ but rather worldly power and preferment. They do not yearn to ascend to the Bridegroom. Bernard calls upon Jesus, "the Bridegroom and defender of the Church," to slay this proud and idolatrous antichrist, which has produced a "sickness of the Church [that] is deeply rooted and incurable."[26]

21. Bernard of Clairvaux, *On the Song of Songs*, Sermon 23.1, 2:26.
22. Bernard of Clairvaux, Sermon 23.1, p. 26.
23. Bernard of Clairvaux, Sermon 23.1, p. 26.
24. Bernard of Clairvaux, Sermon 33.14, p. 157.
25. Bernard of Clairvaux, Sermon 33.15, p. 157.
26. Bernard of Clairvaux, Sermon 33.16, p. 158–59.

Commenting on Song of Songs 2:16 ("My beloved is mine and I am his"), Bernard states that the Bridegroom is God, while believers are the Bride.[27] When the Church is all that it should be, then the Church (the Bride) will be "transported with delight and enraptured by the long-awaited words of the Bridegroom."[28] The Bride will then have been fully made ready for the Bridegroom, and so the marriage of the Lamb can finally take place. Insofar as the Church is holy, the Church is already united to her Bridegroom. The Church as the Bride is known by the fact that she is "aflame with holy love" and "impelled with love," just as the woman in the Song of Songs is.[29]

Bernard admits that he himself does not yet embody what the Church as Bride is called to be. Despite his holy reputation, he is "a sinner" with "a long road" of spiritual discipline and purification ahead of him.[30] His goal, and ours, is to become like the Bride, like the Church under the aspect of holiness. Such transformation will require the grace that comes from Christ. Bernard observes, "She who is the true Bride acknowledges this, and recognizes each grace—first that which is first because it goes before, then that which follows."[31] The spiritual ascent to the Bridegroom proceeds by the power of grace rather than the Bride's own power. Thus, the Bride does not glorify herself; rather, the Bride focuses in faith and love upon Christ. The Bride in this perfected sense is not the Church in its current earthly state, suffering the burden of sinful members, but rather is "the Church of the Saints" or "the Church of the elect."[32] This Bride, which Bernard also calls "the congregation of the righteous," seeks the face of Christ with deep love.[33] God has promised the

27. See Bernard of Clairvaux, *On the Song of Songs IV*, Sermon 68.1, p. 17.

28. Bernard of Clairvaux, Sermon 67.3, p. 6.

29. Bernard of Clairvaux, Sermon 67.3, p. 7.

30. Bernard of Clairvaux, Sermon 67.6, p. 9.

31. Bernard of Clairvaux, Sermon 67.12, p. 15.

32. Bernard of Clairvaux, Sermon 68.2, pp. 18–19.

33. Bernard of Clairvaux, Sermon 68.3, p. 20.

Church that he will purify the Church and make it into Christ's completely holy Bride.

In another sermon, Bernard imagines what it would have been like for the Church to witness the Ascension of Christ. Christ's Ascension, Bernard says, must have so "touched the heart of his household the Church, his newly wedded Bride," as to make the Bride feel almost widowed.[34] It is no wonder that the Bride yearns and begs for the Bridegroom's return. This is not an unseemly lack of faith on the part of the Bride, but rather befits the Bride's love. The Bride's begging for the Bridegroom's return does not constitute an unfaithful refusal to accept God's plan for Christ's Ascension or for human life of earth. On the contrary, a yearning for the fullness of Christ's presence—for the perfection of the marriage of Christ and his Church—is just what we should expect of the Bride. As Bernard says, "Is not this what she asks for every day, when she says in her prayer 'Thy kingdom come'?"[35]

At the same time, Bernard does not wish to minimize the fact that Christ will come *in judgment*. The Bride prays for Christ the Judge to come in the form of mercy, the form that he showed on the cross. Otherwise, even the elect could not be saved. Bernard states, "For if he marks what is done amiss, even by the elect, who can abide it?"[36] The Bride on earth is comprised of members who are sinners. Even the saints, in their earthly lives, commit sins against God. With reference to some passages from Job, Bernard paints a portrait of sin: "In his sight the stars are not clean, and even in the angels he finds corruption. . . . Therefore even the saints have need to ask pardon for their sins, that they may be saved by mercy, not trusting in their own righteousness."[37] The Bride's confidence is in the grace and mercy of Christ crucified, and the Bride rightly relies on him to judge mercifully. Our lack

34. Bernard of Clairvaux, Sermon 73.3, p. 77.
35. Bernard of Clairvaux, Sermon 73.3, p. 78.
36. Bernard of Clairvaux, Sermon 73.4, p. 78.
37. Bernard of Clairvaux, Sermon 73.4, p. 78.

of holiness mars the Church (the Bride), but our confidence is not in our own merits but in Christ. Thus, the Bride/Church proclaims in the Creed that it is the crucified Christ, full of mercy, who "shall be set on high to judge."[38]

In Bernard's reflections on the Church as the Bride of Christ, then, there is a focus not so much on the Church but on Christ. It is by the grace of Christ's Spirit that the Church will fully become the perfect Bride. At present, while the Church on earth is in one sense the holy Bride, in her members she is still in need of the Spirit's purification. The cross of Christ opens up the grace and mercy that the Bride needs. When believers love and serve others, their hearts will be turned to the love of Christ and they will be what the Church should be. Bernard also pays a great deal of attention to Christ's Ascension. The Bride is not to be condemned for begging and yearning to be fully united with Christ the Bridegroom. We should in fact yearn to be with Christ; it is not a sign of unhealthy otherworldliness. If we do not yearn to ascend by grace to where Christ is, this is merely a sign that we do not love our neighbor either: our hearts are cold.

Gregory of Narek

Like Bernard, but a couple centuries before him, the Armenian monk and Doctor of the Church Gregory of Narek wrote a monastic commentary on the Song of Songs that can teach us about the Church as Bride. He remarks, in accord with the Church Fathers, that the Song of Songs is "a parable of the love of Christ and the Church for one another."[39] Commenting on Song of Songs 1:2—"O that you would kiss me with the kisses of your mouth"—Gregory suggests that the kiss here is the one that the (divine) father gives to the prodigal son in Jesus's parable. The

38. Bernard of Clairvaux, Sermon 73.6, p. 80.

39. Gregory of Narek, *The Blessing of Blessings: Gregory of Narek's Commentary on the Song of Songs*, trans. Roberta Ervine (Cistercian, 2007), 83.

Church is in the place of the repentant prodigal son. Christ (or the Father) offers the kiss of peace and of love. Gregory comments that the Bride's imploring the Bridegroom to kiss her means that the Bride begs even more for the transformative divine love.[40]

Like Bernard, Gregory distinguishes between the perfected Bride and the Church as it exists on earth, where its members fall into sin and yearn for an increase of grace and virtue so as to be more deeply united to Christ. He argues that the frequent reference to the "maidens" in the Song of Songs provides a hermeneutical key in this regard. In his view, "the Church and the people are called the *Bride*. And the *maidens* are the angels and saints; those who . . . have become as little children with regard to sin."[41] The fact that the Bride speaks to the maidens shows that the Bride is not yet purified. Some members of the Bride (the "maidens") are purified and everlastingly blessed, but many members are still not particularly holy.

Commenting on Song of Songs 1:5 ("I am very dark"), Gregory suggests that the Bride is here recollecting sins. She recalls "her earlier transgressions and the chastisements which she suffered."[42] Gregory interprets Song of Songs 1:5 completely spiritually, which in his view is the literal meaning. At the outset of the human race, the first humans sinned and lost their communion with God. They were expelled "both from God's presence and from Paradise."[43] The Church, in other words, has existed since Adam and Eve, and its members have committed grave sins. Fortunately, the Bridegroom fully forgave these sins. The Bridegroom Christ was "willing to forget the Bride's wickedness because of His love for her."[44] The Bride is full of love for Christ, who forgives all sins.

40. Gregory of Narek, 90.
41. Gregory of Narek, 92.
42. Gregory of Narek, 94.
43. Gregory of Narek, 94.
44. Gregory of Narek, 95.

Song of Songs 1:8 urges the Bride to find the Bridegroom by following "in the tracks of the flock" that is shepherded by the Bridegroom.[45] Gregory speaks of the Bridegroom as the Good Shepherd, in accordance with John 10. Some sheep leave the flock of the Bridegroom through sin. They become goats, capable of producing no good works—no "wool" or "milk." Other sheep leave the flock of the Bridegroom through heresy. They still think that they belong to the flock (i.e., the Bride), but, tragically, they do not.[46] Gregory also makes much of the image of the dove, as found in Song of Songs 2:14: "O my dove, in the clefts of the rock, in the covert of the cliff, let me see your face, let me hear your voice." According to Gregory, the dove symbolizes purity. The dove obeys God's commandments. The dove's eyes are the Holy Spirit.

Thus, Gregory fully recognizes the Church's mixed character, the fact that it is caught up in sin despite the presence of Christ. Commenting on Song of Songs 2:2 ("As a lily among brambles, so is my love among maidens"), he states that the brambles—or thorns—are the wicked members of the Church, those who claim to belong to the Bride but interiorly do not. As Gregory says, just as in the parable of the wheat and tares Christ insists that the wheat should be allowed to grow with the tares until the harvest, so also the Song of Songs does not claim that the Church is without sinners. Even so, the Church is a beacon of holiness, including holy doctrine and the lives of the saints, in the midst of wicked nonbelievers. Gregory comments, "The Song of Songs . . . considered it appropriate for the righteous to be among the sinners."[47] He adds encouragingly that the brambles or thorns may become lilies. In the Church, the influence and example of the righteous can serve, through God's grace, to

45. Gregory of Narek, 96.
46. See Gregory of Narek, 96.
47. Gregory of Narek, 102.

transform the wicked into saints. By loving the righteous, sinners can come to love Christ who is manifested in them.

More than once, Gregory argues that the Bride is "the Church which is from the gentiles."[48] No doubt in a polemical context, he associates the apostles and the Gospels with the Church of the Gentiles, even though the apostles were Jews. In Song of Songs 2:9, the Bridegroom is standing outside, looking at the Bride through the windows and lattice. The Bridegroom says to the Bride, "Arise, my love, my fair one, and come away" (Song 2:10). Gregory specifies that the Bride is not being invited to come away through the windows and lattice inasmuch as they signify the Law and the prophets. Instead, the Bride, obeying the Bridegroom's call, must ascend with yearning to the heavenly reward where Christ dwells. This requires going through death and Resurrection, as Christ did. Gregory goes on to emphasize that Christ orders his Bride "to conform with the Gospel and its preaching, and not with the Law."[49] He draws this theme, like a number of others, from Gregory of Nyssa's unfinished commentary on the Song of Songs.[50]

Commenting on Song of Songs 2:15, Gregory of Narek suggests that the "foxes" who "spoil the vineyards" represent Satan and the demons.[51] Christ frees the Bride from the dangerous fox. Yet the Bride is never satisfied here on earth; the Bride continually seeks a deeper knowledge of Christ. Specifically, the Bride here is the saints, not every member of the Church. It is the saints who have a "boundless thirst . . . for Christ the Groom."[52] The saints discover that no matter how much knowledge they gain of Christ in this earthly life, it is as nothing in comparison with what they seek—which can only be given in eternal life. More than once, Gregory identifies the Bride with the "faithful,"

48. Gregory of Narek, 107.

49. Gregory of Narek, 112.

50. See Gregory of Narek, 197.

51. Gregory of Narek, 113.

52. Gregory of Narek, 114.

those who are beautiful due to their having put away sin. The Church as Bride consists in those members of the Church who "by a fragrant way of life become the equal of Christ's purity . . . and then become a Bride and ascend to Christ the Groom."[53] He owes a debt in this respect to Gregory of Nyssa, who also defined the Bride in this manner. The desire to ascend to Christ, to attain full union with Christ in charity, is the center of this understanding of the Church. Gregory of Narek describes the Bride—the Church—as having "veiled her face with a virtuous way of life and an unsophisticated and homely manner."[54] Love of the Bridegroom and desire to ascend to him are inseparable from virtue in relation to one's neighbor.

Gregory of Narek's description of the Christian—a description drawn from Gregory of Nyssa—is a description of an elevated soul. He states, "The man who gives himself to God seems to be human, and yet is not human; for if thoughts of fornication trouble him, or of anger, or greed, or any other corporeal passion, he does not entertain them."[55] In other words, the person who belongs to the Bride will treat other people well, rather than using and abusing them through lust, anger, greed, and so on. Real virtue demonstrates the Bride's ascending to where Christ is.

Gregory of Narek praises the power of Baptism, which transforms someone enslaved to sin into "the fragrant Bride of Christ, united with Him in purity of life."[56] Here he is commenting on the praises that the Bridegroom bestows upon the Bride, who is filled "with all chief spices" and who is "a garden fountain" (Song 4:14–15). When the Bride proclaims, "Blow upon my garden, let its fragrance be wafted abroad" (4:16), Gregory comments that the blowing comes from the Holy Spirit and the fragrant spices

53. Gregory of Narek, 118.
54. Gregory of Narek, 126.
55. Gregory of Narek, 135.
56. Gregory of Narek, 135.

are the great saints.[57] The grace of the Spirit enables the virtues that the Bridegroom praises. The Bride ascends to full union with Christ by these means.

Such sanctity, Gregory adds, comes to the Bride through being near the Bridegroom, Christ. The Bride becomes the "abode" of the indwelling Christ, in accordance with John 14 and also in the sense that God dwelt in the Jerusalem temple. The heavenly Jerusalem is the perfect Bride.[58] The Bride is fruitful, full of virtue, like a "nut orchard" with flowers, vines, and pomegranates (Song 6:11). The Bride's fruitfulness comes through "the unity of the Bride with the Groom," especially in humility.[59] On earth, the fruitfulness of the Bride includes her profound concern to seek the "wandering" and the "lost" and to establish or strengthen their faith, through the power of Christ.[60] The Church's works of mercy include evangelization and all else that pertains to uniting God's people in faith and love. As Gregory of Nyssa notes, when members of the Church do not bear such fruit but instead produce disunity, "the form of a wolf hiding under a sheep's skin will show itself."[61]

Again, therefore, we find an ecclesiology of ascent to Christ—not escapism but yearning for full union. The Church as Bride consists in those who are being made perfect by the Spirit in grace and virtue. The intense dynamism toward the ascended Christ does not diminish but rather only increases charity and other virtues toward our neighbor here and now. The greatest thing one can do for one's neighbor is to draw him into the Bride's ascent, not by force or compulsion but by preferential care for those who in whatever way are lost or wandering in this world.

57. See Gregory of Narek, 137.

58. See Gregory of Narek, 163.

59. Gregory of Narek, 186; cf. 190.

60. Gregory of Narek, 187.

61. Gregory of Nyssa, *Anti-Apollinarian Writings*, trans. Robin Orton (The Catholic University of America Press, 2015), 92.

III. YVES CONGAR, OP, AND ANSCAR VONIER, OSB

Yves Congar, OP

Let me now turn to twentieth-century theology of the bridal Church. What more can we come to understand about the Church as Bride? One aspect is the Church's growth in catholicity, as the Church becomes "one flesh" with the catholic fullness of Christ. Another aspect is a greater focus on the Bride's purification and repentance. A third aspect is the extraordinary power of sacramental grace in the world: the Bride is a wondrous sign of the Spirit's presence, despite the sins that afflict believers.

When Yves Congar reflects on the mystery of the Church as the Bride of Christ, he begins with the point that the marriage of God and humanity was understood by the Church Fathers first in terms of the Incarnation. As Congar summarizes the Fathers' perspective, "The Word, the Son, decided to marry human nature through his incarnation. . . . Christ assumed soiled human nature and purified it, by making it his betrothed or bride."[62] Congar also emphasizes the grace of the Holy Spirit and the sacraments, through which humans are united to Christ. He notes that the Bride of Christ is not yet what she will be; the Bride is dynamically ordered to the fullness of holiness, and so the one-flesh marriage is not yet perfect. The Bride's "wedding will only be perfect eschatologically."[63] Congar also draws the link (well known to the Fathers) between God's creation of Eve from Adam's side in Genesis 2 and the creation of the New Eve (the Church) from Christ's side in John 19, where Baptism and the Eucharist are symbolized by the outflowing of blood and water from Jesus's pierced side. On the cross, the marriage of Christ and his Bride is inaugurated.

At present, says Congar, the Church as Bride remains weighed down by sin, without ceasing to be holy in its solemn teachings,

62. Yves Congar, *I Believe in the Holy Spirit*, trans. David Smith (Crossroad, 1997), 2:55.

63. Congar, 2:56.

sacraments, and offices. He argues that the image of the Bride should not become an excuse for Catholics to fail to face the actual reality of sin in the Church. He observes in this vein, "Christians are conscious of the weight of the flesh in the Church, but the Church does not admit it often enough. People's confidence is inhibited by the mass of historical faults and the inadequacies of the Church. The Church . . . has often been proud and hard in history."[64] What is needed is a repentant Church, a Church that faces its flaws. The image of the Church as the Bride answers to this need, Congar thinks, given the biblical connection of this image to ongoing purification. The Holy Spirit operates as a principle of reform and purification, drawing the Church to greater holiness and enabling the Church to renounce its past prudential errors.

For Congar, then, the Church is a Bride that, while holy in one sense, is still deeply burdened by sin. The Bride exists in a dynamic Spirit-guided state of reform and purification. The Bride not only needs to grow in holiness but also needs to grow and develop in catholic fullness. The Bride's catholic fullness comes from her participation in the fullness of Christ through the Holy Spirit. Congar maintains that the Bride enters more and more, through Baptism and the Eucharist (qualitative catholicity) and through inculturation and history (quantitative catholicity), into the fullness of the all-holy Christ. It is in this way that the Bride, at the final consummation, will be truly said to have "made herself ready" (Rev 19:7). The Bride is "prepared" and "adorned" (Rev 21:2) over the course of history by growing in holiness and growing in catholic fullness through sharing in the fullness of Christ and the Spirit.

64. Congar, 2:57.

Anscar Vonier, OSB

Unlike Congar, Anscar Vonier's 1935 *The Spirit and the Bride* argues against drawing attention to the Church's "human infirmities."[65] Vonier firmly distinguishes the Church as the Bride of Christ from all merely human institutions, in light of the unitive power of the Holy Spirit. He states, "The Spirit of God, a divine Person, is to the scattered Christian souls of all times and all climes a bond of life and union that is not thinkable elsewhere."[66]

Vonier's special emphasis consists in the relationship of the Church and the Holy Spirit. More specifically, he seeks to offer a theology of the Holy Spirit *as manifested in* the Church. For Vonier, the Church has existed from Adam onward, inasmuch as "right from the beginning of mankind, salvation has been operative."[67] But he maintains that something different and new happens with the outpouring of the Spirit at Pentecost and the gathering of the visible Spirit-filled community of Christ's disciples from all the nations. No such thing as the universal Church had been seen before in the world's history; there were previously no sacraments of grace. Before Christ breathed out his Spirit and formed a visible community of faith and Baptism, the nations were still pagan.

Vonier does not doubt that "the elect before the coming of Christ formed an innumerable people coming from the Gentiles and the Jewish family."[68] But the revelation of the fullness of Christ and the Spirit established something radically new. At Pentecost, the "principal created sign" of the Spirit's presence in the world was the community of the apostles—namely, "that entirely transformed group of human beings" in the Upper Room.[69] The Church is a visible sign of the Spirit's activity. Vonier comments,

65. Anscar Vonier, OSB, *The Spirit and the Bride* (Assumption Press, 2013), ii.

66. Vonier, iii.

67. Vonier, 53.

68. Vonier, 54.

69. Vonier, 19.

"The Spirit's coming is as literal as the coming of the Word: but instead of His taking flesh, He clothed Himself in signs."[70]

When Vonier lists the ways in which the Spirit-filled Church is a sign of the Spirit's new and permanent presence, he observes that the Church must express "an entirely new life" and communicate "the wonderful things of God."[71] The Church offers a new and unique participation in the things of God, and the Church has a saving message that answers to the needs of every human being across time and space. At the heart of this message are the Resurrection and Ascension of Christ. But other evidences of Christ and the Spirit must also be present in the Church. Vonier states, "[The Church] must work wonders, she must have the faith of miracles, she must have ecstasies, she must, in short, understand that all prophecies have been fulfilled."[72] There must be abundant supernatural gifts among the members of the Church. Were this not the case, then the Church would not be a sign of the Spirit's presence.

As Vonier says, the prophets of Israel had foretold the coming of the Spirit. The outpouring of the Spirit at Pentecost, then, gave the apostolic Church tremendous confidence. The Church shares so fully in the Spirit as to be able to say that its decisions at the Council of Jerusalem "seemed good to the Holy Spirit and to us" (Acts 15:28). Moreover, the Spirit comes upon Gentile believers in Acts 11:15 in the same way that the Spirit had come upon the apostles at Pentecost. The Spirit fills the Church today, as in the apostolic age. Vonier underscores that "the Holy Ghost could not be said to abide in the Church if there were not in the Church those realities which manifested His advent at the beginning."[73] The Holy Spirit fills the Church with a fullness of spiritual life that can only come from God.

70. Vonier, 20.
71. Vonier, 21.
72. Vonier, 21.
73. Vonier, 23.

No wonder, says Vonier, that the book of Revelation closes with the affirmation "The Spirit and the Bride say, 'Come'" (Rev 22:17). The Spirit is joined to the Church in utter intimacy, so that the Church is a sure sign of the Spirit's powerful presence. Christ's humanity manifests the divine Word. The Church is not the incarnation of the Spirit, and the Church in its human dimension is not sinless. But the Church in its visible reality manifests the Spirit. The Bride is manifestly Spirit-filled. The Church is the Bride because the Church—in Vonier's words—"is the fullness of Him who ascended above all the heavens, who has filled all things with the strength of his sanctity."[74]

In other words, the Church is the Bride because the Church shares through the Spirit in the catholic fullness of Christ. Here one sees the influence of Vonier on Congar, an influence the latter acknowledges. The Church contains a vast multitude of diverse peoples and angels, in heaven and on earth, and it draws all these into unity, not by its own power but by Christ's power in the Spirit. This unity is specifically a unity *with Christ*: as Ephraim Radner puts it, "The Church—Israel the Bride—thus yearns to be utterly *with* her Lord, and hence like him."[75]

The measure of the Spirit-filled Church, however, is not perfection. Although he is generally loath to recognize the Church's failures, Vonier does not ignore "the grievous sins . . . which are committed by those who have the faith of Christ."[76] He calls it a "mountain of sin," an all too accurate assessment.[77] Indeed, it is only the sacrament of penance, by uniting repentant believers to the power of Christ's cross, that ensures that the weight of sin does not crush the Church. For Vonier, therefore, it would be a mistake "to enumerate the sins of the Christian people and not to speak of their repentances."[78] His approach has the benefit of

74. Vonier, 32.

75. Radner, *Church*, 173.

76. Vonier, *The Spirit and the Bride*, 65.

77. Vonier, 65.

78. Vonier, 65.

teaching us to praise the bridal Church and to respond to its sacraments and teachings with gratitude. For if the Church as Bride truly shares in the fullness of Christ through the Spirit, then the Church is worthy of praise and its gifts are treasures.[79]

Rejoicing in "the greatness and exaltation of our Christian life," Vonier praises the Spirit for uniting humankind and angels.[80] He urges us not to neglect the Church that now exists in heavenly glory. Emphasizing the unity of the Pilgrim Church and the Church Triumphant, he observes, "The same Spirit vivifies all of us, from the simplest Christian on earth to the Cherub before the throne of God."[81] He comments in 1935 that "there could be no greater community than this"—a particularly striking remark given the fascist nationalisms implicitly in view (Vonier grew up in Germany).[82] He emphasizes that the Church cannot promote nationalism or become a mere instrument for fostering any particular nation's greatness. Vonier sets himself firmly against Nazism: "It is in the fierce conflict between the Church and racialism, between the Church and nationalism, that we see the demarcations between the human spirit . . . and the Holy Ghost who came down from heaven to take men up to heaven."[83] The merely human spirit stirs up the evils of racialism (including anti-Semitism) and nationalism, whereas the Holy

79. See also Jean-Hervé Nicolas, OP, *Catholic Dogmatic Theology: A Synthesis*, bk. 3, *On the Church and the Sacraments*, trans. Matthew K. Minerd (The Catholic University of America Press, 2024), 110–11: "There is room for an equitable judgment that, lucidly assessing her as a historical reality, recognizes her grandeur and beneficence. Does any other human institution exist which has not committed incomparably more evil than she has done, having itself done incomparably less good than her? From the perspective of good and evil, what kind of figure is struck by whatever nation that there is, in whatsoever of our homelands? . . . She has not ceased, does not cease, and will not cease to make the Savior known to the world and to communicate His salvation. And if she is primordially mandated and authorized to communicate eternal salvation to men, through words and sacraments, she has never neglected to contribute efficaciously also, in turn, to their temporal salvation, through her innumerable works of mercy as well as through her teaching. If, undoubtedly, in the course of her long history, she has committed innumerable faults, some that are very substantial, the balance sheet of her benefits (even those that are merely temporal) and her shortcomings is largely positive in the end."

80. Vonier, *The Spirit and the Bride*, 102.

81. Vonier, 103.

82. Vonier, 103.

83. Vonier, 120.

Spirit works to remove such evils and to build up the Church as Christ's Bride.

Vonier goes on to celebrate the sheer "variety of the Bride of Christ," its Spirit-filled unity in a wondrous diversity of "graces and endowments."[84] Not only individuals but also groups in the Church possess a rich variety. The charisms of diverse religious orders complement each other. Out of such broad diversity there could never arise a catholic unity unless the Holy Spirit were the source of the diversity. Vonier states, "The oneness of the Church is the manifest sign of that Spirit who transcends all spirits. It would not be possible for the Church to possess unity if the divine Spirit were not present, as the variety of created spirits would lead to dissension rather than to conformity."[85]

But what about the tragic disunity among Christians, which occupies Congar in his 1937 *Chrétiens désunis*?[86] The unity of the Church has been wounded so often. Is this not a powerful countersign, indicative of a lack of the Spirit's presence?[87] Vonier thinks it more reasonable to look at the Church in terms of what is positively present, while allowing for the sorrow of the divisions. When speaking of faith and doctrinal development, he cautions that "we may pay more attention to the difference than to the identity; such is the human mind, it seizes on differences because they are a phenomenon in opposition to the monotonous substance."[88] Aware of how tenuous any unity is, Vonier is much more struck by the unity of the Church across space and time than he is by the divisions, serious though they be, that have wounded that unity.

84. Vonier, 105.

85. Vonier, 106.

86. See Yves Congar, OP, *Chrétiens désunis: Principes d'un "oecuménisme" catholique* (Cerf, 1937).

87. For an argument along these lines—and much more as well—see Ephraim Radner, *The End of the Church: A Pneumatology of Christian Division in the West* (Eerdmans, 1998). See also, for a bracing look at the sins of Christians, Radner's *A Brutal Unity: The Spiritual Politics of the Christian Church* (Baylor University Press, 2012). I discuss the unity and holiness of the Church at length in my *Engaging the Doctrine of the Holy Spirit: Love and Gift in the Trinity and the Church* (Baker Academic, 2016).

88. Vonier, *The Spirit and the Bride*, 110.

Again, this unity has its source in the Holy Spirit, who communicates the power of Christ's saving work to the Bride. The gifts of the Spirit, says Vonier, make it possible to live out the beatitudes, which "are the morality of an entirely new world, the world of God."[89] He emphasizes that the gifts of the Spirit are not a higher form of Spirit-directed Christianity enjoyed only by mystics. Instead, the history of the whole Church, in its saints and in its general influence, should be read in light of the seven gifts. The Christian virtues are likewise supernaturally transformative. Vonier observes, "The three theological virtues of faith, hope, and charity are those fundamental vitalities [of Christian holiness]; at no time will the Spirit raise a man to a region where the writ of those three great powers would not run."[90] Through faith, hope, and love—aided by the gifts—the Holy Spirit builds up the Bride and enables every member of the Church to taste and "enjoy the sublime things of God."[91]

Vonier repeatedly underscores that the Holy Spirit, not any natural human resource, renders the Church able to be the Bride of Christ. The Church is not merely an institution for serving the world, let alone an institution dependent primarily on the world's gifts. Rather, the Spirit has built up a Bride that lives in the world and has the power to convert the world without being of the world.[92] Evangelization would not succeed unless the Church was attractive, and the Spirit makes the Church attractive. The Spirit

89. Vonier, 119.

90. Vonier, 125.

91. Vonier, 128.

92. Vonier adds, "It is evident, of course, that right through the centuries the Church is helped by the natural wealth—material, intellectual, and moral—which is in this world. Often the impression is created that exclusively human elements have a great part in furthering the prosperity of the Church; that men of learning are precious, nay indispensable defenders of the Church's rights; that the good will of governments is an invaluable asset to the Church's safety; that even material wealth greatly enhances the splendor of the faith. We cannot deny the role of such elements in augmenting the Church's life; they are given to the Church by God's providence as external assets; but none of these things will be of any use to the Church's own life unless she handles them with a talent no one else possesses. By themselves natural advantages can add nothing to the power of the Church; but utilized by her they become the helpers of grace" (145–46).

provides charisms that serve the Church's evangelizing mission, such as, for instance, the ability to do miracles. Vonier argues that there is "no clear line of demarcation between the powers of the Church that build up the Body of Christ and the powers that propagate the Church. One and the same Spirit operates in both directions."[93]

Vonier has much to say about the catholic fullness of Jesus Christ. For example, he states, "Everything . . . in the history of the Church ultimately comes back to something infinitely positive, something immensely actual, something entirely luminous: the life that is in the Incarnate God."[94] The bridal Church is a one-flesh sharing in the living, incarnate Son of God. Vonier holds that this sharing primarily occurs sacramentally. Along these lines, he interprets Ephesians 5:25–26 as referring to the Eucharist and to Baptism. The Church as Bride is always *Christ's* Bride, sharing in Christ. Vonier also finds various references to the sacrament of Confirmation in Acts' descriptions of Pentecost—a descent of the Spirit that is distinct from Baptism (e.g., Acts 19:1–6). He remarks that the Spirit's coming is always "essentially Christological," bringing about not an addition to the Incarnation but the "completion" of the Incarnation by enabling believers to share in Christ's fullness and to become his Bride.[95]

When Vonier discusses the sacraments, he examines them in light of the Spirit's operation in and through them. To say that the sacraments are Spirit-filled makes them more, not less, Christological. For Vonier, "through the presence of the Spirit each sacrament is linked up, through all space and all times, with the cause of all sacramental grace—the death of Christ on the Cross."[96] In the Liturgy of the Eucharist, the Spirit is invoked as the sanctifier. Again, Vonier emphasizes how profoundly the

93. Vonier, 147.

94. Vonier, 150.

95. Vonier, 124.

96. Vonier, 156. See Anscar Vonier, OSB, *A Key to the Doctrine of the Eucharist* (Wipf & Stock, 2002), originally published in 1925.

Church is unlike other institutions.[97] No merely this-worldly institution could have the celebration of the Eucharist at its center. The Church has the power to make Jesus Christ present in her midst on the altar, and the Church sacramentally offers up the sacrifice of Christ. Vonier draws attention to "Christ's profound identification of Himself with the Church's sacramental power."[98] When Bride calls upon the Bridegroom, the Bridegroom will be present in his salvific action. This intimacy of the Church with Christ is nuptial. Quoting Song of Songs 6:3, "I am my beloved's and my beloved is mine," Vonier highlights how fully the Church shares Christ's life.

For Vonier, it is simply amazing how present Christ consents to be. Christ not only allows the Church to offer his sacrifice liturgically, but he remains present in the Eucharistic host. Together, Bride and Bridegroom offer the Eucharistic sacrifice. Christ in the Eucharist stands at the very heart of the Church, enabling the members of the Church to share in the fullness of his love. This sharing is so complete that it is a literal communion, in which believers take Christ into themselves by consuming the sacred host. Vonier terms the Church "the House of the divine Bread," drawing a link to Bethlehem.[99] Similarly, he depicts the Church's bridal communion with Christ in the Eucharist as follows: "She dwells with her Bridegroom for hours and for days; she watches over Him and with Him; she counts her mystical communication with Him in time divisions"—that is, in the durations of periods of adoration.[100] Although the Eucharist is Christ's gift to the Church, the Church is not merely passive but also active in this gift. The Church shares in Christ's life by sharing in the Eucharist, and Christ shares in the Church's life by his presence in the Eucharist.

97. Vonier, *The Spirit and the Bride*, 161.

98. Vonier, 162.

99. Vonier, 164.

100. Vonier, 165.

Vonier's nuptial ecclesiology never tires of extolling the Spirit. Reflecting upon the Trinitarian missions, he comments, "It is the mission of the Holy Ghost to make the Church a fit bride; to give her the heart of a bride, the mind of a bride, the body of a bride."[101] The Holy Spirit does this by sanctifying the Church. Vonier inquires into how the Bride, led by the Holy Spirit, should think of Christ. As he says, Christians have portrayed Jesus Christ in a wide variety of ways. One reason for this is the fact that Christ went through many changes: from the incarnate Lord in the womb, to his infancy and the obscurity of his formative years, to his baptism and preaching and miracles, to his cross and Resurrection and Ascension. If we think of Christ as he was as an infant, we do not think of him as he actually now is in glory at the right hand of the Father.

How then should Christians think of the Bridegroom Christ? Vonier answers that we should think of him as a man filled with virtues—above all, charity and humility. We cannot imagine the extent of his glory at the right hand of the Father; we cannot imagine the glory of his unveiled face. But the Spirit "makes Christ live in the hearts of chosen men and women according to their capacity," so that the saints' diverse portraits of Christ are all true, each in a partial way.[102] The totality of the living Christ, says Vonier, is beyond portrayal; the fullness of Christ can be participated in but not pinned down. His "totality" includes not only his glorified human nature but his infinite divine nature and his divine personhood. Vonier comments, "No one here on earth can make such a totality his own. So the Spirit breaks up that glory, as the prism breaks up the white light, and infinite varieties of the Christ Person are received by the saints as their own share in the boundless mystery of the Son of God."[103]

Thus, the Church as Bride participates in the whole Christ,

101. Vonier, 34.

102. Vonier, 39.

103. Vonier, 40.

but the fullness of Christ cannot be expressed by any member of the Church. Indeed, even a vast number of mystical portraits of the living Christ would not suffice to express the whole. Each Christian encounters Christ and knows and loves him, but no Christian knows him as he is in his totality. Still, the Spirit ensures that each mystic's vision of Christ corresponds to who Christ is, however partially. What the mystics bring the Church is therefore "a genuine communication with Christ Himself, as if His voice were heard from a distance"—a communication with the living, glorified Christ.[104] The Spirit can accomplish this because the Spirit indwells the incarnate Lord. Vonier has in view John 16:14, where Jesus says of the Spirit, "He will glorify me, for he will take what is mine and declare it to you."

Vonier's main point in this discussion is that the Bride knows the Bridegroom, albeit not yet exhaustively. Filled with the Spirit, believers have real knowledge of Christ. As a whole, says Vonier, the Church "will abound in the sense of Christ" and "will see in Him the most varied perfections."[105] The bridal Church will praise the perfections of her Lover, as happens in the Song of Songs, cited in this context by Vonier. Even now, the Spirit enables the Church to see Christ's face, although depicting its fullness would require an infinite number of sketches. Vonier directs attention to Revelation's use of the image of the Lamb. Employing the symbolic number seven, this is an image of fullness: "a Lamb standing, as though it had been slain, with seven horns and seven eyes" (Rev 5:6). The Lamb's Bride, sharing in his fullness, is the Church (see Rev 21:9).

Vonier also explores the significance of Jesus's Resurrection and Ascension. The ascended Lord pours out the Spirit upon his followers. As Vonier notes, Jesus promises this eschatological Spirit in John 7:37–39. Vonier asks an intriguing question in this context: Why did Jesus not pour out the Spirit during his public

104. Vonier, 40.

105. Vonier, 41.

ministry, rather than simply promising it? The answer offered by Vonier accords with the Gospel of John's testimony that "the Spirit had not yet been given, because Jesus was not yet glorified" (John 7:39). Vonier states, "The Spirit is essentially and unalterably the radiation in this world of Christ's glorification."[106] This answer fits with the book of Acts, too, given that Peter proclaims in Acts 2:32–33 that it is the ascended Christ who has poured forth the Spirit. When in Acts 4:31 the disciples are filled with the Spirit after prayer, they boldly praise the Lord Jesus. Vonier even argues that the fact of the Resurrection of Christ became much more important to the disciples once they had received the Spirit, since through the Spirit the incarnate Lord encounters the disciples "in glory and majesty."[107] In other words, it is by the Spirit, sent by the ascended Christ, that the Bride comes to participate in the true fullness of Christ—and thus to recognize him for who he really is.

Prior to his Ascension, the resurrected Christ promised to pour out the Spirit upon his disciples (see Acts 1:4–5). This coming of the eschatological Spirit is so momentous that Vonier counts it as "the crowning event of Christ's own career on this earth."[108] It is through the Spirit that Christ reigns as messianic king, not over a small land but over the entire world in an "empire of the Spirit."[109] The Resurrection of Jesus may seem hidden, but it is made manifest by those who are filled with his Spirit (see John 15:26–27). Spirit-filled believers are so strengthened that they do not fear death, and they know and embrace the "whole mystery of man's salvation in all its aspects."[110] Elevated and instructed by the Spirit, the Bride learns "all those marvels which the Son of God while He was here on earth kept in reserve without showing

106. Vonier, 44.
107. Vonier, 45.
108. Vonier, 46.
109. Vonier, 46.
110. Vonier, 48.

them."[111] Most notably, the Bride manifests to the world "Christ as He is now" by "walk[ing] with the risen Christ in newness of life."[112]

Thus, the Church does not merely point to a Christ who has gone away. The Church does not merely recollect Christ's earthly deeds for our salvation. Instead, the Church as Bride proclaims the fullness of the glorified Christ, because the Holy Spirit enables believers, here and now, to share in that fullness and to live in accordance with Christ's saving work. Through the Spirit, "the very substance of glory takes up its abode with men" and Christ's glory becomes "a reality here on earth" through the Church's catholic sharing in the glorified Lord.[113]

Of course, the Bride's sharing in Christ includes a sharing in his suffering and trials. In the midst of such trials, says Vonier, each believer can count on "the full enjoyment of the whole mystery of Christ as contained in the Church."[114] In Vonier's view, the task of the bridal Church in its trials is to serve as an efficacious engine of supernatural energy and mercy for the whole world, even if the world does not know it. He observes, "God can make provision for the whole of mankind in the supernatural sphere through one portion of mankind. . . . From this sanctified core of humanity there would proceed an endless wave of supernatural magnetism which would leave no one untouched or unenergized."[115] The catholic fullness of the bridal Church is not for itself alone. God ensures that the bridal Church gives off supernatural and saving energy for all those outside the Church's

111. Vonier, 48–49.

112. Vonier, 50–51.

113. Vonier, 50. Vonier adds insightfully, "Unless we consider the Church as being rooted and established in the resurrection from the dead of the Son of God, through the Spirit of glory, our notions of the Church will not exceed human measure. She will be only an assembly of holy people when she ought to be a function of Christ's risen life" (51).

114. Vonier, 170.

115. Vonier, 172.

visible bounds, so that they too may have a participation (in varying degrees) in Christ's fullness.[116]

IV. CONCLUSION

Paul teaches, "Seek the things that are above, where Christ is, seated at the right hand of God. Set your minds on things that are above, not on things that are on earth. For you have died, and your life is hidden with Christ in God" (Col 3:1–3). This is why the image of the Bride should be the starting point for Catholic ecclesiology. As we have seen, it is an image driven by yearning, by ascent to the ascended Bridegroom. It is also a deeply catholic image: in the one-flesh union with the Bridegroom, the Bride shares Christ's catholic fullness. This takes place sacramentally—above all, in the Eucharistic liturgy. The Bride is purified by the Holy Spirit so as to become perfectly configured to Christ. At present, the sins of Catholics may be like a mountain, but even greater are the graces and virtues manifest in the saints, who represent the Bride.

After his discussion of the Church as Bride, Congar turns immediately to a section on "The Struggles of the Holy Church of Sinners."[117] In accord with what we noted above, Congar emphasizes, "The wedding has been celebrated and the Church is the bride, but she is not yet the perfectly pure bride inaugurated by baptism. . . . The union that should be consummated in one spirit (or Spirit) is still imperfect."[118] The bridal fullness of the Church awaits the eschatological consummation. In the present time, the Church is the Bride of Christ, but no one should deny "the mass of historical faults and the inadequacies of the Church."[119] Christ

116. See Vonier, 174. Vonier anticipates Vatican II's *Lumen Gentium*, *Unitatis Redintegratio*, and even *Nostra Aetate* here. In general, however, Vonier is not ecumenically sensitive but instead says such things as (for instance) "the open attack against Catholicism by Protestantism is now four hundred years old" (188–89).

117. Congar, *I Believe in the Holy Spirit*, 2:57.

118. Congar, 2:56.

119. Congar, 2:57.

has not yet fully presented his Bride "to himself in splendor, without spot or wrinkle or any such thing, that she might be holy and without blemish" (Eph 5:27). The Spirit is purifying the Church, intensifying its love for God and neighbor and its yearning for full union with the Bridegroom.

Although Vonier has a way of accounting for the participation (to varying degrees) of non-Catholics in the reality of the Church, the Church that he is rejoicing in is specifically the Catholic Church. Does this make his vision of the Bride overly narrow, given that a non-Catholic Christian such as Sergius Bulgakov, in proclaiming the "love song of the bride and the Lamb" (i.e., the Song of Songs) to be "the crown of the mystical doctrine of the Church as love," has in view a Church constituted differently from Vonier's (Roman) Catholic Church?[120]

My response is no, Vonier's vision of the Bride is not too narrow, even if it is not the final word either. Vonier is correct to affirm that Christ has sustained his Bride as a visible unity by the Spirit. Christ's Spirit ensures the holiness of the Church's offices, sacraments, and solemn teachings, and the Spirit raises up saints and a vast diversity of charisms in the Body of Christ. Recall Gregory of Narek's joyful comments about "those wedded to the Groom."[121] Nevertheless, there is much to mourn, including the lack of fidelity of many Catholic clergy and laity to basic teachings of Christ. Ecumenical work is urgently needed lest divisions fester and grow bigger, as Congar perceived. Even where decisive breakthroughs cannot be achieved, there is the fruitful ecumenical task of "seeking greater depth within the real but limited communion that exists already."[122] As Michael Root observes along lines that helpfully go beyond Vonier (in Congar's direction), the

120. Sergius Bulgakov, *The Bride of the Lamb*, trans. Boris Jakim (Eerdmans, 2002), 264.

121. Gregory of Narek, *The Blessing of Blessings*, 206.

122. Michael Root, "Normal Ecumenism: Ecumenism for the Long Haul," *Pro Ecclesia* 28, no. 1 (2019): 60–77, at 75.

Bride should benefit from the "genuine gifts that other traditions may have received in separation."[123]

Vonier delves deeply into the Church's Spirit-given beauty, which theologians today tend to neglect. The Bride of Christ is visible, a sign of grace for the whole world. The Holy Spirit has been poured out and Christ presently reigns. Even if the perfection of the Bride is an eschatological reality that awaits the consummation of all things, the Church is already the Spirit-filled Bride, the eschatological people inaugurated by the Bridegroom, Jesus Christ, and visibly manifest in the power of its sacraments, the wisdom of its teachings, and the cruciform greatness of its saints. At the same time, the Bride's new-exodus ascent is not a triumphal worldly march, given that, as Paul says, "God chose what is foolish in the world to shame the wise, God chose what is weak in the world to shame the strong" (1 Cor 1:27).

It is "through the Church" that "the manifold wisdom of God" is "now . . . made known" (Eph 3:10). In this bridal Church, Paul invites us "to comprehend with all the saints what is the breadth and length and height and depth, and to know the love of Christ which surpasses knowledge, that you may be filled with all the fulness of God" (Eph 3:18–19). The joy that Vonier takes in the Church, therefore, remains worthy of emulation—and if we lack such joy, we are likely not yet united to Christ in his

123. Root, "Normal Ecumenism," 76. See also Jean-Hervé Nicolas, OP, *Catholic Dogmatic Theology*. Indebted to Congar and Charles Journet, Nicolas offers a helpful approach to ecumenism: "From the perspective of Catholic theology, the entire problem of ecumenism is that of arriving at a union of Christian Churches such that, while recognizing the claims of the Catholic Church in calling herself the Church of Christ (i.e., the Church governed by the authority of Christ, in His name, with the assistance of His Spirit, by the bishop of Rome), she would respect the ecclesial specificity of other confessions that also claim faith in Christ. Thus, the mere fact of posing the problem presupposes a postulate, namely, that the various Christian confessions do not diverge from each other as regards their authentically Christian character but, rather, as regards the limits (indeed, the deviations) that each, through the course of the centuries, has brought to this authentic tradition. Even in the case of the Catholic Church, nothing prevents . . . one from speaking of limits and even particular deviations. However, we believe that she has not deviated in the fundamental direction impressed upon her by Christ because Christ, in accord with His promise, is in her and acts upon and through her, and through the Holy Spirit whom He has sent to her in order to assist her indefectibly, despite the very real and very numerous faults committed through the ages (as well as the errors of her members, particularly of her shepherds)" (129–30).

Bride. Thanks to the ascended Christ, the bridal Church really is an "empire of the Spirit."[124] Likewise, the Bride in her faith and sacraments communicates "an entirely new life" grounded in "the wonderful things of God."[125] The Bride powerfully shares in the Holy Spirit, as evinced by charisms and by miracles. The Spirit enables the Bride to "abound in the sense of Christ."[126] The intimacy of Christ's presence in the Church, not least in the Eucharist, is astounding. As the Catholic biblical scholar and theologian Brant Pitre says, "Jesus is united with his bride through the sacrifice of his own flesh and blood, poured out literally on Calvary and then miraculously in the sacraments of the Church."[127]

Let me also advert here to an insight of Matthias Joseph Scheeben in his *Mysteries of Christianity*. Scheeben insists that the mystery of the Church cannot be perceived without recognizing that its "innermost character" is shaped by supernatural grace.[128] Judging solely by externals, one *might* come to the conclusion that the Church is nothing more than another human institution, marked by the strengths and weaknesses, virtues and vices that characterize all human institutions. But to the eyes of faith, the Church is much more than a merely human institution. The Church, says Scheeben, is Christ's "true bride who, made fruitful by His divine power, has the destiny of bearing heavenly children to Him and His heavenly Father, of nourishing these children with the substance and light of her bridegroom, and of conducting them beyond the whole range of created nature up to the very bosom of His heavenly Father."[129]

Scheeben depicts the bridal Church as grounded in faith and the sacraments, especially Baptism and the Eucharist. To be a

124. Vonier, *The Spirit and the Bride*, 46.

125. Vonier, 21.

126. Vonier, 41.

127. Brant Pitre, *Jesus the Bridegroom: The Greatest Love Story Ever Told* (Image, 2014), 113.

128. Matthias Joseph Scheeben, *The Mysteries of Christianity*, trans. Cyril Vollert, SJ, 2nd. (Emmaus Academic, 2023), 540.

129. Scheeben, 541–42.

member of the Church is, objectively speaking, to have entered through the cross into an extraordinary union with Christ. The Church enjoys "a mystical marriage with the God-man."[130] Each member of the Church attaches himself or herself to Christ the Bridegroom and receives the sacrament of Baptism as "a wedding ring."[131] The Spirit continually enhances this "mystical marriage," as part of his deifying grace. Scheeben states, "With His [the Spirit's] divine fire He must gloriously change Christ's bride into the image of the divine nature, transform her whole being by adding splendor to splendor, and pervade her with His own divine life."[132] Thus, the Bride will share fully in the Bridegroom's life.

At the heart of this nuptial mystery stands the cross. Paul remarks, "All of us who were baptized into Christ Jesus were baptized into his death" (Rom 6:3); and Paul notes that the Eucharist is "a participation in the blood of Christ" (1 Cor 10:16). The bridal Church fully came into being when Christ, on the cross, "loved the Church and gave himself up for her, that he might sanctify her" (Eph 5:25–26). Thus, seeking to share more and more in all that Christ bestows upon his Catholic and catholic Bride, may we learn to obey Christ's nuptial teaching: "If any man would come after me, let him deny himself and take up his cross and follow me. For whoever would save his life will lose it, and whoever loses his life for my sake will find it" (Matt 16:24–25).

130. Scheeben, 543.
131. Scheeben, 543.
132. Scheeben, 544.

2

Family of God

I. INTRODUCTION

Defending the Catholic Church in 1850 against the view that Catholicism must be false because otherwise the European Catholic nations would not be so politically and economically backward and corrupt, John Henry Newman observed that the Catholic Church never has existed to do the work of civil governments. Instead, he argues, it "has a work of its own, and this work is, first, *different* from that of the world; next, *difficult of attainment*, compared with that of the world; and lastly, *secret* from the world in its details and consequences."[1] The purpose of the Church is to make saints, and so the Church's central work is liturgical. Just by being Catholic, therefore, Catholic countries will not necessarily possess good governance or economic prudence, beneficial though a flourishing Catholicism must be to civil government's pursuit of the common good.

At present, almost two centuries later, it is even clearer that many majority-Catholic nations have failed to produce good economic and political governance, especially by comparison with more prosperous majority-Protestant countries. Without denying the truth of the principles of Catholic social teaching, it seems that there has sometimes been naivete in the application of these principles in matters of policy. One thinks for instance of the sorry economic and political condition of many majority-Catholic Latin American countries that have followed

1. John Henry Newman, *Certain Difficulties Felt by Anglicans in Catholic Teaching*, vol. 1 (Longmans, Green, 1897), 241.

the path of socialism.[2] For its part, Italy is not traditionally known for good government and has often relied economically upon help from northern European countries.

Newman's argument that the Church has the primary purpose of making saints, however, cuts against much postconciliar Catholic ecclesiology. It has become theologically popular to suggest that the Church's main task is to foster structures of economic and political justice in the world.[3] Although I think Newman is correct about the Church's purpose, it is understandable that people desire good economic and political structures.[4] In many African nations, for instance, where statism, war, and corruption (in conjunction with other factors, including the impact of colonialism) have led to economic and political injustices,[5] the Church

2. For background from a perspective opposed to the status quo, see Alvaro Vargas Llosa, *Liberty for Latin America: How to Undo Five Hundred Years of State Oppression* (Farrar, Straus and Giroux, 2005).

3. See Avery Dulles, SJ, *The Reshaping of Catholicism: Current Challenges in the Theology of the Church* (Harper & Row, 1988). For background, see Gerd-Rainer Horn, *Western European Liberation Theology: The First Wave (1924–1959)* (Oxford University Press, 2008); and Horn, *The Spirit of Vatican II: Western European Progressive Catholicism in the Long Sixties* (Oxford University Press, 2015).

4. See the nuanced study by Tegha Afuhwi Nji, "*Africae Munus* in the Light of Prophetic Praxis: A Liberation Theology for Africa? A Critical Engagement with Ratzinger," in *Africae Munus: Ten Years Later*, ed. Maurice A. Agbaw-Ebai and Matthew Levering (St. Augustine's, 2022), 225–61. Granting the danger of the "temptation toward historical immanentism," Nji argues that "the human aspiration for a just society constitutes a horizontal hope which finds grounding only in a vertical hope. . . . Liberation . . . must be moved away from a historical immanentist view and away from a political utopia. Liberation is not simply what oppressed people can accomplish alone; it is basically what God has done and will accomplish both in and beyond history. Such a view of liberation at last takes seriously the cross and resurrection of Christ as those mysterious events with ultimate liberative power *in* and *beyond* history, the very events which create the new space of hopeful existence within which a horizontal hope of liberation is made possible" (232, 248). Fittingly, Nji goes on to propose "the category of *Lament* as a fitting expression of an authentic liberation theology within the African context. . . . The prevalence of suffering and oppression on the one hand, and on the other hand, a real human helplessness in the face of that suffering, legitimizes the African's near-natural disposition to lament before God. Lament as a model of liberation is grounded in a *theocentric* spirituality prior to any conceptualization" (249).

5. See Paul Ọlátúbọ̀sún Àdajà, "Catholic Theology in Twenty-First-Century Africa in the Light of the Primacy of the Logos in the Theology of Joseph Ratzinger," in *Joseph Ratzinger and the Future of African Theology*, ed. Maurice Ashley Agbaw-Ebai and Matthew Levering (Pickwick, 2021), 40–62. Àdajà argues that Africa is facing an "anthropological crisis," one that Pentecostal evangelistic emphasis on "material wealth, suppression of demonic forces, healings and miracles, and speaking in tongues" only exemplifies (47, 51). Àdajà is indebted to Emmanuel Katongole, "The Gospel as Politics in Africa," *Theological Studies* 77, no. 3 (2016): 704–20, at 711.

has been heavily involved in uplifting society through education, health care, and other such initiatives. The theologian Joseph Ogbonnaya illustrates this point: "From the days of the missionaries to the present, the Church in Africa has focused its development strategy in Africa in two areas: education and health care," with over 35,000 schools and hundreds of hospitals, orphanages, and homes for the elderly and handicapped.[6] The Catholic Church in the United States of America built up similar institutions in the nineteenth and early twentieth centuries.

Ogbonnaya urges that the Church in (sub-Saharan) Africa needs to do more. He bemoans the fact that African clergy often live better than the people whom they serve. He notes that the laity need to be catechized more with respect to their social responsibilities, HIV/AIDS needs to be more openly addressed, and economic malaise and ecological degradation need more attention.[7] No doubt all this is so, although most people come to church to worship God in Jesus Christ the crucified and risen Redeemer from slavery to sin and death, not to be instructed in the social sciences.

In my view, there is no necessary tension between the primacy of the Church's transcendent purpose (the communion of saints) and the need for social transformation through charity and justice.[8] Ecclesiologically, the two domains can be united

6. Joseph Ogbonnaya, "The Church in Africa: Salt of the Earth?," in *The Church as Salt and Light: Path to an African Ecclesiology of Abundant Life*, ed. Stan Chu Ilo, Joseph Ogbonnaya, and Alex Ojacor (Pickwick, 2011), 65–87, at 74. For brief surveys of African ecclesiology (from perspectives favorable to some aspects of religious liberalism, while also deeply shaped by the African context), see Ogbonnaya, "Ecclesiological Developments in the Majority World," in *T&T Clark Handbook of Ecclesiology*, ed. Kimlyn J. Bender and D. Stephen Long (T&T Clark, 2020), 274–89; and Emmanuel Katongole, "Of Coffins and Churches: Seven Marks of an Emerging African Ecclesiology," in *The Church We Want: African Catholics Look to Vatican III*, ed. Agbonkhianmeghe E. Orobator, SJ (Orbis Books, 2016), 190–202.

7. For a similar concern, see Alex Ojacor, "The Church in Africa and the Search for Abundant Life: Signposts for Renewal and Transformation of God's People in Africa," in Ilo, Ogbonnaya, and Ojacor, *The Church as Salt and Light*, 88–98, at 88. See also Agbonkhianmeghe E. Orobator, SJ, *From Crisis to Kairos: The Mission of the Church in the Time of HIV/AIDS, Refugees and Poverty* (Paulines Publications Africa, 2005).

8. For explorations that adopt an "eschatological reservation"—recognizing that "human salvation and the reign of God are not limited to earthly realities"—see Bede Ukwuije, CSSp., "Political Theology and Liberation Theology in the Works of Elochukwu Uzukwu," in *Under the*

by understanding the Church as the Family of God. As Blessed Columba Marmion says, "Blessed be the Eternal Father who from all eternity has called us to Himself to make us His children and to cause us to share in His own life and His own beatitude."[9]

In African Catholic theology, the image of the Family of God is central, in part because of the strong sense of extended family that Africans traditionally possess. The revered post-colonial Tanzanian president Julius Nyerere made use of this appreciation for extended family in his influential emphasis on *ujamaa*.[10] Regarding the African Church's appreciation for the image of the Church as family, Richard Gaillardetz remarks, "Imaging the church as family offers a helpful path for relating the relationality of familial life to the trinitarian foundations of the church. Africans who see the church as a distinctive form of family readily grasp the sense of reciprocal responsibilities and overarching interdependence that must exist among all church members."[11] For Gaillardetz, the primary value of the image of the Church as the Family of God consists in the fostering of believers' sense of "reciprocal responsibilities and overarching interdependence."

By contrast, I wish to give an especially prominent place in this book to the Church as the Family of God because of believers' adoption as sons and daughters in the Son, sharing in the

Palaver Tree: Doing African Ecclesiology in the Spirit of Vatican II—the Contributions of Elochukwu E. Uzukwu, ed. Stan Chu Ilo and Caroline N. Mbonu (Pickwick, 2023), 179–96, at 191. See also Elochukwu E. Uzukwu, *A Listening Church: Autonomy and Communion in African Churches* (Orbis Books, 1996), although I prefer Ukwuije's synthesis.

9. Columba Marmion, OSB, *Christ, the Life of the Soul*, trans. Alan Bancroft (Zaccheus, 2005), 35.

10. See Julius Nyerere, *Ujamaa: Essays on Socialism* (Oxford University Press, 1968). See also (among other works of scholarship that I will cite below) Oliver Alozie Onwubiko, *The Church as the Family of God*, in his *The Church in Mission in the Light of "Ecclesia in Africa"* (Paulines Publications Africa, 2001), 26–169, previously published as *The Church as the Family of God (ujamaa): In the Light of "Ecclesia in Africa"* (Fulladu, 1999); Joseph Healey and Donald Sybertz, *Towards an African Narrative Theology* (Orbis Books, 1996), 104–67; and Aidan G. Msafiri, "The Church as Family Model: Strengths and Weaknesses," in *African Theology Today*, ed. Emmanuel M. Katongole (University of Scranton Press, 2002), 85–98. These texts are cited in Richard R. Gaillardetz, *Ecclesiology for a Global Church: A People Called and Sent*, rev. ed. (Orbis Books, 2023), 131.

11. Gaillardetz, *Ecclesiology for a Global Church*, 132.

glorious inheritance of the Son.[12] As Ramiro Pellitero observes, the Church as the Family of God—as "the mystery of intimate communion *between human and divine persons*"—arises from our "incorporation into Christ, Son of the Father and firstborn among many brethren, mediating the gift of his Spirit."[13] In his Sermon on the Mount, Jesus describes the "sons of God" as "peacemakers" (Matt 5:9). They are able to bestow the "peace" that is the Spirit of Christ and of the Father (John 14:27). The peace-filled Family of God shares in the Spirit, the bond of Love, that the Father and Son breathe forth eternally and send upon the world.

Thus, there need be no tension between adoption as God's Family and charitable justice for all our neighbors. Configuration to the Lord Jesus requires caring for others in love and mercy, as we would treat our own family members. As the Letter of James says, "If a brother or sister is poorly clothed and in lack of daily food, and one of you says to them, 'Go in peace, be warmed and filled,' without giving them the things needed for the body, what does it profit?" (Jas 2:15–16). At the same time, James insists upon the importance not only of praxis but also of doctrine, by which we "hold the faith of our Lord Jesus Christ" (Jas 2:1). Along these lines, James concludes his letter: "My brethren, if any one among you wanders from the truth and some one brings him back, let

12. These elements are highlighted by Joseph Ogbonnaya, drawing upon the work of Agbonkhianmeghe E. Orobator, SJ, and Elochukwu Uzukwu. See Ogbonnaya, "Ecclesiological Developments in the Majority World," 280–83. Ogbonnaya expresses caution about the ecclesial image of the Family of God: "The events of Africa, especially the genocide in Rwanda, a predominantly Catholic country, while the African synod was going on, shows that the symbol ought to be taken not as a model because of the challenges that could lead to division and violence in the family. The concept of the church as family of God can help in bringing about reconciliation if the African peoples accept the intended image of themselves as brothers and sisters by their priesthood in Christ. But as Archbishop Obiefuna rightly remarked during the first Special Assembly for Africa, the blood of tribes is thicker than the blood of the waters of baptism. Even among the church hierarchy, priests and bishops, ethnic alliances have continued to be obstacles to church administration" (281).

13. Ramiro Pellitero, *Eclesiología*, 2nd ed. (EUNSA, 2019), 88. Pellitero goes on to identify various pastoral implications of the image of the Church as God's Family, including the overcoming of clericalism, the rejection of an individualistic understanding of faith, the deepening of the sense of co-responsibility in evangelization, and "the knowledge that one's own salvation entails preoccupation with the salvation of others" (91). He also speaks of divine filiation, "fraternity among Christians and with all human beings," hospitality and the culture of life, a "civilization of love," the unity of truth and love, and the need for forgiveness (91–92).

him know that whoever brings back a sinner from the error of his way will save his soul from death and will cover a multitude of sins" (Jas 5:19–20). Peace ultimately requires right relationship with the Redeemer in truth.

Inquiring into the Church as God's Family, this chapter undertakes three steps. First, I examine the image of the Church as God's Family as found in the New Testament, drawing upon the recent work of Trevor Burke. Although the Church as God's Family is not a widespread image in ecclesiology today outside Africa, this image has a central place in the New Testament, where it serves to ground our earthly relationships in our sharing in the Trinitarian life through Jesus Christ. The image integrates the transcendent and immanent dimensions of the Church, while insisting upon the Church's utter dependence upon God.

Second, I explore the work of some African theologians on the theme of the Church as God's Family, given that African theologians have generally paid much more attention to this theme than Western theologians, for whom family (beyond the nuclear family) often has less importance as a social category. While recognizing that the category of family can negatively enforce a sense of us-versus-them, African Catholic theologians have much to teach about why the category of family deserves a principal place in Catholic ecclesiology.[14]

14. See the reflections offered by Archbishop Michael Kpakala Francis of Monrovia, Liberia, in his "The Church in Africa Today: Sacrament of Justice, Peace, and Unity," in *The African Synod: Documents, Reflections, Perspectives*, ed. the Africa Faith and Justice Network under the direction of Maura Browne, SND (Orbis Books, 1996), 119–30. Archbishop Francis describes the African perspective both appreciatively and critically: "A man exists as a person, naturally and necessarily enmeshed in a web of relationships. His very existence, his reality is bound up in those relationships. . . . So it is that morality, humaneness, tender and compassionate feelings are largely co-terminal with relationships. Beyond the perimeters of these relationships, the sense of obligation toward another is scarcely perceived. The existence of rights or claims inherent in another upon oneself are not strongly experienced, nor acknowledged apart from relationships. There exists in our culture the very lofty concepts of human dignity and of the respect and obligations due to the human person. A man is perceived as good in proportion to his loyalty to these relationships and to his meticulous fidelity in acquitting himself of all the ensuing requirements. The relationships extend beyond the nuclear family; they include the extended family, the quarter, the clan, and the tribe. But beyond that they dim and fade out completely" (121–22). Archbishop Francis wrote these words within a tragic and terrifying context, which he summarizes as follows: "The Church has suffered very much by the deaths of

Third and lastly, I compare the understanding of the Church as God's Family in Pope Benedict XVI's 2011 apostolic exhortation *Africae Munus* (promulgated after the Second African Synod) to Joseph Ratzinger's ecclesiology in his early work *The Meaning of Christian Brotherhood*. This comparison shows that apprehending the Church as God's Family helps to address a number of urgent issues for ecclesiology, including those arising from liberation theology along with issues related to the doctrine of election and mission. The eternal Father has chosen his people in his Son Jesus Christ "before the foundation of the world, that we should be holy and blameless before him" (Eph 1:4).

Although the *Catechism of the Catholic Church* does not include the image of the Family of God among the various scriptural images of the Church, the *Catechism* does say that the Church is "the house of God in which his *family* dwells" and also that the Church is "the household of God" (1 Tim 3:15).[15] Furthermore, the *Catechism* adds that God, in building up his Church over the generations, ensures that the "'family of God' is gradually formed and takes shape during the stages of human history."[16] Similarly, Vatican II's Dogmatic Constitution on the Church, *Lumen Gentium*, focuses on the Church as the People of God, the Body of Christ, and the Temple of the Spirit. But *Lumen Gentium* also calls for all human beings to "be led into the unity of the family of God."[17]

many of her personnel, by the destruction of her institutions, and the displacement of her flocks. We, the pastors, have suffered physically and mentally at seeing brothers and sisters fighting each other. But what is most painful is the destruction of a whole generation of young boys and girls by warlords" (121).

15. *Catechism of the Catholic Church*, 2nd ed. (Libreria Editrice Vaticana, 1997), §756.

16. *Catechism of the Catholic Church*, §759.

17. Second Vatican Council, *Lumen Gentium* §28, in *Vatican Council II*, vol. 1, *The Conciliar and Postconciliar Documents*, ed. Austin Flannery, OP, rev. ed. (Costello, 1996), 350–426, at 386–87. This phrase appears in the context of *Lumen Gentium*'s teaching on the ordained priesthood. Aloys Grillmeier, SJ, remarks about this teaching of *Lumen Gentium*: "The word of God and the mediation of Christ give the priesthood of the new covenant a fullness without parallel in the history of religions. But since Christ, the mediator and head of the new humanity, wills to unite his brothers to the family of his Father, the task of governing is imposed along with those of preaching and service. . . . When the Church is thought of as the people or the family of God, this service is understood as gathering men and leading them to God, as life, prayer and

Gaillardetz has rightly noted that the image of the Family of God complements the ecclesiological paths favored by Vatican II, including communion ecclesiology, People-of-God ecclesiology, and Eucharistic ecclesiology. He states, "The church-as-family represents a natural development of Vatican II's vision of the church as the people of God, with roots as well in the conciliar theology of the church as communion."[18] I agree with this observation, to which I would add an emphasis on the cross. The Church as the Family of God is no romanticized family, but rather comes into being at the cross and remains firmly grounded in the cross. As the biblical scholar Francis Moloney says (discussing John 19), "Because of the cross and from the moment of the cross a new family of Jesus has been created."[19]

II. SCRIPTURAL BACKGROUND: THE FAMILY OF GOD

Let me begin by providing some scriptural background to the image of the Church as God's Family. In *Adopted into God's Family: Exploring a Pauline Metaphor*, Trevor Burke explores Paul's understanding of our "adoption as sons" in the incarnate Son Jesus Christ (Rom 8:23).[20] Paul is not the only New Testament author

teaching in the midst of their heritage in the land of the Lord." Grillmeier, "Chapter III, Article 28," in *Commentary on the Documents of Vatican II*, vol. 1, ed. Herbert Vorgrimler, trans. Lalit Adolphus, Kevin Smyth, and Richard Strachan (Herder and Herder, 1967), 218–26, at 222–23. For an African reflection on *Lumen Gentium*'s ecclesiology, focusing on the image of the People of God (while also addressing the image of the Family of God), see Gerald Azike, *The People of God in "Lumen Gentium": A Theological Renewal of Institutional Ecclesiology and Its Implications for the Igbo Christians of Nigeria* (Gregorian University Press, 2016).

18. Gaillardetz, *Ecclesiology for a Global Church*, 132.

19. Francis J. Moloney, SDB, *The Gospel of John* (Liturgical, 1998), 504.

20. Trevor J. Burke, *Adopted into God's Family: Exploring a Pauline Metaphor* (InterVarsity, 2006). See also Burke, *Family Matters: A Socio-Historical Study of Kinship Metaphors in 1 Thessalonians* (T&T Clark International, 2003); Jeanne Stevenson-Moessner, *The Spirit of Adoption: At Home in God's Family* (Westminster John Knox, 2003); James M. Scott, *Adoption as Sons of God: An Investigation into the Background of huiothesia in the Pauline Corpus* (Mohr, 1992), whose emphasis upon 2 Samuel 7:11–16 rightly comes in for significant criticism from Burke; and Brendan Byrne, SJ, *"Sons of God"—"Seed of Abraham": A Study of the Idea of the Sonship of God of All Christians in Paul against the Jewish Background* (Biblical Institute, 1979). See also, for discussion of the early Church's understanding of itself as a new family, Joseph H. Hellerman, *The Ancient Church as Family* (Fortress, 2001); Philip E. Esler, "Family Imagery and Christian Identity in Gal. 5:13 to 6:10," in *Constructing Early Christian Families: Family as Social Reality*

to proclaim that believers belong to God's family: John does too, as for instance in 1 John 3:1, "See what love the Father has given us, that we should be called children of God; and so we are." In Christ and through the Spirit, God has made us not only into his friends but into his beloved family, with whom God shares all that he is. Whereas John describes this new familial relationship largely in terms of new birth (see also John 1:12–13 and John 3), Paul describes it in terms of adoption.

As Burke observes, the metaphor of adoption indicates that Christ transfers us from one family to another: we begin in a family caught up in sin and death, the family of the fallen Adam, and we are transferred into the Family of Christ the New Adam.[21] The notion of coming to be part of God's Family in Christ is analogical. The Father's generation of the Son is not a divine instance of human fatherhood, since such an understanding would subordinate the Son to the Father. The Son is not the Father's child. Yet, the bond of intimacy shared by Father and Son—the communication of divine life—is indeed shared in by believers through the power of the Holy Spirit. God's Family the Church is constituted by deifying grace.

Burke points out that the Pauline notion of adoption into God's Family has ethical ramifications. Believers are expected to behave in a manner appropriate to children of God. This manner is cruciform, self-surrendering love, inclusive of justice and all the virtues.[22] As Brant Pitre, Michael Barber, and John Kincaid say in their *Paul, a New Covenant Jew*, for Paul "the righteous act of Christ enables those who are in him to *become* righteous. . . . Those in Christ are so truly united to him that they share in the

and Metaphor, ed. Halvor Moxnes (Routledge, 1997), 121–49; and Karl Olav Sandnes, *A New Family: Conversion and Ecclesiology in the Early Church with Cross-Cultural Comparisons* (Peter Lang, 1994).

21. For the significance and scope of New Adam Christology, see my *Reconfiguring Thomistic Christology* (Cambridge University Press, 2023), chapter 2.

22. See the chapters on Pauline ethics (written by Harrington) in Daniel J. Harrington, SJ and James F. Keenan, SJ, *Paul and Virtue Ethics: Building Bridges between New Testament Studies and Moral Theology* (Rowman & Littlefield, 2010).

Lord Jesus's own divine sonship, becoming adopted children of God in him, living in union with him and in conformity to his character."[23] Paul spells things out lest there be any misunderstanding: "Now the works of flesh are plain: [sexual] immorality, impurity, licentiousness, idolatry, sorcery, enmity, strife, jealousy, anger, selfishness, dissension, party spirit, envy, drunkenness, carousing, and the like. . . . Those who do such things shall not inherit the kingdom of God" (Gal 5:19–21).[24] God's Family must heed this warning.

Left to our own resources, we could not live up to this charge; we would continue to live in accordance with the patterns of the old Adam. Fortunately, adoption into God's Family comes from God's will in Christ and his Spirit—from election and grace—rather than from mere human resources.[25] According to Paul, "In Christ Jesus you are all sons of God, through faith. For as many of you as were baptized into Christ have put on Christ" (Gal 3:26–27). God has chosen us to be his own children—"and if children, then heirs, heirs of God and fellow heirs with Christ" (Rom 8:17). In receiving the Holy Spirit, we receive the "spirit of sonship," and we are enabled to call out with Christ, "Abba! Father!" (Rom 8:15).[26] In Christ the Son, we will receive the

23. Brant Pitre, Michael P. Barber, and John A. Kincaid, *Paul, a New Covenant Jew: Rethinking Pauline Theology* (Eerdmans, 2019), 195, 209.

24. See John M. G. Barclay, *Obeying the Truth: Paul's Ethics in Galatians* (Regent College Publishing, 2005), 152–53; and Frank J. Matera, *New Testament Ethics: The Legacies of Jesus and Paul* (Westminster John Knox, 1996), 171—although Matera interprets sexual immorality as focused on the individual, whereas for Paul and for the later Catholic tradition sexual virtue is crucial for familial and communal flourishing, as I show in my chapter on chastity in *Aquinas's Eschatological Ethics and the Virtue of Temperance* (University of Notre Dame Press, 2019).

25. See John M. G. Barclay, *Paul and the Power of Grace* (Eerdmans, 2020), 150 and elsewhere; and Matera, *New Testament Ethics*, chapter 5: "An Ethic of Election: The Letters to the Thessalonians."

26. Joseph H. Hellerman adds the claim that Paul was seeking to overcome divisions: "The Corinthian and Roman churches can be viewed as archetypical examples of the two ways in which human beings have been divided throughout history. Ethnicity divides us at the horizontal level, so that we gravitate toward those of similar racial and cultural backgrounds, and we fear those who are different. Socio-economic inequalities generate a vertical hierarchy of human persons, so that we look down with disdain, or up with desire, at those who stand on different rungs of the social ladder. The church family model is Paul's divinely inspired solution to these seemingly intractable human issues of race and rank." Hellerman, *When the Church Was a Family: Recapturing Jesus' Vision for Authentic Community* (B&H Academic, 2009), 96.

inheritance that Christ already fully enjoys—namely, the riches of an intimate and everlasting communion with God the Father. Paul proclaims that Christ came "so that we might receive adoption as sons. And because you are sons, God has sent the Spirit of his Son into our hearts, crying, 'Abba! Father!'" (Gal 4:6). In Christ, God has made us into his heirs, with the Church as "our mother" (Gal 4:26).[27]

In the Family of God, Christ is the "first-born," but not for himself alone: he is the "first-born among many brethren" (Rom 8:29). It is Christ who, by his cross and Resurrection and by pouring out his Spirit, brings about the Family of God. This has been the plan of God from the outset of creation. God has eternally elected believers "to be his sons through Jesus Christ" (Eph 1:5).[28] God even now gives us "the riches of his glorious inheritance" (Eph 1:18). Thus, Paul makes clear that "the goal of the Christ-event is familial."[29]

It is noteworthy that the Scriptures of Israel already describe the people of Israel as God's son or sons/children. For instance, in Isaiah 1:2, God bemoans the fact that "sons have I reared and brought up, but they have rebelled against me." Hosea 11:1, cited in Matthew 2:15, portrays God as saying, "When Israel was a child, I loved him, and out of Egypt I called my son." In Exodus 4:22, God instructs Moses to say to Pharaoh, "Thus says the Lord, Israel is my first-born son." Deuteronomy 32:18 rebukes rebellious Israel by appealing to Israel's status as God's son: "You [Israel] were unmindful of the Rock that begot you, and you forgot the God who gave you birth." In Jeremiah 3:19, God mournfully proclaims to his people, "I thought you would call me, My Father, and would not turn from following me." In this same passage, God begs his people, "Return, O faithless sons, I will heal your

27. See also, on ongoing Christian sin, Hellerman, 151.

28. See Rudolf Schnackenburg, *The Epistle to the Ephesians: A Commentary*, trans. Helen Heron (T&T Clark, 1991), 52–54.

29. Pitre, Barber, and Kincaid, *Paul, a New Covenant Jew*, 199.

faithlessness" (Jer 3:22). Further instances along these lines could be cited, demonstrating over and over again that "God's covenant people" are "the family of God"—a point that while already true in the Old Testament, is far truer in the new covenant through the death and Resurrection of the incarnate Son.[30] N.T. Wright affirms, "Messiah-people constitute a *family*, who are to live in practical ways as befits siblings."[31]

In the Pauline understanding of adoptive sonship, as Burke says, believers enjoy "a belonging where God as 'Father' occupies centre stage in his 'family.'"[32] Another relevant point is that the intimate term "*abba*" appears to have been distinctively used by Jesus vis-à-vis God the Father and extended by Paul to the way in which Jesus's followers are to address the divine Father.[33] This use of the term "*abba*" goes beyond the earlier references to God as a Father to his people, whether in the Old Testament or in Second Temple literature. Jesus addresses God as Father in relation to himself, not simply in relation to all Israel.[34] When we are adopted as sons, we share in Jesus's unique relationship with his Father.

Furthermore, Jesus insists that henceforth, adherence to one's blood-family or ancestral family must bow before his own claims. He states in the Gospel of Matthew, "I have come to set a man against his father, and a daughter against her mother, and a daughter-in-law against her mother-in-law; and a man's foes will be those of his own household. He who loves father or mother more than me is not worthy of me; and he who loves son or daughter more than me is not worthy of me" (Matt 10:35–37). Such statements have been taken by some recent scholars to mean

30. Pitre, Barber, and Kincaid, 207. I am turning Pitre, Barber, and Kincaid's sentence about Pauline theology ("those who are justified belong to God's covenant people—that is, the family of God") to my own purposes.

31. N.T. Wright, *Paul and the Faithfulness of God*, bk. 1 (Fortress, 2013), 545.

32. Burke, *Adopted into God's Family*, 73.

33. See Burke, 93–95, addressing concerns raised by James Barr and others.

34. See Burke, 95n55, citing Ben Witherington III and Laura M. Ice, *The Shadow of the Almighty: Father, Son, and Spirit in Biblical Perspective* (Eerdmans, 2002), 60.

that Jesus rejected marriage and family, due to his apocalyptic worldview.[35] Candida Moss and Joel Baden remark that "for Mark, the author of our earliest Gospel, life begins at baptism."[36] On this view, biological familial life is no longer of significance, at least in the sense that the family "is constructed at the foot of the cross."[37] Marianne Blickenstaff puts the matter even more sharply, arguing that the Gospel of Matthew depicts Jesus as "the *only* bridegroom, and all references to weddings are marked by violence."[38] According to Blickenstaff, the choice for the early Christians is "between biological and fictive family ties, between earthly masters and the heavenly kingdom."[39]

Such dichotomies misunderstand Christ's teaching. In proclaiming the imminent arrival of the kingdom of God (which he himself *is* in person), Christ opens up the path of virginity, witnessing to the life of the kingdom. But Christ does not reject marriage or family, so long as they are subordinate to the new Family—the eschatological Israel, the Church—that he is bringing about. He knows that fidelity to the Gospel will strain familial ties in many instances, and these familial ties cannot be set above the Gospel. In this sense, those who do the will of God are indeed the truest family (Matt 12:49–50), since they are adoptive

35. See for instance April D. DeConick, *Holy Misogyny: Why the Sex and Gender Conflicts in the Early Church Still Matter* (Continuum, 2011), 49: "Since Jesus thought that the age of the world was very advanced, and the end so near that God's kingdom was already inbreaking, stories about him suggest that he questioned whether or not it was necessary to continue to procreate in the short interim before the new world fully appeared and sexual behavior was abandoned altogether." On the other hand, DeConick earlier deems Jesus to be "a strong advocate for marriage, and staying married" on the grounds that he rejected divorce entirely (45). For further arguments that Jesus rejected marriage, see Calum Carmichael, *Sex and Religion in the Bible* (Yale University Press, 2010); and David Wheeler-Reed, *Regulating Sex in the Roman Empire: Ideology, the Bible, and the Early Christians* (Yale University Press, 2017).

36. Candida R. Moss and Joel S. Baden, *Reconceiving Infertility: Biblical Perspectives on Procreation and Childlessness* (Princeton University Press, 2015), 169.

37. Moss and Baden, 170. Moss and Baden argue that the New Testament deliberately problematizes the notion that "fertility is a blessing and a good," and they suggest that today we too should consider embracing infertility (including biological infertility) as a blessing and a good (236). In my view, they have missed the point of the New Testament's stories about infertility and about freely chosen virginity.

38. Marianne Blickenstaff, *"While the Bridegroom Is with Them": Marriage, Family, Gender, and Violence in the Gospel of Matthew* (T&T Clark International, 2005), 9.

39. Blickenstaff, 9.

sons and daughters in the Son, sharing through the Spirit in the divine life. To be united to Christ is indeed far greater than any biological familial or ethnic bond, but Christ condemns those who ignore God's commandments about the biological family: "For God commanded, 'Honor your father and your mother,' and, 'He who speaks evil of father or mother, let him surely die'" (Matt 15:4; see Exod 20:12 and 21:17).[40]

In the Gospel of John, Christ on the cross establishes the Church as the Family of God. We read, "Jesus saw his mother, and the disciple whom he loved standing near, [and] he said to his mother, 'Woman, behold, your son!' Then he said to the disciple, 'Behold, your mother!'" (John 19:26–27). This exchange seals the Church as God's Family in Christ. In John 14, too, Jesus promises that believers will receive the indwelling of the Father and the Son and that believers will receive the Holy Spirit. All this is framed by the Evangelist's proclamation in John 1 that those who believe in Jesus are members of God's Family: "To all who received him, who believed in his name, he gave power to become children of God; who were born, not of blood nor of the will of the flesh nor of the will of man, but of God" (John 1:12–13). In light of the whole Gospel of John, Sherri Brown observes that when Jesus on the cross teaches that his own mother is now the mother of the beloved disciple (representative of all believers), the point is to establish the covenantal community as "the family of the new community of God."[41] As Francis Moloney remarks, "As a result of the lifting up of Jesus on the cross the Beloved Disciple and the Mother become one."[42]

40. In his argument with the Pharisees and scribes, Jesus identifies himself as a defender of God's commandments on these matters: see Rudolf Schnackenburg, *The Gospel of Matthew*, trans. Robert R. Barr (Eerdmans, 2002), 148.

41. Sherri Brown, *Gift upon Gift: Covenant through Word in the Gospel of John* (Pickwick, 2010), 196.

42. Moloney, *The Gospel of John*, 503. For discussion of Moloney's and Brown's views, see chapter 5 of my *Engaging the Doctrine of Jesus (and Mary): A Traditional, Historical-Critical, and Mariological Christology* (Cascade, 2025).

At every step—Incarnation, Cross, Resurrection, Eucharist—the profundity of our union with the incarnate Son, so as truly to share in his Sonship vis-à-vis the Father, becomes even more evident. Matthias Joseph Scheeben describes this familial bond by stating, "In the eyes of the eternal Father we are members of His natural Son."[43] The Family of God surpasses all our imagining: we are not merely extrinsic to the Son's relation to his Father, but rather, preeminently in the Eucharistic liturgy, we "truly take part in the infinite glorification which the Son of God gives to His Father. God receives this glorification from us too, because we offer Him Christ as our head, and because Christ who dwells within us presents us to the Father as His members."[44]

III. AFRICAN THEOLOGIANS ON THE CHURCH AS THE FAMILY OF GOD

African bishops and theologians have long emphasized the Church's status as God's Family. In fact, as the theologian Alex Ojacor remarks, African understandings of family profoundly illumine the biblical testimony to the Church as God's Family. Ojacor observes regarding the nature of the family, "The African experience of family is much wider than the word suggests in Europe and America. . . . A family in Africa includes children, parents, grandparents, uncles, aunts, brothers, and sisters. . . . The

43. Matthias Joseph Scheeben, *The Mysteries of Christianity*, trans. Cyril Vollert, SJ, 2nd ed. (Emmaus Academic Press, 2023), 493. Scheeben's language here would need to be very carefully understood, but I think he has captured the truth of the Family of God. Scheeben's full paragraph reads: "As a result of the Incarnation we are no longer merely adopted children of God. Through the sacred humanity we are received into the natural, only-begotten Son of God as His members, and as His members share in His personal relationship to the Father, somewhat as His own humanity does. . . . And the Father extends His hypostatical fatherhood to us, not only by some imitation of it, but as it is in itself, just as He does to Christ's own humanity. For greater clarity we might here again bring in the analogy of marriage in which, especially once it is consummated, a real, and not simply a juridical, kinship arises between the bride and the father of the bridegroom" (493).

44. Scheeben, 495. As Scheeben says, "If Christ were not actually present in the Eucharist, or if He were not present as the sacrificial Lamb, we could not associate ourselves with Him in one sacrifice except by a moral union, a union of affections. We could not even share in the fruits of the sacrifice by any real, true participation" (495).

family also includes departed relatives and unborn members still in the loins of the living."[45] Laurenti Magesa similarly emphasizes the breadth of the word "family." Referencing the work of John Mary Waliggo, Magesa explains that "the authentic family . . . consists of father, mother, brothers and sisters, aunts and uncles, and so on, and so should the authentic Church-family. It is not constituted only of the bishop but is made up of all the faithful in the diocese."[46]

African bishops are well aware that the African understanding of family illuminates the significance of the biblical testimony to the Church as God's Family. The theologian Teresa Okure points out, "The First African Synod adopted the NT and Vatican II's all-inclusive definition of church as God's people by choosing the family as the model for what it means to be church in Africa."[47] Okure identifies not only positive but also negative aspects of this image. On the negative side, she observes that the family in Africa is heavily patriarchal. Positively—and, as she says, theologically fruitful in the ways intended by the First African Synod—"family in Africa embraces all members on equal terms regardless of

45. Ojacor, "The Church in Africa and the Search for Abundant Life," 92. At the same time, Ojacor notes that today "the African family is in mortal danger. The migrant labor system, social and geographical mobility, unemployment, housing shortages, rural-urban migrations, internal displacement due to civil wars (placing people in squalid 'displaced person' camps), refugees, the corrosive influence of the Western neo-pagan culture, and [other] factors are destroying the traditional family and its many positive values" (92–93).

46. Laurenti Magesa, "The Future of the African Synod," in *The African Synod: Documents, Reflections, Perspectives*, ed. Maura Browne, SND, and the Africa Faith and Justice Network (Orbis Books, 1996), 163–71, at 168. Magesa goes on to make the troubling claim, however, that the de facto Church is separated from the "official Church." He argues that "there are in reality two parallel Churches [in Africa], the juridical Church and the Church of the Spirit" (169). This claim implies a mistaken notion of the relationship between Spirit and institution. See also John Mary Waliggo, "'The Synod of Hope' at a Time of Crisis in Africa," in Africa Faith and Justice Network and Browne, *The African Synod*, 199–210. Although critical of the synod's lack of input (in the preparation period) from the laity, Waliggo has many positive things to say about the synod itself. He appreciates the theme of the Church as God's Family, while warning against the patriarchal and overly hierarchical elements of the traditional African family.

47. Teresa Okure, "Becoming the Church of the New Testament," in Orobator, *The Church We Want*, 93–105, at 95. See also Pope John Paul II, *Ecclesia in Africa* §63, apostolic exhortation, September 14, 1995, vatican.va.

personal, social, religious, and other affiliations since one ancestral blood flows in all members and bonds them inseparably."[48]

Okure observes that a number of eminent African theologians have taken up the theme of the Church as family, including Agbonkhianmeghe Orobator in his 2000 book *The Church as Family: African Ecclesiology in Its Social Context*.[49] Indeed, according to the groundbreaking African theologian Bénézet Bujo, "A genuinely African ecclesiology seems to rely on a correct understanding of community and family."[50] Bujo conceives of Jesus as analogously understandable in light of the traditional African view of the tribal father or "primordial ancestor who is the sustaining force for later ancestors, who form a chain of unity and through whom the contemporary generation is able to trace its

48. Okure, "Becoming the Church of the New Testament," 95. However, Okure concludes, "African theologians need to make the call to be Eucharistic church, anchored in the new commandment of love, the soul of their theologizing in service to the church we want to be. We need to help the church hierarchy evolve new practical measures for internalizing this. This requires courageous revision of age-old church structures and the evolution of a new testament ecclesiology and Christology that serve as antidotes to those anti-gospel value systems that infiltrated the church from the empire" (104). I concur with the call to be a Eucharistic Church, but I am skeptical about the revision Okure proposes, given the positions that Okure takes in her "Church-Family of God: The Place of God's Reconciliation, Justice, and Peace," in *Reconciliation, Justice, and Peace: The Second African Synod*, ed. Agbonkhianmeghe E. Orobator, SJ (Orbis Books, 2011), 13–24, at 21. She appears to favor moving away from hierarchy and from the priest/laity distinction, along with including women in the "ministerial priesthood," now understood in functional rather than hierarchical terms.

49. See Agbonkhianmeghe E. Orobator, SJ, *The Church as Family: African Ecclesiology in Its Social Context* (Paulines Publications Africa, 2000). See also Nicholas Fogliacco, "The Family: An African Metaphor for Trinity and Church," in *Inculturating the Church in Africa: Theological and Practical Perspectives*, ed. Cecil McGarry and Patrick Ryan (Paulines Publications Africa, 2001), 120–58; Charles Nyamiti, *Studies in African Christian Theology*, vol. 4, *Christ's Ancestral Mediation Through the Church Understood as God's Family: An Essay on African Ecclesiology* (CUEA, 2010); Joseph G. Healey, *Building the Church as Family of God: Evaluation of Small Christian Communities in Eastern Africa* (AMECEA Gaba Publications, 2012).

50. Bénézet Bujo, "On the Road toward an African Ecclesiology: Reflections on the Synod," trans. T. Allan Smith, in Africa Faith and Justice Network and Browne, *The African Synod*, 139–51, at 140. In the latter part of his essay, Bujo argues for an "African palaver model" of the Church, and he criticizes the "West-European model" of the Catholic Church as "a culturally conditioned concept of Church that arose in the West" (149). What he has in view in speaking of the "West-European model," however, seems to be the understanding of the Church affirmed dogmatically at Trent, Vatican I, and Vatican II—and if so, then he needs to give more place to the Holy Spirit as distinct from "culturally conditioned" influences. For further discussion of Bujo's theology, see my "Natural Law in Bénézet Bujo, Paulinus Odozor, and Stephen L. Brock," in *Continuing the Quest for Morality Truly Christian, Truly African: The Achievement of Paulinus Odozor, C.S.Sp.*, ed. Maurice A. Agbaw-Ebai and Matthew Levering (St. Augustine's, forthcoming).

origins back to the first ancestor."[51] From this perspective, which strikes me as having much ecclesiological value in a time when the communion of saints is often no longer appreciated, Jesus the Last Adam (see 1 Cor 15:45) is accomplishing "the eschatological 'gathering of Israel' [the family of God] . . . as the eschatological tribal father."[52]

For his part, the theologian Idara Otu, in *Communion Ecclesiology and Social Transformation in African Catholicism*, argues that "the Church as Family of God image is an inculturation of the communion ecclesiology of Vatican II."[53] He begins by observing that the 276 African bishops at Vatican II included only six indigenous Africans. The First African Synod, therefore, marked a major step forward for the African Church. Otu praises the First African Synod, arguing that it "galvanized the church in Africa toward a critical reflection and discernment on the content and context of the faith in Africa."[54] At the time of the calling of the Synod, he notes, the African continent was experiencing severe social and economic malaise, including wars, refugee crises, corrupt dictatorships, and the Rwandan genocide.

Reflecting upon Pope John Paul II's apostolic exhortation

51. Bujo, "On the Road Toward an African Ecclesiology," 140.

52. Bujo, 141. Bujo continues, "In many Black African ethnic groups the presence of the ancestors is visually represented by means of a special tree, the ancestor tree. The tree in question is an ever-verdant tree, such as the ficus, which symbolizes the life that never dies. Among the Bahema of eastern Zaire the ficus is planted on the grave of a family father. The father lying in the grave is not dead at all but shoots forth to new life as a ficus tree so that he now becomes shelter and vivifying 'spirit.' The branches and leaves of this tree symbolize the numerous descendants of the deceased. They owe to him their verdure. Separated from him they cannot survive. . . . It is not out of place to transfer this fundamental reality to Jesus Christ. Primarily by means of his cross the murdered Jesus becomes a green tree that dies no more. He owes this new life to God the Father, who raised him up in such a way that he definitively overcame death. The Father, however, operates together with the Holy Spirit, who is the inner vitality represented by the white resin of the ficus. The ficus tree or the cross as the tree of life thereby has a trinitarian dimension. Only if the branches and leaves of the ficus obtain its life-giving energy do they stay green. Similarly, as his members, Christ's disciples are guaranteed the life that never dies when they are rooted in the life of the Trinity through the very same Christ risen to life. . . . The faithful whose life is played out under the tree, which symbolizes the Risen One and the Church simultaneously, receive their vitality and sense of belonging in the Spirit through whom the Father raised the Son" (141–42).

53. Idara Otu, MSP, *Communion Ecclesiology and Social Transformation in African Catholicism: Between Vatican Council II and African Synod II* (Pickwick, 2020), 99.

54. Otu, 105.

Ecclesia in Africa, which emerged out of the First African Synod, Otu observes that the African reception of Vatican II's image of the People of God naturally focused on family. *Ecclesia in Africa* exhorts African theologians to undertake a study of Scripture and Catholic doctrine so as to deepen the place of the image of Family of God in Catholic ecclesiology and Catholic life. Otu provides an extensive presentation of the motif of God's family in the Old and New Testaments, demonstrating (with Orobator) that "Israel as God's people is a family of many families," a family of God that is "chosen and blessed by Yahweh" and that has the responsibility of obeying Torah, loving God and neighbor, and worshipping God rightly.[55] Otu deems significant the first Christians' practice of meeting in private homes for worship, thus further grounding the image of "household of God" (Eph 2:19; 1 Tim 3:15) or Family of God. The Church as God's Family is known by doing God's will, by transcending the ties of blood-kinship, and by willingness to sacrifice even familial bonds in this world in order to build up the kingdom of love.

As Otu says, "In the new family, God is the Father, and the disciples are adopted children of God in Christ, through the Holy Spirit (John 20:17; Matt 3:17)."[56] In God's Family—grounded in Baptism and filial adoption in Christ—all brothers and sisters are equal, deserving of love and care. Otu demonstrates that the best elements of African family life shine a bright light upon the ecclesiological value of the image of Family of God. He also investigates patristic evidence for the significance of understanding the Church as the Family of God, although *Ecclesia in Africa* does not treat the Church Fathers. He shows that the familial image, in various forms (including "brotherhood," the Church as "mother," the family as a "little church," and so on) has importance in the writings of Clement of Rome, Ignatius of Antioch, Tertullian, Cyprian, John Chrysostom, and Augustine. He briefly

55. Otu, 115.
56. Otu, 118.

surveys the image of the Church as Family, or the family as the domestic church, as found in Vatican II and the writings of Popes Paul VI, John Paul II, and Benedict XVI. Pope Francis calls the Church a "family of families, constantly enriched by the lives of all those domestic churches."[57] In his encyclical *Laudato Si'*, Francis describes God's whole creation as "a kind of universal family."[58] Pope Benedict XVI, in his encyclical *Deus Caritas Est*, teaches that "the Church as God's family must be a place where help is given and received, and at the same time, a place where people are also prepared to serve those outside her confines who are in need of help."[59]

As Otu points out, *Ecclesia in Africa* appeals to the traditional African family and its strengths—as distinct from distortions such as "exclusion, paternalism, ethnocentrism, division, subjugation, and domination."[60] The strengths of the traditional African family include, as *Ecclesia in Africa* indicates, "the values of unity, solidarity, fecundity, participation, fraternity, mutual aid, trust, reconciliation, tradition, common good, and hospitality."[61] In Africa, personhood is understood to be intrinsically relational. Traditional African families value the life of children (including the unborn), and traditional African families honor the family's ancestors.

Otu draws out numerous lessons about the above-named familial values and how they apply to the Church as God's Family. He emphasizes the welcoming of each and every person, compassionate care for those in need, and dialogue in pursuit of reconciliation. The model of the Church as Family is ultimately the Trinitarian communion of love. In this regard, Otu observes, "the

57. Pope Francis, *Amoris Laetitia* §29, apostolic exhortation, March 19, 2016, cited in Otu, *Communion Ecclesiology*, 124.

58. Pope Francis, *Laudato Si'* §89, encyclical letter, May 24, 2015, cited in Otu, *Communion Ecclesiology*, 125.

59. Pope Benedict XVI, *Deus Caritas Est* §32, encyclical letter, December 25, 2005, cited in Otu, *Communion Ecclesiology*, 125.

60. Otu, *Communion Ecclesiology*, 126.

61. Otu, 126. Otu is indebted for this list to the work of Orobator.

concept of *perichōrēsis* or *circumincessio* becomes a valuable analogy."[62] He deems the Church as God's Family to be constituted in Baptism, in which believers are incorporated into one Body, the Body of Christ, through the Spirit. The Eucharist sustains and celebrates the unity of the Church in Christ. For Otu, the Trinitarian ground of the Church as God's family means that evangelization includes both the proclamation of Christ crucified and risen as the Savior of the world and an insistence upon justice, peace, and reconciliation. He lifts up in particular the Small Christian Communities that have formed among lay Catholics throughout Africa.

The theologian Paulinus Odozor similarly notes that the African family's unity in ancestral blood is analogous to the Church as "a family made so by one faith, one baptism, one Lord, and sharing a bond on the basis of the blood of Christ into whom we are all baptized."[63] Odozor thereby places the cross at the center of the image of the Church as God's Family. It is the blood of Christ that unites believers, since Christ draws together his followers by his "blood of the covenant" (Mark 14:24). Odozor, like Otu, underlines the necessity of clarifying the family image, so as not to import sins such as patriarchal dominance into African ecclesiology, or to suppose somehow that the Church in Africa is "a collection of clans and peoples who have consanguinity and thus are bonded together" *as Africans* rather than as baptized believers incorporated into Christ.[64]

Odozor adds that the Church as the Family of God is a reality in Africa but not a fully realized reality; there is still a long way to go, and indeed to describe the African Church as God's Family

62. Otu, 134.

63. Paulinus Ikechukwu Odozor, CSSp., *Morality Truly Christian, Truly African: Foundational, Methodological, and Theological Considerations* (University of Notre Dame Press, 2014), 275. See also Odozor's "The Church as Family of God in Africa," in *Handbook of African Catholicism*, ed. Stan Chu Ilo (Orbis Books, 2022), 573–85. He notes, "One of the enduring legacies of the First Synod for Africa was the use of the metaphor of church as 'family of God' as a reality of African life" ("The Church as Family of God in Africa," 573).

64. Odozor, "The Church as Family of God in Africa," 574–75.

is "a statement of theological hope" rather than an empirical assessment.[65] Looking back on his participation in the synod from which *Africae Munus* derived, he remarks, "The Second African Synod was . . . very much an ecclesiological synod" that "spent a lot of time discussing the nature, mission, and spirituality of ecclesial communion in Africa."[66] *Africae Munus* recognizes that many crises, such as the Rwandan genocide, have divided Africans along familial or tribal lines. Since this is so, the image of the Church as God's Family might seem to have unfortunate overtones. The image of the Family of God might seem exclusionary and thus prone to encouraging violence and pride, or it might seem unrealistic in light of ongoing tribal conflicts.

With such concerns in mind, the theologian Stan Chu Ilo comments, "In a continent wounded by ethnocentrism . . . African ecclesiology must show the African faithful the reason to believe that the waters of baptism are stronger than the blood of ethnicity."[67] When the Church is true to itself, the Church as God's Family is marked not by the divisive arrogance of status or by powerful familial connections, but by the self-giving love of Christ and by the witness of martyrdom. Emmanuel Katongole has reflected upon this distinctively Christian family in his work on the martyred Sisters of the Resurrection in Busasamana, Rwanda.[68] Katongole is more optimistic than I am, however,

65. Odozor, 575. Of course, as Odozor says, "African Christians are sometimes as disunited as their societies and sometimes even more so; African churches are sometimes as un-Christlike as the societies in which they are found; and African church men and women can be as sinful as their secular or non-Christian counterparts on the continent" (575).

66. Odozor, *Morality Truly Christian, Truly African*, 280.

67. Stan Chu Ilo, "African Ecclesiologies," in *The Oxford Handbook of Ecclesiology*, ed. Paul Avis (Oxford University Press, 2018), 615–38, at 635.

68. See Emmanuel Katongole, *Born from Lament: The Theology and Politics of Hope in Africa* (Eerdmans, 2017), 256. Katongole remarks, "For the African Church to live into this kind of self-emptying *kenosis* that Paul talks about, it has to sacrifice the elegance and magisterial authority that comes with distance. It has to come down within the confused mess of everydayness and risk becoming less and less churchly, so as to nurture and gestate, to use Éla's expression, 'a different world right here,' which is what the new future in Africa must be about." Katongole, *The Sacrifice of Africa: A Political Theology for Africa* (Eerdmans, 2011), 144. I affirm "everdayness" but, in Catholicism, that includes "magisterial authority." Katongole calls for "a church committed to a new future in Africa" (Katongole, *Born from Lament*, 146). In response, I would emphasize that the Church is committed to Jesus Christ crucified and to his Kingdom,

about the prospects for "a thorough theological reinvention of politics."[69] As noted above, neither the truths of Catholic social teaching nor the sacraments have generally been able to transform majority-Catholic countries into exemplars of political and economic well-being. In this regard, theologians have much to learn from scholars who have studied the political, legal, and economic structures that decrease poverty levels.[70] Even more than Katongole, therefore, I would emphasize that the Church as God's Family is not a competitor of or replacement for the world's structures, but rather is something entirely different—challenging the totalizing claims of both politics and economics.[71] At the

which cannot guarantee a better economic and political future in Africa or anywhere else. Katongole assuages my concerns when he highlights Angelina Atyam's Christ-centered ministry of mercy in the context of the atrocities of Northern Uganda, and when he proclaims that "the new future is a gift grounded in God's forgiveness and reconciliation" in Jesus Christ" (Katongole, *Born from Lament*, 162).

69. Katongole, *Born from Lament*, 262. Few Catholic theologians have practical answers to the problems of political economy in African nations—though an exception surely is Cyril Orji, *Unmasking the African Ghost: Theology, Politics, and the Nightmare of Failed States* (Fortress, 2022), although he does not conceal the complex and seemingly intractable nature of the problems. For theological work that contains much idealism but few real solutions, see the essays in *African Public Theology*, ed. Sunday Bobai Agang (Hippo Books, 2020). Emeka Xris Obiezu, OSA, makes the point that Africans "look beyond economics. They consider issues of division—ethnic and religious—as worse factors militating against sustainable development of the African people. These factors endanger if not peace, at least the pursuit of the common good of society. While Africans do not denigrate economics-based solutions to Africa-specific cases, they insist that any attempt toward a true development of Africa must include the issues of division." Obiezu, "The Church in Africa and the Search for Integral and Sustainable Development of Africa: Toward a Socio-Economic and Politically Responsive Church," in Ilo, Ogbonnaya, and Ojacor, *The Church as Salt and Light*, 34–64, at 35–36. Obiezu directs attention to Stan Chu Ilo, *The Face of Africa: Looking Beyond the Shadows* (Spectrum, 2008).

70. Orji makes an important start, drawing on such works as Jason K. Stearns, *Dancing in the Glory of Monsters: The Collapse of the Congo and the Great War of Africa* (PublicAffairs, 2012) and the essays in *Failed and Failing States: The Challenges to African Reconstruction*, ed. Muna Ndulo and Margaret Grieco (Cambridge Scholars, 2010). See also Paul Collier, *The Bottom Billion: Why the Poorest Countries Are Failing and What Can Be Done About It* (Oxford University Press, 2007); Angus Deaton, *The Great Escape: Health, Wealth, and the Origins of Inequality* (Princeton University Press, 2013); and Daron Acemoglu and James A. Robinson, *Why Nations Fail: The Origins of Power, Prosperity, and Poverty* (Currency, 2012).

71. Katongole emphasizes that "Jesus resists the spiritualization of his ministry. His ministry is not simply about a spiritual message to be listened to and later applied. The Good News that Jesus proclaims is a material vision, which involves a reordering of such material realities as geography, time, food, bodies, and communities" (*The Sacrifice of Africa*, 167). I note that to call the Gospel "a material vision" is true in one sense but not in another, since the Gospel has the Father, Son, and Spirit at its very center. The term "spiritualization" may also be appropriate in certain contexts, insofar as Jesus insists that his "kingship is not of this world" (John 18:36). I concur with Katongole when he observes, "the twelve baskets represent the twelve tribes of Israel, foreshadowing the new Israel, God's new family that is beyond boundaries of race, nation,

same time, as Emeka Xris Obiezu has aptly observed, the Church is "a socially transformative family that seeks to make the Christian moral ideal of love of neighbor part of the common good."[72]

As we will see, just such a perspective finds support in Benedict's *Africae Munus* and Ratzinger's *The Meaning of Christian Brotherhood*, read in light of Scripture's testimony to believers' adoptive sonship. In my view, these texts indicate that Paulinus Odozor is correct when he argues that the main "area in which the church must effect transformation in Africa [as in other continents] is theological. . . . The church, family of God in Africa, must be more intentional in its work as agent of transformation by attending the foundational/theological issues that give credence, grounding, and distinctiveness to its work in society."[73] The Church is the Family of God, and so it must proclaim this God and explain what it means to be the Family of such a God. The primary thing is to come to know God and Christ.

IV. *AFRICAE MUNUS* ON THE CHURCH AS THE FAMILY OF GOD

Pope Benedict XVI's apostolic exhortation *Africae Munus*, which emerged out of the Second African Synod, will help to push this discussion forward. *Africae Munus* first testifies to the connection that believers have with our "forebears in faith," from

tribe, and geography" (168–69). Katongole goes on to tell the extraordinary story of Maggy Barankitse, who has sought in the context of Burundi to raise "children beyond the story of ethnicity" and "into the new story of God's love" (175–76). See also Emmanuel Katongole with Jonathan Wilson-Hartgrove, *Mirror to the Church: Resurrecting Faith after Genocide in Rwanda* (Zondervan, 2009), where he remarks in a Hauerwasian key that "if we know that worship of the true and living God is what we are made for, we will also remember who we are: a community of resident aliens in a world that is both broken and redeemed. Because we know a new creation in Christ, we will live as ambassadors, welcoming strangers as though we belong here while also praying for the heavenly city, our true home, to descend to where we are" (138–39).

72. Obiezu, "The Church in Africa and the Search for Integral and Sustainable Development of Africa," 62. Obiezu is aware of the problems with traditional family life in Africa, including discrimination against women.

73. Odozor, "The Church as Family of God in Africa," 584. See also James Henry Owino Kombo, *The Doctrine of God in African Christian Thought: The Holy Trinity, Theological Hermeneutics and the African Intellectual Culture* (Brill, 2007).

Abraham onward. This insight emphasizes the Church as a Family, grounded in the family of Abraham. In making this point, *Africae Munus* remarks that given the enormous challenges faced by the nations of Africa, "the Church, like Israel, could easily fall prey to discouragement" (*AM* §5). Thus, the trials faced by familial forebears such as Moses (see Heb 11:27) help to illuminate the way forward in hope. Indeed, the family of Israel provides a privileged model for how to get through an onslaught of political, economic, and spiritual disasters. The Family of God must not give up the eschatological hope of entering the Promised Land.

Africae Munus recalls that *Ecclesia in Africa* "made its own the idea of 'the Church as God's Family,' which the Synod Fathers 'acknowledged . . . as an expression of the Church's nature particularly appropriate for Africa'" (*AM* §7; cf. §15). Pope Benedict comments that "to see the Church as a family and a fraternity is to recover one aspect of her heritage" (§8). This is so, he observes, because the Church is comprised of God's adopted sons and daughters in the first-born Son. The reception of the Eucharistic Body and Blood of Christ makes believers to be "truly one," so that believers become "blood relations and thus true brothers and sisters," possessed of a fraternal bond in the Church that "is stronger than that of human families, than that of our tribes" (§152). As members of the Family of Christ, Christians are called to share in Christ's self-sacrificial love. In the midst of "fratricidal conflicts" and poverty, the Church in Africa must bear witness to the "fraternal solidarity" and justice that God intends for all his children (§§8–9; cf. §18), by calling upon "the power of the Spirit to transform the hearts of victims and their persecutors and thus to re-establish fraternity" (§20).

Africae Munus draws a link between Africa and the parable of the prodigal son: not only must the younger son be reconciled to his father (representing the divine Father), but also the younger son must be reconciled to his brother. This is the situation that characterizes some nations in the African Catholic Church, where reconciliation between brothers who have sinned against each other is needed so that "serene coexistence" can be restored (§21). Consciously embracing a familial solidarity with Christ will ensure that a justice grounded in love will truly characterize the Church in Africa (§26). The human family in Africa cries out for assistance in the midst of economic and political suffering. In response, the Family that is the Church must offer "fraternal service" (§29) in accordance with the beatitudes, rising above selfish self-seeking.[74] Christ's Paschal Mystery functions as "the principle and bond of a new fraternity" (§41). All this depends upon encountering Jesus through the proclamation and witness of the Church, an encounter that, when it generates faith, "heals, sets free and reconciles" (§149).

Africae Munus points out that in Africa, the elderly are fully integrated into the family and indeed stand at the head of the family. Among Africans in rural areas, "stability and social order are still frequently entrusted to a council of elders or traditional chiefs" (§49), and their primary task is justice and reconciliation. This example should instruct the bishops in serving the Church as the Family of God. Their leadership must direct the whole people to God in Christ, and they must insist upon and exemplify Christ's selfless love in the service of God's poor.

In light of the Church as God's Family, *Africae Munus* examines the proper roles of Christian men, women, and children. It urges men to ground themselves in prayer and to manifest "God's own fatherhood (cf. Eph 3:15)," not by power but by "guarantee[ing] the personal development of all members of the family" (§53). The equal dignity of women must be promoted, including

74. John Olorunfemi Onaiyekan, commenting on the First African Synod (from which came *Ecclesia in Africa*), states, "The Synod emphasized the political arena, showing its conviction that most of the problems facing our continent result from inept or corrupt governments. Effective government is essential to tackle poverty and disease, civil wars and social unrest, rampant corruption, and blatant abuse of human rights. This is a direct challenge to the laity, whose role it is to make the Gospel values present in these areas" (Onaiyekan, "The Church in Africa Today: Reflections on the African Synod," in Africa Faith and Justice Network and Browne, *The African Synod*, 211–19, at 217).

by protesting ancestral or cultural practices that are contrary to the equality of women.[75] *Africae Munus* calls for initiatives that support women and that recognize women's role in the Church and the world.[76] Inspired by the figure of Mary of Bethany, all believers should read "the Bible daily," so as to increase in "the knowledge of Jesus Christ" and to enable the Word of God to build "up the community of Christ's disciples" (§151).

Regarding the status of children, *Africae Munus* first proclaims that "the Church is Mother and could never abandon a single one of them" (§67). This image of Mother Church fills out the portrait of the Church as God's Family. Believers should

75. For further background, with attention to contemporary developments, see Bosco Ebere Amakwe, HFSN, "Globalization and the African Woman: A Socio-Cultural Analysis of the Effect of Information and Communication Technology (ICT) on Women," in Ilo, Ogbonnaya, and Ojacor, *The Church as Salt and Light*, 99–129.

76. Stan Chu Ilo remarks, "Effective evangelization in Africa calls for greater involvement of African women in African churches, where women are treated as second-class citizens, holding any position at the mercy of a male-dominated hierarchy and leadership across the board. Such treatment of women in the Catholic churches in Africa parallels the patriarchal cultural frameworks that furnish and legitimize the ongoing marginalization of women through various uncritical cultural assumptions" (Ilo, "Conclusion," in Ilo, Ogbonnaya, and Ojacor, *The Church as Salt and Light*, 149–56, at 152). Elsewhere Ilo argues that "the future of the church will be constructed through a learning church that is at home in the world, with women, LGBTQ, the poor, and those on the margins." Ilo, *A Poor and Merciful Church: The Illuminative Ecclesiology of Pope Francis* (Orbis Books, 2018), 287. Ilo's language here gives me pause, since a Church learning from Jesus Christ will have a dialectical relationship with the world, in accordance with Romans 12:2, "Do not be conformed to this world but be transformed by the renewal of your mind." For a fruitful reflection—but one that falls into the mistake of advocating that women perform ministries for which priestly ordination is required—see Bernadette Mbuy-Beya, "Women in the Churches in Africa: Possibilities for Presence and Promises," in Africa Faith and Justice Network and Browne, *The African Synod*, 175–87. See also Agbonkhianmeghe E. Orobator, SJ, *Religion and Faith in Africa: Confessions of an Animist* (Orbis Books, 2018). With reference to the first two African synods (and thus to *Ecclesia in Africa* and *Africae Munus*), Orobator suggests that the claim that the "church as family exists to further the mission of reconciliation, justice, and peace" (130) cannot be sustained unless women are integrated fully into all forms of Catholic ministry. In response, I note that if full participation in the Church is defined in terms of power and if it is assumed that people who lack vocational access to positions of power and sacramental leadership are second-class, then clericalism has taken over. In setting forth his call for the ordination of women, Orobator cites the similar perspectives of Emmanuel Katangole, "The Church of the Future: Pressing Moral Issues from *Ecclesia in Africa*," in Orobator, *The Church We Want*, 172; Tina Beattie, "Maternal Well-Being in Sub-Saharan Africa: From Silent Suffering to Human Flourishing," in Orobator, *The Church We Want*, 176–77; and Marguerite Akossi-Mvongo, "The Church We Want: *Ecclesia* of Women in Africa?," in Orobator, *The Church We Want*, 250–51. For the opposite viewpoint, see Benedict M. Ashley, OP, *Justice in the Church: Gender and Participation* (The Catholic University of America Press, 1996); and Sara Butler, MSBT, *The Catholic Priesthood and Women: A Guide to the Teaching of the Church* (Hillenbrand Books, 2007).

have a child-like "spirit of trusting abandonment," since it is such believers who "find in God a Father and become, through Jesus, children of God"—"adopted children by grace" (§68). Catholics can concur with African traditional religions that life here and now includes the ancestors, as well as those yet to be born and indeed all creation. In the African perspective, the world is "a space of communion where past generations invisibly flank present generations, themselves the mothers of future generations" (§69).

Other ecclesiological motifs, in addition to the theme of the Church as God's Family, are present in *Africae Munus*. The Church is Christ's "Body," united by his gift of the Holy Spirit (§§97, 132). The Church is a sacrament of communion with God and is a sacrament of God's will that the human race be one (§133). *Africae Munus* concludes that believers who truly live the path of charity in the Holy Spirit will find themselves acting as "protagonists of a renewed African society" (§109; cf. §§171–72).[77] Leadership in such renewal would indeed be the fruit of living as God's Family. However, given human fallenness, the brokenness of societies, and the reality that God's grace leads to the eschatological kingdom—often through suffering and even martyrdom rather than through political and economic success—no temporal measure of achievement should be the standard by which the Church is judged.

V. A FAMILY FOR THE SALVATION OF THE WORLD'S FAMILIES: JOSEPH RATZINGER'S *THE MEANING OF CHRISTIAN BROTHERHOOD*

As a final step, let me turn to Ratzinger's 1960 book *The Meaning of Christian Brotherhood*, which Ratzinger's biographer Peter Seewald describes as the place where the young Ratzinger "spoke

77. See Bekeh Utietiang Ukelina, "New Evangelization in Africa: Learning from the Culture of Love in the Early Church," in Ilo, Ogbonnaya, and Ojacor, *The Church as Salt and Light*, 130–48, at 132.

for the first time to a wide readership."[78] This book represents a rich contribution to the theology of the Church as God's Family, along lines that address the danger of a spirit of rivalry and exclusion while emphasizing the ethical imperative that divine filiation brings.

In *The Meaning of Christian Brotherhood*, Ratzinger defines the Christian community—the Church—by citing the Gospel of Matthew, "You have one teacher, and you are all brethren" (Matt 23:8).[79] Christians are brothers due to the Holy Spirit who unites the Church. The status of Christians as brothers (and sisters) in Christ carries with it a moral imperative, which Ratzinger terms the "ethos of brotherliness."[80]

Ratzinger observes that Plato describes *fellow citizens* as brothers, and Xenophon describes *friends* as brothers. Yet, the problem is that by defining a particular group as a brotherhood, one excludes those who do not belong to this group from the circle of brotherhood. Within the brotherhood or "extended family," the members have an ethical responsibility to treat each other as brothers; but often toward people who are outside the brotherhood, no such ethical duty is recognized. Israel understood itself

78. Peter Seewald, *Benedict XVI: A Life*, vol. 1, *Youth in Nazi Germany to the Second Vatican Council, 1927–1965*, trans. Dinah Livingstone (Bloomsbury, 2020), 322. Aidan Nichols, OP, observes, "Christian brotherhood was a theme he had already touched on in Augustine, and Augustine's African predecessor, Optatus. It was also, perhaps, an obvious ecclesiological subject in a self-consciously democratic European world, and especially so on the eve of a great Church council which would underline the fundamental equality of all the baptised." Nichols, *The Thought of Pope Benedict XVI: An Introduction to the Theology of Joseph Ratzinger*, 2nd ed. (Continuum, 2007), 45; see also Emery de Gaál, *The Theology of Pope Benedict XVI: The Christocentric Shift* (Palgrave Macmillan, 2010), 169. It is intriguing—and a missed opportunity—that Vatican II did not really take up this theme. In his *Joseph Ratzinger: Life in the Church and Living Theology; Fundamentals of Ecclesiology with Reference to "Lumen Gentium"*, trans. Michael J. Miller (Ignatius, 2007), Maximilian Heinrich Heim does not discuss *The Meaning of Christian Brotherhood*. In his summary of *The Meaning of Christian Brotherhood*, de Gaál rightly connects "brotherhood" to "communion" (with Christ and each other), and so it is not surprising that Ratzinger's later ecclesiology emphasizes communion. I should note that Nichols's excellent survey of Ratzinger's book is more detailed in certain ways than the one I offer here. See also Fergus Kerr, OP, "Church: Brotherhood and Eschatology," *New Blackfriars* 51, no. 598 (March 1970): 144–54.

79. Joseph Ratzinger, *The Meaning of Christian Brotherhood* (Ignatius, 1993), 3.

80. Ratzinger, 3. In this essay, following *Africae Munus* (and *Ecclesia in Africa*), I employ "family" rather than "brotherhood."

as God's family by contrast to the Gentile nations who lacked divine election and covenant. The Israelites' common father was Jacob-Israel (or Abraham), but their familial unity stemmed most fundamentally from the fact that Israel was the chosen "son" of the divine "father" YHWH. Although they were a family by ancestral blood, their shared relationship to YHWH principally constituted them as a family. Ratzinger observes, "God had a special paternity toward Israel: whereas he was the Father of all the peoples of the world through creation, he was beyond that the Father of Israel through election."[81]

In Ratzinger's view, however, this relationship always had a certain contingency to it.[82] If Israel failed to live as true children of God and as true brothers of each other, God could renounce the election of Israel just as freely as God had once chosen Israel. The prophets dangled this threat over the people of Israel, while at the same time foretelling the ultimate salvation of the people. Ratzinger adds that in later Judaism, the idea would arise that God had offered the Torah to all peoples but only Israel had accepted it. Ratzinger suggests that this viewpoint closes off the circle of brotherhood, whereas in the prophets the circle of brotherhood had remained open due to the fact that Israel's status continued to be dependent upon God's free choice.

Although Israel is uniquely chosen, Israel's story plays out in relation to the nations and to the whole world. The first chapters of Genesis teach that God is the Creator of all humans. All

81. Ratzinger, 8. See also Joseph Ratzinger/Pope Benedict XVI, *Jesus of Nazareth*, vol. 1, *From the Baptism in the Jordan to the Transfiguration*, trans. Adrian J. Walker (Doubleday, 2007), 137–39. For various Jewish accounts of Israel's election (following paths that could only enhance Ratzinger's key idea), see Joel S. Kaminsky, *Yet I Loved Jacob: Reclaiming the Biblical Concept of Election* (Abingdon, 2007); David Novak, *The Election of Israel: The Idea of the Chosen People* (Cambridge University Press, 1995); and Bernard-Henri Lévy, *The Genius of Judaism*, trans. Steven B. Kennedy (Random House, 2017), part 2.

82. For Ratzinger's Israelology, see also his *Many Religions—One Covenant: Israel, the Church, and the World*, trans. Graham Harrison (Ignatius, 1999); Ratzinger, "The Heritage of Abraham," in his *Pilgrim Fellowship of Faith: The Church as Communion*, trans. Henry Taylor (Ignatius, 2005), 270–73; and Pope Emeritus Benedict XVI, "Grace and Vocation without Remorse: Comments on the Treatise *De Iudaeis*," trans. Nicholas J. Healy Jr., *Communio* 45, no. 1 (2018): 163–84.

humans in this sense are one family, sharing "a single humanity because of their single human source and the single creative act of God."[83] The unity of all humans is underlined by Genesis through the story of Noah and the Flood, which entails that all humans descend not only from Adam but also from Noah. Indeed, Israel is not the only people to receive a covenant, since all the nations (including Israel) live under the terms of the Noahide covenant. Humanity has a common divine Father and a common human father (Adam and Noah), and so the unity of humanity as the family of God is clear. Yet, also clear is "the elective exclusiveness of God toward Israel and the exclusive descent from the fathers of the covenant, Abraham, Isaac, and Jacob."[84]

Ratzinger highlights this duality: God's family is exclusively Israel, and yet God's family also includes the entire human race in some way. The duality enables the moral imperative that brotherliness apply not only to fellow Israelites, but to all humanity. Repeatedly, God commands Israel to care for strangers and sojourners. In fact, strangers—those who do not belong to God's family Israel—are shown to be related to Israel by means of pairs of brothers. The nations round about Israel descend from Ishmael and Esau, the brothers of Isaac and Jacob, respectively. The nations are related to Israel, originally speaking, in the relation of a blood brother. Ratzinger comments, "We can . . . see here that even the partners of Israel who were expelled from the election [e.g., Esau] could yet be understood in a wider sense as 'brothers,' that even he who was rejected remained a 'brother.'"[85]

The central issue that Ratzinger is addressing, as will be clear by now, is how God's chosen family—Israel and ultimately all who by grace are adopted sons and daughters in the Son—does not comprise yet another instance of exclusion and division in

83. Ratzinger, *The Meaning of Christian Brotherhood*, 9. See also Joseph Ratzinger, *"In the Beginning . . .": A Catholic Understanding of the Story of Creation and the Fall*, trans. Boniface Ramsey, OP (Eerdmans, 1995).

84. Ratzinger, *The Meaning of Christian Brotherhood*, 10.

85. Ratzinger, 11.

the human race.[86] In his reflections, Ratzinger observes that the claim to be God's family is not limited to Jews (or Christians), but instead has numerous parallels in the ancient world. He states, "In the Syrian Baal cults, the tribes and groups who were united through blood and the unity of the protective deity had long regarded themselves as sons of this god and as brothers of one another."[87] He finds a similar sense of brotherhood among the members of Syrian Jupiter cults and the members of the cult of the Great Mother. The members of the Mithras community and the Qumran sect thought of their fellow community members as their brothers.

Similarly, the Stoics conceived of human beings as God's family, although the Stoics did not limit this status to members of a particular nation or religious group. Ratzinger observes that Roman "political unification had its philosophical parallel in Stoic cosmopolitanism which discovered the unity of the world and of men. Epictetus saw all men as brothers, for all came from God. The ideas of the Stoa, of Seneca, Musonius, and Marcus Aurelius, followed the same direction."[88] According to Ratzinger, perhaps the fullest expression of this Stoic view of the brotherhood of humanity as children of the one Father God is found in the Hermes mystery cult. Even the uninitiated were still brothers, still children of the one Father God, and the initiated prayed to be given the strength to illumine the uninitiated with the truth about the brotherhood of all the Father's children.[89]

Ratzinger attends briefly to the versions of "brotherhood"

86. See the concerns of Regina Schwartz, *The Curse of Cain: The Violent Legacy of Monotheism* (University of Chicago Press, 1997), to which I respond in my *The Betrayal of Charity: The Sins that Sabotage Divine Love* (Baylor University Press, 2011).

87. Ratzinger, *The Meaning of Christian Brotherhood*, 12.

88. Ratzinger, 14.

89. For the above insights, Ratzinger is indebted to encyclopedia articles on "brother" in the ancient world by Hermann von Soden and Karl Schelkle, and he is also indebted to the interests of his teacher Gottlieb Söhngen. See Hermann von Soden, "Adelphos," in *Theologisches Wörterbuch zum Neuen Testament*, ed. Gerhard Kittel, vol. 1 (Kohlhammer, 1964), 144–46; and Karl Hermann Schelkle, "Bruder," in *Reallexikon für Antike und Christentum*, vol. 3, ed. T. Klauser (Hiersemann, 1954), 631–40; Gottlieb Söhngen, "Vom Wesen des Christentums," in *Die Einheit in der Theologie* (Zink, 1952), 288–304. On Söhngen's interests more broadly, see

prevalent during the Enlightenment. By comparison with the ancient viewpoints, God has moved into the background. Enlightenment thinkers derive the brotherhood of humanity simply from the fact that we all share the same human nature. They argue that all humans would be equal were it not for accidental circumstances of history. Against monarchical and feudal systems, they call for recognition of the natural equality of all human beings and for a new social order based upon this equality. They reject Christian brotherhood as insufficient, since it promotes a distinctive ethos for Christians and separates Christians from non-Christians. Ratzinger explains that "in the name of brotherhood all barriers were removed and a unified ethos was proclaimed as binding on all men in equal measure."[90]

The problem with the Enlightenment ideal is that if everyone is a "brother," then the intensity or intimacy of the word "brother" no longer holds. In fact, if everyone is equally a "brother," then no one really is a brother. Unsurprisingly, the Enlightenment ideal was never widely practiced. Those who proclaimed it most prominently were often themselves Freemasons—an esoteric brotherhood—and the Enlightenment ideal easily gave way among the intelligentsia to Marxism, with its sharp division of human beings into the two fiercely opposed groups: the proletariat and the owners of capital. For Marx, the implementation of universal brotherhood necessarily involves crushing some human beings (the owners of capital), just as for the Enlightenment thinkers the implementation of universal brotherhood necessarily involved crushing the nobility and the clergy.

Returning to the Christian understanding of brotherhood, Ratzinger argues that Jesus intentionally changed the meaning of brotherhood among the people of Israel. Specifically, "when Jesus chose twelve disciples, he chose a symbolic number whose

Tracey Rowland, *Beyond Kant and Nietzsche: The Munich Defense of Christian Humanism* (T&T Clark, 2021), chapter 4.

90. Ratzinger, *The Meaning of Christian Brotherhood*, 15. See for example Jean-Jacques Rousseau, *Emile, or On Education*, trans. Allan Bloom (Basic Books, 1979).

significance was obvious for every reader of Scripture. He places himself in the position of Jacob and his twelve sons who became the twelve patriarchs of the Chosen People of Israel."[91] In fulfilling God's covenants with his family Israel, Christ inaugurates the messianic Family of God, with himself at the center. Christ is the one who does the will of God in love, and all who are united to the will of God (and thus to Christ) are his brothers (Mark 3:31–35). Brotherhood in the messianic Israel depends not on literal blood relation but on spiritual relation—not an ethereal spiritual relation but one characterized by Baptism and by shared faith and charity.

The unity of this brotherhood is the Church, and the charity characteristic of this brotherhood is described in Matthew 25 as care for the poor and marginalized. In fact, Matthew 25 suggests that there will be many among "all the nations" (Matt 25:32) who do not consciously know Jesus and who are not consciously members of the brotherhood of the Church, but whom Jesus will nevertheless identify as belonging to the brotherhood due to their works of love. They will be surprised when at the final judgment, Jesus tells them, "Come, O blessed of my Father, inherit the kingdom prepared for you from the foundation of the world" (Matt 25:34).[92] Moreover, the "brothers" of Jesus include all the needy, no matter whether they have faith. Represented by the king in the parable, Jesus states, "Truly, I say to you, as you did it to one of the least of these my brethren, you did it to me" (Matt 25:40). Ratzinger comments, "Nothing suggests that only the faithful, only believers in the gospel of Christ, are meant here . . . but rather all people in need."[93] In a special way, the brothers of Christ are the poor, the lowly, since they make manifest the

91. Ratzinger, *The Meaning of Christian Brotherhood*, 25.

92. For background, see Daniel Daley, *God's Will and Testament: Inheritance in the Gospel of Matthew and Jewish Tradition* (Baylor University Press, 2021). Daley emphasizes that the inheritance is the kingdom of God in its various dimensions. I note that the kingdom is fundamentally a sharing in the everlasting life of Christ with God the Father in the Spirit.

93. Ratzinger, *The Meaning of Christian Brotherhood*, 27.

Lord who himself came as one of them. As the theologian Bede Ukwuije says, Jesus "manifests himself in the faces of the poor, the sick, the stranger, the prisoner (Matt 25:31–41)."[94]

Ratzinger concludes that Christian brotherhood should be conceived in two ways: those who obey God's will (by faith and charity), and those who are lowly and suffering. The latter category indicates again that the circle of brotherhood is not closed. On the one hand, Jesus's brothers are indeed those who, by faith, are adopted sons of the Father; they form "a new fraternal community which will be distinguished from those who do not believe."[95] On the other hand, Jesus's brothers extend far beyond the visible bounds of the Church. In accord with the parable of the Good Samaritan, one's neighbor (or brother) is not simply one's fellow Christian but everyone in need—since everyone in need "is simply a brother of the Master who is always present to me in the lowliest of men."[96] This means that the Enlightenment ideal—the brotherhood of all human beings—is already present in the New Testament, where it is joined to Christology.

Ratzinger also examines how Paul contrasts the fallen human brotherhood of Adam with the glorious human brotherhood of the Second Adam, Jesus. All humans are called into the latter brotherhood. In the Church, all other human distinctions (such as master and slave) are nothing in comparison to the radical unity of brothers and sisters in Christ. In this regard, Paul's vision of God's Family remains exclusive vis-à-vis nonbelievers, who become brothers of Paul in the full sense only when they come to have faith.

For Ratzinger, ecclesiology urgently needs to retrieve the vision of Christian brotherhood found in Scripture, with particular attention to its openness to the non-Christian brother in need.

94. Ukwuije, "Political Theology and Liberation Theology in the Works of Elochukwu Uzukwu," 190.

95. Ratzinger, *The Meaning of Christian Brotherhood*, 29.

96. Ratzinger, 29.

He therefore complements his historical survey with some systematic reflections. First, he notes that Jesus Christ reveals in the most profound way possible the personal character of God the Father. God personally comes to draw humanity into God's Family: God establishes the brotherhood of God and humankind by taking flesh in Jesus Christ and by dying for our salvation. As the incarnate Son and the Messiah of Israel, Jesus represents Israel's status as "son" and brings this status to a wondrous fulfillment. In Christ, believers share in the intimate relationship of Jesus, the divine Son, to his Father. Believers truly, and not merely metaphorically, become brothers of the incarnate Son and sharers in his inheritance in the Family of God. United in Christ, believers can truly call God "Father" as Christ does: "Father" not in the sense of domineering power, but in the sense of radical love and fidelity to his children.

Second, Ratzinger draws a connection between our graced inclusion in God's Family and the Christian moral life. Specifically, the more believers come to share in the "I" of Christ, the more selfless, in the sense of self-giving love, they become. Believers turn away from selfish self-assertion and toward the self-giving love that builds up the Church and that transforms the world.[97] As noted above, Christ's true brothers and sisters are those who do God's will in self-sacrificial love, which becomes possible through faith in Christ as the Redeemer. If it were to be supposed that those who reject Christ and who reject God's will could *fully* be Jesus's brothers within the Family of God, then "brotherhood" and "Family of God" would lose their meaning. In this sense, there is a certain exclusivity to the Family that is the Church. The Church as God's Family, the "brotherly community," does not

97. See Ratzinger, 55. See also Ratzinger/Benedict XVI, *Jesus of Nazareth*, 1:138: "Jesus is 'the Son' in the strict sense—he is of one substance with the Father. He wants to draw all of us into his humanity and so into his Sonship, into his total belonging to God. This gives the concept of being God's children a dynamic quality: We are not ready-made children of God from the start, but we are meant to become so increasingly by growing more and more deeply in communion with Jesus. Our sonship turns out to be identical with following Christ. To name God as Father thus becomes a summons to us to live as a 'child,' as a son or daughter."

for practical purposes include nominal, non-practicing Christians but rather is limited to those "who come with at least a certain regularity to share in the eucharistic celebration."[98] The Eucharist makes the Church, and the Eucharist makes the brotherhood.

Third, regarding outsiders to the Church as God's Family, Ratzinger emphasizes that Christians must love their enemies, care for the poor, and pray for all people. Christians should not judge outsiders (1 Cor 5:12–13). Christians should exhibit both truth and service toward nominal Christians who are not practicing. Indeed, the members of God's Family must, like Christ on the cross, vicariously suffer in love for the salvation of those who are not yet members. The Church's election as God's Family is an "election for others"—namely, for "those who are not God's people."[99] Far from being separated from those outside the Church, the Church exists to serve and save them. To persons in need, Christians must respond as if to Christ. In this sense, all humans must be treated as brothers by Christians. If the members of God's Family are comparatively few, this should merely prompt an increased desire to serve the many. God's Family exists "for the many" and thereby displays its union with Christ who died for all.[100]

98. Ratzinger, *The Meaning of Christian Brotherhood*, 73. For further discussion, see Pope Benedict XVI, *Heart of the Christian Life: Thoughts on the Holy Mass* (Ignatius, 2010), 59, 61: "Through the Eucharist, the Lord not only gives himself to his own but also gives them the reality of a new communion among themselves which is extended in time, 'until he comes' (cf. 1 Cor 11:26). Through the Eucharist, the disciples become his living dwelling place which, as history unfolds, grows like the new and living temple of God in this world. . . . The Church, established in the institution of the Eucharist, in her inmost self is a Eucharistic community, hence, communion in the Body of the Lord."

99. Ratzinger, *The Meaning of Christian Brotherhood*, 79.

100. Ratzinger, 84. For discussion, see Aaron Pidel, SJ, "The Church of the 'Few' for the 'Many': Ratzinger's Missiology of Vicarious Representation," in *Joseph Ratzinger and the Healing of the Reformation-Era Divisions*, ed. Emery de Gaál and Matthew Levering (Emmaus Academic, 2019), 297–318; Christopher Ruddy, "'Smaller but Purer?' Joseph Ratzinger on the 'Little Flock' and Vicarious Representation," *Nova et Vetera* 13, no. 3 (2015): 713–41; Ruddy, "'For the Many': The Vicarious-Representative Heart of Joseph Ratzinger's Theology," *Theological Studies* 75, no. 3 (2014): 564–84; and Anna Elisabeth Meiers, *Eschatos Adam: Zentrale Aspekte der Christologie bei Joseph Ratzinger/Benedikt XVI* (Friedrich Pustet, 2019), 210–20. Pidel draws a connection between Ratzinger's theology of representation and Erich Przywara, SJ's theology of *sacrum commercium*, and he also notes the impact of Karl Barth's theology of election. Other theologians, such as Henri de Lubac, SJ, Yves Congar, OP, and Hans Urs von Balthasar follow

Let me add that if the members of the Family of God in Christ are comparatively few, this should also prompt a desire for evangelization—including a willingness to die, or suffer, for professing the faith in a fallen world. Catholics must be willing to work to re-evangelize stagnant parts of the Church at personal cost (and with charity and patience), so that the salt does not lose its savor (Matt 5:13). Evangelization pertains primarily to the salvation of souls, whom Christ frees from slavery to sin and death.[101]

All societies are fallen ones, marked by significant sins, including structural ones.[102] I think, for example, of the vicious anti-Semitism that has often been present in Christian (and non-Christian) societies.[103] But a strong case can be made for the ability of the Gospel, if embraced, to ameliorate and gradually transform a society's way of life. As the Protestant historian John

a similar path, as Pidel shows. In addition to *The Meaning of Christian Brotherhood*, Pidel cites Ratzinger, "Stellvertretung" and "Die neuen Heiden und die Kirche," in *Das neue Volk Gottes: Entwürfe zur Ekklesiologie* (Patmos, 1969), 566–75 and 325–38.

101. See Ralph Martin, *Will Many Be Saved? What Vatican II Actually Teaches and Its Implications for the New Evangelization* (Eerdmans, 2012).

102. Without denying the reality of "structural" sins (for instance, the way that racism operated in the segregated American South), it is crucial to heed Ratzinger's warning in his "A Christian Orientation in a Pluralistic Democracy? The Indispensability of Christianity in the Modern Age," in *Church, Ecumenism and Politics: New Essays in Ecclesiology*, trans. Robert Nowell (Crossroad, 1988), 204–20, at 206–7: "The idea that the whole of history up till now has been a history of the lack of freedom and that now at last and soon the just society can and must be built is spread in a multitude of slogans among atheists as among Christians today and extends as far as bishops' statements and texts used in worship. . . . Present structures are sinful, future structures will be just, one must simply think them out and build them like one builds pieces of equipment, and then they will be there. For this reason sin becomes social sin, structural sin, and should be labelled as such. For this reason in turn salvation depends on the analysis of structures and the political and economic activity that follows from this."

103. See my *Engaging the Doctrine of Israel: A Christian Israelology in Dialogue with Ongoing Judaism* (Cascade, 2021); and see Cyril Hovorun, *Political Orthodoxies: The Unorthodoxies of the Church Coerced* (Fortress, 2018), chapter 4. Bat Ye'or critiques Catholic ambiguity toward the existence of the State of Israel. She notes that despite Pope John Paul II's "historic pilgrimage to Jerusalem in March 2000, and the intense emotions aroused by his presence at Yad Vashem—and the moving meditation of the ailing and courageous pope at the Western Wall—the pro-Palestinian policy of the Vatican has remained constant. The body of Christendom, represented by the Palestinian *dhimmi* clergies—Catholic, Protestant, and Orthodox—deliberately chose Arafat as the acclaimed protector of Christianity's holy places. This choice of Arafat—Nobel Peace Laureate and erstwhile godfather of international terrorism, champion of *jihad*, and destroyer of Lebanese Christianity—was the culmination of anti-Zionist political choices going back to the nineteenth century. . . . Of all the currents that run through the Vatican and the World Council of Churches, anti-Zionism is the most powerful." Bat Ye'or, *Islam and Dhimmitude: Where Civilizations Collide*, trans. Miriam Kochan and David Littman (Fairleigh Dickinson University Press, 2002), 376–77.

Dickson observes, "Violence has been a universal part of the human story. The demand to *love one's enemies* has not. Division has been a norm. Inherent human dignity has not. Armies, greed, and the politics of power have been constants in history. Hospitals, schools, and charity for all have not. Bullies are common. Saints are not."[104]

Pope Benedict's Regensburg Address is worth noting here for its inquiry into what may rightly be done in the name of God.[105] When religious believers kill people in the name of God due to differences in matters of religious belief—as Christians have too often done—then something has gone very wrong. Such killing can be encouraged by a sense of being God's family. The historian Reuven Firestone has documented the earliest Muslims' shift "from the early impossibility of Muḥammad's followers defining their own kinship group as the enemy, to the materialistic raids conducted even against their own kin, to the total declaration of war against all groups, whether kin or not, who did not accept the truth or the hegemony of Islam."[106] Related problems

104. John Dickson, *Bullies and Saints: An Honest Look at the Good and Evil of Christian History* (Zondervan, 2021), 286. See also the historical narrative of Tom Holland, *Dominion: The Making of the Western Mind* (Little, Brown, 2019).

105. For the text of the Regensburg Lecture, see James V. Schall, SJ, *The Regensburg Lecture* (St. Augustine's, 2007), "Appendix I: The Regensburg Lecture," 130–48. See also the essays in Part 1 of *Kirche und Welt—ein notwendiger Dialog: Stimmen katholischer Theologie*, ed. Johanna Rahner and Thomas Söding (Herder, 2019), which focus on God's solidarity with sufferers, with reference to Pope Francis's rejection of hatred and violence in the name of religion.

106. Reuven Firestone, *Jihād: The Origin of Holy War in Islam* (Oxford University Press, 1999), 134. See also Bernard Lewis, *The Political Language of Islam* (University of Chicago Press, 1988), 77; and James V. Schall, SJ, *On Islam: A Chronological Record, 2002–2018* (Ignatius, 2018). Schall states, "The designated and determined goal of the conquest of the world for Allah has been reinvigorated again and again in world history from the time of Muhammad in the seventh century. These revivals and expansions, which have been only temporarily halted by superior counterforce, have roots in the Qur'an itself and in its commentaries" (*On Islam*, 185). For efforts on the part of scholars (both Muslim and non-Muslim) to show the integration of faith and reason in Islam, see for example Mohammad Hashim Kamali, *Shari'ah Law: An Introduction* (Oneworld, 2008); Anver M. Emon, "Islamic Natural Law Theories," in Anver M. Emon, Matthew Levering, and David Novak, *Natural Law: A Jewish, Christian, and Islamic Trialogue* (Oxford University Press, 2014), 144–87; and Abbas Amanat and Frank Griffel, eds., *Shari'a: Islamic Law in the Contemporary Context*, (University Press, 2007). See also the approach taken by the mid-twentieth century Catholic theologian Louis Massignon, who tried to find a path of reconciliation, but whose views (so far as I can tell) are more attractive to Christians than they are to most Qur'an-believing Muslims: Christian S. Krokus, *The Theology of Louis Massignon: Islam, Christ, and the Church* (The Catholic University of America Press, 2017). For

can be found in Hellenistic pagan religions, African traditional religions, Mayan and Incan religions, and Hinduism. Ratzinger also expresses concern about Christians' recurrent "temptation to leap-frog the limited and imperfect sphere of the nature of the earthly state and to ignore or fight the state," resulting in violent anarchy.[107]

Fortunately, while the image of the Family of God can mutate into an excuse for persecution of outsiders, it should not do so. Adoption into the Trinitarian life requires self-sacrificial lives that make manifest the love that characterizes Christ and the Trinity. In Christ's saving cross, on which he died out of love for every single human being, the Family of God has its greatness.

VI. CONCLUSION

Ratzinger's discussion of Christian brotherhood was not taken up into the ecclesiology of Vatican II or even into Ratzinger's own later ecclesiological work, which emphasized the theme of communion rather than "brotherhood" or the Family of God. Yet, Ratzinger's early book can help to shed light on the relevance of *Africae Munus* for the Church as a whole. He appreciates the biblical understanding of the Church as God's Family,

concerns about "the mutual demonization of the other" by Christians and Muslims, see Sidney H. Griffith, *The Church in the Shadow of the Mosque: Christians and Muslims in the World of Islam* (Princeton University Press, 2008), 178–79.

107. Ratzinger, "A Christian Orientation in a Pluralistic Democracy?," 212. Ratzinger sets forth both Christianity's strength and its weakness: "Christian faith exploded the ancient world's idea of tolerance because it would not let itself be included in the pantheon that formed the sphere of religious live-and-let-live in its exchange and its mutual recognition of gods. From a legal point of view it could not therefore be admitted to enjoy religious tolerance because it refused to let itself be allotted to the sphere of private law where arbitrary forms of religion had their place. . . . In this sense, however small the number of its adherents may have been at first, Christianity from the start laid a claim to public legal status and placed itself on a legal level comparable to that of the state. For this reason the figure of the martyr is to be found in the innermost structure of Christianity. In this is to be found its greatness as the adversary of any and every totalitarianism on the part of the state. But in this too can be found the danger of theocratic exaggeration. Connected with this is the fact that Christianity's claim to truth can rise to the point of political intolerance and has done so more than once" (213–14).

an understanding promoted by many African theologians while often neglected in Catholic ecclesiology.

In the context of ethnic and interreligious conflict worldwide, it is evident that God's adoptive sons and daughters have a moral imperative of self-giving service to all people, in configuration to Christ's cross. As the Catholic theologian Philip Rolnick remarks about the Family of God, "Christian faith will not remove conflict from the social, political, and economic spheres. . . . But Christian faith will mean that people of all classes and races—and even opponents—are to be seen as brothers and sisters."[108] What happens, however, when Catholics go to war against each other, and when Catholics persecute their opponents unjustly? What happens when majority-Catholic countries foster deeply unjust political and economic systems?

This is a concern of many African theologians in their reflections on the Family of God. Emmanuel Katongole challenges the Church in Africa as follows: "Even though there has been much allusion to the growth of Christianity in Africa in the twenty-first century, both the validity and the future prospects of African Christianity will depend greatly on its ability to provide Christians with concrete resources with which to face Africa's social history."[109] For *Africae Munus*, the fundamental "concrete resources" the Church can provide are Christ, his teachings, and his sacraments; but these resources also shape a pattern of charity that makes itself felt throughout all orders of society, including healthcare, education, and politics itself. Through the Holy Spirit, Christ's word and sacraments have the power to conform God's Family to the image of the crucified—and in this way to

108. Philip A. Rolnick, *The Long Battle for the Human Soul*, vol. 1 of *A Post-Christendom Faith* (Baylor University Press, 2021), 122.

109. Katongole, *The Sacrifice of Africa*, 20. Ukelina urges similarly, "The Church must rise and take active roles in society to change the lives of the people. Jesus Christ did not sit on the sidelines when his people were sick, dying, or imprisoned. At each point, he stepped in to set them free" (Ukelina, "New Evangelization in Africa," 145). I note that, although Jesus nourished his people by word and deed, Jesus did not free his people, politically or economically speaking, from Roman domination and corruption.

reshape the world, by reorienting the world toward the Trinitarian life of love.[110] As the theologian Bekeh Utietiang Ukelina says, the members of God's Family will "differentiate themselves from others by the way they love not just each other, but those who do not love them as well," including by "reach[ing] out in love to traditional religionists and Muslims."[111]

When interpreted in light of *The Meaning of Christian Brotherhood*, *Africae Munus* reminds us that if the Church is to have a future in Africa or anywhere else in this power- and wealth-hungry world, it will be the future of the Family of God, living through the Spirit as children of God in love and as the brothers and sisters of Christ crucified, desirous of the full inheritance of the Father.[112] May the retrieval of the Church as God's Family—the Church as radical *Christian brotherhood* with Christ and with one another in Ratzinger's sense—spread throughout the world, so

110. Stan Chu Ilo has rightly remarked about the biblical word, "The scriptural evidence was a testimony of lived experiences, and not a mere invention. . . . The evidence of the Word made flesh is an ongoing testimony attested to in the Church in all that she has and all that she is, including the Word that is written in Scripture" (Ilo, "Beginning Afresh with Christ in the Search for Abundant Life in Africa," in Ilo, Ogbonnaya, and Ojacor, *The Church as Salt and Light*, 1–33, at 3). Ilo goes on to critique Catholic theology for privileging European symbols and for seeking an unhelpful uniformity. He argues that it should be "left to African theologians to articulate a theology that is able to capture the imagination of the ordinary African Christians" (32). This is true within limits, but not in a way that cuts African Catholicism off from the Church's solemn teachings or from Catholics around the world.

111. Ukelina, "New Evangelization in Africa," 145–46. At the same time, Ilo notes with understandable concern that "Radical Islamic advance is also perceived in Kenya, Eritrea, Ethiopia, Chad, Cameroun, Uganda, Sudan, and above all Nigeria" (Ilo, "Conclusion," 155).

112. I agree with Katongole that in a certain sense, "all politics is theological, in that it involves claims about life, reality, and the ultimate meaning of life" (Katongole, *The Sacrifice of Africa*, 22). At the same time, Christ did not come to introduce the Roman Empire to a better political and economic life. Katongole is focused on opposing Christian political quietism: see his commentary on such books as Kwame Bediako, *Christianity in Africa: The Renewal of a Non-Western Religion* (Orbis Books, 1995); Bénézet Bujo, *African Theology in Its Social Context* (Paulines Publications Africa, 1992); and Paul Gifford, *African Christianity: Its Public Role* (Indiana University Press, 1998). Katongole criticizes those who "identify the search for democracy as the essence of Christian mission" (*The Sacrifice of Africa*, 39), and I concur with him in this respect. Katongole goes on to say, "What the different initiatives and programs confirm is that if conditions in Africa have been stressful, it is not because African Christians and the Christian churches have been callous to the plight of the continent. Yet despite the growth of Christianity and the social activism of the churches, Africans in general are 40 percent worse off than they were in the 1980s. One then wonders: What accounts for the dismal social impact of Christianity in Africa? Why has Christianity, despite its overwhelming presence, failed to make a significant dent in the social history of the continent?" (40).

that the whole world in love may praise God in the slain Lamb: "Worthy are you to take the scroll and to open its seals, for you were slain and by your blood you ransomed men for God from every tribe and tongue and people and nation, and have made them a kingdom and priests to our God, and they shall reign on earth" (Rev 5:9–10).

3

Body of Christ

I. INTRODUCTION

After Vatican II, much was made of the differences between a "Mystical Body" ecclesiology and a "People of God" ecclesiology.[1] But what exactly is the Mystical Body of Christ, and why is this image of the Church important?[2] The Catholic theologian Ross McCullough has explored the Mystical Body along lines that I find especially striking, and that will serve to illuminate why I find the image of the Body of Christ to be ecclesiologically important especially in light of the cross.

McCullough observes that the Church as "Christ's body" has a "differentiated relationship to its head."[3] What Christ's Headship means depends upon whether one is talking about goods

1. For distinctions made between "People of God" and "Mystical Body" in the immediate postconciliar period, see Avery Dulles, SJ, *Models of the Church*, exp. ed. (Doubleday, 1987), 52–62; and see also Dulles, "Nature, Mission, and Structure of the Church," in *Vatican II: Renewal within Tradition*, ed. Matthew L. Lamb and Matthew Levering (Oxford University Press, 2008), 25–36. For appreciation of the "Mystical Body," see Yves Congar, OP, "*Lumen Gentium* no. 7, L'Église, Corps mystique du Christ, vu a terme de huit siècles d'histoire de la théologie du Corps mystique," in *Au service de la parole de Dieu: Mélanges offerts à Mgr. A.-M. Charue* (Duculot, 1969), 179–202. Joseph Ratzinger comments broadly, "The Council has laid down no new dogma on any subject. But this does not mean that all the Council says is mere edification, binding no one. . . . This Council is 'pastoral' in its fusion of truth and love, 'doctrine' and pastoral solicitude: it wished to reach beyond the dichotomy between pragmatism and doctrinalism, back to the biblical unity in which practice and doctrine are one, a unity grounded in Christ, who is both the *Logos* and the Shepherd." Ratzinger, "Announcements and Prefatory Notes of Explanation," in *Commentary on the Documents of Vatican II*, vol. 1, ed. Herbert Vorgrimler, trans. Lalit Adolphus, Kevin Smyth, and Richard Strachan (Herder and Herder, 1967), 297–305, at 299.

2. Ecumenically, see the Lutheran theologian Robert W. Jenson's chapter on the Church as the Body of Christ in his *Systematic Theology*, vol. 2, *The Works of God* (Oxford University Press, 1999), 211–27. He includes Eucharistic sacrifice in this chapter. His chapter highlights the theme of communion with Christ and with one another.

3. Ross McCullough, *Freedom and Sin: Evil in a World Created by God* (Eerdmans, 2022), 186.

that come by nature, goods that come by grace, or negations of goods (sorrows, diseases, sins). When McCullough discusses negations of good, he notes that "the cross is a kind of gathering up of all that the world does against itself and its spending upon Christ."[4] Christ suffers, then, in the suffering of his members, because he endured the cross for the redemption of all sin and suffering. McCullough puts it this way: "The suffering of all Christ's mystical members . . . is written upon his physical members, first as wounds and then, and forever, as scars."[5] The body of Christ freely endures what the Body of Christ suffers. The bond between the two is the cross.

Augustine has something similar to say, though from a somewhat different perspective. As James Lee notes, for Augustine, "The church *is* a sacrifice as the one body of Christ, offered under the form of a servant at the eucharistic altar. This is the daily sacrifice of Christians, the sacrifice of the 'whole Christ' (*totus Christus*), head and members, which is pleasing and acceptable to God."[6] Augustine holds that the Body must follow Christ the Head by enduring suffering in the world, journeying toward the fullness of life with the risen and glorified Christ in the kingdom of God. This path is the path of the cross—a path sustained by the Eucharistic sacrifice.[7]

Henri de Lubac makes a similar connection in his *Corpus Mysticum: The Eucharist and the Church in the Middle Ages*. He notes that the medieval *Glossa ordinaria* on 1 Corinthians 10:16–17 refers to the body of Christ in light of the Eucharistic sacrifice that unites believers as one Body. In this sense, says de Lubac,

4. McCullough, 197.

5. McCullough, 198.

6. James K. Lee, "Patristic Ecclesiology in the Latin West," in *T&T Clark Handbook of Ecclesiology*, ed. Kimlyn J. Bender and D. Stephen Long (T&T Clark, 2020), 71–80, at 75.

7. For reflection on the Eucharistic sacrifice that connects it not only with the cross but also with the Passover and the exodus journey, see Brant Pitre, *Jesus and the Last Supper* (Eerdmans, 2015); and Florent Urfels, *La Pâque du Messie: Introduction à une théologie eucharistique du judaïsme* (Parole et Silence, 2013); and my *Sacrifice and Community: Jewish Offering and Christian Eucharist* (Blackwell, 2005).

"the Church is the mystical body of Christ: that is to say . . . it is the body of Christ signified by means of the sacrament."[8] The connection between the Church as the Body of Christ, on the one hand, and the cross (sacramentally represented by the Eucharist), on the other, is clear: the sacrament of the Eucharist signifies the Body.

This relation between the cross and the Body of Christ needs more attention in contemporary ecclesiology. It is all too easy to conceive of the Mystical Body as a Spirit-energized communion of love without ever connecting it explicitly to the suffering body of Christ on the cross. "Communion ecclesiology" or "Mystical Body ecclesiology" does not immediately bring to mind "cruciform ecclesiology."[9] At first glance, the image of People of God seems more connected with the concrete sufferings of Christ and his people than does the image of Mystical Body, which seems more idealized and less historical. The People of God strives and suffers along with Christ crucified, whereas the Mystical Body seems to be united to Christ in a much less agonistic fashion

8. Henri de Lubac, SJ, *Corpus Mysticum: The Eucharist and the Church in the Middle Ages*, trans. Gemma Simmonds, CJ, with Richard Price and Christopher Stephens, ed. Laurence Paul Hemming and Susan Frank Parsons (University of Notre Dame Press, 2007), 250. De Lubac adds, "Eucharistic realism and ecclesial realism: these two realisms support one another, each is the guarantee of the other" (251). I concur fully, although some of de Lubac's claims in this book are doubtful, especially when he is implicitly taking aim at neo-scholasticism. For sympathetic discussion—drawing connections to political theology—see William T. Cavanaugh, *Torture and Eucharist: Theology, Politics, and the Body of Christ* (Blackwell, 1998), 207–14; and for a demonstration that around half of Aquinas's references to "corpus mysticum" are to the Eucharist, see Martin Morard, "Les expressions *Corpus mysticum* et *Persona mystica* dans l'oeuvre de saint Thomas d'Aquin: Références et analyse," *Revue Thomiste* 95, no. 4 (1995): 653–64. See also Gilles Emery, OP, "The Ecclesial Fruit of the Eucharist in St. Thomas Aquinas," trans. Therese C. Scarpelli, in Gilles Emery, *Trinity, Church, and the Human Person: Thomistic Essays* (Sapientia Press, 2007), 155–72. De Lubac's thesis has produced a number of unnuanced portraits, as in John D. Zizioulas, *The Eucharistic Communion and the World*, ed. Luke Ben Tallon (T&T Clark International, 2011), 102–3.

9. For the origins of (immensely fruitful) communion ecclesiology, see Johann Adam Möhler, *Unity in the Church, or, The Principle of Catholicism: Presented in the Spirit of the Church Fathers of the First Three Centuries*, trans. Peter C. Erb (The Catholic University of America Press, 1996). Möhler remarks, "Two extremes are possible in ecclesiastical life, and both are called egoism. They arise if *each as an individual* or *one individual* wishes to be all. In the latter case the bond of unity is so narrow and love so warm that one cannot free oneself of its strangling hold. In the first case everything falls apart, and love grows so cold that one freezes. One egoism begets the other. Neither one nor another must wish to be all. Only all can be all and the unity of all can only be a whole. This is the idea of the Catholic Church" (262).

through the circulation or communion brought about by the grace of the Holy Spirit and the bond of charity.

This contrast between the Body of Christ and the People of God, however, need not be present. As the Anglican theologian Ephraim Radner comments, "Paul speaks of the church as 'the body of Christ,' but it is a body taken up and ever dependent on the creative and re-creative grace of God in Christ, which partakes always of judgment and mercy both, in the cross."[10] Radner recognizes the intrinsic relationship of the cross and the Body of Christ. From a Barthian perspective, too, the young Hans Küng—not yet having broken with the Catholic dogmatic tradition—gave an important place to the cross in his 1967 book *The Church*. Küng remarks, "The application of the concept 'body' to the ecclesia of Christ must have come all the more easily to Paul, since the 'blood of Jesus' (i.e., his sacrificial death) had already, before Paul, been invested with a continuing saving effect for the community of the present."[11] The members of the Church (the Body of Christ), for Paul, are members of Christ crucified.[12]

10. Ephraim Radner, *A Brutal Unity: The Spiritual Politics of the Christian Church* (Baylor University Press, 2012), 162–63.

11. Hans Küng, *The Church*, trans. Ray Ockenden and Rosaleen Ockenden (Sheed and Ward, 1967), 226.

12. Küng, 229. In a Barthian vein, Küng goes on to underscore sharply the distinction between Head and members, arguing that the Church must never put itself (or its magisterial authority) in the place of Christ. He considers that the Church's great temptation is to claim to control God's word rather than to be judged by it. See also Kimlyn J. Bender, "Ecclesiology and Christology," in Bender and Long, *T&T Clark Handbook of Ecclesiology*, 323–41, at 325–26, where he notes, "There is no collapse in Paul between the ascended Christ and the church as his earthly body, and the perfection of the first is set over against the imperfection of the latter. This is evident in the fact that Paul consistently distinguishes between Christ and the Christian (and the church itself) in noting that while the believer dies *with* Christ, it is Christ who has died *for* the believer. . . . While Paul can speak of the intimate union of Christ and his church (and with the believer), this corporate unity retains also an inviolable distinction. . . . [The image of the "body"] points to a real and intimate union of Christ with his church, but one in which the distinctiveness of each and their irreversible and asymmetrical relation is never sacrificed: Christ remains the ascended Lord, and the church remains his servant, even as it is also his earthly body." Bender directs attention here to Ernest Best, *One Body in Christ: A Study in the Relationship of the Church to Christ in the Epistles of the Apostle Paul* (SPCK, 1955); and Ernst Käsemann, *Perspectives on Paul*, trans. Margaret Kohl (Fortress, 1971)—as well as, more broadly, to the concerns of John Webster about Catholic arguments that ecclesiology is co-implicated in Christology: see Webster, *Confessing God: Essays in Christian Dogmatics II* (T&T Clark International, 2005).

Many other theologians and biblical scholars, no doubt, have had this same insight. But in this chapter, I will limit my scope. I will first survey the work of four theologians from the 1930s, 1940s, and 1950s who, in their understandings of the Mystical Body (with reference typically to Aquinas), maintained a place for the cross—that is, for the Body of Christ as participating in the cross and as cruciform. The four theologians are Emile Mersch, Fulton Sheen, Charles Journet, and Pius Parsch. In this first section, I will also examine the place of the cross in Pope Pius XII's 1943 encyclical *Mystici Corporis*. Second, I will take up the approach to the Mystical Body found in five more recent Thomistic theologians: Jérôme Hamer, Marie-Joseph Le Guillou, George Sabra, Jean-Pierre Torrell, and Herwi Rikhof. These interpreters generally leave out the cross in their depiction of Aquinas's understanding of the Body of Christ. I briefly comment upon the place of the cross in Vatican II's *Lumen Gentium*, which I find to be broadly in accord with the portrait given by *Mystici Corporis*. My third and final section will turn to Aquinas himself, in order to display the place of the cross (along with other elements such as the Holy Spirit) in his understanding of the Mystical Body. My argument is that Aquinas's position and that of the above preconciliar theologians as well as *Mystici Corporis* and *Lumen Gentium*, should today be retrieved and accentuated.

II. THE MYSTICAL BODY IN THE 1930S–1950S

Let me begin with the four theologians from the 1930s through the 1950s, in addition to the encyclical *Mystici Corporis*.[13] Emile

13. For an appreciative discussion of Erich Przywara, SJ's 1940 "alternative to mystical body ecclesiology"—in which "organic" analogies are tempered by "a certain priority on the Church 'from above'" in its hierarchical and juridical character—see Aaron Pidel, SJ, *Church of the Ever Greater God: The Ecclesiology of Erich Przywara* (University of Notre Dame Press, 2020), 104. For Przywara in this period, as Pidel says, hierarchy and mission are linked: "Because only divinely representative authority can employ instruments without compromising their freedom . . . a less hierarchical Church will become a less apostolically enterprising, less externally engaged Church" (129). Pidel adds that Przywara's caution regarding "Mystical Body" ecclesiology is not contradicted by Pope Pius XII's encyclical. See Erich Przywara, SJ, "*Corpus Christi*

Mersch, the first of these theologians, remains well known for his 1933 book *The Whole Christ: The Historical Development of the Doctrine of the Mystical Body in Scripture and Tradition*. Mersch argues that in the writings of thirteenth-century theologians such as Aquinas, "the doctrine of the Mystical Body no longer occupies its [biblical and patristic] position of prominence."[14] This is so, Mersch says, due to Aristotelian philosophy, Roman juridical thought, and the difficulty of defining "the Mystical Body in the precise formulas required for syllogistic argumentation."[15] In making this claim, Mersch was reacting against the regnant neo-scholastic theology of his day.

Mersch recognizes, however, that in the thirteenth century, the Mystical Body was hardly ignored. He especially values Aquinas's insistence that Christ, as Head, communicates his own personal grace to the members of his Body. Aquinas thereby presents "the whole life of grace in the members of the Mystical Body as a prolongation of that supreme grace whereby the Head of the body is constituted the very Son of God and the Holy of holies" (although Aquinas differentiates between Christ's grace of union and his habitual grace).[16] Given this view of the Mystical Body, there is a direct connection between Christ's cross and the life of the Church. For Aquinas, all Christ's actions, "especially

Mysticum—Eine Bilanz" (originally published in 1940, and criticized by Congar), in Przywara, *Katholische Krise*, ed. Bernard Gertz (Patmos, 1967), 123–52. As Pidel shows, after World War II, Przywara shifted toward a nuptial (Marian) ecclesiology, emphasizing from a particular angle (centered on Mary's participation in the Cross) the emergence of the global Church from the kenotic ruins of the war-decimated European Church. Pidel sums up this later approach, "Przywara in these writings of the mid-1940s scarcely alludes to the role that specific ecclesial structures, such as the papacy, play in maintaining this creaturely middle. The Church, in short, appears less as a discrete entity, endowed with fixed structures and inalienable privileges, than as a bridge connecting the protological nuptiality of Jesus-Logos and Mary-Wisdom to the eschatological nuptiality of the Spirit and Bride. . . . At the height of his apocalyptic fervor, Przywara's nuptial ecclesiology, to the extent that it generates concrete pastoral directives, certainly assumes a strongly anti-institutional [and decentralizing] edge" (*Church of the Ever Greater God*, 173, 180). See Przywara, *Christentum gemäß Johannes* (Glock und Lutz, 1954).

14. Emile Mersch, SJ, *The Whole Christ: The Historical Development of the Doctrine of the Mystical Body in Scripture and Tradition*, trans. John R. Kelly, SJ (Bruce, 1938), 451.

15. Mersch, 451.

16. Mersch, 455.

his passion and death, His resurrection and ascension, affect us directly."[17]

Aquinas's argument that Christ and his members act as "one mystic person" especially impresses Mersch. Mersch aptly describes Aquinas as teaching that "when Christ suffers, all humanity is redeeming itself in Him."[18] The suffering of the Head is never separated from that of the Body. According to Mersch, then, the redemptive cross is at the center of the Mystical Body, since Christ's sacrifice is not the mere action of an *isolated* individual. Put simply, the Body of Christ shares in the redemption won by Christ because the Body of Christ shares in the Head's sacrifice on Calvary.

In his 1935 *The Mystical Body of Christ*, Fulton Sheen—then a professor of theology at The Catholic University of America, trained in the Thomism of the University of Louvain, and soon to be famous as a television evangelist—approached the Mystical Body from a multitude of angles. These include the "soul" of the Church (i.e., the Holy Spirit, which launches Sheen into a variety of subtopics, such as the Church's catholicity), the relationship between the Church's nature as Christ's Mystical Body and the fact that the Church is marked by sin, the infallibility and authority of the Church, Mary and the Mystical Body, the Eucharist as constitutive of the unity of the Mystical Body, and Catholic social action (social justice), among others.[19] I will focus solely on the role that the cross plays.

Sheen begins by emphasizing that Christ's humanity was, in his earthly life, the instrument of his divinity; and this did not come to an end. It is still the case today that Christ's "life, death, Resurrection, and Ascension are the instruments of Divinity for our sanctification, our life, our resurrection, our ascension."[20]

17. Mersch, 465.

18. Mersch, 470.

19. See Fulton J. Sheen, *The Mystical Body of Christ* (Word on Fire, 2023).

20. Sheen, 19.

Christ acted in the world as priest, prophet, and king. Today, through his Mystical Body the Church, he continues to act in the world as priest, prophet, and king. Moreover, Christ is so intimately bound with the members of his Mystical Body that if they are persecuted, he is persecuted, and when they are cared for, he is cared for. Sheen argues that, as can be recognized in the sacraments, "the Church, . . . the *totus Christus* (the whole Christ), as St. Augustine calls it, is continuing the Incarnation by prolonging the theandric actions of the historical Christ."[21]

One way that the Church prolongs the historical Christ's actions is through the Eucharist, which Sheen identifies as "the sacrifice of the Mystical Body."[22] As Sheen explains, "On the Cross the 'Historical' Christ offered Himself, in the Mass the 'Mystical' Christ which is Christ and us, are associated in the offering."[23] It is through the Church as the Body of Christ that we are able to share in the salvific sacrifice offered by Christ on the cross. The glorious saving power of the cross—its status as the perfect offering—now involves us as we are truly united to and offered in Christ's sacrifice through the liturgical action of the Eucharistic sacrifice.[24] Christ, through his Mystical Body, incorporates us and joins us fully into his one saving cross.

Sheen emphasizes, therefore, that the Body of Christ is not simply the communion of believers incorporated into Christ by the bond of love. At least, this Body cannot be understood unless love is viewed in the context of the cross. To share in the Eucharistic communion, we must possess a "spirit of sacrifice."[25] We must be configured to Christ's dying, through our own dying to our self-centered selves. The love that unites the Body of Christ is the "Incarnate Love [who] emptied Himself of His Life on the

21. Sheen, 37.

22. Sheen, 194.

23. Sheen, 197.

24. For this (then widely shared) understanding of the Eucharist, see also Thomas Merton, *The Living Bread* (Farrar, Straus & Cudahy, 1956).

25. Sheen, *The Mystical Body of Christ*, 212.

Cross."[26] In short, the Church as the Mystical Body consists in those who love as Christ loved us on the cross. The blessed in the state of glory will be those who, as Sheen poetically puts it, "filled up once again with love the Divine Chalice, which God Himself drained in making and redeeming us."[27]

The Thomist theologian Charles Journet's multi-volume *L'Église du Verbe incarné* belongs among the classic works of Catholic theology. In a section written in the late 1940s, he devotes a few hundred pages to the theme of the Body of Christ, which he treats after discussing the uncreated soul of the Church (the Holy Spirit) and the created soul of the Church (organizing principles such as the sacramental characters and jurisdictional structures). The Body of Christ is "the extension of Christ in space and time."[28] Christ is the Head of the Body. The Pauline "body of Christ" includes what Journet distinguishes as soul and body. Journet reflects upon the relationship between Christ's flesh and his Body the Church. Discussing the constitutive elements of the Church as the Body of Christ, Journet approaches the topic from the perspective of the Church's efficient, formal, and final causes. Efficiently, the motion of Christ and the Spirit brings about the Body of Christ, extending and prolonging Christ in time and space. Formally, Christ's capital grace—a "fully Christic grace,"[29] sacramental and cultic—is the inherent cause of the Body of Christ. The final cause is not only Christic grace and the Holy Spirit, but the whole Trinity transforming humans and leading them to glory.

Journet holds that these three causes are aligned with the essential dimensions of the Church as the Body of Christ: the cultic dimension, the prophetic dimension, and the dimension of

26. Sheen, 222.

27. Sheen, 229.

28. Charles Journet, *L'Église du Verbe incarné: Essai de théologie spéculative*, vol. 3, *Sa structure interne et son unité catholique* (Deuxième partie) (Editions Saint-Augustin, 2000), 1437. (I completed my book prior to the publication of the English translation of Journet's work.)

29. Journet, 3:1446.

holiness. According to the Letter to the Hebrews, Christ the supreme high priest accomplishes our salvation by entering with his blood into the heavenly sanctuary. As Journet says, Christ "gave to his death on the Cross the character of a definitive sacrificial offering."[30] This offering cannot be repeated, but it can be participated in, and this was Christ's plan, through Baptism, the Eucharist, and the other sacraments. The importance of sacramental character is found here, because the three sacramental "characters"—imprinted by Baptism, Confirmation, and Holy Orders—participate in and derive from Christ's priesthood. Journet states with respect to Holy Orders, "the hierarchical character of order communicates the power of rendering present and efficacious the redemptive sacrifice" of Christ, a "rendering present" that takes place in the Eucharistic liturgy.[31] Holy Orders ensures that the redemptive power of the cross is able to course through the Body of Christ. For its part, the baptismal character enables the believer to receive the sacrament of the Eucharist and to "co-offer the sacrifice of the Mass."[32]

Journet speaks of "three concentric circles" that are present in the cultic dimension of the Body of Christ,[33] which is the dimension that he discusses first (without denigrating the prophetic dimension and the dimension of sanctity). The first circle is the very heart of the Body of Christ: Christ's own redemptive sacrifice on the cross. Flowing from Christ's cross are the sacraments and the public prayers and liturgical offices. For my purposes in this chapter, the key point is the centrality of the cross for the Body of Christ. The Church, in its cultic dimension, has been "consecrated in order to continue validly in the world the cult inaugurated by Christ the priest."[34] Through the unbloody rite of the Last Supper, the Church is able to make present to all

30. Journet, 3:1447.
31. Journet, 3:1448.
32. Journet, 3:1448.
33. Journet, 3:1449.
34. Journet, 3:1449.

generations Christ's unique sacrifice on the cross—in accordance with numerous biblical passages that affirm the Church's cultic, sacramental, and liturgical work.

Journet notes that the 1947 encyclical *Mediator Dei* highlights the Church's priestly extension of the power of Christ's priestly sacrifice on the cross. After providing a lengthy quotation from *Mediator Dei*, he remarks that the reason the Church is able to exercise the same priestly cult across the ages is because of "Christ's presence in all the acts of the cult of his Church."[35] The blood of Christ, shed on the cross, remains always at the center of the Body of Christ—without overshadowing the fact that the risen, glorious Christ who will come again is always proclaimed as well by this same cult. Eschatological remembrance and promise go together.

Journet goes on to take up a variety of topics, including the "coextensivity" of the soul and body of the Church—which means that where charity is (and thus where the indwelling Spirit is), there is the Church. He pays special attention to the role of the Spirit. He explores the relation of the "visible supernatural society" of the Church to "the nations, visible temporal societies."[36] He investigates the Catholic understanding of the Church's visibility in comparison to Calvin's understanding of this same topic. He treats the hierarchical and non-hierarchical acts of the Church. But, while attending to all these themes (and many others), he keeps in mind the cross's centrality for the Body of Christ, since "the Passion of Christ is the meritorious and redemptive cause of the salvation of all humans without exception," even if this cause is applied differently in accordance with whether people live before or after Christ.[37] Christ acts in his Body in diverse ways, and the Church as Christ's Body shares in Christ's prophetic and royal authority as well as his priesthood. But his

35. Journet, 3:1452.
36. Journet, 3:1573.
37. Journet, 3:1614.

priesthood—his cross—is always central for understanding the Church as the Body of Christ.[38]

Pius Parsch, a priest of the Canons Regular of St. Augustine, was a leader in the liturgical movement. In the early 1950s, he prepared a collection of sermons for all Sundays and feast days of the year, to which he added, as an appendix, ten sermons on the Mystical Body. The first nine sermons do not refer much, if at all, to the cross. Instead, these sermons build upon Pope Pius XII's 1943 encyclical *Mystici Corporis* by focusing on divine grace. The Church mediates to us the grace of the Holy Spirit, "which is an inchoation of glory" or deification.[39] Parsch grounds his account of the Mystical Body in the doctrine of grace. Christ is the source of all grace; Christ the Head fills his Body with the grace of his Spirit. He founded the Church, his Mystical Body, by his preaching and teaching, his redemptive death, and his pouring out the Spirit at Pentecost. Christ dwells in his Body and continues to sustain and build it up.

Parsch grants that the Church has contained not only saints but also many wicked persons and scandals, and he grants that the Church's exercise of political rule and of judicial authority has hardly been spotless, to say the least. But to know the Church properly, one must know it as Christ's Body. Insofar as they are truly members of the Church, possessing the grace of Christ, the Church's many members are one because they share in the one life of grace that comes from the Head. The "soul" of the Body is the Spirit, which Christ breathed into his Church at Pentecost. Believers are temples of the Spirit, and all the various functions

38. Indeed, Journet points out that the law of renunciation and suffering (the pattern of the Cross) is and must be "the supreme rule of the Christian life" for all members of Christ's Body (Journet, 3:1680).

39. Pius Parsch, *We Are Christ's Body*, trans. Clifford Howell, SJ (Fides, 1962), 9. Parsch goes on to say, "When the Second Person of the Blessed Trinity became man he began to possess human, natural life (which was created) and also supernatural life as it exists in man, that is a created participation in the divine life. It is this which we share" (13). For the significant presence of the doctrine of deification in the neo-scholastic period, see Jennifer Newsome Martin, "Neo-Thomist and *Ressourcement* Theology," in *The Oxford Handbook of Deification*, ed. Paul L. Gavrilyuk, Andrew Hofer, OP, and Matthew Levering (Oxford University Press, 2024), 480–98.

of the Body come from grace of the Spirit, mediated by the sacraments. As Parsch says, "Members of Christ's Mystical Body live with Christ's life. And this life is sanctifying grace."[40]

Parsch develops this point in various directions, including by highlighting fraternal charity, the communion of saints, the visibility of the Church as the Mystical Body, the relationship of believers to non-Christians, the relation of non-Catholics to the Mystical Body, the status of Catholics in a state of sin, the "sacramental character" given by Baptism and Confirmation, the nature of the priesthood, Catholic marriage and family life, and so on. But in his final sermon, on "The Mystical Body and the Season of Lent," he makes a strong, though brief, connection to the cross. Although the Church is holy, the Church's members on earth are sinners, with the exception of Mary. To have and dwell in a Body with sinful members, says Parsch, belongs to Christ's emptying of himself in absolute humility, and it entails that the Mystical Body needs purification. Parsch draws a powerful conclusion from this fact. He states, "The Mystical Body of Christ, in passing through this world, must follow the same path as that which was traversed by Christ in his physical body during his earthly life."[41] This path includes the cross: "The body and the members must suffer with their head, must die and rise and attain to glory."[42] Lent requires a tangible participation of the Mystical Body in the cross of Christ through prayer, fasting, and almsgiving or works of mercy.[43]

Lastly in this section, let me briefly mention some aspects of Pius XII's *Mystici Corporis*. The completion of the Mystical Body, *Mystici Corporis* teaches, took place on the cross. The blood and water from the side of Christ established the Church, which, as the New Eve, came forth from the side of the New Adam.

40. Parsch, *We Are Christ's Body*, 39.

41. Parsch, 97.

42. Parsch, 98–99.

43. Parsch goes on to add the Eucharist and its "divine food" as a central part of the Lenten journey, but he does not mention our sacramental sharing in Christ's cross through the Eucharist (i.e., Eucharistic sacrifice).

Through the blood of Christ, the human race was reconciled to God, the gifts of the new covenant were poured out, and the Church was fully formed. On the cross, Christ is the Head of the Church, conquering original sin and uniting human beings to himself. Through Christ's blood, the temple veil was rent and the Church received the fullness of the Holy Spirit. On the cross, Christ gave to his Body the divine gifts that ensure that the Church can always teach, govern, and sanctify its members.

As biblical evidence for the centrality of the cross in constituting the Church, *Mystici Corporis* appeals to Ephesians 2:13–16, where Paul teaches that the Gentile believers "have been brought near in the blood of Christ" because Christ has united Jews and Gentiles by reconciling "us both to God in one body through the cross." It is on this foundation that the encyclical discusses the outpouring of the Spirit at Pentecost.[44] Christ reigns "directly and personally," as well as through the Church's apostolic hierarchy.[45] Christ gives particular graces to each member of his Body. In this way, Christ configures the Body to himself, so that it is truly "his body, the fullness of him who fills all in all" (Eph 1:23) and so that the members "grow up in every way into him who is the head, . . . from whom the whole body, joined and knit together by every joint with which it is supplied, when each part

44. The encyclical does not minimize the Spirit's role. It states, "Christ our Lord wills the Church to live His own supernatural life, and by His divine power permeates His whole Body and nourishes and sustains each of the members according to the place which they occupy in the body, in the same way as the vine nourishes and makes fruitful the branches which are joined to it. If we examine closely this divine principle of life and power given by Christ, insofar as it constitutes the very source of every gift and created grace, we easily perceive that it is nothing else than the Holy Spirit, the Paraclete, who proceeds from the Father and the Son, and who is called in a special way, the 'Spirit of Christ' or the 'Spirit of the Son.' For it was by this Breath of grace and truth that the Son of God anointed His soul in the immaculate womb of the Blessed Virgin; this Spirit delights to dwell in the beloved soul of our Redeemer as in His most cherished shrine; this Spirit Christ merited for us on the Cross by shedding His Own Blood; this Spirit He bestowed on the Church for the remission of sins, when He breathed on the Apostles; and while Christ alone received this Spirit without measure, to the members of the Mystical Body He is imparted only according to the measure of the giving of Christ from Christ's own fulness. But after Christ's glorification on the Cross, His Spirit is communicated to the Church in an abundant outpouring, so that she, and her individual members, may become daily more and more like our Savior" (Pius XII, *Mystici Corporis* §§55–56, encyclical letter, June 29, 1943, vatican.va).

45. *Mystici Corporis* §39.

is working properly, makes bodily growth and upbuilds itself in love" (Eph 4:15–16).

As Head of his Body, *Mystici Corporis* emphasizes, Christ is not merely the leader of a community of people. Rather, "Christ is the Divine Savior of this Body."[46] This explains why the cross must be central to the proper understanding of the Mystical Body. Christ, in and through his saving cross, continually acts for the salvation of his Body. The Mystical Body is comprised of the Savior and those whom he saves. He not only reconciles the members of his Body to God, but he also gives them supernatural and deifying life. He does the latter through the outpouring of his Spirit, who "is the principle of every supernatural act in all parts of the Body."[47]

Furthermore, the Eucharistic sacrifice unites the Body in the saving self-offering of the Head on the cross. In the Eucharistic sacrifice, the priest acts *in persona Christi* on behalf of the whole Mystical Body. In union with the priest's prayers, the faithful—and thus the entire Mystical Body—offer the saving sacrifice of Christ to the Father. In the Eucharistic sacrifice (which is the Church's offering of the one sacrifice of the cross), Christ can be said to offer "to the heavenly Father not only Himself as Head of the Church, but in Himself His mystical members also, since He holds them all, even those who are weak and ailing, in His most loving Heart."[48]

The final paragraphs of *Mystici Corporis* highlight the love of Christ. Christ loves the whole human race, each and every human being. The encyclical reminds us that Christ's cross was for the salvation of the whole world, with the goal of uniting the whole world in the Body of Christ. We must therefore love all human beings as at least potential members of the Body and as "our

46. *Mystici Corporis* §59.
47. *Mystici Corporis* §57.
48. *Mystici Corporis* §82.

brothers in Christ according to the flesh."[49] The Mystical Body involves no cheap grace, no fellowship or communion rooted simply in goodwill rather than in the cross of Christ. Christ freely endured the cross out of love for his Body, and so "it was only at the price of His Blood that He purchased the Church."[50] The members of the Body are members only insofar as they "follow gladly in the bloodstained footsteps" of Christ the Head.[51] By sharing in his cross, the members of his Body will share (and even now share) in his Resurrection.[52]

III. THOMISTIC INTERPRETATIONS OF THE MYSTICAL BODY FROM THE 1960S TO THE 2000S: HAMER, LE GUILLOU, SABRA, TORRELL, AND RIKHOF

The centrality of the cross for the Body of Christ appears to have been lost, due to a shift in theological emphasis, beginning around the late 1950s. I cannot here offer a comprehensive account, and I may have missed some important exceptions (focusing as I do upon Thomistic theologians), but what follows indicates a broadly shared tendency.[53]

49. *Mystici Corporis* §96. With implicit reference to the Nazi slaughter of the Jewish people, whose horrific extent was becoming clear by 1943, the encyclical states, "It is true, unfortunately, especially today, that there are some who extol enmity, hatred and spite as if they enhanced the dignity and the worth of man. Let us, however, while we look with sorrow on the disastrous consequences of this teaching, follow our peaceful King who taught us to love not only those who are of a different nation or race, but even our enemies" (§96).

50. *Mystici Corporis* §106.

51. *Mystici Corporis* §106.

52. *Mystici Corporis* §106.

53. For another example of the tendency to neglect the cross when discussing the Body of Christ, see P. A. Liégé, OP, "The Mystery of the Church," in *The Historical and Mystical Christ*, ed. A. M. Henry, OP, trans. Angeline Bouchard (Fides, 1958), 314–418. Let me add that Liégé quotes a passage from Étienne Borne (a review essay on Yves Congar's *Lay People in the Church* that Borne published in *La Vie Intellectuelle*, December 1953, pp. 21–38) that anticipates the preoccupations of many of the theologians cited in my "People of God" chapter: "Has not the laity long held in the Church the position of a nomadic rather than of an integrated proletariat, that could participate in religious culture and life only through the mediation of a priestly class? And has this not hardened the laity in an intolerable state of hostility?" (Liégé, "The Mystery of the Church," 396).

In his 1962 *The Church Is a Communion*, Jérôme Hamer—an influential voice in the development and promotion of Catholic communion ecclesiology—devoted a chapter to exploring the Mystical Body from the perspective of Thomas Aquinas. Hamer notes that the German theologian Mannes D. Koster, critically reflecting upon Augustine and Aquinas, argued in 1940 that their ecclesiology was primarily spiritual: they interpreted even the expression "body of Christ" non-corporeally, as the invisible Church across the ages. Other students of Aquinas from the 1940s offered a similar criticism that "St. Thomas may have shown the influx of the life of Christ into the Church, but he did not give sufficient place to the corporeity of the 'mystical body.'"[54] In response, Hamer directs attention to the instrumentality of Christ's humanity and, more specifically, to the human actions of Christ as causing grace in us. Since Christ is the incarnate Son, he is our Head not only with respect to our souls but also with respect to our bodies. Although the Church has existed from Abel onward, it has never existed as a merely spiritual communion: it has always been united by corporeal sacraments. The inclusion of the angels does not make the Mystical Body non-corporeal, given that Christ is Head of the angels in a different sense than he is Head of human beings.

Hamer lays particular emphasis upon the Eucharist. For Aquinas, the *res sacramenti* of the Eucharist is the Mystical Body in its unity (united by love).[55] The conclusion that Hamer draws

54. Jérôme Hamer, OP, *The Church Is a Communion*, trans. Ronald Matthews (Geoffrey Chapman, 1964), 73. See Mannes D. Koster, OP, *Ekklesiologie im Werden* (Bonifacius-Druckerei, 1940).

55. Reinhard Hütter observes that Aquinas "regards the ensuing sacramental union of Christ with the faithful in the Eucharist—a surpassing abiding in each other—as the reality of the sacrament, the *res sacramenti*: 'The reality of the sacrament is the unity of the mystical body' [*Summa theologiae* III, q. 73, a. 3]." See Hütter, *Aquinas on Transubstantiation: The Real Presence of Christ in the Eucharist* (The Catholic University of America Press, 2019), 66–67. See also Jan-Heiner Tück, *A Gift of Presence: The Theology and Poetry of the Eucharist in Thomas Aquinas*, trans. Scott Hefelfinger (The Catholic University of America Press, 2018), 156: "The Church as *corpus Christi mysticum* exists on account of the participation of the faithful in the *corpus Christi verum*." Tück has in view here Aquinas's quotation of John of Damascus in *Summa theologiae* III, q. 73, a. 4.

is that, for Aquinas, Christ's real body "is the proper cause of the mystical body as a conjoint instrument [of the Son]."[56]

Although Hamer's book focuses upon "communion" as the basis for ecclesiology, he draws his definition of the Church from the theology of the Mystical Body. He defines the Church as follows: "The Church is the mystical body of Christ, that is to say a communion which is at once inward and external, the life of union with Christ, and established (caused) by the economy of Christ's mediation."[57] Hamer examines the way in which communion with Christ is interior and spiritual and also involves outward forms, including the episcopacy and papacy, as well as the generative causes of communion (the saving mysteries of Christ's life). He thinks of the Mystical Body primarily in terms of interpersonal communion, which governs his ecclesiology. As he says, "Because of its union with Christ, the Church is a mystery of interdependence, a network of relationships between persons. . . . We must restore to the term 'communion,' with all its aura of tradition and meaning, its rightful importance."[58]

I should add that Hamer's investigation of the term "communion" leads him deep into the causes of this communion, including the Father's sending of the Son into the world as messianic priest, prophet, and king.[59] Hamer emphasizes the Eucharist and the common priesthood of the faithful, whose task is to offer worship or spiritual sacrifice to God.[60] In reflecting upon the New Testament meaning of *koinonia* (communion), he recognizes that

56. Hamer, *The Church Is a Communion*, 82.

57. Hamer, 93.

58. Hamer, 93.

59. As Hamer notes, Jesus's possession of these three offices is emphasized by John Calvin in his *Institutes of the Christian Religion* (as early as 1545) and also receives noteworthy attention in the *Roman Catechism* of 1566.

60. See Gilles Emery, OP, "Le sacerdoce spirituel des fidèles chez saint Thomas d'Aquin," *Revue Thomiste* 99, no. 1 (1999): 211–43. According to Hamer, "Any human activity can be the occasion of a spiritual sacrifice, and on these grounds it can be consecrated. The whole life of the Christian is in itself sacred, not profane. Now the relationships which constitute economic, social, cultural and political life are a network of human activities. As such, through the medium of the royal priesthood of the faithful, they revert to God in the form of a sacrifice of praise" (Hamer, *The Church Is a Communion*, 111).

believers "participate in the blood of Christ, in his body, in the Son himself, in his sufferings and in the Spirit."[61] In the patristic Church, "communion" often referred to churches being in Eucharistic communion with each other. Hamer's focus is on communion in the sense of unity of faith, sacraments, and fellowship, inclusive of the apostolic (hierarchical) structure of the Church, and brought about by the Holy Spirit and charity, as well as by Christ's diverse modes of presence in the Church (especially in the Eucharist). While certainly not absent, the cross is not central to Hamer's ecclesiology, either with respect to the Mystical Body or with respect to the Church as communion.

Marie-Joseph Le Guillou's Thomistic study *Christ and Church: A Theology of the Mystery*, originally published in 1963, treats the Mystical Body at length. Drawing upon a wide array of Aquinas's texts, Le Guillou begins by emphasizing, "Absolutely unique, and immediately caused by the assumptive divine action *alone*, the *gratia capitis* of Christ enabled Him to unite all men to Himself through the agency of his humanity."[62] It is because of Christ's grace of Headship that he can, on the cross, merit for all human beings. Likewise, as members of his Body through his grace, we can "merit in Him and through Him."[63] All Christ's acts, not solely his Passion, merit salvation for us. Explicating Aquinas, Le Guillou understands the Incarnation as (from the outset) the redemptive Incarnation. Christ's perfect personal grace is always at the same time his grace of Headship. We, Christ's members, are included in the plan of the Incarnation.

Le Guillou provides a lengthy quotation from *Summa theologiae* III, q. 8, a. 1, where Aquinas treats Christ as Head of his

61. Hamer, *The Church Is a Communion*, 162. In this period, he explains, "communion could be expressed as a whole in terms of faith and of sacramental life, and also in terms of institutional and juridical structures which were still in the making" (168).

62. Marie-Joseph Le Guillou, OP, *Christ and Church: A Theology of the Mystery*, trans. Charles E. Schaldenbrand (Desclee, 1966), 261. For praise of Le Guillou as a theologian, see Joseph Ratzinger, *Milestones: Memoirs, 1927–1977*, trans. Erasmo Leiva-Merikakis (Ignatius, 1998), 143–44.

63. Le Guillou, *Christ and Church*, 262.

Body the Church. He notes that Aquinas draws upon a variety of important biblical texts, many of which can be found also in Aquinas's commentary on Romans 8:29. Among the notable biblical texts are John 1:14 and 1:16, where Jesus is presented as full of grace and as the source of grace to all who receive grace. Romans 8:29 teaches that the purpose of this grace is to configure us to Christ's image, so that we become brothers of Christ and heirs with Christ of the inheritance of God the Father (deification). Indebted to Yves Congar, Le Guillou observes that, according to both Scripture and Aquinas, "through His Body, Christ is the principle of a new creation."[64] Specifically, the Body of Christ is constituted by the sending of the Spirit; where the Spirit dwells, there is the "Church of the baptized, the prophetic, priestly, and royal people, who participate in the anointing of Christ, the prophet, priest, and king."[65] The Body of Christ is the Catholic Church, enlivened by the Spirit and "measured by the mediation of Christ as Head."[66]

Le Guillou directs attention to the centrality of the Eucharist. He argues that the Eucharist constitutes the Church, as "a commemorative participation in the *act* of Christ saving the world and offering to His Father the worship which is due Him."[67] According to Aquinas, every grace proceeds from the Eucharist; and so Le Guillou associates the Eucharist and the Spirit as constituting the Church as the Body of Christ. Faith and Baptism, along with the bond of charity, also play a central role, of course, as do the Church's hierarchical offices. Christ's Body is a visible Body. Through the Eucharist, the members of the Body are united to the salvific "offering made by Christ upon the Cross"; and the effect of sharing in the Eucharist is charity (manifested supremely by Christ in his Passion), building up the Church in unity.[68]

64. Le Guillou, 273.

65. Le Guillou, 274.

66. Le Guillou, 277.

67. Le Guillou, 278.

68. Le Guillou, 284.

For Le Guillou (interpreting Aquinas), the Mystical Body is a particularly important way to understand the Church because the Church is all about the pouring out of the grace of the Holy Spirit by Christ, "the Head of His Body."[69] As Christ's Body, the Church mediates his grace to the world. The Body of Christ also mediates the teachings and sacraments of Christ the Head. After briefly discussing Aquinas on the priesthood (including the episcopacy), Le Guillou emphasizes the spiritual sacrifice offered by the Body of Christ, which grows "in the likeness of its glorious Head."[70] The "Mystery of Christ" is the center of Aquinas's ecclesiology: the Body of Christ manifests Christ. The cross is part of this mystery, and Le Guillou mentions the cross in connection with the Eucharist (and elsewhere), but the cross is not an explicitly central element of Le Guillou's portrayal of the Mystical Body.

In his 1987 *Thomas Aquinas' Vision of the Church*, George Sabra draws attention to a wide range of literature treating Aquinas's understanding of the Mystical Body, including various studies published in the 1930s and 1940s (although he leaves out—as do I in this chapter, unfortunately—the classical commentators such as John of St. Thomas and Cardinal Cajetan).[71] Sabra highlights the Eucharistic dimension of Aquinas's understanding of the Mystical Body,[72] as well as Aquinas's emphasis on Christ's

69. Le Guillou, 280.

70. Le Guillou, 297.

71. See for example Thomas Käppeli, OP, *Zur Lehre des hl. Thomas von Aquin vom Corpus Christi mysticum* (St. Paulusdruckerei, 1931); Joseph Anger, *La Doctrine du corps mystique de Jésus-Christ d'après les principes de la théologie de Saint-Thomas* (Beauchesne, 1929); Friedrich Jürgensmeier, *Der mystische Leib Christi als Grundprinzip der Aszetik* (Schöningh, 1933). Sabra also points out that in E. H. Kantorowicz, *The King's Two Bodies: A Study in Medieval Political Theology* (Princeton University Press, 1957), Kantorowicz wrongly "attributes an important role to Thomas in the development which *corpus mysticum* underwent from being originally sacramental in meaning, then taking on a sociological connotation and finally becoming the purely juridical notion in Boniface VIII." George Sabra, *Thomas Aquinas' Vision of the Church: Fundamentals of an Ecumenical Ecclesiology* (Matthias Grünewald, 1987), 59. Kantorowicz supposes that Aquinas "contributed greatly to the 'juridicalization'" of the Mystical Body, which—in my view and in Sabra's—is an erroneous claim (Sabra, 59).

72. For discussion of various Eucharistic ecclesiologies, see my *Christ and the Catholic Priesthood: Ecclesial Hierarchy and the Pattern of the Trinity* (Hillenbrand Books, 2010), where I examine the positions of Joseph Ratzinger, John Zizioulas, and Nicholas Afanasiev, among others. The central insights of Eucharistic ecclesiologies can be well articulated from the perspective

grace of headship as the source (in the Spirit) of the members' diverse gifts and offices. Sabra recognizes, "The church as *corpus (Christi) mysticum* is a central and characteristic designation in the ecclesiological thought of Thomas Aquinas."[73] Yet, Sabra does not discuss the significance of the cross in Aquinas's doctrine of the Mystical Body.[74]

In *Saint Thomas Aquinas: Spiritual Master*, first published in 1996, Jean-Pierre Torrell reflects at some length on what he calls "the Christological coloration of grace."[75] Torrell observes that Christ, as the Head of his Body, is the source of grace to all those who are joined to him as members of his Body. Christ causes grace in us in a deeply personal way, as our Head rather than as a mere instrumental cause. Torrell emphasizes, therefore, that in Aquinas's mature thought, "the teaching on the Body of Christ reveals itself to be decisive for fully understanding the conformation of

of the Mystical Body, so long as the cross is understood to be central (to both the Mystical Body and the Eucharist).

73. Sabra, *Thomas Aquinas' Vision of the Church*, 64.

74. I think Sabra exaggerates when he argues (with post-Tridentine ecclesiology critically in view), "The idea of society cannot be deduced from Thomas' *corpus mysticum*. In this regard, A. Mitterer was right in pointing to important differences between Thomas' *corpus mysticum* and Pius XII's notion of *mystici corporis* (1943). The latter starts from a sociological and corporative notion of body which includes, and insists on, visibility and juridical organization, while Thomas' *corpus* does not really insist on visibility, and, for the most part, ignores the juridical aspect. Mitterer locates the reason for what he considers Thomas' inadequate *corpus mysticum* conception in the fact that whereas the Encyclical proceeds from the body to the head, Thomas proceeds in the opposite direction, i.e., from the head to the body, from Christ to the church. . . . Thomas always considers *corpus mysticum* as *Christ's* body; he never considers the body in itself apart from the head. Thomas is more interested in the relations of the head to the members and the members to each other rather than in the notion of body as such; in this sense body is a secondary notion" (Sabra, 66–67). As Sabra himself discusses, Aquinas's commentary on 1 Corinthians 12 pays a good deal of attention to Church offices, and Aquinas never imagines the Mystical Body on earth as lacking in juridical structure. In addition, Aquinas attends carefully to the analogy of a body, rather than simply starting with Christ. See Albert Mitterer, *Geheimnisvoller Leib Christi nach St. Thomas von Aquin und nach Papst Pius XII* (Herold, 1950); and see, more broadly, Michael G. Sirilla, *The Ideal Bishop: Aquinas's Commentaries on the Pastoral Epistles* (The Catholic University of America Press, 2017). I recognize, of course, that (in Avery Dulles, SJ's words) "Aquinas attributes the inner unity of the Church with its head and of the members with one another to the influence of the Holy Spirit" and subordinates the visible, external elements of the Church to the interior New Law of the grace of the Holy Spirit. Dulles, "The Church According to Thomas Aquinas," in Avery Dulles, *A Church to Believe In: Discipleship and the Dynamics of Freedom* (Crossroad, 1987), 149–69, at 154–55.

75. Jean-Pierre Torrell, OP, *Saint Thomas Aquinas*, vol. 2, *Spiritual Master*, trans. Robert Royal (The Catholic University of America Press, 2003), 145.

the Christian to Christ through grace. Spiritually, there is no gap between Christ and His members, for he forms with them 'a single mystical person.'"[76] The doctrine of the Body of Christ enables Aquinas to clarify Christ's active and intimate presence in every dimension of the Church. Whereas one might otherwise think of Christ's merit (or his meritorious satisfaction) as applying to others only extrinsically, in fact his merit spreads throughout his whole Body, since grace unites him so intimately with each and every one of his members.[77] Although Torrell does not mention the cross here, he does cite *Summa theologiae* III, q. 48, a. 1, which is about Christ's Passion. Torrell goes on to point out that for Aquinas, Paul's epistles are in diverse ways about Christ's grace in light of the Mystical Body. The Church in Aquinas's vision is "before all else an organism of grace in total dependence on her head, Christ."[78]

Commenting further on Christ and his Body the Church, Torrell notes that Aquinas conceives of Christ as priest, prophet, and king, and Christ's members share in his priestly, prophetic, and royal offices. Indeed, Aquinas is quite clear, in Torrell's words, that "since the Church-Body of Christ is an expression of his capital grace, all who are linked to him through baptism become kings, priests, and prophets with him."[79] Torrell also treats the Body of Christ in the context of Aquinas's theology of the Holy Spirit, in which the Spirit is the bond of love both in the Trinity and in the Church. In this context, he observes not only that Aquinas's ecclesiology centers around the doctrine of the Mystical Body, but also that the grace of the Holy Spirit is therefore at the heart of Aquinas's ecclesiology. The Church is formed by the grace flowing from the Head and constituting the Body.

76. Torrell, 2:147.

77. See also, on Christ's substitutionary satisfaction, Emmanuel Rousselin, *Nouvel Adam et Serviteur souffrant: La substitution du Christ au pécheur à la lumière de saint Thomas d'Aquin* (Cerf, 2022).

78. Torrell, *Saint Thomas Aquinas*, 2:148.

79. Torrell, 2:150.

Torrell remarks that the Spirit perfectly unites the Head and the Body. He states that for Aquinas, "the role of the Holy Spirit is precisely to establish the 'continuity' between Christ the Head and the faithful members, for he [the Spirit] has the property of remaining numerically *one and the same* in the Head and in the members."[80] The Spirit plays the role of the soul in the Mystical Body. Like the soul in the human body, the Spirit in the Body of Christ is present "entirely in the Whole and entirely in each of its parts," and the Spirit serves as the principle of the Body's unity and its source of holiness, and thus as the principle of the Body's spiritual life and fecundity.[81] Torrell reiterates that the Spirit, as the bond of love in the Trinity, unites the Mystical Body in the charity of Christ. Like blood in a corporeal body, charity is the "vital current" that connects the whole Mystical Body as one "communion of saints."[82] While it is clear that Torrell has a rich and subtle understanding of Aquinas's theology of the Mystical Body, Torrell rarely alludes to the cross in relation to the Mystical Body and never mentions the cross as such.

In a notable essay published in 2004, Herwi Rikhof argued persuasively for "the relevance of Thomas' thought for present discussion of the Church."[83] As Rikhof observes, the one image of the Church that Aquinas systematically develops is the image of the Body of Christ. Rikhof notes that when Aquinas attends to the Mystical Body, he focuses on unity and plurality, the role of the Holy Spirit (the "soul" of the Body), and Christ as the Head. Rikhof does not mention the cross of Christ. He argues that for

80. Torrell, 2:189.

81. Torrell, 2:190.

82. Torrell, 2:194.

83. Herwi Rikhof, "Thomas on the Church: Reflections on a Sermon," in *Aquinas on Doctrine: A Critical Introduction*, ed. Thomas G. Weinandy, OFM Cap., Daniel A. Keating, and John P. Yocum (T&T Clark International, 2004), 199–223, at 201. For Aquinas on the Church (and for the various images most frequently employed by Aquinas in discussing the Church), see also Yves Congar, OP, "The Idea of the Church in St. Thomas Aquinas," *The Thomist* 1 (1939): 331–59; Congar, "Vision de l'Église chez s. Thomas d'Aquin," *Revue des sciences philosophiques et théologiques* 62 (1978): 523–41; and Otto Hermann Pesch, *Thomas von Aquin: Grenze und Größe mittelalterlicher Theologie* (Matthias Grünewald, 1989), 373–80. Pesch is heavily indebted to Sabra, who in turn is indebted to Congar.

Aquinas, the Church is first of all a Trinitarian reality—the indwelling of the Trinity—and secondly "the Church is, basically, the community of believers."[84]

Lastly from this period, let me briefly examine the portrait of the Mystical Body found in Vatican II's Dogmatic Constitution on the Church, *Lumen Gentium.*[85] After his death and Resurrection, says *Lumen Gentium* in paragraph 7, Christ poured out his Spirit and thereby constituted his Mystical Body. All who receive the sacraments, specifically Baptism and the Eucharist, are united to Christ "in his passion and glorification" and comprise his Body.[86] Through the Eucharist, believers "are taken up into communion with him and with one another."[87] *Lumen Gentium* speaks about the diversity of members, functions, ministries, and gifts. The Holy Spirit functions analogously to how the soul functions in a human body, insofar as the Spirit unifies the diverse members into one Body by bestowing charity. Christ reigns as the Head of the Body. The members of the Body must be configured to him by "suffering with him, that with him we may be glorified (cf. Rom 8:17)."[88] In this context, paragraph 7 draws its closest link between the cross and the Mystical Body, stating that "following in trial and in oppression the paths that he trod, we are associated with his sufferings as the body with its head."[89] The paragraph concludes by noting that Christ fills his Body and Bride with his gifts, especially his Holy Spirit.

Paragraph 7 of *Lumen Gentium* should be read in light of paragraph 3. Paragraph 3 states about the cross, the Eucharist, and the Body of Christ,

84. Rikhof, "Thomas on the Church," 220.

85. For further discussion, see Alexandra Diriart, SASJ, *Ses frontières sont la charité: L'Église Corps du Christ et "Lumen Gentium"* (Lethielleux, 2011).

86. Second Vatican Council, *Lumen Gentium* §7, in *Vatican Council II*, vol. 1, *The Conciliar and Post Conciliar Documents*, ed. Austin Flannery, OP, rev. ed. (Costello, 1996), 350–426, at 355.

87. *Lumen Gentium* §7, in *Vatican Council II*, 1:355.

88. *Lumen Gentium* §7, in *Vatican Council II*, 1:355.

89. *Lumen Gentium* §7, in *Vatican Council II*, 1:356.

> The Church—that is, the kingdom of Christ already present in mystery—grows visibly through the power of God in the world. The origin and growth of the Church are symbolized by the blood and water which flowed from the open side of a crucified Jesus (cf. John 19:34), and are foretold in the words of the Lord referring to his death on the cross: "And I, if I be lifted up from the earth, will draw all men to myself" (John 12:32; Gk.). As often as the sacrifice of the cross by which "Christ our Pasch is sacrificed" (1 Cor 5:7) is celebrated on the altar, the work of our redemption is carried out. Likewise, in the sacrament of the eucharistic bread, the unity of believers, who form one body in Christ (cf. 1 Cor 10:17), is both expressed and brought about. All men are called to this union with Christ, who is the light of the world, from whom we go forth, through whom we live, and toward whom our whole life is directed.[90]

Reading paragraphs 3 and 7 together, with the former as the foundation of the latter, one sees that *Lumen Gentium* portrays the sacrifice of the cross, celebrated in the Eucharist, as bringing about the unity of the Body of Christ. On this basis, one can conclude that, overall, the cross receives an important place in *Lumen Gentium*'s theology of the Mystical Body.[91]

IV. THOMAS AQUINAS ON THE CROSS AND THE MYSTICAL BODY

The postconciliar authors noted above understandably chose to focus on other constitutive elements of the Mystical Body (such

90. *Lumen Gentium* §3, in *Vatican Council II*, 1:351.

91. Pope John Paul II interprets *Lumen Gentium* §3 in the above way in his 2003 encyclical *Ecclesia de Eucharistia*: "After stating that 'the Church, as the Kingdom of Christ already present in mystery, grows visibly in the world through the power of God,' [footnote to LG 3] then, as if in answer to the question: 'How does the Church grow?,' the Council adds: 'as often as the sacrifice of the Cross by which "Christ our pasch is sacrificed" (1 Cor 5:7) is celebrated on the altar, the work of our redemption is carried out. At the same time in the sacrament of the Eucharistic bread, the unity of the faithful, who form one body in Christ (cf. 1 Cor 10:17), is both expressed and brought about.'" John Paul II, *Ecclesia de Eucharistia* §21, encyclical letter,

as the Holy Spirit). I do not think they *intended* to downplay the cross in their interpretations of Aquinas on the Body of Christ. This final section will directly address Aquinas's theology. I will first treat some passages from his biblical commentaries and then turn to the *tertia pars* of the *Summa theologiae*. My purpose is to display the cross at the center of the Mystical Body, although Aquinas draws out other themes as well.

Commenting on Ephesians 2:16, where Paul praises Christ for reconciling Jews and Gentiles "in one body through the cross," Aquinas observes that this "one body" is the Church, the Body of Christ.[92] Aquinas cites Romans 12:5 as supporting evidence: "We, though many, are one body in Christ"—and in his commentary on Romans 12:5, Aquinas in turn cites Ephesians 2:16 as supporting evidence. Thus, Aquinas emphasizes that it is through the cross that human beings have been reconciled to God and united *as one Body*. Aquinas also credits the Holy Spirit, poured out by Christ. He states, "This mystical body has a spiritual unity through which we are united to one another and to God by faith and love."[93] In this regard he cites Ephesians 4:4, "There is one body and one Spirit." This passage from Ephesians carries forward Paul's earlier discussion of "the blood of Christ" by which Christ reconciled Jews and Gentiles "to God in one body through the cross" (Eph 2:13, 16).

Another aspect of the Mystical Body is the diversity of the members' gifts and functions. When Aquinas comments on 1 Corinthians 12, he focuses upon the diversity of gifts in the Body of Christ. As context for 1 Corinthians 12, recall 1 Corinthians

April 17, 2003, vatican.va. I owe this insight about *Lumen Gentium* §3 and *Ecclesia de Eucharistia* to an anonymous reviewer.

92. Thomas Aquinas, *Commentary on Ephesians* §118, trans. M.L. Lamb, in *Commentary on the Letters of Saint Paul to the Galatians and Ephesians*, trans. F.R. Larcher, OP, and M.L. Lamb, ed. J. Mortensen and E. Alarcón (The Aquinas Institute for the Study of Sacred Doctrine, 2012), 234.

93. Thomas Aquinas, *Commentary on Letter of Saint Paul to the Romans* §974, trans. F.R. Larcher, OP, ed. J. Mortensen and E. Alarcón (The Aquinas Institute for the Study of Sacred Doctrine, 2012), 333.

1–2, where Paul discusses the power of the cross. Commenting on 1 Corinthians 1:18—"For the word of the cross is folly to those who are perishing, but to us who are being saved it is the power of God"—Aquinas explains what it means to be in Christ. Specifically, believers have discovered "in the cross of Christ God's power, by which he overcame the devil and the world: *the lion of the tribe of Judah, has conquered* (Rev 5:5)."[94]

When Aquinas turns to 1 Corinthians 12:12—"For just as the body is one and has many members, and all the members of the body, though many, are one body, so it is with Christ"—he first reflects upon what it means to be "one." He notes that a body is made perfect by the presence of its diverse members, and therefore a body has perfect unity when it has all its diverse members or organs. Analogously, Christ's Body has perfect unity through its many members. These members perform all the diverse functions needed for the Church's witness to Christ. In the sacrament of Baptism, the Holy Spirit unites diverse human beings to Christ and establishes "the unity of the Church, which is the body of Christ."[95] Some members follow the active life, some the contemplative; some are farmers, some teachers. Aquinas discusses offices in the Church, including the apostolic office, the office of prophecy, and the office of teachers, as well as those who perform miracles or speak in foreign tongues.

In the *tertia pars* of the *Summa theologiae*, Aquinas treats Christ as the Head of the Mystical Body. He inquires first into Christ's grace in relation to the hypostatic union, observing that "the habitual grace of Christ is understood to follow this union, as light follows the sun."[96] Since the habitual grace of Christ perfects him as an individual, the question is how Christ can be the

94. Thomas Aquinas, *Commentary on 1 Corinthians* §47, in *Commentary on the Letters of Saint Paul to the Corinthians*, trans. F.R. Larcher, OP, B. Mortensen, and D. Keating, ed. J. Mortensen and E. Alarcón (The Aquinas Institute for the Study of Sacred Doctrine, 2012), 19.

95. Aquinas, *Commentary on 1 Corinthians* §734, p. 277.

96. Aquinas, *Summa theologiae* III, q. 7, a. 13. See the discussion of this point in Dominic Legge, OP, *The Trinitarian Christology of St Thomas Aquinas* (Oxford University Press, 2017).

source of grace for all his members. Citing John 1:14–16 and Romans 8:29, Aquinas emphasizes that Christ is in fact the source of our grace. If he were not the source of grace for each of us, then he could not be the Head of the whole human race. His habitual grace is of such plenitude that it serves as his grace of headship, overflowing onto the members of his Body. Aquinas comments that in an exterior manner, people can be the cause of the communication of grace to others through their leadership roles in the Church, as "heads" of dioceses or of the whole Church. But no human can communicate interior grace other than Christ.[97]

As Head of the Mystical Body, Christ aims to perfect his Body. The ultimate source of this perfecting is the cross. Aquinas explains, "To be a *glorious Church not having spot or wrinkle* is the ultimate end to which we are brought by the Passion of Christ."[98] The reference here is to Ephesians 5:25–27, where Paul states that "Christ loved the Church and gave himself up for her, that he might sanctify her . . . [and] that he might present the Church to himself in splendor, without spot or wrinkle or any such thing, that she might be holy and without blemish." According to Paul in Ephesians 5, just as husband and wife become one body or one flesh (Gen 2:24), so Christ and the Church are one body: "For no man ever hates his own flesh, but nourishes and cherishes it, as Christ does the Church, because we are members of his body" (Eph 5:29–30). Aquinas states in commenting on Ephesians 5:25, "The sign of Christ's love for the Church is that 'he delivered himself up for it'"; and he adds that Christ's sanctifying of the Church "is the effect of Christ's death," not least because Baptism has its "power from the passion of Christ."[99]

In his discussion in the *Summa theologiae* of the effects of Christ's Passion, Aquinas makes reference to the Mystical Body. Christ's Passion accomplishes its effects not for Christ (since

97. See Aquinas, *Summa theologiae* III, q. 8, a. 6.

98. Aquinas, *Summa theologiae* III, q. 8, a. 3, ad 2.

99. Aquinas, *Commentary on Ephesians* §§323–24, p. 320.

Christ does not need healing from sin) but for us. Aquinas states, "Christ's Passion causes forgiveness of sins by way of redemption. For since he is our head, then, by the Passion which He endured from love and obedience, He delivered us as His members from our sins."[100] Aquinas compares this to the way in which, in a human body, the hands may work to redeem an offense committed by the feet. He further explains, "For, just as the natural body is one, though made up of diverse members, so the whole Church, Christ's mystic body, is reckoned as one person with its head, which is Christ."[101] Therefore, what the members have done—namely, sinned—is redeemed by what the Head does on the cross. The action of the Head justifies the members, because the members have been united to the Head as his Body, through the grace of the Holy Spirit. Christ and his members have become "one person." As Aquinas says somewhat further on, even though Christ's Passion in itself is superabundantly sufficient for the salvation of all human beings, "Christ's Passion works its effect in them to whom it is applied, through faith and charity and the sacraments of faith."[102] Not only must sinners be joined to Christ's Body (and thereby share in the redemptive power of his Passion), but also sinners must be configured to Christ, as members to the Head.[103] This begins through Baptism.

Aquinas treats these matters sometimes without mentioning the Mystical Body, but he mentions it often enough. For instance, in a reply to an objection, he remarks, "Christ's satisfaction [on the cross] works its effect in us inasmuch as we are incorporated with Him, as the members with their head. . . . Now the members must be conformed to their head."[104] Our configuration to Christ the Head is complex. Christ had a passible body and a graced soul, and through his Passion, he attained to immortality

100. Aquinas, *Summa theologiae* III, q. 49, a. 1.

101. Aquinas, *Summa theologiae* III, q. 49, a. 1.

102. Aquinas, *Summa theologiae* III, q. 49, a. 3, ad 1.

103. See Aquinas, *Summa theologiae* III, q. 49, a. 3, ad 2.

104. Aquinas, *Summa theologiae* III, q. 49, a. 3, ad 3.

and glory. We, as his members, receive the salvific effects of his Passion, but we are not yet made immortal. This is because we must be configured to his Passion in our passible bodies. Aquinas states that we, "who are His members, are freed by His Passion from all debt of punishment"—which might seem to entail that we no longer will suffer or die.[105] But, in fact, we still do suffer and die, because it is through being configured "to the sufferings and death of Christ" that "we are brought into immortal glory."[106] The members must follow the path taken by the Head. In this vein, Aquinas cites Romans 8:17, where Paul promises that we will be "fellow heirs with Christ, provided we suffer with him in order that we may also be glorified with him."

In addition to the cross, the Resurrection and Ascension are also central to the Mystical Body. Meditating upon the risen and ascended Christ's sitting at the right hand of the Father, Aquinas directs attention to Romans 8:11, where Paul states, "If the Spirit of him who raised Jesus from the dead dwells in you, he who raised Christ Jesus from the dead will give life to your mortal bodies also through his Spirit who dwells in you." Aquinas here finds a connection between the Mystical Body—our union with Christ through the Spirit—and the exaltation (Resurrection/ Ascension) of Christ. He avers, "Since Christ is our Head, then what was bestowed on Christ is bestowed on us through Him."[107]

Paul maintains in Ephesians 2:6 that God has "raised us up with him [i.e., Christ], and made us sit with him in the heavenly places in Christ Jesus." Discussing the Ascension, Aquinas comments that if our Head is "already raised up," then, in a sense, we are already raised up with him, as his Body.[108] We have a foretaste of his risen life insofar as we are even now "in Christ." In faith, we know that we will be raised and will ascend with Christ so as to

105. Aquinas, *Summa theologiae* III, q. 49, a. 3, ad 3.
106. Aquinas, *Summa theologiae* III, q. 49, a. 3, ad 3.
107. Aquinas, *Summa theologiae* III, q. 58, a. 4, ad 1.
108. Aquinas, *Summa theologiae* III, q. 58, a. 4, ad 1.

sit with him at the right hand of the Father—that is, "in the heavenly places." This will happen, says Aquinas, "for the very reason that Christ our Head sits there."[109] For Aquinas, sitting at the right hand of the Father means being taken up into the Father's power and glory.[110] Here we should recall Christ's promise to the church in Laodicea: "He who conquers, I will grant him to sit with me on my throne, as I myself conquered and sat down with my Father on his throne" (Rev 3:21). The members of Christ's Body will share in what the Head possesses.

Aquinas also treats the Mystical Body in his account of Christ the Judge. At the Final Judgment, Christ will judge all humankind. While the entire Trinity will judge the world, wisdom is appropriated to the Word, and so judiciary power is attributed to Christ in particular. Drawing upon Augustine, Aquinas remarks that "judiciary authority is attributed to the Father, inasmuch as He is the Principle of the Son, but the very rule of judgment is attributed to the Son who is the art and wisdom of the Father."[111] As man, Christ will judge the world, communicating the Trinity's judgment. Aquinas cites John 5:26–27, "For as the Father has life in himself, so he has granted the Son also to have life in himself, and has given him authority to execute judgment, because he is the Son of man."[112] Aquinas contests Chrysostom's suggestion that Christ is Judge only as the divine Son, not as man. In this regard, Aquinas appeals to Christ's Headship of the Mystical Body. He states, "Christ even in His human nature is Head of the entire Church. . . . Consequently, it belongs to Him, even according to His human nature, to exercise judiciary power."[113]

Christ judges in accordance with his priestly sacrifice and intercession. Citing Hebrews 4:15—"For we have not a high priest who is unable to sympathize with our weaknesses"—Aquinas

109. Aquinas, *Summa theologiae* III, q. 58, a. 4, ad 1.

110. Aquinas, *Summa theologiae* III, q. 58, a. 3.

111. Aquinas, *Summa theologiae* III, q. 59, a. 1, ad 2.

112. Aquinas, *Summa theologiae* III, q. 59, a. 2, *sed contra*.

113. Aquinas, *Summa theologiae* III, q. 59, a. 2.

highlights the point that Christ the Judge is not aloof from other humans but rather has shown intimate solidarity with them, preeminently through his suffering on the cross. As the supreme high priest, Christ "appeared once for all at the end of the age to put away sin by the sacrifice of himself" (Heb 9:26). In the context of Hebrews, Aquinas affirms that "judiciary power belongs to the man Christ on account of both His divine personality, and the dignity of His headship, and the fulness of His habitual grace."[114] Thus, although Aquinas does not say it explicitly here, Christ's Headship is that of the "high priest" who, on the cross, offered his life for our sins.

Let me add a word regarding the Eucharistic dimension of the Mystical Body. For Aquinas, at the heart of the sacramental order is Christ's Passion. It follows that the cross is the "final cause" of the "sacraments" of the Mosaic law.[115] With respect to the sacraments of the New Law of grace, Aquinas portrays the sacraments in terms of the distinction between a united instrument (Christ's humanity) and a separated instrument (the sacraments, moved by the united instrument). To understand the sacraments of the New Law, says Aquinas, we must recognize that "Christ delivered us from our sins principally through His Passion."[116] Sacraments unite us to the cross's reconciling and deifying power. Aquinas comments that "the sacraments of the Church derive their power specially from Christ's Passion, the virtue [i.e. power] of which is in a manner united to us by our receiving the sacraments."[117]

Among the sacraments, the Eucharist has preeminence as the one to which all the others are directed.[118] Taken together, however, the seven sacraments are an integrated organism. Aquinas compares their role in the spiritual life to our bodily needs: Baptism corresponds to generation and birth, Confirmation to

114. Aquinas, *Summa theologiae* III, q. 59, a. 3.

115. Aquinas, *Summa theologiae* III, q. 61, a. 3, ad 1.

116. Aquinas, *Summa theologiae* III, q. 62, a. 5.

117. Aquinas, *Summa theologiae* III, q. 62, a. 5.

118. See Aquinas, *Summa theologiae* III, q. 65, a. 3.

growing to maturity, the Eucharist to our daily nourishment, and so on.[119] In Baptism, Aquinas says, the grace of the Holy Spirit and the fullness of the virtues are infused into the baptized person's soul, inaugurating the fullness of supernatural life and making the person a member of Christ's Body. Aquinas here again cites John 1:16, combined with a text in which Augustine credits Baptism with incorporating people into Christ's Body. Reiterating that "the fulness of grace and virtues flows from Christ the Head to all His members," Aquinas explores what this means for Baptism.[120] He underscores Baptism's constitutive relation to the Mystical Body. As he states, "By Baptism man is born again unto the spiritual life. . . . Now life is only in those members that are united to the head, from which they derive sense and movement. And therefore it follows of necessity that by Baptism man is incorporated in Christ, as one of His members."[121] Aquinas describes this "sense and movement" as knowledge of the true faith ("sense") and the "instinct of grace" ("movement") making it possible to perform virtuous acts.[122] To be a member of Christ's Body is to have this supernatural life.

Baptism incorporates us into Christ's Body, and the Eucharist completes our fellowship or communion with Christ, since we receive Christ himself and are changed, as it were, into Christ.[123] Through Baptism we are "born anew in Christ in virtue of His Passion," and through the Eucharist we are "made perfect in union with Christ who suffered."[124] In these sacraments, the

119. See Aquinas, *Summa theologiae* III, q. 65, a. 1.

120. Aquinas, *Summa theologiae* III, q. 69, a. 4.

121. Aquinas, *Summa theologiae* III, q. 69, a. 5. See Colman O'Neill, OP, "St. Thomas on the Membership of the Church," *The Thomist* 27 (1963): 88–140.

122. Aquinas, *Summa theologiae* III, q. 69, a. 5. See Servais Pinckaers, OP, "La morale et l'Église Corps du Christ," *Revue Thomiste* 100, no. 2 (2000): 239–58.

123. See Aquinas, *Summa theologiae* III, q. 73, a. 3, ad 1 and 2.

124. Aquinas, *Summa theologiae* III, q. 73, a. 3, ad 3. See Bruce D. Marshall, "The Whole Mystery of Our Salvation: Saint Thomas Aquinas on the Eucharist as Sacrifice," in *Rediscovering Aquinas and the Sacraments: Studies in Sacramental Theology*, ed. Matthew Levering and Michael Dauphinais (Hillenbrand Books, 2009), 39–64. See also Avery Dulles, SJ, "The Eucharist as Sacrifice," in *Rediscovering the Eucharist: Ecumenical Conversations*, ed. Roch Kereszty, O.Cist.

cross is at the center of our incorporation into and union with Christ as members of his Mystical Body.

Let me conclude this discussion of Aquinas on Christ's Mystical Body by directing attention to Aquinas's discussion of the efficient causality of Christ's Passion—question 48 of the *tertia pars*. Aquinas reiterates that "grace was bestowed upon Christ, not only as an individual, but inasmuch as He is the Head of the Church, so that it might overflow into His members."[125] To this point, he adds a somewhat surprising claim. He says that the unity of the Mystical Body is so profound that "Christ's works are referred to Himself and to His members in the same way as the works of any other man in a state of grace are referred to himself."[126] When Christ died on the cross, his action belonged (in its merit) not only to Christ, but also to his members. He acts on our behalf in the fullest possible sense, in such a way that, because we are members of his Body, *we* can be said to merit *in his action*. Aquinas lays down a radical principle, one that is indebted to Augustine (and St. Paul): "The head and members are as one mystic person; and therefore Christ's satisfaction belongs to all the faithful as being His members."[127] The cross is at the center of the Mystical Body, because believers are "one mystic person" with Christ on the cross.

V. CONCLUSION

This chapter has argued that the image of the "Mystical Body" or "Body of Christ" is intelligible only in light of the cross. The Mystical Body is, in a real sense, a cruciform Body. The Body of

(Paulist, 2003), 175–87; and Dulles, "The Theology of Worship: Saint Thomas," in Levering and Dauphinais, *Rediscovering Aquinas and the Sacraments*, 1–13.

125. Aquinas, *Summa theologiae* III, q. 48, a. 1. For discussion, see Tück, *A Gift of Presence*, 114–15.

126. Aquinas, *Summa theologiae* III, q. 48, a. 1.

127. Aquinas, *Summa theologiae* III, q. 48, a. 2, ad 1. See Dulles, "The Church According to Thomas Aquinas," 154; and Jean-Pierre Torrell, OP, *Jésus le Christ chez saint Thomas d'Aquin* (Cerf, 2008), 809; cf. 807.

Christ is configured not simply to the risen Christ and his glory, but to the risen Christ who bears his scars and intercedes for us in the presence of the Father. Embodied self-sacrificial love is the mark of the Mystical Body. It is not an idealized or ahistorical Body, but rather it is the Body of Christ crucified and risen, whose members are presently being configured to Christ through self-sacrificial love. As Philippe de la Trinité remarks in a book published just before the Council, "[Christ's] heart keeps the stigmata of suffering after his victorious Resurrection because they are the living symbols of those bonds of merciful love, which, in the Mystical Body, bind Head to members in the unity of the Holy Spirit."[128]

By means of some representative commentators on Aquinas's ecclesiology, I have suggested in this chapter that, beginning in the late 1950s, the place of the cross in the theology of the Body of Christ came to be relatively neglected by comparison with earlier treatments. There are evident reasons why such neglect would occur. It is difficult to attend equally to all the many dimensions of the Mystical Body. The centrality of the grace of the Holy Spirit and charity are undeniable; and other issues, such as the Mystical Body's corporeity and Christ's Resurrection and Ascension, also needed to be addressed. The Mystical Body is a glorious fellowship of grace, a communion of persons sharing in all good things.

128. Philippe de la Trinité, OCD, *What Is Redemption? How Christ's Suffering Saves Us*, trans. Anthony Armstrong, OSB (Emmaus Road, 2021), 115. See also Rowan Williams, *Passions of the Soul* (Bloomsbury, 2024), reminding us about the divine mercy: "One of the most striking images of redemption in the whole of Christian Scripture is Paul's language in his letter to the Colossians about God striking through the list of what we owe him and nailing it up in public on the cross, as someone might nail up a cancelled bill in a public place: an extraordinary metaphor, that the crucified body of Jesus on the cross is the certification of our debts to God being cleared" (51). Williams goes on to emphasize that this does not mean that human beings, having been forgiven, no longer need worry about reparations in the order of justice toward those who have been oppressed: "Jesus himself, in his most vivid parable about debt (Mt. 18), depicts a slave whose immense debt to his royal master is written off and who then decides to exercise his own limited power in insisting, with threats and violence, on the payment of a small debt to himself: he has failed to grasp that his master has, paradoxically, paid him the debt of grace and respect and has not understood that, even with his limited power and security, he now has to show the same 'just' attention to someone even less powerful. The fact that he has been shown mercy is not a privilege that enables him to live without cost but a gift that enables him to create justice in his turn" (53).

Nevertheless, the place of the cross at the center of the Mystical Body needs emphasis. To insist upon the cross's importance, in accordance with the truth that "the head of the body, the Church" makes "peace by the blood of his cross" (Col 1:18, 20), does not take away from the other elements such as the Holy Spirit, grace, and charity. Instead, this approach simply highlights what the biblical scholar Michael Gorman calls "cruciformity." As Gorman says, "Cruciformity summons people to adopt a posture before God of radical self-offering (faith), to become a sort of Christ for others (love), to accept weakness as strength (power), and to yearn confidently for their own bodily resurrection and for the transformation of the entire creation (hope)."[129] It is this cross-centered stance that characterizes the Church as the Body of Christ. The Body, without emphasis on the cross, loses touch with what grounds it in all times and places. Catholic ecclesiology needs to accentuate the cross, and the image of the Body of Christ is the place to do this. In this way, the image of the Body of Christ offers a hermeneutical key to images such as Bride and Family. For the Church, led by Christ the Head, is on "a journey through humility to participation in the life of God that can be best understood in terms of the knowledge that is also love—knowing Christ crucified, and moving through his death and resurrection, Good Friday and Easter, towards knowing him in glory."[130]

129. Michael J. Gorman, *Cruciformity: Paul's Narrative Spiritual of the Cross* (Eerdmans, 2001), 400.

130. Brian E. Daley, SJ, *Christology in Early Christianity: Collected Essays* (Eerdmans, 2025), 200. Daley has the theologies of Origen and Augustine in view here.

4

People of God

I. INTRODUCTION

That the Church is the "People of God" is a theologically complex, but necessary and irreplaceable, truth. Discussing the ecclesiology of Vatican II's *Lumen Gentium*, Joseph Ratzinger has pointed out, "Purely empirically no people is the people of God. To set God up as an indicator of descent or as a sociological label could only ever be an intolerable presumption and indeed ultimately blasphemy. Israel is described by the term people of God to the extent that it is turned towards the Lord."[1] Ratzinger says something similar with respect to the Church. He states, "The people of the New Covenant takes its origin as a people from the Body and Blood of Christ; solely in terms of this center does it have the status of a people."[2] In this precise sense, the Church is

1. Joseph Ratzinger, "The Ecclesiology of the Second Vatican Council," in *Church, Ecumenism and Politics: New Essays in Ecclesiology*, trans. Robert Nowell (Crossroad, 1988), 3–28, at 18–19. Ratzinger is here indebted to the Old Testament scholar Norbert Lohfink. For further background, see Pablo Blanco Sarto, *Benedict XVI y el Concilio Vaticano II: De la historia a la hermenéutica* (EUNSA, 2022). Regarding Israel, Benoît-Dominique de La Soujeole, OP aptly comments, "Although the covenants by which God bound himself to men in history have a successive aspect, in the sense that the previous covenant was to announce and prepare the following one that replaces it—and in this case the covenant sealed by Christ is the new, definitive, perfect, and eternal covenant—it is commonly admitted today that the earlier covenants were not revoked. They coexist today for the benefit of those who, by no fault of their own, do not have access to the fullness of Christianity. This survival is a divine mercy. . . . This mercy on behalf of Israel is also a gift for the Church, which thus possesses a living testimony of its origins and of its future, its 'root' on which it is 'grafted' (Rom 11:16ff.)." De La Soujeole, *Introduction to the Mystery of the Church*, trans. Michael J. Miller (The Catholic University of America Press, 2014), 145.

2. Joseph Ratzinger, *Called to Communion: Understanding the Church Today*, trans. Adrian Walker (Ignatius, 1996), 29. Ratzinger goes on to observe, "By itself, however, the term 'people of God' signifies almost without exception the people of Israel and not the Church" (30). See also Henri de Lubac, SJ's remark in 1969: "Now, on various sides, some seem to want to retain from this doctrine [*Lumen Gentium*'s doctrine of the Church] only the idea, or, rather, the

wondrously God's People, led by Jesus Christ as King and High Priest. Thus, 1 Peter 2:9–10 states, "But you are a chosen race, a royal priesthood, a holy nation, God's own people. . . . Once you were no people but now you are God's people; once you had not received mercy but now you have received mercy." These verses hearken back to God's election of his people Israel, as described in Exodus 19 and many other places. In the New Testament, "the church is the messianic people of God, foreshadowed in God's covenant with David, promised by the prophets, realized in Jesus, the Christ."[3] Granted that this is so, what more does the image of the Church as the People of God add to Catholic ecclesiology?

In his *Models of the Church*, originally published in 1974, Avery Dulles associates the image of the People of God with certain emphases that typically have characterized Protestant ecclesiology. He observes that the image of the People of God "differs from that of the Body of Christ in that it allows for a greater distance between the Church and its divine head. . . . In stressing the continual mercy of God and the continual need of the Church for repentance, the People of God model picks up many favorite themes of Protestant theology."[4] As he goes on to

expression, of 'People of God', in order to transform the Church into a vast democracy. By a similar misinterpretation, the idea of episcopal collegiality is corrupted by some who want to extend it to every sphere and who confuse it with the collegiality of a parliamentary government." De Lubac, *The Church: Paradox and Mystery*, trans. James R. Dunne and Anne Englund Nash (Ignatius, 2021), 193.

3. Guy Mansini, OSB, *Ecclesiology* (The Catholic University of America Press, 2021), 91. For a rich Evangelical Protestant biblical theology of the people of God—ranging widely, including some points with which I disagree but many more that I find deeply insightful—see Benjamin L. Gladd, *From Adam and Israel to the Church: A Biblical Theology of the People of God* (IVP Academic, 2019). Gladd centers his reflections upon the triad priest, prophet, and king. Jesus himself, Gladd argues, is "the true people of God" (75). See also the instructive biblical theology of the people of God offered by Gerhard Lohfink, *Does God Need the Church? Toward a Theology of the People of God*, trans. Linda M. Maloney (Liturgical, 1999),

4. Avery Dulles, SJ, *Models of the Church*, exp. ed. (Doubleday, 1987), 53. For the view that "People of God" fits better with Protestant ecclesiology and "Mystical Body" fits better with Catholic ecclesiology, see Lesslie Newbigin, *The Household of God: Lectures on the Nature of the Church* (SCM, 1953). Karl Barth portrays the Church as both "body of Christ" and "people of God." He ensures that the latter is theocentric and Christocentric. He states in a representative passage, "What does the people of God see in world-occurrence around it? . . . This new thing—and this is what makes the community what it is as the people of God created in world his-

say, the themes of divine mercy and corporate repentance belong to Catholicism as well, and the image of the People of God has a central place in Vatican II's Dogmatic Constitution on the Church, *Lumen Gentium*.

Indeed, Dulles deems the image of the messianic People of God to be as valuable for Catholicism as it is for Protestantism. Among Catholics, as Dulles recognizes, no one did more than Yves Congar to promote the image of the Church as the People of God. In his 1965 essay "The Church: The People of God," Congar provides some background to the twentieth-century retrieval among Catholics and Protestants of this biblical image. With reference to his own book *The Mystery of the Church* (written in 1937 and published in 1941) as well as to studies by other theologians, he remarks, "Between 1937 and 1942 the idea of the People of God was firmly reestablished in Catholic theology. This rediscovery was the work of men who wished to go beyond the rather juridical concept of the foundation of the Church made once by Christ, and they sought in the whole Bible a development of God's Plan."[5] These scholars found that the New Testament conceived of the Church as the messianically reconfigured Israel and thus as the eschatological People of God.

In addition to Congar, these scholars included some of the more notable Catholic theologians of the first half of the

tory—has revealed and made itself known to it as the work of God for the world and His Word to it. . . . The new thing in Jesus Christ, in the power and truth of which He is the new person, consists quite simply in the fact that in Him—as the people of God in the world may know even though the world itself does not—we are concerned in the strictest sense with God, with His work and Word." Barth, *Church Dogmatics*, vol. 4, pt. 3.2: *The Doctrine of Reconciliation*, trans. G.W. Bromiley, ed. G.W. Bromiley and T.F. Torrance (T&T Clark, 1961), 708–9, 711. For discussion, see Kimlyn J. Bender, *Karl Barth's Christological Ecclesiology* (Cascade, 2013), chapter 8.

5. Yves Congar, OP, "The Church: The People of God," trans. Kathryn Sullivan, RSCJ, in *The Church and Mankind*, vol. 1 of *Concilium: Theology in the Age of Renewal* (Paulist, 1965), 11–37, at 14. See also Congar, *The Mystery of the Church*, trans. A. V. Littledale (Helicon, 1960). Although in the early 1970s Congar became in certain ways even more enthusiastic about "People of God"—see his *Un peuple messianique: Salut et libération* (Cerf, 1975) and his *Ministères et communion ecclésiale* (Cerf, 1971), 18–19, 34–35—in 1965 he warned that (in Gerd-Rainer Horn's words) "the eschatological and messianic potential of the church cannot be adequately expressed by the anthropocentric notion of the people of God." Horn, *The Spirit of Vatican II: Western European Progressive Catholicism in the Long Sixties* (Oxford University Press, 2015), 23.

twentieth century. For example, after publishing his study of the Church as the Bride of Christ, Anscar Vonier in 1937 published *The People of God*, emphasizing the presence of the divine life in God's People and thus the historical, communal character of salvation. The German Dominican Mannes Koster devoted significant attention to the image of the People of God, contrasting it with the Mystical Body, in his 1940 book *Ekklesiologie im Werden*. The prominent French theologian and biblical exegete Lucien Cerfaux, in his 1947 book *The Church in the Theology of St. Paul*, argued that the central Pauline image for understanding the Church was not the Mystical Body but rather the People of God, with the Church as the new Israel and the new People of God (with "new" here meaning "eschatological").[6] Congar observes that eminent Protestant biblical scholars and theologians such as H.F. Hamilton (1912), Gerhard von Rad (1929), Ernst Käsemann (1938), and Nils Dahl (1941) highlighted the image of the People of God.[7] Works from the late 1950s and early 1960s cited by Congar as representative of the growing Catholic appreciation for the image of the People of God include studies by Michael Schmaus, Frank Norris, and Ignaz Backes.[8]

Congar identifies numerous valuable elements in the image of the People of God. First, the Church's continuity with Israel is highlighted, thereby associating the Church with the constitutive aspects of Israel's life: election (for mission), covenant, dedication

6. See Anscar Vonier, OSB, *The People of God* (Burns, Oates & Washbourne, 1937); Mannes D. Koster, OP, *Ekklesiologie im Werden* (Bonifacius-Druckerei, 1940); and Lucien Cerfaux, *The Church in the Theology of St. Paul*, trans. Geoffrey Webb and Adrian Walker (Herder and Herder, 1959).

7. See H.F. Hamilton, *The People of God*, 2 vols. (Oxford University Press, 1912); Gerhard von Rad, *Das Gottesvolk im Deuteronomium* (Kohlhammer, 1929); Ernst Käsemann, *Die wandernde Gottesvolk: Eine Untersuchung zum Hebräerbrief* (Vandenhoeck & Ruprecht, 1938); and Nils Dahl, *Das Volk Gottes: Eine Untersuchung zum Kirchenbewusstsein des Urchristentums*, 2nd ed. (Wissenschaftliche Buchgesellschaft, 1963).

8. See Michael Schmaus, *Katholische Dogmatik*, vol. 3 (Max Hueber, 1958), 204–39; Frank B. Norris, *God's Own People: An Introductory Study of the Church* (Helicon Press, 1962); and Ignaz Backes, "Die Kirche ist das Volk Gottes im Neuen Bund," *Trierer theologische Zeitschrift* 69 (1960): 111–17.

to praise and service of God, and God's eschatological promises.[9] The Church as the eschatological People of God is dynamically ordered toward the consummation of the kingdom, which God will bring about. As such, the Church is "the sacrament of salvation," an efficacious sign of the world's ultimate transformation.[10] In addition, the image of the People of God allows for deeper reflection upon Israel according to the flesh (the Jewish people), "who continue to be the people chosen and loved by God," and who must be understood in light of God's will for salvation and God's eschatological purposes for Jews and Gentiles.[11] When the Church is understood as the People of God, furthermore, the fact that the Church consists of actual human beings journeying toward salvation becomes clearer. Congar observes that here we can account for "failures and sins, the struggle for a more perfect fidelity, the permanent need for reform and for the efforts this involves."[12] Moreover, in the Church understood as the People of God, believers' inequality of offices and equality of dignity can be easily squared; and God (or Christ) stands as the Head. The diversity of cultures and local churches can also be appreciated. The central point is that "in the midst of all the peoples of the world, God assembles a People that is his."[13]

9. See, however, the point made by Rudolf Schnackenburg in his *The Church in the New Testament*, trans. W. J. O'Hara (Seabury, 1965), 154–55: "The people of God of the new Covenant is no longer in any respect the same as in the old, even though fundamental ideas of gracious election to be God's possession, of Covenant and of God's community are preserved. . . . The originality of the eschatological covenant of grace and of the eschatological people of God is seen in the fact that it is no longer the old sign of the Covenant, circumcision, but faith in Jesus Christ and the 'circumcision of Christ' (Col 2:11), that is to say, baptism, which is decisive for admission into the people of God and membership of God's Church. Jews and gentiles have equal access if they take this new way of salvation opened up by God."

10. Congar, "The Church," 20.

11. Congar, 21.

12. Congar, 23–24.

13. Congar, 27. Congar adds, "The ecumenical interest of the idea of the People of God is obvious, especially in the dialogue with Protestants. Let us speak of this dialogue. This idea provides many points of agreement and encounter. What Protestants like about the category of the People of God is first, the idea of election and of call, everything depends on God's initiative. Then it is the historicity that it involves in the sense of incompletion and of movement toward eschatology. It suggests less sharply defined frontiers, because it is composed of a multitude assembled by God himself. On the one hand, Protestants are happy to find in the frank use of People of God, a way of avoiding institutionalism with its intemperate use of ideas of 'power'

There are also some weaknesses that Congar associates with the ecclesiological image of the People of God. One weakness is something that Congar considers to be a deficiency of Protestant ecclesiology more generally: "There is a tendency to reduce the Church of the Word Incarnate to the conditions of the People of God under the old Dispensation," insofar as the dimension of "not yet" overshadows the dimension of "already."[14] Congar insists that there is much that is new in the Church and that is not found in biblical Israel as God's People. Even now, Christian believers dwell with Christ in heaven, incorporated into his Body as sons and daughters in the Son and as true temples of the Spirit. This dimension can go missing from People-of-God ecclesiology, and it is more clearly present in Mystical-Body ecclesiology.

A second weakness noted by Congar consists in the fact that, now that Christ has poured out his Spirit, the Church is more than what may be recognized in a People-of-God ecclesiology, which emphasizes the sinfulness of the journeying people (just as Israel was continually sinning and repenting). Congar observes that the Church truly is indefectible and infallible. The Church is holy, even if its earthly members are sinful, since the Church possesses holy sacraments, doctrine, and offices.

A third weakness consists in the ambiguity of the term "people." The Church is not a "people" in the same way that biblical Israel was a people or in the same way that the nations are peoples. As the eschatological People of God led by Christ and formed by his Spirit, the Church's visibility and structure transcends that of any other "people." This aspect can be better appreciated in a Mystical-Body ecclesiology. Congar sums up, "Under the new Dispensation, that of the promises realized through the incarnation of the Son and the gift of the Spirit (the

and infallibility, and on the other hand, the romanticism of a biological concept of the Mystical Body whose favorite expression is that of 'continued incarnation'; just as if the Church were literally 'Jesus Christ extended and communicated'" (28).

14. Congar, 29.

'Promised One'), the People of God was given a status that can be expressed only in the categories and in the theology of the Body of Christ."[15] Thus, Congar emphasizes the complementarity of the descriptions of the Church as People of God and as Mystical Body. He cites a number of biblical scholars and theologians who articulate this complementarity, including Ratzinger in his 1954 book *Volk und Haus Gottes in Augustins Lehre von der Kirche*, where Ratzinger states, "The Church is the New Testament People of God, founded by Jesus Christ, hierarchically structured, ministering to the advance of God's kingdom and the salvation of men, and this is the Mystical Body of Christ."[16]

In this chapter, I will not argue for the complementarity of the images of the Mystical Body and the People of God, since I presume this complementarity. Instead, I will further explore the meaning of the Church as the People of God, in light of postconciliar ecclesiology. Benoît-Dominique de La Soujeole notes that "in our day the theology of the People of God in particular has been distorted and misunderstood in ways that are fraught with consequences."[17] The nature of this distortion or misunderstanding is hotly contested today, since opposite viewpoints claim to possess the true interpretation. Anthony Gilles argues, "The Council moved away from the static conception of the Church that had dominated Catholic thought for fifteen centuries. No

15. Congar, 35.

16. Joseph Ratzinger, *Volk und Haus Gottes in Augustins Lehre von der Kirche* (Karl Zink, 1954), 48. For discussion, see Emery de Gaál, "Augustine of Hippo: The Reciprocal Dependence of Faith and World," in *Joseph Ratzinger in Dialogue with Philosophical Traditions: From Plato to Vattimo*, ed. Alejandro Sada, Tracey Rowland, and Rudy Albino de Assunção (T&T Clark, 2024), 22–41, at 24–30; Tracey Rowland, "Joseph Ratzinger on Democracy within the Church," *Communio* 50, no. 4 (2023): 635–56, at 649–50. On the complementarity of the People of God and Mystical Body, see also Rudolph Schnackenburg and Jacques Dupont, OSB, "The Church as the People of God," trans. Herbert A. Musurillo, SJ, in *The Church and Mankind*, 117–29; Schnackenburg, *The Church in the New Testament*, 149–57, 165–76.

17. De La Soujeole, *Introduction to the Mystery of the Church*, 199. For de La Soujeole, "The People of God theme is a key theme in *explaining* many aspects of the Body of Christ theme. For example, whereas we say . . . that the Christian *is* a member of this Body, we specify with the People of God theology the *activity* to which these members are called (priest, prophet, king). Moreover, the Church as Body of Christ appears to us initially in its fundamental *being* (the great organism of grace), and the Church as People of God appears to us initially in its fundamental *activity* (the acts proper to this organism by which it grows)" (253).

longer was the Church to be thought of as an 'it,' but as an 'us.' The Church is a community. It is the 'people of God.'"[18] Similarly, Richard Gaillardetz in his *Ecclesiology for a Global Church* sums up the import of the image in terms of equality of power in the Church. In his view, the Church as the People of God involves "a renewed emphasis on the equality of all God's people" and enables "the shift away from a hierarchical conception of the church to the priority of baptism, discipleship, and mission."[19]

This emphasis on equality is present—though not in an anti-hierarchical way—in the final document of the Synod for Synodality, titled "For a Synodal Church: Communion, Participation, Mission" (October 2024). The document strongly privileges the image of the People of God as befitting a synodal Church, although the images of Body of Christ and Temple of the Spirit appear as well. The document also draws connections between the image of the People of God and communion ecclesiology or Eucharistic ecclesiology.[20] In addition, Baptism in the Trinitarian name receives a prominent place. The document

18. Anthony E. Gilles, *People of God: The History of Catholic Christianity* (Franciscan Media, 2000), 184.

19. Richard R. Gaillardetz, *Ecclesiology for a Global Church: A People Called and Sent*, rev. ed. (Orbis Books, 2023), 198. I do not emphasize discipleship enough in the present book; on this topic, see Luke Timothy Johnson, *Imitating Christ: The Disputed Character of Christian Discipleship* (Eerdmans, 2024); and my *Why I Am Roman Catholic* (IVP Academic, 2024). Johnson contrasts two models of discipleship: "In the traditional model of discipleship, salvation is both present and future and in both dimensions is thoroughly *extra nos*, brought about by God through the grace of Jesus Christ. Salvation in the present is being liberated from the power of sin and being empowered to live according to the will of God in imitation of Jesus. Being saved in this sense means also turning away from the snares of the devil in the secular world and joining other disciples in the body of Christ, the church. Together, such disciples seek to learn Jesus through their shared participation in the Holy Spirit, in a process of personal and communal transformation that is called sanctification. Salvation in the future means to be freed from the bondage of death through resurrection and a share in God's eternal life. This is all accomplished through the presence and power of God and, although demanding the cooperation of human effort, does not derive from any work done by believers themselves. . . . [By contrast] the second vision of discipleship minimizes personal salvation, whereas the salvation/liberation of entire populations under oppressive systems is emphasized" (Johnson, *Imitating Christ*, 146). Johnson adds all too accurately: "The appeal to Jesus in the newer version of discipleship, sadly, amounts to not much more than rhetoric" (146; cf. 182–83).

20. XVI Ordinary General Assembly of the Synod of Bishops, "For a Synodal Church: Communion, Participation, Mission," §§16–18, https://www.synod.va/content/dam/synod/news/2024-10-26_final-document/ENG---Documento-finale.pdf, accessed on January 22, 2025.

teaches, "The identity of the People of God flows from Baptism in the name of the Father and of the Son and of the Holy Spirit. This identity is lived out as a call to holiness and a sending out in mission, inviting all peoples to accept the gift of salvation. . . . The missionary synodal Church springs from Baptism, in which Christ clothes us with Himself."[21] This is a beautiful summation of the truth about the People of God.

In this chapter, I will not survey "For a Synodal Church" or reflect upon synodality as such.[22] Rather, I propose to do four things in this chapter, with the aim of highlighting the reception of Vatican II's teaching on the People of God by theologians sympathetic to the project of the journal *Concilium*—a reception that is now receiving a significant degree of approbation by the Magisterium.[23]

First, I will set the scene by briefly discussing some currently influential theologians on People-of-God ecclesiology (and synodality), including Rafael Luciani, Bradford Hinze, and Massimo Faggioli.[24] I examine their views in the context of the influential work of Yves Congar. Second, I will survey what *Lumen Gentium* includes in its chapter on the "People of God." Third, I will

21. "For a Synodal Church," §15.

22. For an effort to undertake this task, see Kristin M. Colberg and Jos Moons, SJ, *The Future of Synodality: How We Move Forward from Here* (Liturgical, 2025). Much depends upon which elements of "For a Synodal Church" are pursued and in what manner in the years to come. One key element will be the interpretation of the *sensus fidei*. As noted by "For a Synodal Church," *Lumen Gentium* teaches that "the holy People of God cannot err in matters of belief. They manifest this special property when they show universal agreement in matters of faith and morals" ("For a Synodal Church," §22). The document "For a Synodal Church" goes on to say, "The *sensus fidei* aims at reaching a consensus of the faithful (*consensus fidelium*), which constitutes 'a sure criterion for determining whether a particular doctrine or practice belongs to the apostolic faith' (International Theological Commission, *Sensus fidei in the life of the Church*, 2014, 3)" ("For a Synodal Church," §22). I note that equal attention needs to be paid to the other criteria for determining the status of Church teachings about faith and morals.

23. For discussion of the reception of Vatican II led by Pope John Paul II and Pope Benedict XVI, see Matthew L. Lamb and Matthew Levering, eds., *Vatican II: Renewal within Tradition* (Oxford University Press, 2008); Matthew L. Lamb and Matthew Levering, eds., *The Reception of Vatican II* (Oxford University Press, 2017); and Matthew Levering, *An Introduction to Vatican II as an Ongoing Theological Event* (The Catholic University of America Press, 2017).

24. For further background, see the essays in *Autorität und Synodalität": Eine interdisziplinäre und interkonfessionelle Umschau nach ökumenischen Chancen und ekklesiologischen Desideraten*, ed. Christoph Böttigheimer and Johannes Hofmann (Lembeck, 2008).

examine some representative usages of the image of the People of God in *Concilium*-oriented Catholic ecclesiology from the late 1960s and early 1970s.[25] This ecclesiology has reemerged today as the manifestation of a supposedly "new ecclesial hermeneutics of . . . reciprocity among all ecclesial subjects" in service to the Church's progress "in the hermeneutics and the reception of the Church as people of God."[26] The theologian (now Cardinal) Timothy Radcliffe wrote in preparation for the October 2023 Synod on Synodality that "we must let the Holy Spirit work creatively in our midst with new ways of being Church that now we cannot imagine but perhaps the young can!"[27]—but in fact

25. Gerd-Rainer Horn describes the immediate postconciliar period as follows: "Soon a classic mechanism which frequently operates within social movements began to click in: a radicalization process, a virtuous circle of ever-larger expectations and ever-more-daring demands. Progressive priests often began their mobilization cycle over the issue of celibacy. Yet, in the process of addressing this topic, they rapidly began to draw ever-larger circles and more far-reaching conclusions, soon agitating for democratization of the church, eventually advocating the declericalization of the priesthood. . . . As the cycle of activism propelled by Christian inspirations got under way, Vatican II soon was used as a metaphor for any number of possible blueprints for radical actions" (Horn, *The Spirit of Vatican II*, 253). For a better postconciliar approach, see Ratzinger's *Das neue Volk Gottes: Entwürfe zur Ekklesiologie* (Patmos, 1969), building constructively upon his dissertation *Volk und Haus Gottes in Augustins Lehre von der Kirche.* For Horn, Ratzinger—along with Daniélou, de Lubac, Balthasar, and Pope Paul VI—represents the reaction on the part of some previously reform-minded Catholic theologians to the cycle of radicalization. Horn bemoans this reaction. After complaining about the dominance in the Church since the mid-1970s of "conservative and traditionalist forces," Horn, writing in 2015, states: "By no means insignificant numbers of individuals, loose associations, and organized groups continue to profess—and to live in accordance with—Left Catholic convictions. . . . In fact, there are grounds for optimism. The recent surprise election of Pope Francis has created a new dynamic which is, if anything, on balance rather favourable to many of the designs of today's Catholic Left" (Horn, *The Spirit of Vatican II*, 259). See also Mariusz Biliniewicz, *"Amoris Laetitia" and the Spirit of Vatican II: The Source of Controversy* (Routledge, 2018).

26. Rafael Luciani, *Synodality: A New Way of Proceeding in the Church*, trans. Joseph Owens, SJ (Paulist, 2022), 144–45. Luciani is aware that this "new way" dates to the immediate postconciliar period. He blames the "clericalized institutional model," characteristic of the postconciliar pontificates until the arrival of Pope Francis, for the current worldwide crisis of faith (9). Luciani cites Ronaldo Muñoz, *Nueva conciencia de la Iglesia en América Latina* (Sígueme, 1974), arguing that the Church must become "a community of free and open persons who cooperate responsibly. The Church should be a community in which all unite in solidarity and participate actively in an attitude of ongoing searching and self-criticism. At all levels there should be *structures of participation* for lay people, religious, and priests and the possibility of choosing the representatives and leaders" (362–63, quoted in Luciani, *Synodality*, 13).

27. Timothy Radcliffe, OP, *Listening Together: Meditations on Synodality* (Liturgical, 2024), 85. Radcliffe comments rather uncharitably—despite the charitable tone of his work overall—that "we have a profound instinct to hang on to control, which is why the synod is feared by many" (82). The fear was actually rooted, it seems to me, in sincere love for the Catholic Church and concern that the synod, being fallible, might steer the Church wrongly. See also Radcliffe's *What Is the Point of Being a Christian?* (Burns & Oates, 2005), arguing in chapters 9

the "new ways" that are being promoted go back to the period 1965–1975, when Radcliffe himself was young. I focus in this third section on such figures as Richard McBrien, Léon-Joseph Cardinal Suenens, and Gregory Baum. These figures interpreted the Church as the People of God largely in terms of power and participation, and they envisioned significant changes in the life of the Church. In different ways and to different degrees, these figures held that the renewal of the Church requires not only doctrinal changes (especially regarding sexual morality and the role of women in the Church), but also—to ensure that the changes are made—the participation of all members of the Church in decision-making. Their reception of the council's teaching on the People of God emphasized what the International Theological Commission's 2018 document "Synodality in the Life and Mission of the Church" calls "the brotherhood of communion and the co-responsibility and participation of the whole People of God in its life and mission."[28]

and 10 that Catholics should reject the division between liberals and conservatives or between *Concilium* and *Communio*. He argues that both sides can be right, since they emphasize different things. He denies that the two sides manifest "a conflict between those who are faithful to the tradition and those who wish to surrender to the modern world" (168). In his view, the polarization in the Church can be overcome "if we have the imagination to understand the other's sense of exile and work to build a community in which they may feel that they too belong" (171). He calls for embracing change and supporting a "dynamic" tension, "as the Church is becoming, for the first time, truly global" (177). Unfortunately, he implies that those who would disagree with him are too narrow to allow for such fruitful tension: "We are bound together as this particular community by communion with the See of Rome. But we are also Catholic, which means that we reach out to universality, eager to be open to the unimaginable diversity of human cultures and wisdom. This means that we are always impatient with any identity which seems closed and finished and defined"—a "walled Fortress Church" in which believers have "to toe the party line, to stick to precise formulations of dogmatic positions in the face of the enemy" (177, 181). He instances *Humanae Vitae* and the ordination of women as two areas where he hopes for rethinking (of the Church's two-thousand-year tradition). Johanna Rahner appreciatively cites Radcliffe's 2005 book in "Glaubenskrise?—Gotteskrise?—Kirchenkrise? Versuch einer aktuellen Standortbestimmung," in *Begegnungen—Entgegnungen: Beiträge zur modernen Gottesfrage, kontextuellen Theologie und Ökumene; Festgabe für Ulrike Link-Wieczorek zum 60. Geburtstag*, ed. Johanna Rahner and Andrea Strübind (Evangelische Verlagsanstalt, 2015), 93–109. She suggests that no faith that promises absolute certainty can be credible in the modern, historically conscious world; faith must take a stance of questing and searching, not a stance of closed dogmatic certitude.

28. "For a Synodal Church," §30, quoting the International Theological Commission, "Synodality in the Life and Mission of the Church," March 2, 2018, §70, https://www.vatican.va/roman_curia/congregations/cfaith/cti_documents/rc_cti_20180302_sinodalita_en.html, accessed January 22, 2025. Both documents carefully add (to the end of the sentence I have

In my view, the approaches advocated by the theologians whom I discuss in this chapter contain both opportunities (as the International Theological Commission and the Synod on Synodality, joined by Pope Francis, have argued) and potential pitfalls regarding both doctrine and ecclesial life. Fourth and finally, therefore, I explore the work of the Anglican theologian Ephraim Radner, whose work provides antidotes to such pitfalls. Among contemporary English-speaking theologians, Radner stands out for combining an insistence on the centrality of the image of the People of God with a keen sensitivity to the sinfulness of the People of God and to the Church's relation to the people of Israel.[29] Radner's work provides a buffer against notions of the People of God that are not sufficiently grounded in divine revelation but that instead reflect the tradition of religious liberalism.[30] Through his realistic and Christ-centered portraits of the Church in various

quoted) the following words: "distinguishing between various ministries and roles." See also Keith Lemna, "The Synod on Synodality in Light of Pope Francis's Theology of Mission," *Nova et Vetera* 21, no. 2 (2023): 509-39.

29. For further background, see George A. Lindbeck, *The Church in a Postliberal Age*, ed. James J. Buckley (Eerdmans, 2003), 274n15. A key point made by Lindbeck is that a lot of the modern uses of "people of God" are connotative, pointing to a particular *way* of being Church, whereas in Scripture, the usage is more denotative: *this particular people*. Radner follows Lindbeck on this point. For my disagreements with Radner on the Church's unity and holiness, see the final two chapters of my *Engaging the Doctrine of the Holy Spirit: Love and Gift in the Trinity and the Church* (Baker Academic, 2016). In his commentary on Leviticus, however, he remarks along lines with which I strongly concur: "What God has given—himself in the fire of the Holy Spirit—dwells within his people, as a formative love that offers itself in return." Ephraim Radner, *Leviticus* (Brazos, 2008), 86.

30. For historical background to Protestant and Catholic religious liberalism, see my Introduction to *Catholic Modernism: Tyrrell, Loisy, and the Ongoing Challenge to Dogmatic Christianity*, ed. Matthew Levering and Jeffrey L. Morrow (Emmaus Academic, forthcoming). For the view that critique of post-Vatican II versions of Catholic religious liberalism undermines the Church's ability to engage with the world, thereby turning Catholicism into a fundamentalist relic (as, in his view, the post-Tridentine Church largely was), see Neil Ormerod, *Re-Visioning the Church: An Experiment in Systematic Historical Ecclesiology* (Fortress, 2014). Writing during the pontificate of Pope Benedict XVI, Ormerod states, "The present danger the Church faces is that it was in an oppositional stance for so long that some people presume that such a stance is both normal and normative, and are seeking to return the Church to its earlier sectarian position" (354). Ormerod fears that the Church (under Pope Benedict, continuing the post-Tridentine model that Pope John XXIII sought to dislodge) "has lost its sense of world-transforming mission" and has been outpaced by the world, while retreating to a static vision of "the purity of the tradition" and to a "rigidity of social organization" that limit "mission" to the Church's "own religious, moral, cultural, and social reproduction and . . . expansion" (351).

writings, he demonstrates the abiding significance of the image of the People of God.[31]

II. SYNODALITY AND THE PEOPLE OF GOD

In his 2022 *Synodality: A New Way of Proceeding in the Church*, Rafael Luciani laments John Paul II's Extraordinary Synod of 1985, which codified the proper mode of the reception of the Second Vatican Council. According to Luciani, the main problem with the 1985 synod was a failure to challenge hierarchy by means of further steps of power-sharing, as the key to Christian discipleship and mission.[32] Luciani argues that decentralization and democratization would have prevented the homogenization of doctrine that one finds in the *Catechism of the Catholic Church*.[33] In 1970, Karl Rahner laid down the key principle: "It is . . . no

31. In this chapter, I do not discuss Radner's critique of Anglican/Episcopalian versions of religious liberalism, since his major theological works (as distinct from his popular-level writings) generally leave the critique implicit.

32. Mission here is understood primarily in terms of addressing unjust economic and political structures, supporting ecological initiatives, and so on. See also the essays in *For a Missionary Reform of the Church: The Civiltà Cattolica Seminar*, ed. Antonio Spadaro, SJ, and Carlos María Galli, trans. Demetrio S. Yocum (Paulist, 2017). Massimo Faggioli deems that centralized Church government has its place, so long as the right pope is in charge: "The pontificate of Francis has revealed the paradox that the decentralization of the global governance of the Catholic Church needs heavy Vatican inputs." Faggioli, *The Liminal Papacy of Pope Francis: Moving toward Global Catholicity* (Orbis Books, 2020), 145. For a critique in principle of such heavy inputs, see Yves Congar, OP, *Diversity and Communion*, trans. John Bowden (Twenty-Third Publications, 1985), 29: "This principle of variety in unity, affirmed so many times by the popes and still to be found today, has been misunderstood by popes themselves. In my view, the beginnings of the assertion by the Bishop of Rome of his authority to regulate the life of the churches are to be found with Damasus (366–384), Siricius (384–399) and Innocent I (401–417). These popes began to identify unity of discipline with unity of faith and then to interpret unity in terms of uniformity."

33. For theological protests against the *Catechism* before it was completed, see the essays in *The Universal Catechism Reader: Reflections and Responses*, ed. Thomas Reese, SJ (HarperCollins, 1990); and see also Claude Geffré, OP's claim: "The importance given to practice as a *locus theologicus*, then, involves a real change in the way in which theological work should be understood. As a theology of praxis, theology cannot simply be satisfied with a different interpretation of the Christian message. It creates new possibilities of existence. As soon as we begin to take seriously the practice that is peculiar to each church insofar as it is conditioned by an original culture and by specific historical movements, we have to abandon the illusory ideal of a universal theology that is valid for the whole of the Church. From then onward, we begin to live in a situation of insurmountable theological pluralism." Geffré, *The Risk of Interpretation: On Being Faithful to the Christian Tradition in a Non-Christian Age*, trans. David Smith (Paulist, 1987), 268.

longer possible to conceive of any such single formula [i.e., a particular creed] finding universal acceptance. . . . There will no longer be any one single and universal basic formula of the Christian faith applicable to the whole Church and, indeed, prescribed for her as authoritatively binding."[34] Rahner repeats this point frequently in the early 1970s, arguing that all official decisions regarding doctrinal and pastoral conflicts must be regarded as provisional unless Church officials are responding to an explicit rejection of indisputable dogma. Even then, Rahner suggests, the new reality of radical theological and contextual pluralism entails that it is no longer possible for the Vatican to interpret with any confidence what a given theologian—who may appear to be contradicting an indisputable dogma—really means. Furthermore, he says, valid interpretations of core dogmas may be irreducibly plural and even seemingly contradictory.[35] Rahner affirms that

34. Karl Rahner, SJ, "Reflections on the Problems Involved in Devising a Short Formula of the Faith," in *Theological Investigations*, vol. 11, *Confrontations 1*, trans. David Bourke (Seabury, 1974), 230–44, at 233. Rahner goes on to say, "To show how impossible it is to produce any such new, single and universal basic formula of the faith we may begin by pointing to the fact that certain attempts which have been made to compose and officially introduce a world catechism to be enforced throughout the world have failed and have met with unanimous resistance on the part of preachers and exponents of catechetical theory. . . . Against all such attempts it is justifiable to point out again and again that the differences between the individual peoples, cultures, and social milieux, and also those which arise from the different mentalities of the hearers, all have a bearing on the concrete situation in which the faith has to be preached. And nowadays these differences are too great for us to be able to address these hearers in all parts of the world through the medium of one and the same monotonous and uniform catechism" (233). See also Nicholas Lash, "Theologies at the Service of a Common Tradition," in *Different Theologies, Common Responsibility: Babel or Pentecost?*, ed. Claude Geffré, Gustavo Gutiérrez, and Virgil Elizondo, English edition ed. Marcus Lefébure, *Concilium* 171 (T&T Clark, 1984), 74–83, at 80: "In these circumstances, the unity of the Creed, no longer maintained by subscription to a single formula, will be maintained by continual quest for *mutual recognition*. The stories that differently express different experiences will not be verbally identical. But, if each creed, each 'abbreviated statement' of faith, containing what are taken to be the essential elements of the Christian narrative, is to be a *Christian* creed, a 'catholic' and 'orthodox' creed . . . then it must be offered as, and be capable of being accepted by others as, a different version of the same story, not a different story. The temptation is to suppose that such mutual recognition can only occur if there is, somewhere, some neutral 'standard of measurement' by which the adequacy of particular creeds could be assessed. But, on non-classicist assumptions, there is not, nor could there be, any such standard."

35. See Karl Rahner, SJ, "Toleration in the Church," trans. Cecily Bennett, in *Meditations on Freedom and the Spirit* (Seabury, 1978), 91, 101; Rahner, "The Changing Church," trans. W.J. O'Hara, in *The Christian of the Future* (Herder and Herder, 1967), 9–38, at 33–34. Rahner thus undermines any practical consequences of his claim that "there is something we must be quite clear and firm about: it is part of the self-understanding of the Catholic Church that the

the Church teaches enduringly true dogmas about Christ and the Trinity, but he suggests that, in other domains, it is difficult to know where the line is between the unchangeable dogmatic truth and the fallible historical expression, and it is impossible to discern with certitude whether particular doctrines taught by the ordinary Magisterium are infallible or provisional.[36]

Luciani considers the Extraordinary Synod of 1985 to represent John Paul II's (and Joseph Ratzinger's, since Ratzinger was heavily involved) betrayal of the Second Vatican Council's teachings on the People of God, reasserting the universalizing model of papal dominance. He states, "The Extraordinary Synod of 1985—the Twentieth Anniversary of the Conclusion of the Second Vatican Council—represented an inflection point that discounted the ecclesiology of the people of God and assumed the model of *hierarchical communion* as central to the interpretation and implementation of the conciliar event."[37] For Luciani as for

substance of the faith is binding in character and constitutive both of the Church itself and of individual membership of it; that it follows from the nature of the Church and the mission of Christ that its proclamation of this message is authoritative; and that when it is offered to the individual, for his free assent, it is objectively, morally binding" ("Toleration in the Church," 98).

36. See Karl Rahner, SJ, "Does the Church Offer Any Ultimate Certainties?" (originally published in 1970), in *Theological Investigations*, vol. 14, *Ecclesiology, Questions in the Church, the Church in the World*, trans. David Bourke (Seabury, 1976), 47–65. Rahner sums up, "Dogma, even in its most ultimate and binding form, is open to the future. That which is truly signified in a given dogmatic proposition is open to a further course of development in terms of truth in the Church's awareness of her faith, even after it has been defined. And this course of development extends outwards into a future which it is quite impossible to calculate. In the light of this let us consider, then, a situation in which one man holds that, with the reservations and due distinctions mentioned above, a dogmatic proposition is certainly true and incapable of retrospective revision, and another who regards such a proposition as possibly erroneous while still acknowledging that the Church herself abides in the truth. It would almost be possible to say that judgment in the light of our foregoing observations the disagreement between these two amounts to little more than an argument over words, because neither side can define precisely enough whether the boundary is to be drawn in such propositions between one that is erroneous and one which all Catholic theologians would concede to be inadequate and capable of subsequent reform" (64).

37. Luciani, 108. Luciani is well versed in Pope Francis's theological background and vision; see his *Pope Francis and the Theology of the People* (Orbis Books, 2017). For the 1985 synod's documents, see *The Extraordinary Synod—1985: Message to the People of God* (St. Paul Editions, 1986). For a defense of the 1985 Synod's interpretation of Vatican II, see my *An Introduction to Vatican II as an Ongoing Theological Event*. For critiques of the 1985 synod from theologians who (in the main) share Luciani's viewpoint, see *Concilium* 188, which appeared as *Synod 1985—An Evaluation*, ed. Giuseppe Alberigo and James Provost (SCM, 1986). In his essay in this volume, "New Balances in the Church since the Synod," trans. Paul Burns, 138–46,

the influential Italian theologian Dario Vitali, the Second Vatican Council's teachings on collegiality were never truly received prior to Pope Francis's pontificate.[38]

For his part, the ecclesiologist Bradford Hinze argues that priestly ministry will need to be transformed in light of the true significance of the image of the People of God. Appealing to Pope Francis's vision, he states, "Synodality demands courageous, honest speech and priestly power-sharing with the faithful people of God in their shared efforts to advance sacramental communion and missiological discipleship."[39] As Karl Rahner warned immediately after the council—an event that he judged to be the most significant council thus far in the Church's history, although the council in his view did nothing more than make a beginning toward the radically renewed, global Church of the future—"it would be very difficult at this point to predict precisely how or

Alberigo concludes with the hope that "the Gospel—and therefore the Incarnation, the Cross, the Resurrection, the Trinity, *koinonia*, the poor and hope of the Kingdom—will be able fully to recover its role as nucleus and unifying norm of the nature of the Church and its life, while the experiences and structures of the People of God on their way will take on characteristics of variability and instrumentality. To take up an old distinction, the *status ecclesiae*, that is, Christ and faith in him, will form the common and permanent element of the Church, while the *statute ecclesiae*, that is all that concerns the life of the community, will be the place for pluriformity" (144). See also Peter Hebblethwaite's *Synod Extraordinary: The Inside Story of the Rome Synod, November/December 1985* (Doubleday, 1986); and Stan Chu Ilo, "Depolarizing Catholic Ecclesiology: Mediation between the Theologies of *Communio* and *Concilium* in Uzukwu," in *Under the Palaver Tree: Doing African Ecclesiology in the Spirit of Vatican II—the Contributions of Elochukwu E. Uzukwu*, ed. Stan Chu Ilo and Caroline N. Mbonu (Pickwick, 2023), 120–46, at 132–33, along lines that hardly seem "depolarizing": "Proponents of *communio* ecclesiology developed an image of the Church as an ahistorical subject of holiness. . . . *Communio* ecclesiology initiated this endless culture war between the defenders of those traditions and structural appurtenances for maintaining this kind of ecclesiology, and those who wanted a more diffuse interpretation that employs other images and symbols of the Church employed by *Lumen Gentium*. What emerges subsequently in the Church, particularly after the 1985 Synod, is clericalism, absolutization of the Church's teachings, undue hierarchism, centrism, and deliberate appointment of bishops amenable to a restorationist agenda through the enforcement of this visibilism and universalism in local churches." Ilo argues that what is emerging under Pope Francis is "a new recovery of the reforming and renewing agenda of Vatican II" (132), forgotten since the 1970s. On this basis he calls for opening the Eucharistic table to non-Catholics.

38. See Dario Vitali, *Verso la sinodalità* (Qiqajon, 2014).

39. Bradford E. Hinze, "Transforming Priestly Identity and Ministry," in *Priestly Ministry and the People of God: Hopes and Horizons*, ed. Richard R. Gaillardetz, Thomas H. Groome, and Richard Lennan (Orbis Books, 2022), 101–8, at 102. The reference to "courageous, honest speech" means continuance of the "dissent"—now receiving significant ecclesiastical approval—that predominated in academic circles under Popes John Paul II and Benedict XVI.

whether the recent proclamation of the collegial-synodal principle of the Church will take concrete form and be put into actual operation."[40] For Rahner in the late 1960s and early 1970s, implementing synodality and a series of changes in the Church's teaching and practice was a priority, beginning with the program for the German Würzburg Synod, at which he took a leading part.[41] He advocated for the election of bishops and for giving "all members of a synod," including laity, "an active voice in the taking of decisions," so that bishops would no longer exercise a monopoly on doctrinal and pastoral decision-making, but instead a permanent elected synod (comprised of bishops, priests, and laity) would govern the Church in Germany, with binding authority.[42] Against the fear that "'democratization' in the Church" would threaten "the purity of faith, the truth of the gospel, and the abiding nature of the Church," Rahner responds that episcopal office is not strictly needed for such decision-making or for the integrity of the Catholic faith because "God's grace can . . . just as well preserve the people of God in the truth of the gospel as popes and bishops."[43]

Rahner's perspective on doctrinal decision-making was contested by Joseph Ratzinger and others, and the Würzburg Synod eventually disbanded without achieving its aims. Of course, understanding "People of God" in terms of increased lay power in the Church can lay claim to uncontroversial roots: lay people, as Yves Congar emphasizes, should not be and, over the course of history, have not been powerless in the Church. In *Lay People in the Church*, whose original edition appeared in 1951, Congar

40. Karl Rahner, SJ, *The Church after the Council*, trans. Davis C. Herron and Rodelinde Albrecht (Herder and Herder, 1966), 11.

41. For background, see Stefan Voges, *Konzil, Dialog und Demokratie: Der Weg zur Würzburger Synode, 1965-1971* (Ferdinand Schöningh, 2015); and Manfred Plate, *Das deutsche Konzil: Die Würzburger Synode; Bericht und Deutung* (Herder, 1975). See also the essays in *Wege der Kirche in die Zukunft der Menschen: 50 Jahre nach Beginn der Würzburger Synode*, ed. Herbert Haslinger (Herder, 2021).

42. Karl Rahner, SJ, "On the Theology of a 'Pastoral Synod'," in *Theological Investigations*, vol. 14, 116–31, at 130–31.

43. Rahner, "On the Theology of a 'Pastoral Synod'," 129.

explores "lay people's part in Christ's kingship, in its aspect of power properly so called, of governing authority [within the Church]."[44] He shows that Church history, beginning with the early Fathers, exhibits the presence of real lay power within the Church. There has been lay participation in the election or appointment of bishops; lay participation in councils and synods (beginning with the Council of Jerusalem, as shown by Acts 15:4 and Acts 15:22); the participation of emperors and rulers, generally representing the unity of "Christendom"; the framing of initiatives and reforms "from below"; and participation in some judicial functions—for example, as advocates in ecclesiastical trials.[45] Congar distinguishes all these instances from the congregationalist or feudal claim of a lay person or the lay community to have "proprietorship of the parish church."[46]

Congar argues that the key is to distinguish between the

44. Yves Congar, OP, *Lay People in the Church: A Study for a Theology of the Laity*, trans. Donald Attwater (Geoffrey Chapman, 1965), 243.

45. Congar comments, "Laity do not form part of councils habitually and by right, but as St Cyprian and others show, they can do so when they are able to supply useful information or when the matters to be discussed concern them: e.g., restoration to the Church's communion, mixed questions, marriage, abuses to be reformed" (250). He adds that at the center of his book is "the necessity of a twofold consent in the Church: the radically necessary consent of life to incorporate itself in the structure, lacking which we run in vain and life is not the life *of the Church*; and the consent of the structure to welcome life's needs and developments, lacking which the bases remain firm but there is no movement at all, and the Church, while faithful to her fundamental constitution, fails to fulfil her mission" (258).

46. Congar, 259. He strongly rejects the view that "it would be a good thing were the whole temporal administration of the Church in the hands of the laity," and he insists: "There can be no mistake about it: the Church's constitution is fundamentally hierarchical, not democratic. The Church is first of all, in the strong sense, an institution: a man is incorporated with her by baptism, and thus acquires certain rights. She is not in the first place a society formed by the faithful joining together, and as such the subject of rights laid down for itself. Therefore, in the various juridical forms through which she shapes her life, the Church has always been careful jealously to safeguard the fundamental right of the hierarchical principle" (260–61). See, by comparison, Edward Schillebeeckx, OP, *Church: The Human Story of God*, trans. John Bowden (Crossroad, 1990), chapter 4: "Towards Democratic Rule of the Church as a Community of God." For Schillebeeckx, "Vatican II was a catching up manoeuvre of the church which came too late (in relation to what was happening in the world). By that time the developed and critical consciousness of the world and general human consciousness had already moved on much further than the late feudal dreams that the church still cherished" (206). Schillebeeckx affirms "co-responsibility" and calls for "the participation of all believers in decisions relating to church government" (209). He contends, "The rejection by the official church of the possibility of a democratically governed community of faith in fact has nothing to do with subjection to the Word of God, which is under no one's sovereign control (i.e., neither that of the community of faith or the hierarchy)" (219).

Church's "structure" and "life."[47] He suggests that within the domain of the Church's "life," lay people should have power, in appropriate ways; but within the domain of the Church's "structure," lay people should not control things. This is because the Church's "structure" pertains to what has been given by Jesus Christ, described by Congar as "the deposit of faith, the deposit of the sacraments of faith, and the apostolical powers whereby the one and the other are transmitted."[48]

Whereas Congar tends to assume that changes today in the Church's "life" will not affect that which belongs to the Church's "structure," I am less optimistic. The wall between "life" and "structure" turns out to be rather porous. The legitimate lay power that Congar seeks to retrieve is not limitable in the specific way that he supposes in *Lay People in the Church*. Once the "People of God" becomes an image of lay people taking back power in the Church, then ecclesiology tends to come to revolve around power rather than around the gifts, wisdom, and will of Christ as witnessed to in Scripture and Tradition. This is an inverse, but equally baneful, hierarchology.

47. For background, see the (rather unfortunate) distinctions between "life" and "speculation" and between "life" and "hierarchy," in Johann Adam Möhler, *Unity in the Church, or, The Principle of Catholicism: Presented in the Spirit of the Church Fathers of the First Three Centuries*, trans. Peter C. Erb (The Catholic University of America Press, 1996), 185, 266, and elsewhere. See also Congar, *Diversity and Communion*, 13–14.

48. Congar, *Lay People in the Church*, 262. See also Hans Küng, *Structures of the Church*, trans. Salvator Attanasio (Thomas Nelson & Sons, 1964), especially chapter 5 on "Church, Council, and Laity." Küng repeats much of what Congar outlined, including his account of Acts 15 and the Council of Jerusalem. In support of his position, he cites Congar's book and Piet Fransen, SJ's "Das Konzil und die Laien," *Orientierung* 25 (1961): 1–5, along with (including some perspectives that differ from his own) such works as Schmaus, *Katholische Dogmatik*, 3:732; Hans Urs von Balthasar, "The Layman and the Church," trans. Brian McNeil, CRV, in *Explorations in Theology*, vol. 2, *Spouse of the Word* (Ignatius, 1991), 315–31; Gérard Philips, *The Role of the Laity in the Church*, trans John R. Gilbert and James W. Moudry (Fides Publishers, 1955); Karl Rahner, SJ, "The Consecration of the Layman to the Care of Souls," in *Theological Investigations*, vol. 3, *The Theology of the Spiritual Life*, trans. Karl-H. Kruger and Boniface Kruger (Helicon, 1967), 263–76; and Rahner, "Notes on the Lay Apostolate," in *Theological Investigations*, vol. 2, *Man in the Church*, trans. Karl-H. Kruger (Helicon, 1963), 319–52. In "Notes on the Lay Apostolate," Rahner states (cautiously but already envisioning serious changes), "Once relations between priests, bishops, and laymen within the hierarchical apostolate are governed by the right outlook and attitude, and once this attitude takes ever deeper roots, it will perhaps be possible gradually to give a more precise *legal* formulation to everything involved in this" (351).

In his *Liminal Papacy of Pope Francis*, Massimo Faggioli argues that Pope Francis has found a middle ground between the hierarchical-sacramental model and a power-focused model "based on a liberal and individualistic idea of a right of the baptized to be consulted and to be part of the decision-making process."[49] In Faggioli's view, this middle ground is a People-of-God "missionary ecclesiology."[50] But when Faggioli spells out the meaning of "missionary," it becomes clear that power remains central. The supernatural truth and grace of the Gospel are little in view. Faggioli states that the purpose of Pope Francis's synodality is to ensure that the Church is not governed by a small group (whether in Rome or advocacy groups elsewhere), but instead governance is shared throughout the world (the "peripheries"), through intensive local dialogues and participatory decision-making, and with a focus on mercy, the poor, and a truly communal (rather than priest-centered) liturgy. On this view, synodality is an attempt "to see how much of modern efforts toward fair representation can become part of the institutional church," even while synodality also stands against demagogic populism. A synodal Church is able "to deal with a vertical crisis of the 'intermediate bodies' between the individual and power, in politics and in the economic system," and to assist in political and interreligious peace and reconciliation.[51] The emphasis is on adjusting and improving

49. Faggioli, *The Liminal Papacy of Pope Francis*, 134. I have criticized Faggioli's prior work at length in the fifth chapter of my *An Introduction to Vatican II as an Ongoing Theological Event.*

50. Faggioli, 134.

51. Faggioli, 174. Not only Trump and other populist leaders, but also Evangelical Protestantism as a whole, along with Catholics sympathetic to Evangelicals in any way, are a regular target of Faggioli, including in *The Liminal Papacy of Pope Francis*. See also Antonio Spadaro, SJ, and Marcelo Figueroa, "Evangelical Fundamentalism and Catholic Integralism: A Surprising Ecumenism," *La Civiltà Cattolica* 4010 (July 13, 2017). By contrast, Faggioli is optimistic about American Catholic Democrats: see Massimo Faggioli, *Joe Biden and Catholicism in the United States* (Bayard, 2021). Faggioli compares Pope Francis's dealing with "Brexit and the election of Donald Trump" to "John Paul II's fight against communism or Benedict XVI's responsibilities in a post–9/11 world" (Faggioli, *The Liminal Papacy of Pope Francis*, 12). Displaying the limits of his support for dialogue and participation, he bemoans the fact that "from the very beginning of Francis's pontificate, the militant, neoconservative, and neo-traditionalist factions of American Catholicism felt the need to ensure a hermeneutic of absolute literal continuity with John Paul II and Benedict XVI" (20). See also Massimo Borghesi's *Catholic Discordance: Neoconservatism*

power relationships and political situations in the Church and in the world.

Faggioli's *Liminal Papacy of Pope Francis* largely avoids the image of the Church as the People of God.[52] Yet, his viewpoint largely mirrors that expressed by T. P. O'Mahony on the back cover of his *Why the Catholic Church Needs Vatican III*: "Do we need to radically rethink our notion of 'church' and how leadership is exercised within it? Ought we all to be seeking a reformed church so that it better expresses and serves the 'People of God' and especially that people's 'ownership' of it?"[53] As Hans Küng put the matter

vs. the Field Hospital Church of Pope Francis, trans. Barry Hudock (Liturgical, 2021), a work marked by a fawning account of Joe Biden.

52. He frequently implies that Pope Francis is deeply influenced by the postconciliar *Concilium* theologians. For example, he states, "What is also typical of Francis is the idea that the interpretation of Vatican II as an exercise of textual exegesis made in a historical vacuum is not only a reduction of its meaning, but it is also the subtlest form of rejection of the council"; and he remarks, "unlike Benedict XVI, Francis sees a consistency between Vatican II and the post–Vatican II period—his defense of the council does not require him to distance himself from the tumultuous postconciliar period." Faggioli, *The Liminal Papacy of Pope Francis*, 71; for a survey of the postconciliar tumult by a religiously liberal Catholic thinker, see Peter Hebblethwaite, *The Runaway Church*, 2nd ed. (Fount, 1978). In Faggioli's view, Pope Francis is restarting the Church's reception of Vatican II, now along the lines of those who were John Paul II's and Benedict XVI's theological opponents. Faggioli depicts Pope Francis's opponents as hidebound, ahistorical, and lacking concern for the poor. He writes, "The opposition to Pope Francis is made up of different streams. There is a *theological* opposition that is nostalgic of a supposedly unchanging and immutable John Paul II–Benedict XVI paradigm. Then there is an *institutional* opposition that is trying to defend the ecclesiastical status quo. Finally, there is a *social-political* opposition that is concerned with the political, economic, and ideological sustainability of the Roman Catholic Church after a pontificate that is radically on the side of the poor, a fear that Francis's global Catholicism could be disastrous for Western civilization and for Catholicism as a Western religion" (Faggioli, *The Liminal Papacy of Pope Francis*, 183). For a related critique of the pontificate of John Paul II, see Hans Küng, "Is the Second Vatican Council Forgotten?," trans. Natalie K. Watson, in *Vatican II: A Forgotten Future*, ed. Alberto Melloni and Christoph Theobald, *Concilium* 2005/4 (SCM, 2005), 108–17. Küng bemoans such things as the condemnation of birth control, the reservation of the priesthood to men, clerical celibacy, the rejection of Eucharistic intercommunion, the absolute prohibition of abortion, and the failure to institute the election of bishops and (by a universally representative body rather than simply by the cardinals) the election of the pope. He looks with hope toward a near-future pontificate that takes his position on these matters and on other related matters, turning the Church away from "rigorous moral encyclicals and traditionalist catechisms" and finally appreciating the modern world rather than complaining about the "Zeitgeist" (116). See also Lieven Boeve, "'La vraie réception de Vatican II n'a pas encore commencé': Joseph Ratzinger, révélation et autorité de Vatican II," in *L'autorité et les autorités: L'herméneutique théologique de Vatican II*, ed. G. Routhier and G. Jobin (Cerf, 2010), 13–50.

53. See T. P. O'Mahony, *Why the Catholic Church Needs Vatican III* (Columba Press, 2010). O'Mahony is not aware of the possibility that each national group will claim ownership in a different way. For this possibility, see Jean-Marie Tillard, OP, "Theological Pluralism and the Mystery of the Church," in *Different Theologies, Common Responsibility*, 62–73, at 71.

in a 1962 book dedicated to Karl Rahner: "The oft-cited 'hour of the laity'—the awakening of the laity to active participation in the liturgy and the apostolate is one of the most hopeful signs in the Church of our century—even with respect to ecumenical councils, must not remain a mere slogan by which one at best understands new duties but no new corresponding rights."[54]

III. *LUMEN GENTIUM* ON THE CHURCH AS THE PEOPLE OF GOD

It is striking how distant *Lumen Gentium*'s chapter on the People of God is from the above emphases, although *Lumen Gentium*, like all the documents of Vatican II, deeply values the participation of the laity.

Lumen Gentium begins by observing that, in an important sense, *all* people are God's.[55] It quotes Peter's speech in Acts to the household of the Roman centurion Cornelius, where Peter says, "God shows no partiality, but in every nation any one who fears him and does what is right is acceptable to him" (Acts 10:34–35). Yet, God does not wish simply to draw to himself people as individuals scattered among the nations. He intends, rather, to constitute a holy people, visible in the world. God has done this in forming his people Israel over the course of history. God "chose the Israelite race to be his own people and established a covenant with it."[56] God taught the people and prepared them, but the

54. Küng, *Structures of the Church*, 100. Küng calls for the laity to possess full voting rights at councils. He remarks, "There is scarcely a problem area in the Church—not the least of which is that of the dogmas—which would not also affect lay persons" (104). The result of Küng's proposal is the clericalization of the laity: an ecclesiological "hierarchology" in the name of representative government.

55. See Lohfink, *Does God Need the Church?*, 21: "The Bible does not begin with the election of the people of God, but with the creation of the world. Its first figure is not Abraham, but *'ādām*, the human being. . . . The Bible begins with humanity. This observation, banal in itself, is of serious theological import, for it makes clear that everything the Bible goes on to describe is not only an action between God and God's people; it is aimed toward the nations, the world, the universe."

56. Second Vatican Council, *Lumen Gentium* §9, in *Vatican Council II*, vol. 1, *The Conciliar and Post Conciliar Documents*, ed. Austin Flannery, OP, rev. ed. (Costello, 1996), 350–426,

people (as God foreknew) were not able to be holy and to live up to their side of the covenants.

From the outset, therefore, God planned to come as Redeemer and to establish the new covenant in Christ, through whom God would fully reveal himself and his merciful love. *Lumen Gentium* cites Jeremiah 31:31–34's prophecy of the new covenant and observes that Christ brought about the new covenant on the cross. Christ "called a race made up of Jews and Gentiles which would be one, not according to the flesh, but in the Spirit, and this race would be the new People of God," born from water and the Spirit and grounded in faith in God's Word.[57] *Lumen Gentium* makes clear that this usage of "People of God" is not new, but rather comes from 1 Peter 2:9–10.[58]

The Church as the People of God is theocentric and Christocentric, according to *Lumen Gentium*. The People of God is messianic, and at its head is the true Davidic king, Jesus. He leads the People of God because he has conquered sin and death by his cross and Resurrection, and he now reigns at the right hand of the Father, having poured out the Spirit to draw his people to himself. The People of God have their "dignity and freedom" not autonomously, but as "the sons of God, in whose hearts the Holy Spirit dwells as in a temple."[59] Their law is Jesus's new commandment of cruciform love. Their destiny is the consummated kingdom of God, which has been inaugurated and must be spread throughout the world, until Christ comes in glory. *Lumen Gentium* teaches that the Church, the People of God, is the seed of the unity of the human race. Filled with love and truth, the People of God is

at 359. For historical-critical and theological discussion, focused upon Exodus 19, Isaiah, Ezekiel, Genesis 12:1–4, and 1 Peter 2:4–10, see Jo Bailey Wells, *God's Holy People: A Theme in Biblical Theology* (Sheffield Academic, 2000).

57. *Lumen Gentium* §9, in *Vatican Council II*, 1:359. See Áron Fejérdy, *L'Église de l'Esprit du Christ: La relation ordonnée du Christ et de l'Esprit au mystère ecclésial; Une lecture de Vatican II* (Academic Press Fribourg, 2013).

58. For the "People of God" in the Church Fathers, see de La Soujeole, *Introduction to the Mystery of the Church*, 217–19.

59. *Lumen Gentium* §9, in *Vatican Council II*, 1:360.

God's instrument for evangelizing the world. It is the light and salt of the world, as Jesus proclaimed (see Matt 5:13–16). It is the "new Israel," journeying toward the consummated kingdom that God will bring about.[60]

Lumen Gentium emphasizes that the People of God is what it is because of Jesus Christ. Christ redeemed the people by his cross and filled the people with his Spirit. Christ gave the People of God its apostolic structure and sacraments. Christ stands as the People's "principle of unity and peace."[61] The Church is a sacrament of the unity of the human race, and, through the grace of the Holy Spirit, the Church will not fail to teach the truth of faith and to sanctify believers. Indeed, *Lumen Gentium* goes so far as to say that the Church as the People of God will "not waver from perfect fidelity" but rather will "remain the worthy bride of the Lord, ceaselessly renewing herself through the action of the Holy Spirit" until Christ comes in glory.[62]

Just as Christ offered himself up as the perfect sacrifice for sin, so also his people are called to be configured to his cruciform love. The People of God is recognizable through its prayer, spiritual sacrifices, works of mercy, and evangelization. *Lumen Gentium* mentions that the People of God includes both the common priesthood (shared by all) and the hierarchical priesthood.[63] The latter sanctifies and governs the Church. In the Eucharistic celebration, the priest acts *in persona Christi* to consecrate and offer the Eucharist, and the whole congregation participates in this offering. The common priesthood is exercised, too, in "the witness of a holy life, abnegation and active charity."[64] All believers have a duty to worship God and to profess and spread the faith by

60. *Lumen Gentium* §9, in *Vatican Council II*, 1:360.

61. *Lumen Gentium* §9, in *Vatican Council II*, 1:360.

62. *Lumen Gentium* §9, in *Vatican Council II*, 1:360. I should note that just prior to the chapter on "The People of God," *Lumen Gentium* describes the Church as always "holy and always in need of purification" and as following "constantly the path of penance and renewal" (*Lumen Gentium* §8, in *Vatican Council II*, 1:358).

63. For discussion, see de La Soujeole, *Introduction to the Mystery of the Church*, 268–78.

64. *Lumen Gentium* §10, in *Vatican Council II*, 1:361.

word and deed. As the People of God, believers find their highest vocation in worship: "In the eucharistic sacrifice, the source and summit of the Christian life, they offer the divine victim to God and themselves along with it."[65] The People of God also partake in the other sacraments, including Penance and Anointing of the Sick; and certain believers are called to receive Holy Orders or Matrimony. The People of God is known by its families, as "Christian married couples help one another to attain holiness in their married life and in the rearing of their children."[66] The good of children is also the main means by which the People of God extends to new generations, since clearly without people there could be no People of God. Parents must have their children baptized and teach them the faith. All members of the People of God are called to the fullness of holiness.

In discussing the People of God, *Lumen Gentium* amplifies the theme of the Church's perfect fidelity in the truth of the Gospel. The whole People of God, both lay and cleric, cannot err when they are universally agreed upon the truth of a matter of doctrine. *Lumen Gentium* affirms "the supernatural appreciation of the faith (*sensus fidei*) of the whole people, when, 'from the bishops to the last of the faithful' they manifest a universal consent in matters of faith and morals."[67] Sometimes this vision of

65. *Lumen Gentium* §11, in *Vatican Council II,* 1:362.

66. *Lumen Gentium* §11, in *Vatican Council II,* 1:362.

67. *Lumen Gentium* §12, in *Vatican Council II,* 1:363. In *Theology of the People: The Pastoral and Theological Roots of Pope Francis,* trans. Kris Fankhouser and Carmen Fernandez-Aguinaco (Paulist, 2021), Juan Carlos Scannone, SJ, remarks that for the Argentine "theology of the people" that influenced Pope Francis—Scannone (who did his doctorate under Rahner) was a key figure in the development of this theology—"the people of God, here and now, are the *subject of theological wisdom* and of a *sensus fidei,* which tends to inculturate, in communion with the universal people of God and the universal tradition of the Church. This theological wisdom can be articulated in a reflective, critical, and methodical way in theological *science.* In this way, the *sensus fidei* of the faithful is revalued as a 'theological locus' or *source* of theological knowledge, and it is interpreted contextually, at the level of the particular Church in communion with the *whole* Church. The local cultural-historical perspective *does not* lead to expressions of different or new truths, but rather it influences the 'style' or way of believing. . . . The faithful people are not only the subject, however, but also the *recipient* of this theological task. Therefore, it is one of its *norms.* This allows for a reinterpretation of the *function of the theologian,* since it is part of his or her mission and charism, as a member of that inculturated faithful people, 'to bring to concept,' that is, to express reflectively, articulately, and systematically such theological wisdom

the *sensus fidei* is imagined to provide a basis for rejecting the solemn teachings of the Magisterium or for supposing that doctrine must be renegotiated in every era to fit the current worldview of Catholics, but *Lumen Gentium* shows that this would be a misunderstanding. When the People of God (inclusive of the Magisterium) receives and professes truths of faith under the Holy Spirit's guidance, the People of God can be sure that these truths are not merely human truths, but rather are divinely revealed.[68]

as that people of God" (108; cf. 69). For a similar perspective, see Víctor Manuel Fernández, "El 'sensus populi': Legitimidad de una teología 'desde' el Pueblo," *Teología* 72 (1998): 133–64. I wonder, however, whether in practice the local cultural-historical perspective *does* likely lead to some "different or new truths" (divergent from the Church's Tradition and from other local perspectives. *Lumen Gentium*'s understanding of the *sensus fidei* rests upon an understanding of Tradition that requires continuity in the moral and doctrinal truths professed infallibly by the *sensus fidei* over the generations. See Robert Dodaro, OSA, "*Sensus Fidelium*: Sense of the Faithful," in *The Faith Once and for All Delivered: Doctrinal Authority in Catholic Theology*, ed. Kevin L. Flannery, SJ (Emmaus Academic, 2023), 229–49; and, in the same volume, Guy Mansini, OSB, "Episcopal Conferences and the Local Renewal of Sacramental Doctrine," 283–305, at 295–300. Dodaro responds to Ormond Rush's notion that the *sensus fidelium* can legitimately be different in different localities: see Rush, *The Eyes of Faith: The Sense of the Faithful and the Church's Reception of Tradition* (The Catholic University of America Press, 2009), 243. Mansini emphasizes that the *sensus fidei* is "dependent on the prior word of the Gospel, the Scriptures recorded in the Bible and hammered out in Church teaching. . . . So whatever the *sensus fidei* is and however it is imagined it operates, it brings no new hitherto unheard-of truth into the consciousness of the Church" ("Episcopal Conferences," 296). Mansini responds directly to Scannone's perspective, without naming him, on pp. 298–99, showing that the problem is that the *sensus fidei* has here been confused with religious experience.

68. In his *Revelation, Hermeneutics, and Doctrinal Development in Joseph Ratzinger* (Emmaus Academic, 2024), Mauro Gagliardi observes that Joseph "Ratzinger . . . specifies that once approved councils have positively established doctrine, nobody, not even the pope, can contradict them. If the episcopal body expressed itself definitively in communion with the pope, and the latter confirmed these decisions, then the doctrinal development manifested remains forever, as the inalienable patrimony of the Ecclesial Community. The pope cannot nullify defined doctrines or even doctrines that, although not defined, have always been proposed by the universal ordinary magisterium and, for that reason, are held by the Church as infallibly taught" (145–46). This is the perspective of *Lumen Gentium* as well. For insight into the deposit of faith and the hierarchy of truths, see the Congregation for the Doctrine of the Faith, *Profession of Faith*, January 9, 1989, vatican.va, a profession of faith that consists of the Niceno-Constantinopolitan Creed plus three paragraphs that serve to distinguish the order of truths that the faithful are called to embrace. See also Pope John Paul II, *Ad Tuendam Fidem*, apostolic letter, May 18 1998, vatican.va, which adds further clarifications and directs attention to Canons 750 and 752; and Congregation for the Doctrine of the Faith, "Doctrinal Commentary on the Concluding Formula of the *Professio fidei*," June 29, 1998, vatican.va. In *The Liminal Papacy of Pope Francis*, Faggioli dismisses theological efforts to assess the weight and authority of Magisterial teaching: "This Jesuit global ethos is visible also in Francis's attention to the diversity and plurality of languages and forms of communications and embodiments of the Christian experience in the church, and he is not afraid of the accusations of a theological lack of clarity in his teaching. As Ghislain Lafont writes, 'The attempts to establish whether one or the other assertion of the magisterium is infallible, definitive, irreformable, etc.—they are a kind of ecclesiastical gymnas-

As support for its vision of faith, *Lumen Gentium* cites 1 Thessalonians 2:13, where Paul praises the Thessalonians as follows: "When you received the word of God which you heard from us, you accepted it not as the word of men but as what it really is, the word of God, which is at work in you believers." *Lumen Gentium* also makes reference to the existence of a stable deposit of faith received by the People of God, as found in Jude 3: "Beloved, being very eager to write to you of our common salvation, I found it necessary to write appealing to you to contend for the faith which was once for all delivered to the saints."

The People of God receive special graces or charisms that foster diverse missions. Here 1 Corinthians 12 has a central place, as do the injunctions that Paul delivers in 1 Thessalonians 5 regarding respect for Church leaders and the requirement that these leaders "test everything" and "hold fast to what is good" (1 Thess 5:21). Since God calls all human beings into the unity of the Church, Christians must evangelize the whole world so that Christ might be known by all peoples as "teacher, king, and priest of all, the head of the new and universal People of God's sons."[69] In every land, the Church establishes the kingdom of God, but not in a manner that aims to take over the duties of earthly kingdoms or to entirely negate or displace particular cultures. The Church is catholic or universal, focused upon the true king of all creation, Christ the Head of his People. But at the same time, the Church appreciates and fosters the good elements of "the abilities, the resources and customs of peoples."[70]

According to *Lumen Gentium*, the Church's catholicity as the People of God allows for true diversity, including a diversity of rite and governance—as in the case of Eastern Catholic

tics that is quite recent in the history of the church.' As such, Francis is not troubled by them" (43–44, citing Lafont, *Piccolo saggio sul tempo di papa Francesco* (EDB, 2017).

69. *Lumen Gentium* §13, in *Vatican Council II*, 1:364. On Christ and his followers as priest, prophet, and king, see de La Soujeole, *Introduction to the Mystery of the Church*, 214–17.

70. *Lumen Gentium* §13, in *Vatican Council II*, 1:364. For discussion of §§13–17, see de La Soujeole, *Introduction to the Mystery of the Church*, 247–52.

Churches. So long as there is communion with the bishop of Rome, the communion of the Church retains universality. This catholicity or universality is never an autonomous achievement of the Church; it is always Christ's gift. Believers should recognize that God himself calls us into a "catholic unity."[71] This unity follows from the nature of divine revelation. Without negating or compromising the diversity of peoples and of vocations, "the Catholic Church ceaselessly and efficaciously seeks for the return of all humanity and all its goods under Christ the Head in the unity of his Spirit."[72] The Catholic Church possesses unity and catholicity (though these can be deepened), while other Christians and all humankind are related to this catholic unity or participate in it to different degrees.

Lumen Gentium maintains that belonging to the Church of Christ, the People of God, is necessary for salvation because only Christ is the Mediator and Savior. Nevertheless, a person can belong to the Catholic Church through implicit faith or by receiving the means of salvation (such as the Gospel) through other Christian communities without knowing that these means properly lead to the Catholic Church. Treating the situation of non-Christians, *Lumen Gentium* explains, "Those who, through no fault of their own, do not know the Gospel of Christ or his Church, but who nevertheless seek God with a sincere heart, and, moved by grace, try in their actions to do his will as they know it through the dictates of their conscience—those too may achieve eternal salvation."[73] Salvation is even possible for atheists who are sincerely seeking and who strive to lead a morally good life, since such seeking and striving may reflect an interior response to grace. But evangelization remains urgently necessary because, lacking the guidance of the Gospel and absent the healing and

71. *Lumen Gentium* §13, in *Vatican Council II*, 1:365.

72. *Lumen Gentium* §13, in *Vatican Council II*, 1:364–65.

73. *Lumen Gentium* §16, in *Vatican Council II*, 1:367. On the possibility of salvation for those outside the visible bounds of the Church—who nevertheless are not outside Christ's Body—see the discussion in de La Soujeole, *Introduction to the Mystery of the Church*, 254–68.

strengthening provided by the sacraments, it is easy to go astray. For the sake of the world's salvation, therefore, the Church as God's People works assiduously to proclaim the Gospel, to baptize, to purify cultures, and to ensure that honor and glory are given to God.

Lumen Gentium's chapter on the People of God ends there. It is a highly positive portrait, depicting the People of God as faithful without fail to the revealed deposit of faith due to the power of the Holy Spirit. According to *Lumen Gentium*, the People of God has spread throughout the whole world and is profoundly one without undermining distinctive cultures or impeding the expression of diverse vocations. Christ structures the People of God and gives sacraments to it. The People of God is the new Israel, a messianic and theocentric community filled with the charity of God's adopted sons and daughters.

I embrace *Lumen Gentium*'s vision of the catholicity of the People of God, the indefectibility of the *sensus fidei* in proclaiming the realities contained in the apostolic deposit of faith, and the Holy Spirit's provision of the People of God with charity, self-sacrifice, and virtue configured to Christ. The sinfulness of Catholics, however, needs further attention. Bishop Robert Barron, reflecting in 2019 upon the sex abuse scandals and other problems facing the Catholic Church today, remarked aptly that "a deep and abiding corruption has invaded the Mystical Body of Christ"—and not for the first time.[74] To understand this corruption theologically, more needs to be said about the People of God than is said in *Lumen Gentium*'s chapter. Radner's writings will assist in this task, while also helping to show why the image of the People of God remains so necessary for ecclesiology.

Before turning to Radner, however, let me first explore the image of the People of God in Catholic ecclesiology of the late

74. Robert Barron, *Letter to a Suffering Church: A Bishop Speaks on the Sexual Abuse Crisis* (Word on Fire, 2019), 96. See also the astute essays in *Clerical Sexual Misconduct: An Interdisciplinary Analysis*, ed. Jane F. Adolphe and Ronald J. Rychlak (Cluny, 2020).

1960s and early 1970s. This ecclesiology exhibits an anthropocentric and power-centered (in the name of democratic participation) pattern of thought about the People of God that today has reemerged.

IV. THE PEOPLE OF GOD IN THE LATE 1960S AND EARLY 1970S

In his 1970 book *Church: The Continuing Quest*, Richard McBrien examines the responses to the first draft of the document that became *Lumen Gentium*. He highlights the concerns of Bishop Léon-Arthur Elchinger, who requested that "the People of God be the controlling image over against the hierarchy."[75] Elchinger proposed that it is best to emphasize the whole people, the community, and the open relationship of the whole community with all other Christians and with the whole world. In the second draft of the document, however, the hierarchy was still discussed prior to the People of God. Yves Congar contended against this ordering, and his intervention succeeded. McBrien sums up the result: "The Church was no longer to be seen initially or primarily as the scholastic-doctrinal method saw it—as a juridically, hierarchically constituted society which exists to communicate the grace of redemption to all mankind. Rather, it is first and foremost a community of people on march in history, a pilgrim people, the very People of God."[76]

This emphasis on "a community of people" marching through history (in McBrien's portrait at least) is arguably more triumphalist than the notion of a hierarchical institution constituted by Christ and the Spirit to communicate Christ's redemptive grace to the world. As McBrien describes it, the People of God marching through history possesses a confidence borne of recognition of certain fundamental democratic values that God

75. Richard P. McBrien, *Church: The Continuing Quest* (Newman, 1970), 32.
76. McBrien, 33.

has inscribed into his Church. McBrien specifies that God has elected his Church; the Church is not a Pelagian work of human beings. He also specifies, "Within this People of God, there is a fundamental equality of vocation, of commitment, and of dignity."[77] The Church as the People of God does not have degrees of dignity but rather is marked by equality. In history, therefore, this people is on the march because God has made it a beacon of equality.

McBrien does not wish to fall into triumphalism, which in his view flows mainly from the identification of the Church with the kingdom of God. He criticizes chapter 7 of *Lumen Gentium*, on "The Eschatological Nature of the Pilgrim Church and Its Union with the Heavenly Church," in part because *Lumen Gentium* still contains the idea that all humans are called to enter into the Church. He bemoans the fact that *Lumen Gentium* includes the detail that those who refuse to enter the Church, even while knowing that Jesus Christ established the Church, cannot be saved. Against this view, he highlights the historical march of God's people who are witnessing to the value of human equality in God's sight.[78]

77. McBrien, 33.

78. Somewhat similarly, while speaking of Vatican II's "authentic and binding interpretation of the faith," Peter Hünermann redefines what "authentic and binding" means. Hünermann, "The Ignored 'Text': On the Hermeneutics of the Second Vatican Council," trans. Natalie K. Watson, in Melloni and Theobald, *Vatican II: A Forgotten Future*, 118–36, at 123. For Hünermann, the texts of Vatican II represent a "fundamental consensus" of the Church about what constitutes "faithful ecclesial life" (126, 128), and this consensus or "constitution" is the measure of all reception of the council. Since the council gave rise to (and, in certain ways, intended to give rise to) "transformations among the People of God, in the unfolding of their consciousness of having come of age, of being able to think for themselves and of their own responsibility, especially among the laity," Hünermann concludes that what is "authentic and binding" in Vatican II is above all that which accords with the laity's consciousness of co-responsibility and of "being able to think for themselves" (130). He thus grounds future radical changes in doctrine and morality (including radical change to things taught by Vatican II itself) precisely in adherence to Vatican II as "authentic and binding." See also the similarly dubious ingeniousness of Christoph Theobald, SJ, who concludes that "the pastoral principle of Vatican II called not just for a simple application but for a real learning process, even for a capacity to envisage the *transformations* . . . produced at the heart of the constitutive interplay between those who proclaim the Good News and those who receive it, and to allow them to reflect the whole apparatus back on each other, thereby steering it toward a new 'doctrinal' balance. The normativeness of the Council texts would then consist not in their theological or juridical literalness, nor in a spirit that sees nothing more to be gained from them; *it would rather appear concretely*

For McBrien, hierarchy is associated with papal domination, priestly celibacy, the reservation of priesthood to men, and other offenses against equality. He suggests that the reality of human sinfulness is on display in the hierarchical Church with its sins of exclusion, high-handedness, and domination.[79] The image of the People of God reflects a Church that is beginning to overcome these sinful warts, without thereby being a Pelagian enterprise.[80]

Nevertheless, McBrien is not content with the image of "People of God." Although he deems it to be the predominant image of the Church at Vatican II, he argues that it is ultimately too conservative. He states, "It is many strides beyond the more scholastic and doctrinal emphasis conveyed by 'Mystical Body of Christ,' but it remains so closely allied to the kerygmatic way of viewing the Church that it is not fully open to the eschatological implications worked out, in part at least, by *Gaudium*

in pastoral or missionary applications that—guided by the Spirit—go right to the point where fresh formulations of such and such a text become evidently necessary . . . thereby awakening expectations of a new council" (Theobald, "The Theological Options of Vatican II: Seeking an 'Internal' Principle of Interpretation," trans. Paul Burns, in Melloni and Theobald, *Vatican II: A Forgotten Future*, 87–107, at 105). For further examples of this historicist and praxis-centered approach to doctrine, see Hünermann, "On the Specific Theological Character of the Sacrament of Matrimony," in *Authentic Voices, Discerning Hearts: New Resources for the Church on Marriage and Family*, ed. Thomas Knieps-Port le Roi and Aldegonde Brenninkmeijer-Werhahn (LIT, 2016), 133–50; and Theobald, "The Principle of Pastorality at Vatican II: Challenges of a Prospective Interpretation of the Council," in *The Legacy of Vatican II*, ed. Massimo Faggioli and Andrea Vicini, SJ (Paulist, 2015), 26–37.

79. For more recent charges of exclusion (in an ecumenical context, and along lines that are commonplace now), see Tobias Nicklas, "Together with the Lord on the Way to the Lord," in Stefan Alkier, Christos Karakolis, and Tobias Nicklas, *The Promise of Ecumenical Interpretation: Protestant, Catholic, Orthodox*, trans. Jacob N. Cerone and David M. Moffitt (Fortress, 2024), 188–95, at 195: "The final horizon described by the Bible is the grace of the Lord Jesus. And again it must be stressed that this grace comes within the horizon of the 'in spite of everything' and is therefore something incomprehensible, immeasurable, and wonderful in the truest sense of these words. In light of this grace, no form of exclusionary mercilessness can be accepted among those who want to stand for the body of Christ in this world. Such a stance cannot be held to be in accordance with the will of Christ." The problem is that "mercy" is here unmoored from charity and faith—and their full moral and creedal dimensions.

80. I note that McBrien distances himself from the view that "the Church exists wherever the Kingdom exists, i.e., wherever human beings are doing good, wherever people are becoming friends" (McBrien, *Church*, 38). He responds, "This view tends to blur the distinctive character of the Church as a community which specifically acknowledges the Lordship of Jesus and gives praise and thanksgiving to the Father through its sacraments, and through the Eucharist in particular" (38). McBrien also denies "that the Church can eventually get along without a college of bishops or the Pope" (39).

et Spes."[81] For McBrien, these "eschatological" implications are essentially the idea that Christ came to establish the kingdom, not the Church. The Church's purpose is to serve and support the establishment of the (eschatological) kingdom in the world. Thus, the Church itself is far more provisional than is supposed by those who hold that Christ came to found his Church on the apostles and to bestow sacraments imbued with the grace of the Holy Spirit. The Church supports the emergence of the kingdom in this world rather than being "the ordinary means of salvation."[82]

McBrien deems that the postconciliar Congar remained too conservative in his view of the Church, despite his important preconciliar contributions.[83] What is needed now, says McBrien, is to move beyond the council, following hints laid down in *Gaudium et Spes*. He agrees with Eugene Bianchi that the Church must not be "inward-oriented" but rather must understand itself as comprised of "communities of reconciliation" that are "outer-oriented," serving the formation of the kingdom in the

81. McBrien, 46.

82. McBrien, 49.

83. See for example Yves Congar, OP, "Theology's Tasks after Vatican II," in *Renewal of Religious Thought: Proceedings of the Congress on the Theology of the Renewal of the Church Centenary of Canada, 1867–1967*, ed. L.K. Shook, CSB, vol. 1 (Palm, 1968), 47–65. Congar states, "What hitherto was considered unchangeable now seems to be opened up for change. . . . The Council did not create the questions but lifted the barrier which had prevented them from being asked freely. It has officially opened the way to change, not the foundations, but the forms, the expressions. . . . I, too, feel almost every day a temptation of uneasiness in the face of all that has changed or is being called into question. Secondly, it is easy to say—and there is good reason for saying—that these forms are all relative. But the absolute has been delivered, communicated, to us in these relative forms. . . . The example of the sixteenth century may illustrate, and cast tragic light upon, what we are saying. It is averred that in those times it was necessary not only to reform a number of abuses, but also to disengage Christian life and religion from many superstitions. This is what the [Protestant] reformers set out to do. But they were not careful to salvage the valuable substance covered by these blameworthy forms. . . . A warning sign should be posted for our present day reformers: Beware! Do not repeat the old mistake when you envisage the replacement, legitimate *per se* and sometimes even necessary, of liturgical, theological, institutional forms by others that are more in accord with our world, our culture, our conditions" (49–50). Congar places a strong emphasis on continuity: "Surely there is every reason for theological renewal. But this novelty will be such in a relative sense only. The aspect of continuity, and even of identity, is incomparably weightier. The task of theology remains what it always has been. It is still a reflection on the mysteries of faith. . . . Moreover, theology today draws its decisive teachings from the same source, that is, from the very same faith, which nourished it yesterday and from its beginnings. . . . [Theology] remains in depth and substance the same 'discourse' about God and the mysteries of salvation which it was in the time of Gregory of Nazianzus, Augustine, or Thomas Aquinas" (59).

world.[84] At the same time, the Church is shaped by Christ and stands as Christ's instrument for bringing about the kingdom. McBrien agrees with Charles Davis that the Church is Christ's vanguard in the work of the accomplishment of the kingdom. As he puts it—indebted also to Johann Baptist Metz and Karl Rahner—the Church is not primarily "a community of proclamation" but rather is a community of "socio-political *diakonia*," building the kingdom through justice and righteousness in the world here and now.[85] As such, the Church must be flexible in its structure and its self-understanding: "The Church of the future will have more of the quality of a movement: informal, flexible, adaptable—an open structure."[86]

84. McBrien, *Church*, 51.

85. McBrien, 58. For Metz's perspective, see his *Theology of the World*, trans. William Glen-Doepel (Seabury, 1969), especially "An Eschatological View of the Church and the World," 81–97, at 96: "An eschatologically oriented theology must place itself in communication with the prevailing political, social and technical utopias and with the contemporary maturing promises of a universal peace and justice. . . . In obeying its eschatological vocation Christianity should not establish itself as a ghetto-society or become the ideological protective shell for the existing society. Rather it should become the liberating and critical force of this one society." See also in the same volume Metz's "The Church and the World in the Light of a 'Political Theology,'" 107–36, where Metz highlights "the difference, consciously accepted in Christian hope, between the institutional Church and the eschatological 'kingdom of God' proclaimed by it. Where this difference or this gap is retained, that is, where the Church itself is consciously perceived in its own eschatological provisionalness, there is always present a critical element to question and destroy all those tendencies to which the Church, in its institutional character, is exposed and is constantly in danger of succumbing; for example, the tendency to mere preservation and stabilization, to accept only what has grown up and now exists, to keep only to what is well tried and to have a fundamental distrust of what is new and has never before existed, to canonize a custom and then see it as an image of one's own invincibleness. . . . In this sense there arises out of the difference between the Church and the 'kingdom of God,' thematized in hope, the impulse towards creating a critical freedom within the Church" (134–35). For Rahner's perspective, McBrien directs attention to Rahner, "Church and World," in *Sacramentum Mundi: An Encyclopedia of Theology*, 6 vols. (Herder and Herder, 1968–70), 1:346–57; and Rahner, "Christianity and the New Earth," *Theology Digest* 15 (1967): 275–82. McBrien also expresses a debt to Carl E. Braaten's eschatological ecclesiology—a book that Braaten later rightly renounced: Braaten, *The Future of God: The Revolutionary Dynamics of Hope* (Harper & Row, 1969). See also the discussion of Rahner, Metz, McBrien, and Gustavo Gútierrez in Patrick Lynch, SJ's largely appreciative "Servant Ecclesiologies: A Challenge to Rahner's Understanding of Church and World," *Irish Theological Quarterly* 57, no. 4 (1991): 277–98; and see Michael Kirwan, SJ, "'Speaking Well': Euphemistic Theology and the Synodal Way," in *Synodality and the Recovery of Vatican II: A New Way for Catholics*, ed. Stephen J. McKinney, Thomas O'Loughlin, and Beáta Tóth (Messenger, 2024), 135–47, which follows Metz and Rahner on the theological dignity of the world and highlights (as the key "signs of the times") the institutional role of women, LGBTQ+ acceptance, and the rot exposed by the clergy sex abuse crisis.

86. McBrien, *Church*, 55.

Thus, although McBrien argues that he is moving beyond the Church as People of God, in another sense he is simply repackaging and accentuating this image as he understands it. The Church's role, he contends (with the theology of Edward Schillebeeckx in view), is to take part in humanizing the world, bringing about liberation so that people can finally become the people God created them to be. The Church exists to transform history and the world—which means, for McBrien, to replicate the social movements of the 1960s and to jettison anything that does not cohere with them.[87] On this view, from a condition of

87. See Edward Schillebeeckx, OP, "The Church as the Sacrament of Dialogue," in his *God the Future of Man*, trans. N.D. Smith (Sheed and Ward, 1968), 117–40, at 136–37, arguing for "a new self-definition on the part of the Church's teaching office, the prophetic (that is, critical and constructive) power of which is also dependent on continued *dialogue* with the world. . . . In social and political issues the ecclesiastical authorities no longer seek merely to safeguard humanity's ethical past achievements; they seek rather to let the authoritative voice of the Church community be heard in the guidance of humanity towards a better, more humane world—which, for the faith and hope of Christians, can truly be called an ascent, in Christ, towards the definitive kingdom. The Pastoral Constitution [*Gaudium et Spes*] has already formulated this principle: 'To carry out such a task, the Church has always had the duty of scrutinizing the signs of the times and of interpreting them in the light of the Gospel.'" For background, see M.-D. Chenu, OP, *Peuple de Dieu dans le monde* (Cerf, 1966), especially chapter 2, "Les signes des temps" (but the whole book is pertinent, and much more biblically rich than Schillebeeckx's essay); and Chenu, "The History of Salvation and the Historicity of Man in the Renewal of Theology," in Shook, *Renewal of Religious Thought*, 1:153–66, at 162–64: "To understand the 'places' of the Word of God in the world, the first requirement is not to deduce its applications from an abstract and extratemporal analysis, as we have long done, but 'to scrutinize, to discern, to interpret' in history, in the Church in act, 'the multiple languages of our time' (*Gaudium et spes*, art. 44), or in the now classic expression of John XXIII, taken up by Paul VI and expressly recorded by the Council (*ibid.*, art. 4) 'to scrutinize the signs of the times.' 'Signs of the times': here without a doubt we have the key phrase, the theological category which will function as a pivot, not only for analysis of the pastoral *aggiornamento* of the Church, but much more for the renewal of a theology conscious of the historical dimension of its object. . . . It is not by chance that the Christian is becoming more attentive to the peculiar character of the economy of salvation at the moment when man is becoming vitally aware of the historicity of his own nature. This is a normal convergence, if it is true that faith, incarnate in the human subject, adjusts itself to man's structures and evolutions." See also the development of the "signs of the times" hermeneutic—indebted both to Chenu and (even more) to Schillebeeckx—that has been spearheaded by, among others, the German theologian Hans-Joachim Sander. For discussion, see Thomas Marschler, "Zeichen der Zeit als neuer *locus theologicus*?," in *Jesus Christus—Alpha und Omega: Festschrift für Helmut Hoping zum 65. Geburtstag*, ed. Jan-Heiner Tück and Magnus Striet (Herder, 2021), 38–56; and Richard Schenk, OP, "Places and Times: Searching for a Theological *Topica*," *Nova et Vetera* 19, no. 1 (2021): 163–89. The result of the hermeneutic of the "signs of the times" is to destabilize the Church's teachings, given that whenever it seems that the Church's doctrine impedes human flourishing (measured by current secular standards), the "signs of the times" hermeneutic calls for a change in doctrine. Among Sander's many works, see for example "Vom religionsgemeinschaftlichen Urbi et Orbi zu pastoralgemeinschaftlichen Heterotopien: Eine Topologie Gottes in den Zeichen der Zeit," in *Zweites Vatikanisches Konzil: Programmatik—Rezeption—Vision*, ed. Christopher Böttigheimer (Herder, 2014), 157–79.

large-scale oppression and domination, humanity is now emerging—through the Church's "dialogue" with the world—into a new, liberated, fully human existence. The Church is not "the center of history," as it is in visions of the Church that focus on sacramental grace.[88] But the Church plays a pivotal role, in dialogue with the world, in the establishment of the kingdom through liberation. The Church thereby finally will bring about the true "People of God," a liberated, fully human people. The Church is called to be "an active and aggressive instrument of the realization of the human brotherhood as an achievement of history."[89] The true People of God is coming to be even now, in history understood as "in process of becoming the Kingdom of God," of which reality the Church—a community of faith, baptism, transformation, and mission—is "sign, instrument, and herald."[90] Although McBrien argues that he has moved beyond the image of the Church as People of God (and even farther past the image of the Church as "Mystical Body"), in my view McBrien is actually promoting a new vision of the Church as the People of God, not *Lumen Gentium*'s understanding of this image but one that is focused on power and on transforming the world in a worldly way.

This new People of God will bear testimony, in word and deed, to "the process of human history as it is moving toward the promised future of God."[91] Whereas (for McBrien) the old hierarchical People of God was inward-focused, organized around the sacraments and around sharing in Christ's Paschal Mystery,

88. McBrien, *Church*, 61.

89. McBrien, 63.

90. McBrien, 68. McBrien defines the Church as follows: "The Church is the community of those who confess the Lordship of Jesus Christ, who ratify that faith in baptism, and who thereby commit themselves to membership and mission within that sacramental community of faith. But the primary reality is the Kingdom of God, and the existence and function of the Church makes no sense apart from it. That mission is threefold in relationship to the reign of God: to proclaim in word and sacrament the definitive arrival of the Kingdom in Jesus of Nazareth (*kerygma*), to offer itself as a test case of its own proclamation, as a group of people transformed by the Spirit into a community of faith, hope love, and truthfulness—a sign of the Kingdom on earth and an anticipation of the Kingdom of the future (*koinonia*), and finally to realize and extend the reign of God through service in the socio-political order (*diakonia*)" (73).

91. McBrien, 85.

the new People of God will be a virtuous agent of economic, political, and social liberation, building up the coming kingdom. McBrien concludes in this vein, "The Church must offer itself as one of the principal agents whereby the human community is made to stand under the judgment of the enduring values of the Gospel of Jesus Christ and to see itself against the horizon of its eschatological expectation: the time of freedom, justice, righteousness, peace, charity, compassion, reconciliation."[92] McBrien's Church, in dialogue with the world, stands at the vanguard of this historical-eschatological process.[93]

Let me offer further examples of this postconciliar spirit (inverse hierarchology at its most optimistic). In his 1967 edited volume *We, the People of God . . . : A Study of Constitutional Government for the Church*, James Coriden and his fellow contributors emphasize the necessity of the Church's internal political reform. They hold that Vatican II's "People of God" is distinctive because the laity are now coming to share in the clergy's power of governance.[94] A similar perspective on the People of God char-

92. McBrien, 85.

93. See the similar vision of John Sullivan, "Reflections on Engaging with Synodality," in McKinney, O'Loughlin, and Tóth, *Synodality and the Recovery of Vatican II*, 85–96, at 95: "The synodal way also seems to herald a shift from institutional, Church-centred starting points and orientation to a more God-centred outlook. That is, although Church is a major site for God's communication of life and love for creation, it is not the only one. My experience of synodality is helping me to ask myself more often, where is God already at work in the world? Where is God calling us to join in his creative and healing work? Rather than assuming that the Church already possesses in full what God has to say to her, the synodal way prompts her to open herself to receive the communication of the Holy Spirit—a communication which is ongoing, unending, continuing, unfinished, ever-new and creative, surprising and profoundly disturbing. This means that, instead of a backward-looking emphasis on preserving and reiterating something she already owns—and is often tempted to think that she controls—the Church recognises the need to be open and vulnerable to what God still has to say and to require of us today: new learning and deeper conversion is required from all of us. Two particular shifts in emphasis are required if synodality is to take off as intended: first, a much stronger emphasis on consultation, cooperation and co-responsibility in the Church; second, the development of the local Churches and their theologies." It is clear that the "profoundly disturbing" and "surprising" "new learning" will be solely on the part of those who have adhered to the teachings of the Church under Pope John Paul II and Pope Benedict XVI—since Sullivan's proposals simply rehash, in a "backward-looking" way, ideas from the early 1970s that he has long supported.

94. See *We, the People of God . . . : A Study of Constitutional Government for the Church*, ed. James A. Coriden (Our Sunday Visitor, 1967). Vatican II's Dogmatic Constitution *Lumen Gentium*, along with its Decrees *Christus Dominus* (on bishops) and *Apostolicam Actuositatem* (on the laity), does not envision such lay participation in decision-making through voting. For

acterizes Léon-Joseph Cardinal Suenens's 1968 book *Coresponsibility in the Church.* Suenens was an influential figure from the late 1950s onward, including during the Second Vatican Council.[95] As M.-D. Chenu commented in an essay delivered in 1967, "Everyone remembers the intervention of Cardinal Suenens at the end of the first session (December 4, 1962). . . . Out of a confused and unwieldy agenda paper, he extracted the decisive line of the Council: the Church has to define herself within herself, but also outside herself in a 'dialogue' with the world."[96] From this intervention came *Gaudium et Spes.* Suenens's impact upon postconciliar discussions up to the present day has been notable. In a 2005 essay on the future of Vatican II, the theologian Andrés Torres Queiruga credits Suenens for perceiving from the outset that "in strict adherence to the gospel . . . it has to be admitted that an appropriate 'democratization' is necessary for the life of

further discussion, see my "*Christus Dominus,*" in Lamb and Levering, *The Reception of Vatican II*, 147–69; and see the astute observation of Guy Mansini, OSB: "In Pope Francis's challenging image, we stand the pyramidal Church on its apex. This is to remind us that priests and bishops and pope stand 'under' the baptized faithful in order to serve them. They are ministers ('servants') not only of the Gospel and of Christ, but of Christ's people. The Holy Father's point is doubtless true and imaginatively expressed. But in what does this service consist? . . . Stand the Church on its apex as you will, this does not alter the dependence of the Church as a whole on episcopal teaching authority, itself dependent on the authority and word of Christ, which is the perfect embodiment of the word of God and which alone is the foundation of faith" (Mansini, "Episcopal Conferences and the Local Renewal of Sacramental Doctrine," 300).

95. See Gérard Philips, "The Church in the Modern World," in *The Church and the World*, ed. Johannes B. Metz, *Concilium* 6 (Paulist, 1965), 5–22, at 5. Suenens, who apparently was almost elected pope after the death of Pope John XXIII, was already a leader in the Church prior to the council. François Houtart, OSB, who directed the Center for Socio-Religious Research in Brussels, makes this clear in his *The Challenge to Change: The Church Confronts the Future*, ed. Mary Anne Chouteau (Sheed and Ward, 1964). Houtart states, "New discoveries in the world have given new dimensions to moral problems such as those of birth control, psychological and emotional disorders, nuclear war, civil rights, and so on. Not nearly enough progress has been made in our approach to these problems. But some steps have been taken. Cardinal Suenens, in 1958, called together a group of Catholic biologists, theologians, and doctors to discuss and reflect upon some of these new problems and to keep up with the fresh discoveries. This group still meets regularly. Not long ago a meeting was organized with Protestant leaders and leaders of the Population Council to discuss birth control and population questions with the end in mind of reaching an understanding of one another's point of view" (*The Challenge to Change*, 205–6; cf. 26–33).

96. Chenu, "The History of Salvation and the Historicity of Man in the Renewal of Theology," 155. See also Karl Rahner, SJ, "The Present Situation of Christians: A Theological Interpretation of the Position of Christians in the Modern World," in *The Christian Commitment: Essays in Pastoral Theology*, trans. Cecily Hastings (Sheed and Ward, 1963), 3–37, at 23–24.

the Church. Those who do not like the word or even mistrust the symbol 'people of God' can replace them with others such as 'communion' or 'synodality,' but disagreements over names should not obscure the question of real values."[97]

Karl Rahner argued similarly for democratization in various writings from the period 1965–75. In Rahner's view, the modern understanding of freedom stands as a contribution not simply to secular history but to the history of salvation. He calls for a variety of democratic structures in the Church, including a new awareness that office in the Church is a functional rather than sacred power, the installation of term limits for bishops and the pope, the involvement of laity in the appointment of bishops and the pope, the implementation of a system of checks and balances or "counter-authorities" in the Church, and a "continuing process of change" marked by national synods inclusive of laity and empowered to make binding doctrinal and pastoral decisions.[98] For his part, Yves Congar wrote in 1972 with a striking confidence in modern man: "We must ask ourselves whether *aggiornamento* is enough or whether something else will not be necessary. . . . Our epoch requires a revision of 'traditional' forms that goes beyond the plans for adaptation or *aggiornamento*; it requires a new creation. It is not enough simply to maintain and adapt what

97. Andrés Torres Queiruga, "Vatican II and Theology," in Melloni and Theobald, *Vatican II: A Forgotten Future*, 21–33, at 30. Queiruga spells out this democratization: "With regard to the *base of the Church*, this is urgently in need of a revitalization of egalitarian communion, doing away with the scandalous circumstance—in modern consciousness—that in the Church all deliberation should have only a consultative character, and, of course, bringing in full equality of *women*, thereby redeeming, against all historical inertia, the shining and foundational Pauline principle that in Christ 'there is no longer male and female' (Gal. 3.28). And with regard to *hierarchical government*, the autonomy of society forces us to undertake an honest and forceful rethinking of the divine origin of authority, parallel to that done for civil authority . . . showing that this does not prevent it from being founded, transmitted, elected, and defended through the community" (30). On this question, see also Heribert Heinemann, "Demokratisierung oder Synodalisierung? Ein Beitrag zur Diskussion," in *Kirche sein: Nachkonziliare Theologie im Dienst der Kirchenreform*, ed. W. Geerlings and Max Seckler (Herder, 1994), 349–60.

98. See Karl Rahner, SJ, "Freedom and Manipulation in Society and the Church," trans. David Smith, in *Meditations on Freedom and the Spirit*, 61–71; and see also Rahner, *The Shape of the Church to Come*, trans. Edward Quinn (Seabury, 1974). For an application of the same solvent to the authority structures in the New Testament, see Gordon Shaw, *The Cost of Authority: Manipulation and Freedom in the New Testament* (Fortress, 1983).

has existed until now; it is necessary to create something new."[99] Although Congar limits this "reinvention" to the "forms" as distinct from the offices, sacraments, and doctrines, this limitation is difficult to maintain in practice. He, too, was often focused on power-sharing in his understanding of the People of God. He remarks in a passage quoted by Luciani, "We are still far from understanding the consequences of discovering . . . that the entire Church is a single People of God and that it is made up of the faithful along with the clergy."[100]

In *Coresponsibility in the Church*, Suenens interprets the image "People of God" largely in terms of sharing leadership roles so that all believers have a participation in leadership. To be the People of God requires, on this view, democratic or quasi-democratic participation in ecclesial leadership. Suenens states, "History will render glory to the council for having beautifully defined the nature of the church, the people of God, and for having boldly sketched the place and role of the laity in the church. History will no doubt also accuse us of not having sufficiently put into practice that which is so well defined [by the council]—the coresponsibility of the laity."[101] All the council's voting members were bishops,

99. Yves Congar, OP, "Renewal of the Spirit and Reform of the Institution," trans. John Griffiths, *Concilium* 73 (1972): 39–49, quoted in Luciani, *Synodality*, 145; cf. Möhler, *Unity in the Church*, 265: "When the beautiful seeds planted in the constitution of the Church at the time ripened, the stiff form of the hierarchy should have changed with the circumstances that had been changed *by it*, and those forms of unity that had fallen away should have again stepped into the foreground. However, since human beings attempted by principles to give generality and necessity to a form, limited by the individuality of [a specific] time, life disappeared from the principles and the school."

100. Yves Congar, OP, *Pour une église servante et pauvre* (Cerf, 2014), quoted in Luciani, *Synodality*, 143. Overall, I agree with Bernhard Blankenhorn, OP's positive assessment of Congar's ecclesiology: see Blankenhorn, "The *Sensus Fidei* and Synodality: Theological Epistemology and the *Munus Propheticum*," *The Thomist* 87, no. 2 (2023): 311–38, at 338. See also Michael Bredeck, *Das Zweite Vatikanum als Konzil des Aggiornamento: Zur hermeneutischen Grundlegung einer theologischen Konzilsinterpretation* (Schöningh, 2007).

101. Léon-Joseph Cardinal Suenens, *Coresponsibility in the Church*, trans. Francis Martin (Herder and Herder, 1968), 187. See also Cardinal Suenens's May 15, 1969, interview and related interventions and essays, published in *The Suenens Dossier: The Case for Collegiality*, ed. Jose de Broucker (Fides, 1970). For cognate views, see Elochukwu E. Uzukwu, *A Listening Church: Autonomy and Communion in African Churches* (Orbis Books, 1996); Charles A. Ebelebe, CSSp., "An Inculturated Church in Africa: Lessons and Failings since *Ecclesia in Africa*," in *Faith in Action*, vol. 2, *Pastoral Renewal, Public Health and the Prophetic Mission of the Church in Africa Since the Two African Synods*, ed. Stan Chu Ilo, Justin Clemency Nabushawo, and

and their assistants were almost all priests. For Suenens, the answer is not to make laity into a pressure group or into "judges in matters of faith."[102] But the laity nevertheless should have real participation so as to be, in a real (political) sense, co-responsible.

In Suenens's view, the Catholic Church's authority structures have tended to mirror those of the surrounding society. A democratic Church would not have made sense in a Roman Empire ruled by Constantine, but a democratic Church makes ample sense today. Suenens denies that he is using the term "democracy" in any simple sense, but he does not doubt that the image of the People of God tends in a democratic direction.[103] He maintains

Ikenna U. Okafor (Pickwick, 2020), 27–52; Dennis P. McCann, *New Experiment in Democracy: The Challenge for American Catholicism* (Sheed & Ward, 1987); Thomas P. Rausch, SJ, *Authority and Leadership in the Church: Past Directions and Future Possibilities* (Michael Glazier, 1989); and the essays in *A Democratic Catholic Church: The Reconstruction of Roman Catholicism*, ed. Eugene C. Bianchi and Rosemary Radford Ruether (Crossroad, 1992). McCann proposes that co-responsibility will mean not only structural reform but also a reversal of much of the Church's moral and sacramental teaching. In his "What Catholic Ecclesiology Can Learn from Official Catholic Social Teaching," in *A Democratic Catholic Church*, 94–112, Charles E. Curran takes a similar line: "Classicism tends to think in terms of the eternal, the immutable, and the unchanging, whereas historical consciousness recognizes continuity and discontinuity but gives importance to the particular, the individual, the contingent, and the changing. While classicism employs a deductive approach, historical consciousness sees a greater but not absolute role for inductive reasoning. . . . Catholic social teaching was able to change its approach to freedom, equality, participation, human rights, and democratic forms of government. . . . A more rigorously consistent historically conscious methodology in ecclesiology will share with official Catholic social teaching the importance of freedom, equality, participation, basic human rights, and democratic forms of government" (108–9).

102. Suenens, *Coresponsibility in the Church*, 188.

103. For opposition to democratization of Church structures, see Joseph Ratzinger and Hans Maier, *Demokratie in der Kirche: Möglichen und Grenzen* (Lahn, 2000). With reference to *Demokratie in der Kirche*, Tracey Rowland has discussed Ratzinger's critique of "Karl Rahner's idea of an all-German (or a national) synod of bishops, priests, and lay people, which would be the governing body of the individual national churches, to which the bishops should also be subject." Rowland, "Between the Theory and the Praxis of the Synodal Process," *The Thomist* 87, no. 2 (2023): 233–54, at 247. John C. Cavadini observes that Ratzinger, as Pope Benedict XVI, attempted in two allocutions—in 2009 and 2012, respectively—to reorient the concept of "co-responsibility" in accordance with communion (or Eucharistic) ecclesiology. See Cavadini, "An Antidote to Clericalizing the Laity?," *Church Life Journal*, March 26, 2020, https://churchlifejournal.nd.edu/articles/co-responsibility-is-the-remedy-for-lay-clericalism/; and Cavadini, "Could 'Synodality' Defeat 'Co-Responsibility'?," *The Thomist* 87, no. 2 (2023): 289–309. Cavadini notes that Pope Francis's 2013 apostolic exhortation *Evangelii Gaudium*, in paragraphs 102, 120, and 122 and elsewhere, fits with Pope Benedict's perspective on the responsibilities of the baptized. As Cavadini recognizes, Suenens, too, builds upon Baptism, although as Cavadini says, Suenens "seems completely to ignore the way in which both *Lumen Gentium* and *Presbyterorum Ordinis* locate communion in the Church as ultimately the fruit of the Eucharist, with baptism itself ordered towards the Eucharist" ("Could 'Synodality' Defeat 'Co-Responsibility'?," 299; cf. 300–301). Cavadini shows that Suenens blurs the co-responsibility that flows from

that "the Second Vatican Council certainly was characterized by a move in the direction of 'democratization' because of the accent it placed on the people of God."[104] In making this point, Suenens is careful to clarify that he is not suggesting that doctrine be put to popular vote, nor is he denying the apostolic and thus hierarchical character of the Church of Christ. But the Church as the People of God requires that the gifts of all the people be incorporated. Suenens foretells, "Resolutely utilizing all the charismatic wealth of the people of God, the church will be more authentically than ever before the church of Pentecost."[105] When the Church includes the participatory leadership or co-responsibility of all its members, the People of God will experience a new Pentecost.[106]

Baptism with the co-responsibility that flows from Holy Orders, to the detriment of both. See also, for insight into *Evangelii Gaudium*—and further connections to the perspective represented by Suenens—the volume *Pope Francis and the Future of Catholicism: "Evangelii Gaudium" and the Papal Agenda*, ed. Gerard Mannion (Cambridge University Press, 2017); and see Christoph Theobald, SJ, "L'exhortation apostolique *Evangelii Gaudium*: Esquisse d'une interprétation originale du Concile Vatican II," *Revue théologique de Louvain* 46 (2015): 321–40; Luc Forestier, "Le pape François et la synodalité: *Evangelii gaudium*, nouvelle étape dans la réception de Vatican II," *Nouvelle revue théologique* 137, no. 4 (2015): 597–614; and Dario Vitali, *"Un Popolo in cammino verso Dio": La sinodalità in "Evangelii Gaudium"* (San Paolo, 2018).

104. Suenens, *Coresponsibility in the Church*, 191. He adds that the council tended in a democratic direction because of its understanding of hierarchy as service and because of "its creation of certain organisms within the church which favor democratic methods of government" (191).

105. Suenens, 212.

106. Suenens is a key source of Pope Francis's vision of synodality, as Christopher Ruddy shows in his "Synodality and the Second Vatican Council," *The Thomist* 87, no. 2 (2023): 211–32—although Suenens is not mentioned in Massimo Borghesi's informative *The Mind of Pope Francis: Jorge Mario Bergoglio's Intellectual Journey*, trans. Barry Hudock (Liturgical, 2018). Ruddy directs attention also to Salvador Pié-Ninot, *Eclesiología: La Sacramentalidad de la Comunidad Cristiana*, 3rd ed. (Sígueme, 2006), 565–75, which offers an account of synodality that is deeply indebted to Suenens's book, both directly and through a number of mediating sources. See Giuseppe Alberigo, "Conciliarità, future delle chiese," in *Synod and Synodality: Theology, History, Canon Law and Ecumenism in New Contact*, ed. Alberto Melloni and S. Scatena (LIT Verlag, 2005), 463–88—a volume to which Massimo Faggioli, Ladislas Örsy, Gilles Routhier, and others also contributed; Alberigo, "La sinodalità dopo il Vaticano II," in *Vescovi per la Speranza del mondo*, ed. M. Fabri dos Anjos (EDB, 2004), 99–113; Gilles Routhier, *Le défi de la communion: Une relecture de Vatican II* (Médiaspaul, 1994), which treats synodality at 115–210; Routhier, "Marcher ensemble et vivre la synodalité," in *Précis de Théologie Pratique*, ed. Gilles Routhier and M. Viau (Lumen Vitae, 2004), 637–49; Hervé Legrand, "La sinodalità, dimensione inerente alla vita ecclesiale: Fondamenti e attualità," *Vivens Homo* 15 (2005): 5–42; and M. Rivella, ed., *Partecipazione e corresponsabilità nella Chiesa: I Consigli diocesani e parrochiali* (Àncora, 2000), taking up the path of Archbishop Carlo Martini. See also Pié-Ninot's *La Sinodalitat Eclesial: "L'Església té nom de Sínode"* (Facultat de Teologia de Catalunya, 1993). Ruddy points out, "Authentic synodality depends upon a correct understanding of faith and doctrine. The six dispositions for an authentic participation in the *sensus fidei* outlined in the

Let me briefly mention a second book edited by James Coriden, *The Case for Freedom: Human Rights in the Church* (1969). Again we find the claim that the New Testament lacks a plan for the Church's structure—with the result that the Church in various eras has mirrored the regnant culture. At the outset, Christians understood themselves in terms of the pattern of the synagogue, led by elders or presbyters. The Roman Empire's structures shaped the Constantinian Church. The medieval Church's structure impacted the development of the modern state. The key to finding a good structure, the authors suggest, is to determine whether it upholds Christian freedom. The list of Christian rights that they propose includes freedom to dissent from non-infallibly taught doctrine and "the right to participate, according to their gift from the Spirit, in the teaching, government, and sanctification of the Church."[107] The basic idea is that the hierarchical Church is now undergoing structural change so that the members all enjoy the rights that, at the outset of the Church's life, believers enjoyed. The People of God will be itself again once the laity's liturgical, governing (e.g., through episcopal elections), and prophetic functions are restored. As José Comblin articulates the

ITC's *Sensus fidei in the Life of the Church*—and largely reprised in the ITC's 2018 document on synodality—are effectively absent in the [2021–22] *Preparatory Document*, *Vademecum*, and *Working Document for the Continental Stage*, as well as in recent papal teaching and preaching on the synodal process" (Ruddy, "Synodality and the Second Vatican Council," 227–28). See also Blankenhorn's "The *Sensus Fidei* and Synodality," which also includes the point that "connatural knowledge does not leave behind concept-bound cognition derived from Scripture and Tradition" (333). Ruddy identifies what is at stake: "Synodality must not be conscripted into service as a cover for doctrinal change—likely tacit and gradual at first, 'holding the form of religion but denying the power of it' (2 Tim 3:5)—on matters of human sexuality, sacramental discipline and doctrine, and ordained ministry" (Ruddy, "Synodality and the Second Vatican Council," 231). For further discussion, from a perspective contrasting with that of Ruddy and Blankenhorn (and the ITC), see Jean-François Chiron, "*Sensus fidei* et vision de l'Église chez le pape François," *Recherches de science religieuse* 104, no. 2 (2016): 187–205, arguing that for Pope Francis the "sensus fidei" manifests itself dynamically in dialogue and should not be understood in terms of holding to doctrinal givens. Chiron's essay is cited in Faggioli, *The Liminal Papacy of Pope Francis*, 133. For further discussion, see the special issue on the "Synodale Kirche" in *Internationale Katholische Zeitschrift Communio* 51, no. 4 (2022), which contains essays by eminent figures such as Rowan Williams and Walter Kasper; the volume *La Synodalité: La participation au gouvernement dans l'Église*, ed. E. Corecco (Unesco, 1992); and Jean-Marie R. Tillard, OP, *L'Église locale: Ecclésiologie de communion et catholicité* (Cerf, 1995), 331, 557.

107. "Toward a Declaration of Christian Rights: A Position Paper," in *The Case for Freedom: Human Rights in the Church*, ed. James A. Coriden (Corpus Books, 1969), 5–14, at 13.

basic solution in a 2005 essay—with liberation theology in view, inclusive of liberation from the priestly caste—true Catholic faith "is a matter of recognizing the march of the people of God in our times."[108]

At the height of his theological reputation in 1968, the Canadian Catholic theologian Gregory Baum published a book-length response to Charles Davis's 1967 *A Question of Conscience*, in which Davis (who had been a rising star in the Catholic world) explained his recent, shocking decision to leave the Catholic Church due to its retrograde faith and practice.[109] As a final contribution to this section, let me examine Baum's arguments.

In Baum's view, Davis paradoxically remains constrained by the preconciliar juridical understanding of the Church. According to Baum, Vatican II in fact produced a doctrinal development that he calls "the Open Church." This phrase means that "Church" now names other Christian communities and indeed

108. José Comblin, "The Signs of the Times," trans. Paul Burns, in Melloni and Theobald, *Vatican II: A Forgotten Future*, 73–85, at 83. Comblin explains, "Faith does not consist in intellectual acceptance of specific truths drawn from the Bible. Faith consists in recognizing God's plan, or the coming of the kingdom of God" (83). We recognize this coming when we side with the oppressed. Jesus himself—according to Comblin—identified his fellow (Jewish) believers as oppressed by priests and their wealthy allies. At the council, Comblin says, few understood that the real "signs of the times" (in *Gaudium et Spes*'s phrase) were the need for the liberation of God's people from (among other oppressors) the priestly caste. Comblin directs attention to the work of the (then-)liberation theologian Clodovis Boff, *Sinais dos Tempos: Princípios de Leitura* (Edições Loyola, 1979), a notable work in the development of "signs of the times" theology.

109. See Charles Davis, *A Question of Conscience* (Harper & Row, 1967); and Gregory Baum, *The Credibility of the Church Today: A Reply to Charles Davis* (Herder and Herder, 1968). See also Davis's response to Baum's book: Davis, "A Loving Defense of a Church That Never Was," *National Catholic Reporter,* June 26, 1968, p. 9; as well as, for background, Davis's *Theology for Today* (Sheed and Ward, 1962), in which he exhorts, "We should not be content to ask theology and theologians questions that can be answered by simply turning up the index of a theological manual. . . . We must ask real questions, questions that cannot be met without fresh theological thought" (23–24). Francis Oakley's brief survey of the Davis-Baum exchange, in Oakley's *Council Over Pope? Towards a Provisional Ecclesiology* (Herder and Herder, 1969), is noteworthy because of Oakley's own strong conciliarist viewpoint and his dismay about Pope Paul VI's postconciliar actions. For Oakley, Paul VI's promulgation of *Humanae Vitae* (1968) without consulting the body of bishops, along with Paul VI's Credo (1968) with its inclusion of numerous dogmatic claims (such as Mary's Assumption, papal infallibility, original sin) that Oakley wished to see repudiated, demonstrated that Paul VI failed to implement *Lumen Gentium*'s teaching on collegiality. For analysis of Davis's 1966 repudiation of the Catholic faith, with particular attention to Herbert McCabe, OP's response to Davis and McCabe's own experience of ecclesiastical censure in 1967, see Jay P. Corrin, *Catholic Progressives in England after Vatican II* (University of Notre Dame Press, 2013), chapter 12.

"the entire human race as redeemed by Christ."[110] As such, the Church is hardly the monolithic institution that Davis imagines when he rejects it. As Baum sees it, Vatican II also corrected the Church's understand[illegible]g of the hierarchy. Instead of engaging in top-down teachin[illegible] the hierarchy now should embody what Baum calls "represen[illegible]ive authority" in which the members of the hierarchy "try to [illegible]mulate the convictions the Spirit is producing in the comm[illegible]y and to detect the directions in which the Church is being m[illegible]d by this Spirit."[111]

Baum perceives t[illegible]ituation of the Church in 1968 as being quite fluid. With r[illegible]rd to doctrine and structure, he argues against a "primitivism" [illegible] would tie the Church strictly to a past mode of being Church[illegible] likewise rejects Newmanian views of homogeneous doctrina[illegible]velopment on the grounds that such views are not historicall[illegible]stifiable. Instead, indebted to Schillebeeckx, he proposes tha[illegible]ch epoch engages in the "re-focusing of the Gospel" to fit th[illegible]ew spiritual-cultural climate," while preserving "the unchang[illegible] Gospel."[112] The content of the unchanging Gospel is not p[illegible]ositional but personal: namely, God discloses himself and us, [illegible] this self-disclosure unfolds its meaning in an ongoing dialog[illegible] The "salvation" brought by Christ in every epoch consists in w[illegible]ever serves life and unity.[113]

110. Baum, *The Credibility of [illegible]urch Today*, 27; cf. 47.

111. Baum, 141.

112. Baum, 153–54; cf. 164–[illegible]

113. This is exactly the path c[illegible]sical religious liberalism. For his part, Oakley argues that the Church must accept the fact [illegible] dogmatic statements can and have been contradicted and reversed by later dogmatic stater[illegible], which means that even Church dogmas can be false and can be reversed. On the basis o[illegible]nderstanding of *Haec Sancta*, he states, "The decrees and the ecclesiologies of Constance a[illegible]atican I are in direct conflict one with another—and this despite the fact that both have [illegible] regarded as meeting the requirements for dogmatic validity. What does this mean? . . . It [illegible]ans that the claim to attach infallibility to *particular* conciliar or papal pronouncements m[illegible]imply be dropped" (Oakley, *Council over Pope?*, 176). Oakley then sets forth the implications[illegible] It means, again, that conservatives no longer have to twist or reject the findings of the majori[illegible]f biblical exegetes or to continue to manipulate scriptural texts in order to hold them to con[illegible]rmity with the obvious meaning of conciliar or papal doctrinal pronouncements in the past. . . . It means . . . that theologians, bishops and popes can slough away their obsessive preoccupation with protecting the 'continuity' of papal and conciliar teaching, that no unsurmountable barrier need now divide the Roman Church from the other Christian churches" (176–77). See also *The Crisis of Authority in Catholic Modernity*, ed. Michael

In our day, says Baum, there is much work to be done. Baum states that the work of "re-focusing" or re-envisioning the totality of Christian faith will demand that the whole Church undertake "dialogue, research, [and] reflection."[114] He argues that the late 1960s have produced a new human self-understanding, grounded in listening, dialogue, and re-orientation toward reality. In this situation, the Church's task is to bring to bear the Gospel. He describes the purpose of "the Gospel" as follows: "The Gospel does not offer a ready-made blueprint of the good life. . . . It leaves many moral and intellectual questions unsolved. What the Gospel lays bare are the forces that could destroy man and what it offers as a remedy are the sources that enable a man to become a listener, to enter into dialogue, to be ready for conversion and growth, and to participate in the life of the community."[115] No longer is the Gospel or divine revelation conceived of as a static and impersonal body of truth—"divine teaching on faith and morals."[116] Instead, the Gospel as a liberative dialogue

J. Lacey and Francis Oakley (Oxford University Press, 2011); and *Governance, Accountability, and the Future of the Catholic Church*, ed. Francis Oakley and Bruce Russett (Continuum, 2004). In their "Introduction: How Did We Get Here and Where Do We Go?" to the latter volume (pp. 7–12), Oakley and Russett call for the "assembly of an initial general council and one at which, not only bishops, but also representatives of the lower clergy and laity, women as well as men, would be proudly present and permitted to have their say. Rights to participation in church institutions and procedures are 'fundamental rights of a people both holy and free'" (11).

114. Baum, *The Credibility of the Church Today*, 170.

115. Baum, 185.

116. Baum, 186. Thus, theology must be contextual/experiential rather than doctrinal in its starting points. See the remarks of another leading figure from this period, Bernard J. Cooke: "Traditional theology presumes faith (in the Church, in its teaching authority, in its doctrines) and seeks to deepen it through intelligent reflection. . . . Even today in some circles, the task of theology has been and continues to be much like Anselm's: theology provides explanations and defenses of official Church teaching. The starting point of theological reflection in this system is the doctrinal teaching of popes and the hierarchy. Most modern theologians, however, begin from a different place. Slowly over the last fifty years, a paradigm shift in [Catholic] theological method and outlook has occurred, which stresses shared faith experience and memory as a starting point. . . . Today, theology is not primarily a means of explaining doctrine. It understands itself as a ministry to the intellectual life, mature faith, and informed pastoral practice of the Church." Cooke, "Progressive Approaches to Ministry," in *What's Left? Liberal American Catholics*, ed. Mary Jo Weaver (Indiana University Press, 1999), 135–46, at 144. Cooke directs attention to the essays in *Paradigm Change in Theology*, ed. Hans Küng and David Tracy (Crossroad, 1989).

(with God and with the world) befits the new humanity and the Open Church.

For Baum, the Church as an institution must now change radically. Many Catholics fear such change because there is as yet no rigorous theology of change. But in fact, says Baum, the main principles of this change have already been laid down by Vatican II through its emphasis on dialogue, participation, and co-responsibility in the Church as the People of God. He predicts that, with regard to ecclesiastical structures, "many experiments in social living" will be needed and the Church "will have to develop a greater sense of the provisional."[117]

Baum also presents in some detail what he calls "the third man," neither progressive nor traditionalist. This ideal Catholic sits loose to the teachings of the Church but loves the Church. The "third man" experiences the Church not so much as an institution or society but as "an outer-oriented movement" grounded in the Gospel.[118] Without being a rebel, the "third man" recognizes that the precise teachings of the Church are no longer so important. Baum argues, "As Catholics we accept the Church's teaching, but as we adjust to the new focus of the Gospel, there are many doctrinal positions to which we are, at this time, unable to assign a clear meaning. These doctrinal positions were formulated with a reference to a previous focus. Because the focus has been shifted, these positions no longer make the sense they once did."[119] At present, the future of many previously true (within their own context) doctrines is doubtful. As Baum sees it, the solution will involve thoroughgoing re-interpretation of Catholic doctrine, and this is to be done through "more reflection, more dialogue, more theological research, more vital engagement in Christian life."[120]

117. Baum, 188. Baum does not adopt the sociological path of instituting democratic structures.

118. Baum, 205.

119. Baum, 203.

120. Baum, 203.

Baum's notion of "the Gospel" depends on its relationship to "life," but, as contextual theology shows, this can mean almost anything depending upon a person's or people's situation.[121] Baum assumes that 1968's new understanding of the human being provides a solid foundation upon which to build, rather than presaging further breakdown. The connection between the Church—or the "Open Church"—and any real divine revelation worthy of the name is highly tenuous in Baum's book.[122]

121. See for example Andrew Prevot, *The Mysticism of Ordinary Life: Theology, Philosophy, and Feminism* (Oxford University Press, 2023), 192–93: "[Ada María] Isasi-Díaz develops this intersectional feminist argument by defining *mestizaje* as 'a symbol of Hispanic women's moral truth-praxis.' . . . The hyphenated phrase 'moral truth-praxis' expresses Isasi-Díaz's belief that in order to discern the truth about the common good and to achieve it one must engage in reflective social practices such as 'evaluating existing moral norms of our communities, adapting them, and producing new ones in order to survive.' She does not understand truth to be a cognitive object in an individual's mind but a living process manifest in the bodily acts of interconnected human beings." See Ada María Isasi-Díaz, *En La Lucha/In the Struggle: Elaborating a Mujerista Theology* (Fortress, 2004), 203–5. For background to contextual theology—recently promoted by Pope Francis in his 2023 motu proprio *Ad Theologiam Promovendam*, calling for a "cultural revolution" in Catholic theology to bring about a "fundamentally contextual theology" suited to a synodal Church—see Stephen B. Bevans, SVD, *Models of Contextual Theology*, 2nd ed. (Orbis Books, 2002). Bevans maintains that Scripture is fundamentally a compendium of various contextual theologies, without intrinsic unity; that the tradition of the Church is likewise a set of radically diverse contextual receptions of Scripture's contextual theologies; and that today our task is to recognize that our Catholic theologies, too, are contextual and must be measured, as regards their truth, by their ability to be relevant to the experiences of Catholics in diverse contemporary contexts, with special attention to the experiences of those "in situations of marginality such as among women, people of color, or homosexuals" (7). For a better approach, see Thomas Joseph White, OP, "The Precarity of Wisdom: Modern Dominican Theology, Perspectivalism, and the Tasks of Reconstruction," in *Ressourcement Thomism: Sacred Doctrine, the Sacraments, and the Moral Life*, ed. Reinhard Hütter and Matthew Levering (The Catholic University of America Press, 2010), 92–123.

122. From a broadly similar perspective to Baum's, Edward Schillebeeckx, OP arrived at the conclusion in the 1970s that (in Eric Borgman's words) "what is normative, from the perspective of faith, are not Jesus' words and actions but the relationship between the words and deeds of Jesus on the one hand and their context on the other. Believers here and now are not asked to imitate what Jesus said or did, rather they are to relate to their context as Jesus related to his" (Borgman, "*Gaudium et Spes*: The Forgotten Future of a Revolutionary Document," trans. Natalie K. Watson, in Melloni and Theobald, *Vatican II: A Forgotten Future*, 48–56, at 54). Our "life" is in some way to be correlated to Jesus's "life," as distinct from propositionally knowable revelation to which the Church is accountable and which the Church faithfully preserves and hands down, as *Dei Verbum* affirms. See also, for a similar emphasis on "life" (or "pastorality of doctrine," which allows for rupture in the propositional truth content of a doctrine but not in its "core values" or essential praxis, grounded in the Gospel of divine love), Theobald, "The Theological Options of Vatican II" and Richard Gaillardetz, *An Unfinished Council: Vatican II, Pope Francis, and the Renewal of Catholicism* (Liturgical, 2015), 134–35—both cited in Eduardo Echeverria, "Saint Vincent of Lerins and the Development of Christian Doctrine," in *The Faith Once for All Delivered: Doctrinal Authority in Catholic Theology*, ed. Kevin L. Flannery, SJ (Emmaus Academic, 2023), 171–98, at 184–85.

Regarding the Church's hierarchical structures, Baum thinks they will be re-envisioned, although they may continue for a period. Henceforth, the purpose of the hierarchy will be to work toward "the establishment and formulation of consensus."[123] Baum looks forward to the coming Church in which the ministers will no longer conceive of power in a juridical fashion as power to command. Instead, in this new, law-free religious world, "the people will associate themselves in the movement freely and responsibly, as they decide in the Spirit."[124] The fact that the Church is even now becoming a movement, says Baum, "will eventually demand an adaptation of the Church's sacramental and collegial structure," but what this adaptation will look like does not need to be decided yet.[125] Regarding the Church's mission, Baum presumes that evangelization is no longer about salvation from eternal damnation, but instead can only now be about helping "the redemptive presence of God among people to triumph in terms of unity, reconciliation, social justice, and peace."[126] Although Baum does not focus on the image of the People of God—instead preferring to speak about the brotherhood of man or the unity of the human family—the core content that other postconciliar

123. Baum, *The Credibility of the Church Today*, 206.

124. Baum, 207.

125. Baum, 207. See also Gerald A. Arbuckle, *Refounding the Church: Dissent for Leadership* (Orbis Books, 1993). I agree with Baum when he writes, "I do not think it would be desirable to have a Church that is a spiritual republic in which all members are involved in policy-making and the perfection of the ecclesiastical organization. In such a situation every Christian would be involved in ecclesiastical life—he would spend much of his time and ingenuity in making decisions regarding the organizational life of the Church" (Baum, *The Credibility of the Church Today*, 195).

126. Baum, 198. Baum similarly observes, "Faith means to believe that evil is not the only force at work in the human situation. The Good News is that God is graciously present to human life. Wherever people are they are summoned to enter more deeply into their humanity; wherever people are they are called to move forward to their destiny. This is the message of Jesus" (16–17; cf. 13). See also Metz, *Theology of the World*, 16: "A theologian who thinks historically will not so readily accept the imputation that the modern process of secularization is, in essence, unchristian. . . . The 'spirit' of Christianity is permanently embedded in the 'flesh' of world history and must maintain and prove itself in the irreversible course of the latter." Metz does not deny the power of sin or the cross as a sign of contradiction, but he argues that once Christians understand that Christ has accepted the world in its own integrity as world (as "secular"), Christians will be able to learn much from the world.

thinkers such as Suenens associate with this image is fully present in Baum's work.[127]

In short, the image of the People of God, in its postconciliar Catholic form, took on anthropocentric and democratic implications that were not present in the biblical or conciliar image of God's People. Many of the most influential Catholic theologians of the postconciliar period, responsible for shaping academic trends around the world, adopted this perspective. Today, People-of-God ecclesiology needs renewing by re-introducing the biblical image and its understanding of God, Christ, and the fallen but redeemed members of God's People—along lines that will complement and enrich the vision of *Lumen Gentium*.

V. EPHRAIM RADNER ON THE PEOPLE OF GOD

Let me now turn to the alternative provided by the work of Ephraim Radner. His Anglican ecclesiology—which has recently been the subject of Amy Erickson's *Ephraim Radner, Hosean Wilderness, and the Church in the Post-Christendom West*—exhibits in a sophisticated theological manner a number of the core elements of the biblical image of the People of God.[128] In this section, I discuss relevant portions of four of Radner's books: *A Time to Keep* (2016), *A Profound Ignorance* (2019), *A Brutal Unity* (2012), and *Church* (2017). The first two books examine the human condition, or more specifically the condition of Christians in the world today. They offer a biblically and anthropologically informed diagnosis of our condition that has significant bearing upon the Church understood as the People of God. The final two books are explicitly ecclesiological. *A Brutal Unity* addresses the divided and sinful Church that nevertheless may receive, in repentance,

127. See also Baum's *New Horizon: Theological Essays* (Paulist, 1972). Although Baum credits his perspective on Christianity to the insights of Maurice Blondel—whose insights he considers foundational for Vatican II—in my view he owes more to Alfred Loisy.

128. See Amy J. Erickson, *Ephraim Radner, Hosean Wilderness, and the Church in the Post-Christendom West: A Dialogue on the Shape of Waiting* (Brill, 2020).

the gifts of unity and holiness. *Church* centers around the image of the People of God in connection with the people of Israel. My suggestion is that, when taken together, these four books help to illumine what it means for the Church to be a "people" that is "God's," under the fallen conditions of the present life. Radner connects the image of the People of God with its deepest meanings, including election, sin, death, vulnerability, redemption, sanctification, Israel and the Church, the new exodus, and redemptive suffering.

Radner's A Time to Keep

The focus of *A Time to Keep* is the human (Christian) situation after the nineteenth century's extraordinary increase in human lifespan, at least in countries that have modern education, medicine, and technology. According to Radner, the result of the change in lifespan has been a forgetfulness of or dissociation from our need for the power of the cross. We are now often able to conceal our creatureliness from ourselves, so that we no longer feel so radically dependent upon God and no longer fully appreciate the miracle of life, its character as a sheer divine gift. Life's greatest miracle is self-giving love in the context of sharp mortal limits; and this fact points us to the cross as the source of life for God's People, inasmuch as Christ gives up his life to God in love. As Radner says, "To the one who gives life, all that the creature can offer is some measure of that life. . . . It is a 'life' that is bound to this kind of service, bound and bowed, 'decreasing' that the life giver in his mercy might 'increase' (John 3:30)."[129]

Our need for the cross is even more evident, Radner suggests, when a consideration of the deeper impulses of our nature alerts us to our fallenness as a people, despite the veneer of optimistic technological civilization. Radner examines Sigmund Freud's

129. Ephraim Radner, *A Time to Keep: Theology, Mortality, and the Shape of a Human Life* (Baylor University Press, 2016), 35.

view that our repressed sexual desires indicate that "human beings are driven by things that are frightening and violent."[130] Freud perceived that our self-knowledge is weak and that we harbor impulses that easily lead to anti-social behavior. As a result, the orderliness of civilization cannot be taken for granted—as Freud knew experientially due to living through World War I. God's People, in our fallen humanness, have the capacity as individuals and as communities to commit terrible wrongs.

When we look closely, we also perceive the murky channels and costly consequences of our fierce will-to-live. The result is not wholly negative, however, because we thereby perceive anew our "vulnerable givenness," our closeness to death.[131] We discover how much our lives are not our own; our lives are deeply integrated in those of others. Individuals are inevitably part of a people, though a people marked by highly troubling tendencies toward (and acts of) sin. Nevertheless, we discover not only our lack of goodness but, even more fundamentally, God's goodness or God's gifting. There is something very good about God's People, grounded in the goodness of God.

Reflecting upon the temptation to despair and to commit suicide, a temptation with which he himself has struggled, Radner explores "life" through the work of Michel Henry, including life's grounding in (divine) Life, and he explores "givenness" through the work of Jean-Luc Marion. He concludes that suicide, objectively speaking, is a form of blasphemy. If we are a people—and we are—we are a people *of God*, constituted by radical divine gift, which we must embrace, share, and celebrate through our own gifting to others (above all God). For Radner, then, "mortal creaturehood is defined by its generative and ramifying context and responsibilities."[132] We are inscribed in a wide array of sets

130. Radner, 45.
131. Radner, 48.
132. Radner, 75.

of relations, which suicide attempts to deny and destroy. We are created to be the People of our Creator.

A Time to Keep underscores that we are not morally good individuals whose death is far off. Rather, we are sinners who are profoundly vulnerable to death, and our lives are inscribed in sets of relations that entail our belonging to a people. In this light, says Radner, redemption through the cross and incorporation into the cross as God's People make sense. The cross is at the center of our Peoplehood, which is not a matter of claiming our power or of resisting hierarchy, but rather is about following the crucified Lord of Israel on the ascent of the new exodus.[133]

Radner's A Profound Ignorance

Radner deepens this point pneumatologically in *A Profound Ignorance*. A crucial concern of his is that in modern times, the study of the Holy Spirit has not sufficiently allowed for the fallenness of the world. He argues that modern "pneumatology" has led Christians to suppose that "the world 'as it is,' as a creation by God in all its intrinsic moral limits, is without hope unless and until it is left behind."[134] He has in view the world of finitude, filled with suffering, with physical limitations, and with various barriers that prevent us from achieving or attaining what we wish we could. Radner puts his main concern another way: "The Holy Spirit does not resolve the world as it is."[135] As is all too evident, our

133. Attention to this point helps keep Christianity from being instrumentalized. Karl Rahner, SJ, describes such instrumentalization in his "Christianity and Ideology," where he discusses "the historical fact that Christianity has actually often been misused, sometimes for revolutionary purposes, but, for the most part in conservative, reactionary ways as a means of justifying a social, economic, political, cultural, or scientific condition, which can claim no permanent reality. To be sure, such a misuse of Christianity is difficult to avoid and for the most part is only overcome gradually by the slow processes of history, but where such a misuse has been made, Christianity is indeed changed into an ideology." "Christianity and Ideology," in *The Church and the World* (*Concilium* 6), 41–58, at 44–45. Rahner has in view conservative-reactionary misuse. But the other extreme of religiously liberal misuse was on the Catholic horizon in 1965.

134. Ephraim Radner, *A Profound Ignorance: Modern Pneumatology and Its Anti-Modern Redemption* (Baylor University Press, 2019), 7.

135. Radner, 7.

lives continue to be marked by the limits and pain of this finite and fallen world. Since this is so, the task of theologians is not to create utopias, but rather is to be attuned to the real "character of human life," to "the hard and opaque work of bodily existence."[136] While he accepts that death as we experience it is caused by sin, his point is that redemption does not "do away with sin and its effects."[137] The kind of life that Christians lead is a *mortal* life that is filled with sufferings, struggles, limitations, and disappointments, and that ends when "we physically die and lose all."[138]

Insightfully, Radner contrasts this realism with modern pneumatology's frequent focus upon experiences of liberation from our limits and struggles. Modern pneumatology, he argues, has generated "the Pneumatic Human Being."[139] Advocates of this (false) "Pneumatic Human Being" hold that the Spirit's presence and salvific activity will be empirically measurable. On this view, the Spirit-filled person will always demonstrably manifest an increasing sanctification and perfection. Advocates of this optimistic pneumatology, in Radner's reading, include George Fox and John Wesley, who are joined by secularized forms of the same pneumatology in such figures as Ralph Waldo Emerson and Walt Whitman.

Thus, according to modern pneumatology, the spread of the Gospel necessarily results in measurable, visible spiritual transformation of God's People. Christians will experience in themselves a strong assurance of salvation due to the evident, transformative work of the Spirit in them. Whole societies will be transformed and will manifest the Gospel's world-changing power, as the kingdom comes ever closer. In John Wesley, Radner finds this view joined to various treatises on health: "Making use of the 'world soul' of electricity and special rubs and disciplines, Wesley

136. Radner, 9. See also Radner's *Mortal Goods: Reimagining Christian Political Duty* (Baker Academic, 2024).

137. Radner, *A Profound Ignorance*, 9.

138. Radner, 9.

139. Radner, 10.

believed that the physical form of human creatures can be responsibly pressed into the beneficent current of divine power. Human beings are perfectible, deeply in the spirit, more superficially (but significantly) in the body."[140]

Radner's argument is that such a vision of the Spirit's work is not realistic. He denies that "everything can be fixed—if not immediately, very soon."[141] He much prefers Charles Wesley's emphasis on ongoing suffering and struggle, because he finds here the real (rather than idealized) People of God. As he sharpens his critique of the Pneumatic Human Being, Radner examines various responses to World War I, comparing descriptions of heroic and noble martyrs, on the one hand, with descriptions of the actual suffering, on the other. The Great Litany of the Church of England's Book of Common Prayer provides Radner with an alternative to modern pneumatology. Aware of the existential threats that we experience, the Great Litany invites us to pray to God *from within* those threats rather than assuming that God is present solely in erasing the threats. Radner comments that in the Great Litany, "God is *bound up with* the limits to our lives—including suffering, disease, violence, and death. God's grace is given *within* and through these realities, not simply over and against them."[142]

Radner observes that the Great Litany begs God for ongoing deliverance from vices, as well as from physical diseases. The Litany carries forward what Radner deems to be a medieval realism about the world as inhabited by Christians. The world is strange and dangerous, a place of mystery and struggle, even if also of joy. God's People encounter God most fully in Jesus at Gethsemane and on the cross, where Jesus struggles with sorrow, suffering, abandonment, and death due to our sins. Radner states, "Our need is the place God acts, not only by eliminating the hard forms

140. Radner, 138.
141. Radner, 137.
142. Radner, 168.

of our lives, but by somehow communicating mercy just there."[143] The Spirit does not spare us from the experience of death or illness, but the Spirit makes it bearable; the Spirit does not spare us from struggle with vices, but enables us not to despair.

On this basis, Radner expresses doubt that the People of God—Christians—can be empirically identified due to the Spirit's work in them. He considers this to be a triumphalism that does not connect with real Christian life, since Christians, too, experience profound struggles and not only physical ones. His opponents are Wesleyans, Pentecostals, and Catholic charismatics. But these perspectives represent a much broader current. The Spirit-filled Church imagined by Romantic ecclesiology, he argues, must be visibly marked by liberation and fullness of life. The evolutionary spiritualization of the world, due to the Spirit, characterized Pierre Teilhard de Chardin's writings, which were enormously influential from the 1940s onward.[144] Such perspectives claim that the Spirit transforms our world in a manner that, in fact, the Spirit *does not do*. The claim that new modes of power-sharing will result in a new Pentecost for the People of God is, I note, deeply suspect from this perspective.

As an example of a better twentieth-century path, Radner turns to the German Jesuit Alfred Delp, martyred for his anti-Nazi activities. Delp's spiritual vision had its roots in devotion to the Sacred Heart. Thus, Delp did not allow the Spirit to float free from Christ's cross or from embodied struggle and

143. Radner, 173.

144. For further background, discussing the portrait of Teilhard found in Jacques Maritain's *The Peasant of the Garonne: An Old Layman Questions Himself about the Present Time*, trans. Michael Cuddihy and Elizabeth Hughes (Holt, Rinehart and Winston, 1968), see Corrin, *Catholic Progressives in England After Vatican II*, 351. Corrin's book offers a fascinating portrait of the Catholic Church in England from the late 1950s through the early 1970s, demonstrating "the increasing radicalism that swept the Catholic community by the late 1960s" (168) and that made preconciliar liberal Catholicism look conservative, due to the postconciliar theological demands related to the sexual revolution and to democratization in the Church (as well as to Marxism). Corrin, however, sees the pontificate of John Paul II as a dark period in which *First Things* and other groups, "along with the revival of conservative forces in the Roman Curia, helped to reimpose the centralized and authoritarian tendencies of an earlier brand of Catholicism" (378).

death. Radner also has positive words for Adolphe Tanquerey's neo-scholastic manual on ascetical theology (or spirituality), which tightly links the Spirit's work with Christ's own life and especially with Christ's sacrificial suffering and death on the cross.[145] The domain of suffering and struggle does not become transfigured by life in the Spirit; instead, the Spirit makes our suffering and struggle redemptive, by joining it to the cross. Dietrich Bonhoeffer, too, insists upon the Spirit's work precisely in our pain, rather than imagining the Spirit delivering us from pain. Christ had the Spirit in full, but Christ sorrowed far more profoundly than any of us can.

Radner's purpose in making these arguments is to insist upon attention to concrete human life, with its reality of struggle, suffering, confusion, and brokenness. He wants to emphasize the troubles of mortal flesh, whose pain-filled experience the outpouring of the Spirit does not resolve. The Spirit meets us in our limitations and even our foulness—a point that Radner finds highlighted by Paul and by Tertullian. By contrast, he argues that the Scholastic tying of the Spirit to virtues and gifts (and so on) in a systematic fashion led eventually, even if not perhaps inevitably, to the Spirit's separation from the embodied suffering and struggle of Christ.[146] In his view, our bodies are united to Christ's body by the Spirit, and this reality can be described in terms of virtues and gifts. But he argues that *habitus* and *motus*, virtues and gifts, must be held together rather than distinguished too firmly, lest a

145. See Adolphe Tanquerey, SS, *The Spiritual Life: A Treatise on Ascetical and Mystical Theology*, trans. Herman Branderis, SS (Desclée, 1930).

146. Although this is a good warning, I do not think it corresponds to the actual development of Scholastic and Thomistic ascetical and moral theology, as found in John of the Cross, Teresa of Avila, and Francis de Sales through Adolphe Tanquerey and Réginald Garrigou-Lagrange—deeply attuned to redemptive suffering and trials, even while affirming the presence of a foretaste of eternal life and the possibility of spiritual growth. Yet, Radner's warning fits with the tendencies of some contemporary Thomistic virtue theory, with its celebration of the infused virtues, gifts of the Spirit, and the beatitudes, and its neglect of the ongoing reality of sins, vices, and profound struggle.

clear "framework of progress, demand, and achievement" result in a neglect of the actual reality of embodied life.[147]

For Radner, the sanctification of the People of God is to be found not in theories of the Spirit's work, but in cleaving to Christ's embodied suffering on the cross, to the Spirit's meeting us in the very midst of suffering and death from which the Spirit does not liberate us. What this means for our interior sanctification is something that we cannot judge. Only God knows the heart. Even the person cannot see his or her own heart clearly. The bottom line is that we must avoid constructing "projections of unrealized and unrealizable desires," and we must not deem "normal life" unworthy of God's presence.[148] Yet when this is understood, we do find sanctification in the Church. A Church of patient endurance, united in the Spirit to Christ's patient endurance, will manifest its goodness to the world. Radner states that the "pneumatic fruits" in such a Church "include patience, joy, gentleness, self-control, just as they are founded upon or shaped by a stark Christological obedience, which . . . is determined by a final bodily self-sacrifice."[149]

Obedience in the Spirit produces configuration to and union with Jesus's body. Believers draw close to Christ in a self-gift that "is bound up with the Spirit's gifts and fruits enacted in the complex and underdetermined morass of discernment and uncertainties."[150] In those who draw close to Jesus's suffering and mortal body, Radner finds an enactment of "openness, extravagance, generosity, spontaneity."[151] Mutual subjection is another crucial element, as are bearing others' burdens, avoiding discord or a disputatious spirit, and offering forgiveness and love to others. These are signs of the Spirit's presence and activity in the People of God. The key is that none of these elements neglect or seek to

147. Radner, *A Profound Ignorance*, 230.

148. Radner, 281.

149. Radner, 286.

150. Radner, 286.

151. Radner, 287.

transcend "the Spirit's mysterious ordering of our actual bodies in time—their coming-to-be, growth, burdens, generative strivings, suffering, weakening, and death."[152] Bodiliness is the matrix of Spirit-filled life, because Jesus's body is the source and goal of such life. As Radner says, "All the limitations of human creatureliness are thus, in their intractable obscurities and faithful self-offerings, the basis for the unimaginable risk of obedience. . . . While the martyr's body stands as that risk's pneumatic attestation, the risk and its pneumatic center partake of the inscrutable character of created life itself."[153]

In the end, then, it does seem that for Radner the People of God will be, as *Lumen Gentium* contends, truly sanctified and even "holy"—so long as one is looking for the right thing. The People of God will manifest "Christian self-offering."[154] God's People will do so in ways that accept bodily limitations, sufferings, and struggles, rather than supposing the Spirit removes such troubles. Put simply, the cross cannot be bypassed; it is the true politics of the Church. God's People have hoped that the Spirit will relieve them of the cross, rather than pressing them ever closer to the cross in their own bodies. God's People today have abandoned the power of the cross, have abandoned the task of glorifying God in the flesh. Radner diagnoses this ecclesial failure while reassuring us that sanctification—even if it may be hidden and unmeasurable by the metrics of the world—is still possible, because God in Christ crucified is faithful to his Church.

Radner's A Brutal Unity

Radner considers that modern Christians have suppressed sin and death, neglected the cross, and imagined the Spirit along lines that no longer allow for real suffering and struggle but instead

152. Radner, 280.
153. Radner, 281.
154. Radner, 281.

insist upon an illusory ideal. This rebellion against Christ and the Spirit has resulted in a deeply wounded Church. *A Brutal Unity* discusses this wounding. In this book, Radner offers a powerful account of "the woefulness of Christian witness in this world" and of "the Church's life of disordered failure."[155] Radner strips away any temptation toward triumphalism on the part of those who have been constituted as God's People.

Divided Christians, he notes in *A Brutal Unity*, insist that their own communities are in fact the one Church, against all others. Divided Christians do so both in order to forget the divisions that besmirch Christianity and in order to continue fighting their fellow Christians. Furthermore, Christian violence is more than intramural. Radner shows that Christians have been deeply implicated in violence undertaken on religious or quasi-religious grounds. The Rwandan genocide, which was committed by Catholics, is an example. Although the Catholic Church long favored the Tutsis, in the twentieth century many younger Catholic missionaries turned toward the Hutus. The Hutu rule that took hold in the 1950s was mirrored by the Catholic Church's installation of a Hutu bishop with authority over Tutsi priests. Radner points to "anti-Tutsi propaganda" that described Tutsi "dominance as 'Old Testament,'" in need of Hutu supersession.[156] Even worse than the Hutu government's appropriation of Catholic propaganda was the uselessness of the postconciliar Catholic Church in preventing the genocide.

Turning to the Reformation era, Radner remarks that Catholics in Paris heard sermons denouncing Protestants in the years leading up to the St. Bartholomew's Day Massacre. Catholics then carried out these sermons by attempting to rid France of heretics by murdering the Protestants. Radner adduces numerous shameful details, such as the fact that "papal masses of thanksgiving

155. Ephraim Radner, *A Brutal Unity: The Spiritual Politics of the Christian Church* (Baylor University Press, 2012), 2.

156. Radner, 36.

for the slaughter, along with commemorative medals and murals . . . , joined a throng of celebrative material, even as the hatred of Protestants was stoked and expressed in the most scripturally vivid of terms."[157] It is evident that this was religiously motivated violence, even if it had other motivations as well. Profoundly religious Catholics participated in the violence, and prominent Catholics defended and applauded it. Such religious violence, Radner believes, caused disgusted French Catholics later to shift toward favoring a non-doctrinal religion, a response that Radner repudiates. Likewise, Cromwell's Puritan wars were fought by people with religious motivations. In response, during the next century, English society sought religious toleration and showed much less concern about doctrinal differences—although wars, of course, did not cease.

Similarly, Christian vilification of Jews has a very long history. Radner tells some of it. For instance, discussing anti-Semitism in the nineteenth and twentieth centuries, Radner makes clear that Nazi anti-Semitism's "coherence with earlier theological categories and their coincidence within ecclesial networks of communication meant that [Nazi] novelty was easily assimilated into [anti-Semitic] tradition through dynamics of ecclesial order."[158] Pogroms, persecution, and inflammatory rhetoric against Jews were widely supported by Christian leaders in the nineteenth century and, of course, for centuries earlier. Christian kings, with the support of the Catholic Church, all too frequently expelled the

157. Radner, 46–47.

158. Radner, 94–95. For more details, see some of the sources cited in my *Engaging the Doctrine of Israel: A Christian Israelology in Dialogue with Ongoing Judaism* (Cascade, 2021). The effort to dissociate earlier Christian anti-Judaism from nineteenth-century anti-Semitism is, as Radner would expect, not very persuasive, as can be seen in Irven M. Resnick, *Marks of Distinction: Christian Perceptions of Jews in the High Middle Ages* (The Catholic University of America Press, 2022). Neither Radner nor I aim to depict Jews solely as passive victims: on this topic see Elliott Horowitz, *Reckless Rites: Purim and the Legacy of Jewish Violence* (Princeton University Press, 2008). Jacques Maritain states, "The conduct of the Holy See with regard to the Jews has varied with the epochs. The Popes, even the ones most severe in their legislation, never knew this hatred. They knew how to read St. Paul without making him say the contrary of what he wrote." Maritain, *On the Church of Christ: The Person of the Church and Her Personnel*, trans. Joseph W. Evans (University of Notre Dame Press, 1973), 167. This seems an exaggeration of the popes' beneficence, unfortunately.

Jews living in their domains. Christian leaders often, though certainly not always, showed little concern for Jews as human beings.

In *A Brutal Unity*, Radner speaks of the Church as a "person" rather than as a "people." Grounded in the biblical fact that "Israel" was the name given by God to the patriarch Jacob, the idea of the corporate personality of the Church strikes Radner as valuable. As he points out, Mary serves as a figure of the Church for Catholics, but he considers that Catholic Mariology separates her from the "historical forms of human life" (for example, sinfulness) that Christ came to redeem.[159] Karl Rahner compared the Church figurally to Mary Magdalene. Peter—as distinct from the Petrine office—can also serve as a figure of the Church. For Radner, the important thing is that whatever figure we choose for the Church, the figure must personify the Church in a manner that does not hide the sins of the Church. If the Church is a "person," the Church cannot claim to be an innocent person. The People of God cannot rightly claim to be innocent.

I affirm the holiness and unity of the Church, as I discuss in dialogue with Radner's *A Brutal Unity* in my *Engaging the Doctrine of the Holy Spirit*. But Radner's realism ensures that one cannot delude oneself into thinking that if the Church makes structural changes, the kingdom will be in reach and the ideal community of Acts 2 will flower into being. The Spirit does not work in this way.

Radner's Church

In *Church*, Radner sets forth a strong People-of-God ecclesiology, while anticipating or drawing upon many of the insights of his books surveyed above. He observes that all Christian ecclesiologies begin with a notion of a true Church grounded in God's action and in the biblical witness: "God gathers a people; they are

159. Radner, *A Brutal Unity*, 161.

God's people; and Scripture tells us what that means."[160] Because of Scripture's emphasis on God's gathering a people—whether Israel or the reconfigured Israel gathered by Christ—Radner contends that "the clearest way to engage the Church is through the human reality of peoplehood."[161]

God establishes his People first and foremost through election and covenant, which make Israel to be a corporate "person." More broadly, God makes peoples, in the sense that "peoples are . . . the divinely given form of experienced history."[162] To be created by God, for human beings, means to be more than individuals. Israel, then, receives from God an exalted place among the peoples or nations. In Christ, the Church is the messianic Israel, "a divinely shaped people."[163]

Yet, as Radner says, this talk of the Church as God's particular People may seem too abstract, as opposed to defining the Church in terms of local practices. It also may seem indebted to Enlightenment and Romantic ideas about nations and races, each with its own "character or destiny."[164] Rather than exalting a people or nation separated from other peoples and nations, it might be better to valorize the whole human community. Biblically speaking, however, it is impossible to do without peoples or nations. Even when nations in the Bible are wicked, they are linked with particular peoples.

The Church is comprised of many individuals in many places, and so identifying its "singular reality" can be difficult. Radner appreciatively examines Bonhoeffer's efforts to do so, focusing upon Christ as the New Adam and upon existence "in Christ." The corporate person of the Church is ultimately Christ, as Christ (in his human members) proceeds through history. Radner also contends that peoples or nations correspond to

160. Ephraim Radner, *Church* (Cascade, 2017), 64.

161. Radner, 65.

162. Radner, 72.

163. Radner, 73.

164. Radner, 73.

God's command in Genesis to be fruitful and multiply and to fill the earth—something that comes to fulfillment in Christ. The Church unites all peoples or nations in Christ, while standing as a "nation for the nations."[165] The nations come forth from Adam's side, and the Church comes forth from the New Adam's side. In the New Adam, the (Gentile) nations are called to join Jews in worshipping God.

Radner defines the Church as "a people in the process of being peopled and peopling in the life of Christ."[166] Sent to the nations, the apostles bear witness to them about Christ, while baptizing them in the Trinitarian name. Well before Christ, the prophets of Israel had recognized the existence of a God-given Jewish mission to the nations that would convert the nations to the worship of the true God. The prophet Amos also describes Israel in relation to the nations as (in Radner's words) "one nation among many, liable to the same judgments from God."[167] This is a dimension that Radner highlights with respect to the Church. He notes that some theologians have mistakenly thought that the Church was no nation, and therefore they imagined that the Church could not fall under judgment as nations do.

The Church can imagine itself to have replaced Israel and therefore to lack the national identity that Israel has, but Radner argues that Israel's way of relating to the nations should be the Church's. In fact, for Radner, the Church is precisely *how* Israel is "for the nations."[168] The Church overcomes national divisions while being distinctive itself. Radner hearkens back to the story of Babel, where God scattered the one human community into many, separated by languages. In Christ, Babel's oppositions are intended to be resolved. Within the Church, diverse peoples are intended to learn to live as one without denying or annulling

165. Radner, 90.

166. Radner, 92.

167. Radner, 96. Radner points to Amos 2:1–5 and Amos 9:7–10.

168. Radner, 99.

their diversity. An example of this diversity consists in the multiplicity of languages and, correspondingly, the possibility of the one Gospel being proclaimed in diverse languages. Radner's vision here is a hopeful one, grounded in Israel's vocation to be a light to the nations. He states, "Chosen among nations by its assumption in the being of Christ, this one nation would lead human particularity away from cacophony into a divine resolution of common praise."[169]

Moving from "nation" back to "people," Radner observes that the mid-twentieth-century ecumenical interest in the Church as the People of God was inspired by a desire to think about the Church in non-institutional, humble, missionary terms. The image of the People of God sought to highlight the people's exodus journey from slavery in Egypt to the Promised Land, empowered by God. The Church was conceived as not a powerful institution but rather as God's eschatological people on the new exodus, pilgrims in the world. According to Joseph Ratzinger, early twentieth-century biblical theology highlighted this image, and Vatican II adopted it because it appeared more historical, or less static, than the image of the Mystical Body. Ratzinger added that the image of a People allows for an easier grasp of the ways in which non-Catholics and non-Christians are related to the Church.[170] Lastly, the image of the People of God emphasizes that Christians are not autonomous self-rulers, but are God's.

Even so, the problems that have beset the image of the People of God are twofold: first, the People can easily be assimilated in believers' imaginations to whatever a particular society or culture wants; and second, a People-of-God ecclesiology can spawn the sense that the people now stand in opposition to the authority and need to claim their power. Radner summarizes Ratzinger's concerns: "From a practical or moral standpoint, when 'people'

169. Radner, 111.

170. Radner cites Joseph Ratzinger, "The Ecclesiology of Vatican II," *Conference of Cardinal Ratzinger at the Opening of the Pastoral Congress of the Diocese of Aversa (Italy)*, September 15, 2001, *L'Osservatore Romano*, weekly edition in English, January 23, 2002, 5.

becomes the focus in the Church's self-understanding, it is too easy for the Church to succumb to the enclosing web of competing human interests and organizations."[171] In Radner's view, however, the benefits outweigh the drawbacks. God has become man; therefore, human nature ("peoplehood") truly has become God's. The Church is indeed a "people" among the peoples, or, better, a people *for the sake of* all peoples. It is not theologically possible, therefore, for the Church to renounce a political task.

Radner notes that the ecumenical movement turned in the 1960s from People-of-God ecclesiology toward "communion ecclesiology," as part of the ecumenical quest for visible sacramental communion and shared witness to the world. The Eucharist receives a central place in communion ecclesiology, as do the intra-Trinitarian relations in which believers share. But for Radner, this ecclesiological model represents a step backward, since its emphasis on "mutuality" and "relationality" (which, after all, are abstractions) has no political weight, and since its goal of shared sacraments and order is not feasible. The decades in which "communion" has dominated ecumenically have been marked, in fact, by new and greater separations. Radner observes that the Father, Son, and Holy Spirit, in their inner life, have no need to do many things that characterize ecclesiastical life (for instance, negotiate, compromise, mend internal divisions), and so divine mutuality does not really provide a model for the Church. He concludes, "To be the Church, one must figure out how to be, and at least submit to being, an actual people."[172]

Yet, although the Church *must* be a people, the People of God is sinful. Contemporary theologians freely acknowledge "Christian division, rancor, and sometimes gross complicity in social suffering and violence."[173] When Christians are seen up close, the

171. Radner, *Church*, 117. For analysis of how this happens (and how it is affecting the Catholic Church today), see Tracey Rowland, *Unconformed to the Age: Essays in Catholic Ecclesiology* (Emmaus Academic, 2024).

172. Radner, *Church*, 121.

173. Radner, 123.

picture is often not pretty. In *Church*, Radner argues that the solution here may be George Lindbeck's idea that the Church should think of itself in terms of Israel. This answer is embedded in Radner's love of figural reading.[174] The idea is to avoid the temptation to "timelessly identify the Church apart from the actual life of Israel, scripturally described."[175] In other words, talk about the Church as *a* People must be subordinated to its figural identification with *this* people—namely, Israel. The timeless identification of the Church as "one, holy, catholic, and apostolic" does not reckon adequately with failure, in Radner's view. If the Church is figuratively identified with Israel, then we do not have to defend it, but rather we have to participate in its historical journey, notwithstanding its failures. Just as worship, trust in God, teaching, scriptural proclamation, and the moral life mattered for Israel, so must they matter for the Church. The Church lives Israel's vocation for the nations. The one people (Israel/Church) is dispersed among the nations and called to bear witness to the living God and to do the works of mercy.

The Church must struggle politically in order to be faithful to this call rather than merely assimilating to the nations. Just as Israel failed, sinned terribly, endured punishment, and repented and experienced renewal, so has the Church over the course of the centuries. As the New Israel, the Church does not need to conceal these sins but instead simply needs to repent for them and turn again to the Lord. The Church can be Israel—God's one, holy people by God's faithful covenantal election—and yet, at the same time, the Church can be neither one nor holy empirically speaking, just as Israel itself was rent apart by sin.

On this basis, Radner returns to his definition of the Church as a people, expanding it somewhat: "The Church is a people,

174. See Lindbeck, *The Church in a Postliberal Age*, chapter 1; and see Ephraim Radner, *Time and the Word: Figural Reading of the Christian Scriptures* (Eerdmans, 2016); *All Thy Lights Combine: Figural Reading in the Anglican Tradition*, ed. Ephraim Radner and David Ney (Lexham, 2022).

175. Radner, *Church*, 124.

a nation of a certain kind, that exists on behalf of all nations in their distinctive kinds, and for their multiplied reconciliation."[176] Here, his emphasis is that the nations remain distinct from each other. The Church does not swallow up the nations' distinctiveness, even in gathering them into Christ. Yet, the Church must reconcile the nations. As a matter of historical fact, the Church has not done so.

The first and most consequential unreconciled division is that between Jew and Gentile. Radner argues that this division came about when the Church began (as it quickly did) to envision itself as a Gentile reality. This is Lindbeck's argument as well: the Church gradually separated itself from Israel in its self-understanding.[177] The result was that "Israel" became simply a spiritual figure, or something from the biblical past, rather than being a concrete reality with an actual historical life as "Church." Old and New Testaments were thereby bifurcated. The Gentile Church looked upon the Jews as alien. Supposedly, the Jews were carnal and of the past, while the Gentile Christians were spiritual and of the present. The Gentile Church did not see itself as a historical people in the way that Israel did; instead, the "Church" was an idealized reality in its own self-understanding, or else the Church in a particular nation became fully assimilated to the nation's interests, betraying Christ in the process.[178] The Gentile Church became poisoned by the terrible sin of anti-Semitism.

If the solution is to understand the Church as the People of God and the messianic Israel, what does this mean for Christians' relation to the Jewish people? Radner rejects the idea that the Church should no longer offer the Gospel to Jews, as though the Church and the Gospel were meant to be solely for the Gentiles. Nevertheless, it is evident to Radner that "the statement 'the

176. Radner, 125.

177. See Shaun C. Brown, *George Lindbeck and The Israel of God: Scripture, Ecclesiology, and Ecumenism* (Palgrave Macmillan, 2021).

178. Radner, *Church*, 134.

Church is Israel' somehow needs to take into account the fact that the Israel that is made up of Jews is not self-evidently a part of the Christian Church in experiential terms, and that Christians (Jewish and Gentile in national origin) and Jews are clearly two distinct groups with respect to theological claims and the order of common life before God."[179] Seeking to make progress, Radner notes that some Christians begin by conceiving of "Israel" as one but divided—with a Jewish part and a Gentile Christian part, analogous to the division between Judah and Israel after Solomon. But he resists beginning with sin and division. He is not sure quite how to resolve the problem, but he suggests that conceiving of the Church as Israel "involves a relationship of Jew (believing or non-Christian) and Christian believer (whether Gentile or Jewish) that is ordered *together* to an obedience of God that will finally give rise to a common praise."[180]

I do not agree with all that Radner says in *Church*. To my mind, many of the insights of Vonier and Congar need to be incorporated more fully by Radner; and, of course, Radner is not Catholic, so there are bound to be ecclesiological differences. But his explanation of why the Church must be a People among the peoples—and why any attempt to describe the Church as the People of God must hew closely to the witness of the Old Testament and its realism about God's judgment and the need for the Messiah's work, rather than falling into triumphalist optimism about new modes of power-sharing that are at best loosely related to the apostolic reality—strikes me as not only correct but urgently necessary.

VI. CONCLUSION

Lumen Gentium emphasizes that the People of God receives from Christ and the Spirit a "perfect fidelity" in doctrine—inclusive of

179. Radner, 128.
180. Radner, 130.

the infallibility of the *sensus fidei*—as well as unity and holiness. As *Lumen Gentium* says, the People of God is sanctified through the sacraments, above all Baptism and the Eucharist. The People of God is a "worthy bride" of Christ, constantly being renewed by the Spirit. Christ ensures that the People of God is one. The Spirit makes the members of the People of God to be adoptive sons in the incarnate Son, obeying Christ's new commandment of love. The People of God stands as the "seed" of the human race's ultimate unity. The People of God is constituted by the new covenant in Christ's cross, joining together Jews and Gentiles. There are various modes and degrees of belonging to the People of God, and the unity of the People of God allows for a wide diversity of vocations and cultures.

All these elements are true, and all make clear that the image of the People of God is not merely about the empowerment of the laity but rather possesses an extraordinary Christological and pneumatological richness. Yet, more must be said. Radner instructs us on how to say it. He ponders the way in which Christians are not good, due to deep impulses that can lead to violent and anti-social behavior. He attends to the deep vulnerability to sin and death that characterizes human creaturehood after the fall. From this perspective, he highlights our relationships to others and our need for the self-sacrificial love that Christ enacts. He observes that the Spirit's grace comes to us precisely within our neediness and struggle, which the Spirit does not do away with.

The People of God, then, is one and holy, yet—as Radner emphasizes much more than *Lumen Gentium*—sinful and broken too.[181] As we saw, Radner also makes clear that since the Church

181. See the exposition of the Church's holiness (in relation to sinfulness) in Mansini, *Ecclesiology*, chapter 12. Mansini contrasts the views of Congar and Charles Journet on this topic. As he notes, "Congar distinguishes four senses of the church: the church taken according to the divine principles of faith, the sacraments of faith, and hierarchical power that actively and formally constitute her; the church as the *congregatio fidelium*, the material cause of the church informed by the church taken in the first way; the church of the hierarchy—the churchmen who teach, sanctify, and govern; church as the synthesis of the foregoing three aspects. In the first sense, the church is infallible and cannot sin. . . . If 'church' means the assembly of the baptized faithful, however, the church sins. . . . In the third sense, the church of churchmen, the church

has a historical life, the Church must be a people. And since the Church is the messianically reconfigured Israel, the Church must be the People of God, gathered by God for divine praise and for the reconciliation of the peoples or nations of the world. Division remains, however; and this is nowhere clearer than in the division and enmity between Christians and Jews. Radner perceives that the existence of such divisions means that the People of God must be a repentant people, continually calling out for the salvation that comes from the cross, even while living in the light of the Resurrection and the promise of Christ's glorious coming.

Further attention to the biblical theme of the new exodus may enrich the emphases of both *Lumen Gentium* and Radner regarding the Church as the People of God. The Catholic biblical scholar Brant Pitre has argued on historical-critical grounds that it is likely that "Jesus saw himself as both the new and greater Mosaic prophet and the heavenly Son of Man from the book of Daniel, whose coming would bring about a new exodus, the final unleashing of the heavenly kingdom of God in this world, and the ingathering of the new Israel."[182] Here and now, the People of God is on the new exodus journey. While still suffering with Christ, the People is already also sharing in his arrival at the glorious right hand of the Father. As Benoît-Dominique de La Soujeole says, "The theme of the People of God allows one to underscore properly the progressive character of the manifestation of the ecclesial mystery in time as the Church marches toward her eschatological end."[183] The Church does so as a hierarchical people, with

is sinful, just insofar as hierarchs, even in the acts of their official capacity, are vain, rash, violent, and unjust" (234–35).

182. Brant Pitre, *Jesus and the Last Supper* (Eerdmans, 2015), 515. See also Richard Ounsworth, OP, *Joshua Typology in the New Testament* (Mohr Siebeck, 2012), 175.

183. De La Soujeole, *Introduction to the Mystery of the Church*, 200. He adds, "This is the perspective of final causality, eternal beatitude, which the people of God theme expresses well" (200). He goes on to unite the image of the People of God to those of the Mystical Body and the Temple of the Holy Spirit: "The more specifically New Testament themes (Body of Christ and Temple of the Spirit) present the Church along a more 'essential' line (*in facto esse*): what the Church is and does not cease to be in her perfection, which is brought about by the accomplishment of the mission of the Son and the Spirit. The theme of the People of God, because it directly takes up the historical dimension, presents the same Church along a more 'existential'

Christ as Head, and with the apostles and their successors sharing uniquely, though certainly not exclusively, in Christ's roles of prophet, priest, and king.[184]

Moira McQueen represents a widespread view of the People of God and of synodality when she looks forward to equal ecclesiastical voting rights. From this perspective, it is hard to see how anything other than a purely ceremonial hierarchy could serve the People of God, whose progress is here measured by power-sharing and by reassessing divine revelation through new collaborative mechanisms. Reflecting upon her experience at the 2015 synod, McQueen states, "One thing lay people cannot do at synods is vote on the issues. . . . A wise person pointed out that some moves to include lay people further were progressing, perhaps *piano piano*, gently, gently, but still progressing!"[185] In McQueen's work,

line (*in fieri*): what the Church becomes during the time of her earthly pilgrimage. Hence the sequence in which the Constitution *Lumen gentium* presents things is explained. The first thing to be taught is what the Church is, her 'fundamental ontology,' with the accent on her note or mark of unity; this is the subject of the first chapter (mainly paragraphs 7 and 8), with the help of typically New Testament themes, since Christ is the one who gave the community of salvation its essential perfection" (200–201).

184. For "hierarchical" as a negative word, see Moira McQueen, *Walking Together: A Primer on the New Synodality* (Novalis, 2022), 32. See also the alarm bells in José Antonio Ureta and Julio Loredo de Izcue, *The Synodal Process Is a Pandora's Box: 100 Questions and Answers*, trans. José A. Schelini (The Foundation for a Christian Civilization, 2023), which—written prior to the 2023 and 2024 synods—exhibits strong familiarity with the German *Synodaler Weg* and points with concern to *Evangelii Gaudium*'s observation that "a juridical status of episcopal conferences which would see them as subjects of specific attributions, *including genuine doctrinal authority*, has not yet been sufficiently elaborated" (Pope Francis, *Evangelii Gaudium* §32, November 13, 2013, vatican.va; emphasis added). Ureta and Loredo de Izcue express concern that "Cardinal Hollerich was confirmed in the decisive role of relator general of the Synod even after his scandalous statements on the need to change the Church's magisterium on homosexuality" (*The Synodal Process Is a Pandora's Box*, 74).

185. McQueen, 34. She adds, "as the Pope has frequently observed in his teachings, 'Time is greater than space. . . .' The synodal process itself, once begun, is part of the gradual change" (34). In her afterword, she notes that her proposal for lay voting at a Synod of Bishops was not enthusiastically received by most participants at the 2015 Synod, and she reiterates that "I did not mean my proposal as a political statement on the rights of the laity. Rather, I see it as a natural outcome of the concept of synodality, if 'walking together' is to be taken seriously. In no way was the proposal meant to challenge the authority of the bishops or their collegial role in exercising that authority" (59). As she points out, lay voting took place at the Synod on Synodality, as ensured by the appointment of Sister Nathalie Bequart as Under-Secretary at the Secretariat of the Synod. See also Pope Francis's Apostolic Constitution *Episcopalis Communio* (September 15, 2018, vatican.va); and see Salvador Pié-Ninot, *La Sinodalidad como el "Caminar Juntos" en la Iglesia* (Centre de Pastoral Litúrgica, 2021), 45, where (like Pope Francis) he distinguishes between the process of "decision-making" and the action of "decision-taking," the latter of which belongs to the bishops (and the pope). For background, see the account of synods

the phrase "People of God" consistently functions to denote "what the people want," which is linked with the infallibility of the *sensus fidei*. She underscores that "the whole People of God . . . must be consulted on important matters. . . . Modern maxims that make sense to many people, such as 'Nothing about us without us,' are long preceded by the Church's maxim 'That which touches upon all must be approved by all.' This ancient wisdom still applies in the present day, and the People of God can surely appreciate its authenticity."[186] Indebted to Maltese cardinal Mario Grech, Secretary General of the 2021–24 Synod on Synodality, she adds that the Synod on Synodality's second phase will involve "focused listening to what the People of God request."[187] Although McQueen goes on to say that synodality "is not intended as a reallocation of power by the hierarchy, or as a struggle for equal rights for the laity in a legalistic, political way,"[188] this claim comes too late. It is clear that the phrase "People of God" has here been turned—as in many of the postconciliar approaches examined above—into a vehicle for efforts to clericalize the laity and to bring about changes in currently unpopular or countercultural Catholic doctrines.

Pope Francis made the image of the People of God central to his seminal 2013 apostolic exhortation *Evangelii Gaudium*. He emphasizes that the Church as God's People is open to everyone, not simply to an elite. Those who belong to God's People must be

of bishops offered by Antonio Viana, *Organización del gobierno en la Iglesia: Según el Derecho Canónico Latino*, 3rd ed. (EUNSA, 2010), 157–64.

186. McQueen, *Walking Together*, 51.

187. McQueen, 51. See also the Final Document of the Synod of Bishops, "The Amazon: New Paths for the Church and for an Integral Ecology," §88, October 26, 2019, vatican.va: "In order to walk together, the Church today needs a conversion to the synodal experience. It needs to strengthen a culture of dialogue, reciprocal listening, spiritual discernment, consensus and communion in order to find areas and ways of joint decision-making and to respond to pastoral challenges. In this way, co-responsibility in the life of the Church will be fostered in a spirit of service. It is urgent to go forward to make proposals and take on responsibilities to overcome clericalism and arbitrary impositions. Synodality is a constitutive dimension of the Church. We cannot be Church without recognizing a real practice of the *sensus fidei* of all the People of God." See also §92 of the same document, which speaks of synodality in terms of co-responsibility and emphasizes lay participation (especially that of women) in decision-making and in ecclesial discernment.

188. McQueen, *Walking Together*, 54.

"God's leaven in the midst of humanity."[189] Pope Francis defines this task in terms of ensuring that the Church is a place "where everyone can feel welcomed, loved, forgiven, and encouraged to live the good life of the Gospel."[190] Radner's perspective fits well here. Nevertheless, doctrinal and moral divisions mean that not everyone will feel fully "welcomed," and this, too, is part of the journey of the People of God.

Pope Francis adds along lines that correspond to Radner's, "The People of God is incarnate in the peoples of the earth, each of which has its own culture."[191] What Radner can add here is the explicit insistence that the Holy Spirit does not overcome all tensions in finite and fallen life. Despite Pope Francis's emphasis (correct so far as it goes) that "when properly understood, cultural diversity is not a threat to Church unity,"[192] it seems clear that the differences between cultures can and often do threaten the Church's unity in faith and morals. In his book on the People of God according to *Evangelii Gaudium*, Dario Vitali astutely observes, "Without the discernment of the Church's pastors, the prophetic office of the People of God would be reduced to a clash

189. *Evangelii Gaudium* §114.

190. *Evangelii Gaudium* §114. For an analysis and critique of the kinds of pastoral (and doctrinal-moral) reasoning that tend to arise in this context, see Mansini, "Episcopal Conferences and the Local Renewal of Sacramental Doctrine."

191. *Evangelii Gaudium* §115.

192. *Evangelii Gaudium* §117. For discussion of these paragraphs of *Evangelii Gaudium* in light of Suenens's theology—focusing on the Church as an "inverted pyramid"—see Pié-Ninot, *La Sinodalidad como el "Caminar Juntos" en la Iglesia*, 12–15. See also Pié-Ninot, *Hacia el "primado sinodal y diaconal" del papa Francisco: Documentos histórico-eclesiológicos del ministerio petrino* (BAC, 2021), in which Pié-Ninot compiles texts from the history of the Church that he hopes can soon be employed to support a new "synodal" mode of exercising papal primacy, in accordance with the hint given in *Evangelii Gaudium* §32 (where Pope Francis says, "Since I am called to put into practice what I ask of others, I too must think about a conversion of the papacy. It is my duty, as the Bishop of Rome, to be open to suggestions which can help make the exercise of my ministry more faithful to the meaning which Jesus Christ wished to give it and to the present needs of evangelization"). Pié-Ninot, like many others, links synodality with the Council of Jerusalem in Acts 15, and thereby also with Acts 2:42–47 and 4:32–35 with their reference to the "breaking of the bread" or the Eucharist. See Pié-Ninot, *La Sinodalidad como el "Caminar Juntos" en la Iglesia*, 22–32. In my view, Pié-Ninot draws some mistaken conclusions on the basis of his reading of Acts 15, which he interprets—along with various other passages from Acts—as supporting the ecclesiological perspectives of the opponents of Ratzinger. See also Stephen J. McKinney, "The Council of Jerusalem in Acts 15 and Synodality," in McKinney, O'Loughlin, and Tóth, *Synodality and the Recovery of Vatican II*, 17–28.

of partisan viewpoints driven by the rule of those who shout the loudest."[193]

For Vitali, however, shared decision-making in a synodal Church can avoid such partisanship by means of mutual listening and commitment to a process of discernment. I think something more is needed: a valorization of Scripture and Tradition in the communication of dogmatic and moral truth, grounded in Christ's outpouring of his Spirit to ensure that his People, on their new exodus journey, are illuminated by the enduring truth of the Gospel in their faith and life. This will enable a proper interpretation of diversity in the (synodal) Church and in the cultures of the world, so that the People of God can truly be "God's leaven" through whom Christ acts. The theologian Douglas Bushman states, "As Vatican II taught, the Church is a sacrament through which Christ continues his mission as Prophet, Priest, and King. Christ, the Servant, the Good Samaritan, and the Physician continues to exercise his merciful love in behalf of all those in need, and he does this through those whose hearts are conformed to his."[194] It is repentant conversion to Christ in truth, embracing him as Lord and Savior, that configures us to Christ's "paschal charity" in our cultural diversity, enabling us to leaven the fallen world with the mercy of Christ rather than with our best approximation of what is right.[195] We must look "to Jesus the pioneer and perfecter of our faith, who for the joy that was set before him endured the cross, despising the shame" (Heb 12:2).[196]

193. Vitali, *"Un Popolo in cammino verso Dio,"* 144. Vitali argues that there is a "virtuous circle" here, because—as he continues just after the words I have quoted—"without listening to the People of God, the discernment of the pastors would be a form of power grounded in a religious justification and therefore even more exposed to the danger of self-referentiality" (144).

194. Douglas G. Bushman, *The Theology of Renewal for "His Church": The Logic of Vatican II's Renewal in Paul VI's Encyclical "Ecclesiam Suam" and Its Reception in John Paul II and Benedict XVI* (Pickwick, 2024), 234.

195. Bushman, 234.

196. Schnackenburg and Dupont rightly praise "the rich treasures of the epistle to the Hebrews for the idea of the People of God. Here the wandering people of the Old Testament crossing the desert to the Promised Land becomes the type of the eschatological People of the New Law, who already experience the fulfillment of the promise, yet are still on the way to perfection and require divine protection" ("The Church as the People of God," 128).

5

Mother

I. INTRODUCTION

In the mid-twentieth century, Henri de Lubac, Hugo Rahner, and numerous other scholars showed how richly the Church Fathers and medieval theologians celebrated the Church as our Mother.[1] As Henri de Lubac says with Galatians 4 in view—and

1. See especially Henri de Lubac, SJ, *The Motherhood of the Church*, trans. Sergia Englund, OCD (Ignatius, 1982); Hugo Rahner, SJ, *Mater Ecclesiae: Lobpreis der Kirche aus dem ersten Jahrtausend christlicher Literatur* (Benzinger, 1944). See also such studies as Karl Delahaye, *Ecclesia Mater: Chez les pères des trois premiers siècles; Pour un renouvellement de la pastorale d'aujourd'hui* (Cerf, 1964); J.C. Plumpe, *Mater Ecclesia: An Inquiry into the Concept of the Church as Mother in Early Christianity* (The Catholic University of America Press, 1943); Deyanira Flores, "Virgin Mother of Christ: Mary, the Church, the Faithful Soul—Patristic and Medieval Testimonies on This Inseparable Trio," *Marian Studies* 57 (2006): 97–172; and, focusing on de Lubac's approach, Denis Dupont-Fauville, *L'Église mère chez Henri de Lubac* (Parole et Silence, 2009). By comparison, the image of the Church as Mother has had a mixed—at best—reception in the decades following the Second Vatican Council. On the one hand, Gilberte Baril, OP, argues in *The Feminine Face of the People of God* that the "maternal commitment of the ecclesial bride and of her members cannot be understood in any other way except in terms of participation in [the] *kenosis* of love of the Son, the only true salvific 'birth' of the new world." Baril, *The Feminine Face of the People of God: Biblical Symbols of the Church as Bride and Mother* (Liturgical, 1990), 203. For Baril, the image of the Church as Mother is a liberative image, evoking radical solidarity with the poor and with those who are suffering. On the other hand, Cristina Lledo Gomez holds that the image of Mother Church reflects what she calls "the 'Good Mother' myth," which "continues to affect women all over the world in insidious but also overtly dangerous ways." Gomez, *The Church as Woman and Mother: Historical and Theological Foundations* (Paulist, 2018), xvii–xviii. In Gomez's view, appreciation for "Mother Church" tends to idealize motherhood and to reify the notion of "two genders" (181). Gomez perceives Pope Francis as trying to rectify this situation but as still falling into gendered stereotypes at times. For a sharper critique of Pope Francis's understanding of gender, see Elyse J. Raby, "Beyond 'Women in the Church': Gender and Ecclesiology since Vatican II," in *Vatican II at 60: Re-Energizing the Renewal*, ed. Catherine E. Clifford with Stephen Lampe (Orbis Books, 2024), 115–34, although Raby is deeply hopeful about the Synod on Synodality and the synodal process, as are all the essays in *Vatican II at 60*, which concludes with Cardinal Robert W. McElroy's "Synodality: An Enduring Legacy of the Council," 173–91, an essay that lays emphasis on LGBTQ+ acceptance and women's ordination. See also Natalie K. Watson, *Introducing Feminist Ecclesiology* (Sheffield Academic, 1996), 40–41: "The use of Mary, after all a real childbearing woman, as the supreme personification of the church, is also a reminder of the exclusion of women and their suffering from traditional ecclesiological reflections. . . . Personification perpetuates oppressive hierarchical gender patterns and deters attention from the reality and diversity of the lives of those who

in preparation for quoting Irenaeus, Origen, Cyprian, Basil, Augustine, and others on this theme—"She [the Church] summons all men so that as their mother she may bring them forth to divine life and eternal light."[2] De Lubac wrote extensively on Mother Church while in the midst of a wrenching conflict with the Magisterium of the Church, a conflict that caused him to be removed by his Jesuit superiors from his professorship in Lyon and from his editorial duties for *Recherches de science religieuse*. This conflict was even more noteworthy given the fact that Ignatius of Loyola understood obedience to the pope to be especially important for Catholics and for Jesuits. In the midst of his ecclesiastical sanction, de Lubac strove to show that he loved the Church as his spiritual Mother, a Mother who gives us the nourishing gifts of divinely revealed truth and to whom obedience is owed.

Indeed, de Lubac was so concerned with not being perceived as a rebel that he has been sharply criticized for this aspect of his ecclesiology. In *The Suspended Middle*, while praising de Lubac as one of the two great theologians of the twentieth century, the Anglican theologian John Milbank argues that de Lubac fell into the trap of conceiving of the "Marian" and "Female" (and "Lay") Church in strictly responsive and receptive terms.[3] In Milbank's view, this gendered portrait ensured that de Lubac cast the Petrine office—the Magisterium, representing the clergy and grace—strictly in terms of "active authority" that must be obeyed.[4] Milbank refers to de Lubac's "perhaps insufficient critique of modern centralized papal control," and he underscores that the Marian dimension of the Church "is not simply receptive, but 'actively receptive.'"[5] Although I will make clear that de Lubac valued

are church. . . . Motherhood is in itself an ambiguous experience, as is the experience of being mothered."

2. Henri de Lubac, SJ, *Catholicism: Christ and the Common Destiny of Man*, trans. Lancelot C. Sheppard and Elizabeth Englund, OCD (Ignatius, 1988), 65.

3. John Milbank, *The Suspended Middle: Henri de Lubac and the Renewed Split in Modern Catholic Theology*, 2nd ed. (Eerdmans, 2014), 111.

4. Milbank, 111.

5. Milbank, 109, 112.

active receptivity and had a nuanced view of the Magisterium, Milbank's critique nevertheless rightly shines light on de Lubac's commitment to obeying Mother Church.

In the years following the Second Vatican Council, de Lubac entered into the inner circle of magisterial authority. Whereas in 1950 de Lubac was under the condemnatory gaze of the Magisterium, after the council he joined with the Magisterium to shine condemnatory light upon other theologians. His good friend Joseph Ratzinger, as head of the Congregation for the Doctrine of the Faith, assisted in the 1990 promulgation of *Donum Veritatis*, "On the Ecclesial Vocation of the Theologian." This Instruction teaches that the role of the Magisterium is to "protect God's People from the danger of deviations and confusion, guaranteeing them the objective possibility of professing the authentic faith free from error, at all times and in diverse situations."[6] In part, the Instruction was written against theologians then known as "dissenters," due to their vocal and public dissent from *Humanae Vitae* and indeed from almost every initiative of Pope John Paul II's pontificate, including (later in the 1990s) the *Catechism of the Catholic Church* and the encyclical *Veritatis Splendor*. In the decades following the council, these "dissenting" theologians dominated most Catholic universities and colleges around the world, and many seminaries as well. They were associated with the journal *Concilium*, from which de Lubac and Ratzinger had broken off to form *Communio*. The dissenting theologians' guiding lights included Karl Rahner, Edward Schillebeeckx, Bernard Häring, and Jon Sobrino, among others.[7]

6. Congregation for the Doctrine of the Faith, *Donum Veritatis* §14, May 24, 1990, vatican.va.

7. For a critique of Rahner's theology, see Christopher J. Malloy, "Rahner: The Withering of Faith," in *The Faith Once and for All Delivered: Doctrinal Authority in Catholic Theology*, ed. Kevin L. Flannery, SJ (Emmaus Academic, 2023), 31–68. The same volume contains a critique of Walter Kasper's theology: see Thomas Heinrich Stark, "The Historicity of Truth: On the Premises and Foundations of Walter Kasper's Theology," 69–100. Malloy and Stark show—in Stark's case by quoting Kasper at length—that the warrants of dogma collapse in Rahner's and Kasper's theological systems. See also Karl Rahner, SJ, "Yesterday's History of Dogma and Theology for Tomorrow," in *Theological Investigations*, vol. 18, *God and Revelation*, trans. Edward

Donum Veritatis avers that even non-infallible "magisterial decisions in matters of discipline . . . are not without divine assistance and call for the adherence of the faithful."[8] Everything that the Magisterium teaches "in a definitive way" about faith and morals "must be firmly accepted and held," while non-definitive teaching requires "religious submission of will and intellect."[9] The dissenters agreed to none of the above as it pertained to the teachings that they opposed (i.e., teachings about the authority of the Magisterium, birth control, remarriage after divorce, homosexual acts, the reservation of the priesthood to men, and so on).

Even so, *Donum Veritatis* allows for some forms of what I would describe as resistance within receptivity. The Instruction states, "The willingness to submit loyally to the teaching of the Magisterium on matters *per se* not irreformable must be the rule. It can happen, however, that a theologian may, according to the case, raise questions regarding the timeliness, the form, or even the contents of magisterial interventions."[10] In such cases, says

Quinn (Crossroad, 1983), 3–34; and the trenchant response by Hans Urs von Balthasar in his *New Elucidations*, trans. Mary Theresilde Skerry (Ignatius, 1986), 74–87. For praise of Schillebeeckx's critique of dogma, see Daniel Speed Thompson, *The Language of Dissent: Edward Schillebeeckx on the Crisis of Authority in the Catholic Church* (University of Notre Dame Press, 2003). Thompson explains that for the postconciliar Schillebeeckx, who rejects "a developmental model of doctrine" in favor of "*a hermeneutical, critical, and practical translation of Christian experience from one historical era to the next*," it is the case that "any purely theoretical understanding of the faith, whether simply conceptual or even hermeneutically nuanced, is impossible within the epistemological conditions of human historicity. Because the criterion for orthodoxy does not rest in such a theoretical construction, or even with the idea that there is one essence of faith which is simply clothed in different conceptual forms, Schillebeeckx argues that continuity in the understanding of faith comes from the act or intentionality of faith itself in relationship to the various referential contexts in which that act occurs. There is only one saving mystery of Christ that elicits the inward act of faith, but that saving mystery both expresses itself (through the biblical *kerygma*) and is received and understood in the course of the church's history in a variety of different contexts and through a diversity of 'structurising elements.' The constant factor, therefore, is neither the act or intentionality of faith itself nor the 'structurising' elements that are used to express it, but rather it is the proportional relationship between the two, as they both shape the understanding of the one saving mystery of Christ" (117–18). The bottom line is that to articulate any enduring propositional truth about "the one saving mystery of Christ" becomes impossible. Any particular past dogmatic formulation is at best "the true expression of an earlier experience of faith" and "must be valued within the context of its particular time and recognized also as a bearer of that experience of faith to the next era" (126–27).

8. *Donum Veritatis* §17.

9. *Donum Veritatis* §23.

10. *Donum Veritatis* §24.

the Instruction, theologians first need to assess the weight and degree of authoritativeness of the Magisterial teaching. Theologians also should strive to abide by the following rule: "When there is a question of the communion of faith, the principle of the 'unity of truth' (*unitas veritatis*) applies. When it is a question of differences which do not jeopardize this communion, the 'unity of charity' (*unitas caritatis*) should be safeguarded."[11]

On this basis, *Donum Veritatis* proceeds to undertake a lengthy analysis of the phenomenon of dissent as found since the Second Vatican Council. As the Instruction observes, dissenters justify their positions on various grounds, including conscience, Christian freedom, the fact that numerous Catholics oppose a particular teaching, and the notion that Magisterial teaching is as debatable as any theological intervention. For example, in his 1973 *The Remaking of the Church: An Agenda for Reform*, published the year before he became president of the Catholic Theological Society of America, Richard McBrien suggested that "the Church must . . . demythologize its understanding of the papacy," rejected the consistent practice of the Church regarding the reservation of the priesthood to men, and urged that all Catholics need to become resisters of the Church's teaching

11. *Donum Veritatis* §26. The Instruction adds, "The preceding considerations have a particular application to the case of the theologian who might have serious difficulties, for reasons which appear to him well founded, in accepting a non-irreformable magisterial teaching. Such a disagreement could not be justified if it were based solely upon the fact that the validity of the given teaching is not evident or upon the opinion that the opposite position would be the more probable. Nor, furthermore, would the judgment of the subjective conscience of the theologian justify it because conscience does not constitute an autonomous and exclusive authority for deciding the truth of a doctrine. In any case there should never be a diminishment of that fundamental openness loyally to accept the teaching of the Magisterium as is fitting for every believer by reason of the obedience of faith. The theologian will strive then to understand this teaching in its contents, arguments, and purposes. This will mean an intense and patient reflection on his part and a readiness, if need be, to revise his own opinions and examine the objections which his colleagues might offer him. . . . It can also happen that at the conclusion of a serious study, undertaken with the desire to heed the Magisterium's teaching without hesitation, the theologian's difficulty remains because the arguments to the contrary seem more persuasive to him. Faced with a proposition to which he feels he cannot give his intellectual assent, the theologian nevertheless has the duty to remain open to a deeper examination of the question. For a loyal spirit, animated by love for the Church, such a situation can certainly prove a difficult trial. It can be a call to suffer for the truth, in silence and prayer, but with the certainty, that if the truth really is at stake, it will ultimately prevail" (*Donum Veritatis* §§28–31).

office as part of "summoning the whole Church along the path of self-determination and thereby toward continued growth in Christ."[12] Echoing a March 31, 1972, statement signed by many internationally prominent Catholic theologians, McBrien argues that no one may rightly remain silent and that everyone must participate in "applying constant pressure from below."[13]

Similarly, the eminent dissenter Bernard Häring differentiates resistance—which he approves—from rebellion. In his 1997 *My Hope for the Church*, he holds that he and other theologians like him are responding directly to the "Magisterium of Jesus Christ," bypassing (on the contested matters) the faulty current Magisterium of the Church. He maintains that theologians are doing so under the impulse of Christ's Spirit and with attention to prophetic voices and to "the poor, the rejected, the cry of the plundered planet earth"—endangered especially by "the fact that the human population explosion, along with global migration, has skyrocketed the crime rate and the inclination to violence."[14] Häring considers that theologians who adhere to the Magisterium of Christ in opposition to the Magisterium of the Church in areas where Catholic moral teaching has been consistent for two millennia are not a negative "counter-magisterium." Rather, such theologians listen critically but respectfully to the papal Magisterium, which they then resist and reject where they deem

12. Richard P. McBrien, *The Remaking of the Church: An Agenda for Reform* (Harper & Row, 1973), 92, 101.

13. McBrien, 146. In his book's concluding paragraph, McBrien offers a summary of his vision of what matters for true Christianity: "For after we have obeyed the Lord, and in his Spirit nurtured on earth the values of co-responsibility, accountability, unpretentious service, individual rights, freedom, human dignity, equal justice for all regardless of sex or race, truthfulness, fraternal love of all Christians, and indeed all the good fruits of our ecclesial nature and enterprise, we will find them again, but freed of stain, burnished and transfigured. This will be so when Christ hands over to the Father a Kingdom eternal and universal" (147–48).

14. Bernard Häring, CSsR, *My Hope for the Church: Critical Encouragement for the Twenty-First Century*, trans. Peter Heinegg (Liguori, 1999), 102, 64. For further discussion of Häring's project, see my *The Abuse of Conscience: A Century of Catholic Moral Theology* (Eerdmans, 2021). See also John T. Noonan Jr., *A Church That Can and Cannot Change: The Development of Catholic Moral Teaching* (University of Notre Dame Press, 2005). Noonan raises three issues where he argues the Church has reversed its longstanding moral teaching: slavery, usury, and religious freedom. He thinks that other consistent Catholic moral teachings will undergo similar reversal.

necessary in conscience, under the Spirit's guidance and out of a direct fidelity to Christ, bypassing the papal Magisterium.[15]

Today, those whom *Donum Veritatis* and (later) *Veritatis Splendor* identified as dissenters—and their disciples, holding views like McBrien's and Häring's—are still vocal and influential. Increasingly, however, their views are not condemned as dissent

15. See also Peter A. Kwasniewski's *Bound by Truth: Authority, Obedience, Tradition, and the Common Good* (Angelico, 2023). Kwasniewski's book contains a section on "Faithful Resistance." Kwasniewski's fundamental argument is as follows:

> Protestants exalt Scripture to the extent of denying or minimizing the other two [i.e., Tradition and Magisterium]. As a result, even Scripture is eventually corrupted in them. Eastern Orthodox, on the other hand, exalt Tradition, to the extent of denying a universal Magisterium and teaching authority in the Church, and even to the extent of denying some premises of Sacred Scripture (e.g., the teaching on marriage and divorce). But what does their devotion to Tradition mean, if some of their most respected theologians can accept universalism, contraception, and homosexual 'marriage' (as apparently Kallistos Ware did)? A disordered devotion to 'Tradition' can result, ironically, in its cancellation. But the third group is the most interesting: I shall call them Reductive Catholics (although one could also say Magisterialist Catholics or Hyperpapalist Catholics, etc). *These* exalt Magisterium—and, practically speaking, the papal office—above Scripture and Tradition, so that it becomes the sole principle by which we know truth. It becomes, in a sense, *all* truth, so that it would never be possible to challenge assertions of the Magisterium . . . on the basis of Scripture and Tradition. As with the behavior of the other two groups, so with this one too: the exaggerated exaltation of the Magisterium ends up canceling out the Magisterium of preceding popes and councils. It turns into a 'Magisterium of the moment' (3–4).

I agree that theologians, and non-theologians for that matter, may "challenge assertions of the Magisterium," but, given the possibility of doctrinal development and the fact that not all doctrines have been definitively taught, theologians cannot assume that everything that *truly* belongs to the contents of Scripture and Tradition can today be known with infallible certitude without the assistance of the living Magisterium. To my mind, Kwasniewski has fallen into the error of "private judgment," much as the immensely erudite Ignaz von Döllinger did in the nineteenth century in ruling out papal infallibility. Drawing an analogy from Newman, Kwasniewski states,

> In our time . . . the pope's magisterium, analogously to that of the Arian or Semi-Arian or complicit bishops, is in a 'state of suspension.' In regard to matters on which the pope has gone astray, his teaching and his decrees are without standing or force; they are prevented by intrinsic defects from taking effect. A large number of statements and actions of Pope Francis meet this description (108).

I do not agree with this, or with Kwasniewski's claim that Pope St. John Paul II was guilty of a number of grave doctrinal errors, including religious indifferentism: see Kwasniewski, *The Road from Hyperpapalism to Catholicism: Rethinking the Papacy in a Time of Ecclesial Disintegration*, vol. 1, *Theological Reflections on the Rock of the Church* (Arouca, 2022), 39. For appropriate (and accurate) ways of raising concerns, see Emmanuel Perrier, OP, "Fiducia supplicans face au sens de la foi," https://revuethomiste.fr/contenu-editorial/chroniques/lumieres-et-grains-de-sel/fiducia-supplicans-face-au-sens-de-la-foi, accessed January 6, 2025; and Jarosław Kupczak, OP, *Before "Amoris Laetitia": The Sources of the Controversy*, trans. Grzegorz Ignatik (The Catholic University of America Press, 2021).

by the Magisterium. In fact, the dissenters' perspective arguably predominated at the 2023 Synod on Synodality, which focused to a significant degree on matters that *Donum Veritatis* understood to have been settled by definitive magisterial teaching.[16] A large majority of academic theologians in the West adhere to the perspective of the dissenters. For example, discussing John Paul II's solemn teaching about the impossibility of women's ordination, the theologian Thomas Groome voiced the opinion of many theologians when he argued in 2022 that "*Ordinatio Sacerdotalis* does not fulfill the necessary conditions to be a universal infallible statement." He went on to say, "Might the recent appointment by Pope Francis of another commission to study ordaining women to the diaconate imply such openness? While the diaconate is an ordained ministry in its own right—as evident in the restoration in 1967 of the Permanent Diaconate for men—if women are admitted to one holy order, why not the other two?"[17] The

16. Timothy Radcliffe, OP, reports on the Synod on Synodality: "I saw the smiles and the laughter, barriers falling. Does it sound crazy to assert that one of the fruits of this first part of the synod was that people who had regarded each other with mutual incomprehension were learning to smile at each other? . . . I had been a member of three previous synods and was often treated with suspicion and even hostility by members of the Roman Curia, with the exception of Cardinal Ratzinger, who was unfailingly friendly. What a change now! With the exception of a very small number of people who kept their distance, I was caught up in the joy and warmth of a community that was open to the fresh breathing of the Spirit." Radcliffe, *Listening Together: Meditations on Synodality* (Liturgical, 2024), 124–25. In the previous synods, Radcliffe's published views about the Church's sexual morality, women priests, and so on, were not shared by many of the participants. In the 2023 synod, his viewpoint was widely shared.

17. Thomas H. Groome, "The Catechesis of Priesthood," in *Priestly Ministry and the People of God: Hopes and Horizons*, ed. Richard R. Gaillardetz, Thomas H. Groome, and Richard Lennan (Orbis Books, 2022), 168–76, at 172–73. For perspectives like Groome's, see—among many other examples—Karl Rahner, SJ, *Theological Investigations*, vol. 20, *Concern for the Church*, trans. Edward Quinn (Crossroad, 1981), chap. 3; and Richard R. Gaillardetz, "Infallibility and the Ordination of Women," *Louvain Studies* 21, no. 1 (1996): 3–24. See also the Statement by the Boston College Seminar on Priesthood and Ministry for the Contemporary Church (from which *Priestly Ministry and the People of God* emerged), "To Serve the People of God: Renewing the Conversation on Priesthood and Ministry," *Origins* 48, no. 31 (2018): 484–93, at 486, which awaits "the *consensus fidelium*, the 'breathing together' of the whole church" on these matters; and see the essays in *Christusrepräsentanz: Zur aktuellen Debatte um die Zulassung von Frauen zum priesterlichen Amt*, ed. Margit Eckholt and Johanna Rahner (Herder, 2021), which take up a multitude of issues, preeminently sacramental representation, generally with the goal of supporting women's ordination. In his apostolic letter *Ordinatio Sacerdotalis* (May 22, 1994, vatican.va), Pope John Paul II solemnly teaches the following: "Although the teaching that priestly ordination is to be reserved to men alone has been preserved by the constant and universal Tradition of the Church and firmly taught by the Magisterium in its more recent documents, at the present time in some places it is nonetheless considered still open to debate,

Final Document of the Synod on Synodality, published in October 2024 as part of Pope Francis's ordinary Magisterium, affirms that "the question of women's access to the diaconal ministry remains open" and "the discernment needs to continue."[18] Rather ironically, sharp critiques of the papal Magisterium have in recent years arisen from John Paul II Institutes around the world, known for their longtime opposition to the views of the dissenters. As a result, one John Paul II Institute for Marriage and the Family has been radically restructured by the Vatican, and another has been shut down.

Are the theologians who in 1990 embraced *Donum Veritatis* now the "dissenters," reversing places with the theologians who rejected *Donum Veritatis* and whose views now seem more in favor?[19] If so, is the whole thing arbitrary, depending simply

or the Church's judgment that women are not to be admitted to ordination is considered to have a merely disciplinary force. Wherefore, in order that all doubt may be removed regarding a matter of great importance, a matter which pertains to the Church's divine constitution itself, in virtue of my ministry of confirming the brethren (cf. Lk 22:32) I declare that the Church has no authority whatsoever to confer priestly ordination on women and that this judgment is to be definitively held by all the Church's faithful" (§4). For the Congregation for the Doctrine of the Faith's affirmation that the teaching of *Ordinatio Sacerdotalis* has been taught infallibly by the ordinary universal Magisterium, see "Doctrinal Congregation, 'Inadmissibility of Women to Ministerial Priesthood,'" *Origins* 25, no. 24 (1995): 401. See also Sara Butler, MSBT, *The Catholic Priesthood and Women: A Guide to the Teaching of the Church* (Hillenbrand Books, 2007).

18. See the XVI Ordinary General Assembly of the Synod of Bishops, "For a Synodal Church: Communion, Participation, Mission," §60, https://www.synod.va/content/dam/synod/news/2024-10-26_final-document/ENG---Documento-finale.pdf. In summer 2023, Pope Francis answered a *dubium* posed by five cardinals regarding whether *Ordinatio Sacerdotalis* "is still valid" so that "this teaching is no longer subject to change." In his answer, Pope Francis emphasizes the ministerial priesthood must be understood as service, not as domination. He observes, "If this is not understood and the practical consequences of these distinctions are not drawn, it will be difficult to accept that the priesthood is reserved only to men and we will not be able to recognize the rights of women or the need for them to participate, in various ways, in the leadership of the Church. On the other hand, to be rigorous, let us recognize that a clear and authoritative doctrine has not yet been exhaustively developed about the exact nature of a 'definitive statement.' It is not a dogmatic definition, and yet it must be observed by all. No one can publicly contradict it and yet it can be the object of study, as is the case with the validity of ordinations in the Anglican Communion" (Daniel Payne, "Read Pope Francis' Response to the 'Dubia' Presented to Him by 5 Cardinals," *National Catholic Register*, October 2, 2023, www.ncregister.com/cna/pope-francis-response-to-the-dubia). For background to what Pope Francis has in view here, see Richard R. Gaillardetz, *By What Authority? Foundations for Understanding Authority in the Church*, 2nd ed. (Liturgical, 2018), 169–70.

19. In this regard, Tracey Rowland directs attention to Charles Davis's "Theology and Praxis," *Cross Currents* 23, no. 2 (1973): 154–68. Davis's final paragraph raises the fundamental question (with Davis agreeing with Schillebeeckx): "Is theology, as [Edward] Schillebeeckx says, the critical self-consciousness of Christian *praxis*, or is [Leszek] Kołakowski right when he says:

upon who holds papal power at the moment? Given that the previous dissenters spent nearly five decades decrying and vocally undermining papal authority—prior to coming to appreciate the value of strong papal authority under Pope Francis—should their opponents today imitate their mode of resistance?[20]

The present chapter addresses these issues, guided by de Lubac's instructive insistence in *The Motherhood of the Church* upon differentiating his resistance in 1950 from the kind of resistance undertaken by the postconciliar dissenters. I grant that, as Joseph Ratzinger observes in his 1969 *Das neue Volk Gottes*,

'For theology begins with the belief that truth has already been given to us, and its intellectual effort consists not of an attrition against reality but of an assimilation of something which exists already in its entirety'?" "Theology and Praxis," 167, quoted in Rowland, "Between the Theory and the Praxis of the Synodal Process," *The Thomist* 87, no. 2 (2023): 233–54, at 237. Rowland correctly observes, "The reason Davis's question is so important is that if Critical Theory or some other version of a priority of *praxis* theory becomes the intellectual partner for theology, then almost every branch of theology is open for a radical revision" (237, with reference to a similar conclusion drawn by Joseph Ratzinger in his late-1970s essay "Questions about the Structure of Theology," in his *Principles of Catholic Theology: Building Stones for a Fundamental Theology*, trans. Mary Frances McCarthy [Ignatius, 1987], 315–31, at 318). A key element of Davis's rationale for leaving the Catholic Church was his rejection of its "hierarchical structure of power, centred on the papal monarchy"—not least due to its being "inappropriate for Christian mission." Davis, *A Question of Conscience* (Harper & Row, 1967), 119–21; cf. 178. Davis sums up: "In its present social structure the Church is unable to allow a consistent acceptance of the change in man's self-understanding. . . . Men, however, have had enough. They want to grow and be themselves. If the Church will not allow this: well, so much the worse for the Church" (218).

20. The problem is compounded by the tendency of theologians to amplify the praise of popes who share their favored perspectives, as for example Juan Carlos Scannone, SJ's remark in concluding his *Theology of the People: The Pastoral and Theological Roots of Pope Francis*, trans. Kris Fankhouser and Carmen Fernandez-Aguinaco (Paulist, 2021): "For Bergoglio is not only the 'pope of the people' (of the faithful people of God and of the peoples of the earth) but also the 'pope of discernment' of the signs of our times" (201). Having taught Bergoglio, Scannone highlights Pope Francis's debts to the Argentine "theology of the people" and to Karl Rahner, Scannone's doctoral director: "Rahner, though he was not personally familiar with Latin America, had a fine sense for the new theological contributions and therefore edited two books about what was coming from the continent: *Teología liberadora* and *Religión popular-religión del pueblo*" (168). In Scannone's view, Catholic philosophy even before the council "had already overcome the mere classic paradigm of substance and was overcoming the modern one of subject, moving toward a new paradigm that was not only theological but also historical-cultural. While the first two paradigms privileged identity, need, intelligibility, and eternity as characteristic traits of the first principle and therefore of the understanding of God, the emerging paradigm, which implies a reassessment of the category of relationship over that of substance, without denying those characteristics, rethinks them from the basis of difference of alterity (the relationship), the mystery revealed *as* mystery, the gratuitousness of the gift, and therefore the unpredictable historical novelty" (127; cf. 107–9). See also Gerard Mannion, "A Teaching Church That Learns? Discerning 'Authentic' Teaching in Our Times," in *The Crisis of Authority in Catholic Modernity*, ed. Michael J. Lacey and Francis Oakley (Oxford University Press, 2011), 161–92.

"Criticism of papal statements will be possible and even necessary to the extent that they lack support in Scripture and Creed, or in the faith of the Church as a whole."[21] But I argue that Catholics must adopt a firm stance of receptivity to the ecclesial mediation of the Word of God by the Magisterium of the Church—and not only when the Magisterium's teaching is congenial to one's own understanding of Scripture and Tradition. Guided by the Holy Spirit, the Church nourishes us with true sacraments and true teachings, thereby giving us spiritual birth in Christ and guiding us to eternal life with Christ and the blessed. The Church, therefore, is our Mother, whose unique teaching office must be respected and reverenced.

I will also maintain that some kinds of resistance can be appropriate. Let me explain my use of the term "resistance" by reference to a 2001 document of the Congregation of the Doctrine of the Faith. This document addresses the fact that some theologians have justified their dissent by noting that theologians such as de Lubac conflicted with the Magisterium and later were vindicated. The document replies by distinguishing between an acceptable "tension" and an unacceptable "opposition." The latter comes about "when the search for truth is undertaken without regard for the Church's doctrinal inheritance and becomes hardened into ambiguous or patently erroneous positions."[22] The conflict between the Magisterium of Pope Pius XII and the *ressourcement* theologians who were silenced in the 1950s did not involve such opposition, and therefore rose solely to the level of acceptable tension.

Accepting this distinction between tension and opposition, I note that tension intrinsically involves—as both a reality of physics and an intellectual reality—*some* form of resistance. It is

21. Joseph Ratzinger, *Das neue Volk Gottes: Entwürfe zur Ekklesiologie* (Patmos, 1969), 144 (my translation); cf. 356.

22. Congregation for the Doctrine of the Faith, "Some Comments on the Notification of the Congregation for the Doctrine of the Faith regarding Certain Writings of Fr. Marciano Vidal, CSsR," §5, May 15, 2001, vatican.va.

such resistance, as distinct from opposition, that I ascribe to de Lubac in this chapter. It is a resistance or tension that maintains a firm stance of receptivity to Mother Church. It allows for raising concerns and, in certain ways, for resisting a line of teaching set forth by the Magisterium. It cannot become opposition without ceasing to be what de Lubac and other members of the *ressourcement* movement sought to practice. They maintained obedience toward the papacy and the Church's moral and doctrinal inheritance, while critiquing (often in implicit ways, but clear enough to everyone at the time) both the Vatican and some aspects of some papal documents. John Henry Newman did the same in his day vis-à-vis the Magisterium of Pope Pius IX. I have chosen to use the term "resistance" because "tension" sounds less serious than what actually occurred. There was tension because there was real resistance. But there was no "opposition" in the sense defined above, and there was a no lack of commitment in faith to the Church's solemn dogmatic and moral teaching, grounded in the authority of God revealing.[23]

My chapter will begin with two sections that set forth the foundations of Mother Church in Scripture and Tradition. First, I briefly examine Galatians 4's complex image of the Church as Mother. Second, I explore receptivity and Mother Church, in light of the Virgin Mary as the actively receptive and obedient archetype of the Church. Marian receptivity often garners little respect in contemporary Western society. But members of Mother Church, including the pope and bishops, must faithfully receive the Gospel that they hand on. All members of (Marian) Mother Church must therefore exhibit Marian receptivity, and

23. See also Pope Francis, *Gaudete et Exsultate* §44 (Our Sunday Visitor, 2018): "Doctrine, or, better, our understanding and expression of it, 'is not a closed system, devoid of the dynamic capacity to pose questions, doubts, inquiries. . . . The questions of our people, their suffering, their struggles, their dreams, their trials and their worries, all possess an interpretational value that we cannot ignore if we want to take the principle of the Incarnation seriously. Their wondering helps us to wonder, their questions question us.'" Pope Francis is here quoting his own "Video Message to Participants in an International Theological Congress Held at the Pontifical Catholic University of Argentina (1–3 September, 2015)," *AAS* 107 (2015): 980.

this is particularly evident in receiving the teachings of the Magisterium. My third and final section then examines the perspective and practice of de Lubac. As noted above, while emphasizing the importance of receptivity to Mother Church, de Lubac found himself in serious conflict with the Magisterium of Pope Pius XII and therefore in a stance of resistance (producing "tensions") to some of what Mother Church was teaching. After being rehabilitated and largely triumphing at Vatican II,[24] de Lubac presaged conflicts that the Church faces today when, in 1971, he published *The Motherhood of the Church* as a sorrowful response to the postconciliar emergence of a powerful strain of Catholic religious liberalism.[25]

My argument in this third section is that de Lubac has much to teach us about how Marian receptivity to Mother Church can be united with a certain kind of resistance, different from that of the postconciliar dissenters and different from "opposition." De Lubac did not knowingly resist weighty and consistent Church teachings, nor did he publicly and vociferously denounce the pope (as the postconciliar dissenters did for five decades). Instead, he repeatedly affirmed that Mother Church, through the Magisterium, truly mediates Christ's truth in the Holy Spirit; and he lived this commitment. But he resisted the Magisterium in his scholarly work when he perceived the pope to be repressing a legitimate movement in theology. He understood his resistance to be done in accordance with the truth of Mother Church, never in opposition to the Church's teaching.

After the council, de Lubac sounded the alarm regarding

24. See Henri de Lubac, SJ, *Vatican Council Notebooks*, 2 vols., trans. Andrew Stefanelli and Anne Englund Nash (Ignatius, 2015–16). See also Karl Heinz Neufeld, "Henri de Lubac SJ als Konzilstheologe," *Theologisch-Praktische Quartalschrift* 134 (1986): 149–59; Aaron Riches, "Henri de Lubac and the Second Vatican Council," in *T&T Clark Companion to Henri de Lubac*, ed. Jordan Hillebert (Bloomsbury T&T Clark, 2017), 121–56.

25. See also de Lubac's massive two-volume response to the French spirit of Marxist revolution in the late 1960s, published originally in 1979 and 1981, in which de Lubac charts a middle path between Lefebvrist Traditionalism and postconciliar Progressivism: Henri de Lubac, SJ, *La postérité spirituelle de Joachim de Flore: De Joachim à nos jours*, ed. Michael Sutton (Cerf, 2014).

Catholic religious liberalism of the kind that I noted above in McBrien and Häring. According to de Lubac—and I agree with him—religious liberalism cannot be a path down which the Church's Magisterium could authoritatively go. This is so because religious liberalism, logically speaking, undermines the very basis of magisterial authority and the notion of a trustworthy Mother Church. In his condemnation of Modernism in the early twentieth century, Pope Pius X already solemnly made this point.[26] The dogmatic and moral reversals called for by the postconciliar dissenters, if ever they were to occur, would surely have to be "resisted," because they undermine solemn teaching and have only a flimsy foundation in Scripture and Tradition. But such reversals could only be rightly resisted in full communion with Mother Church, and thus from a stance of receptivity and obedience to Church authority.

II. GALATIANS 4: THE CHURCH AS MOTHER

The apostle Paul, in his Letter to the Galatians, interprets Genesis's story of Sarah and Hagar, with their respective sons Isaac and Ishmael, as an allegory.[27] Although Genesis itself does not give notice of an allegorical meaning, Paul reads it in this way in

26. See Pius X, *Pascendi Dominici Gregis*, encyclical letter, September 8, 1907, vatican.va, and his "*Lamentabili Sane*: Syllabus Condemning the Errors of the Modernists." 1907, https://www.papalencyclicals.net/pius10/p10lamen.htm.

27. For background and interpretation, see Ben Witherington III, *Grace in Galatia: A Commentary on Paul's Letter to the Galatians* (Eerdmans, 1998), 321–40; and, from the perspective of the "Apocalyptic Paul" school, J. Louis Martyn, *Galatians: A New Translation with Introduction and Commentary* (Yale University Press, 1997), 432–66. Martyn argues speculatively that Paul draws many of the terms of this text from the teachers who led the Galatians astray. He states, "The word 'mother' is applied neither to Hagar nor to Sarah in the Genesis texts. . . . The Teachers have very probably employed it to refer to the church in Jerusalem, perhaps drawing on two strands of tradition. One of these speaks of Jerusalem as the mother of her inhabitants. The other amalgamates the figure of mother Jerusalem with that of mother Sarah. According to this tradition, Sarah/Jerusalem will one day nourish with her milk not only her native children but also the Gentiles. The Teachers, apparently say, then, that the Jerusalem church, in spearheading the Law-observant mission, is properly mothering the Gentiles in the end-time. In contrast, Paul insists that the mother of the Galatians—and of himself—is the Sarah/Jerusalem church in heaven. . . . The Galatians' birth identity is analogous to Paul's apostolic identity, for their mother is God's promissory church in heaven . . . in the sense that they were born by the power of God's promise in the circumcision-free mission to the Gentiles" (441).

order to drive home a theological argument. His case is that Jesus Christ has saved us not through the Mosaic law but through the power of his cross and Resurrection. As a result, Christians do not need to obey the fine points of Torah (as distinct from the Decalogue).

Paul's allegory is a polemical one since he argues that the Jewish people who have not confessed Jesus to be the Messiah are in slavery to sin, whereas those who have faith (whether Jew or Gentile) have fulfilled the Torah and belong to the heavenly Jerusalem, the true and free Church. As Paul points out, in Genesis's story about Sarah and her slave Hagar, "the son of the slave was born according to the flesh, the son of the free woman through promise" (Gal 4:23). The latter (Sarah's son, Isaac) involves a covenantal promise that points to Jesus. The "flesh" in Paul's allegory stands for Torah observance and, more specifically, circumcision. Whereas Jews understand themselves to descend from Sarah and to be grounded in God's promise, Paul contends that Christians (whether Jewish or Gentile) are now the true descendants of Sarah because they have embraced the true child of the promise—Jesus, the Messiah and New Isaac. According to Paul, non-Christian Jews, having rejected the true child of the promise, are now descendants of the child of the flesh (Ishmael) and remain in slavery to sin, due to the impossibility of salvation through Torah observance as such.[28]

Thus, Paul holds that the Abrahamic covenant of promise is now associated not with the present Jerusalem or the bounded land of Israel but with the cosmic and transcendent kingdom that Jesus has inaugurated.[29] Jesus presently reigns at the right hand

28. For explanation that this does not mean that the ongoing Jewish people cannot be saved or have lost their covenantal election, see my *Engaging the Doctrine of Israel: A Christian Israelology in Dialogue with Ongoing Judaism* (Cascade, 2021). For Jesus as the New Isaac, see Leroy A. Huizenga, *The New Isaac: Tradition and Intertextuality in the Gospel of Matthew* (Brill, 2009).

29. For further discussion, including the point that this claim should not entail Christian rejection of the Jewish state of Israel, see my "The Christian Bible and the Promised Land," in *The Challenge of Catholic-Jewish Theological Dialogue*, ed. Matthew Tapie, Alan Brill, and Matthew Levering (The Catholic University of America Press, 2025), 275–300.

of the Father. Drawing upon Second Temple imagery, Paul calls this inaugurated kingdom "the Jerusalem above" (Gal 4:26; cf. Rev 21:10; Heb 12:22–24; and Col 3:1–4). Christians have their faith-existence not in "the present Jerusalem" but instead in "the Jerusalem above" (Gal 4:25–26).[30] This heavenly Jerusalem, mediating the saving work of the Messiah, is free of the crushing burden of sin and death. Regarding "the Jerusalem above," Paul says that "she is our mother" (Gal 4:26). The identification of the heavenly Jerusalem as "our mother" justifies later Christian identification of the Church as our Mother. Paul makes clear that the heavenly Jerusalem is the Church of Christ with respect to which he himself "mothers" believers: "My little children, with whom I am again in travail until Christ be formed in you!" (Gal 4:19).

The Church is like Sarah, greatly desiring to bear children, and doing so by the power of the promise that God has fulfilled (in Christ). The Church brings about children of God in the order of grace, adopted sons and daughters in the Son, Jesus Christ. As noted in chapter 2 above, Paul regularly tells the story of salvation in terms of spiritual children. God has sent his Son so that we might be freed from slavery to sin and become his adopted sons and daughters. Paul states, "God sent forth his Son, born of woman, born under the law, to redeem those who were under the

30. Witherington comments that Paul "is here drawing on early Jewish apocalyptic ideas which he has reshaped for his own ends. It is clear enough from a text like Phil. 3.20 that Paul can speak of this entity in several ways. It is instructive to compare 4 Ezr. 10.53ff. and 13.35ff. which speaks of the new Jerusalem appearing from heaven which is visible at present only to the apocalyptic seer. . . . Especially interesting is the fourth vision in 4 Ezra where the earthly Jerusalem is depicted as a barren woman . . . who is given a son only through divine intervention. Less compelling but worth mention is 2 Bar. 4.2–7, which speaks of the heavenly Jerusalem as pre-existing and also as the eternal home of the saints. Notice that this does not cause the writer to give up on the present Jerusalem. Rather he believes it will be transformed in the age to come (2 Bar. 6.9; 32.4). Finally we may refer to the heavenly journey of Enoch as recorded in 2 En. 55.2 which speaks of him going up into the highest heaven, the highest Jerusalem" (*Grace in Galatia*, 334). Richard B. Hays directs attention to Isaiah 54:1, "Sing, O barren one, who did not bear; break forth into singing and cry aloud, you who have not had labor pains! For the children of the desolate one will be more than the children of her that is married, says the Lord"; and 51:2, "Look to Abraham your father and to Sarah who bore you." See Hays, *Echoes of Scripture in the Letters of Paul* (Yale University Press, 1989), 111–21. Hays notes that "the latent sense [of Genesis] is disclosed, according to Paul, only when the narrative is correlated with the present experience of the community of those whom Paul now addresses as 'brothers' (vv. 28, 31)—that is, the church" (116).

law, to receive adoption as sons. And because you are sons, God has sent the Spirit of his Son into our hearts, crying, 'Abba! Father!' So through God you are no longer a slave but a son, and if a son then an heir" (Gal 4:4–7; cf. Rom 8:14–17). God is our Father, and just as God commanded the Israelites to "look . . . to Sarah who bore you" (Isa 51:2), Paul maintains that Christians are also children of "Sarah" insofar as she represents the Church as "the Jerusalem above" who is "free" and "is our mother" (Gal 4:26).

The fundamental purpose of Mother Church is to enable human beings to become God's adopted children in Christ through the power of Christ's death and Resurrection and by the grace of the Holy Spirit. Where Christ is, there is the Church, the Spirit-filled inaugurated kingdom and inbreaking new creation. The Church is an eschatological and heavenly reality, fully present "above" where Christ dwells with the Father in the Spirit. Mother Church gives us birth and nourishes us with the saving truth of the Word of God, with the sacraments, and with all the things that we need in order to flourish in faith, hope, and love as God's adopted children. Mother Church carries us in her secure womb—so that our "life is hid with Christ in God" (Col 3:3)—until we are born fully into eternal life: "When Christ who is our life appears, then you also will appear with him in glory" (Col 3:4). Christ himself also shows motherly virtues, as for instance when he says sorrowfully over Jerusalem, "How often would I have gathered your children together as a hen gathers her brood under her wings, and you would not!" (Luke 13:34). Christ's Church, therefore, is our Mother.

III. RECEPTIVITY AND THE MARIAN MOTHER CHURCH

Receptivity

In the Church's theological tradition, calling the Church "our mother" has been a constant. One reason for valuing the motherhood of the Church is our need to receive divine nourishment and instruction. If people simply ignored or rejected their pastors, then Christ's intention that the Church mediate his teaching and sacraments would fail. The situation would be that of the period of the Judges (of Israel), in which—disastrously—"every man did what was right in his own eyes" (Judg 21:25).

Indebted to Hans Urs von Balthasar, the theologian David L. Schindler describes creaturely receptivity as an ontological perfection rooted in the "receptivity" of the Son to the Father—that is, the fact that the only begotten Son receives everything from the Father in the Trinity.[31] Sonship can instruct us about the goodness of receptivity, including creaturely receptivity. Discussing the ontology of the creature, Schindler observes, "What the creature first 'does' is receive its be-ing (being): what it first 'does' is 'be.' In technical philosophical terms, the creature's '*agere*' (or 'second act') thus consists most properly in its freely taking over and recapitulating the receptive feature that is always-already inscribed in its *esse* (or 'first act')."[32] The very *esse* of the creature—while

31. Schindler is drawing upon Balthasar here. Thomas Joseph White, OP, helpfully distinguishes Balthasar's emphasis on the Son's receptivity from some of Balthasar's other reflections on the Son and on Trinitarian ontology. White remarks, "Balthasar . . . follows Barth unambiguously in ascribing to the Son of God a capacity for obedience even in his divine essence. In fact, Balthasar goes further than Barth does explicitly, in speaking of a divine self-emptying, passivity, or receptivity within the Godhead. This is something distinct from the receptivity of the person of the Son (who receives his personal being from the Father through eternal generation). A notion of receptivity of this kind is traditional and proper to any coherent Trinitarian theology. By contrast, self-emptying or passivity in the essence of the Godhead itself is something else. Such a receptivity would suggest diverse modes of being (as gift on the one hand and receptivity on the other) *within* the simple, immutable, eternal essence of God." White, *The Incarnate Lord: A Study in Thomistic Christology* (The Catholic University of America Press, 2015), 432.

32. David L. Schindler, "Catholic Theology, Gender, and the Future of Western Civilization," *Communio* 20, no. 2 (1993): 200–239, at 220.

comprising a real substance or essence—is relational, receptive toward the divine Giver of all finite being.[33] Schindler argues that all good creaturely acts bear the mark of the creature's relational act-of-being, and thus in some way must be informed by receptivity. Put in terms of classical Greek philosophy, the human creature must be fundamentally shaped not by autonomous, active *technē* but by contemplative, receptive *theōria*.

Balthasar emphasizes that being receptive does not mean being less active. The example of bearing a child, which only women can do, confirms this. There is a fundamentally receptive fruitfulness involved in the conception of a child, but the egg is fully "active" in the process of conception, and, when one factors in pregnancy (and lactation), "the woman exhibits an activity which is significantly superior to the man's."[34] The point is that receptivity can be active, and indeed, Mother Church is actively receptive vis-à-vis Christ and the Spirit. Believers, in receiving the Word and sacraments from Mother Church, should likewise exhibit an active receptivity, working to receive and incorporate Christ's gifts in the Spirit.

Balthasar's valuation of receptivity is taken up by Schindler in his emphasis that creaturely being is primarily receptive. Schindler underlines that the true nature of human existence is not primarily revealed by human works, human making, or human doing. Rather, the deepest nature of human existence is revealed by active receptivity to divine gift, a receptivity that is fruitful.

33. I note here that receptivity does not have ontological priority to substantial being in creatures. Steven A. Long puts the matter well: "It may sound good to say that the creature is constituted by its relation to God, but this is not true: the creature is not constituted by its relation to God, but by God; and for God to constitute or cause is not for God to change or be really related, but for the creature to be. The effect of God is the very being of the creature; insofar and inasmuch as the creature exists, it is therefore related to God as its cause. . . . Hence the analogical formality of being is prior to and the basis of the real relations of creatures to God, and it is necessarily ontologically prior to the relation of createdness, prior to the relation of causal participation (the creature participates nothing until it exists)." Long, *Analogia Entis: On the Analogy of Being, Metaphysics, and the Act of Faith* (University of Notre Dame Press, 2011), 9–10. Schindler's broader point holds even with this clarification.

34. Hans Urs von Balthasar, "A Word on *Humanae Vitae*," in *New Elucidations*, 204–28, at 213.

It may seem that by associating the Church with *maternal* active receptivity and fruitfulness (in relation to Christ's gifting), theologians have downgraded male Christians—since they are not Christ and are not representative of Mother Church. This issue goes back to Ephesians 5, with its presentation of the Church as Christ's spouse, and it goes back as well to the Old Testament's frequent presentation of Israel as the bride or spouse of YHWH. In response, Schindler notes that men and women share a common human nature. Even so, human creaturely and ecclesial being is fundamentally receptive and therefore "feminine" in relation to God. In her response to the angel Gabriel at the Annunciation—"Behold, I am the handmaid of the Lord; let it be to me according to your word" (Luke 1:38)—Mary articulates her graced openness to the Word and Spirit. By contrast, the notion of the self-made man or, more radically, of human technological progress toward a form of deification, cuts against Marian receptivity. It undermines the willingness of persons to receive the Word and sacrament from the Church that authoritatively hands on and interprets Scripture and Tradition through the Magisterium. Efficiency, mastery, and specialization are privileged in a culture that values knowledge as power. By contrast, a Marian culture of love gives primacy to receptivity and contemplation.

For Balthasar and Schindler, one danger facing the Church and culture today is the extinction of receptivity, which would mean the end of the creature's fundamental "receptive" or "feminine" posture in the light of the divine gifting. Both theologians understand that it is mistaken to romanticize motherhood or to limit women's societal roles to motherhood and domesticity. Their focus, however, is on the disastrous restriction of human dignity to productive agency. As they say, active receptivity, not power, is the real measure of human dignity.

The centrality of receptivity for the Church's mediation of Christ's saving work should be evident. The Church must receive from Christ in the Spirit. Believers, as members of the Church, must receive from the Church the gifts of Word and sacrament. Without receptivity at its very center, the Church collapses into a human construction that is merely about power. The knowledge claimed by the Church would be exposed as simply an excuse for exercising power, not love.

Mary and Mother Church

The Virgin Mary exemplifies active receptivity in the economy of salvation. It is not for nothing that Vatican II's Dogmatic Constitution on the Church, *Lumen Gentium*, locates Mariology as the capstone of ecclesiology. *Lumen Gentium* states, "The blessed Virgin, through the gift and office of the divine motherhood which unites her with the Son the redeemer, and by reason of her singular graces and gifts, is also intimately united to the church: the mother of God is the type of the church."[35] *Lumen Gentium* goes on to describe the Church as "mother."[36] Mary carries out a motherly role in the Church, cooperating in the spiritual birth and the raising to maturity of believers.[37] *Lumen Gentium* clarifies that "the maternal role of Mary toward humanity in no way obscures or diminishes this unique mediation of Christ; rather, it shows forth its power. For every saving influence that the blessed Virgin has on humanity arises not from any natural necessity but from the divine good pleasure."[38]

Quoting both Galatians 4:26 and John Calvin, the Protestant theologian Max Thurian commented around the same time that *Lumen Gentium* was promulgated, "The Church . . . has no truer

35. Second Vatican Council, *Lumen Gentium* §63, in *Decrees of the Ecumenical Councils*, vol. 2, *Trent–Vatican II*, ed. Norman P. Tanner, SJ (Georgetown University Press, 1990), 849–98, at 896. For extensive discussion of the theme of Mary's motherhood of the Church, from Scripture and the Church Fathers onward (including *Lumen Gentium*, and with a focus on Mary's mediation), see Pierre Kocian, OSB, *Marie et l'Église: Compénétration des deux mystères* (Parole et Silence, 2018), 449–524.

36. *Lumen Gentium* §63, in *Decrees of the Ecumenical Councils*, 2:896.

37. *Lumen Gentium* §63, in *Decrees of the Ecumenical Councils*, 2:896.

38. *Lumen Gentium* §60, in *Decrees of the Ecumenical Councils*, 2:895.

or greater title than that of 'Mother.'"[39] Thurian argues that this title best articulates the vocation of the Church—namely, to give spiritual birth to sons and daughters in the Son. Mary is, therefore, an image of Mother Church. As he says, "Neither the Gospel nor past Christian tradition has been able to separate Mary and the Church. To speak of Mary is to speak of the Church. The two are united in one fundamental vocation—maternity."[40] Mary is physically and spiritually the Mother of her Son by the grace of the Spirit; the Church is spiritually the Mother of sons and daughters in the Son by the grace of the Spirit. Mary's "messianic motherhood" makes her "the symbol of the Church, the Mother of the Faithful."[41]

Many Catholic theologians contemporaneous with Thurian also drew connections between Mary and Mother Church. For example, Hugo Rahner's *Maria und die Kirche* begins with reflections that are quite similar to Thurian's. He states, "The early Christians' devotion to Mother Church always went hand-in-hand with their devotion to the Mother of God, and this was because they still realized that the whole mystery as presented in the Scriptures shows Mary, the virgin mother, to be essentially the symbol of the Church, our mother."[42] Mother Mary and Mother Church reflect each other. Mary's graced openness to God's will, her faith and humility, and her cooperation in the saving mysteries of her Son have ecclesiological correlates. Hugo Rahner contends that "in the inspired Scriptures, what is said in the widest sense of the Virgin Mother the Church, is said in a special sense of the

39. Max Thurian, *Mary: Mother of the Lord, Figure of the Church*, trans. Neville B. Cryer (Mowbray, 1985), 9. For Calvin's presentation of the Church as Mother, insisting on the necessity of the Church's mediation of the Gospel, see John Calvin, *Institutes of the Christian Religion* 4.1.1, trans. Henry Beveridge (Eerdmans, 1989), 281–85.

40. Thurian, *Mary*, 9.

41. Thurian, 25.

42. Hugo Rahner, SJ, *Our Lady and the Church*, trans. Sebastian Bullough, OP (Zaccheus, 2004), x. See also Alois Müller, *Ecclesia—Maria: Die Einheit Marias und der Kirche* (Universitätsverlag, 1951); Otto Semmelroth, SJ, *Mary, Archetype of the Church*, trans. Maria von Eroes and John Devlin (Sheed & Ward, 1963); and Gérard Philips, "Mariologische Perspectieven: Maria en de Kerk," *Mariale Dagen* 12 (1953): 9–78.

Virgin Mary. And what is spoken of the Virgin Mother Mary in a personal way, can rightly be applied in a general way to the Virgin Mother of the Church."[43] Mary's motherhood of her Son is paralleled by the Church's motherhood, in the spiritual order, of sons and daughters in the incarnate Son who are destined to share in the life of God. Jean-Hervé Nicolas specifies Mary's motherhood vis-à-vis other members of the Church in terms of her prayer, and he also notes that she "plays a role (symbolized by her maternity) in the very birth of the Church," due to her presence at the foot of the cross, representing faithful Israel.[44] Louis Bouyer comments, "The motherhood of the Church is actual because the Church has found her anticipated perfection: the supreme created holiness, a unique communication of the holiness of Christ to her [Mary], who is not only our Mother… but first of all *his* Mother."[45]

For his part, Hans Urs von Balthasar highlights the "freedom of Mary's Yes from all hesitation" and her "guileless openness to every disposition of God."[46] He expands upon this openness or receptivity by drawing upon the category of childlikeness, rooted in Matthew 18:3–4, where Jesus teaches that "unless you turn and become like children, you will never enter the kingdom of heaven. Whoever humbles himself like this child, he is the greatest in the kingdom of heaven." Mary's humility is the greatest and most childlike receptivity. Aware of the cruciform character of

43. Rahner, *Our Lady and the Church*, xii.

44. Jean-Hervé Nicolas, OP, *Catholic Dogmatic Theology: A Synthesis*, bk. 3, *On the Church and the Sacraments*, trans. Matthew K. Minerd (The Catholic University of America Press, 2024), 139. For Nicolas, "the communal personality of the Church is in some way condensed and realized in her [Mary's] unique personality," although he also emphasizes that "from the time that the Church was constituted at Pentecost, it is quite clear that Mary becomes a member of this Church, indeed, her most eminent member" (135, 139). He observes, "If one were to object that Mary cannot be the 'mother of the Church' because she is a member of the Church, one would thus make a rigid and univocal use of metaphor, contrary to its own proper fluidity" (140). See also M.-J. Nicolas, OP, *Théotokos: Le mystère de Marie* (Desclée, 1965); and Jean Galot, SJ, "Mère de l'Église," *Nouvelle revue théologique* 86, no. 11 (1964): 1163–85.

45. Louis Bouyer, *The Church of God: Body of Christ and Temple of the Spirit*, trans. Charles Underhill Quinn (Ignatius, 2011), 588.

46. Hans Urs von Balthasar, "Mary in the Church's Doctrine and Devotion," in Joseph Ratzinger and Hans Urs von Balthasar, *Mary: The Church at the Source*, trans. Adrian Walker (Ignatius, 2005), 99–124, at 105. See also Hans Urs von Balthasar, *Unless You Become Like This Child*, trans. Erasmo Leiva-Merikakis (Ignatius, 1991).

Mary's vocation (which he does not romanticize), Balthasar comments, "Mary's humility is not that of the contrite sinner; rather, it is a blithe, unselfconscious, childlike humility that would never get the idea that anything she had was her property instead of God's gift."[47] Because she knows that everything she possesses is divine gift, she is like a "child"—she is "greatest in the kingdom of heaven." In her graced receptivity, says Balthasar, she is "the archetypal Church, whose form we have to take as our pattern."[48]

According to Balthasar, as noted above, receptivity involves amazement, gratitude, and thanksgiving for the gift of being. To be actively receptive to God's gifting means to desire to share these gifts with others. Balthasar comments that the believer "must show that he has understood God's gesture of gift-giving by taking it over and becoming a giver: not only in the generation of children, but in every kind of human communication and fruitfulness."[49] Grace has a radical newness that amplifies the natural requisite of thanksgiving.[50]

Balthasar emphasizes that the Church—and thus all the members of the Church (including the Petrine office)—is always marked by a Marian stance of receptivity or "ontological gratitude," insofar as we receive divine gifts.[51] This stance, Balthasar thinks, justifies the feminine imagery that surrounds the Church (and Israel) in Scripture. He affirms Matthias Joseph Scheeben's dictum that "the mystery of Mary and the mystery of the Church

47. Balthasar, "Mary in the Church's Doctrine and Devotion," 123.

48. Balthasar, 123. See also Jean-Miguel Garrigues, *L'épouse du Dieu vivant: Marie plenitude trinitaire de l'Église* (Parole et Silence, 2000).

49. Hans Urs von Balthasar, "The Marian Mold of the Church," in Ratzinger and Balthasar, *Mary: The Church at the Source*, 125–44, at 129.

50. Regarding nature and grace, Balthasar comments, "Grace does something new. It elevates man, in Christ, to an immediate filiation vis-à-vis God the Father, gives him birth 'from God,' and liberates him from the entanglements of sin, in which he lives turned away from God. In this respect, grace clearly stands apart from the realm of nature. True, in the concrete the two domains intimately penetrate each other because of the Incarnation of God in Christ. Nevertheless, we cannot infer from this that they are no longer distinct principles" (129).

51. Balthasar, 140. See also Balthasar's reflections in *The Office of Peter and the Structure of the Church*, trans. Andrée Emery (Ignatius, 1986). Balthasar includes a lengthy section in this book on "The All-Embracing Motherhood of the Church," 183–225.

penetrate and illuminate each other perichoretically, [so] that neither can be correctly situated and explained without the other."[52] Scheeben uses the word "perichoresis" and explains that it means an "intrinsic union and similarity."[53] Mary's motherhood and the Church's motherhood are grounded in the work of the Holy Spirit. It is the Spirit who enables Mary and the Church to be fruitful. And, although Mary's motherhood is greater than the Church's, the Church's fruitfulness is analogous to Mary's bearing of her Son Jesus Christ, since the Church bears "the Eucharistic Christ."[54]

In his emphasis on Marian receptivity and fruitfulness at the heart of Mother Church, Balthasar's work in the late 1970s recalls Henri de Lubac's *Méditation sur l'Église*, originally published in 1953. In addition to a chapter on "Ecclesia Mater," *Méditation sur l'Église* includes a final chapter on "The Church and Our Lady." Mary is a type of the Church, as de Lubac shows through his characteristic method of stringing together citations from patristic and medieval authors. He states, "Our Lady is in all ways the image of the maternity of the Church."[55] As John Nepil notes, for de Lubac the mission of Mary illuminates the Church decisively: "Mary and the Church are incomprehensible apart from each other."[56] De Lubac explains this relation by reference to var-

52. Balthasar, "Marian Mold of the Church," 141, with reference to Matthias Joseph Scheeben, *Handbook of Catholic Dogmatics*, bk. 5, *Soteriology*, part 2, *The Work of Christ the Redeemer and the Role of His Virgin Mother*, trans. Michael J. Miller (Emmaus Academic, 2021), no. 1819, p. 645. For discussion, see John L. Nepil, *A Bride Adorned: Mary-Church Perichoresis in Modern Catholic Theology* (Emmaus Academic, 2023), chapters 2 and 4. Nepil states in his conclusion, "The total and mutual relationship between Mary and the Church, the bond of which is *perichoresis*, is established by one specific reality—their shared motherhood. . . . Because their intrinsic relationality is a shared motherhood, Mary and the Church exist in mutual indwelling and dynamic interpenetration. . . . Though their generative fecundity is derived from the Spirit, their shared maternity is entirely centered upon the Son" (*A Bride Adorned*, 241).

53. Scheeben, *Handbook of Catholic Dogmatics*, 5.2, no. 1819, p. 645.

54. Scheeben, 5.2, no. 1819, p. 645.

55. Henri de Lubac, SJ, *The Splendor of the Church*, trans. Michael Mason (Ignatius, 1986), 321. See also Charles Journet, "Sancta Mater Ecclesia," in *Dictionnaire de spiritualité*, vol. 4.1 (Beauchesne, 1961), col. 460–68.

56. See Nepil, *A Bride Adorned*, 31. Mariology is not, however, simply reducible to ecclesiology, as Nepil goes on to make clear, with reference to Joseph Ratzinger, "On the Position

ious early medieval thinkers, who observe that Mother Church, as a Marian reality, continues to spiritually conceive the incarnate Word in faith and to bear him in sound doctrine and holy action. Like Scheeben and Balthasar, de Lubac emphasizes the Eucharist: "Just as the maternal function of Mary is to give the God-Man to the world, so the maternal function of the Church, which culminates . . . in the celebration of the Eucharist, is to give us Christ."[57]

IV. RECEPTIVITY AND RESISTANCE? THE EXAMPLE OF HENRI DE LUBAC

Thus far, I have emphasized the Marian receptivity that Mother Church and all members of Mother Church must exemplify. Mother Church mediates Christ's saving work. All the members of Mother Church must be receptive in a Marian mode, and this involves receptivity to the ascended Christ teaching and acting through his Spirit-filled Body, the Church. In her graced receptivity, relying upon God rather than upon her own resources and bringing forth Christ to the world, Mary is the model of Mother Church.

But what if the Church, through the Magisterium, calls upon believers to receive something that is not adequate to the full truth of the Gospel or that is pastorally misguided, as sometimes happens? What happens to Marian receptivity then? In this regard, de Lubac's personal story is helpful. He published *Méditation sur l'Église* in the early 1950s, when he was in his mid-fifties.[58] Ever

of Mariology and Marian Spirituality in the Totality of Faith and Theology," in *The Church and Women: A Compendium*, ed. H. Moll (Ignatius, 1988), 67–81, at 73.

57. De Lubac, *Splendor of the Church*, 329.

58. For background to the purposes and influence of this work, see Theresa Marie Chau Nguyen, OP, *The Splendor of the Church in Mary: Henri de Lubac, Vatican II, and Marian Ressourcement* (The Catholic University of America Press, 2023). See also, more broadly, Brian E. Daley, SJ, "Sign and Source of the Church: Mary in the *Ressourcement* and at Vatican II," in *Mary on the Eve of the Second Vatican Council*, ed. John Cavadini and Danielle Peters (University of Notre Dame Press, 2017), 31–54; René Laurentin, *La Vierge au concile* (Éditions du Seuil, 1965); and Brian Graebe, *Vessel of Honor: The Virgin Birth and the Ecclesiology of Vatican II* (Emmaus Academic, 2021).

since his formative studies in the Jesuit novitiate, he had been working to promote a different approach to theology than that taken by the neo-Thomistic school that had been at the theological and philosophical center of the Church since Pope Leo XIII's publication of the encyclical *Aeterni Patris* in 1879 (a school with which I have much sympathy). In 1929, de Lubac was appointed to the chair of fundamental theology at the Université Catholique de Lyon. In his inaugural lecture on "Apologetics and Theology," he sought boldly (in Jordan Hillebert's words) "to subvert what he believe[d] to be the common methodological and metaphysical commitments underwriting both contemporary atheism and Roman Catholic neo-Scholasticism."[59]

Méditation sur l'Église appeared three years after de Lubac, in May 1950, had been removed from teaching and ordered to cease his editorial work with *Recherches de science religieuse*. That same year, on August 12, 1950, Pope Pius XII published the encyclical *Humani Generis*, in which he noted that some theologians were seeking "to bring about a return in the explanation of Catholic doctrine to the way of speaking used in Holy Scripture and by the Fathers of the Church."[60] Pope Pius XII grants, of course, that return to the sources is not in itself bad. He observes in this vein that "theologians must always return to the sources of divine revelation: for it belongs to them to point out how the doctrine of the living Magisterium is to be found either explicitly or implicitly in the Scriptures and in Tradition. Besides, each source of divinely revealed doctrine contains so many rich treasures of truth, that they can really never be exhausted."[61] But it remains the case that neo-scholastic (or simply Scholastic) language belongs to the magisterial presentation of dogma and cannot be responsibly neglected. Targeting a position close to that taken by

59. Jordan Hillebert, *Henri de Lubac and the Drama of Human Existence* (University of Notre Dame Press, 2021), 4.

60. Pius XII, *Humani Generis* §14, encyclical letter, August 12, 1950, trans. N. C. W. C. (Pauline Books, 1950).

61. *Humani Generis* §21.

de Lubac in *Surnaturel* (although in response de Lubac strove to differentiate himself from *Humani Generis*'s critique, arguing that he was speaking only about this world and its *actual* economy), Pius XII has this to say about nature and grace: "Others [i.e., some contemporary theologians] destroy the gratuity of the supernatural order, since God, they say, cannot create intellectual beings without ordering and calling them to the beatific vision."[62]

In 1951, the Jesuit superior general, Jean-Baptiste Janssens, issued a letter providing a correct interpretation of various topics on which de Lubac had written, including the proofs of God's existence, the credibility of Christian revelation (apologetics), and the relationship of nature and grace.[63] On Janssens's orders, three of de Lubac's most important books, *Surnaturel*, *Corpus Mysticum*, and *De la connaissance de Dieu*, were removed from Jesuit libraries. Suffice it to say that at the age of fifty-five, de Lubac's career and reputation were under a very dark cloud, due to serious conflict with the Magisterium.

In de Lubac's 1954 preface to the second edition of *Méditation sur l'Église*, he refuses to retract any of the conclusions of his previous works. He notes that one of the reviewers of the book's first edition had commented, "This book is closely connected with several previous books by the same author."[64] De Lubac gladly confirms that this is the case. In his preface, de Lubac explains that in preparing *Méditation sur l'Église* he was not breaking new ground but rather was *extending* his "efforts—however insignificant these may have been—between the years 1945 and 1950 in particular," which, notably, were the very years in which he

62. *Humani Generis* §26. For further discussion, see the chapter on *Gaudium et Spes* in my *An Introduction to Vatican II as an Ongoing Theological Event* (The Catholic University of America Press, 2017), 134–73.

63. See Joseph A. Komonchak, "*Humani Generis* and *Nouvelle Théologie*," in *Ressourcement: A Movement for Renewal in Twentieth-Century Catholic Theology*, ed. Gabriel Flynn and Paul D. Murray (Oxford University Press, 2012), 138–56, at 154.

64. Henri de Lubac, SJ, "Preface to the Second Edition," in *Splendor of the Church*, 11–13, at 11.

published and defended *Surnaturel.*[65] He alludes to the crack-down on him and others that took place in 1950 and that, in 1954, was still fully in effect. In the period between 1945 and 1950, he says, he already "felt, too strongly for comfort, the gathering of those dangers which have in some cases, unfortunately, since become only too clear to all."[66]

Was de Lubac exhibiting Marian receptivity to Mother Church when, in 1954, he reaffirmed the contents of his earlier works, including the controversial publications that had been removed from ecclesiastical libraries and subjected to magisterial critique, and when he announced himself to be presently *extending* the very work that led to his ecclesiastical punishment? Or was de Lubac in open dissent? Certainly, de Lubac professes Marian receptivity toward Mother Church. He does so not only by writing in the final chapter of *Méditation sur l'Église* about the Church as our (Marian) Mother, but also by his remarks in the remainder of his 1954 preface. After referring again to the accusations that led in 1950 to his removal from teaching—and after granting that if there really existed the kind of clique that *Humani Generis* portrays, it would be a matter for serious concern—de Lubac professes his abiding, deep love for the Church. He describes "the pricelessness of that good which consists, quite simply, in belonging to the Church at all."[67] He rejoices in the Church despite the cloud overshadowing him: "Once you have got your eyes in focus, you cannot miss the wonderful blossoming that goes on everywhere in her garden. . . . Joy is still triumphant, breaking through the most somber of appearances and flourishing on everything that should, humanly speaking, snuff it out. Joy is over everything and the foundation of everything."[68] He concludes by asking his readers to pray for him.

65. De Lubac, 11.

66. De Lubac, 11.

67. De Lubac, 12.

68. De Lubac, 12.

In this preface, he seems to sense—as was in fact the case—that the younger theologians and bishops were taking up his cause, reading his books, and siding with him and his colleagues. If I read him correctly, he has significant hope that things will get better for him and for his perspective. In fact, in his mid-sixties, he emerged as a preeminent light of the Second Vatican Council and then became, in his seventies, a cardinal of the Catholic Church and friend of popes.[69] Posthumously, he was appreciatively cited by name in Pope Benedict XVI's encyclical *Deus Caritas Est,* and today, he is under consideration to be raised to the stature of a "Servant of God."

In 1971, in the aftermath of Vatican II, a period in which de Lubac (and many others, including Balthasar and Ratzinger) were shocked by the rapid disintegration of faith and the rise of a strong variant of Catholic religious liberalism, de Lubac published another book about the Church. This new book, titled in English *The Motherhood of the Church,* was comprised of two parts: a part on *Les églises particulières dans l'Église universelle* and a part on *La maternité de l'Église.*[70] The first sentence of the book's introduction quotes a 1913 letter from Jules-Émile Roberty to Charles Péguy, in which Roberty states, "The Gospel existed before the Church. It is about the only thing of which we can be certain in this world."[71]

De Lubac strenuously disagrees with Roberty's claim. In his view, while the Gospel had priority when Jesus was preaching in Galilee and Judea, for us the Church inevitably has a certain priority: We receive the Gospel from Mother Church. Jesus came to unite his disciples in one Body. There is thus no Gospel (and

69. See, for example, Georges Chantraine, SJ, "Cardinal Henri de Lubac (1896–1991)," *Communio* 18, no. 3 (1991): 297–303; Xavier Tilliette, SJ, "Henri de Lubac: The Legacy of a Theologian," *Communio* 19, no. 3 (1992): 332–41. See also Aidan Nichols, OP, "Henri de Lubac: Panorama and Proposal," *New Blackfriars* 93 (2012): 3–33; Rudolf Voderholzer, *Meet Henri de Lubac: His Life and Work,* trans. Michael J. Miller (Ignatius, 2008).

70. See also, from the same time period, Georges Chantraine, SJ's "Catholicité et maternité de l'Église: À propos d'un livre récent," *Nouvelle revue théologique* 94, no. 5 (1972): 520–36.

71. De Lubac, *Motherhood of the Church,* 7.

no Christianity) without the Church. De Lubac is contending here against Catholic religious liberalism as well as Protestantism, in both of which the Church is often sharply contrasted with the Gospel. He expresses horror that Vatican II, whose most essential doctrinal teaching is contained in the Dogmatic Constitution on the Church (*Lumen Gentium*), has given rise not to "a new start . . . in the accomplishment of the great mission of unity received from Christ" but instead to a surge of Catholic religious liberalism, fully evident by 1971.[72] He depicts the situation as follows: "The old seeds of dissolution gaining in virulence—a certain para-conciliar agitation foisting itself on public opinion as the only authentic interpreter of the Council's spirit—a resentment against the abuses of yesterday producing blindness to the benefits received from the Church—the opening up to the world to be evangelized turning into a mediocre and sometimes scandalous worldliness."[73] Priests and religious are abandoning their mission and vocation; theologians are demanding that their arbitrary dictates be embraced by the Church; the Church's tradition is treated with disdain and neglect; "moral laxity" is "presented as the adult man's irreversible progress which the Church must confirm"; and dogma is rejected under the pretext of rejecting dogmatism, thereby threatening to destroy "the Christian faith in its original twofold character comprising an objective content received from authority."[74]

De Lubac knows that he will be accused by his opponents of nostalgia, unreasonable opposition to modernity, and failure to read the "signs of the times"[75]—all because he is defending core

72. De Lubac, 25. For further discussion, see Walsh, "De Lubac's Critique of the Postconciliar Church," *Communio* 19, no. 3 (1992): 404–32. See also Walsh, "Henri de Lubac in Connecticut: Unpublished Conferences on Renewal in the Postconciliar Period," *Communio* 23, no. 4 (1996): 786–805.

73. De Lubac, *Motherhood of the Church*, 25–26.

74. De Lubac, 26.

75. For a critique along these lines, arguing that de Lubac invented an idealized past in part due to his upbringing in a family of French nobility (and in the context of the destruction wrought by World War I), see Robin Darling Young, "An Imagined Unity: Henri de Lubac and the Ironies of Ressourcement," *Commonweal* 15 (2012): 13–18; Young, "A Soldier of the Great

Catholic teachings that Vatican II strongly affirmed. He expresses hope for the future, but he is also well aware that "the Catholic framework has been completely shaken" and that there has been "a loss of awareness among Catholics themselves of what constitutes the unique originality of their Church."[76] While appreciating the importance of social justice, integral human development, and the Spirit's opening up of new doors, he points out that appeals to these things are useless "if faith grows tepid or disappears" and "if the fabric of the Church disintegrates."[77] Large swaths of Catholic priests and laity in Europe in 1971 were demanding "structural reforms" beyond those dictated by Vatican II, whereas de Lubac

War: Henri de Lubac and the Patristic Sources for a Premodern Theology," in *After Vatican II: Trajectories and Hermeneutics*, ed. James L. Heft with John O'Malley, SJ (Eerdmans, 2012), 134–63. For the opposite claim, suggesting that de Lubac helped to lead a quasi-Modernist (i.e., Catholic religious liberal) movement and then was later dismayed by the postconciliar outcome, see Jon Kirwan, *An Avant-garde Theological Generation: The Nouvelle Théologie and the French Crisis of Modernity* (Oxford University Press, 2018). See also Jon Kirwan and Matthew K. Minerd, "Translators' Introduction: A Dialogue Delayed," in *The Thomistic Response to the Nouvelle Théologie: Concerning the Truth of Dogma and the Nature of Theology*, ed. and trans. Jon Kirwan and Matthew K. Minerd (The Catholic University of America Press, 2023), 1–85. For the main concerns of the *nouvelle théologie*, see the essays in *Ressourcement after Vatican II: Essays in Honor of Joseph Fessio, SJ*, ed. Nicholas J. Healy Jr. and Matthew Levering (Ignatius, 2019); and *Ressourcement: A Movement for Renewal in Twentieth-Century Catholic Theology*, ed. Gabriel Flynn and Paul D. Murray (Oxford University Press, 2012). On de Lubac's motivations, see also Joseph S. Flipper, *Between Apocalypse and Eschaton: History and Eternity in Henri de Lubac* (Fortress, 2015); and Andrew Prevot, "Henri de Lubac (1896–1991) and Contemporary Mystical Theology," in *A Companion to Jesuit Mysticism*, ed. Robert A. Maryks (Brill, 2017), 279–309.

76. De Lubac, *Motherhood of the Church*, 29. Already in 1945, de Lubac had the following to say: "Everyone can see plainly that unbelief and indifference, in spite of some contrary trends, are spreading almost everywhere. Do we realize that one of the causes of this fact is that each year, through a series of obscure tragedies, deep within the *khagnes* of the provinces or of Paris, or in similar milieux, many of our young élite lose their faith while discovering a universe where Christianity seems to have no place? Tomorrow they will be the educators of our youth, the molders of opinion, the most popular of our writers" (*Paradoxes of Faith*, 46).

77. De Lubac, *Motherhood of the Church*, 30. Already in 1945, de Lubac had warned against politicizing Christianity along purely immanent lines: "We must avoid a certain confusion which would be fatal. Some of those who speak today of adapting Christianity would like, at bottom, to change it. Some of those who would like, they say, to 'incarnate' it more would like, at bottom, to bury it. Christianity must not become 'the religion of which one can make what one wills' (Franz Overbeck). A wish to 'incarnate' Christianity sometimes actually leads to disincarnating it, emptying it of its substance. It becomes lost, buried in politics or in sociology or, at best, in morality" (*Paradoxes of Faith*, 64). He adds against Catholic religious liberalism: "We do not want a religion that is outside of life. All right. But what is life? We must take it as a whole. What life would be worth our love and our attention that would not reach eternal life? . . . Accordingly, the resurrection is succeeded by the ascension, to show us what it meant and to force us finally to turn our eyes upward, to go beyond the earthly horizon and all that pertains to man in his natural state" (68–69).

denies that such reforms can ever be "the main part of a program that must aim at the only true renewal, spiritual renewal."[78]

In his introduction to *The Motherhood of the Church*, de Lubac posits that what has been forgotten by many Catholics in the few years since the ending of the council is the Church's receptive mediation of the Gospel of Jesus Christ. After all, "the mystery of faith, which is a mystery of life, is entrusted to 'the living Church of God, pillar and support of the truth,' which is herself included within this mystery."[79] The very heart of the Church—the *sine qua non*—is receptivity to the *mysterium fidei*. The Church lives to uphold and communicate, through faithful mediation, the *mysterium fidei*. Receptivity to divine revelation in Christ is the ground on which everything else stands. Communion in revealed and received truth is what enables authoritative dogmatic teaching about the salvific realities of faith.

At the present historical moment, suggests de Lubac, it is necessary to defend strenuously "the nature and role of authority in the Church" along with "the objectivity of dogma and the value of the sacrament."[80] According to de Lubac, the problem with religiously liberal construals of the Catholic Church's life is that they neglect and even negate receptivity and mediation of the Gospel given by God in and through Jesus Christ. They show little awareness that "the Christian life is a life received from above, a life to which we are begotten and in which we are nourished by a ministry coming from Jesus himself and which realizes historically a communion victorious over all history."[81]

What would de Lubac have done if the Magisterium had attempted to implement the religiously liberal construal of the Church's life that he excoriated in 1971? Arguably, we can find the answer in what de Lubac did in the early 1950s, when he found

78. De Lubac, *Motherhood of the Church*, 33. I have removed the italics from these quotations.

79. De Lubac, 34.

80. De Lubac, 35.

81. De Lubac, 35.

himself at odds in certain ways with Pope Pius XII. De Lubac believed that his positions did not fall under the condemnations articulated by Pius XII. He therefore felt comfortable maintaining his core positions—clarifying certain elements, but not backing down. Even so, he carefully expressed his complete devotion to and submission to Mother Church, from whence he received the saving Word of God and the sacraments.

On the one hand, de Lubac did not engage publicly in vocal critique of Pope Pius XII and his magisterial teachings. He made his viewpoint known, but not by hurling anathemas. His obedient acceptance of the Church's sanctions and his refusal to react strongly, in a public way, against Pope Pius XII was wise. Had he reacted more strongly, he would have undermined precisely what in his life and writings he sought to defend—namely, that the Church is our Mother, through whom Christ wills in the Spirit to give us his saving gifts. He would have fomented an attitude of suspicion toward Mother Church's mediation. In sum, he would have undermined the filial and Marian virtues that ensure Mother Church's ability to teach, sanctify, and govern.

On the other hand, he recognized that Mother Church, as represented by human agents, is capable of some error. Arguably, de Lubac's approach to his disagreement with *Humani Generis* exemplifies what theologians should do in such a situation. If de Lubac had been insisting against Vatican I (and against Scripture and Tradition) that nature and grace are identical in their dynamism, or if de Lubac had contended against the Church's consistent and solemn teaching in some other manifest way, then de Lubac would have been in a position of unwarranted *opposition* to Mother Church. But de Lubac was not denying the distinction between nature and grace or the radical difference between the power of grace and what nature can accomplish on its own. De Lubac's position on nature and grace was not unprecedented in the history of Catholic theology,[82] and his viewpoint (as he understood it) had not been condemned, let alone consistently or irreversibly condemned. De Lubac never denied the enduring truth-status of dogma, even though he sharply challenged neo-scholastic theology.

In his essay "Ecclesia Mater" in *Méditation sur l'Église*, de Lubac provides an instructive portrait of the true Catholic, the *homo catholicus*—without claiming that he always has measured up to this ideal. He remarks that the true Catholic "will have fallen in love with the beauty of the House of God; the Church will have stolen his heart."[83] The true Catholic will allow himself to be configured by the Church so as to be in the likeness not only of Christ but also of the Church (Mary)—since the Church is in the likeness of Christ. The true Catholic will want to embrace all the riches of the Church. The true Catholic "will be aware that through her [i.e., the Church] and through her alone he participates in the unshakeableness of God."[84] The true Catholic will make sacrifices to be in unity with the Church. The true Catholic "will allow her to judge him, and he will agree gladly to all the sacrifices demanded by her unity."[85]

Still more, de Lubac states that the true Catholic will engage in no nostalgic or corrosive critique of the present Church. Although the true Catholic will reverence tradition and go deep into it, "the last thing he will do will be to devote himself to a cult of nostalgia, either in order to escape into an antiquity he can reshape as he likes or in order to condemn the Church of his own day."[86] The true Catholic will listen reverently to the Magisterium of the Church. De Lubac even states, "He will, of course, never take it into his head to appeal from the present teaching of the

82. See Jacob Wood, *To Stir a Restless Heart: Thomas Aquinas and Henri de Lubac on Nature, Grace, and the Desire for God* (The Catholic University of America Press, 2019).

83. De Lubac, "Ecclesia Mater," in *Splendor of the Church*, 236–278, at 241.

84. De Lubac, 241.

85. De Lubac, 241–42.

86. De Lubac, 242.

Magisterium to some past situation, doctrinal or institutional, or invoke such things in order to apply to that teaching an interpretation that would in fact be an evasion; for he will always accept the teaching of the Magisterium as the absolute norm."[87]

De Lubac says all this in "Ecclesia Mater," but can it really be applied to his actions at that time? After all, de Lubac knew that he was pushing against—indeed involved in a "battle" with—the perspective that was dominant in Rome and that Pope Pius XII firmly favored.[88] At the time of publishing "Ecclesia Mater" in his *Méditation sur l'Église*, de Lubac was under ecclesiastical penalty, and he had not repented of his perspectives. He later remarked, "The decisions made in Rome in June 1950 officially emanated solely from the General of the Society. The latter was motivated to make them, however, by the fact of 'pernicious errors on essential points of dogma' maintained by the five professors in question . . . : Fathers Emile Delaye, Henri Bouillard, Alexandre Durand, Pierre Ganne and I."[89] De Lubac did not back down or denounce the theological movement of which he was a leading member. He knew that his sincerity was doubted, including by Pope Pius XII, who (according to de Lubac's friend Cardinal Gerlier) said in 1950, "What is annoying about him [i.e., de Lubac] is that one never knows if what he says or writes corresponds to what he thinks."[90] This charge of craftiness is present in *Humani Generis*, although de Lubac is not named.

Was de Lubac receptive to Mother Church, as given voice by the authoritative encyclical of Pius XII, an encyclical that was implemented through ecclesiastical penalties? On the one hand, as

87. De Lubac, 243–44.

88. See Henri de Lubac, SJ, *At the Service of the Church: Henri de Lubac Reflects on the Circumstances that Occasioned His Writings*, trans. Anne Elizabeth Englund (Ignatius, 1993), 64. De Lubac protests against the title *The Splendor of the Church*: "The English translation dressed it up with the pompous title 'The Splendour of the Church,' which seems to rank it among the 'triumphalist' writings and thereby to accelerate its obsolescence. It is no more a treatise on the Church than was *Catholicisme*" (77).

89. De Lubac, 68.

90. De Lubac, 68.

noted above, he did not think that any doctrine the encyclical defended was one that, strictly speaking, he denied.[91] On the other hand, he did not renounce his theological perspectives—which certainly were close to the ones the encyclical deemed dangerous—and he never tried to take as his own the lines promoted by the encyclical. In 1953 and 1954, he published two editions of *Méditation sur l'Église* despite the fact that at this time he was generally banned from publishing theological works. In his later memoir, de Lubac recounts that his effort to publish *Méditation sur l'Église* was "strangely crowned with success," given that Rome approved it at the same time (1952) that Rome was rejecting permission for him to publish various other things.[92] The essays had all been written by 1949, but de Lubac augmented them with "several new pages," along with (in the second edition, published very quickly after the first one) the preface from which I have quoted.[93] De Lubac explains in his memoir that *Méditation sur l'Église* got through the Roman censors largely by chance, due to the absence of the censor normally in charge. Indeed, the 1954 Italian translation was denied an imprimatur by the Vicariate of Rome, but the Italian edition nevertheless ended up appearing in print due to the patronage of Milan's archbishop Giovanni Montini, the future Pope Paul VI.

How do we square de Lubac's actions with his insistence in *Méditation sur l'Église* on receptivity to the authority of the present-day Magisterium? To my mind, the answer is simple, and I have already adumbrated most of it above. Marian receptivity to Mother Church means listening reverently to the teachings of the present-day Magisterium and not trying to evade their binding doctrinal and moral content. But such receptivity does not mean agreeing with the present pope's judgments in respect to every matter. In his memoir, *At the Service of the Church*, de

91. See de Lubac, 71.
92. De Lubac, 74.
93. De Lubac, 75.

Lubac rejects the view that "one is less free to the degree that one is more respectful of the Magisterium."[94] All magisterial teachings must be attended to with reverence and respect. Nevertheless, not everything has the same weight.[95]

I should add that my perspective does not require that de Lubac be always consistent or always in the right. To take positions that cut against the grain of (reversible) magisterial teaching, even if one believes that one's positions do not strictly fall under an encyclical's condemnations or can be justified in other ways, is a risk. De Lubac suggests in his memoir that he both respected Pope Pius XII's Magisterium and felt free to cut against it, so long as he was not denying the doctrinal truths insisted upon by *Humani Generis*. Whether he succeeded in maintaining the respect for Pius XII's Magisterium that he wanted to have is an open question. I think he maintained enough respect for it, since he was never bound to agree with Pope Pius XII on everything. Had he strongly attacked (as distinct from querying or respectfully challenging) Pius XII in print, or had he dissented from the consistently taught doctrines of the Church that the pope sought to defend, I think he would have violated his commitment to embody receptivity toward Mother Church and would have harmed others' ability to perceive the Church's motherhood. But given the fact that he remained obedient, even while continuing to argue against the grain of Pope Pius XII's Magisterium in favor of positions held by himself and his colleagues, I think his receptivity to Mother Church was made manifest.

The point is that publicly differing from the current pope or thinking that the current pope has erred in certain ways—assuming that one is not rejecting weighty doctrines of faith and

94. De Lubac, 77.

95. De Lubac had commented in 1945, along lines that I find questionable (since dogmatic statements express the truth of the Gospel) but that correctly underscore that not all papal teaching is infallible: "The only 'gospel truth' is the words of the Gospel. The words of encyclicals are but encyclical words: assuredly very worthy, extremely important, but another thing" (*Paradoxes of Faith*, 53–54).

morality—is not the same thing as lacking a Marian receptivity toward Mother Church's mediation of the Gospel of Christ.[96] If this were not the case, then John Henry Newman—well known for his carefully worded disagreements with Pope Pius IX's Magisterium (as well as for his more passionate and explicit private letters in this regard, even though in matters of dogmatic teaching Newman affirmed all that Pius IX taught)—could never have been a saint of the Church. As de Lubac puts the point in "Ecclesia Mater," "Whether we like it or not, there are many non-essential things that change according to time and place."[97] This fact need not get in the way of "being enlightened, guided, and shaped . . . by dogmatic truth," which is binding and cannot be reversed by Mother Church.[98]

Thus, de Lubac's commitment to receptivity to Mother Church was not just lip service. He sincerely argues in "Ecclesia Mater" that "all action that deserves to be called 'Christian' is

96. It should go without saying, given the above, that I disagree with Jürgen Mettepenningen's *Nouvelle Théologie—New Theology: Inheritor of Modernism, Precursor of Vatican II* (Continuum, 2010), which argues that de Lubac and the other members of the *nouvelle théologie* were essentially Modernists.

97. De Lubac, *Splendor of the Church*, 246.

98. De Lubac, 248. I grant—as does de Lubac himself—that de Lubac did not always live up to the ideals that he set for himself, as, for instance, when he says of the true Catholic: "He will hold himself apart from all coteries and all intrigue, maintaining a firm resistance against those passionate reactions from which theological circles are not always free" (250). De Lubac demonstrably indulged occasionally in intrigue and passionate reactions. He goes on to say, among other things, that the true Catholic "will always direct his accusations against himself first and foremost; yet he will not resign himself to Christ's disciples' settling down in the all-too-human or stagnating outside the great currents of humanity. He will see the good, be glad of it, and set himself to making it visible to others, but without blinding himself to the faults and sufferings that some try to deny while others are scandalized by them; he will not consider that loyalty or simply experience of human nature obliges him to condone every abuse. And he will, moreover, be aware that the mere passing of time wears out many things, so that many innovations are necessary if dangerous novelty is to be avoided" (254–55). This seems to describe both de Lubac's ideal and his practice. De Lubac concludes his portrait of the theologian who is a man of the Church by stating, "This picture of the Catholic in whom the consciousness of churchmanship is lively is, of course, altogether too meager and abstract an affair, besides being—obviously—overidealized. Here, as in all things, there is normally a big gap between the most sincere faith and the most loving disposition, on the one hand, and effective practice, on the other; for man is always inconsequential. But the important thing to take note of is not the tribute we all pay, more or less heavily, to human weakness but, rather, the nature and scope of our desires. The mystery of the Church and the good things she brings are always beyond what we manage to live of them in actual practice. We never draw upon more than a meager part of the wealth that our Mother has at her disposal" (273).

necessarily deployed on a basis of passivity. The Spirit from whom it derives is a Spirit received from God."[99] This theocentric and Marian receptivity is the ground of Christian faith, since God gives us the gift of faith, whose ground is not our own rational reflection or private judgment. Submission to the Church's Magisterium nourishes this spirit of receptivity. What I have called receptivity, de Lubac with biblical and Ignatian warrant calls obedience: "the obedience of faith" (Rom 1:5).

De Lubac did not rebel, break with the Church, or denounce the pope publicly when he was removed from teaching and when he and his close colleagues were accused of grave errors and were assigned to write on non-theological topics. As he says in *Méditation sur l'Église*, the man of the Church (or the true Catholic) must accept the "acts of the hierarchy" "as obedience demands," while "never adopting an argumentative attitude where obedience is concerned, as if there were some question of defending at all costs a threatened autonomy."[100] De Lubac rejects the very notion of entering into a contest "with those who represent God."[101] De Lubac—perhaps giving himself a pep talk—describes the interior attitude of a person who has been reprimanded and penalized by legitimate Catholic authority as an attitude of interior peace, assurance that the Spirit is at work, and acceptance of God's will. Nevertheless, neither does de Lubac renounce "common sense"; he does not assume that a member of the Church's hierarchy

99. De Lubac, 257.

100. De Lubac, 260. See also the nuances found in de Lubac, *Paradoxes of Faith*, from a section first published in 1945: "To impose conditions on the exercise of authority, to justify it only as a means of pedagogy, instead of recognizing it simply as a right; to look upon it first of all as functional: does not this, they ask, slacken obedience? Not at all. For if this does occasionally counteract certain abuses of power, it also shows, above all, that a purely external submission, a mere return of everything to *order*, is not yet true obedience, but only its prerequisite. It indicates that ideal submission extends to obedience of the judgment, until the time comes when it will freely expand into the liberty of the children of God. An obedience which only recognizes orders—even if, to assure the perfect execution of those orders, it calls on the will and on the judgment—is utterly insufficient. Especially in the spiritual life, which does not consist in gestures. To fulfill the prescriptions of religious authority faithfully, strictly, without any omission, is good. But if you are satisfied with that, you have not begun to *obey*. You take for an end what is still only a means" (26–27).

101. De Lubac, *Splendor of the Church*, 260.

never acts obtusely or never teaches erroneously.[102] The man of the Church "will make the appropriate evaluation of the scope of each one of the acts of the hierarchy" and "will accept them all as obedience demands and understand them as obedience demands."[103] Obedience, yes, but not a blind obedience devoid of reflection.

In *Méditation sur l'Église*, without being explicit about it, de Lubac indicates why he thought it appropriate to continue with the work that he and his colleagues were attempting to achieve in the Church, despite the fact that this cut against the will of Pope Pius XII, who would have liked the *ressourcement* movement to come to an end. De Lubac states that "as long as the order is not final, [the man of the Church] will not abandon the responsibilities with which he has been invested by his office or circumstances. He will, if it should be necessary, do all that he can to enlighten authority; that is something which is not merely a right but also a duty, the discharge of which will sometimes oblige him to heroism."[104] This statement again expresses the truth that receptivity toward Mother Church does not mean pure passivity or the assumption that the representatives of the Church are correct about everything. De Lubac's point that sometimes one must make a heroic effort to "enlighten authority" bears not only upon his situation in 1953 but also upon his situation in 1971, when he faced the spread of a version of Catholic religious liberalism.

More than once in *Méditation sur l'Église*, de Lubac emphasizes that God is in charge and God's legitimate representatives must be obeyed (in "conformity with the obedient Christ").[105] The

102. De Lubac, 261.

103. De Lubac, 261.

104. De Lubac, 262. See also *Paradoxes of Faith*, 58, describing (in 1945) de Lubac's hopes for *ressourcement*: "But how should we rediscover Christianity if not by going back to its sources, trying to recapture it in its periods of explosive vitality? How should we rediscover the meaning of so many doctrines and institutions which always tend toward dead abstraction and formalism in us, if not by trying to touch anew the creative thought that achieved them?"

105. De Lubac, *Splendor of the Church*, 263. See also the inspiring words of Richard R. Gaillardetz, *While I Breathe, I Hope: A Mystagogy of Dying* (Liturgical, 2024), who, in the midst of struggling with his terminal cancer, writes (indebted to an insight of Karl Rahner),

man of the Church will not suppress his mind, but he will recognize that he might be wrong and he will obey when commanded. De Lubac states, "Even where he has a duty to act, and in consequence a duty to judge, he will on principle maintain a certain distrust with regard to his own judgment."[106] The true Catholic will maintain a firm awareness that his fallible actions and judgments must be grounded in receptivity to Mother Church. De Lubac remarks, "He cannot be an active member of this Body if he is not, first and foremost, a submissive member," accepting everything that the obedience of faith requires.[107] Mother Church is hierarchical, and we owe obedience to the actual hierarchs who exist now, although this does not mean that we need to think or act as though they must be correct in a particular non-definitive matter. We must love and submit to Mother Church not as an ideal but as she is, with her current pope, even when disagreements arise.[108] After all, it is Mother Church "who daily teaches us the law of Christ, giving us his Gospel and helping us to understand its meaning."[109]

"Such hope gives me courage to accept the uncontrollable features of my present life as a way of embracing God's own radical uncontrollability. It may seem odd to speak of God's 'uncontrollability,' at least until we consider the many ways in which we endeavor to control God through a certain instrumentalist or transactional approach to prayer, or with a selective appeal to biblical proof texts or Hallmark card sentiments that conveniently align God's desires to our fervent wishes. True hope can free me to surrender before the uncontrollability of God only to the extent that I trust that this divine uncontrollability is not capricious but is in fact Love itself graciously enfolding me in God's tender embrace" (146–47).

106. De Lubac, *Splendor of the Church*, 264.

107. De Lubac, 264.

108. De Lubac notes that "the Catholic will not be content merely to grant and grasp that in the last analysis the Church is, so to speak, concentrated whole in Peter; the seeing of the fact will be an occasion of joy to him. He will not be worried by those who try to persuade him that he has 'lost the sense of the totality of the Church' and that in submitting himself to the power of the pope he has resigned himself to a belief that is, as it were, merely belief at the word of command" (de Lubac, 270). De Lubac, of course, was not enthusiastic about the pontificates of Pope Pius XI and Pius XII, and so to some degree he is presenting an ideal; but he was in fact joyful that the Church is led by the successor of Peter.

109. De Lubac, 275. Joseph Ratzinger comments—in response to the concept of freedom prevalent in the late 1960s and 1970s—that "to live the law of Christ therefore means to live according to the status of being of a spiritual person, in the manner of the Spirit. That includes the crucifixion of the flesh 'with its passions and desires' (Gal 5:24); what this excludes is indicated by Paul in a catalogue of fifteen vices which, he notes, could be extended (Gal 5:19–21). Undemanding, therefore, is something this freedom is not, nor is it a matter of doing what you want. Its obligations extend to the point that it can be called 'crucifixion.'" Ratzinger, "Freedom

De Lubac ends "Ecclesia Mater" with a string of praises. He praises Mother Church for her doctrine, her liturgy, her consecrated religious, her traditions of spiritual life, her rejection of heresies and false paths, her fruitfulness, her bringing forth things old and new, her rejection of sectarianism, her missionary work, her catechetical labors, her witness to Christ, her sacraments, her holiness, and many other things.[110] All these praises show that de Lubac, while enduring his ecclesiastical penalty and while leading the *ressourcement* movement, remained committed to living and helping others to live within the trustworthy nourishment of Mother Church, rather than vociferously claiming to be the representative of Christ against the current Magisterium.

Let me return one more time to de Lubac's 1971 *The Motherhood of the Church*, written in a situation of ecclesiastical chaos. In his analysis of the Church's motherhood in this book, he reflects upon how each individual member participates in this motherhood, so that every member exercises a (Marian) spiritual maternity. He notes that "the maternal action of the Church toward us never ceases, and it is always in her womb that this action is accomplished for us. . . . Her mission of giving birth always remains."[111] In addition to Galatians 4, de Lubac identifies another New Testament passage bearing testimony to the Church as our Mother: "The elder to the elect lady and her children, whom I love in the truth, and not only I but also all who know the truth" (2 John 1:1). This "elect lady" is none other than Mother Church. To be nourished in Christ's truth is to receive the truth of the Gospel, the truth of Scripture, from the "elect lady."

and Constraint in the Church," in *Church, Ecumenism and Politics: New Essays in Ecclesiology*, trans. Robert Nowell (Crossroad, 1988), 183–203, at 198.

110. See also the point added in de Lubac, *Paradoxes of Faith*, 29: "The maternal bosom of the Church is vast enough to contain the greatest minds—and the most diverse. All can find in it the shelter necessary for all. Each according to his needs, as well, life-giving forces."

111. De Lubac, *Motherhood of the Church*, 71.

V. CONCLUSION

It remains to sum up constructively the main lines of this chapter. First, the Catholic Church is our Mother. We owe reverence to our Mother, and thus we owe reverence to the teaching office or Magisterium of the Church. Mother Church can be relied upon to nourish her children with the truth of Christ, both doctrinally and sacramentally. Here is where I part ways with the resistance—that is, the opposition—modeled by Richard McBrien and Bernard Häring, since they embodied the widespread postconciliar dissent from doctrines of faith and morality that have been taught consistently and in a weighty matter over the centuries by the Church's Magisterium.[112] If any weighty or consistently taught doctrine is today to be reversed, it would be incumbent upon advocates of such reversal to demonstrate that this step does not undermine the entire body of dogma, including prior dogmatic teaching about the Magisterium itself. Although postconciliar dissenting theologians have tended to speak as though rupture with weighty and consistently taught doctrine would be a minor problem and has happened before (they often name slavery, religious freedom, and usury as examples[113]), the weakness of their examples—all of which can be understood satisfactorily in terms of Newmanian doctrinal development—indicates the true scope of the problem such rupture would pose.

112. Häring tends to argue that he and other moral theologians who follow his positions are not contradicting any irreversible teaching. I disagree with him, but to make this case requires more space than I have here. For further background, see my discussion of Häring in *The Abuse of Conscience*; and see also Edmund Waldstein, O.Cist., "Bernhard Häring's Moral Theology," in *The Faith Once for All Delivered: Doctrinal Authority in Catholic Theology*, ed. Kevin L. Flannery, SJ (Emmaus Academic, 2023), 101–24. For his part, McBrien shows a willingness to reverse (if only occasionally) solemn magisterial teaching.

113. For discussion of these examples, see the chapter on doctrinal development in my *Engaging the Doctrine of Revelation: The Mediation of the Gospel through Church and Scripture* (Baker Academic, 2014). See also Francis Oakley's argument—despite the murky status of elements of the Council of Constance, due to the Great Schism—that Vatican I reversed the Council of Constance's conciliarist decree *Haec Sancta* and that this constitutes an example of reversing an "irreversible" teaching: Oakley, "History and the Return of the Repressed in Catholic Modernity: The Dilemma Posed by Constance," in Lacey and Oakley, *The Crisis of Authority in Catholic Modernity*, 29–56.

A real rupture with weighty and consistently taught doctrine would cast into doubt the Magisterium itself and all its decisions: On what grounds do we know that the Church's present judgment is true, if the Church in a weighty and consistent manner taught the very opposite until now? An arbitrary Magisterium would be merely the human will-to-power, no matter what claims it might make to be channeling the "Spirit." In such a situation, the Church's hierarchical structure would be threatened with collapse—an outcome, indeed, that many postconciliar dissenting theologians have explicitly wished for. If the rupture could be defended as a rupture of a weighty but still reversible teaching, then the best that could be said, in my view, is that this present-day reversal would itself be a likely candidate for reversal in the future, given the likelihood that the Magisterium of today (rather than the consistent Magisterium of multiple popes in the past) is in error. The motherhood of the Church requires a Magisterium that holds fast to divine revelation as handed down by the Church. In faith, de Lubac believes that Christ and the Holy Spirit will sustain Mother Church and her Magisterium in this regard, although the Church may err in some ways.

Second, believers must have a strong spiritual attitude of receptivity to Mother Church, just as de Lubac makes clear. The alternative would be a spirituality of private judgment (in the Newmanian sense of this reality). Filled with the Spirit, the whole Church receives Christ; the whole Church shares in Christ's salvific self-offering to the Father in the Eucharist. The Church is built upon Marian receptivity to Christ and his salvific gifts, and this receptivity is at the heart of Scripture and Tradition. Ontologically, every creature stands in a fundamental relation of receptivity to God. Everything that we are and have, insofar as it is good and real, comes from God. The grace of the Holy Spirit elevates this receptivity so that we can open our minds to receive all that Christ wants us to receive. We receive Christ through the mediation of the Church built up by his Spirit. If we refuse to be open to Mother Church (and thus to the Magisterium, which itself is bound to Marian receptivity) as the Church mediates Christ to us, then we will not be able to receive Christ's gifts, since one of his biblically attested gifts *is* the Church. We are not in charge, and we must be truly receptive rather than only accepting what we deem fit.[114]

Third, we can distinguish between cases where the hierarchical representatives of Mother Church communicate doctrinal and moral truth in a weighty, consistent, and solemn way and cases where the Magisterium puts forward non-definitive teaching, as for instance (to refer again to de Lubac) about what can be said speculatively about the human desire for beatitude given that grace and nature are distinct.[115] We owe the full assent of faith to all magisterial teaching that is presented to us solemnly as the faith of Mother Church. Not all magisterial teaching is at this level. But, as de Lubac notes, we owe respect to all magisterial teaching; we must pray to receive it in a spirit of reverent openness.

As the life of de Lubac suggests (and as the life of John Henry Newman shows as well), there may be times when it is permissible to cut against the grain of the present-day Magisterium, even to the point of significant resistance. In such cases, public denunciations—as distinct from raising concerns in a less polemical

114. For further discussion, see my "What God qua God Must Do: Providence, Predestination, and the Limits of *Sacra Doctrina*," in *Love Become Incarnate: Essays in Honor of Bruce D. Marshall*, ed. Justus H. Hunter, T. Adam Van Wart, and David L. Whidden III (Emmaus Academic, 2023), 193–213.

115. For further discussion of the distinction between non-definitive and definitive teaching (with respect to the ordinary magisterium), see Avery Dulles, SJ, "The Magisterium and Theological Dissent," in *The Craft of Theology: From Symbol to System*, exp. ed. (Crossroad, 1995), 105–18; and Dulles, *Magisterium: Teacher and Guardian of the Faith* (Sapientia, 2007), chapter 7. As Dulles points out, "The problem of dissent within the Church was acutely raised when Vatican II seemed to modify, and even perhaps to reverse, previous papal teaching on several subjects such as biblical inerrancy, the ecumenical movement, religious freedom, and criteria for membership in the Church" ("The Magisterium and Theological Dissent," 112). Dissent became widespread after the Council, and of course the Church over the centuries has undergone convulsions of dissent, as for instance the Reformation. Dulles recommends that the Magisterium should "avoid issuing too many statements, especially statements that appear to carry with them an obligation to assent" (116–17).

fashion—should be avoided by theologians, since public denunciations undermine believers' appreciation for the Church's motherhood and impair Marian receptivity in oneself and others, paving the way for the reign of private judgment. But when dealing with a non-definitive teaching that pastorally undermines weighty and consistent prior Catholic teaching, theologians have a duty to Mother Church to raise concerns in light of the sources of faith, Scripture and Tradition.

Thus, theologians may be required to publish works that call into question some aspects of the teaching of the contemporary Magisterium. In so doing, theologians' attitudes must remain receptive and Marian, willing to suffer ecclesiastical penalty obediently and refusing to enter into "opposition." A theologian who publishes such critiques can only do so with sorrow, recognizing that he or she may be wrong and avoiding vituperative rhetoric. Again, such valid "tension" or resistance cannot be to teachings that bear the evident marks of having been infallibly taught. The undermining of dogma—by which the risen Christ instructs believers, enlightening them in the Spirit about the truth of Scripture and Tradition—would call down the Lord's condemnation: "It would be better for him if a millstone were hung round his neck and he were cast into the sea, than that he should cause one of these little ones to sin" (Luke 17:2).

If ever we find ourselves in a time in which some resistance is required precisely in order to love Mother Church, let us, like de Lubac, "turn to God, acknowledging our dependence on Him and giving thanks"[116]—especially for Mother Church and for the Magisterium of the reigning pontiff. The alternative attitude would be unthinkable for a Catholic, who cannot proceed by "forging alliances of hate" against the pastors of Mother Church.[117] As Paul instructs his Philippian congregation during the difficult

116. Alan Noble, *On Getting Out of Bed: The Burden and Gift of Living* (InterVarsity, 2023), 101.

117. Tom Hiney, "The New Agnosticism," *First Things* 338 (December 2023): 17–22, at 21.

years of his imprisonment, "In everything by prayer and supplication with thanksgiving let your requests be made known to God. And the peace of God, which passes all understanding, will keep your hearts and your minds in Christ Jesus. . . . Whatever is true, whatever is honorable, whatever is just, whatever is pure, whatever is lovely, whatever is gracious, . . . if there is anything worthy of praise, think about these things" (Phil 4:6–8). One such thing is the Marian motherhood of the Church—never separated, let us note, from Simeon's prophetic word to Mary about her sharing in her Son's cross: "A sword will pierce through your own soul also" (Luke 2:35).

6

Apostolic

I. INTRODUCTION

When Catholics recite the Nicene Creed during Mass and profess that the Church is "apostolic," relatively few know what this term actually means—other than that it is a claim that the first members of the Church were Jesus's apostles and that the inspired books of the New Testament originate with them. What, then, does apostolicity mean?

Catholics and Protestants can generally agree on a baseline definition, despite a tragic history of polemics that led the Lutheran theologian Warren Quanbeck to remark in 1970, "Between 1520 and the present Lutherans and Catholics have on this topic addressed to each other language of such violence that humanly speaking it seems unforgiveable."[1] In his *Apostolicity: The Ecumenical Question in World Christian Perspective*, John Flett provides this baseline definition: "Apostolicity is identified first with the cultivation of the faith and so in relation to historical

1. Warren A. Quanbeck, "A Contemporary View of Apostolic Succession," in *Lutherans and Catholics in Dialogue*, vol. 4, *Eucharist and Ministry*, ed. Paul C. Empie and T. Austin Murphy (USA National Committee of the Lutheran World Federation, 1970), 178–88, at 178. Quanbeck goes on to offer an ecumenically fruitful account of Luther and the early Lutherans' protest: "He and his friends did not turn away from the traditional authorities because of historical amnesia or a radical distaste for everything from the past. When they stressed the importance of faith, of justification by grace alone, of the priesthood of the faithful, they thought of themselves not as innovators but as men who stood on scriptural and apostolic ground. . . . It is this crisis of faith and obedience that underlies the Lutheran objections to apostolic succession. When authorities whose duty it is to hand on the gospel, to safeguard sound doctrine, and to tend the flock of God refuse free course to the word of God, defend patent misunderstandings of doctrine, and excommunicate those who refuse to recant their defense of the gospel, it is understandable that earnest men should raise questions about the true authority of the bishops and the effectiveness of their relationship with the apostles" (179).

continuity, stability, order and office."[2] This definition is on display in the *Catechism of the Catholic Church*. The *Catechism* portrays the Church as "apostolic" because of three elements, all of which relate to "historical continuity, stability, order and office." These three elements are the following (and here one finds some differences with Protestant understandings): the Church is built upon the "foundation of the apostles" (Eph 2:20); the Church faithfully hands on the apostolic teaching or deposit of faith; and the apostles' successors, the bishops led by the pope, ensure that the apostolic deposit is handed on correctly.

For the *Catechism*, then, the core elements of the Church's apostolicity are the apostolic deposit of faith and apostolic succession, inclusive of the Petrine office. In his *Introduction to the Mystery of the Church*, Benoît-Dominique de La Soujeole approaches apostolicity from this perspective. He distinguishes between the "being" and the "action" of the Church, specifying that he intends to treat apostolicity in light of the Church's "being." He then argues that the apostolicity of the Church involves apostolic Tradition and the churches founded by the apostles. Faith and the handing on of faith in the Church, therefore, are at the heart of apostolicity. Grounding himself in the early Fathers, de La Soujeole explains that "there is something called *the apostolicity of faith*—in other words, the fact that we take our faith from the

2. John G. Flett, *Apostolicity: The Ecumenical Question in World Christian Perspective* (IVP Academic, 2016), 16. This definition does not, of course, entail agreement on particulars. Quanbeck reports that traditional Lutherans, for instance, deny "the necessity or even the advisability of apostolic succession through episcopal consecration. . . . [In this sense] apostolic succession can mean only an empty formality which in no way guarantees the apostolic heritage" (Quanbeck, "A Contemporary View of Apostolic Succession," 182). For Quanbeck, too, "Apostolic succession in the narrower sense as succession through episcopal ordination is not a *sine qua non* of the apostolic succession of church and ministry" (187). He adds, however, that "ordination by episcopal imposition of hands should be seen as a sign of the apostolic succession of the ministry and of the church, and therefore as a sign of the unity and catholicity of the church. Lutherans should for this reason acknowledge the usefulness of ordination by bishops through the history of the church as a sign of apostolicity, and where the sign is absent, recognize that it is right to work for its introduction" (187). His fundamental concern is the one shared by Luther and the early Lutherans: "The sign should never be separated from the reality which it signifies, namely the apostolic tradition. The sign of apostolic succession cannot take away the necessity of a constantly renewed submission to the gospel as it is communicated in the apostolic tradition, nor can it devalue the pastoral ministry which exists without episcopal ordination" (187).

witness of the apostles. . . . This is so-called *formal* apostolicity. And then there is the fact that this true faith is preserved thanks to the apostolic succession, for which it is the decisive criterion: the pastor is subject to what he must preserve in order to transmit it."[3] These two interrelated dimensions of apostolicity—the apostolic deposit and apostolic succession—are also the heart of the matter for Yves Congar, as can be seen in his "Apostolicité de ministère et apostolicité de doctrine."[4] Charles Journet is the source of the highly traditional discussion of apostolicity that de La Soujeole largely adopts in his book.[5]

Flett, a Presbyterian theologian, warns sharply against the above views of apostolicity. He thinks they treat the missionary spread of the faith as secondary. As a result, he argues, institutional structures become overly rigid, and institutional claims (including claims about how to understand Scripture) too expansive.[6] A particular historico-cultural expression of the Church is made normative for all time. When Christian faith takes on new forms in new places and times, such forms are condemned merely because they are not the canonized or normative form. The forms that Christianity took in the Roman Empire, or in the Byzantine Empire, or in sixteenth-century Germany, become sacrosanct. According to Flett, this harms inculturation in Africa or Asia. He suggests the following solution: "Might apostolicity be defined in terms of, and not in contest with, the diverse expressions of

3. Benoît-Dominique de La Soujeole, OP, *Introduction to the Mystery of the Church*, trans. Michael J. Miller (The Catholic University of America Press, 2014), 593. Regarding what de La Soujeole terms "formal apostolicity," Quanbeck observes, "There is no continuation of the apostolic office in the narrow sense of the term. Apostolic office as the foundation of the church comes to an end with the death of the last apostle. The two decisive qualifications for apostolic office are no longer possible, namely, that he be a witness of the resurrection, and that he has been appointed immediately by Jesus Christ" (Quanbeck, "A Contemporary View of Apostolic Succession," 185).

4. Yves Congar, OP, "Apostolicité de ministère et apostolicité de doctrine," in his *Ministères et communion ecclésiale* (Cerf, 1971), 51–94.

5. See Charles Journet, *The Church of the Word Incarnate: An Essay in Speculative Theology*, vol. 1, *The Apostolic Hierarchy*, trans. A. H. C. Downes, ed. Matthew K. Minerd (Emmaus Academic Press, 2025), 697–743.

6. Flett, *Apostolicity*, 16.

world Christianity? In this approach, apostolicity would cease to be an issue of how these communions correspond to a supposedly 'timeless' gospel expressed through the given language and institution of the church universal."[7] Instead, apostolicity would become a way of testifying to the importance of inculturation through diverse structures that fit with diverse places and times. Apostolicity would describe the *flexibility* of the apostles in their efforts to bear witness to Christ.

Flett quotes the Catholic theologian William Burrows, who complains that, due to the conflation of certain culture-specific norms with apostolicity, the Church presumes "the normativity of the 'European experience' and attempts to 'exercise control' over non-Western appropriations of the gospel through the insistence on 'the binding character of [the Western church's] formulation of the meaning of the Christian fact and Euro-American patterns of fellowship and worship.'"[8] According to Flett and Burrows, people who are filled with faith in Christ must be allowed to adapt and transform "apostolic" ecclesial structures, including with respect to ministerial office and to the liturgy, so that these structures fit with local cultures. Failure to recognize the need for such adaptation as part of missionary inculturation, Flett thinks, is the fatal flaw of Vatican II's *Ad Gentes* and Pope John Paul II's encyclical *Redemptoris Missio*.[9]

7. Flett, 19.

8. William R. Burrows, *New Ministries: The Global Context* (Orbis Books, 1980), 31–32 (cf. 79–80), quoted in Flett, *Apostolicity*, 27. Flett also cites José Comblin, *Called for Freedom: The Changing Context of Liberation Theology*, trans. Phillip Berryman (Orbis Books, 1998); Teresa Okure, "The Church in the World: A Dialogue on Ecclesiology," in *Theology and Conversation: Towards a Relational Theology*, ed. Jacques Haers and P. De Mey (Peeters, 2003), 393–438; and Edward Schillebeeckx, OP, *The Church with a Human Face: A New and Expanded Theology of Ministry* (Crossroad, 1987). Many other such books could be cited.

9. Flett also raises concerns about Jean Daniélou, SJ's *The Lord of History: Reflections on the Inner Meaning of History*, trans. Nigel Abercrombie (Longmans, 1958). He notes that for Daniélou, "the church embodies an international culture unified around a Hellenistic and, by extension, Latin core. All necessary authority for this position, according to Daniélou, rests in the church's historical origins and the persistence of the associated forms to the contemporary period. What he leaves unexamined is the extent to which the observed entanglement of Western culture with the social patterns of the church might, in fact, be revised given that mission mediates this cultural heritage to other cultures" (Flett, *Apostolicity*, 42). Daniélou is indebted to the work of Georges Florovsky on Hellenism and Christianity.

Even so, Flett rejects both "an unlimited freedom in relation to structures" and "an extreme form of cultural relativism in relation to theological affirmations."[10] He argues that a *proper* theology of apostolicity will show us what the "controls" are that can ensure a basic harmony between different valid structures and different sets of doctrinal claims. In his view, there is in fact a fundamental apostolic "doctrine" or, rather, a person: "Jesus Christ and him crucified."[11] "Apostolicity" therefore consists in constantly converting to Jesus Christ and being open to his ever-new authority in the Spirit.[12] Heavily indebted to Karl Barth, Flett remarks that the communities founded by the apostles have no foundation other than Christ, and so particular ecclesial structures and interpretations of Scripture are replaceable as the Spirit continues to blow where he will, under the reign of Christ. In sum, apostolicity is best defined as "the movement of the community beyond itself, the movement of the body toward its head," Jesus Christ.[13]

Flett's position is not persuasive to me. By arguing that apostolicity need not involve a body of definitive teaching (an apostolic deposit of faith) and episcopal order (an apostolic succession), he cuts off elements that I consider to be fundamental. The task of this chapter is ultimately to show why these elements are necessary. The first two sections of the chapter will investigate Karth Barth's discussion of apostolicity in *Church Dogmatics* 4.1 in comparison with John D. Zizioulas's Orthodox proposal, with

10. Flett, *Apostolicity*, 47.

11. Flett, 56.

12. Flett approvingly quotes the Catholic theologian Peter Phan's protest against traditional Catholic ecclesiology and dogma: "Appeals to unity masked 'diversity and multiplicity in favor of an imagined and often enforced uniformity. There is not, nor has there ever been, one Christianity; rather there exist Christianities (in the plural), all over the world and all the time.'" See Flett, *Apostolicity*, 287, quoting Peter C. Phan, "World Christianity: Its Implications for History, Religious Studies, and Theology," *Horizons* 39, no. 2 (2012): 171–88.

13. Flett, *Apostolicity*, 320. For Flett and Barth, apostolicity simply means that the Church is grounded in Christ; apostolicity is not about the Church's claim to possess a true deposit or a true ministry on its own, as though Christ could not change it. There is no secure "continuity" in the Church other than the continuity found in Christ, who makes free to manifest himself in multiple ecclesiastical forms and cultures, against any ecclesiastical "petrification" that turns the Church's gaze inward.

which I largely agree. My final section will then set forth a Catholic view of apostolicity, building especially on Irenaeus.

II. KARL BARTH'S REFORMED ACCOUNT OF APOSTOLICITY

For Karl Barth, apostolicity involves being disciples of Christ *in the same way that the apostles were disciples*. They received the Holy Spirit who came upon them, and they preached Christ by the Spirit's power. They bore witness not to a Church controlled by men but to the glory of the Father attested by the Son. They testified to the freedom of the Spirit, who can indeed work through men but who cannot be transferred from man to man automatically. A Church that is apostolic, then, will ensure the freedom of Jesus Christ and his Spirit. On this view, there can be no "institutional and ritual mediation and transference of the Holy Spirit and therefore of apostolicity."[14]

Barth adds that Christ manifested himself to his apostles in a unique way, since they saw him in his glory (and in his flesh). Thus, they cannot transfer their authoritative witness to any successors. All that can be done by the later community is to *accept* their written witness, without daring to augment or replace it. The later community must maintain and confirm the apostles' witness to what Christ himself manifested and allowed to be understood. The apostles' unique witness is contained in Scripture and is not contained elsewhere. The Church, however, can never pin down with *absolute* definitiveness what the scriptural word means, since Christ and his Spirit remain free always to speak afresh through the scriptural word. Therefore, while the apostles' witness can never be augmented or replaced and always remains the witness through which Christ manifests himself in every era, the apostles

14. Karl Barth, *Church Dogmatics*, vol. 4, part 1, *The Doctrine of Reconciliation*, trans. G.W. Bromiley, ed. G.W. Bromiley and T.F. Torrance (T&T Clark, 1956), 718.

themselves (let alone any later Christians) never become "lords of the community" or possess "any autonomous role."[15]

According to Barth, all the apostles—and not only Peter—stand as the "rock" (Matt 16:18) upon which Christ builds his Church. But they do so only in the sense that Christ makes use of them to manifest himself and to build his community: "They are only servants."[16] The apostles are uniquely Christ's servants, and so they are uniquely great. Their witness, found in Scripture, must be "sounded out and received and accepted and reproduced" at all times.[17] The Church is "apostolic" when it confesses that it has no power of its own and must serve Christ, allowing for Christ's absolute freedom and authority over the Church. Apostolic "succession" can only be apostolic service and obedience, not any kind of authority that can be juridically or ritually handed down to the next generation. The Church is not even subject to the authority of the apostles' (scriptural) witness. Rather, the Church, like the apostles, is radically subject to Christ himself. The Church only has ministerial authority, not dominion of any kind. In the school of the apostles, learning from their witness, the Church gains an "apostolic succession" of obedience, but none of transmitted authority.

At every point in history and at various places, therefore, the Church becomes the true "apostolic" Church when "by the ministry of the apostles He [Christ] speaks in it and to it and it accepts Him as the One who speaks in it and to it."[18] The Church practices this through hearing and obeying Christ through the biblical word. The Church is apostolic—and thus the true Church—whenever and wherever it "hears the apostolic witness of the New Testament, which implies that of the Old, and recognises and puts this witness into effect as the source and norm of its

15. Barth, *Church Dogmatics*, 4.1:718.
16. Barth, *Church Dogmatics*, 4.1:719.
17. Barth, *Church Dogmatics*, 4.1:719.
18. Barth, *Church Dogmatics*, 4.1:721.

existence."[19] When the Church does this, it is the servant-Church and it is apostolic; when it does not do this, it falsely lays claim to being apostolic. To be fully "apostolic," the Church does not need to conform to any particular outward structure. Instead, the Church is apostolic in encountering Scripture's witness to Christ and, in light of this witness, conforming itself solely to Christ, without trusting in anything else. Guided by the Spirit, the Church is "apostolic" when it looks toward the risen Christ and obeys him totally.

Apostolicity, then, is not about an episcopal structure or a doctrinal deposit, but rather is about constantly turning toward the Lord Jesus to whom the Scriptures (heard in the Spirit) testify. Wherever this turning toward the Lord happens—wherever we find obedient conversion to Jesus through his word that he always speaks freely to his people anew—"Scripture then works in the service of its Lord, and the Church becomes and is apostolic and therefore the true Church."[20] Again, neither hierarchical succession nor enduring doctrine signals the presence of apostolicity; only turning obediently toward Christ through the words of Scripture suffices for this.

Nevertheless, Barth maintains that the above insights have implications for what the structure of the apostolic Church should be. Namely, the structure should be loose enough with respect to Church government that "all encroachment on the lordship of the One who is alone the Lord is either avoided or so suppressed and eliminated in practice that there is place for his rule."[21] The Lord Jesus must be free to speak authoritative new words to the Church through Scripture. Clearly, this is quite the opposite of a dogmatic, hierarchical Church that takes control away from Christ by supposing that apostolicity means a succession of authoritative hierarchs handing on (and further developing)

19. Barth, *Church Dogmatics*, 4.1:722.
20. Barth, *Church Dogmatics*, 4.1:723.
21. Barth, *Church Dogmatics*, 4.1:723.

immutable dogmas. Barth does not wish to pin down a particular structure as the right one, since this would remove freedom from Christ to decide in different ways and at different times.

Understood in this way, apostolicity entails that the Church's "preaching, doctrine, instruction and theology" will always strictly concentrate upon "Jesus Christ as God revealed and speaking and acting."[22] The Church will set up nothing of its own, whether dogma or ordained ministry, that threatens to take the place of the sole Head. In this context, Barth warns against becoming attached to an immutable "orthodoxy," since we can control the contents of orthodoxy, whereas for any security we must look solely toward Jesus Christ, who cannot be captured by us. Certainly there is such a thing as "orthodoxy": it consists in rightly confessing the Christ who manifests himself in the witness of his apostles (Scripture). But no set of human formulas will be able to pin this down once and for all.

Therefore, the Church will always and above all be "a listening Church," listening not to itself but to Christ who continues to speak.[23] The Church is recognizably apostolic when seeking to hear Christ and to proclaim Christ, rather than focusing on any other "neighbouring centres and truths and priorities and directions."[24] The Church that is "apostolic" will never focus itself on its own experience or its own insight or decisions, but rather will always focus on Christ and allow itself to be governed by the One who is above any "Christian feeling or power of thought or activity."[25] All confidence, all security, will be in the living Christ, to whom apostolic Scripture bears witness, rather than in any human resource or authority.

Barth observes that even the apostles are not important in themselves. As mere heralds in service to Christ, they "renounce

22. Barth, *Church Dogmatics*, 4.1:723.
23. Barth, *Church Dogmatics*, 4.1:724.
24. Barth, *Church Dogmatics*, 4.1:724.
25. Barth, *Church Dogmatics*, 4.1:724.

any self-grounded or self-reposing rightness or importance of their distinctive being and activity," and instead they look resolutely toward Christ.[26] In renouncing themselves and their own resources in favor of Christ, the apostles established what "apostolic" means. Their perspective is normative for the Church. No doubt, the Church performs actions that build it up, such as gathering to hear the scriptural word, as well as baptism, the Lord's Supper, common prayer, and theology. But such things are done only as part of proclaiming Jesus Christ to the world as its crucified and risen Savior. The Church, as such, can never be what is proclaimed; the Church is always under the judgment of Christ, and exists only in service to Christ, without anything that is securely its own. Its being is pure (apostolic) mission: proclaiming Christ.

In my view, the apostolic Scriptures have more definitive truths to teach than Barth allows—including more about the Church. The Church, for 1 Timothy 3:15, is "the pillar and bulwark of the truth." The apostle Peter receives "the keys of the kingdom of heaven," and Jesus tells him, "Whatever you bind on earth shall be bound in heaven, and whatever you loose on earth shall be loosed in heaven" (Matt 16:19). Jesus prays in his Farewell Discourse that his disciples "may be consecrated in truth" (John 17:19). He tells his disciples earlier in John's Gospel, "You will know the truth, and the truth will make you free" (John 8:32). The "glorious gospel of the blessed God" (1 Tim 1:11) includes moral teachings, and it includes teachings such as that "there is one God" (1 Tim 2:5). Paul urges Timothy to "guard what has been entrusted to you," including "the sound words of our Lord Jesus Christ and the teaching which accords with godliness" (1 Tim 6:3, 20).[27] Titus, too, received a commission directly from Paul. Paul tells Titus, "This is why I left you in Crete, that you might amend

26. Barth, *Church Dogmatics*, 4.1:724.

27. Luke Timothy Johnson has defended Pauline authorship of these letters in various publications, most powerfully in his *The First and Second Letters to Timothy: A New Translation with Introduction and Commentary* (Yale University Press, 2001).

what was defective, and appoint elders in every town as I directed you" (Titus 1:5). Paul describes himself and the other apostles as "servants of Christ and stewards of the mysteries of God" (1 Cor 4:1). Paul likewise describes the "bishop," appointed by Paul (or by Titus), as "God's steward" (Titus 1:7).

In the book of Acts, "the apostles and the elders" gather to discuss whether the Gospel requires the Gentiles to be circumcised and obey the Mosaic law (Acts 15:6). Arguing that the answer is no, Paul is at the center of the debate. In Galatians, he describes a conflict that ended only when the apostles met together in council in Jerusalem. He remembers that "when they perceived the grace that was given to me, James and Cephas and John, who were reputed to be pillars, gave to me and Barnabas the right hand of fellowship, that we should go to the Gentiles and they to the circumcised; only they would have us remember the poor, which was the very thing I was eager to do" (Gal 2:9–10). This memory crackles with tension in the way that Paul frames it, and it is no surprise when he proceeds to recount a conflict he had with Peter in Antioch over the fact that Peter at first felt free to eat with Gentiles, whereas after James's intervention Peter separated himself from eating with Gentiles. On behalf of his own understanding of the status of the Mosaic law in the light of Christ's saving work, Paul "opposed [Peter] to his face" (Gal 2:11).

The book of Acts describes how such doctrinal conflicts are handled. Acts 15:4 remarks, "When they [Paul and Barnabas] came to Jerusalem, they were welcomed by the Church and the apostles and the elders." These "elders" are associates of the apostles, and they provide a basis for successors of the apostles in the local churches, as found in Acts 20:17–38, Titus 1:5, and elsewhere. Acts 15:6 describes the controversy being addressed by "the apostles and the elders" gathering to discern the truth of the Gospel. There are speeches by Peter, Barnabas, Paul, and James. James articulates the solution, but he does so along lines prompted by Peter and in accord with the ministry of Paul and Barnabas. In their letter communicating their solution, the apostles and elders affirm the authority of the gathering to represent "the whole Church" (Acts 15:22). The conclusion of the letter states explicitly that the gathering speaks in the power of the Holy Spirit and with the Spirit's divine authority: "It has seemed good to the Holy Spirit and to us to lay upon you no greater burden than these necessary things: that you abstain from what has been sacrificed to idols and from blood and from what is strangled and from unchastity" (Acts 15:28–29).

I mention the above to indicate why I think that Barth's portrait of apostolicity is too simple. Certainly, the apostles proclaim Christ and rely upon him rather than upon themselves for salvation. Certainly, the Gospel is about Jesus Christ crucified and risen. But there are aspects of Scripture's apostolic witness that are not sufficiently present in Barth's account. These aspects include the transmission of authority in the Church and the indications that the Spirit-filled Church will not fail in communicating the truth about the realities of salvation. These realities include God, Christ, the Holy Spirit, Baptism, the Eucharist, the Church as the Body of Christ, the laying on of hands, marriage, the resurrection of the dead, eternal life, and so on. I do not think that the development of Church government is simply indeterminate. According to the New Testament, the apostles possess authority, exercise it in the Spirit's name, and transmit it to others by the laying on of hands. Apostolicity has to do with the deposit of faith and the governance and authority of the Church.

Such a claim does not require a Church that lacks humility or deems itself to be in charge of the Holy Spirit. For the Catholic Church in particular, a lack of humility about the transmission of authority and the transmission of dogma would be unseemly at this stage of history. One need only think of the terrible tenth-century popes, or of the many scandals involving bishops across the centuries and today, or even of Gregory of Nazianzus's disgust with the mode of proceeding that characterized the Council of Constantinople—let alone the Great Schism, the corrupt Renaissance popes who laid the seeds of the Reformation, and, more recently, the rejection by many nominal Catholics of core truths of the Gospel. After Christ identified Peter as the rock on which Christ would build his Church, Peter reacted vehemently against Christ's next words, which were about Christ's coming death. Christ had to correct him in the strongest possible terms: "Get behind me, Satan!" (Matt 16:22–23). Apostolicity does not entail arrogance. Indeed, it is an exercise in faith and hope, since only the Holy Spirit could ensure an "apostolic succession" that hands on the "apostolic deposit of faith," given the sinfulness, foolishness, and ever-present urge to capitulate to the spirit of the age that one finds in Christ's Church and in oneself.

III. JOHN D. ZIZIOULAS'S EASTERN ORTHODOX ACCOUNT OF APOSTOLICITY

Along lines quite different from Barth's, the Orthodox theologian John D. Zizioulas is notable for his distinction between, on the one hand, Christ's sending of the apostles to evangelize—apostles who then send others, who send still others, in a continuous and ongoing chain—and, on the other hand, the apostles' presence *here and now* in the eschatological gathering of each Eucharistic community.[28] I note that from a Catholic perspective, making the eschatological (and Eucharistic) dimension of the Church central to apostolicity makes a lot of sense. Let me, therefore, set forth Zizioulas's perspective by surveying chapters 4 and 5 of *Being as Communion*, respectively titled "Eucharist and Catholicity" and "Apostolic Continuity and Succession."

28. Flett contends, however, that Zizioulas makes his preferred, culturally inflected hierarchical and liturgical Church structures permanent and universally binding. In Flett's view, this makes mission into other cultures, which in Flett's view requires shaping Church structures to reflect the new cultures, a truly secondary or even impossible thing. See Flett, *Apostolicity*, 302.

Zizioulas emphasizes "the catholic character of the eucharist."[29] The Eucharist enables us to see that for the Church to be "catholic" means to share fully in Christ, through the Holy Spirit. The Eucharist also makes manifest the eschatological dimension of catholicity, which is measured not quantitatively through power but qualitatively through humility and love. If the existence of hierarchical orders is thought to be an uncatholic dichotomy (between clergy and laity), Zizioulas reminds us that ordination takes place within the context of the Eucharistic liturgy.

In this light, Zizioulas makes some remarks about apostolicity. He notes that apostolic succession is not merely a list of bishops separated from the laity. Rather, apostolic succession has its vital center in the Eucharistic liturgy, in which bishops are ordained. Zizioulas grants the possibility that the lists are incomplete, and he grants that the notion of apostolic succession (of bishops) may have only emerged in the mid-second century. His key point is that apostolic succession carries the weight that it does because the bishops represented (Eucharistic) communities. Understood in this way, the notion of apostolic succession serves to identify "the *continuity of the Church's historical life in its entirety*, as it was realized in each community."[30]

Therefore, apostolicity—understood in terms of apostolic succession—and catholicity go together. Each bishop was thought to be a successor of the whole group of apostles rather than of a particular apostle. Apostolicity, inclusive of apostolic succession, confirms the catholic wholeness of the Church, and each local church is "*fully apostolic*."[31] Each local church is connected, through the bishop at the head of the Eucharistic community (united to all other bishops and all Eucharistic communities), to the presence of the apostles. Moreover, the past and present are

29. John D. Zizioulas, *Being as Communion: Studies in Personhood and the Church* (St. Vladimir's Seminary Press, 1985), 157.

30. Zizioulas, 168.

31. Zizioulas, 168.

joined in the Eucharistic liturgy, so that apostolic succession is more than just a linear historical list.

Zizioulas goes on to define apostolicity in terms of two aspects: a *historical* mission carried forth in the world that has its origins in Christ's sending of the apostles and in the apostles sending their successors; and an *eschatological* presence of the apostles (as the "Twelve") that stands at the heart of the living Church in every era. According to Zizioulas, among the early Fathers, Clement of Rome presents apostolicity in a historical manner, while Ignatius of Antioch presents apostolicity in an eschatological manner.

Both the historical and the eschatological approaches are necessary. Regarding the historical approach, Zizioulas notes that Christ anchors apostolicity by pouring out his Spirit and sending his apostles. The apostolic period provides a past norm for the present Church. The Church recognizes itself to be connected to the apostles, and Christ makes this possible through his Spirit and according to established modes of the transmission of apostolic authority and testimony. Regarding the eschatological approach, Zizioulas notes that it has its anchor in the risen Christ, around whom the apostles are uniquely gathered. The presence of eschatological apostolicity is felt here and now, insofar as the Church already participates in the final fullness. The Holy Spirit makes possible this participation in the midst of history. The community of the apostles becomes not past but present.

How can these two aspects of apostolicity be brought together? Zizioulas proposes an answer consisting in five steps. First, he notes that Christ's existence is pneumatological and relational, which means that Christ never exists without his Body. We are radically in Christ, and all future time and the eschaton itself are already in Christ. In Christ and the Spirit, therefore, history is never purely linear; it always participates in the eschaton, which is constantly breaking into the linear dimension of history. Thus, we do not simply get farther away from Christ and from the apostles as time passes. Our continuity with Christ and the apostles involves not only historical transmission but also eschatological participation. Second, we experience a real communion with the apostles even now; the reality of the apostolic communion is not simply transmitted from the past but rather is also experienced "from" the eschatological fullness.

This second point expands the meaning of apostolic succession and the transmission of the apostolic deposit of faith. Zizioulas affirms that the Petrine keys (see Matt 16:19) are transmitted in apostolic succession over the course of history—though he thinks that all bishops share equally in the keys. Zizioulas also affirms that there is an "apostolic kerygma" that the Church faithfully preserves and hands on, and that originated with the apostles (who received it from Christ).[32] But the linear-historical dimension of apostolicity is not the sole dimension. The "apostolic kerygma," after all, has the risen Christ as its living center; and the keys are "keys of the [eschatological] kingdom." Thus, says Zizioulas, "in both cases historical prerogatives are eschatologized."[33] The Church is not only moving through history as part of history but also is already the judge of all creation as the embodiment of the inbreaking of the eschaton.

Third, the Holy Spirit's constitution of the Church means that the identification of the Church with the inbreaking kingdom is not absurd. If apostolicity is understood solely historically, then the Church's claim to be apostolic may seem to imply that apostolicity is the secure and mechanical possession of the Church, despite the Church's failures and with no reference to the Church's constant dependence on the Spirit's gifting. From an eschatological perspective, however, the Church's apostolicity can be recognized to be an "epicletic" reality, requiring that the Church always ask the Holy Spirit to bestow what, in its historical dimension, the Church already is. Thus, there is no mechanical security in the historical transmission. The historical transmission

32. Zizioulas, 184.

33. Zizioulas, 184.

will not fail, but neither is it understandable without the eschatological dimension of the Spirit's outpouring, the constant renewal of Pentecost coming from the risen Christ and his eschatological fullness. Without denying historical continuity with the apostles via faithful historical transmission, the eschatological dimension grounds apostolicity in the Spirit's gifting to the Church here and now. Zizioulas puts the matter strongly (in a manner that answers some of Barth's concerns, though Zizioulas does not mention Barth): "The epicletic life of the Church shows only one thing: That there is no security for her to be found in any historical guarantee as such—be it ministry or word or sacrament or even the historical Christ Himself. Her constant dependence on the Spirit proves that her history is to be constantly eschatological."[34] At the same time, since the Spirit is Christ's Spirit, the Church's apostolicity is also historical, originating in Christ's life with and his sending of the apostles.

Fourth, given that Christ himself is filled with the Spirit, there need be no opposition (for those who are "in Christ") between history-as-linear-progression and history-as-the-space-of-eschatological-inbreaking. Both are true "in Christ." The kingdom is present already but not yet. We have a yearning for the fullness of the kingdom, and we receive a foretaste of it through the eschatological dimension of apostolicity. But this foretaste is rooted in the historical Christ (who is also eschatological), and therefore it is rooted in his historical life with and sending of the apostles. The Eucharist brings the two dimensions together.

Fifth, concentrated reflection on the Eucharist reveals that it is where apostolicity comes into its own and can be perceived fully for what it is. The Eucharist intrinsically involves the historical apostolic succession and the handing on and proclamation of the apostolic deposit of faith; and yet the Eucharist is also the eschatological inbreaking of the kingdom and the union of the

34. Zizioulas, 185–86.

many into one in Christ, as a foretaste of eternal life. Eschatological past (Christ and his apostles) and eschatological future (the fullness of the kingdom) are united. This happens, says Zizioulas, through the epiclesis, where the Spirit is called upon to work the Eucharistic mystery. Uniting historical past and eschatological future, the Eucharist is "the context in which the basic concrete manifestation of apostolic continuity" takes place.[35]

In light of the above, Zizioulas draws some conclusions about apostolicity's historical dimension. The more complicated aspect is apostolic succession, but the handing on of the apostolic deposit of faith also has complications. For one thing, the Spirit's work must be present at all times, if the words of Jesus (and of the Scriptures) are to be received in faith. Zizioulas states, "In the New Testament itself we can find an idea of *paradosis* or *logia* which are historically transmitted from place to place and time to time. And yet, it is the Spirit that vivifies the words."[36] The transmission of the apostolic deposit of faith takes place within the Spirit-filled community and thus can never be separated from the "eschatological" dimension of apostolicity. In Zizioulas's view, Irenaeus comes close to overemphasizing the "historically transmitted norm" as though it could suffice on its own, but fortunately Irenaeus also gives a strong place to the Spirit and the Eucharist.[37] In the patristic liturgy, too, the placement of the Liturgy of the Word ensured that the Eucharist was the preeminent context for receiving the apostolic deposit of faith as communicated by the Scriptures.

Insofar as the apostolic deposit of faith is articulated dogmatically, Zizioulas warns against viewing dogma solely in a "historical" manner—as truths that must be handed on intact—and not also in an "eschatological" manner in which the constant re-reception of dogmatic truth in the Spirit enables dogmas to

35. Zizioulas, 188.

36. Zizioulas, 189.

37. Zizioulas, 189.

be truly alive in the Church, "in new forms of experience and with a constant openness to the future."[38] Zizioulas is contending against a doctrinal antiquarianism that separates doctrinal propositions from the ongoing life of the Church in the Spirit. But the "historical" apostolic deposit of faith—apostolicity understood with a strong valuation of the Church's past—needs equal emphasis alongside the eschatological.[39]

With respect to apostolic succession in episcopal ministry, Catholics highlight the role of Peter among the apostles—that is, the special leadership role that Peter receives according to Scripture and that pertains to the office of the bishop of Rome. Catholics and Orthodox can agree, however, on the basic point that (as Zizioulas says) "already in *1 Clement* the missionary or historical scheme of continuity implies the idea of apostolic succession through an instituted ministry."[40] Zizioulas emphasizes that apostolic succession has to do not simply with the individual bishops (as such) in the list, but rather with these same bishops in relation to the whole, especially the presbyterate in the local church. Apostolic succession is, in this sense, the "succession of communities," for which the bishops serve as instruments.[41]

Apostolic succession also involves the particular churches that trace their origins back to the founding work of the apostles. These churches help to ground continuity with the apostles. Zizioulas cautions that not only the historical lineage but also (once again) the eschatological dimension needs attention here. From the eschatological perspective, each local church is an image of the apostle Peter (symbolized by the bishop) surrounded by the whole apostolic college, so that the eschatological fullness of apostolicity is present in each local church. Zizioulas warns against following Cyprian in conceiving of the apostolic college

38. Zizioulas, 191–92.

39. See Reinhard Hütter, *John Henry Newman on Truth and Its Counterfeits: A Guide for Our Times* (The Catholic University of America Press, 2020).

40. Zizioulas, *Being as Communion*, 192.

41. Zizioulas, 198.

without Christ, which leads inevitably to the search for a "vicar of Christ" along Catholic lines. Zizioulas adds that Catholic ecclesiology does not give sufficient significance to the bishop's relation to his local church. The local church (including that of Rome) tends to get overlooked, and instead the pope (as the "vicar of Christ") leads the whole Church from Rome. For Zizioulas, the local churches that were founded by the apostles have a special status, but in fact all local churches are fully apostolic, given the eschatological dimension of apostolicity.

Although the historical understanding of apostolicity has been central for Orthodox (and Catholic) theology for centuries, Zizioulas thinks it is seriously flawed. First, the notion that the Church's episcopal ministry is "*derived*" from the apostles (and their appointing of successors) needs revision, given what we know of the late first-century Church.[42] Second, the notion of (dogmatic and liturgical) Tradition is overly static. In actual fact, the faith has never been handed on without constantly being "re-enacted and re-received in the Spirit."[43] There is an opening to doctrinal development here, even if Zizioulas does not mention the term.

IV. AN IRENAEAN CATHOLIC PERSPECTIVE

In my view, Zizioulas is correct about the two dimensions of apostolicity, but he risks allowing the eschatological dimension to dominate the historical one, and he is too critical of the papacy. In this section, therefore, I will foreground the historical dimension of apostolicity.

As is well known, the Reformation raised a number of serious questions about the origins of Roman Catholic ministries and doctrines. After all, Timothy and Titus hardly seem to be bishops in the later sense. If Christ established Peter as the bishop

42. Zizioulas, 207.
43. Zizioulas, 207.

of Rome with the jurisdiction claimed by the later popes, then how is it that the successors of Peter in Rome (if at first there even was *one* appointed successor, rather than a set of elders) did not exercise their authority in anything like the way that medieval and modern popes do? John Henry Newman addresses such questions in describing doctrinal development, as distinct from doctrinal corruption, in his *Essay on the Development of Christian Doctrine*. But some religiously liberal Catholics—joining Protestants in this respect—have proposed a different answer: namely, that the offices of the bishops and the pope were invented to suit the times and can now be reversed or radically changed.[44]

I have argued in an earlier work that the apostles understood themselves to have a participation in Christ's priestly, prophetic, and royal authority, as an apostolic ministerial order handing on the deposit of faith.[45] Even if this is true, however, it is evident that there has been a significant (Newmanian) development of ministerial order and, even more so, of the papacy. John Rist states that in Rome in the early second century, "presbyter-bishops were to be found . . . and even presumably a chairman, the successor of Clement in that role, elected by the local community."[46] But, in Rist's view, the authoritative episcopal office that was then developing in the Greek East was not yet present in Rome. Even Ignatius of Antioch was not a bishop in the later sense of the term, according to Rist, although Rist takes note that, for Ignatius, Baptism and the Eucharist "can only be performed in (or with reference to) a community where there is a bishop."[47] Rist

44. See, for example, Terrence W. Tilley, *Inventing Catholic Tradition* (Orbis Books, 2000).

45. See chapter 3 of my *Christ and the Catholic Priesthood: Ecclesial Hierarchy and the Pattern of the Trinity* (Hillenbrand Books, 2010), where I critique such works as James Tunstead Burtchaell, CSC, *From Synagogue to Church: Public Services and Offices in the Earliest Christian Communities* (Cambridge University Press, 1992); and Francis Sullivan, SJ, *From Apostles to Bishops: The Development of the Episcopacy in the Early Church* (Newman, 2001). See also, more recently, Alistair C. Stewart, *The Original Bishops: Office and Order in the First Christian Communities* (Baker Academic, 2014).

46. John M. Rist, *What Is Truth? From the Academy to the Vatican* (Cambridge University Press, 2008), 219. For Newman and Ignaz von Döllinger on the development of the papacy, see chapter 5 of my *Newman on Doctrinal Corruption* (Word on Fire Academic, 2022).

47. Rist, *What Is Truth?*, 217.

thinks that the New Testament indicates that, when a Christian community lacked an itinerant apostle, it was governed by a set of "presbyters," some of whom could be called "bishops," but certainly not "monarchical" bishops of the kind that emerged later.[48]

All this is speculative, but it is easily squared with Zizioulas's proposal that, until perhaps the mid-second century, apostolic succession pertained to communities (led by a "bishop") rather than necessarily to a monarchical bishop who handed on his authority to a successor. Historical apostolic succession does not require the absence of doctrinal development regarding office in the Church. That there was an apostolic succession in local churches (as the apostles grew old and died), and that this succession involved some kinds of doctrinal and cultic authority that were understood as apostolic, seems clear. Joseph Ratzinger observes, "In those writings of the New Testament that stand on the cusp of the second generation or else already belong to it . . . the principle of succession does in fact take on concrete shape. The Protestant notion that the 'succession' consists solely in the word as such, but not in any 'structures,' is proved to be anachronistic in light of . . . the New Testament."[49] Ratzinger especially has in view the laying on of hands, which gives the recipient a share in Christ's (and the apostles') authority in the local church by the Spirit's power. Ratzinger also notes that there is testimony in Irenaeus to the emergence of Roman primacy, prior to the time when the New Testament was canonized.

I see no reason to doubt Irenaeus when in book 3 of *Against the Heresies* he writes about apostolic succession, in the context of an apostolic Gospel that was "first preached orally" and later

48. For the standard view, see Ernst Dassmann, "Zur Entstehung des Monepiskopats" and "Bichofsbestellung in der frühen Kirche," in *Ämter und Dienste in den frühchristlichen Gemeinden* (Verlag Nobert M. Borengässer, 1994), 49–73 and 190–211.

49. Joseph Ratzinger, *Called to Communion: Understanding the Church Today*, trans. Adrian Walker (Ignatius, 1996), 67. Arguably, early apostolic succession especially had to do with the apostolic sees associated with Peter—namely, Rome, Antioch, and Alexandria. See Vincent Twomey, SVD, *Apostolikos Thronos: Rival Accounts of Roman Primacy in Eusebius and Athanasius* (Emmaus Academic, 2023).

handed on in Scripture.[50] Irenaeus argues that the core contents of this apostolic Gospel allow for no correction. The apostles who delivered it did so not only individually but also collectively, as the one Church. As Irenaeus points out, the Gnostics reject apostolic mediation. They reject the truth of much of the Scriptures and instead claim to have been taught "by a living voice" or to have discovered the truth for themselves.[51] Irenaeus counters the Gnostics with an apostolic "rule of truth" to which the Scriptures testify.[52] He states that what he believes about the Gospel of Christ has been handed on by bishops in apostolic succession and is known to be the apostles' doctrine—that is, "the tradition that derives from the apostles and is guarded in the Churches by the

50. Irenaeus of Lyons, *Against the Heresies* 3.1, trans. Dominic J. Unger, OFM Cap., with Irenaeus M. Steenberg (Paulist, 2012), 30. For succinct background to Irenaeus's theology and his understanding of the "Gnostics," see John Anthony McGuckin, *The Path of Christianity: The First Thousand Years* (IVP Academic, 2017), 48–53. See also John Behr, *The Way to Nicaea*, vol. 1 of *The Formation of Christian Theology* (St. Vladimir's Seminary Press, 2001), 29–46.

51. Irenaeus of Lyons, *Against the Heresies* 3.2, p. 31. For the argument (against Irenaeus) that there was no "single thing called 'Christianity'" and that there was no "single, original orthodoxy and . . . single, multifaceted Gnosticism," see David Brakke, *The Gnostics: Myth, Ritual, and Diversity in Early Christianity* (Harvard University Press, 2010) (quotations from pp. 3 and 5). In the tradition of Walter Bauer (which he and others have developed and enriched), Brakke argues more fully: "Any conception of 'the varieties of early Christianity' that places a single proto-orthodoxy within a plurality of 'other groups' retains one key aspect of the Irenaean view: that proto-orthodoxy was single and consistent wherever it was found, while other forms of Christianity were multiple and diverse. But, as we shall see, in several important ways such proto-orthodox teachers as Justin Martyr and Clement of Alexandria had more in common with, say, Valentinus than they did with Bishop Irenaeus. There was no single and uniform proto-orthodoxy, but multiple modes of piety, authority, and theology that later orthodox represents as its forerunners" (10). See Walter Bauer, *Orthodoxy and Heresy in Earliest Christianity* (Fortress, 1971), originally published in 1934; and see also Karen L. King, *What Is Gnosticism?* (Harvard University Press, 2003); and Denise Kimber Buell, *Why This New Race: Ethnic Reasoning in Early Christianity* (Columbia University Press, 2005). More recently, see Markus Vinzent, *Resetting the Origins of Christianity: A New Theory of Sources and Beginnings* (Cambridge University Press, 2023), which contends not only that "Christianity did not begin with the [putative] appearances of the risen Christ" (x) but also that, in fact, the New Testament texts are not first-century products but rather were re-written (in the forms we now possess) much later—for instance, "the Gospels were pseudonymous rewritings of an earlier and no longer extant gospel-narrative, produced on oral material by a certain Marcion of Sinope" (xiv). For Vinzent on Irenaeus, see *Resetting the Origins of Christianity*, 154–91, arguing for "the dependence of Irenaeus' collection of Christian writings on its shorter predecessor—Marcion's 'New Testament'" (184). For his part, Congar responds to Bauer by eschewing "the simplistic idea of 'rediscovering' a unity which is supposed to have been 'lost.' And that allows us to look for a unity which allows of diversity, a unity which has existed despite the fact of divisions." Yves Congar, OP, *Diversity and Communion*, trans. John Bowden (Twenty-Third Publications, 1985), 21.

52. Irenaeus of Lyons, *Against the Heresies* 3.2, p. 31.

succession of the presbyters."[53] The "succession" described here is plausibly a succession of communities led by presbyter-bishops (as Zizioulas suggests); one need not claim that there was no development in understanding the office of the "bishops" or "presbyters." Although Irenaeus may mean more, he means at least that the communities founded by the apostles heard and believed the apostolic preaching and carefully handed on that preaching.

Irenaeus insists strongly upon his own historical connection to the apostles and their successors. He claims that "the tradition of the apostles" is available to anyone who wishes to receive it.[54] It is not esoteric. Rather, the "bishops" who have handed on the apostolic tradition are known by name. Irenaeus testifies to their chain of succession. He notes that they have upheld the apostolic doctrine and have never affirmed anything like the Gnostic teaching. Sent into the world by the crucified and risen Christ, the apostles bestowed "their own teaching office" upon their successors, whom the apostles hoped would "be perfect and blameless in every respect."[55]

Rather than detailing the list of succession in each of the churches established by the apostles, Irenaeus focuses on the church of Rome on the grounds that it is "the greatest and most ancient Church," having been founded by Peter and Paul.[56] This community received the apostolic tradition whose content has been passed down "through the successions of the bishops."[57] Moreover, because of its standing and its "greater authority," all other churches must be in accord with the church of Rome.[58] Irenaeus claims that in the church of Rome above all, "the apostolic tradition has always been safeguarded."[59]

53. Irenaeus of Lyons, 3.2, p. 31.
54. Irenaeus of Lyons, 3.3, p. 32.
55. Irenaeus of Lyons, 3.3, p. 32.
56. Irenaeus of Lyons, 3.3, p. 32.
57. Irenaeus of Lyons, 3.3, p. 32.
58. Irenaeus of Lyons, 3.3, p. 32.
59. Irenaeus of Lyons, 3.3, p. 32.

After the deaths of the apostles Peter and Paul, says Irenaeus, the administration of the church of Rome was given to Linus as bishop. Anacletus came after Linus, and then came Clement. Clement had seen the apostles and heard their teaching, and he knew the apostolic tradition of faith and practice. Indeed, at the time of Clement, there were still many alive who had seen and heard the apostles. Irenaeus explains that the Clement to whom he is referring is the author of the "forceful letter to the Corinthians" in which the apostolic tradition (the content of apostolic faith and practice) is reaffirmed.[60]

According to Irenaeus, then, the Christian community of Rome in the first century had a series of bishops who succeeded the apostles and who personally had heard the apostolic teaching. Their understanding of that teaching, he notes, can be found in Clement's letter. Thus, apostolicity in the shape of a historical succession of bishops and an apostolic deposit of faith are perfectly real things for Irenaeus. His explanation should embolden us to insist upon the historical connection, via communities led by their "bishops," to the apostles and the apostolic tradition. After Clement, says Irenaeus, there followed Evaristus, Alexander, Xystus, Telesphorus the martyr, Hyginus, Pius, Anicetus, Soter, and Eleutherus. Irenaeus observes that Eleutherus is presently bishop of Rome, which means Irenaeus was writing around 180. There must have been living memory of many earlier bishops of Rome at the time when Irenaeus wrote.

The basic idea of the apostles having successors who, as "bishops," administered the major churches and who knew and upheld the teaching of the apostolic founders of the churches is plausible. If the teaching of the later bishops cohered with the teaching of Clement's letter to the Corinthians—and there is no reason to doubt this (certainly Irenaeus, who knew and had met

60. Irenaeus of Lyons, 3.3, p. 33. For this letter, see *The Epistles of St. Clement of Rome and St. Ignatius of Antioch*, trans. James A. Kleist, SJ (Newman Bookshop, 1946). See also Kenneth J. Howell's interpretive essays, and the scholarship cited therein, in *Clement of Rome and the Didache: A New Translation and Theological Commentary* (CHResources, 2012), chapters 1–5.

Eleutherus, had every reason to affirm it)—then the existence of an apostolic deposit of faith is confirmed, since Clement's letter fits with the New Testament's teachings.

Irenaeus emphasizes how important this historical succession is, and I think we should follow his lead. For Irenaeus, the list of successors to Peter serves as a guarantee of a connection to the apostolic teaching. It is evident why this would have been important to the church of Rome, and it would be surprising had there been no such historical memory. It makes sense that the earliest "presbyter-bishops" understood themselves to be successors of the apostles carrying forward what they, and many others in their community, had heard from the apostles. Apostolic succession, Irenaeus argues, "is the fullest proof that it is one and the same life-giving faith that has been preserved in the Church from the apostles until now, and has been handed down in truth."[61]

As further evidence for apostolic succession, Irenaeus mentions people whom he says he knew when he was young. Above all, he knew Polycarp, who was the bishop of Smyrna. Irenaeus recalls that Polycarp told stories of listening to the apostles and to others who had heard the Lord. This historical element of continuity was a crucial part of the early Church, and Irenaeus is right to highlight it. By the time he knew Polycarp—decades before writing *Against the Heresies*—Polycarp was a very old man, approaching his death by martyrdom (which took place in the late 150s). Polycarp and others at Smyrna testified that apostles had appointed Polycarp to be "bishop" of Smyrna. He was a living exemplar of apostolic succession at its original root. According to Irenaeus, whose arguments against the Gnostics show him to be grounded in the same faith that one finds in the New Testament, Polycarp "always taught the things that he had learned from the apostles, which he also handed on to the Church and which alone are true."[62] Irenaeus observes that Polycarp's successors as bishop

61. Irenaeus of Lyons, 3.3, p. 33.

62. Irenaeus of Lyons, 3.3, p. 33.

of Smyrna, all of whom Irenaeus seems to have known, have followed in Polycarp's steps by seeking to communicate the apostolic tradition. And Irenaeus makes clear that Polycarp as bishop of Smyrna was not alone. There was a network of churches in "Asia" that sought to do the same thing and that helped each other to ensure that their teaching handed on what, in living memory, they had received from the apostles.

According to Irenaeus, then, the bishops of the earliest Church knew one another and shared with one another their memories of the apostles. He mentions that Polycarp lived for a time in Rome, when Anicetus was bishop. Irenaeus relates a story of Polycarp's, one that Irenaeus did not hear directly but that he received from sources: "There are those who heard him say that when John the disciple of the Lord was at Ephesus and went to take a bath, on seeing Cerinthus there, he rushed out of the bath-house without having bathed."[63] Irenaeus also relates a story from Polycarp's own life, in which the bishop stood in opposition to the Gnostic Marcion, refusing to be in communion with him. Like the apostles, Polycarp is present in Irenaeus's day not only through oral stories but also through writings. Irenaeus references Polycarp's letter to the Philippians as evidence of the (apostolic) "standard of his faith and the preaching of the truth."[64]

Thus, Irenaeus contends that the apostles bestowed upon the Church a substantial body of truths. He states that "the apostles most abundantly placed in her [the Church], as in a rich receptacle, every thing that belongs to the truth."[65] This is what theologians call the apostolic deposit of faith. It is by receiving this apostolic deposit, this "tradition of the truth," that the Church is "the entrance to life."[66] Irenaeus goes on to imagine a situation in which the apostles had left no writings. There still would have

63. Irenaeus of Lyons, 3.3, p. 34.
64. Irenaeus of Lyons, 3.3, p. 34.
65. Irenaeus of Lyons, 3.4, p. 34.
66. Irenaeus of Lyons, 3.4, p. 34.

been available to early Christians such as Polycarp—and therefore to Irenaeus who knew Polycarp—some apostolic teaching about faith and practice. Irenaeus calls this latter teaching, distinct from written Scriptures, "tradition." He states, "What if the apostles had not left us the Scriptures; ought we not, then, to follow the disposition of tradition, which they handed down to those to whom they entrusted the Churches?"[67] Having linked the apostolic "tradition" with apostolic succession (the apostles' entrusting bishops with authority over the churches they founded), Irenaeus adds the logical point that the oral teachings of the apostles are most likely to have shaped, and to be found in, the churches that the apostles themselves directly founded. He describes these churches as "the most ancient Churches, in which the apostles had lived."[68] Rome is preeminent among these churches, as we have seen.

Irenaeus summarizes the content of the apostolic deposit of faith by offering a summary that we now call the Apostles' Creed. Some people have believed in this faith without even being able to read, thus demonstrating the power of the oral apostolic tradition, which Irenaeus holds to have had the same essential content as the apostolic writings. Turning to the apostolic writings, Irenaeus offers a demonstration from Scripture against the Gnostic claims. This proof is lengthy and rich, tapping into the doctrinal content of the Scriptures with respect to such realities as God, Christ, the Father and the Son, the Holy Spirit, the moral life, idolatry, the Mosaic law, and so on.

Contemporary biblical scholars have addressed the importance of the personal memories of the apostles and the resulting efforts to remain in accord with the apostolic tradition. The Anglican biblical scholar Markus Bockmuehl observes, "Irenaeus affirms a harmony of Scripture and its tradition of interpretation, which the church has inherited from the apostles. And this

67. Irenaeus of Lyons, 3.4, p. 35.

68. Irenaeus of Lyons, 3.4, pp. 34–35.

tradition for him is no mere ideological figment of a 'collective memory,' but it is vouchsafed by an unbroken and identifiable chain of *personal* recollection reaching back to the apostles themselves."[69] I note that although Irenaeus knows of various New Testament texts, he is not working with a canonized Scripture. Instead, Irenaeus knows of men—bishops and others—whose memories of hearing the apostles fit with the written apostolic texts that the Church possesses. He has a living connection to the apostles, and this connection manifests itself both in apostolic succession of "bishops" or leaders of communities established by the apostles, and in testimony to the apostolic faith. As Bockmuehl observes, "It is highly significant to observe the extent to which even Irenaeus [writing in the late second century] can still justify his condemnation of Valentinian Gnosticism on the grounds that it is repugnant to the living memory of the apostolic teaching as expounded in keeping with Scripture."[70]

This point highlights the value of what Zizioulas calls the "historical" dimension of apostolicity. Apostolicity—apostolic succession and the apostolic deposit of faith—is no mere abstraction or idea. It is a concrete reality that Irenaeus has personally experienced, and it characterizes the Church in its difference from other claimants such as the Gnostics. Bockmuehl comments that this dimension illustrates "the indispensable realism of an incarnational faith,"[71] and he is correct. The apostles and others of their generation knew and heard Jesus, and there were many people who knew and heard the apostles—and who even received the laying on of hands from them. Some of these people enjoyed lengthy lives and were remembered by people living in the late second century. What Bockmuehl calls "the vital urgency of memory" is at the core of the Church's apostolicity.[72]

69. Markus Bockmuehl, *Seeing the Word: Refocusing New Testament Study* (Baker Academic, 2006), 184.

70. Bockmuehl, 186.

71. Bockmuehl, 187.

72. Bockmuehl, 187.

In a complementary fashion to Bockmuehl's work, the biblical scholar Richard Bauckham has reclaimed the significance of community memory. In *Jesus and the Eyewitnesses*, Bauckham emphasizes that, at the time when the Gospels were written, a significant number of people still alive in Galilee and Judea had seen and heard Jesus or had seen and heard the testimony of the apostles. The evangelists would have been constrained, to some degree at least, by the fact that there were eyewitnesses to Jesus and/or the apostles in the communities in which the Gospels were read. As Bauckham says (speaking about form criticism), "We have been accustomed to working with models of oral tradition as it is passed down through the generations in traditional communities. We imagine the traditions passing through many minds and mouths before they reached the writers of the Gospels. But the period in question is actually that of a relatively (for that period) long lifetime."[73] This renewed valuation of memory supports a much deeper appreciation for the historical dimension of the Church's apostolicity.

Another recent work deserving of mention is the Catholic biblical scholar Gregory Vall's *Learning Christ: Ignatius of Antioch and the Mystery of Redemption*. Vall shows the significance of the apostles' writings and oral teachings (as well as what Zizioulas would call their "eschatological" presence in the Church at every time and place) for Ignatius's ecclesiology. Vall remarks, "It is far too simplistic to make Ignatius the early church's 'spokesman' for a 'vertical' and 'charismatic' understanding of apostolic authority over against the 'horizontal' model of apostolic succession advocated by Clement of Rome and Cyprian, leaving it to Hippolytus

73. Richard Bauckham, *Jesus and the Eyewitnesses: The Gospels as Eyewitness Testimony*, 2nd ed. (Eerdmans, 2017), 7. Bauckham is not the lone voice, although his book—originally published in 2006—has stimulated a booming industry of memory-studies among New Testament scholars. He cites Martin Hengel, *The Four Gospels and the One Gospel of Jesus Christ*, trans. John Bowden (SCM, 2000), 143; and, from an earlier generation, Vincent Taylor, *The Formation of the Gospel Tradition*, 2nd ed. (Macmillan, 1935), 41. For discussion of Bauckham's book and others like it, see my *Did Jesus Rise from the Dead? Historical and Theological Reflections* (Oxford University Press, 2019).

and Irenaeus to achieve the desired Hegelian synthesis of the two."[74] Vall notes that Ignatius praises the church of Ephesus for living according to the pattern of the apostles, which Ignatius knew from the writings of Paul, Matthew, and John—and which Ignatius must have also known by encountering people such as Polycarp of Smyrna who had known and heard the apostles.

As a final step, let me say a few words about Irenaeus's *On the Apostolic Preaching*, which complements the portion of book 3 of *Against the Heresies* that I have discussed above. Irenaeus presents *On the Apostolic Preaching* as a "summary memorandum" to his friend Marcianus about the contents of Christian faith, intended for Marcianus's use in teaching the faith and refuting heretics.[75] At the outset, Irenaeus emphasizes the connection between true doctrine and salvation. Those who do immoral deeds cannot profit from the truth of the Gospel—what Irenaeus calls the "rule [κανών] of faith."[76]

Irenaeus sets forth the basic contents of faith. He begins with our Baptism in the name of the Father, Son, and Holy Spirit, for the purpose of the forgiveness of sins and rebirth in God. He describes the incarnate Son Jesus Christ and his death and Resurrection. He portrays God as the Creator, and he explains the role of the Word and Spirit in creating. He discusses how the Spirit configures us to Christ. He maintains that Christ recapitulated all things and died to conquer death and to reconcile humankind to God. He presents the Spirit's outpouring and the Spirit's work of instruction, sanctification, and renewal.

74. Gregory Vall, *Learning Christ: Ignatius of Antioch and the Mystery of Redemption* (The Catholic University of America Press, 2013), 330–31. Vall here has in view (critically) the perspective of Niels Christian Hvidt, *Christian Prophecy: The Post-Biblical Tradition* (Oxford University Press, 2007), 231. On the relationship of the local Church and the universal Church according to Ignatius, see also the trenchant criticisms that Vall directs (*Learning Christ*, 333–40) toward Zizioulas's *Eucharist, Bishop, Church: The Unity of the Church in the Divine Eucharist and the Bishop during the First Three Centuries*, trans. Elizabeth Theokritoff (Holy Cross Orthodox Press, 2001), 107–20.

75. Irenaeus of Lyons, *On the Apostolic Preaching*, trans. John Behr (St. Vladimir's Seminary Press, 1997), 39.

76. Irenaeus of Lyons, 41.

There is much more, since Irenaeus proceeds slowly through the Old Testament, beginning with Adam and Eve and continuing through Cain and Abel, Noah, Babel, the covenantal calling of Abraham, Moses and the Passover, the giving of the Law at Sinai, the entrance into the Promised Land, the prophets, the Incarnation and virgin birth, the Crucifixion, Christ's fulfillment of the covenants with Abraham and David, the Resurrection, our communion with God and "participation in incorruptibility,"[77] the outpouring of the Spirit and sending of the apostles into the world, and the coming general resurrection. The whole Bible, or at least large portions of it, is summarized by Irenaeus in broad strokes. Part 2 of Irenaeus's book treats prophetic testimonies to Jesus, not solely from the prophets but also from Abraham, Jacob, and Moses. The divinity of the Son receives attention, as does the meaning of "Christ" or "Messiah." Much attention goes to prophecies that point to Christ, including those found in Isaiah and the Psalms, and also in texts such as Genesis 49 (with its prophecy about the descendants of Judah). Irenaeus examines "the witness of the apostles [the New Testament], who, sent by the Lord, preached to the whole world the Son of God."[78] He portrays Scripture as the work of the prophets and apostles, cohering marvelously around the figure of Christ.

At the conclusion of *On the Apostolic Preaching*, Irenaeus adds a note on the Church's apostolicity. Summing up his work, he states, "This, beloved, is the preaching of the truth, and this is the character of our salvation, and this is the way of life, which the prophets announced and Christ confirmed and the apostles handed over and the Church, in the whole world, hands down to her children."[79] Although the Greek words translated by "handed over" and "hands down" are different, the point is clear enough: Christ, fulfilling the Old Testament, revealed the truth of the

77. Irenaeus of Lyons, 65.
78. Irenaeus of Lyons, 92.
79. Irenaeus of Lyons, 100.

Gospel to his apostles, who in turn, under the Spirit's guidance, bestowed it upon the communities they founded and upon their successors, so as to enable the Church to spread throughout the (known) world and to deliver the truth of the Gospel to all who have ears to hear. In Irenaeus's perspective, the Church continues to share the truth received from Christ by the apostles, and so the Church is apostolic.

The importance of the historical connection to the apostles does not override the "eschatological" dimension, which Irenaeus (arguably) frames in terms of Christ's "recapitulation of mankind."[80] At all points of human history, Christ is present as the interpretive key. The apostolic witness to Christ is always present through the "prophetic grace" of the Holy Spirit that enables human beings to share in "the life of God."[81] Irenaeus also highlights the Father who sends, the Son who becomes incarnate, and the Spirit who enlightens.[82] Even so, the truth and life possessed by the Church is always concretely mediated or handed down. Apostolicity requires this historical dimension as the ground of the eschatological dimension, notwithstanding the fact that without the latter, the historical dimension would not fully be the sharing in Christ that it truly is.

V. CONCLUSION

Let me sum up this chapter's perspective. In his *Apostolicity Then and Now*, the Catholic theologian John Burkhard astutely lays out four aspects of apostolicity according to the early Fathers: origin, doctrine, life, and succession. The aspect of origin has to

80. Irenaeus of Lyons, 101.

81. Irenaeus of Lyons, 101.

82. For further discussion, see Michel René Barnes, "Irenaeus's Trinitarian Theology," *Nova et Vetera* 7, no. 1 (2009): 67–106; and, for Irenaeus on divine simplicity, the production of the Word, and the Incarnation, see Anthony Briggman, *God and Christ in Irenaeus* (Oxford University Press, 2019).

do with the apostolic sees, the churches founded by the apostles.[83] Doctrine has to do with the continuity of the faith, so that the apostolic deposit of faith is preserved by the Church—with the Scriptures at the center. The aspect of life or praxis became a central part of apostolicity in some texts of Vatican II and in the work of some theologians after Vatican II. Certain practices, disciplines, and works of charity characterize apostolic "life." "Life" also accentuates "the authentic witness of the whole of the local church, and not simply the isolated authoritative witness of its leadership, however important or indispensable."[84] Lastly, succession involves the historical dimension of leadership in the Eucharistic community.

I concur with this fourfold presentation of apostolicity. All four aspects belong to apostolicity, and Zizioulas's eschatological (Eucharistic) emphasis adds a fifth aspect—and, I have argued, a particularly valuable one. I agree with Zizioulas, Burkhard, and Congar that apostolic succession is not a merely mechanical historical chain in which the meaning of "bishop" must always be the same, given that development clearly occurs in the early centuries regarding the meaning of "bishop."[85] Burkhard observes that the Holy Spirit can act directly to confer the grace of the sacrament, thereby preserving the apostolic succession whenever an invalid episcopal ordination (for instance, due to simony) would jeopardize the later chain of succession.[86] This point further con-

83. See John J. Burkhard, OFM Conv., *Apostolicity Then and Now: An Ecumenical Church in a Postmodern World* (Liturgical, 2004), 26–28, drawing upon James F. McCue, "Apostles and Apostolic Succession in the Patristic Era," in *Eucharist and Ministry*, ed. Paul C. Empie and T. Austin Murphy (United States Catholic Conference, 1970), 138–77.

84. Burkhard, *Apostolicity Then and Now*, 35.

85. Burkhard finds that the bishops expanded their role widely in the third century, with the development of regional synods of bishops and of the ritual for the ordination of the bishop; and Burkhard decries the resulting "clericalization of the ministry" (here he agrees firmly with Martin Luther and John Calvin that the Church focused on the bishops to the detriment of the laity and of the contents of faith). See Burkhard, *Apostolicity Then and Now*, 31.

86. Burkhard is here following Congar's reflections on the principle of "economy." See Kamiel Duchatelez, "La notion d'économie et ses richesses théologiques," *Nouvelle revue théologique* 92, no. 3 (1970): 267–92; Yves Congar, OP, "Composantes et idée de la Succession Apostolique," *Oecumenica* 1 (1966): 61–78; Joseph Ratzinger, *Principles of Catholic Theology: Building Stones for a Fundamental Theology*, trans. Mary Frances McCarthy (Ignatius, 1987),

firms that apostolic succession is not a mechanical process, but rather is a complex historical reality in which the Spirit is active.

There is evident ecumenical fruit, too, in Burkhard's point that apostolicity involves the transmission of the *whole pattern of life* of the apostles—an "apostolicity" that can be shared in by Christians whose communities lack apostolic succession in the stricter sense. Of course, the fact that apostolicity involves the transmission of the apostolic deposit of faith, which is found richly in Scripture, means that Protestants already have an evident share in apostolicity, according to the Catholic perspective.[87] In this regard, Burkhard is right that it helps to consider apostolicity in conjunction with (qualitative) catholicity, which I will treat in the next chapter.

Nevertheless, the proper emphasis in the doctrine of apostolicity must fall upon apostolic succession and the apostolic deposit of faith—even if all things come together eschatologically in the

245–46. If a pope or council erroneously began the process of the ordination of women, the principle of "economy" would apply.

87. See also Burkhard, *Apostolicity Then and Now*, chapter 7: "Apostolicity in Ecumenical Dialogue." Burkhard highlights the texts of the Anglican-Roman Catholic Dialogue (especially ARCIC-II). See especially "Church as Communion," in *Growth in Agreement II: Reports and Agreed Statements of Ecumenical Conversations on a World Level, 1982–1998*, ed. Jeffrey Gros, Harding Meyer, and William G. Rusch (Eerdmans, 2000), 328–43. Somewhat more briefly, he attends to Orthodox-Catholic dialogue. See Orthodox-Roman Catholic Consultation in the USA, "Apostolicity as God's Gift in the Life of the Church," in *The Quest for Unity: Orthodox and Catholics in Dialogue: Documents of the Joint International Commission and Official Dialogues in the United States 1965–1995*, ed. John Borelli and John H. Erickson (St. Vladimir's Seminary Press, 1996), 125–30; Johannes Oeldermann, *Die Apostolizität der Kirche im ökumenischen Dialog mit der Orthodoxie: Der Beitrug russicher orthodoxer Theologen zum ökumenischen Gespräch über die apostolische Tradition und die Sukzession in der Kirche* (Bonifatius Verlag, 2000). Attending to Lutheran-Catholic dialogue, he points to some significant studies, including Margaret O'Gara, "Apostolicity in Ecumenical Dialogue," *Mid-Stream* 37 (1998): 175–212; Walter Kasper, "The Apostolic Succession: An Ecumenical Problem," in *Leadership in the Church: How Traditional Roles Can Serve the Christian Community Today*, trans. Brian McNeil (Crossroad, 2003), 114–43; Ola Tjørhom, "Apostolic Continuity and Apostolic Succession in the Porvoo Common Statement: A Challenge to the Nordic Lutheran Churches?," *Louvain Studies* 21, no. 2 (1996): 126–37; Henrik Roelvink, "The Apostolic Succession in the Porvoo Statement," *One in Christ* 30, no. 4 (1994): 344–54; and Mary Tanner, "The Anglican Position on Apostolic Continuity and Apostolic Succession in the Porvoo Statement," *Louvain Studies* 21, no. 2 (1996): 114–25. See also the essays in *The Plurality of Ministries*, Concilium 74, ed. Hans Küng and Walter Kasper (Herder and Herder, 1972); Avery Dulles, SJ, "Church, Ministry, and Sacraments in Catholic-Evangelical Dialogue," in *Catholics and Evangelicals: Do They Share a Common Future?*, ed. Thomas P. Rausch (InterVarsity, 2000), 101–21; and Thomas M. Kocik, *Apostolic Succession in an Ecumenical Context* (Alba House, 1996).

Eucharistic celebration. Simply put, the Church cannot give up the memory of the apostles that Irenaeus, like many contemporary biblical scholars, recognizes to be crucial for the true Christian faith. This apostolic memory includes doctrinal and moral contents. It also includes the ministerial succession through the laying on of hands. The two elements are not separable, either for Irenaeus or for the New Testament. To attempt to get around this fact, as Flett and Barth do by defining apostolicity as solely the imitation of the apostles' absolute dependence upon Christ, is to ignore the actual apostolic testimony to a deposit of faith and to succession by the laying on of hands. It is also to ignore the early Church's memory of the apostles and their work in the churches.

For his part, Burkhard ends up placing too much weight upon what he calls, following Bernard Lonergan (though Lonergan is no historicist), the transition from naive classicism to historical consciousness. The result is that whereas I have emphasized the historical dimension of apostolicity (without minimizing the eschatological dimension), Burkhard emphasizes the historicity of apostolicity—by which emphasis he aims to undermine doctrinally rich accounts of apostolic tradition. He defines apostolicity in a historicist manner: "The church's apostolic character then is defined by the church's historicity. It pertains not only to the stable factor of the church's nature—its identity—but also to its changeable factor—its historicity. When the church defines itself as apostolic, in our contemporary situation we are referring primarily to the church's inherent historicity."[88] On this view, the Church's apostolicity and the Church's identity are fluid and contextual. Everything becomes "apostolic" except for what Irenaeus himself would have recognized as such.[89]

88. Burkhard, *Apostolicity Then and Now*, 162. He draws here upon the influential work of Wolfgang Beinert, "Die Apostolizität der Kirche als Kategorie der Theologie," *Theologie und Philosophie* 52, no. 2 (1977): 161–81.

89. For Burkhard's amorphous vision of "ecclesiality," see *Apostolicity Then and Now*, 244–45.

Burkhard appeals in this regard to Walter Kasper's theology. In Kasper's "The Apostolic Succession: An Ecumenical Problem," as Burkhard accurately reports, "Kasper recasts episcopal succession in terms of the succession of the college of bishops. Gone is the insistence on the bishop as a successor to an apostle or to the apostles in some generic sense. The bishop 'succeeds to' the apostles by being incorporated, through the sacrament of episcopal ordination, into the college of bishops."[90] Against Kasper's reimagining, I note that in the Church's actual history, there really were successors of the apostles, men upon whom the apostles laid hands in order to bestow upon them a share in their authority in the Church (through the power of Christ and his Spirit) and who were commanded to uphold the apostolic tradition, including the cultic tradition to which the evangelists testify and to which Paul testifies in 1 Corinthians 11.[91]

Once these "bishops" are no longer significant for "apostolic succession," then apostolic succession loses its grounding in the apostolic tradition—and also, arguably, its grounding in the eschatological community of the Eucharist. The "body of bishops" floats free of a particular transmission of authority in particular churches; the commissioning of particular "bishops" by the apostles themselves is forgotten. No longer rooted in the wisdom and will of Christ and his actual apostles, the "body of bishops" manifests merely what Burkhard vaguely calls "the mystery of human being-with-others (co-being)," a mystery that enables

90. Burkhard, 247.

91. Burkhard argues, in accordance with a widespread view, that in Irenaeus's day, people "wouldn't spontaneously have associated the office of bishop with something sacerdotal or cultic. The bishop was the master teacher who taught his community about Jesus Christ, and that knowledge came to him within the *traditio*" (Burkhard, 54). Surely the latter point is true (the bishop was indeed expected to be a master teacher who taught the apostolic tradition), but I think that the early Christians were not nearly so separated from cult—and from ministry associated with cult—as this majority view maintains. For further discussion, see for example Stefan Heid, *Altar and Church: Principles of Liturgy from Early Christianity*, trans. Susan Johnson (The Catholic University of America Press, 2023); Anthony Giambrone, OP, *The Bible and the Priesthood: Priestly Participation in the One Sacrifice for Sins* (Baker Academic, 2022); Jean-Pierre Torrell, OP, *A Priestly People: Baptismal Priesthood and Priestly Ministry*, trans. Peter Heinegg (Paulist, 2013); and Daniel Cardó, *The Cross and the Eucharist in Early Christianity: A Theological and Liturgical Investigation* (Cambridge University Press, 2019).

us to embrace "other churches for the reality of their otherness" and no longer to lay claim to possessing an apostolic mark lacking in "other churches."[92] This tragically impoverished language amounts simply to giving up real apostolicity.

Retrieving Irenaeus offers an antidote to such perspectives. The Catholic Church would be making a grave mistake if it cut off apostolicity from the actual work done by the apostles—that is, from what appears in 1 Timothy and Titus and, as we have seen, in Irenaeus. For Irenaeus, there is nothing amorphous about apostolic succession. He connects it directly to the apostles, and he highlights the importance of this not only for Church governance but also for the faithful teaching of the apostolic tradition. We must not lose this concrete link to the apostles. The Church is grounded in Christ's sending of the apostles and their sharing their authority (whose source is always Christ) with chosen successors. The body of bishops is not a self-defining entity. The Church has a structure from the outset, and that structure, even while it develops significantly, is more than a simple turning toward Christ.

Again, this is not to discount the eschatological and Eucharistic sense of apostolicity. On the contrary, it grounds this sense. An Irenaean understanding of apostolicity, with a concrete apostolic succession and apostolic deposit of faith, insists upon the real importance of the apostles, gathered and sent by Christ in the Spirit. Understood in this way, apostolicity reveals its power through its witness to Christ. As Paul says to his rebellious Corinthian flock, "I think that God has exhibited us apostles as last of all, like men sentenced to death. . . . When reviled, we bless; when persecuted, we endure; when slandered, we try to conciliate; we have become, and are now, as the refuse of the world, the dregs of all things" (1 Cor 4:9, 12–13). Here we see the apostle as imitator of Christ, sharing in the *kenosis* of the crucified one for the salvation of the world—a participation enacted preeminently

92. Burkhard, *Apostolicity Then and Now*, 250.

in the Eucharist: "For as often as you eat this bread and drink the chalice, you proclaim the Lord's death until he comes" (1 Cor 11:26). Insofar as the Church lives its apostolicity, the bishops and pope, joined by the whole community of believers, participate in and hand on the apostolic Gospel, whose center is "Christ crucified," the "foolishness" and "weakness" of God (1 Cor 1:23, 25).

7

Catholic

I. INTRODUCTION

In an essay published shortly before his death, the Catholic theologian Roch Kereszty remarked aptly, "The key to understand the Church's nature is her participation in the mysteries of the Holy Trinity and the Incarnation."[1] This participation is the heart of the Church's catholicity. For much of the Church's history, however, the mark of catholicity—joined to the other three marks of the Church, unity, holiness, and apostolicity[2]—was associated primarily with visible universality. Thomas Aquinas, for example, taught that the Church is catholic (or universal) because it extends throughout the world, includes people from all social conditions, and has existed since Abel.[3] From this angle, the catholicity of

1. Roch Kereszty, O.Cist., "Synodality, the Magisterium, and the Faith of the People of God," *Communio* 48, no. 4 (2021): 638–62, at 643.

2. Thomas Prügl comments, "Pope Francis has elevated the concept of 'synodality' to the status of a new ecclesiological guiding concept, comparable to a *nota ecclesiae*, which captures the essence of the Church as comprehensively as do the traditional characteristics of the Church, namely, unity, holiness, catholicity, and apostolicity." Prügl, "Synodality and the Conciliar Tradition of the Church: Medieval and Early Modern Experiences of Synodality," *The Thomist* 87, no. 2 (2023): 191–210, at 191. After appreciatively exploring the medieval tradition of reform synods focusing on pastoral issues, Prügl observes, "It would be a step back to understand the concept of synodality only in terms of authority and organization, instead of keeping in mind the main task and only purpose of the Church, which is to continue the mission of Jesus Christ, or in the words of *Lumen Gentium*, to be 'sign and instrument of union with God and of the unity of the whole human race' (*LG*, 1)" (Prügl, "Synodality and the Conciliar Tradition of the Church," 209–10).

3. Thomas Aquinas, *The Sermon-Conferences of St. Thomas Aquinas on the Apostles' Creed*, trans. and ed. Nicholas Ayo, CSC (University of Notre Dame Press, 1988), 129. I note that Aquinas has a rich appreciation of the election of Israel, however, by comparison to the warning about "texts in the Hebrew Scriptures that stressed the ethnic purity of God's people" and "the exclusivism that preoccupied much of Second Temple Judaism" voiced by Richard R. Gaillardetz in his analysis of catholicity; see Gaillardetz, *Ecclesiology for a Global Church: A People Called and Sent*, rev. ed. (Orbis Books, 2023), 37. Gaillardetz goes on to say, along lines that connect with Richard McBrien's argument that the Church's purpose is to serve the upbuilding

the Church clearly relates to the ministry of the bishop of Rome, whose purpose is to foster unity in faith in a culturally, intellectually, and geographically diverse Church that otherwise would break into various regional groups following different doctrinal and moral paths.

This visible universality under the primacy of the bishop of Rome has been contested for more than a millennium, first by Orthodox and then, in a different way, by Protestants.[4] Claims about catholicity have therefore long been an ecumenical sore spot. While in a certain way it is true that, as Richard Gaillardetz says, "the Holy Spirit does not erase difference but renders difference nondivisive,"[5] this is only true for some differences. Other differences inevitably divide. This sad experience of "divided Christendom" or "Chrétiens désunis"—to cite the title of Yves Congar's book[6]—prompts the question of whether the Spirit has ensured that the Church's mark of catholicity still exists.

Protestants have understood the Church and its ongoing catholicity in diverse ways, but, like the Orthodox, they have been united in holding that the (Roman) Catholic Church's catholicity has been gravely impaired by the strong, indeed in their view overbearing and doctrinally deleterious, role of the church of Rome. For their part, the Orthodox have often considered that their Church alone has catholicity.

Congar reflects at length upon catholicity in his *Chrétiens désunis*. Well aware that the Church Fathers and the medievals emphasized visible universality, he observes that in the Fathers prior

of the kingdom (with only the latter having perduring significance), "Stephen Bevans and Roger Schroeder write: 'One of the most important things Christians need to know about the church is that the *church* is not of ultimate importance.' According to Acts, the church was constituted by the Spirit in the upper room, but only as a community sent forth in mission." *Ecclesiology for a Global Church*, 38, quoting Bevans and Schroeder, *Constants in Context: A Theology of Mission for Today* (Orbis Books, 2004), 7.

4. See the summary offered by the Protestant writer Hartzell Spence in his *The Clergy and What They Do* (Franklin Watts, 1961), 159.

5. Gaillardetz, *Ecclesiology for a Global Church*, 39.

6. Yves Congar, OP, *Divided Christendom: A Catholic Study of the Problem of Reunion*, trans. M. A. Bousfield (Geoffrey Bles, 1939).

to Augustine, at least, "this quantitative aspect is never affirmed in isolation, it is enumerated among other elements: *universality of truth*—the Church propounds all dogma on every subject, she sets forth principles true for all: *universality of redemption* and healing for humanity, . . . *universality of gifts*, virtues and spiritual endowment, and . . . *universality in time*."[7] Since this is so, Congar is able to show that the quantitative dimension of catholicity is in fact grounded in the qualitative dimension of catholicity: the Church's Christological and Trinitarian fullness enables real universality. The Church is Catholic because the Church's Head, King, and sole Mediator is Jesus Christ, the incarnate Lord who accomplished our salvation, drawing us into union with God. As Congar says (citing various biblical texts), "All the new order, which is the Church—the gathering together in the oneness of God—exists in Christ as in its Principle: all that we are called

7. Congar, *Divided Christendom*, 94. For an attempt to interpret "catholicity" in terms of the immense complexities and interconnectedness accessible to psychology and natural science, through which one can perceive the presence of divine Spirit at the core of all things, see Edwin E. Olson, *And God Created Wholeness: A Spirituality of Catholicity* (Orbis Books, 2018). Olson's well-intentioned book exemplifies the reduction of grace to nature, since he holds that natural reason and natural faith—open to the depths of the unconscious and to emergent and transformative dynamisms, and capable of a Jungian "transcendent function"—are equivalent to the mysteries of catholicity that Christianity describes. Olson is indebted to the perspectives of Matthew Fox, Ilia Delio, and Richard Rohr, among others. See also Ilia Delio, OSF, *Making All Things New: Catholicity, Cosmology, Consciousness* (Orbis Books, 2015). Offering a historical sketch of the word "catholicity," Delio comments, "If the Greeks understood catholicity as human consciousness of the wider cosmos, Christians appropriated catholicity as a consciousness of the whole centered in Christ. . . . Catholicity, for Irenaeus, is attentiveness to the Spirit of God, that is, the Spirit of healing and wholeness. When we are inwardly whole, we can attend to the cosmos in all its beauty" (Delio, *Making All Things New*, 10, 12). For Delio, Nicaea was a tragedy for the Church's catholicity: "The Arian controversy created such an embattled church at Nicaea that consciousness of the whole—catholicity—was broken. After Nicaea the Church became defined as *Catholic* not with a sense of the whole but with a sense of the true. Catholicity was no longer a function of cosmology but orthodoxy. The embroiled Christian religion became ensnared by political factions to the extent that catholicity lost its noumenal dimension and was reduced to the constraints of orthodoxy. Nicaea disconnected cosmos from anthropos" (14–15). Delio sets forth a list of changes, mainly having to do with a new distribution of power in the Church and the end of dogmatic faith, that the Church must embrace, on the grounds that "a system open to the environment is affected by the environment; when the environment changes, so does the system, given a sufficient amount of time. The ability of a system to change in tandem with the environment *is* the viability of the system. . . . Human consciousness finds itself on the threshold of a new age that requires entirely new dimensions and values. The deepest beliefs of human beings must find new forms of expression" (127, 131). Delio portrays Pope Francis as the exemplar of this vision: "The pope bears a 'catholic' spirit, open to the whole and a desire to create new christic wholes. However, his openness of gospel life in history cannot be supported by the closed, mechanistic structures of the Church" (131).

to become, to receive and to inherit is established in Christ, so that the Church, His Body, His *Pleroma*, may manifest it and make it explicit."[8] The catholicity of the Body of Christ comes from the Head. This catholicity exhibits itself in the universality of dogmatic truth, the universality of the sacraments, and the universality of the Church's fellowship.[9]

Congar's brief sketch of catholicity in *Chrétiens désunis*—whose antecedents can be found in the nineteenth-century Tübingen School—coheres with an observation by Henri de Lubac in his 1939 book, *Catholicisme*: "The Church is not Catholic because she is spread abroad over the whole of the earth and can reckon on a large number of members. She was already Catholic on the morning of Pentecost, when her members could be contained in a small room."[10] Congar and de Lubac, of course, are not alone in

8. Congar, *Divided Christendom*, 96.

9. See Congar, 98–99. It follows that there can be no catholicity without the Church's unity, which means that the Church of Rome has a role in ensuring catholicity (via unity). Of course, it is Christ and the Spirit who unite the Church, but the pope has an instrumental role in service to this unity. Congar critiques a mere uniformity governed by the Vatican, as though local bishops and local contexts were not important. He suggests the formation of something like episcopal conferences, as well as liturgical use of local languages and culture-specific programs of priestly formation. In Nikolai Berdyaev's view, Congar notes, "the Catholic Church, attaching chief importance to numbers and quantity, desires to organize the world under one system of jurisdiction in a kind of imperialism of temporal rather than spiritual inspiration, aiming at domination over the greatest number with the maximum of uniformity to be obtained by means of authority and coercion. Against this Berdyaev sets out the idea of a more spiritual and interior Church, one, though not unique, in the sense that its profound unity can be accommodated to several forms of confessional organization" (107). Congar replies astutely, "The notion of a Church spiritually one and confessionally diverse implies a failure to recognize the essential and organic link which binds together the Church as a confessional entity with the Church as a spiritual and mystical unity of life" (107–8).

10. Henri de Lubac, SJ, *Catholicism: Christ and the Common Destiny of Man*, trans. Lancelot C. Sheppard and Elizabeth Englund, OCD (Ignatius, 1988), 48–49. De Lubac goes on to grant that "when the treatises on the marks of the Church came to be written too much importance was attached to geographical considerations. St. Ambrose contemplating the Church saw her embracing both earth and sky with Christ set above for sun. He sees her including the whole *orbis terrarum* because he is aware that all, whatever their origin, race or condition, are called on to become one in Christ, and that thenceforeward the Church is fundamentally that unity. From another point of view the same may be said of Origen, Tertullian and St. Augustine. In such expressions as *per orbem terrae ecclesiae latitude diffusa* Origen states what is a requirement arising from his idea of the Church rather than actual statement of fact. Tertullian, mistaken in this like so many others, celebrated the actual extensive universality of the Church in phrases that were far too oratorical; but over and beyond this he describes that universality 'in depth' which he explained by showing its relation with the human soul, everywhere the same and everywhere 'naturally Christian.' In the same way there is not a little of the same illusion in St. Augustine's *Chorus Christi jam totus mundus est.* And yet, though it is not so accurate an estimate

their emphasis on qualitative catholicity. The same move characterizes the great Lutheran bishop and theologian Gustaf Aulén's 1956 book *Eucharist and Sacrifice*. Drawing on the work of the Anglican theologian Arthur Ramsey, Aulén contends that "catholicity is no longer a quantitative but a qualitative idea. . . . A departure from the 'true' catholicity involves therefore a departure from that which is 'genuine' and 'essential' Christianity."[11] In Aulén's view (which I consider overhasty in dismissing the "quantitative" dimension entirely), the emphasis on qualitative catholicity is an ecumenical breakthrough. He remarks along lines that I share and that the present chapter will underline: "In this meaning catholicity ceases to be a term which divides Christendom. Instead it creates fellowship. In other words, it becomes ecumenical."[12]

Yet, in some contemporary ecumenical circles (especially, I will suggest, in Evangelical-Catholic dialogue), the emphasis on qualitative catholicity has not been given its due. For some prominent Evangelical theologians, the role of the church of Rome still seems to render suspect any (Roman) Catholic claim to catholicity. There is also confusion about whether, from a (Roman) Catholic perspective, other Christian communions that do not submit to the bishop of Rome have any catholicity at all.

In order to identify and address these concerns and questions—and in order to clarify further how ecumenical advances might best take place—this chapter has two main sections. The first sets forth some criticisms put forward in the past few years by the Wesleyan and Reformed theologians Kenneth Collins, Jerry

of the reality, it was a sound view of the nature of the Church that made the holy doctor add *Chorus Christi ab oriente ad occidentem consonat.* Whatever the number of members . . . and however great or small the part of the earth on which she was to be found, the Church still sings the canticle that is never old, the canticle of universal charity. . . . It is not, then, the small extent of their territory that produces St. Augustine's censure of the Donatists but their claim to self-sufficiency, to restrict the Church to their own bounds" (50–52).

11. Gustaf Aulén, *Eucharist and Sacrifice*, trans. Eric H. Wahlstrom (Muhlenberg, 1958), 198.

12. Aulén, 198.

Walls, and Kevin Vanhoozer, whose viewpoints have had wide impact in contemporary Evangelical Protestantism.[13] These theologians, whose ecumenical credentials are not in doubt, deny that the (Roman) Catholic Church is "catholic."[14] They recognize that their perspective is not new. In the past century, the same concerns were raised by, among many others, the Lutherans Friedrich Heiler in his *Der Katholizismus: Seine Idee und seine Erscheinung* and Wilhelm Stählin in his "Katholizität, Protestantismus, und Katholizismus." Avery Dulles sums up Heiler's argument along lines that are precisely those of Collins, Walls, and Vanhoozer: "[Heiler] assailed the Roman practice of identifying Roman with Catholic, and argued that Rome commits the anti-Catholic heresy of making the particular into the universal. . . . Rome . . . is not Catholic, for it wants to rule in the spirit of the Caesars rather than serve in the spirit of the gospel."[15]

13. See for example Matthew Barrett, *The Reformation as Renewal: Retrieving the One, Holy, Catholic, and Apostolic Church* (Zondervan, 2023).

14. Throughout this chapter, I will generally place "Roman" in parentheses because the term is not typically used by the Catholic Church today, although Vatican I spoke of "the holy, catholic, apostolic, and Roman Church," indicating the role of Roman primacy in maintaining the unity of Christ's Church. See First Vatican Council, Dogmatic Constitution on the Catholic Faith, *Dei Filius* §1, in *Decrees of the Ecumenical Councils*, vol. 2, *Trent–Vatican II*, ed. Norman P. Tanner, SJ (Georgetown University Press, 1990), 804–11, at 805. Avery Dulles, SJ, points out, "Some apologists of the Roman school in the nineteenth and early twentieth centuries did actually use submission to the authority of Rome as a criterion of the true Church. Gustave Thils, in surveying the apologetics of this period, observes that many of the authors reduced the other three notes to that of unity, and then reduced the argument from unity to one from Roman primacy." Dulles, *The Catholicity of the Church* (Oxford University Press, 1985), 132, citing Gustave Thils, *Les Notes de l'Église dans l'apologétique catholique depuis la Réforme* (Duculot, 1937), 248; and see also Giovanni Perrone, SJ's deployment of "Romana Ecclesia" in his *Praelectiones Theologicae*, vol. 1 (Leroux, Jouby, 1854), especially part 1, chaps. 2 and 3. Dulles adds approvingly that both Vatican I and Vatican II "avoided the term 'Roman Catholic,'" and Vatican II avoided "the rather inflated title 'holy, catholic, apostolic, and Roman Church'" and deliberately chose instead to speak of the "Catholic Church" (Dulles, *The Catholicity of the Church*, 132). Dulles gives a twofold reason why the Catholic Church today does not use "Roman." First, Eastern Catholics are not properly identified as "Roman Catholics," even though they are in full communion with Rome. Second, the local church of Rome, not the whole Church, is properly described as the "Roman" Church.

15. Dulles, *The Catholicity of the Church*, 130. See Friedrich Heiler, *Der Katholizismus: Seine Idee und seine Erscheinung* (E. Reinhardt, 1970), 633–57; Wilhelm Stählin, "Katholizität, Protestantismus, und Katholizismus," in *Die Katholizität der Kirche* (Evangelisches Verlagswerk, 1957), 179–204. Dulles notes that some other Lutherans in Germany—and, he could have added, some ecumenically inclined Lutherans in the United States as well—have argued that "there can be no true Catholicism without union with Rome as the visible center of the universal Church. The papacy, according to these theologians, could properly be criticized, but not

In this first section, I will also discuss the concerns of the Anglican theologian Hans Boersma. Boersma argues that the (Roman) Catholic position flies in the face of empirical reality. In his view, the Church is manifestly divided and none of the existing churches today possess either unity or catholicity. For Boersma, what is needed for true ecumenical dialogue is for all churches to recognize in repentance and humility that Christ's Church has been fragmented into parts. From this perspective, which is characteristically Anglican (and which can also fit with some Reformed ecclesiologies), all Christians should implore the Spirit's aid to restore the lost unity and catholicity that Christ wills for his followers.

In the chapter's second section, then, I examine some post-conciliar Catholic perspectives on catholicity, corresponding to Congar's and de Lubac's insights above. I focus in this section on the work of Aidan Nichols, Hans Urs von Balthasar, and Avery Dulles.[16] My goal is to strengthen and confirm Congar's suggestion that when catholicity is understood primarily as the Church's

discarded. The intention of the Reformers, as they interpreted it, was not to form a new Church but to reform the existing Church" (Dulles, *The Catholicity of the Church*, 130). See for example the essays in *The Catholicity of the Reformation*, ed. Carl E. Braaten and Robert W. Jenson (Eerdmans, 1996). I should add that Heiler, a convert to Lutheranism from Catholicism, was (to say the least) not particularly representative of German Lutherans of his day. For concerns about "Rome," see also Martin Luther, *On the Councils and the Church*, trans. Charles M. Jacobs with revisions by Eric W. Gritsch, in *Luther's Works*, vol. 41, *Church and Ministry III*, ed. Eric W. Gritsch (Fortress, 1966), 9–178, at 145.

16. See also Joseph Ratzinger, "Catholicity as the Formal Structure of Christianity," in his *Principles of Catholic Theology: Building Stones for a Fundamental Theology*, trans. Mary Frances McCarthy (Ignatius, 1987), 285–311. Ratzinger observes, "The new view of the relationship between theory and practice that is widely accepted today under the influence of neo-Marxist thought undoubtedly shares the responsibility for the emphasis that is being placed on the subject of 'local ecumenism.' In its most radical form, this view holds that truth is not the measure but the product of practice; change produces truth by turning future potential into reality and freeing mankind from the past. Even in its less radical form, this view destroys faith in a truth that constantly bears witness to itself and in terms of which facts can be measured in a binding way" (309). See Robert J. Schreiter, CPPS, *The New Catholicity: Theology between the Global and the Local* (Orbis Books, 1997), arguing that "the Christian Tradition itself might be seen as a series of local theologies" (*The New Catholicity*, 2). Schreiter treats "catholicity" mainly in his book's final chapter, where he reflects upon the emergent "World Church" (marked by "intercultural communication and hermeneutics") and concurs with Siegfried Wiedenhofer in understanding "catholicity" as "wholeness and fullness through exchange and communication" and as grounded in "truth as orthopraxis." Wiedenhofer, *Das katholische Kirchenverständnis* (Styria, 1992), 279, quoted in *The New Catholicity*, 128.

participation in Christ and the Trinity, there is a possibility for better ecumenical understanding and appreciation—just as Aulén likewise perceives. I should note that Congar's approach to catholicity owes a significant debt to Anscar Vonier, as we saw in chapter 1.

The chapter's conclusion suggests a threefold path for moving forward. First, recognizing that catholicity in its fullness is an eschatological reality, Christians can grant that in a real sense we are *all* striving for it. Second, Christians should highlight the qualitative dimension of the Church's catholicity—its character as a sharing in the catholicity of Christ and the Trinity—without dismissing the quantitative dimension found in Jesus's command to "make disciples of all nations" in accordance with Christ's possession of "all authority in heaven and on earth" (Matt 28:18–19). Real ecumenical fruit is found along these non-competitive qualitative lines, since we are all called to be more catholic in Christ-like wisdom and love, imaging the Father through the power of the Holy Spirit.[17] Third, divided Christians can recognize each other as equals at the ecumenical table precisely in our task of striving for deeper personal and ecclesial catholicity.

For Catholic ecclesiology, my chapter primarily underlines the need for a renewed sense of the Church's Christocentric character, which is not at odds with appreciation of the Spirit's work.[18]

17. See also the insights in Robert Barron, "The Metaphysics of Coinherence: A Meditation on the Essence of the Christian Message," in *Exploring Catholic Theology: Essays on God, Liturgy, and Evangelization* (Baker Academic, 2015), 31–43; and Peter J. Leithart, *Traces of the Trinity: Signs of God in Creation and Human Experience* (Brazos, 2015).

18. Ilia Delio articulates a Catholic position that I find inadequate due to its conflation of grace with nature (among other problems). She states, "In a fixed, stable cosmology, the Eucharist is placed over and above the world as an object of adoration and worship, hence, the Church as center of the world. When the Eucharist is situated in the context of the world, undergirding a world in evolution, we are in an expanding cosmos. The first catholicity has a vertical direction and the second catholicity a horizontal one. Jesus of Nazareth lived the second catholicity" (*Making All Things New*, 181). In Delio's vision, God univocally becomes part of "the whole." She writes, "What we see in the lives of the LCWR women, the Dalai Lama, Barbara Marx Hubbard, and Pope Francis is the unquenchable fire of the Spirit. The Spirit *is* the 'trinitization' of God in history, the unmasking of divine love in the evolution of life, the deepening of relationality, and a consciousness of being part of a whole that empowers action toward unity" (188). For cognate perspectives, in which the influence of a popularized version of the thought of Pierre Teilhard de Chardin is ever present, see Donald C. Maldari, SJ, *Christian*

The Church's reality and mission have to do with nothing less than deifying salvation from sin and death. Catholics need to move away from the postconciliar temptation to understand the Church as our own world-improving project and return firmly to understanding the Church as having Jesus Christ as, in Congar's words, its "Head or Source of life in God."[19] As the Catholic theologian Wolfgang Beinert comments in a Christocentric vein, "Jesus is the entire salvation of God for the entire world. From the perspective of salvation history, the property of catholicity belongs to him in an original and primary way. He and he alone is already 'catholicity' in its fullness."[20]

II. PROTESTANT CONCERNS

Kenneth Collins and Jerry Walls

In *Roman but Not Catholic*, Kenneth Collins and Jerry Walls contend, among other things, that the (Roman) Catholic Church is not catholic—that is, does not bear the mark of catholicity. They define "catholic" as follows: "universal, comprehensive, ecumenical, global, extensive, and whole."[21] They quote the *Catechism*

Ministry in the Divine Milieu: Catholicity, Evolution, and the Reign of God (Orbis Books, 2019); and Thomas E. Hosinski, CSC, *The Image of the Unseen God: Catholicity, Science, and Our Evolving Understanding of God* (Orbis Books, 2017). For Maldari, "The Church's catholicity is essentially a participation in the catholicity of the universe," which is marked by diversity and flexibility (*Christian Ministry in the Divine Milieu*, 167).

19. Congar, *Divided Christendom*, 97.

20. Wolfgang Beinert, "Catholicity as a Property of the Church," *The Jurist* 52 (1992): 455–83, at 469, cited in Gaillardetz, *Ecclesiology for a Global Church*, 40. Gaillardetz interprets Beinert's statement to mean that "the catholicity of the Christian faith lies in the tension between the universal and the particular" (Gaillardetz, *Ecclesiology for a Global Church*, 40). The meaning that I draw from Beinert's statement, however, is not about a generalized "tension" but about the uniqueness of Christ, the incarnate Son. Beinert and I disagree about some important ecclesiological matters, including the *sensus fidei*: see Wolfgang Beinert, "Einstimmen oder Übereinstimmen? Die Aufgabe des Glaubenssinnes der Gläubigen," in *Zerreißprobe Ehe: Das Ringen der katholischen Kirche um die Familie*, ed. Ulrich Ruh and Myriam Wijlens (Herder, 2015), 27–44. See also Beinert, "Der Glaubenssinn der Gläubigen in Theologie und Dogmengeschichte: Ein Überblick," in *Der Glaubenssinn des Gottesvolkes: Konkurrent oder Partner des Lehramts?*, ed. Dietrich Wiederkehr (Herder, 1994), 66–131.

21. Kenneth J. Collins and Jerry L. Walls, *Roman but Not Catholic: What Remains at Stake 500 Years after the Reformation* (Baker Academic, 2017), 97.

of the Catholic Church to the effect that the Church is "catholic" because Jesus Christ is present in the Church. According to the *Catechism*, it follows from the fullness of Christ's presence that the (Roman) Catholic Church possesses all the means of salvation that unite the Church to Christ. These include the teachings of the faith, the seven sacraments, and the offices of the Church in accordance with apostolic succession. The *Catechism* adds that the Church is also "catholic" insofar as the Church possesses a universal mission to spread the Gospel.

In response, Collins and Walls comment, "The authors of the *Catechism* have defined the universality of the church in terms of the particular form that the church has taken in the Roman Catholic tradition."[22] They contend that according to this definition, the Church only bears the mark of catholicity when it confesses the Creed with the *filioque*, when it celebrates the seven sacraments, and when it is led by the pope. Since these elements all developed in the (Roman) Catholic Church over centuries—the *filioque* was a late patristic (Western) addition to the Creed, the explicit recognition of seven sacraments did not take place in the West until the twelfth century, and the pope's role gradually expanded over the centuries—it would appear that the early Church itself was not "catholic." Moreover, Christian communities that do not accept the authority of the pope are simply excluded, according to Collins and Walls's reading of the *Catechism*, from catholicity.

It follows that the (Roman) Catholic Church has limited the mark of catholicity to those ecclesial communities that are in union with Rome. Although many Christians worship in such churches, a majority of Christians do not do so. Collins and Walls draw the conclusion that "catholicity" has thereby become its opposite. Rather than truly involving universality, the (Roman) Catholic definition of catholicity only pertains to a minority of the world's Christians. The "universal" Church turns out to be

22. Collins and Walls, 97.

only the segment of the Christian community that is in communion with Rome.

Collins and Walls explain that the *Catechism* has indulged in "a confusing and, in the end, contradictory twofold process: first, it maintains that the word 'catholic' refers to the universal, comprehensive church; second, it then identifies that universal catholic church specifically with itself in a move of generalization in which a part, that is, a particular theological tradition, is mistaken for the whole."[23] In fact, the "universal" Church, comprised of the majority of all Christians, rejects the (Roman) Catholic Church's claims about the requirements of catholicity. Protestants reject the papacy and most of the seven sacraments along with many other (Roman) Catholic doctrines. The Orthodox reject the papacy and some doctrines. The Church prior to the fourth century lacked much of what supposedly belongs to catholicity. But the *Catechism* nevertheless declares, "Particular Churches are fully catholic through their communion with one of them, the Church of Rome, 'which presides in charity.' 'For with this church, by reason of its pre-eminence, the whole Church, that is the faithful everywhere, must be in accord.'"[24] The *Catechism* goes on to cite a similar sentence from Maximus the Confessor. Collins and Walls point out that the (Roman) Catholic Church judges the Eastern Orthodox Church "to be not completely catholic simply because this historic church is not in full communion with the Vatican."[25] Despite the fact that the Orthodox Church is just as ancient as the (Roman) Catholic Church, and despite the fact that it was the (Roman) Catholic Church that altered the Creed, the rejection of the papacy is enough to render the Orthodox Church deficient in catholicity.

Collins and Walls conclude that "catholicity" for the

23. Collins and Walls, 98.

24. *Catechism of the Catholic Church*, 2nd ed. (Libreria Editrice Vaticana, 1997), §834, quoting Ignatius of Antioch, *To the Romans* 1.1, and Irenaeus of Lyons, *Against Heresies* 3.3.2; cited in Collins and Walls, *Roman but Not Catholic*, 98.

25. Collins and Walls, *Roman but Not Catholic*, 99.

(Roman) Catholic Church really means "in full communion with the Pope." Such a definition of catholicity inscribes into the definition of "universal" precisely one of the most contested claims in all Christianity, the claim that elevates the See of Rome above all else and that makes acceptance of papal authority to be the measure of universality. Surely this is one of the most self-serving, divisive, and dubious definitions of Christian ecclesial "universality" that could be imagined. In its replacement of true universality with a universality based upon its own status, then, the Church led by the bishop of Rome has shown itself to be an exponent of division. In other words, while it lays claim to the name Catholic, it is not catholic.

The real "universal" or "catholic" Church, say Collins and Walls, can be seen around the world wherever there are Christians. Collins and Walls affirm that there really is today a universal or catholic Church, existing "under the power, authority, and sovereignty of Christ, the head of the church."[26] (Roman) Catholic Christians make up a part of that universal Church, but the universal Church is much broader than (Roman) Catholicism imagines. Collins and Walls explain that this is why, unlike (Roman) Catholics themselves, Collins and Walls always and only refer to the "*Roman* Catholic Church."[27] To do otherwise would be implicitly to accept the (Roman) Catholic claim to be catholic or universal, thereby insulting and diminishing all other Christians. They especially wish to avoid insulting Orthodox Christians who, during the eleventh century, had the catholicity of their Churches called into question by (Roman) Catholics laying claim to the term, as though a mere part of the Church (i.e., the Latin Church) could reasonably claim to be the "universal" Church.

Since they recognize (Roman) Catholics to be Christians, Collins and Walls argue that their perspective is more ecumenical and generous than is the (Roman) Catholic position, with

26. Collins and Walls, 99.

27. Collins and Walls, 99.

its seizing of catholicity to itself. Granted, in their view the (Roman) Catholic Church has developed traditions and practices that "may at times detract from both the power and the clarity of the gospel," but (Roman) Catholics should still be recognized as Christians.[28] By allowing that the universal or catholic Church includes (Roman) Catholics and Orthodox along with Protestants of all stripes, Collins and Walls aim to have "the good sense not to make any one of these traditions the heart of the church," although of course their ecclesiology is Protestant rather than (Roman) Catholic or Orthodox.[29] For Collins and Walls, the central point consists in "the theological and ecclesiastical trouble that emerges when any one communion insists on being the center."[30]

They are aware that Orthodox Churches, too, claim catholicity or universality and believe that (Roman) Catholicism and Protestantism have, to different degrees, fallen away from the fullness of catholicity. The fact that both (Roman) Catholics and Orthodox make the same divisive claim in the name of a supposed universality that ceased to exist when they split from each other in the eleventh century makes clear that a more ecumenical ecclesiology is needed—which Collins and Walls find in Protestant ecclesiology, once stripped of the classical Protestant claim that (Roman) Catholics are not actually Christians. Collins and Walls accentuate their emphasis on (Roman) Catholic narrowness by employing "the term 'Rome' to refer to the Roman Catholic Church."[31]

In pressing their case against (Roman) Catholicism on multiple fronts—not only on the matter of catholicity—Collins and Walls remark that they have deliberately chosen to "read and learn even from Roman Catholic dogmatists, that is, from those authors who have already made up their minds that whatever Rome

28. Collins and Walls, xvi.

29. Collins and Walls, xvi.

30. Collins and Walls, xvii.

31. Collins and Walls, xviii.

affirms is the gospel truth."[32] I am among the "Roman Catholic dogmatists" whom they have in view, both appreciatively and critically.[33] While I will provide a fuller response to their critique of the (Roman) Catholic doctrine of catholicity in the second section of my chapter, where I underline the significance of qualitative catholicity, let me begin a response here. Given that both Catholics and Orthodox assert that the fullness of catholicity is in their respective communions, Collins and Walls are in fact asserting that only a Protestant ecclesiology is correct about catholicity. They are consigning those who do not agree with them to the status of those who distort true catholicity. Ironically, they offer a Protestant version of what they think (Roman) Catholics are doing, by insisting that only their own ecclesiology is compatible with true catholicity today. They make room for (Roman) Catholics and Orthodox within their Protestant ecclesiological understanding of catholicity, but not fully, due to the false doctrines they believe these traditions maintain—especially, in the case of (Roman) Catholics, the doctrines about the papacy.

Kevin Vanhoozer

Kevin Vanhoozer pushes further along these problematic lines. Writing from a "Mere Evangelical" (or "Mere Protestant") perspective focused upon developing strategies by which Protestants from various traditions can come to see each other as full partners, Vanhoozer argues that "part of the process of producing mature disciples is coming to accept your own interpretations of Scripture as one of the riches of the royal priesthood rather than the whole

32. Collins and Walls, xviii.

33. They devote a couple pages to my *Engaging the Doctrine of Revelation: The Mediation of the Gospel through Church and Scripture* (Baker Academic, 2014). They are kind to my work, noting that "we largely agree with Levering's account of revelation, even as we profoundly disagree with him about a number of particular doctrinal claims" (Collins and Walls, *Roman but Not Catholic*, 78).

treasury."[34] The whole treasury is contained in Scripture alone.[35] Only Scripture is reliable and authoritative in an absolute sense, as God's Word.[36] Yet Christ-centered, Spirit-filled interpreters (both as individuals and collectively, i.e., in creedal confessions) across the ages have much to teach us through their readings of Scripture. To broaden our perspective, says Vanhoozer, we need "to attend to the broader pattern of Protestant authority and to listen for the Spirit speaking in the history of the church's interpretation of Scripture."[37]

In this context, Vanhoozer explains that every Protestant should be a "catholic Christian" attuned to the "communion of saints"—but not in the (Roman) Catholic (or, for that matter, the Orthodox) understanding of "catholic" or "saints." All believers in Christ are "saints," as the apostle Paul's usage of the term indicates. This does not mean they are sinless or holy in every way, but it means that they have accepted Christ as Lord, their sins have been forgiven, and they are being sanctified by the Holy Spirit. The communion of such "saints" extends across generations, and so the insights of past Spirit-guided Christians help Christian communities today to understand God's authoritative Word. Vanhoozer emphasizes that "Protestants too care about

34. Kevin J. Vanhoozer, *Hearers and Doers: A Pastor's Guide to Making Disciples Through Scripture and Doctrine* (Lexham, 2019), 184.

35. Vanhoozer comments, "One of the concerns about *sola Scriptura* is that it encourages interpretive pride: every individual can act as if they are a chief priest of the Bible's meaning. I see *sola Scriptura* working rather differently, namely, as a standing challenge to this tendency toward prideful certainty. Properly understood, *sola Scriptura* teaches us that Scripture *alone* is authoritative, not our interpretation of it. Jesus Christ alone is Lord, but there are other masters who teach us how to read his word. Scripture clearly shows us the Way of Jesus Christ *and* affords us opportunity to discuss with others what discipleship means for today. What the Protestant Reformers discovered is that reading the Bible with others is itself a means of learning humility" (177).

36. As Vanhoozer explains, "As Creator, God is the ultimate 'expert,' the all-knowing one, because he is the author of all domains. . . . This gives him right of say-so: ultimate authority over all things. The crucial question is whether God has *expressed* his authority and, if so, where. Authority must be verbally expressed—*said*—because, apart from meaningful content, there is nothing else that holds persons accountable. Protestants confess that God expresses his authority verbally, and that the Old and New Testaments are God's last will and testament, as it were" (175).

37. Vanhoozer, 183.

catholicity. Protestants propose a kind of wholeness, unity, and universality centered not on an imperial structure (the domain of Rome) but an imperial gospel (the domain of God's word)."[38]

Unfortunately, says Vanhoozer, (Roman) Catholics trust in the "imperial structure" or imperial power of "Rome" or the papacy in order to establish and ensure catholicity—that is, the universal fullness, breadth, and mission of the Church. Vanhoozer compares this artifact of the Roman Empire with the Protestant recognition that catholicity or Christian fullness flows from the universality and fullness of the Gospel or the Word of God. If one is choosing between a universality based upon a powerful leader in the Church and a universality based upon the fullness of God's Word, the correct choice is clear.

In an earlier work co-authored with Daniel Treier, Vanhoozer suggests that Evangelical theology has traditionally been focused on resources from America, Great Britain, and (to a degree) Germany. Vanhoozer and Treier identify "a deficit of catholicity: evangelical theology has not yet reckoned adequately with either time or place."[39] They therefore advocate for a "Protestant catholicity" grounded in Jesus Christ calling to himself a holy people ("saints" or all people who profess him with a sincere heart as Lord and Savior) and sending them on mission. The Gospel itself is what has "catholicity" or fullness, since the Gospel is the Word of God, Jesus Christ. The Church receives and embodies catholicity insofar as baptized believers proclaim the Gospel of Jesus Christ. As members of the "catholic" Church, believers are by divine grace "sharers in all that Christ is," and Christ calls believers to share what they have received with the whole world.[40]

Vanhoozer and Treier define "catholicity" as sharing in what the whole Church believes "about the gospel of God and the God

38. Vanhoozer, 199.

39. Kevin J. Vanhoozer and Daniel J. Treier, *Theology and the Mirror of Scripture: A Mere Evangelical Account* (IVP Academic, 2015), 37.

40. Vanhoozer and Treier, 136.

of the gospel," and thereby being united to "the catholic tradition" or "the consensus tradition passed down through the centuries."[41] This includes the fact that Jesus is the incarnate Lord, the consubstantiality of the Son and the Father, the reality of the Triune God, the salvific Crucifixion and Resurrection of Jesus, and so on. The catholic tradition is catholic because it reflects Scripture truly. It is the *consensus* tradition rather than merely what a part of the Christian world teaches. Doctrines that are taught only by a part of the Christian world are not "catholic" or at least *not yet* catholic; Christians as a whole have not perceived them to be a true reflection of the Word of God. The catholic tradition exhibits continuity over time and is extended across the world rather than being merely a local or twenty-first-century phenomenon. Believers should appreciate "the ministerial authority of the catholic tradition" in light of the "magisterial authority of the canonical Scriptures."[42] When this is done, Vanhoozer and Treier argue, the catholic essentials of the Gospel can be distinguished from the nonessentials with regard to which Christian diversity should be permitted and respected. Nonessentials include the nature of the Lord's Supper, the nature of offices in the Church, and so on.[43]

Ultimately, Vanhoozer is confident about what the fullness

41. Vanhoozer and Treier, 116. Vanhoozer and Treier go on to say, "Theology is the attempt to set forth in speech (and eventually in individual and corporate life) *what is in Christ*. There is true deity (*homoousios*); there is the forgiveness of sins (atonement); there is true humanity (the *imago Dei*). There is much else besides, so much so that no one denomination or theological system exhausts everything there is to be said" (119). Or as they put it shortly afterward: "All the treasures of wisdom are in Jesus Christ. However, just as it took four Gospels to set forth his narrative identity in speech, so it may take many interpretations—communicated and lived—to embody the wisdom potential that is in Christ. Mere evangelical theology does not result in a cacophony of conflicting interpretations—that way lies pervasive interpretive pluralism—but rather in a distinct 'Pentecostal' plurality. As many members with different gifts make up the one body of Christ (Rom 12:4; 1 Cor 12:12), so many anchored (apostolic) readings make up the fullness (catholicity) of evangelical theology. Scripture is sufficient, yet it takes four Evangelists to tell the story of Jesus Christ. In similar fashion, could it not take a number of different voices (denominations, cultures, even eras) to articulate all the wisdoms and blessings that are in Christ?" (121–22).

42. Vanhoozer and Treier, 123.

43. On this basis, Vanhoozer and Treier distinguish level-one doctrines from level-two doctrines. Their purpose is to unite Reformed, Wesleyan, Lutheran, and Anglican Evangelicals, since (in my view at least) many of the doctrines they deem to be "level-two" would be considered by (Roman) Catholics and Orthodox to be "level-one."

of Jesus Christ—the fullness that catholic Christians receive—consists in. It consists in whatever the large majority of Evangelical Protestants today agree is contained in Scripture, leaving room for future development of doctrine within Evangelical Protestant communities.[44] Fortunately, Evangelical Protestants find much agreement with (Roman) Catholics and Orthodox on this content—for instance, on core doctrines about Christ and the Trinity. In Vanhoozer's view, wherever Evangelical Protestants disagree with (Roman) Catholics and Orthodox, or with one another, these are either disagreements about nonessentials (second-level doctrines) or disagreements that demonstrate how far Catholics and Orthodox have diverged from the Word of God as communicated in Scripture. Vanhoozer is confident that Evangelical Protestants have the right, biblically warranted methods for interpreting Scripture correctly, and that (Roman) Catholics employ some wrong, biblically unwarranted methods that arrive at unacceptable doctrinal conclusions.[45] Vanhoozer urges Catholics to reject the notion of catholicity rooted in "Rome" and its power, and instead to embrace "an evangelical catholicity bounded by the gospel, not by Rome"—and thus to embrace a "catholicity . . . as deep and wide as the gospel itself."[46] This sharp contrast between a catholicity based on "Rome" and a catholicity based on "the gospel," as we will see, does not even begin to do justice to Catholic understandings of catholicity.

44. For a recent Protestant account of development of doctrine, see Alister E. McGrath, *The Nature of Christian Doctrine: Its Origins, Development, and Function* (Oxford University Press, 2024). McGrath argues that we should "envisage early Christianity as a period of theory development and testing [much like parallel procedures in the natural sciences], rather than accepting Walter Bauer's influential (though under-evidenced) theory of the suppression of early 'orthodoxies.' Early Christian writers . . . set out what they considered to be viable doctrinal proposals for evaluation; these only became 'orthodox' if and when their merits had been evaluated over an extended period of time by the community of faith, which then received them as communally reliable and authoritative" (vii–viii).

45. See Kevin J. Vanhoozer, "A Mere Protestant Response," in *Was the Reformation a Mistake? Why Catholic Doctrine Is Not Unbiblical*, by Matthew Levering (Zondervan, 2017), 191–231.

46. Vanhoozer, 231.

Hans Boersma

In a recent contribution to an ecumenical symposium on Vatican II, Hans Boersma points out that according to *Lumen Gentium* and *Unitatis Redintegratio*, "the various ways in which people belong to or are related to the people of God may be depicted by a widening set of concentric circles, with Catholic believers in the center, and moving outward via other Christians to Jews, Muslims, and non-believers."[47] The fact is that in the Catholic view, the "people of God," or the "one, holy, catholic, and apostolic Church," really "subsists in" the visible Catholic Church.[48] This position excludes Protestant communions from possessing, in a strict sense, catholicity or fullness, although Protestant communions can and do participate in catholic fullness insofar as they possess the means of salvation. On the positive side, Boersma notes that *Unitatis Redintegratio* recognizes that there is a hierarchy of truths and that Catholics and Protestants share the highest revealed truths. *Unitatis Redintegratio* also grants that, due to Christian divisions, the Catholic Church "finds it more difficult to express in actual life her full catholicity in all its aspects," even though the Catholic Church possesses catholicity.[49]

The problem that Boersma highlights is this: if the unity and catholicity that Christ wills are properly present in the Catholic Church alone—even if these marks of the Church can be increased

47. Hans Boersma, "Meeting *par cum pari*: *Unitatis Redintegratio* and Ecumenical Progress," in *Dogma and Ecumenism: Vatican II and Karl Barth's "Ad Limina Apostolorum,"* ed. Matthew Levering, Bruce L. McCormack, and Thomas Joseph White, OP (The Catholic University of America Press, 2020), 245–67, at 252.

48. For discussion of "subsistit in" in relation to "est," see Stephen A. Hipp, *The One Church of Christ: Understanding Vatican II* (Emmaus Academic, 2018), chapters 1 and 2. Hipp goes on to remark, "In *Unitatis Redintegratio*… the Catholic Church is described as possessing the *totality* of the means of salvation as well as the fullness of the ecclesial unity intended by Christ. . . . Reference to the fullness of the Church's being or ecclesiality, and to its counterpart, incomplete or partial realizations of the same, is an acknowledgment of *degrees* of ecclesiality. Different degrees of ecclesiality thus differentiate different ecclesial communities" (97).

49. Second Vatican Council, *Unitatis Redintegratio* §4, in *Vatican Council II*, vol. 1, *The Conciliar and Post Conciliar Documents*, ed. Austin Flannery, OP, rev. ed. (Costello, 1996), 452–70, at 458–59.

and enriched—then it appears that the Catholic Church understands itself to be radically different from all other churches or ecclesial communities that have a place at the ecumenical table. Whereas from an Anglican perspective one can suppose that each church or ecclesial community brings something to the fullness of the whole—since the fullness of the whole, which visibly existed in the early Church, now does not exist in any one of the numerous divided churches—from a Catholic perspective (in this regard comparable to the Orthodox one[50]) the Catholic Church alone properly possesses the fullness, and the other churches or ecclesial communities may enhance or enrich that fullness. As a result, says Boersma, Catholics at the ecumenical table do not meet non-Catholic Christians as equals.

Boersma adds that according to *Unitatis Redintegratio*, "restoration of unity can come about only through unity with Rome, since it alone has the *plenitudo* of the means of salvation."[51] This

50. Indeed, the Orthodox position is sometimes stronger, to the extent of denying that the Roman Catholic Church possesses valid sacraments (even valid Baptism). John D. Zizioulas, who presumably considered the Orthodox Eucharist to be valid, makes the following strong claim, but he does so for ecumenical purposes: "If two or more Churches are in schism, the eucharistic life (and perhaps also 'validity'?) of *all* local Churches is upset. Conciliarity as an expression of the unity of the local Churches in *one* Church, constitutes a fundamental condition for the Eucharist. Just as the many individual members of a local Church must be united in and through the ministry of the One (the bishop, representing Christ), in the same way the many local Churches must be united into one for their Eucharist to be proper ecclesiologically. Ecclesial unity on a universal level is essential for the Eucharist. . . . The *validity* of the Eucharist depends on the following conditions: i) the presidency (direct or indirect) of the Bishop; ii) Communion with the other Churches in the world (both in terms of space and time, that is, Apostolic succession, and conciliarity); and iii) the presence of the community with all its members and orders, including the *laity*. . . . It would appear that no attempt to restore eucharistic communion among divided Churches would ignore the above mentioned ecclesiological presuppositions of the Eucharist. This would mean that all Churches wishing such a restoration of communion should ask themselves whether not only in theory but *also in practice* they fulfil the above mentioned principles. It may well be that many Churches who do not accept these principles in theory (e.g. the episcopal office, Apostolic succession etc.) in fact practice them, while other Churches who profess these principles in their doctrine fall in fact short of applying them in their liturgical and canonical practice. No progress towards full eucharistic communion can be made without some kind of reformation of existing practices taking place in all Churches in one form or another. . . . These observations apply particularly to the relations between Roman Catholic and Orthodox Churches." Zizioulas, *The Eucharistic Communion and the World*, ed. Luke Ben Tallon (T&T Clark International, 2011), 109. Above, I discussed Zizioulas on apostolicity, but I am unsure what he means when he says that some Churches that reject apostolic succession and episcopacy "in fact practice them."

51. Boersma, "Meeting *par cum pari*," 261.

is true even though Catholics would insist that it is not "Rome" alone that has the *plenitudo*, but the Catholic Church in communion with the bishop of Rome, and more fundamentally Christ and the Trinity. Benoît-Dominique de La Soujeole devotes most of his recent discussion of the Church's catholicity to insisting that "the Church 'is neither Latin [i.e., Roman], nor Greek, nor Slavonic, but Catholic.'"[52] This is so even though—and here de La Soujeole treats the problem of inculturation and the relationship between the universal Church and the particular churches—"this catholicity is realized concretely among the Latins, the Greeks, the Slavs . . . who nevertheless do not cease to be Latins, Greeks, or Slavs."[53]

Boersma observes that despite *Unitatis Redintegratio*'s laudable concern for increasing or perfecting ecclesial unity and catholicity, the decree holds that the Protestant communions are separated from ecclesial unity (and thus from catholicity), while the Catholic Church truly possesses these realities and cannot lose them. As Boersma remarks with some dismay, according to *Unitatis Redintegratio*, "only the separated brethren are lacking in terms of the fullness of the catholicity of the church," even though this fullness is in certain regards still imperfect in the Catholic Church and can be enhanced.[54] With reference to unity, but along lines that apply also to catholicity (which, of course, is closely connected with unity), Boersma asks, "If unity was never lost—except from the side of those who are separated from the

52. Benoît-Dominique de La Soujeole, OP, *Introduction to the Mystery of the Church*, trans. Michael J. Miller (The Catholic University of America Press, 2014), 567, quoting Pope Benedict XV, *Dei providentis*, Motu proprio, May 1, 1917, creating the Congregation for the Oriental Churches, *Acta Apostolicae Sedis* 9:530. De La Soujeole emphasizes, "The property of *catholicity* indicates the idea of fullness, one that is not solely quantitative ('Go into all the world'), but also and essentially qualitative. The two aspects are connected: the qualitative fullness is for everyone. This worldwide destination of God's gifts is not brought about, however, in a sort of totalitarianism, as though the whole world had to abandon its local peculiarities" (de La Soujeole, *Introduction to the Mystery of the Church*, 567).

53. De La Soujeole, *Introduction to the Mystery of the Church*, 567.

54. Boersma, "Meeting *par cum pari*," 262.

Catholic Church and except for certain expressions of the unity of the Catholic Church—what is there to restore?"[55]

In Boersma's view, the Catholic Church has gravely underestimated the impact of the East-West division and the Reformation. The wounds to unity (and thus to catholicity) have been such that no one institutional church, at present, can claim either unity or catholicity. The notion that the Catholic Church possesses the catholic fullness of revealed truth is implausible to Boersma. He states, "It strains credulity that brothers and sisters in Christ, who love and care for one another, must either continue in their divided paths or accept that the uniquely Roman Catholic representations of certain doctrines are essential to Christian unity."[56]

Unlike Collins, Walls, and Vanhoozer, Boersma does not suggest that (Roman) Catholicism has built an ecclesiology or a doctrine of catholicity upon a Roman imperial model. He simply thinks that it is implausible that the Catholic Church is not in the same mess that all Christian communities are in. It is empirically clear that baptized Christians, meant to be united, are divided. The supposed solution of communion with the bishop of Rome, and acceptance of (Roman) Catholic dogmatic and moral teaching, only further illuminates the intractable divisions, which

55. Boersma, 263. Boersma goes on to say, "Perhaps I can best illustrate my concern by means of a question that Charles Morerod raises in his discussion of the document. He asks: 'Since all Christian communities are divided, should we not say that the Catholic Church is also not blessed with "that unity which Jesus Christ wished to bestow"?' Though Morerod recognizes the strength of this argument, he counters it with two comments, from Pope Paul VI and Pope John Paul II respectively, in which they affirm the fullness of the unity of the Catholic Church, and Morerod concludes from this: 'Catholic theologians must deal with a paradox: All Christians are divided, and Catholics are in this situation of division, but the Catholic Church alone has never lost full unity.' While I appreciate the appeal to the two pontiffs, it is not enough to appeal to the Catholic magisterium in support for the full and perduring unity of the Catholic Church. The paradox on which Morerod insists needs not just a formal but also a material theological argument," 264–65, quoting Charles Morerod, OP, "The Decree on Ecumenism, *Unitatis Redintegratio*," in *Vatican II: Renewal within Tradition*, ed. Matthew L. Lamb and Matthew Levering (Oxford University Press, 2008), 311–42, at 317.

56. Boersma, "Meeting *par cum pari*," 265. He adds that in his view, "the church's unity is an eschatological reality, which, although it breaks into this world and allows us provisionally to share in it through the preaching of the gospel and the sharing of the Eucharist, does not visibly take shape today as fully as it will in the hereafter" (265).

common sense suggests *must* break down the Church's unity and catholicity.

I note that the logical conclusion to draw from Boersma's argument is that the Church exists today, insofar as it does exist, wherever Christians gather in fact to hear the true Word of God proclaimed and to celebrate the true sacraments. Divided Christian communities are at best branches or parts of the one and catholic Church that Jesus founded. This viewpoint reflects a Reformed or Anglican ecclesiology. The problem thus persists: the case against the catholicity of (Roman) Catholicism hinges upon compelling Catholics to accept Protestant ecclesiology.

III. CATHOLIC THEOLOGIES OF CATHOLICITY

Let me now turn to what twentieth-century Catholic theology had to say about the Church's catholicity. I will begin briefly with the *Catechism* and Vatican II. The first point that the *Catechism* makes is that "the Church is catholic because Christ is present in her."[57] The *Catechism* goes on to explain that what makes the Church "catholic" is the fact that the Church is Christ's Body and possesses all the means of salvation, so as to be able to share in Christ fully, just as Christ wills to be shared in. Although among the means of salvation is the Petrine office, established by Christ (see Matt 16; John 21), the *Catechism* makes clear that the Church does not depend upon the developed doctrine of the papacy in order to be "catholic." On the contrary, already on the day of the first Pentecost the Church was fully catholic.

Vatican II's Decree on Ecumenism, *Unitatis Redintegratio*, accepts that Christian divisions make it difficult for the Catholic Church "to express in actual life her full catholicity in all its aspects."[58] Yet, the fact of these divisions does not negate the value of the Petrine office, which does clearly play a unifying role—even

57. *Catechism of the Catholic Church*, §830.

58. *Unitatis Redintegratio* §3, in *Vatican Council II*, 458–59.

if the exercise of its authority, with its inevitable imperfections, also results regularly in what Hans Urs von Balthasar calls the "anti-Roman attitude."[59] The Catholic Church maintains that local churches, which in their diverse cultures and traditions display the Church's catholicity, must be in communion with Rome, as appears for instance in *Lumen Gentium*'s statement that "there are also particular Churches that retain their own traditions [i.e., Eastern Catholic Churches], without prejudice to the Chair of Peter which presides over the whole assembly of charity."[60] *Unitatis Redintegratio* teaches that although the Orthodox Churches are indeed Churches, still the *fullness* of unity and catholicity is lacking to these Churches, since they do not possess "the fullness of the means of salvation" inclusive of the apostolic college headed by Peter and his successors.[61] This lack of fullness is present even though the mark of catholicity remains in a real sense, given the true ecclesial status of these Churches and the corresponding fact that "through the celebration of the Eucharist of the Lord in each of these [Eastern Orthodox] Churches, the Church of God is built up and grows in stature."[62]

Aidan Nichols, OP

In his *Figuring Out the Church*, Aidan Nichols first distinguishes between qualitative and quantitative catholicity. The latter consists in the expansion of the Church around the globe; the former consists in the fullness of the Church's faith. As a representative of the qualitative understanding of catholicity, he cites Cyril of

59. Hans Urs von Balthasar, *The Office of Peter and the Structure of the Church*, trans. Andrée Emery (Ignatius, 1986).

60. Second Vatican Council, *Lumen Gentium* §13, in Flannery, *Vatican Council II*, 1:350–426, at 365.

61. *Unitatis Redintegratio* §3, in *Vatican Council II*, 1:456.

62. *Unitatis Redintegratio* §15, in *Vatican Council II*, 1:465. *Unitatis Redintegratio* goes on to say, "These Churches, although separated from us, yet possess true sacraments, above all—by apostolic succession—the priesthood and the Eucharist, whereby they are still joined to us in closest intimacy" (*Unitatis Redintegratio* §15, in *Vatican Council II*, 1:465).

Jerusalem's *Mystagogical Catecheses* 18.23, where Cyril identifies catholicity with possession of the means of salvation (doctrine and sacraments) and with holiness.[63] Cyril also offers a quantitative reason for catholicity—namely, the Church's geographical breadth. Nichols observes that in the post-Tridentine Catholic Church up until the Second Vatican Council, with a few exceptions, catholicity was defined in terms of "the wide geographical extent of a single sacramental society, which is plainly one thanks to the unity of its governance."[64]

Nichols emphasizes that a proper understanding of catholicity will relate it "to the Church's own triune source in Jesus Christ."[65] He thinks Avery Dulles does a particularly good job of this, and I will briefly summarize Dulles's contributions below. Suffice it to say here that Dulles highlights the divine plenitude and the unity and distinction of the divine persons, and that Dulles presents the incarnate Word (in the unity of his person and the diversity of his two natures) as "catholic" in himself and in his mission to "fill all things" (Eph 4:10) with his own glorious life. Dulles identifies the image of the Church as Christ's Body as crucial to the catholicity of the Church, insofar as the Body participates in its Head's catholicity through Christ's gift of himself to his Body. Thus, the Church possesses catholicity, but not yet in the fullness that the consummated Church will one day enjoy (see Eph 4:13).

Having emphasized that the Church's catholicity comes from Christ's catholicity, which he shares with his Body, Nichols reflects upon how the Holy Spirit sustains the Church's catholicity by "foster[ing] communion without effacing differences," both with respect to diverse individuals and with respect to diverse

63. See Cyril of Jerusalem, *Catechetical Lectures*, trans. Edwin Hamilton Gifford, in *Nicene and Post-Nicene Fathers*, Second Series, vol. 7 (Hendrickson, 1994), 1–157, at 139.

64. Aidan Nichols, OP, *Figuring Out the Church: Her Marks, and Her Masters* (Ignatius, 2013), 59.

65. Nichols, 59.

cultures.[66] Here, he takes up not only the differences between Latin and Eastern Catholic Churches, but also the distinction between the universal Church and the particular churches.[67] The particular churches manifest the "universal Church" in accordance with their specific charisms. Ultimately, Baptism and the Eucharist have the universal Church in view, as do "such institutions as ecumenical councils, the Petrine office, the episcopate considered as a college, and worldwide religious orders of the globally unified variety."[68]

Nichols then addresses "quantitative" catholicity—that is, the spread of the Church throughout the world. This spread fulfills the Old Testament's prophetic testimony that Israel's election was for all nations. Christ commands his disciples to spread the Gospel to all nations (see Matt 28:19). The Church is possessed of a message that is universal and of sacraments that are intended to mediate the Paschal Mystery of Christ to all peoples. There can be no purely "national" Church, since this can result in dangerous distortions. Nichols's vision seems quite reasonable to me.

66. Nichols, 65.

67. For differences among diverse instantiations of the Catholic Church in the first millennium, see Gaillardetz, *Ecclesiology for a Global Church*, 41–43. Gaillardetz also provides a discussion of post-Tridentine Catholic missionary work. He criticizes the missions for rejecting inculturation in favor of cultural conquest, although he notes some exceptions such as Matteo Ricci in China. He praises some aspects of Pope Benedict XV's 1919 apostolic letter on the missions, *Maximum Illud*; Pope Pius XI's 1926 encyclical on the missions, *Rerum Ecclesiae*; and Pope Pius XII's 1951 encyclical on the missions, *Evangelii Praecones*. See also the debate over the proper meaning of inculturation between Bénézet Bujo and Paulinus Ikechukwu Odozor, CSSp.: see Bujo, *Foundations of an African Ethic: Beyond the Universal Claims of Western Morality*, trans. Brian McNeil (Crossroad, 2001); and Odozor, *Morality Truly Christian, Truly African: Foundational, Methodological, and Theological Considerations* (University of Notre Dame Press, 2014). Additional insight is found in Emery de Gaál, "Mission, Inculturation, and 'Interculturality' in the Thinking of Joseph Ratzinger / Benedict XVI in Relation to Africa," in *Joseph Ratzinger and the Future of African Theology*, ed. Maurice Ashley Agbaw-Ebai and Matthew Levering (Pickwick, 2021), 183–213. Gaillardetz's perspective reflects David Bosch's *Transforming Missions: Paradigm Shifts in Theology of Mission* (Orbis Books, 1991); and Peter C. Phan's *In Our Own Tongues: Perspectives from Asia on Mission and Inculturation* (Orbis Books, 2003).

68. Nichols, *Figuring Out the Church*, 70.

Hans Urs von Balthasar

In his book, Nichols directs attention to Hans Urs von Balthasar's short but striking 1975 work *Katholisch*, which in English appeared as *In the Fullness of Faith: On the Centrality of the Distinctively Catholic*. Let me briefly discuss its contributions. Balthasar observes that unless one is entranced by the sheer mystery of catholicity, one is likely to construe the Catholic Church—and all other Christian traditions—along merely institutional lines, on the assumption that the sheer variety of Christian claimants to be the Church means that there no longer is (if there ever was) a truly "catholic" visible, institutional Church. In response, he argues that "the measure of its [the Church's] catholicity, which permeates and informs it, is found, not in itself, but above it, in the mystery of Christ"—a mystery that is inseparable from the Church's testimony to Christ.[69]

Balthasar does not hesitate to defend the Petrine office as fundamental to the Church's catholicity, but he notes that the Petrine office relies for its intelligibility upon the higher principle of sacramental or apostolic office in the Church, and thus upon "the pneumatic and eucharistic Christ and his ever-living presence" in the Church.[70] The Petrine office is intelligible, too, only in light of the Church's indefectibility—the holiness of the communion of saints—as symbolized by Mary's holy *fiat* in her participation in the work of redemption. The presence of the glorified and eucharistic Christ and the Spirit-guided indefectibility of the Church ground the Church's catholicity. Balthasar argues that "these deeper principles could not exercise their unity-creating power right to the end without the external reference-point of the Roman bishop."[71]

69. Hans Urs von Balthasar, *In the Fullness of Faith: On the Centrality of the Distinctively Catholic*, trans. Graham Harrison (Ignatius, 1988), 16.

70. Balthasar, 104.

71. Balthasar, 104. He continues in this vein, "And the more worldwide the Church becomes, the more threatened she is in the modern states with their fascism of the right and of

Balthasar posits that Jesus is catholic or else his Church could not be catholic. He defines "catholic" as "embracing everything, leaving nothing out."[72] Yet, how can a single man, even the God-man, embrace everything, given that Jesus was a late-Second-Temple Jew who lived and died in a very particular context? Balthasar suggests that Jesus's catholicity is manifested in his revelation of the Father. In every way, Jesus makes himself transparent to the divine love of the Father. His lowliness, his mercy, his severity, his compassion—all point toward the Father. Jesus unites paradoxical attributes, and he thereby reveals the plenitude of God; Jesus sends the Spirit, and he thereby reveals the diversity and bond of unity within God. Balthasar adds, "Jesus' catholicity is not only 'vertical,' as it were, doing God's will on earth as in Heaven and revealing God in the world: it is also 'horizontal,' recapitulating the history of Adam's race."[73] Jesus fulfills—or "full"-fills by his plenitude—the whole of the Old Testament, which he reinterprets in light of himself. By the Spirit, Jesus speaks his catholic word, inclusive of his Church, through the Scriptures.

Balthasar offers a rich account of the catholicity of the cross. He meditates upon how Jesus's catholic fullness "has room for us to enter right inside it," since it is "a fullness that creates space within it, not a mere flowing outward (*bonum diffusivum sui*) but a fullness that opens up its inner riches."[74] Jesus wants to give us his catholic fullness and to take away our brokenness, enriching rather than suppressing our individuality within the catholicity of

the left, the more she is called upon to incarnate herself in the most diverse, non-Mediterranean cultures, and the wider theological and episcopal pluralism she contains, the more indispensable this reference-point becomes" (104–5). Earlier he similarly appealed to "the qualitative difference between the unity of life and doctrine within the 'Roman' Catholic Church and the unity that exists within all other Christian communions. For, if we begin with the Orthodox, no ecumenical council has been able to unite them since their separation from Rome. And if we turn to the innumerable ecclesial communities that arose from the Reformation and subsequently, even though they are members of the World Council of Churches, they have scarcely managed to get any further than a 'convergence' toward unity" (103–4).

72. Balthasar, 27.

73. Balthasar, 33.

74. Balthasar, 41.

the Triune God. In love, the Son Jesus surrenders himself utterly to the Father; and "because he surrenders himself, he receives himself."[75] The Father eternally gives his whole being to the Son in begetting the Son. Christ's *kenosis* enables us to share in the Trinity's catholicity by sharing in the self-surrendering love of the Father and the Son in the Holy Spirit. Thus, Balthasar identifies the Trinity's catholicity as the source of the Church's catholicity. He suggests that this can be interpreted in terms of both the image of Body and the image of Bride: "'body' in that the Church is made into a vessel, an organ, an extension of Christ through his self-communication, and 'bride' or 'spouse' in that it is fashioned by the Bridegroom's self-surrender and thus presented by him to himself (Eph 1:23; 5:25–27)."[76]

Balthasar argues that on the cross, Christ manifests the mutual self-surrendering love of Father and Son, united by the bond of the Spirit (a bond that is self-surrendering love), "who draws men into the divine fullness of both [Father and Son] that is prodigally squandered on the world."[77] The Eucharist, the charisms and vocations of the members of Christ's Body, and the catholic "we" are all manifestations of our incorporation into the catholic fullness (infinite self-surrendering love) of the Father in the Son through the Spirit. The Church shares in the self-surrendering mission of Christ for the sake of the world. Balthasar states, "The reiterated 'all' at the end of Saint Matthew's Gospel shows that Christ's catholicity is opened up, in the catholicity of his Church, to a future catholicity of the world."[78]

Balthasar contends that the Petrine office is not an affront to Christ's sharing of his catholicity with the Church. The Church is a "constellation around Christ within which the Petrine constitutes

75. Balthasar, 41.
76. Balthasar, 42.
77. Balthasar, 43.
78. Balthasar, 54.

one element."[79] The Petrine office—precisely as an office of authority—is modeled upon the cross, due to the ever-humiliating difficulty of the papal task.[80] In combination with other elements in the Church, the Petrine office serves the unity of the Church, grounded in the Gospel of catholic self-surrendering love.[81]

In a 1972 essay on "The Catholicity of the Church," published a few years before *In the Fullness of Faith*, Balthasar distinguishes between "anthropological catholicity" and "Christological catholicity." Christ's gift of catholic fullness, he emphasizes, remains Christ's even when the Church possesses it. We can never claim it as our own. Indeed, Balthasar portrays the Church's catholicity as a "paradox" and, for many, a "scandal," given the evident humanness and limitedness of the Church.[82] Christ's catholic fullness is defensible, but the Church's claim to catholic fullness can appear absurd. As Balthasar says, "A church that claims to be catholic would have to have a very special relationship to the universal experience of humanity and a very special relationship to the God-man."[83]

Balthasar, therefore, first examines the Church's relationship to humanity—that is, the Church's anthropological catholicity. The Church is built in a certain sense upon Abraham—specifically,

79. Balthasar, *The Office of Peter and the Structure of the Church*, 290. In this context, Balthasar criticizes Congar for making "a fundamental distinction between 'structure', even 'skeleton' (the bones mentioned by Ezekiel, which wait for the coming Spirit), and 'life,' whereby he [Congar] reduces the aspect of office to a purely 'instrumental' function. Such a distinction can be made only at a superficial level. Looking deeper, one can see the living organism, nailed to the hard wood of the so-called institution, as the very proof of divine love" (289–90). See Yves Congar, OP, *Vraie et fausse réforme dans l'Église* (Cerf, 1950), 96; Congar, *Jalons pour une théologie du laïcat* (Cerf, 1953), 148. Balthasar observes that Congar achieves a better balance in *Ministères et communion ecclésiale* (Cerf, 1971); and Balthasar also has positive things to say about Congar's understanding of catholicity in Yves Congar, OP, *Chrétiens désunis: Principes d'un "oecumenisme" catholique* (Cerf, 1937) and Yves Congar, OP, *Esquisse du mystère de l'Église*, rev. ed. (Cerf, 1953).

80. See Balthasar, *The Office of Peter and the Structure of the Church*, 353–56; cf. 153–54.

81. See also Balthasar's discussion of the Catholic Church in relation to the Roman Empire in 331–49, with an emphasis on Augustine's critique of Rome.

82. Hans Urs von Balthasar, "The Catholicity of the Church," in Joseph Ratzinger and Hans Urs von Balthasar, *Mary: The Church at the Source*, trans. Adrian Walker (Ignatius, 2005), 157–76, at 157–58.

83. Balthasar, 158.

upon Abraham's absolute dependence upon and faith in God, to the point of obedient self-surrender to God's will. The people of Israel on the exodus have to learn to enact such self-surrender. Finally, Jesus fulfills and perfects this attitude.[84] All human religious experience is bound up in Jesus's graced self-surrender to God the Father, since human *religio* is the work of being related to God. Besides, Jesus's self-surrendering trust in God the Father consists fundamentally in love. This trust encompasses all history, from human origins to the eschaton. In Jesus Christ, we trust that the whole of reality, ourselves included, originates in God and providentially returns to God.

Second, the Church has Christological catholicity. In Mary, the Church receives the fullness of God. This is possible because Mary's *fiat* is, by grace, completely open to the Incarnation of the Word. Her yes establishes the Church in its catholic fullness, because she receives the fullness of Christ. Her yes includes prayer and cooperation, each of which contains manifold dimensions. It is a "child-like" yes, in the sense of the humility that Jesus requires of his followers in Matthew 18:3–4. It is a yes made possible by the Holy Spirit, a yes that makes possible true action (or cooperation) "within the unlimited, universal, catholic mission of Jesus Christ."[85] This Marian yes goes beyond the limits of human understanding; it makes itself apparent in a truly catholic or full "identification" with Christ's own mode of self-surrendering action.[86]

There is a temptation, says Balthasar, to make this ecclesial catholicity merely ideal rather than concrete. It is for this reason that ecclesiastical office cannot be separated from true catholicity. Jesus cannot be detached from his own historical time and place or from the testimony of his followers, given that it is only through that testimony that he can be known at all. It is

84. See Balthasar, 159.

85. Balthasar, 165.

86. See Brendan Leahy, *The Marian Profile: In the Ecclesiology of Hans Urs von Balthasar* (New City, 2000).

therefore impossible to know Jesus without the concrete apostolic Church, led by Peter and the Twelve (and by Paul), that gave testimony to him.[87]

Paul especially shows how the office in the Church upholds the Church's catholicity. For the Church to exist concretely (as the Pauline churches do), the Church must possess a structure, an order that sustains its teaching, sanctifying, and governing. Office should therefore not be dismissed as mere "institution." The living Eucharistic Church, the Body of Christ, requires office or concrete structure in order to be the catholic entity it is. Paul has concrete authority, and he hands this on.[88] Balthasar points to the concrete authority exercised by Paul, as reflected in his Corinthian correspondence. The purpose of this authority, in Paul's hands, is to direct the Corinthians back to the fullness of the yes to Christ, in self-surrendering love.[89] Without the service

87. By comparison, drawing upon Lamin Sanneh's work and also upon that of Stephen Bevans and Robert Schreiter, Gaillardetz argues that the task of translating the Gospels into new languages (reflective of the translation of Jesus's own Aramaic words into Greek) inevitably "gave rise to Christian forms quite different from those championed by the missionaries themselves" (Gaillardetz, *Ecclesiology for a Global Church*, 70). He finds that while divine revelation took place in the person Jesus Christ, there is no way for any particular words about Jesus (including scriptural words) to be other than fully and inextricably culturally embedded: "There is no transcultural kernel" (73). If so, then there is also no transcultural dogma, but only contextual expressions that can and should change whenever cultures change. For a helpful critique of such a viewpoint, see Thomas Joseph White, OP, *The Incarnate Lord: A Thomistic Study in Christology* (The Catholic University of America, 2015), especially 470–86, in dialogue with Edward Schillebeeckx, OP, Claude Geffré, and others. Gaillardetz tries to propose a solution based upon intercultural overlap, but I do not see how this overlap, which itself would be culturally contingent, could suffice for dogmatic truth (that is, universally true claims about God, Christ, the Church, and so on); see Gaillardetz, *Ecclesiology for a Global Church*, 75. Gaillardetz continues to appeal to "the gospel" and to affirm its "transcendence," but, since what "the gospel" is cannot be articulated in anything but contingent and changeable expressions, the claim that "the gospel" has "transcendence" is of little import.

88. Balthasar comments, "The objection that the Church structure depicted in Paul's letters cannot serve as a model for the postapostolic period because later officeholders no longer possess the fullness of apostolic authority does not hold water. If this were the case, then a vital portion of the New Testament canon would have no more than antiquarian value for us. Paul makes a point of calling, not only himself, but also his collaborators and successors 'servants of Christ,' 'co-workers of God,' and he demands (in Corinth, no less) the very same reverent reception, the very same obedience for them as he does for himself. . . . Of course, the successors do not have the apostles' Church-founding functions and the special powers belonging to them. Nor do they need them, for the structure has already been established and must only be kept alive" (Balthasar, "The Catholicity of the Church," 169–70).

89. See also Hans Urs von Balthasar, *Paul Struggles with His Congregation: The Pastoral Message of the Letters to the Corinthians*, trans. Brigitte L. Bojarska (Ignatius, 1992).

performed by hierarchical office (including the Petrine office), the unity of the Church with Christ would not be embodied; the pluralism of charisms, practices, time, and place would find no sustained point of catholic unity.

Balthasar thus conceives of the Church's catholicity in terms of the relationships of Mary and Peter to Christ. Both relationships involve humility and self-surrender, and Peter's office does not take precedence over the Marian dimension of the Church. Peter's office stands in service to Johannine love. The Marian and Petrine dimensions of catholicity are complementary: both are "pure service," both point to Christ, both are "supernaturally fruitful," both have the cross and Resurrection at their center.[90] The Church is catholic not because of itself—though it needs both the Marian and Petrine dimensions to be catholic—but because of Christ.

Avery Dulles, SJ

Avery Dulles points out that after the council, Karl Rahner rejoiced that "the era of Eurocentrism is coming to an end and . . . Catholicism is at length becoming, for the first time in history, a *de facto* planetary Church."[91] Rahner was greatly taken with the

90. Balthasar, "The Catholicity of the Church," 174. For Gaillardetz, by contrast, the Church cannot be "catholic" without the ordination of women; see Gaillardetz, *Ecclesiology for a Global Church*, 84–85. Balthasar himself makes matters more concrete in his *Two Sisters in the Spirit: Thérèse of Lisieux and Elizabeth of the Trinity*, trans. Donald Nichols, Anne Englund Nash, and Dennis Martin (Ignatius, 1992); and see Balthasar's reflections on women priests and on the pitfalls facing modern theology in his *New Elucidations*, trans. Mary Theresilde Skerry (Ignatius, 1986). See also Josephine Lombardi, *Marian Approaches to Synodality* (Paulist, 2024). Unlike Balthasar, Lombardi argues that the Marian dimension of the Church should be institutionalized in terms of concrete participation in leadership: "What would it look like to have women, in a more formal role, accompanying the magisterium in prayer and discernment? Is the Holy Spirit calling us to discern a formal institutional expression of another Mary, revealing the deeper meaning of Church, walking with the people of God as Mother and Teacher? Is the Synod on Synodality providing this opportunity?" (Lombardi, 146). For guideposts for the task of answering such questions, see Thomas Michelet, OP, "Deaconesses and Diaconate," forthcoming in *Nova et Vetera* 23 (2025).

91. Dulles, *The Catholicity of the Church*, 174. See Karl Rahner, SJ, "Towards a Fundamental Theological Interpretation of Vatican II," *Theological Studies* 40, no. 4 (1979): 716–27. For further discussion, see Dulles, "The Emerging World Church: A Theological Reflection," *Proceedings of the Catholic Theological Society of America* 39 (1984): 1–12. Dulles comments

Swiss Capuchin missiologist Walbert Bühlmann's 1974 book *The Coming of the Third Church: An Analysis of the Present and Future of the Church.*[92] Its core idea is that a "Third Church" is now emerging from the global South—Latin America, Africa, and Asia—to renew and stand alongside the Churches of East (the "First Church") and West (the "Second Church").[93] In support of Bühlmann's vision, Rahner wrote an essay appended to

regarding a danger with false (but increasingly popular) notions of inculturation, "When the Bible, dogmas, sacraments and ecclesiastical structures are branded as culture-bound, the sources of continuity and communion in the church are weakened. The idea of a visible world church is undercut, and its place is taken by an invisible fellowship of an elite who have undergone intellectual, moral, and religious conversion within their own cultures and religions" ("The Emerging World Church," 8). For his part, Gaillardetz warns (in 2008, under Pope Benedict), "Whenever the need for control leads church leadership to be suspicious of new forms of Christian life emerging daily throughout the world, there the church's catholicity suffers" (Gaillardetz, *Ecclesiology for a Global Church*, 85–86).

92. See Walbert Bühlmann, OFM Cap., *The Coming of the Third Church: An Analysis of the Present and Future of the Church* (Orbis Books, 1977). See also, for preconciliar reflections that point in the same direction (in a mild-mannered way), Joseph Folliet, *World Catholicism Today*, trans. Edmond Bonin (Newman, 1961). Folliet observes, "Now, although the very nature of the Church precludes her being linked to any one civilization or type of culture, historically she appears to non-Europeans as essentially bound up with the West. Consequently, since her relations with any country or culture are historical and, therefore, contingent and accidental, she must strive to free her fundamental self from whatever elements in those relations would seem to impugn her universality. Harmless and obvious as it seems, that statement presupposes a heroic program of work, study and abnegation. . . . A new order is coming into being—one which will differ radically from the old ones and, very likely, from the dreams of those who think they are shaping it. Under the circumstances, there is no room for complacence. Any saint today must be a revolutionary" (*World Catholicism Today*, 107, 158).

93. In Bühlmann's view, "In spite of all difficulties, the Council went much further than Pope John had imagined possible. . . . The euphoric period of openness was followed (typically for the western Church, that is, for our Second Church) by a period of contestation. The Fathers of the Council, in their speeches and behaviour, had presented a new image of the Church, belying former impressions of closedness, regimentation and servile obedience. This shift of public image was confirmed by the Council's openness towards the laity, typical of its general openness, which led to an awareness of lay people's maturity and co-responsibility in the Church. And so, immediately after the Council, many lay people, priests and even bishops began to show increasing impatience and anger when reforms were presumed to be or really were obstructed" (*The Coming of the Third Church*, 13). The result of this obstruction, Bühlmann thinks, was a collapse of Catholic faith and practice in Europe. He conceives of a "death and resurrection" of the Church in Europe that now requires Europeans to embrace the task of "carrying through with courage the transition from Western Church to world-wide Church" (19). Part of this task will be assisting with economic and political transformation in the name of justice. Another part will involve structural reform; Bühlmann proposes "radical decentralizing, to give the regions [of the world] more responsibility and a chance to work out their own Christian life" (188). He encourages Catholics to imitate Jesus's courage in criticizing the leaders of God's people by "going against laws, structures and institutions (in so far as they are opposed to the Spirit)" (210), while also imitating Jesus's kenotic humility. He generally favors married priests, admission to the Eucharist of the divorced and remarried without annulment, and acceptance of birth control in situations of overpopulation and poverty.

Bühlmann's 1984 *Welt Kirche: Neue Dimensionen—Modell für das Jahr 2001*, a book translated into English as *Church of the Future: A Model for the Year 2001*.[94] This essay, "Perspectives for Pastoral Theology in the Future," builds upon Rahner's programmatic 1979 essay announcing the World Church, "Basic Theological Interpretation of the Second Vatican Council."[95]

Bühlmann considered humanity and the Church to be poised to progress beyond national and religious divisions to a declericalized and decentralized *catholic* fellowship, modeled by St. Francis.[96] He states in 1974, "Nothing damages the Church and her mission more than the desire to cling to historically conditioned forms. If we have the courage to let go of structures that are out of date, God will enable us to find new structures through

94. For Bühlmann's book and Rahner's afterword, see Karl Rahner, SJ, "Perspektiven der Pastoral in der Zukunft," in *Welt Kirche: Neue Dimensionen—Modell fur das Jahr 2001*, by Walbert Bühlmann, OFM Cap. (Styria, 1984), 220–34—an essay that appears as "Perspectives for Pastoral Theology in the Future," in Rahner, *Theological Investigations*, vol. 22, *Humane Society and the Church of Tomorrow*, trans. Joseph Donceel (Crossroad, 1991), 106–19. See also Bühlmann, *Church of the Future: A Model for the Year 2001* (Orbis Books, 1986), where he looks back with sorrow to the role of Capuchins in preaching the Counter-Reformation. He argues that today's Catholics are reclaiming the spirit of St. Francis and "coming to understand [ecumenically] that the differences of constituent elements and traditions that still remain scarcely any longer justify rifts between the churches and that in basic communities, for example, we are already living in a practical unity. Francis would not in any case lay much stress on structures but on the one Spirit, the one gospel, the one Lord Jesus Christ, the one baptism" (Bühlmann, *Church of the Future*, 107).

95. See Karl Rahner, SJ, "Basic Theological Interpretation of the Second Vatican Council," in *Theological Investigations*, vol. 20, *Concern for the Church*, trans. Edward Quinn (Crossroad, 1981), 77–89.

96. This point is made by Peter Joseph Fritz, "Catholicity and Translatability: Renewing Rahner on the World Church," *Theological Studies* 83, no. 3 (2022): 400–423, at 407–8; see Bühlmann, *Church of the Future*, 110. Bühlmann deems that the Church under the pontificate of Pope John Paul II has stifled the implementation of the Council: "Despite Vatican II, not everything is right with the church. The interests of the church as a church of the Spirit, of love, of the good news, continually conflict with the interests of the institutional church, which has resisted change. The problem for the contemporary period of the church consists precisely in that the concepts having to do with the new image of the church—concepts propounded in many conciliar and postconciliar documents—have not yet been translated into structures" (132). He blames the European loss of faith upon the Church's slowness in radically reforming itself: "For the last hundred years the church has lost one social class after another in the Western world . . . first the workers, because it did not take their problem seriously enough; then the intellectuals, because it would not accept the autonomy of science; then the men, because they grew tired of being treated like children; then the young, because they had no patience with the ecclesiastical mentality; and finally the women, because they form the main contingent at the basis of the church but have no voice at the top" (*Church of the Future*, 133).

observing the signs of the times."[97] Rahner agrees with this while recognizing (as does Bühlmann) that, due to sin and to the sheer "unpredictability of history," the unification of all humanity in the new Church will come about fully only in the eschaton.[98] In Rahner's view—well summed up by Peter Joseph Fritz, who is critical of Rahner in this regard—"the historical trappings of former ecclesial forms [will] fall away in the development of the world church and, presumably, its global pastoral-strategic plan."[99] Like Bühlmann and many others, Rahner understands Vatican II to have inaugurated something radically new, beyond merely updating the Church in *aggiornamento*. He underscores that "the coming-to-be of the world-Church as such does not mean merely a quantitative augmentation of the earlier Church, but contains a theological caesura in church history which has not by any means been clearly considered, which can be compared perhaps only with the transition from Judaeo-Christianity to Gentile Christianity."[100]

97. Bühlmann, *The Coming of the Third Church*, 407.

98. See Karl Rahner, SJ, "Unity of the Church—Unity of Mankind," in *Concern for the Church*, 154–72, at 164. He observes, "What then might seem to be a purely secular task for Christians and their Churches—working to achieve the unity of mankind—has for them also a Christian aspect. By this work they create conditions to enable Christianity to become concretely a true world-religion or increasingly so, for the Church to become increasingly a true world-Church" (172). See also Folliet, *World Catholicism Today*, 194–95, 197: "We are living in an age of catholicity. . . . Catholicism is the religion of an age dedicated to the universal. A unified world will need a new culture, one that will be universally shared and will gather the attainments of all previous cultures into a living synthesis. . . . To a world which, for the first time in history, is laying the foundations for oneness, Catholicism offers the ideal and the experience of universality."

99. Fritz, "Catholicity and Translatability," 409–10. This will impact papal governance first and foremost, since, in Rahner's view, "a world-Church simply cannot be ruled by that Roman centralism which was usual in the time of Pius XII" (Rahner, "Basic Theological Interpretation of the Second Vatican Council," 89). Rahner appeals to a "basic substance of the Christian message"—identifiable in universal or transcendental terms—that must be inculturated in unpredictable and untranslatable ways in the diverse categorial historical contexts found across the world (87). Rahner envisions a thoroughgoing reassessment of the contents of the Catholic dogmatic tradition in light of this "basic substance" and the process of a truly pluralist inculturation.

100. Rahner, "Basic Theological Interpretation of the Second Vatican Council," 88. Rahner adapts Bühlmann's tripartite division: "The suggested tripartite division is the only right one. It means that the transition from one historical and theological situation into an essentially new one happened only once before in the history of Christianity and is now set to occur for the second time in the transition from the Christianity of Europe (with its American appendages) to an actual world-religion" (84). In his writings after World War II, Erich Przywara moved in the

Dulles pushes back firmly against some of Rahner's suggestions, insofar as they impact the understanding of catholicity. Today, says Dulles in 1985 during the height of the first wave of Rahner's influence, catholicity is thought to entail openness, while Catholicism under Pope John Paul II is thought to entail a narrow dogmatism. In defense of dogma and structure, Dulles aims to reconnect "catholicity" and "Catholicism."[101] To be "catholic" is not to be open to anything and everything but rather is to be open to the fullness of God's gifts in Christ, a fullness that includes the Church's teachings, sacraments, and offices. These latter entities are the ways in which Christ wills for us to know and commune with him intimately. They enable us to receive "the plenitude of divine life" that is in Christ and the Holy Spirit.[102]

Dulles's historical survey of the concept of catholicity indicates that, indebted to Augustine, medieval theologians such as Aquinas associated catholicity primarily with geographical breadth and with the presence in the Church of people from all social ranks. Post-Tridentine Catholic theologians did the same, up until the Tübingen School and the retrieval of the Greek Fathers. Vatican II moved in an ecumenical direction, affirming in paragraph 17 of *Unitatis Redintegratio* that the heritage of the Orthodox Churches belongs to full catholicity. Vatican II also recognized that, while

same direction, though largely with different implications. For Przywara, European Catholicism imploded in World War II, and its demise can and will kenotically bear fruit in a newly global Church. For discussion, see Aaron Pidel, SJ, *Church of the Ever Greater God: The Ecclesiology of Erich Przywara* (University of Notre Dame Press, 2020).

101. See Dulles's discussion of the term "Catholicism" in "The Meaning of Catholicism: Adventures of an Idea," chapter 4 of his *Reshaping of Catholicism: Current Challenges in the Theology of the Church* (Harper & Row, 1988), 51–74. Dulles directs attention to Hans Urs von Balthasar's "Die Absolutheit des Christentums und die Katholizität der Kirche," in *Absolutheit des Christentums*, ed. Walter Kasper (Herder, 1977), 131–56. As Dulles sums up: "Influenced both by [Henri] de Lubac and by the German Jesuit Erich Przywara, von Balthasar advocates a tension-filled 'Catholicism of fullness.' The concept of *pleroma*, he points out, was a major theme of the New Testament and one that continued to appear in the writings of the fathers. Catholicism is the fullness of the incarnate love of God, which in Jesus Christ divests itself of all possessiveness and thereby opens itself to every positive and authentic human value. To be Catholic, for the church, means to receive the fullness of God paradoxically present under the forms of poverty and nakedness, the signs of total and selfless giving" (Dulles, "The Meaning of Catholicism," 66).

102. Dulles, *The Catholicity of the Church*, 9.

the Catholic Church possesses catholicity, it does not do so in a perfect or complete way. There is plenty of room for growth, not only through an increase in the unity and devotion of Catholics, but also through the increase of the unity of Christians and through the evangelization of non-Christian peoples.[103]

Dulles emphasizes Jesus Christ in his definition of catholicity.[104] Christ is catholic because he possesses the divine fullness as the incarnate Lord. Christ is also catholic because he is the head of all Christians across time and space and because of his primacy over all creatures. Dulles observes that the Church participates in Christ's catholicity as his Body, since Christ is present in his Body. Dulles turns also to the image of the Church as Christ's Bride. He states, "Like the marriage bond, the union between Christ and the Church is indissoluble. Thanks to his sanctifying action, the Church has a definitive share in his fullness of life."[105] The Church's catholicity is never her own as such, but is always a participation in Christ's catholicity, which is infinitely fuller than the Church's.[106] Dulles adds that the communication of Christ's catholicity (the fullness of divine love) to the Church is the work of the Holy Spirit, who unites us to Christ. The Trinity is the ultimate source of catholicity.

The "quantitative" measure of catholicity is also important for Dulles. He argues that Jesus repeatedly makes clear in the Gospels that he intends to draw in all nations. He underlines Paul's teachings about the breaking down of the wall of separation between Jews and Gentiles. Since the early Christians were

103. For background, see the essays collected in Augustin Cardinal Bea, SJ, *The Unity of Christians*, ed. Bernard Leeming, SJ (Herder and Herder, 1963).

104. See Dulles, *The Catholicity of the Church*, 31. See also Dulles, "The Meaning of Catholicism," 71: "Narrowness and particularism have no place in the true church of Christ. As we have seen, catholicity means more than numerical or geographical inclusiveness. To be qualitatively catholic the church must be receptive to the sound achievements of every race and culture." For Dulles's presentation and critique of the Catholic Modernist understanding of Tradition, see his "Vatican II and the Recovery of Tradition," chapter 5 in *The Reshaping of Catholicism*, 75–92.

105. Dulles, *The Catholicity of the Church*, 41.

106. Dulles states, "It may be called a *catholicitas aliena*, and yet it does belong to the Church, for Christ lives in her and identifies himself with her" (44).

committed to spreading the Gospel far and wide, the Church must be missionary, and therefore geographical breadth will be a measure of catholicity. Dulles urges that true catholicity allows for significant diversity across different cultures, and he suggests that "reconciled diversity" may provide a basis for ecumenical movement toward unity.[107] Catholicity means that the Church stands at the service of all human beings. The Church is not a club for a spiritual elite, but rather is an instrument through which God cares for the whole of humanity.[108] Dulles states, "Loving every human being in Christ, the Church labours for all, prays for all, suffers for all. Only thus can it remain Catholic."[109] The catholicity of the Church, Dulles adds, includes the blessed in heaven, who pray for and with the Church on earth.

Dulles examines catholicity across time, arguing that "continuity in the temporal dimension corresponds to communion in the spatial."[110] In his view, the Church began with Abel. He notes that Vatican II has retrieved this perspective, which had become less prominent due to the post-Tridentine emphasis on the Church as a structured institution. He adds that the final, consummated Church will have no need of structures or sacraments, because God will be all in all. But this does not mean that the consummated kingdom will replace the Church, as though the institutional Church were a mere instrument. As Dulles says,

107. Dulles, 82.

108. Here, Dulles quotes from Joseph Ratzinger's *The Open Circle: The Meaning of Christian Brotherhood* (Sheed & Ward, 1966), 120—a book later republished by Ignatius Press as *The Meaning of Christian Brotherhood.*

109. Dulles, *The Catholicity of the Church*, 83.

110. Dulles, 88. Dulles comments that "Catholic Christianity is committed to a fundamental continuity. It holds that the Holy Spirit, having inspired the apostolic Scriptures, continues to be with the Church at every stage of her development preventing her from betraying the apostolic heritage. Hence it must be possible to trace a direct line from past to present. Tradition is not infinitely fluid" (98). Such continuity, as Dulles goes on to say, is not immutability—*pace* the claims of Jacques-Bénigne Bossuet, *The History of the Variations of the Protestant Churches* (R. Coyne, 1829), 2:388. In this sense, "catholicity in time . . . includes an element of discontinuity. Just as the Church's geographical catholicity requires a variety of cultural forms, so her temporal catholicity calls for responsiveness to the times and seasons" (Dulles, *The Catholicity of the Church*, 102). See also Avery Dulles, SJ, "Nature, Mission, and Structure of the Church," in Lamb and Levering, *Vatican II: Renewal Within Tradition*, 25–36.

both Catholics and Orthodox insist that the present-day Church truly possesses the marks of unity, holiness, catholicity, and apostolicity that will be perfected in the consummated Church. The Catholic Church possesses these marks in an imperfect way, given that the Church is presently still being built up into Christ by the Spirit.[111] Nevertheless, the catholic Bride is already here: "The catholic fullness or *plērōma* of Christ's living presence really inheres in the Church. Christ has suffered and has by the shedding of his blood gained for himself his beloved Bride."[112] Christ's Bride is catholic through its sacramental structures, including Baptism, the Eucharist, and Holy Orders.

For Dulles, catholicity can be apprehended in terms of height (the Triune God's fullness), depth (the filling of all things by Christ), breadth (enabling the Church to be a worldwide institution), and length (continuity across the centuries). These dimensions are sacramentally sustained in the Catholic Church. Believers receive the Word of God through the mediation of the Church. Dulles notes that whereas Protestants emphasize the Word and faith, Catholics emphasize the sacraments; but in the end, Word and sacrament are inseparable. The Scriptures are not independent of the Church that, in Christ and by the Spirit, unites the faithful through Baptism and the Eucharist. The Eucharist has an eschatological and cosmic dimension that makes it a catholic sacrament, a sacrament of unity and charity. In celebrating the Eucharist, each local church in communion with the whole Church is catholic. The Church was first united under the

111. Dulles sums up his position with regard to the Church between Pentecost and the final consummation: "In the Catholic view, the Church at this stage already participates in a real, definitive, though imperfect manner, in the fullness of God's gift in Christ," and "this participation brings about a real continuity or communion between different generations of Christians" (Dulles, *The Catholicity of the Church*, 92). Dulles adds a third point (which could go without saying), namely that each different period of the Church possesses its own distinctiveness.

112. Dulles, 92. Dulles reports that numerous Protestant theologians, influenced by Barth, disagree with this perspective, arguing that the Church does not have anything that inheres in it (as distinct from its response to the Word of God, ever new in each moment). For Dulles, *Unitatis Redintegratio* is correct that "the unity of the Church is given to her 'as something she can never lose,' but still capable of being increased in the course of time (*UR* 4). The same may be said of the Church's holiness and catholicity" (*The Catholicity of the Church*, 94).

leadership of the apostles, and the successors of the apostles serve that purpose now. Christ acts through these ordained leaders as his authorized witnesses in each generation. Apostolic succession grounds not only the ministry of the sacraments, but also the proclamation of the Word.

With regard to papal primacy, Dulles offers a brief historical sketch suggesting that in the first millennium it was associated with witness and apostolicity, while in the second millennium it was associated with power and unity. Dulles observes that Vatican II connects papal primacy with service and catholicity—but not with catholicity understood in terms of power. Dulles argues that we should make a distinction between "papalism," which has sometimes afflicted the Catholic Church, and the papacy as such.[113] Our participation in the fullness of Christ is served by papal primacy, which, although it cannot prevent all divisions (and may indeed foment some), nevertheless greatly assists in the operational reality of a global Church that is constantly threatening to break apart for various reasons.[114]

Dulles defends "the collegial understanding of the papacy, which emerges from Vatican II."[115] As he suggests, if a pope (John Paul II) can come from Kraków, it is not exactly fair to describe the Catholic Church as "Rome." The pope does not simply represent "Rome," and the doctrines of the Catholic Church are not simply those of "Rome"—indeed, very few doctrines of the Catholic Church originated in Rome. If there were no collegial head among the bishops, this absence would not serve participation in

113. See Dulles, *The Catholicity of the Church*, 145.

114. See also Dulles, "The Meaning of Catholicism," 73–74: "The question of the relationship between Catholicism and Rome may be fittingly discussed under the heading of apostolicity. In some Catholic ecclesiologies prior to Vatican II the primacy of the pope was so emphasized that *romanitas*, in effect, became a fifth mark of the true church, swallowing up the other four. Complaints were heard, especially from non–Roman Catholics, that catholicity was being explained in such a way that it resided in the pope alone. Some rejected the authority of Rome because they saw no other way of escaping from the excesses of papalism. . . . Vatican II has helped to restore the balance."

115. Dulles, *The Catholicity of the Church*, 138. Dulles is indebted in this discussion to J. M. R. Tillard, OP, *The Bishop of Rome* (Michael Glazier, 1983).

catholic fullness, given the fallen human tendency toward fragmentation. Nor does the existence of the papacy entail uniformity among the local churches around the world; the evidence of history and of the present day shows the falsity of that view.[116] In Dulles's view, the papacy serves diversity-in-unity and thereby serves catholicity, which values diversity. Catholicity consists in fullness and universality, and therefore is necessarily broad.[117]

As Dulles notes, some time periods have seen more appreciation for ecumenical convergence than have other time periods. He identifies the period 1840–1920 as among the low points in Catholic-Protestant relations, while deeming that things have improved since that time. He affirms, "The [Catholic] Church can certainly profit from external criticism, whether from friendly or from hostile sources."[118] He rejects "exorbitant claims" regarding "the institutional Church and its hierarchical leadership," and he bemoans the fact that "in certain periods the Church has been seen as a quasi-incarnation of the divine."[119] Fortunately, he says, there have been Catholics in every age who have been bold enough to check "institutionalism" by castigating all too accurately "the sins

116. Dulles discusses various ecumenical advances regarding the papacy since Vatican II, including Raymond E. Brown, SS, Karl P. Donfried, and John Reumann, eds., *Peter in the New Testament: A Collaborative Assessment by Protestant and Roman Catholic Scholars* (Augsburg, 1973), and some Lutheran-Catholic and Anglican-Catholic formal ecumenical dialogues. He also mentions two books by John Macquarrie: *Principles of Christian Theology*, rev. ed. (SCM, 1979) and *Christian Unity and Christian Diversity* (SCM, 1975).

117. Dulles notes that in the sixteenth- and seventeenth-century controversies, "While claiming catholicity for themselves, the two sides differed somewhat in their interpretation of the term. On the Protestant side, Luther and Calvin saw the Church as catholic in the sense of universal. There could be only one true faith, and hence only one Church in which that faith was believed, confessed, and practised. The true Church was present wherever the gospel was purely preached and the sacraments were rightly administered, and nowhere else. Early Lutherans such as Philipp Melanchthon and Johann Gerhard, taking up this line of argument, held that the Church was catholic in so far as it was faithful to the gospel as attested by the Scriptures and the early Christian authorities. The Roman Church, with its medieval doctrines and practices, had allegedly departed from the original patrimony, and was thus no longer catholic" (Dulles, *The Catholicity of the Church*, 148). Collins and Walls, for their part, offer a sharp critique of Newmanian doctrinal development, on the grounds that it is a model of doctrinal "evolution" that implausibly assumes that "all the 'large accretions' to the Christian revelation in Roman Catholic theology are likely to be true developments" (Collins and Walls, *Roman but Not Catholic*, 53).

118. Dulles, *The Catholicity of the Church*, 158.

119. Dulles, 159.

and blindness of popes and bishops."[120] Reform and discontinuity of certain kinds will be needed in order to renew and energize the Church. Catholics must hold fast to the Word of God and give Scripture its central and authoritative place, just as Vatican II repeatedly insisted. The act of faith is an assent to Christ, not to the Church, even while mediated by the Church.

Dulles appreciates that Christians can learn from each other in ecumenical exchange. Vatican II displayed a Catholic willingness to learn from Protestant concerns without renouncing the Church's "full sacramental, hierarchical, and dogmatic structures."[121] The Catholic Church possesses catholicity as Christ's Bride, sharing in his fullness, but, again, this does not mean that the Catholic Church embodies catholicity perfectly. On the contrary, both Orthodox and Protestants can help the Catholic Church by their example and by their criticisms to live up to catholicity. Even if, in the Catholic and Orthodox view, Protestant communions do not possess catholic fullness (since they have renounced some of the ways in which Christ wills for his fullness to be participated in the Spirit), they possess many catholic elements, including the Word of God, Baptism, numerous creedal affirmations, and so on. Indeed, the Catholic view of Protestantism vis-à-vis catholicity is much like Collins and Walls' position that Catholics possess a part of catholicity but lack other parts. The difference is that Catholics (like Orthodox) consider that there exists a visible, institutional Church that truly is one, holy, catholic, and apostolic, even though that Church is still imperfect and can increase in the fullness of its participation in Christ's fullness.

120. Dulles, 159.
121. Dulles, 166.

IV. CONCLUSION

At the end of this chapter, what common ground can be found? Must we simply choose between asking Catholics (and Orthodox) to adopt a Protestant ecclesiology and a Protestant account of catholicity, on the one hand, or asking Protestants (and Orthodox) to adopt a Catholic ecclesiology and a Catholic account of catholicity, on the other? Or perhaps Rahner's claim that the Church has begun anew with Vatican II, so that dogma and offices can be rethought almost entirely in a newly unified and pluralist World Church, shows the catholic path?

Rahner's path is the one trod, along somewhat different lines but in the same direction, by liberal Protestantism since the eighteenth century. Nichols, Balthasar, and Dulles concur in rejecting this path. From their perspective, which is the perspective of Vatican II's documents and the *Catechism of the Catholic Church*, Catholics rightly hold that Protestants do not properly possess catholicity because they are not in communion with Rome and, more importantly, are not possessed of certain doctrines, sacraments, and offices that pertain to the way in which Christ, through the Spirit, wills to share his catholic fullness with his Church. In turn, Evangelical Protestants argue today that (Roman) Catholicism lacks catholicity because it makes communion with Rome a requirement of full catholicity—and because Catholicism teaches numerous false doctrines, in addition to practicing a number of false sacraments.

Biblically speaking, I think the disputed question is what has happened to the Church to which Jesus refers in the Gospel of Matthew when he says, "On this rock I will build my Church" (Matt 16:18), and also when he commands, "Tell it to the church; and if he refuses to listen even to the church, let him be to you as a Gentile and a tax collector" (Matt 18:17). This is the same visible, institutional Church about which Acts 5:11 says, "And great fear came upon the whole church." At first, the whole Church is centered in Jerusalem. It then spreads out due to "a great persecution . . . against the church in Jerusalem," which led the first Christians (except for the apostles) to scatter "throughout the region of Judea and Samaria" (Acts 8:1). Although Paul writes letters to various churches around the Mediterranean, he does not relinquish the notion of a universal visible Church. On the contrary, he insists that the Church is one: "For by one Spirit we were all baptized into one body" (1 Cor 12:13). When he says that "Christ is the head of the church" (Eph 5:23), he means the whole Church—the visible, institutional Church, wherever it has existed, does now exist, or will exist in the future. Paul invites us "to comprehend with all the saints what is the breadth and length and height and depth, and to know the love of Christ which surpasses knowledge, that you may be filled with all the fulness of God" (Eph 3:18–19). God "has made him [Christ] the head over all things for the church, which is his body, the fulness of him who fills all in all" (Eph 1:22–23).

From the Catholic perspective, the Petrine office—grounded in Peter's leadership among the apostles and in Christ's words to Peter—is a biblical datum about the Church founded by Christ. The Catholic Church in communion with the bishop of Rome possesses the mark of catholicity because this pertains to how Christ wills for us to share in his fullness. Without the Petrine office (and the hierarchical constitution of the Church), which stands in service to Christ's fullness, the diversity-in-unity that characterizes catholicity could not be maintained but would fragment and no longer be concretely expressed. A sign of catholicity is that the Catholic Church can still meet in council, as did the Jerusalem Church in Acts.

Yet, as Yves Congar says, "The Scriptures do not surrender their meaning by the bare text; they surrender it to a mind that is living, and living in the conditions of the Covenant. This mind, or living subject, is . . . the Church."[122] Granting Congar's point, the problem is that one of the most contested meanings of Scripture is where the Church today is. Christians are not likely soon to cease to be divided about where and how to find the catholicity of Christ and the Trinity in the Church. Inevitably, Wesleyan, Reformed, and Anglican Christians will feel closer to one another, in certain ways at least, than they do to Catholics such as Balthasar and Dulles who insist upon the Petrine office's role in ensuring the Church's catholicity.[123] This is clear when Collins and Walls argue that the *Catechism* (in defining the unity of the Church) has shifted attention "from Christ, in whom all union rightly subsists, to a particular theological tradition, the Roman church."[124] To focus attention upon "the Roman church" rather than the incarnate Lord would be a horrific sin indeed (and I hope to have shown that Catholic theology of catholicity does not fall into it). Catholics will think similarly that Protestants have distorted or discarded important aspects of how Christ makes himself present. Catholics believe, for instance, that the Eucharist builds the Church, and that the Eucharist is necessarily consecrated by recipients of the sacrament of Holy Orders in accordance with apostolic succession.[125]

How then might such painful and intractable divisions be addressed, especially in situations where Protestants or Catholics do not find one another's ecclesiology well represented in the other's understanding of the catholicity of the Church? In light of the above discussion, I suggest three ways forward.

First, Catholics and Protestants (and Orthodox) can agree that the *perfection* of catholicity and unity is an eschatological

122. Yves Congar, OP, *The Meaning of Tradition*, trans. A. N. Woodrow (Ignatius, 2004), 91.

123. For a Wesleyan perspective deeply sympathetic to the Catholic Church, however, see Edgardo Colón-Emeric, *Wesley, Aquinas, and Christian Perfection: An Ecumenical Dialogue* (Baylor University Press, 2009).

124. Collins and Walls, *Roman but Not Catholic*, 89.

125. See Ezra Sullivan, OP, *Alter Christus: Priestly Holiness on Earth and in Eternity* (Sophia Institute, 2022).

reality that awaits the consummation of all things. Without doubt, this perfection will be vastly greater than that which we see in any ecclesial body today. Since this is so, no Christian community can afford to ignore or dismiss other Christian communities, since no Christian community perfectly expresses catholicity, and we all have much to learn.

Second, Catholics and Protestants (and Orthodox) can together appreciate the qualitative dimension of catholicity. Christ is catholic; the Triune God is catholic. This catholicity is the divine fullness of wisdom and self-surrendering love, in utter humility. The ecclesial mark of catholicity, therefore, involves being turned toward the other in Christ-like love. For this reason, the fact that Catholics and Protestants (and Orthodox) now recognize each other as fellow Christians is a wonderful thing. Deepening this mutual recognition will not involve requiring Catholics to adopt a Protestant ecclesiology. Nor will it mean requiring Protestants to think that the papacy and the seven sacraments enhance (rather than detract from) the catholic fullness of the Church's participation in Christ. Instead, the deepening that I have in view will proceed from Catholics and Protestants together directing ourselves Godward, seeking always to participate more fully in the catholicity of Christ and the Trinity.

Third, Catholics and Protestants (and Orthodox) can therefore meet each other as equals, indeed as partners, in a real *quest* to partake in the catholicity of Christ and the Trinity, without Catholics and Orthodox needing to deny that Christ has indeed given this catholicity to the Church. Pouring forth his Spirit, Christ will encounter us in his catholic fullness. He will do so, surely, through the Scriptures and through the Eucharist; through those who are poor and through our own existential poverty; through "the mystics, saints, and scholars of the classical Christian tradition"; through the "windows, towers, vaults, naves, roses, labyrinths, altars, and façades" of the great cathedrals about which Robert Barron has written so eloquently; and through much more.[126] Protestants and Catholics can rejoice together in these encounters with Christ and can rightly hope that their fruit will be deeper ecclesial communion.

As we Catholics and Protestants (and Orthodox) strive to participate more fully in the catholicity that Christ gives to his people, we should be on the alert for aspects of catholicity that we might share with one another as friends of Christ through his Spirit. While we are in certain important respects divided, we are in other (even more) important respects united. As Collins and Walls say, "The common ground we share is far more important than any disagreements that distinguish and even divide us," since this common ground is "profound and far reaching."[127] Most importantly, Catholics and Protestants today recognize that we are united by belief in Jesus Christ as our Savior and Lord. Since this is so, we can encourage each other. For as Paul remarks, "What then shall we say to this? If God is for us, who is against

126. Robert Barron, *The Strangest Way: Walking the Christian Path* (Orbis Books, 2002), 11; Barron, *Heaven in Stone and Glass: Experiencing the Spirituality of the Great Cathedrals* (Crossroad, 2000), 10. Barron opposes the reduction of grace and the supernatural order to our natural (even our highest natural) capacities and connections, even though grace suffuses, heals, and elevates the created order, which was created for the goal of deification. For an instance of this reduction of grace to nature, see Daniel P. Horan, OFM's criticism of the view that humanity is "insufficient for [i.e., in need of supernatural or elevating grace to attain] its divinely intended end or goal, which demeans human beings while further distancing the Creator from creation." Horan, *Catholicity and Emerging Personhood: A Contemporary Theological Anthropology* (Orbis Books, 2019), 240. I am not denying, of course, what Heidi Russell calls "our interconnectedness and unity in creation itself," a theme prominent in Pope Francis's encyclical *Laudato Si'* and that is reflected in the cosmic dimension of Christ and the Eucharist. Russell, *The Source of All Love: Catholicity and the Trinity* (Orbis Books, 2017), 170. Russell includes a beautiful meditation on the fact that "living in relationship to the Triune God is about how we respond to the call to love more than we do now" (173). As Russell says, "With that recognition of what it means to live in love comes the recognition of my own constant failure, my own sinfulness, and my own need for mercy and forgiveness. This awareness of sin is not a scrupulous and shame-centered mindset, but rather the healthy guilt of being called to love more. . . . Jesus asks us to give our lives over to love, to give up our lives for the sake of love. That awes me. That makes me fall to my knees and realize that I can never do enough, and that I am loved anyway" (175).

127. Collins and Walls, *Roman but Not Catholic*, 3. They add that Protestants and (Roman) Catholics "share convictions that profoundly unite us in heart and mind against the secular worldview that predominates in much contemporary culture. . . .We reject the attitude of some evangelicals who do not consider Roman Catholics true Christians or doubt that they have genuine faith. We forthrightly affirm our Roman Catholic brothers and sisters as full members of the body of Christ, and we celebrate our common convictions that unite us as the family of God" (5, 7).

us? He who did not spare his own Son but gave him up for us all, will he not also give us all things with him?" (Rom 8:31–32).

I will give the final word to reflection on Hans Boersma's concern, one that many Catholic theologians, too, have raised since Vatican II. The viewpoint of the Catholic theologian Richard McBrien, writing in 1973, is representative. He states that the marks of the Church are *not* possessed by the Church but rather are simply goals toward which the Church strives. In his view, as in Boersma's, to the extent that diverse Christian "communities within the one Body of Christ" have "divisions over doctrine, liturgy, morality, and church order"—that is, to the extent that Catholics, Reformed, Orthodox, Anglicans, Lutherans and so on are divided—"the Church cannot be called 'one.' Rather, the Church is always on the road to the unity which it does not yet possess."[128] On this view, just as unity does not exist today, so neither does catholicity. McBrien describes the Catholic Church as a "part" of the divided Body of Christ.[129] The Body of Christ may possess catholicity in some sense, but the Catholic Church (while an important part of the Body) cannot claim to possess it. The fullness or catholicity of the Body requires all the parts of the Body, including but not limited to the Catholic Church.

Heinrich Fries and Karl Rahner, in their 1983 *Unity of the Churches: An Actual Possibility*, express a similar perspective. They argue that while the Church today is not one, it can become one by healing the divisions between Catholics, Orthodox, and the main bodies of Protestants. They describe these various churches as "the uniting churches" or "partner churches," which, taken together, will become the "one Church of Jesus Christ."[130] Commenting on this claim, Rahner argues that the Catholic Church

128. Richard P. McBrien, *The Remaking of the Church: An Agenda for Reform* (Harper & Row, 1973), 132. He adds, "The Catholic Church certainly could not participate in a movement which is designed to foster unity if the Catholic Church were convinced that the unity already exists" (132).

129. McBrien, 132.

130. Heinrich Fries and Karl Rahner, SJ, *Unity of the Churches: An Actual Possibility*, trans. Ruth C. L. Gritsch and Eric W. Gritsch (Paulist, 1985), 7.

must acknowledge that not only the Orthodox but also the Protestant communions are in fact true "churches." He goes on to say, "The churches of the Reformation enlarge the one Church not only quantitatively but qualitatively if they unite with Rome."[131] On the accurate ground that there are dimensions of catholicity that are presently being lived out more richly outside the (Roman) Catholic Church, Rahner concludes that the "treasure" or fullness is found only partially in each of the churches, and thus if the churches come together as partners, the catholicity of the unified Church will be greater in quantity (not simply in quality) than that found at present in any church.[132] This means that the catholicity of the Catholic Church, in terms of its quantity, is a part to which can be added the parts found in other churches, so as to produce a truly catholic whole.

This perspective is widespread in Catholic theological circles today, although it is not found in the *Catechism* and contradicts the Church's self-understanding as found in Vatican II. It can be extended still further—as it is by the Catholic biblical scholar Dianne Bergant. She remarks, "In the realms of theology and religious identity, *catholic* usually has come to signify what is identifiably separate—as in Catholic Church or Catholic teaching—in contrast to what is Protestant, Jewish, or Islamic. This is almost the reverse of its foremost meanings."[133] She extends the meaning of "catholicity," therefore, to include not only Protestants, Jews, and Muslims, but also all of creation, the whole Earth and the whole universe. She opposes what she deems to be the reduction of "catholicity" that inevitably occurs through any claim to truth that is "sectarian, factional, tribal, or exclusive."[134]

131. Fries and Rahner, 48. This section was written by Rahner (see p. 6 of *Unity of the Churches* for an explanation).

132. Fries and Rahner, 48.

133. Dianne Bergant, CSA, *A New Heaven, A New Earth: The Bible and Catholicity* (Orbis Books, 2016), 4.

134. Bergant, 4. Bergant's biblical hermeneutic is as follows: "In order to read biblical passages with an appreciation of the community of Earth, two methodological principles come into play: the hermeneutic of suspicion and the hermeneutic of retrieval. Suspicion is necessary

As Bergant knows, however, Scripture tells of God revealing himself to a particular people whom he covenantally elected. God redeems us through a particular man, Jesus of Nazareth, who is the one Mediator and who alone is the perfect image of the Father and the true divine Son, incarnate in God's people Israel as the Messiah. Having messianically reconfigured Israel (Torah, temple, land, and so on) around himself, Jesus opens up adoptive filiation for us. In him, we share in the inheritance of the Son, an inheritance that is nothing less than the fullness of the Trinitarian life, far greater than any fullness we could desire or give ourselves on the basis of our own creaturely resources. Jesus establishes his community or Church hierarchically upon his apostles, chosen from among the much larger community of his followers. He promises that this Church will not fail, and he gives it the mission of spreading the Gospel, baptizing, and obeying his commandment of love, preparing for his return in glory to consummate the kingdom of God.

In this light, the catholicity of the Catholic Church need not be deemed exclusive or sectarian in any negative sense. Rather, it is an invitation to enter into the fullness of Christ and the Trinity, mediated by a divinely constituted human community with Christ at its head. Jesus prayed that the members of his Church would be sanctified in the truth and would be "one even as we [Father and Son] are one" (John 17:22), by the power of the Holy Spirit. This Church shares in the catholic fullness of the Trinity and of Christ. This Church still exists and does so not merely as many separated parts that together form a catholic unity. Yet elements of this catholic fullness exist outside the Catholic Church, and the Catholic Church has much to gain and learn, deepening

lest one uncritically accept the message of the passage without questioning whether the customs, behaviors, and values portrayed therein value or devalue the Earth. If they value Earth, the message can be retrieved and retained or developed further. If they devalue Earth, the message will be deemed lacking in revelatory significance and set aside, or might be retrieved and its objectionable meaning be somehow subverted so that the message can still act in a revelatory fashion. The goal here is to develop an Earth consciousness in reading the Bible, an advocacy stand in support of the community of Earth" (5–6).

its catholicity, through ecumenical dialogue and (for that matter) through Jewish-Christian dialogue, in addition to welcoming all truth and wisdom wherever it is found.[135]

The catholic fullness of the Church can be described as the Church's "foundation." In this sense, Paul remarks, "For no other foundation can any one lay than that which is laid, which is Jesus Christ" (1 Cor 3:11). Different people in the Church will lay diverse foundations and will build upon these foundations, but when all is said and done, nothing will thereby be added to the foundation that has already been laid, since Christ contains all fullness within himself and has enabled his Church, from the outset, to share in this catholic fullness. As Paul says of this fullness, "Far be it from me to glory except in the cross of our Lord Jesus Christ, by which the world has been crucified to me, and I to the world" (Gal 6:14). This is not mere renunciation; it is a rejoicing in the glory of catholicity. Let us join in this joy.

135. For helpful introductions to ecumenical dialogue and its value, see (from a Catholic perspective) Philip Goyret, *Church and Communion: An Introduction to Ecumenical Theology*, 2nd ed., ed. Joseph Thomas, trans. Philip Goyret and Joseph Thomas (The Catholic University of America Press, 2022); and (from a Protestant perspective) R. David Nelson and Charles Raith II, *Ecumenism: A Guide for the Perplexed* (Bloomsbury, 2017). See also the comparative work of Carol Bakhos, *The Family of Abraham: Jewish, Christian, and Muslim Interpretations* (Harvard University Press, 2014).

Conclusion

Not long before his death, Hans Urs von Balthasar titled the final volume of his *Theo-Logic*—the final volume of his massive trilogy—*The Spirit of Truth*. Jesus Christ, says Balthasar, "faithfully declares the Father, not only by reproducing his Logos exactly in human words, but also by being 'the true light' (John 1:9), 'the true bread' (John 6:32), the 'true judgment' (8:16), and the 'true vine' (15:1). In all this he is the truth of God in earthly form."[1] The "Spirit of truth" (John 15:26) enables us to know the truth of Christ. Thus, "the Spirit is the indispensable Declarer of trinitarian truth," and the Spirit makes the Church possible.[2] Balthasar states, "Without the Spirit's operation . . . there would be no *communio* of the ecclesial Body of Christ."[3] The Spirit builds up the Church in the communion of Christ's truth, working through both institutional offices and the charisms of Spirit-filled persons.

The view that the Spirit-filled Church bears the truth of Christ is, of course, nothing new. In favor of the Holy Spirit's guidance of the Church in the proclamation of the truth about the Gospel, the Tübingen theologian Johann Adam Möhler cites John 15:26 and 16:13, which he paraphrases as "I will send the Spirit of truth, who will lead you into all truth."[4] Even more strongly, Matthias Joseph Scheeben remarks, "In all its members the Church is a temple of the Holy Spirit, who dwells in it as the soul in its own

1. Balthasar, *Theo-Logic*, vol. 3, *The Spirit of Truth*, trans. Graham Harrison (Ignatius, 2005), 24. For the first two paragraphs of this chapter, see my "The Church as Temple of the Spirit: Is There Room for Magisterial Error?," *Communio* 50, no. 1 (2023): 7–36.

2. Balthasar, *Theo-Logic*, 3:24.

3. Balthasar, 3:189.

4. See Johann Adam Möhler, *Symbolism: Exposition of the Doctrinal Differences between Catholics and Protestants as Evidenced by Their Symbolical Writings*, trans. James Burton Robertson (Crossroad, 1997), 265.

body, and manifests His divine and divinizing power in it."[5] Louis Bouyer, in *The Church of God*, emphasizes similarly that it is as the Temple of the Holy Spirit that the Church draws believers into Christ's kingdom, where the ascended Christ presently reigns in mercy and love. The Spirit makes us sons and daughters in the Son; and Christ's own fullness fills the Church (despite its troubles), a fullness of love and of truth.[6] For his part, Yves Congar highlights the role of the Spirit in leading us toward God, enriching our prayer, enabling us to recognize Jesus as Lord, giving us true freedom, and making us a temple of right worship.[7] In his recent *Ecclesiology*, Guy Mansini cites various additional biblical passages that point toward the theme of the Church as the Temple of the Holy Spirit, including numerous passages from the book of Acts. He concludes, "The church which is the body of Christ is, then, also the new temple, the temple of the Holy Spirit. So, Charles Journet can say, the church 'is the Holy Spirit insofar as he is manifested visibly in the world.' And for Anscar Vonier, the church precisely in her visibility is the visible mission of the Spirit."[8] Journet holds that the Church's uncreated soul is the Holy Spirit, and its created soul is Christoform grace and charity.[9]

These lovers of the Church have experienced the power and presence of Christ and the Holy Spirit through the Church. Their

5. Matthias Joseph Scheeben, *The Mysteries of Christianity*, trans. Cyril Vollert, SJ, 2nd ed. (Emmaus Academic, 2023), 544.

6. See Louis Bouyer, *The Church of God: Body of Christ and Temple of the Spirit*, trans. Charles Underhill Quinn (Ignatius, 2011), 271–77.

7. See Yves Congar, OP, "The Spirit is the Source of Life in Us Personally and in the Church," in *Spirit of God: Short Writings on the Holy Spirit*, trans. Susan Mader Brown, Mark E. Ginter, Joseph G. Mueller, SJ, and Catherine E. Clifford, ed. Mark E. Ginter with Susan Mader Brown and Joseph G. Mueller, SJ (The Catholic University of America Press, 2018), 36–51, at 40–41.

8. Guy Mansini, OSB, *Ecclesiology* (The Catholic University of America Press, 2021), 121, citing Charles Journet, *Théologie de l'Église* (Desclée, 1958), 359; and Anscar Vonier, OSB, *The Spirit and the Bride* (Burns, Oates and Washbourne, 1935), 26–27. See also See Sebastian Tromp, SJ, *De Spiritu Sancto anima Corporis mystici*, 2 vols., 2nd ed. (Pontificia Universitas Gregoriana, 1948–52).

9. See Charles Journet, *The Church of the Word Incarnate*, vol. 2, *The Internal Structure of the Church*, trans. Matthew K. Minerd (Emmaus Academic, 2025).

theologies of the Catholic Church manifest a living bond with the prophets and apostles and with the Church Fathers, medieval masters, and post-Tridentine tradition. They have not been blind to the errors and difficulties that have plagued Christ's eschatological community over the centuries, but they have perceived the Church's faithful mediation of the Gospel's truth, mercy, reconciliation, and deification.

In this book, my desire has been to join these lovers of the Church, while heeding Henri de Lubac's postconciliar exhortation that "the whole future of the Church, all the fruitfulness of her mission, all that she can and must bring to the world, depends today on an energetic awakening of the faith."[10] My book has involved a stream of interlocutors and controversies, unified by the main images and marks of the Church. In the opening chapter on the Bride of Christ, I proposed an eschatological ecclesiology oriented toward the fullness of the marriage of God and his people, due to Christ's inauguration of the kingdom of God and his pouring out of his Spirit on his bridal Church. The chapter on the Family of God placed adoptive filiation at the center of the meaning of this eschatological Church: through the Spirit, we share even now in the inheritance of the Son—we share in all that the Father is. The chapter on the Body of Christ argued that the path of the cross, cleaving to the crucified King, stands at the center of ecclesiology. The chapter on the People of God insisted upon the theocentric and Christocentric character of the Church on the new exodus, as befits a fallen and finite (but redeemed) people. The chapter on Mother Church emphasized that the Church is characterized by Marian receptivity to the Word of God, even when resistance to certain kinds of magisterial teaching is needed. The chapter on apostolicity clarified the importance of apostolic succession and the apostolic deposit of faith, both of which are made fully present in the Eucharist. The chapter on catholicity

10. Henri de Lubac, SJ, *The Church: Paradox and Mystery*, trans. James R. Dunne and Anne Englund Nash (Ignatius, 2021), 191.

portrayed the Church as sharing in the fullness of Christ and the Trinity. Christ calls believers into "the tribulation and the kingdom and the patient endurance" (Rev 1:9).

In sum, the Church is nuptial, familial, cross-centered, Spirit-filled, on the new exodus, full of truth, Marian, united to the apostles, and sharing with the saints and angels in the divine life and love. With Ida Görres, I can say that "I believe 'because' the faith of the Church lives in me. I believe because faith is a vital process of life within the Church like breathing is a vital process of life in the flesh."[11] At the same time, the Church is also yearning to be perfected and is terribly afflicted by conflict, controversy, and worldliness. Although ecumenical debates continue apace, the main controversies facing Catholic Christians today have to do with the purpose (and therefore also the source and structure) of the Catholic Church. At bottom, the issue is whether the modern world has leapt ahead of the Church in the pursuit of justice and equality, so that the Church must radically restructure and reorient itself in order to be a full partner with the world in God's redemptive work.

In his 1988 *The Reshaping of Catholicism*, Avery Dulles combed through a variety of postconciliar proposals regarding the Church's purpose. As he notes, after the council Jean Daniélou continued to affirm that "the purpose of the church is to produce saints and to make sanctity possible."[12] Other postconciliar

11. Ida Friederike Görres, *The Church in the Flesh*, trans. Jennifer S. Bryson (Cluny, 2023), 71.

12. Avery Dulles, SJ, "Vatican II and the Purpose of the Church," in *The Reshaping of Catholicism: Current Challenges in the Theology of the Church* (Harper & Row, 1988), 132–53, at 133. See Jean Daniélou, SJ, *Why the Church?* (Franciscan Herald, 1974); and see also the arguments against Marxism (and, implicitly, nascent liberation theology) in Daniélou, *The Lord of History: An Essay on the Mystery of History*, trans. Nigel Abercrombie (Cluny, 2022). For background, see Sarah Shortall, *Soldiers of God in a Secular World: Catholic Theology and Twentieth-Century French Politics* (Harvard University Press, 2021), especially 180–83 contrasting the positions of Marie-Dominique Chenu, OP, and Daniélou—both sharply critical of the French Catholic right—in light of the French bishops' 1952 rebuke of *La Quinzaine* and the Holy Office's 1949 decree against Communism. Gerd-Rainer Horn aptly remarks, "The suddenly unfolding signs of the times in the course of the long sixties pushed Chenu further along a road he had already entered when he first ascribed redemptive powers to the working class within the social conflicts of the twentieth century." Horn, *The Spirit of Vatican II: Western European Pro-*

theologians saw the fundamental purpose of the Church as offering true worship to God, or fostering intimate bonds between persons and bearing witness to Trinitarian love, or evangelizing. All these things have to do with saints and sanctity, since holiness entails worship, communion, and proclamation. Still other influential postconciliar theologians, such as Jon Sobrino, argue that "the church achieves its goal when it effectively proclaims the gospel to the poor by word and by deed."[13] Sobrino measures the Church by whether it is actively transforming the economic situation of the poor and oppressed. A similar perspective is held by Roger Haight, who, in Dulles's words, believes "that the church exists in order to turn outward to the world by participating in the mission of God and of Jesus, especially through evangelization and human development."[14] For liberation theologians such

gressive Catholicism in the Long Sixties (Oxford University Press, 2015), 31. For Congar's similar (postconciliar) embrace of liberation theology, while continuing to maintain that "salvation" is more than human terrestrial "liberation," see *The Spirit of Vatican II*, 24–25; and Congar, *Un peuple messianique: Salut et libération* (Cerf, 1975). For further background see Horn, *Western European Liberation Theology: The First Wave (1924–1959)* (Oxford University Press, 2008); and Horn, *The Spirit of '68: Rebellion in Western Europe and North America, 1956–1976* (Oxford University Press, 2007).

13. Dulles, "Vatican II and the Purpose of the Church," 133–34. See Jon Sobrino, SJ, *The True Church and the Poor*, trans. Matthew J. O'Connell (Orbis Books, 1974)—and works such as José Porfirio Miranda, *Communism in the Bible*, trans. Robert R. Barr (Orbis Books, 1982); and Roman A. Montero, *All Things in Common: The Economic Practices of the Early Christians* (Resource, 2017), arguing that "Christianity is about the kingdom of God and the working out of the Jubilee and Sabbatical ideals both in the here and now as well as in the *eschaton*" (*All Things in Common*, 123). See also John C. Peet, *The Politics of the Crucified: The Cross in the Political Theology of Yoder, Boff, and Sobrino* (Pickwick, 2021). I agree with Peet that "political theology, ecclesiology, and Christology are inextricably entwined" (259), and to this I would add eschatology as an important check (when properly conceived) upon political theology. Peet and I strongly agree that (as I indicated in chapter 3) "the church's cruciformity is an inescapable consequence of its nature as the body of Christ. It is no exaggeration to state that the very genuineness of the church is recognized by such cruciformity. . . . A Pauline *theologia crucis* leads inescapably to an *ecclesia crucis*, and a kenotic Christology to a kenotic ecclesiology. If the church's identity is found elsewhere than in the vulnerability of the crucified Christ, it foregoes its right to be called, in any meaningful way, the body of Christ" (261). See also William T. Cavanaugh, *Torture and Eucharist: Theology, Politics, and the Body of Christ* (Blackwell, 1998), 27: "The true body of Christ is wounded, marked by the cross."

14. Dulles, "Vatican II and the Purpose of the Church," 134. See Roger D. Haight, SJ, "The 'Established' Church as Mission: The Relation of the Church to the Modern World," *The Jurist* 39 (1979): 4–39. See also the autobiographical remark of Gregory Baum, *Man Becoming: God in Secular Experience* (Herder and Herder, 1970), vii-viii: "A Christian meets his crisis when the spiritual experience of his culture is no longer reconcilable with the religious outlook he has inherited and God seems to be more powerfully present in the former than the latter. Such a crisis often results in what is called, superficially, a loss of faith. The Christian then gives up his

as Gustavo Gutiérrez and Juan Luis Segundo, the Church exists to make visible God's presence with the poor through participating in the struggle for social justice and liberation from political and economic oppression.[15] On this basis, Eugene Bianchi and Richard McBrien (representing, unfortunately, a mainstream view) propose that the Church must be reconceived. Whereas in preconciliar epochs the Church was understood to mediate sacramental grace necessary for salvation, now the Church must be understood as an agent helping the world to make manifest the liberative values of the Gospel, through service work and through reconciliation in justice.[16]

As Dulles says, a series of questions arises from these postconciliar paths. For example: "Should the church continue to work for goals that are religious and supernatural? . . . Does the church have any mission that is uniquely its own, or is it one of a number of agencies devoted to common human betterment? Was the church before Vatican II ecclesiocentric or even narcissistic?"[17] Dulles's answer first of all involves turning to the texts

religion. But if there are available to him theological methods by which he may reinterpret and reassimilate the inherited religion, he may discover a new unity of religious experience, where the Gospel celebrated in the Church sheds light on and intensifies the Spirit-created, redemptive values present in the culture to which he belongs. He may then, as a Christian, transform this culture along the line of its own deepest dimension."

15. The rapidity of the international spread of these perspectives is striking. The eminent African theologian Paulinus Odozor reports about his seminary training in Nigeria in the 1970s, "In my seminary days . . . I read a lot of Liberation theologians like Segundo. . . . In fact, one of our professors was nicknamed Segundo. I read a lot of Karl Rahner, Raimundo Panikkar." James Nkemngong, *Odozor: The Man, the Priest and the Scholar: Interview with Rev. Fr. Paulinus I. Odozor* (privately printed, 2024), 36.

16. See Eugene C. Bianchi, *Reconciliation: The Function of the Church* (Sheed & Ward, 1969); Richard P. McBrien, *Do We Need the Church?* (Harper & Row, 1969); Gustavo Gútierrez, *A Theology of Liberation: History, Politics, and Salvation*, trans. Caridad Inda and John Eagleson (Orbis Books, 1973); Juan Luis Segundo, *The Community Called Church* (Orbis Books, 1973); Segundo, *The Sacraments Today* (Orbis Books, 1974). Regarding McBrien's sharp distinction between Church and Kingdom, with the Church conceived of as an agent to build up the Kingdom of justice in this world, see Gerald O'Collins, SJ, "On Richard P. McBrien's *Do We Need the Church?*," *Heythrop Journal* 10, no. 4 (1969): 416–19, at 418: "The New Testament nowhere speaks clearly of people who are called to the Kingdom without being elected to the Church."

17. Dulles, "Vatican II and the Purpose of the Church," 134–35. In the next essay in the same book, "The Church, Society, and Politics," 154–83, Dulles notes: "A number of recent theologians would wish to add . . . that the official leadership of the church should intervene prophetically in certain concrete situations in which there are not sufficient doctrinal warrants for a clear magisterial teaching. As an example, Edward Schillebeeckx suggests issuing a directive

of the council. He sets forth the relationship of the Church to the kingdom, and he argues that in the ecclesiology of the council—just as was the case before the council—"eschatological salvation, to be fully attained in the world to come, is the ultimate aim of the church."[18] According to the council, the Church mediates the grace of Christ and salvation, even if it is possible to receive this grace and to be united to the Church through an implicit intention without being a visible member of the Church.[19] He demonstrates that "the council repeatedly and emphatically taught that the procurement of salvation is the most important task of the church."[20]

Dulles does not downplay the importance of apostolic works in the service of justice. Even so, the primary purpose of the Church is worship and sanctification in Christ, in which the whole world is called to share, and which is already a foretaste of the deified life of the world to come.[21] As *Gaudium et Spes* says,

that certain large estates in a particular region should be broken up, if necessary, by expropriation. In taking such action, he holds, the official church, functioning under the charismatic guidance of the Spirit, could speak out decisively. Even though the directive in question lay beyond the scope of the church's teaching office, it would merit the obedience due to the church's pastoral function" (181). Dulles responds, "I think that the charismatic assistance might appropriately be given to the political rather than to the ecclesiastical authorities in a case of this kind. In any case I would want rather clear assurances that purportedly prophetic utterances about contingent secular issues were in fact divinely prompted" (181). Dulles here has in view Edward Schillebeeckx, OP, *God the Future of Man* (Sheed & Ward, 1968), 163; and he points also to Karl Rahner, SJ, *The Shape of the Church to Come*, trans. Edward Quinn (Seabury, 1974), 76–81.

18. Dulles, "Vatican II and the Purpose of the Church," 138. He cites *Gaudium et Spes* §40 and *Apostolicam Actuositatem* §6.

19. For an account of how this is so—alongside a trenchant critique of the particulars of Rahner's theory of the "anonymous Christian"—see Anthony R. Lusvardi, SJ, *Baptism of Desire and Christian Salvation* (The Catholic University of America Press, 2024).

20. Dulles, "Vatican II and the Purpose of the Church," 141. Dulles adds, "According to the postconciliar trend to which we have alluded, the church should no longer be viewed as administering means of grace to its own members. The sacraments are signs intended to remind Christians of what God is doing and wills to have done throughout the world" (141). In response to this Rahnerian viewpoint, Dulles states, "In my judgment, the council cannot fairly be taken as supporting this doctrine. It did indeed rehabilitate the sign aspect of the church and of its sacraments, and it stressed the links between worship and mission, but it did not for all that minimize the church's ministries as means of grace" (142).

21. By contrast, Baum rejects the distinction between nature and grace, and he states, "The pretense to have access to a higher life not available elsewhere [tends] to make Catholics blind to the holiness present in others and, with more damaging effects, insensitive to their own failings and vices." Baum, *Man Becoming*, ix; see also Lauren F. Winner, *The Dangers of Christian Practice: On Wayward Gifts, Characteristic Damage, and Sin* (Yale University Press, 2018). No

"The specific mission (*missio propria*) that Christ entrusted to his church is not in the political, economic, or social order. The purpose which he set before her is a religious one."[22] Dulles concludes that the Church has a "hierarchy of ends," with its proper and primary end being salvation, sharing in the life of God in Christ Jesus through the grace of word and sacrament, above all in the liturgy of the Eucharist.[23]

But what does it matter if the Church's primary purpose is worship, if today people are being oppressed? How can the Church not turn its full attention to rectifying all such oppression, as a necessary preliminary to worship? In his 1977 essay "Eschatology and Utopia," Joseph Ratzinger rejects the call to revolutionary

doubt this blindness can happen, but, in my view, Baum has failed to see the impact of grace. I should note that Baum does not fall into a triumphalist view of the world and its future progress, although he holds out hope for such progress and considers it to be the Church's primary goal. He observes, "Since Christ is the pivotal point of history and since he has made available forces of reconciliation able to overcome, in time, the destructive processes of society, it may well be that human history now moves in a direction of greater institutional sanity and hence of an evolution to a superior kind of humanity. But it may also happen that the social pathologies will destroy mankind on this earth and that the total victory of Christ will only take place in the new life which God creates out of death" (Baum, *Man Becoming*, 123).

22. Second Vatican Council, *Gaudium et Spes* §42, December 7, 1965, as quoted in Dulles, "Vatican II and the Purpose of the Church," 146–47. Of course, the council is certainly "aware that the religious mission of the church has ramifications in the temporal sphere" (Dulles, "Vatican II and the Purpose of the Church," 147).

23. Dulles, "Vatican II and the Purpose of the Church," 150. Dulles further explains, "It may be objected that the council's teaching . . . is ecclesiocentric. In a certain sense this is the case. The council does not regard the world as the center and the church as peripheral, but rather the reverse. . . . The material world was made for the sake of humanity (*GS* 12), but human beings exist in order to be brought by grace into the life of the triune God (*GS* 18). Christian revelation irreversibly accomplished a kind of Copernican revolution by presenting the world as taken up into the orbit of Christ and no longer being centered on itself. The church is the place in which the human community participates in the life of God. It is the people of God, the body of Christ, and the temple of the Holy Spirit (*LG* 17). This outlook does not absolve the church from humble service (*GS* 3). Its aim, like that of its divine Master, is to serve and not be served (*GS* 3). It seeks to liberate rather than dominate, to give rather than take. While the members of the church are summoned to many kinds of giving, depending on their personal talents and assets, the church itself is especially called to render the spiritual service of bringing the world into union with its Creator and Lord" (151). See also Virgil Michel, OSB, *Christian Social Reconstruction: Some Fundamentals of the Quadragesimo Anno* (Bruce, 1937), especially chapter 8. Dulles is responding, I assume, to the widespread claim that liberal Catholicism stands out in part due to its foregrounding of justice. As Anne E. Patrick, Bernard J. Cooke, and Diana L. Hayes put it, for liberal Catholics "spirituality is no longer relegated to the cloister, and matters of ecological, racial, gender, and economic justice are increasingly seen as central to Christian discipleship." Patrick, Cooke, and Hayes, "Worship in the Spirit: A Renewed Vision of Liturgy and Spirituality," in *What's Left? Liberal American Catholics*, ed. Mary Jo Weaver (Indiana University Press, 1999), 155–75, at 167.

action promoted by much liberation theology. He notes that whereas God's action can bring about the consummation of history, human politics will always be ambiguous and unable to fulfill human persons, created for a transcendent end. Without the redeeming God (and without worship) at the center of communal life, humans can have no enduring or satisfying hope. In this sense, says Ratzinger, "eschatology functions as the guarantee of meaning in history precisely because it does not become a political goal itself."[24] In his 1986 essay "Freedom and Liberation: The Anthropological Vision of the 1986 [CDF] Instruction *Libertatis Conscientia*," Ratzinger presses further into the nature of "liberation." For much liberation theology, says Ratzinger, "Baptism becomes the symbol of the exodus, while the exodus becomes a symbol of political revolutionary action in general."[25] In fact, the truth is the other way around: the exodus is a symbol of Baptism, through which we share in Christ's eschatological new exodus to the true promised land, the new creation. Recall *Lumen Gentium*'s statement—echoed in *Sacrosanctum Concilium*—that "in the eucharistic sacrifice, the source and summit of the Christian

24. Joseph Ratzinger, "Eschatology and Utopia," in Ratzinger, *Church, Ecumenism and Politics: New Essays in Ecclesiology*, trans. Robert Nowell (Crossroad, 1988), 237–54, at 248.

25. Joseph Ratzinger, "Freedom and Liberation: The Anthropological Vision of the 1986 [CDF] Instruction *Libertatis conscientia*," in *Church, Ecumenism and Politics*, 255–75, at 265. For a (fairly anodyne) example, see Anthony R. Ceresko, OSFS, *Introduction to the Old Testament: A Liberation Perspective*, rev. ed. (Orbis Books, 2001), 85; cf. 115. See the critique of liberation theologians' exegesis in Jon D. Levenson, "Exodus and Liberation," in *The Hebrew Bible, the Old Testament, and Historical Criticism: Jews and Christians in Biblical Studies* (Westminster John Knox, 1993), 127–59. As examples of liberation theology's characteristic exegesis of Exodus, Levenson points to J. Severino Croatto, *Exodus: A Hermeneutics of Freedom*, trans. Salvator Attanasio (Orbis Books, 1981); and George V. Pixley, *On Exodus: A Liberation Perspective* (Orbis Books, 1987); and he directs attention to earlier Marxist-inspired exegesis, such as Lincoln Steffens's *Moses in Red: The Revolt of Israel as a Typical Revolution* (Dorrance, 1926). See also, more broadly, Levenson's *The Love of God: Divine Gift, Human Gratitude, and Mutual Faithfulness in Judaism* (Princeton University Press, 2016). For the International Theological Commission's *Human Development and Christian Salvation* (1976) and Hans Urs von Balthasar's "Liberation Theology in the Light of Salvation History" (trans. Erasmo Leiva), see James V. Schall, SJ, *Liberation Theology in Latin America: With Selected Essays and Documents* (Ignatius, 1982), 363–83 and 131–46. Schall's reflections in this book—reflections that he titles "Liberation Theology in Latin America" (1–126)—underscore the importance of Hannah Arendt's distinction between "social questions" and "political questions" in her *On Revolution* (Viking, 1965). See also Álvaro Vargas Llosa, *Rumbo a la Libertad: Por Qué la izquierda y el "neoliberalismo" fracasan en América latina* (Planeta, 2005).

life, they [believers] offer the divine victim to God and themselves along with it."[26] Eucharistic worship is the center and pinnacle of the Church as the Bride, Family, Body, and People of God.

Fundamentally, the Church's worship is a sharing in the self-offering of Jesus on the cross, and a communion in his risen life. The Church's worship participates in Christ's self-giving love and is characterized, as an eschatological act, by reconciliation and redemption. Drawn into the heavenly liturgy and the Trinitarian life, the Church's worship pulses with the Spirit-filled energy of charity. Through the grace of the sacraments, the Church is enabled to share this energy and life with the world (despite the Church's—and our own—failures), both by inviting the whole world to conversion in Christ and to the Eucharistic worship, and by living out this conversion ourselves through eucharistic self-sacrificial love and mercy.

What is the Church, then? We know it by its worship and by sharing in its worship, united in faith, hope, and charity. This is what defines the royal and priestly community, with God in Christ at the center, joined by all Spirit-filled believers and by the whole groaning creation. Alexander Schmemann describes it this way: "He [i.e., man] stands in the center of the world and

26. Second Vatican Council, *Lumen Gentium* §11, November 21, 1964, in *Vatican Council II*, vol. 1, *The Conciliar and Post Conciliar Documents*, ed. Austin Flannery, OP, rev. ed. (Costello, 1996), 350–426, at 362. Let me quote Baum once more, representing a perspective opposite, in my view, to *Lumen Gentium*'s, although not without some insight: "At worship the Church celebrates the redemptive mystery that takes place everywhere. For this reason the sacred does not sever men from the ordinary things of life happening every day; on the contrary, the sacred as the celebration of the depth dimension of human life enables men to lay hold of the ordinary daily reality in a new way. Worship, understood in this way, unites a man more closely to his entire life. Word and sacrament enable him to interpret the meaning of secular life and discern the divine presence in his relationship with people and the building of the human world. . . . The first means of grace is life itself. It is here that God is redemptively present to man. This divine presence, fully disclosed in Jesus Christ, is celebrated in worship. Liturgy understood in this way should teach Christians to discern God's redemptive call and gifts in the ordinary situations of life and hence, in a sense, make them more independent of the liturgy" (*Man Becoming*, 252–53). See also, in a similar vein, Karl Rahner's argument (in the early 1970s) that "the sacraments constitute the manifestation of the holiness and the redeemed state of the secular dimension of human life and of the world" and thereby are "a symbolic manifestation of the liturgy of the world." Rahner, "Considerations of the Active Role of the Person in the Sacramental Event," in Karl Rahner, SJ, and Johann Baptist Metz, *Finding God in a World Come of Age*, ed. Roger Haight, SJ, Alfred Pach III, and Amanda Avila Kaminski (Fordham University Press, 2024), 49–80, at 59.

unifies it in his act of blessing God, of both receiving the world from God and offering it to God—and by filling the world with this eucharist, he transforms his life, the one he receives from the world, into life in God, into communion with Him."[27] Worship, on this view, is to receive everything from God and to offer one's transformed, Eucharistic life to God in Christ. In this sense, as John Zizioulas says, "the Church constitutes the Eucharist while being constituted by it."[28]

Once more, let me accentuate the place of the cross. Mary, the model of the Church, stands at the foot of the cross (see John 19:25–27), in fulfillment of Simeon's prophetic words to her: "A sword will pierce through your own soul also" (Luke 2:35). It is to the cross that we cleave in worship, because the cross is Christ's (and therefore, Eucharistically, our) perfect worship in love. This is how I interpret Schmemann's words of warning, "Christianity has forgotten itself, forgotten that always it must first of all stand at the cross."[29] Grounded in the cross, the Eucharistic liturgy enacts the new exodus, from death to life at the right hand of the Father. In the liturgical action, says Schmemann, believers "*constitute the Church*" or, more precisely, are "transformed into the Church of God."[30] Ascending to where Christ has ascended,

27. Alexander Schmemann, *For the Life of the World: Sacraments and Orthodoxy*, 3rd ed. (St. Vladimir's Seminary Press, 1973), 15.

28. John D. Zizioulas, *The Eucharistic Communion and the World*, ed. Luke Ben Tallon (T&T Clark International, 2011), 105; emphasis in original. For Zizioulas, "The body of Christ, which is the body of the Eucharist and of the Church at the same time, is the body of the *risen*, the eschatological Christ. This means that the ecclesiological presuppositions of the Eucharist are to be found in a consideration of the eschatological Christ and the eschatological community" (106). But Zizioulas also states clearly, "The Divine Eucharist is a *sacrifice*. The patristic tradition in both East and West lays great stress on this aspect of the Eucharist. . . . So when Christ says at the Last Supper, and the Church repeats in the course of the Eucharist, that 'this is my blood, the blood of the new covenant,' our thoughts are directed towards the coming and establishment of the Kingdom of God, and not simply towards an event which took place in the past. The sacrifice of the Lord upon the cross cannot be isolated from its eschatological significance" (51–52). In the Eucharist, Zizioulas points out, the Cross is interpreted in light of the Resurrection "as the first realization in history of the Kingdom which is to come. . . . In the Eucharist, we move within the space of the age to come, of the Kingdom" (54, 57).

29. Schmemann, *For the Life of the World*, 23.

30. Schmemann, 27.

sharing in "the new life of the Kingdom," believers "become the temple of the Holy Spirit."[31]

The intimacy of the Church's union with Christ does not spare the Church on earth from blundering, as we have seen. In his *Icon of the Kingdom of God: An Orthodox Ecclesiology*, Radu Bordeianu rightly cautions against "an idealized, ontological description of the Church" that allows theologians to turn a blind eye to concrete reality.[32] He urges theologians to take stock of "the reality of generalized misperceptions, faulty understandings, and sinful practices in the Church."[33] He defines the Church by considering its relation to the kingdom of God that Christ proclaimed: The Church is an "icon" in which God is present and through which God is building up his eschatological kingdom. As he puts it, "The Church is the community of disciples that enacts the values of the Kingdom of God, while striving to be closer and closer to the eschatological Kingdom."[34] In my view, much more than this needs to be said, lest the Church be seen merely as an ethical enterprise. Bordeianu, however, is less than enthusiastic about the lofty titles of the Church. He remarks rather caustically that for some Catholics, "the Church is the clergy or an undefined teaching authority with clearly defined answers to every modern question imaginable. The Church—especially for theologians—is the Body of Christ, People of God, Bride of Christ, Temple of the Spirit, Pilgrim People."[35] While he does not reject these titles, he focuses on the Church as "the assembly of worshippers gathered in *the Liturgy* as an icon of the Kingdom of God manifested visibly in the sacred space of the church building."[36]

I share Bordeianu's insistence on the centrality of the liturgy.

31. Schmemann, 28.

32. Radu Bordeianu, *Icon of the Kingdom of God: An Orthodox Ecclesiology* (The Catholic University of America Press, 2023), 4.

33. Bordeianu, 4.

34. Bordeianu, 5.

35. Bordeianu, 336.

36. Bordeianu, 337.

But the biblical titles of the Church support this centrality and provide a true vision of the Church. As Bride, Family, Body, People, and Mother, the Church cleaves to the crucified Lord and thereby shares in his fruitful exaltation, as liturgically enacted. Such a Church breaks free from the chains of worldliness in the Johannine sense of the term (see John 15:18–19).[37] For it is self-sacrificial love, inseparable in the Church from faith and hope, that takes us up into the life that is truly ecclesial: glorifying God and glorifying one another (as images of God) "by being included," in Eucharistic worship, "in Christ's human extension of his divine glorification of the Father."[38]

This divine-human communion of glorification *is* the Church, "the Bride, the wife of the Lamb" (Rev 21:9). It is Christ's cruciform love that delivers true liberation, by which humans are led into a deifying "participation in being itself," since divine being is none other than infinite love.[39] Let this, then, be the final word of Catholic ecclesiology, a word (or incarnate Word) that measures everything by the Spirit unto the glory of God.

37. See Serena Noceti, *Reforming the Church: A Synodal Way of Proceeding*, trans. Joseph Owens, SJ (Paulist, 2023), 155. Noceti makes a number of valuable observations, but I miss an equal emphasis on the revealed givens that are the heart of faith and of being a Christian.

38. Khaled Anatolios, *Deification through the Cross: An Eastern Christian Theology of Salvation* (Eerdmans, 2020), 428.

39. Joseph Ratzinger, "Freedom and Constraint in the Church," in *Church, Ecumenism and Politics: New Essays in Ecclesiology*, 183–203, at 198. Ratzinger comments with liberation theology in view, "'Being like God' is doubtless also the goal of radical emancipatory theories of education which have in their sights an unrestricted god-like freedom that has everything at its disposal. The goal is right: it is only the image of God that is wrong. Being like God means being like the trinitarian God. The education of love as education of θείωσις is necessarily the education of the cross, which does not for nothing form the key concept of the Pauline doctrine of freedom" (198–99). Along lines that I would underscore, Ratzinger concludes: "In the Church it is a matter of freedom in the profoundest sense of that word, of opening up the possibility of sharing in the divine being. The fundamental organization of the Church's freedom must therefore be to ensure that faith and sacrament, in which this sharing in the divine being is mediated, are accessible without diminution or adulteration. The fundamental right of the Christian is the right to the whole faith. . . . All remaining freedoms in the Church are directed towards and subordinate to this fundamental freedom. Ultimately it will be a question of making active and fervent participation in the Church's life of faith possible in the most comprehensive and varied way possible without letting this turn into compulsion towards congregational activity" (201–2).

Bibliography

Ables, Travis E. *The Body of the Cross: Holy Victims and the Invention of the Atonement*. Fordham University Press, 2022.

Acemoglu, Daron, and James A. Robinson. *Why Nations Fail: The Origins of Power, Prosperity, and Poverty*. Penguin Random House, 2012.

Àdajà, Paul Ọlátúbọ̀sún. "Catholic Theology in Twenty-First Century Africa in the Light of the Primacy of the Logos in the Theology of Joseph Ratzinger." In *Joseph Ratzinger and the Future of African Theology*, edited by Maurice Ashley Agbaw-Ebai and Matthew Levering, 40–62. Pickwick, 2021.

Adolphe, Jane F., and Ronald J. Rychlak. *Clerical Sexual Misconduct: An Interdisciplinary Analysis*. Cluny, 2020.

Agang, Sunday Bobai, ed. *African Public Theology*. Hippo Books, 2020.

Akossi-Mvongo, Marguerite. "The Church We Want: Ecclesia of Women in Africa." In *The Church We Want: African Catholics Look to Vatican III*, edited by Agbonkhianmeghe E. Orobator, SJ. Orbis, 2016.

Alberigo, Giuseppe. "Conciliarità, future delle chiese." In *Synod and Synodality: Theology, History, Canon Law and Ecumenism in New Contact*, edited by Alberto Melloni and S. Scatena, 463–88. Lit Verlag, 2005.

———. "La sinodalità dopo il Vaticano II." In *Vescovi per la Speranza del mondo*, edited by M. Fabri dos Anjos, 99–113. EDB, 2004.

Alberigo, Giuseppe, and James Provost, eds. *Synod 1985—An Evaluation*. SCM, 1986.

Allen, Michael. *The Fear of the Lord: Essays on Theological Method*. T&T Clark, 2022.

Amakwe, Bosco Ebere, HFSN. "Globalization and the African Woman: A Socio-Cultural Analysis of the Effect of Information and Communication Technology (ICT) on Women." In *The Church as Salt and Light: Path to an African Ecclesiology of Abundant Life*, edited by Stan Chu Ilo, Joseph Ogbonnaya, and Alex Ojacor, 99–129. Pickwick, 2011.

Amanat, Abbas, and Frank Griffel, eds. *Shari'a: Islamic Law in the Contemporary Context*. University Press, 2007.

Anatolios, Khaled. *Deification through the Cross: An Eastern Christian Theology of Salvation*. Eerdmans, 2020.

Anger, Joseph. *La Doctrine du corps mystique de Jésus-Christ d'après les principes de la théologie de s. Thomas*. Beauchesne, 1929.

Anglican-Roman Catholic Dialogue. "Church as Communion." In *Growth in Agreement II: Reports and Agreed Statements of Ecumenical Conversations on a World Level, 1982–1998*, edited by Jeffrey Gros, Harding Meyer, and William G. Rusch, 328–43. Eerdmans, 2000.

Arangüena, José Ramón Pérez. *La Iglesia: Iniciación a la Eclesiología*. 4th ed. Rialp, 2001.

Arbuckle, Gerald A. *Refounding the Church: Dissent for Leadership*. Orbis Books, 1993.

Arendt, Hannah. *On Revolution*. Viking, 1965.

Ashley, Benedict M., OP. *Justice in the Church: Gender and Participation*. The Catholic University of America Press, 1996.

Aulén, Gustaf. *Eucharist and Sacrifice*. Translated by Eric H. Wahlstrom. Muhlenberg, 1958.

Azike, Gerald. *The People of God in* Lumen Gentium*: A Theological Renewal of Institutional Ecclesiology and Its Implications*. Gregorian University Press, 2016.

Backes, Ignaz. "Die Kirche ist das Volk Gottes im Neuen Bund." *Trierer theologische Zeitschrift* 69 (1960): 111–17.

Bakhos, Carol. *The Family of Abraham: Jewish, Christian, and Muslim Interpretations*. Harvard University Press, 2014.

Balthasar, Hans Urs von. "Die Absolutheit des Christentums und die Katholizität der Kirche." In *Absolutheit des Christentums*, edited by Walter Kasper, 131–56. Herder, 1977.

———. *Explorations in Theology*. Vol. 2, *Spouse of the Word*. Ignatius, 1991.

———. *In the Fullness of Faith: On the Centrality of the Distinctively Catholic*. Translated by Graham Harrison. Ignatius, 1988.

———. *New Elucidations*. Translated by Mary Theresilde Skerry. Ignatius, 1986.

———. *The Office of Peter and the Structure of the Church*. Translated by Andrée Emery. Ignatius, 1986.

———. *Paul Struggles with His Congregation: The Pastoral Message of the Letters to the Corinthians*. Translated by Brigitte L. Bojarska. Ignatius, 1992.

———. *Theo-Logic*. Vol. 3, *The Spirit of Truth*. Translated by Graham Harrison. Ignatius, 2005.

———. *Two Sisters in the Spirit: Thérèse of Lisieux and Elizabeth of the Trinity*. Translated by Donald Nichols, Anne Elizabeth Englund, and Dennis Martin. Ignatius, 1992.

———. *Unless You Become Like This Child*. Translated by Erasmo Leiva-Merikakis. Ignatius, 1991.

Balthasar, Hans Urs von, and Joseph Ratzinger. *Mary: The Church at the Source*. Translated by Adrian Walker. Ignatius, 2005.

Barclay, John M. G. *Obeying the Truth: Paul's Ethics in Galatians*. Regent College Publishing, 2005.

———. *Paul and the Power of Grace*. Eerdmans, 2020.

Baril, Gilberte, OP. *The Feminine Face of the People of God: Biblical Symbols of the Church as Bride and Mother*. Liturgical, 1990.

Barnes, Michel René. "Irenaeus's Trinitarian Theology." *Nova et Vetera* 7, no. 1 (2009): 67–106.

Barón, María García-Nieto. *La Presencia de la Mujer en el Gobierno de la Iglesia: Perspectiva Jurídica*. EUNSA, 2023.

Barrett, Matthew. *The Reformation as Renewal: Retrieving the One, Holy, Catholic, and Apostolic Church*. Zondervan, 2023.

Barron, Robert. *Exploring Catholic Theology: Essays on God, Liturgy, and Evangelization*. Baker Academic, 2015.

———. *Heaven in Stone and Glass: Experiencing the Spirituality of the Great Cathedrals*. Crossroad, 2000.

———. *Letter to a Suffering Church: A Bishop Speaks on the Sexual Abuse Crisis*. Word on Fire, 2019.

———. *The Priority of Christ: Toward a Postliberal Catholicism*. Brazos, 2007.

———. *The Strangest Way: Walking the Christian Path*. Orbis Books, 2002.

Barth, Karl. *Church Dogmatics*. Vol. 4, *The Doctrine of Reconciliation*. Edited by G. W. Bromiley and T. F. Torrance. Translated by G. W. Bromiley. T&T Clark, 1961.

Bauckham, Richard. *Jesus and the Eyewitnesses: The Gospels as Eyewitness Testimony*. 2nd ed. Eerdmans, 2017.

Bauer, Walter. *Orthodoxy and Heresy in Earliest Christianity*. Fortress, 1971.

Baum, Gregory. *The Credibility of the Church Today: A Reply to Charles Davis*. Herder and Herder, 1968.

———. *Man Becoming: God in Secular Experience*. Herder and Herder, 1970.

———. *New Horizon*. Paulist, 1972.

Bea, Augustin, SJ. *The Unity of Christians*. Edited by Bernard Leeming, SJ. Herder and Herder, 1963.

Beattie, Tina. "Maternal Well-Being in Sub-Saharan Africa: From Silent Suffering to Human Flourishing." In *The Church We Want: African Catholics Look to Vatican III*, edited by Agbonkhianmeghe E. Orobator, SJ. Orbis, 2016.

Behr, John. *The Way to Nicaea*. Vol. 1 of *The Formation of Christian Theology*. St. Vladimir's Seminary Press, 2001.

Beinert, Wolfgang. "Catholicity as a Property of the Church." *The Jurist* 52 (1992): 455–83.

Beinert, Wolfgang. "Der Glaubenssinn der Gläubigen in Theologie und Dogmengeschichte: Ein Überblick." In *Der Gaubenssinn des Gottesvolkes: Konkurrent oder Partner des Lehramts?*, edited by Dietrich Widerkehr, 66–131. Herder, 1994.

———. "Die Apostolizität der Kirche als Kategorie der Theologie." *Theologie und Philosophie* 52 (1977): 161–81.

———. "Einstimmen oder Übereinstimmen? Die Aufgabe des Glaubenssinnes der Gläubigen." In *Zerreißprobe Ehe: Das Ringen der katholischen Kirche um die Familie*, edited by Ulrich Ruh and Myriam Wijlens. Herder, 2015.

Bender, Kimlyn J. "Ecclesiology and Christology." In *T&T Clark Handbook of Ecclesiology*, edited by Kimlyn J. Bender and D. Stephen Long, 323–41. Bloomsbury, 2020.

———. *Karl Barth's Christological Ecclesiology*. Cascade, 2013.

Benedict XVI. "Address to Catholics Engaged in the Life of the Church and Society." September 25, 2011, vatican.va.

———. *Africae Munus*. Apostolic exhortation, November 19, 2011, vatican.va.

———. *Deus Caritas Est*. Encyclical letter, December 25, 2005, vatican.va.

———. "Grace and Vocation without Remorse: Comments on the Treatise *De Iudaeis*." Translated by Nicholas J. Healy Jr. *Communio* 45 (2018): 163–84.

———. *Heart of the Christian Life: Thoughts on the Holy Mass*. Ignatius, 2010.

———. *Jesus of Nazareth*. Vol. 1, *From the Baptism in the Jordan to the Transfiguration*. Translated by Adrian J. Walker. Doubleday, 2007.

Bergant, Dianne, CSA. *A New Heaven, A New Earth: The Bible and Catholicity*. Orbis, 2016.

Bernard of Clairvaux. *Five Books on Consideration: Advice to a Pope*. Translated by John D. Anderson and Elizabeth T. Kennan. Cistercian Publications, 1976.

Bernard of Clairvaux. *On Baptism and the Office of Bishops*. Translated by Pauline Matarasso. Cistercian Publications, 2004.

———. *On the Song of Songs I: Sermons 1–20*. Translated by Kilian Walsh, OCSO. Cistercian Publications, 1971.

———. *On the Song of Songs II: Sermons 21–46*. Translated by Kilian Walsh, OCSO. Cistercian Publications, 1983.

———. *On the Song of Songs IV: Sermons 67–86*. Translated by Irene Edmonds. Cistercian Publications, 1980.

Bevans, Stephen B., SVD. *Models of Contextual Theology*. 2nd ed. Orbis Books, 2002.

Bianchi, Eugene C. *Reconciliation: The Function of the Church*. Sheed & Ward, 1969.

Bianchi, Eugene C., and Rosemary Radford Ruether, eds. *A Democratic Catholic Church: The Reconstruction of Roman Catholicism*. Crossroad, 1992.

Biliniewicz, Mariusz. *Amoris Laetitia and the Spirit of Vatican II: The Source of Controversy*. Routledge, 2018.

Blankenhorn, Bernhard, OP. "The *Sensus Fidei* and Synodality: Theological Epistemology and the *Munus Propheticum*." *The Thomist* 87 (2023): 311–38.

Blickenstaff, Marianne. *"While the Bridegroom Is with Them": Marriage, Family, Gender, and Violence in the Gospel of Matthew*. T&T Clark, 2005.

Blowers, Paul M. *Maximus the Confessor: Jesus Christ and the Transfiguration of the World*. Oxford University Press, 2016.

Bockmuehl, Markus. *Seeing the Word: Refocusing New Testament Study*. Baker Academic, 2006.

Boersma, Hans. "Meeting *par cum pari*: *Unitatis Redintegratio* and Ecumenical Progress." In *Dogma and Ecumenism: Vatican II and Karl Barth's* Ad Limina Apostolorum, edited by Matthew Levering, Bruce L. McCormack, and Thomas Joseph White, OP, 245–67. The Catholic University of America Press, 2020.

Boeve, Lieven. "'La vrai reception de Vatican II n'a pas encore commence.' Joseph Ratzinger, revelation et autorité de Vatican II." In *L'autorité et les autorités: L'hermeneutique théologique de Vatican II*, edited by G. Routhier and G. Jobin, 13–50. Cerf, 2000.

Bordeianu, Radu. *Icon of the Kingdom of God: An Orthodox Ecclesiology*. The Catholic University of America Press, 2023.

Borghesi, Massimo. *Catholic Discordance: Neoconservatism vs. the Field Hospital of Pope Francis*. Translated by Barry Hudock. Liturgical, 2021.

———. *The Mind of Pope Francis: Jorge Mario Bergoglio's Intellectual Journey*. Translated by Barry Hudock. Liturgical, 2018.

Borgman, Eric. "*Gaudium et Spes*: The Forgotten Future of a Revolutionary Document." Translated by Natalie K. Watson. In *Vatican II: A Forgotten Future*, edited by Alberto Melloni and Christoph Theobald, *Concilium* 2005/4, 48–56. SCM, 2005.

Bosch, David. *Transforming Missions: Paradigm Shifts in Theology of Mission*. Orbis Books, 1991.

Bossuet, Jacques-Bénigne. *The History of the Variations of the Protestant Churches*. Vol. 2. R. Coyne, 1829.

Boston College Seminar on Priesthood and Ministry for the Contemporary Church. "To Serve the People of God: Renewing the Conversation on Priesthood and Ministry." *Origins* 48, no. 31 (December 27, 2018): 484–93.

Böttigheimer, Christoph, and Johannes Hofmann, eds. *Autorität und Synodalität: Eine interdisziplinäre und interkonfessionelle Umschau nach ökumenischen Chancen und ekklesiologischen Desideraten*. Lembeck, 2008.

Bouyer, Louis. *The Church of God: Body of Christ and Temple of the Spirit*. Translated by Charles Underhill Quinn. Ignatius, 2011.

Braaten, Carl E. *The Future of God: The Revolutionary Dynamics of Hope*. Harper & Row, 1969.

Braaten, Carl E., and Robert W. Jenson, eds. *The Catholicity of the Reformation*. Eerdmans, 1996.

Brakke, David. *The Gnostics: Myth, Ritual, and Diversity in Early Christianity*. Harvard University Press, 2010.

Bredeck, Michael. *Das Zweite Vatikanum als Konzil des Aggiornamento: Zur hermeneutischen Grundlegung einer theologischen Konzilsinterpretation*. Schöningh, 2007.

Bredero, Adriaan H. *Bernard of Clairvaux: Between Cult and History*. Eerdmans, 1996.

Briggman, Anthony. *God and Christ in Irenaeus*. Oxford University Press, 2019.

Brown, Shaun C. *George Lindbeck and The Israel of God: Scripture, Ecclesiology, and Ecumenism*. Palgrave Macmillan, 2021.

Brown, Sherri. *Gift upon Gift: Covenant through Word in the Gospel of John*. Pickwick, 2010.

Buell, Denise Kimber. *Why This New Race: Ethnic Reasoning in Early Christianity*. Columbia University Press, 2005.

Bühlmann, Walbert, OFM Cap. *Church of the Future: A Model for the Year 2001*. Orbis Books, 1986.

———. *The Coming of the Third Church: An Analysis of the Present and Future of the Church*. Orbis Books, 1977.

Bujo, Bénézet. *Foundations of an African Ethic: Beyond the Universal Claims of Western Morality*. Translated by Brian McNeil. Crossroad, 2001.

———. "On the Road toward an African Ecclesiology: Reflections on the Synod." Translated by T. Allan Smith. In *The African Synod: Documents, Reflections, Perspectives*, edited by Maura Browne, SND, and the Africa Faith and Justice Network, 139–51. Orbis, 1996.

Bulgakov, Sergius. *The Bride of the Lamb*. Translated by Boris Jakim. Eerdmans, 2002.

Burke, Trevor J. *Adopted into God's Family: Exploring a Pauline Metaphor*. InterVarsity, 2006.

———. *Family Matters: A Socio-historical Study of Kinship Metaphors in 1 Thessalonians*. T&T Clark, 2003.

Burkhard, John J., OFM Conv. *Apostolicity Then and Now: An Ecumenical Church in a Postmodern World*. Liturgical, 2004.

Burrell, David B., CSC. "The Church and Individual Life." In *Toward Vatican III: The Work That Needs to Be Done*, edited by David Tracy with Hans Küng and Johann B. Metz, 124–33. Seabury, 1978.

Burrows, William R. *New Ministries: The Global Context*. Orbis Books, 1980.

Bushman, Douglas G. *The Theology of Renewal for* His Church*: The Logic of Vatican II's Renewal in Paul VI's Encyclical* Ecclesiam Suam *and Its Reception in John Paul II and Benedict XVI*. Pickwick, 2024.

Butler, Sara, MSBT. *The Catholic Priesthood and Women: A Guide to the Teaching of the Church*. Hillenbrand, 2007.

Byrne, Brendan, SJ. *'Sons of God'—'Seed of Abraham': A Study of the Idea of the Sonship of God of All Christians in Paul against the Jewish Background*. Biblical Institute, 1979.

Calvin, John. *Institutes of the Christian Religion*. Translated by Henry Beveridge. Eerdmans, 1989.

Cardó, Daniel. *The Cross and the Eucharist in Early Christianity: A Theological and Liturgical Investigation*. Cambridge University Press, 2019.

Carmichael, Calum. *Sex and Religion in the Bible*. Yale University Press, 2010.

Catechism of the Catholic Church. 2nd ed. Libreria Editrice Vaticana, 1997.

Catherine of Siena. *The Dialogue*. Translated by Suzanne Noffke, OP. Paulist, 1980.

Cavadini, John C. "Co-Responsibility: An Antidote to Clericalizing the Laity?" *Church Life Journal*, March 26, 2020, https://churchlifejournal.nd.edu/articles/co-responsibility-is-the-remedy-for-lay-clericalism/.

———. "Could 'Synodality' Defeat 'Co-Responsibility'?" *The Thomist* 87 (2023): 289–309.

Cavanaugh, William T. *Torture and Eucharist: Theology, Politics, and the Body of Christ*. Blackwell, 1998.

Ceresko, Anthony R., OSFS. *Introduction to the Old Testament: A Liberation Perspective*. Rev. ed. Orbis, 2001.

Cerfaux, Lucien. *The Church in the Theology of St. Paul*. Translated by Geoffrey Webb and Adrian Walker. Herder and Herder, 1959.

Chantraine, Georges, SJ. "Cardinal Henri de Lubac (1896–1991)." *Communio* 18 (1991): 297–303.

———. "Catholicité et maternité de l'Église." *Nouvelle revue théologique* 94, no. 5 (1972): 520–36.

Chenu, M.-D., OP. "The History of Salvation and the Historicity of Man in the Renewal of Theology." In *Renewal of Religious Thought: Proceedings of the Congress on the Theology of the Renewal of the Church*, edited by L. K. Shook, CSB, 153–66. Palm, 1968.

———. *Peuple de Dieu dans le monde*. Cerf, 1966.

Chiron, Jean-François. "Sensus fidei et vision de l'Église chez le pape François." *Recherches de science religieuse* 104 (2016): 187–205.

Clement of Rome. "Epistle to the Corinthians." In *The Epistles of St. Clement of Rome and St. Ignatius of Antioch*, translated by James A. Kleist, SJ. The Newman Bookshop, 1946.

Colberg, Kristin M., and Jos Moons, SJ. *The Future of Synodality: How We Move Forward from Here*. Liturgical, 2025.

Collier, Paul. *The Bottom Billion: Why the Poorest Countries Are Failing and What Can Be Done About It*. Oxford University Press, 2007.

Collins, Kenneth J., and Jerry L. Walls. *Roman but Not Catholic: What Remains at Stake 500 Years after the Reformation*. Baker Academic, 2017.

Colón-Emeric, Edgardo. *Wesley, Aquinas, and Christian Perfection: An Ecumenical Dialogue*. Baylor University Press, 2009.

Comblin, José. "The Signs of the Times." Translated by Paul Burns. In *Vatican II: A Forgotten Future*, edited by Alberto Melloni and Christoph Theobald, *Concilium* 2005/4, 73–85. SCM, 2005.

Congar, Yves, OP. *Chrétiens désunis: Principes d'un "oecuménisme" catholique*. Cerf, 1937.

———. "The Church: The People of God." Translated by Kathryn Sullivan, RSCJ. In *The Church and Mankind*, vol. 1 of *Concilium: Theology in the Age of Renewal*, 11–37. Paulist, 1965.

———. "Composantes et idée de la Succession Apostolique." *Oecumenica* 1 (1966): 61–78.

———. *Diversity and Communion*. Translated by John Bowden. Twenty-Third Publications, 1985.

———. *Divided Christendom: A Catholic Study of the Problem of Reunion*. Translated by M. A. Bousfield. Geoffrey Bles, 1939.

———. *Esquisse du mystère de l'Église*. Rev. ed. Cerf, 1953.

———. *I Believe in the Holy Spirit*. Translated by David Smith. Crossroad, 1997.

———. "The Idea of the Church in St. Thomas Aquinas." *The Thomist* 1 (1939): 331–59.

———. *Jalons pour une théologie du laïcat*. Cerf, 1953.

———. *Lay People in the Church: A Study for a Theology of the Laity*. Translated by Donald Attwater. Geoffrey Chapman, 1965.

Congar, Yves, OP. "*Lumen Gentium* no. 7, L'Eglise, Corps mystique du Christ, vu a terme de huit siècles d'histoire de la théologie du Corps mystique." In *Au service de la parole de Dieu: Mélanges offerts à Mgr. A.-M. Charue*, 179–202. Duculot, 1969.

———. *The Meaning of Tradition*. Translated by A. N. Woodrow. Ignatius, 2004.

———. *Ministères et communion ecclésiale*. Cerf, 1971.

———. *The Mystery of the Church*. Translated by A. V. Littledale. Helicon, 1960.

———. *Un people messianique: Salut et liberation*. Cerf, 1975.

———. *Pour une église servant et pauvre*. Cerf, 2014.

———. "Renewal of the Spirit and Reform of the Institution." Translated by John Griffiths. *Concilium* 73 (1972): 39–49.

———. *Spirit of God: Short Writings on the Holy Spirit*. Edited by Susan Mader Brown, Mark E. Ginter, and Joseph G. Mueller, SJ. Translated by Susan Mader Brown, Mark E. Ginter, Joseph G. Mueller, SJ, and Catherine E. Clifford. The Catholic University of America Press, 2018.

———. "Theology's Tasks after Vatican II." In *Renewal of Religious Thought: Proceedings of the Congress on the Theology of the Renewal of the Church*, edited by L. K. Shook, CSB, 47–65. Palm, 1968.

———. "Vision de l'Église chez s. Thomas d'Aquin." *Revue des sciences philosophiques et théologiques* 62 (1978): 523–41.

———. *Vraie et fausse réforme dans l'Église*. Cerf, 1950.

Congregation for the Doctrine of the Faith. "Doctrinal Commentary on the Concluding Formula of the *Professio fidei*." June 29, 1998, vatican.va.

———. "Doctrinal Congregation, 'Inadmissibility of Women to Ministerial Priesthood.'" *Origins* 25, no. 24 (1995): 401.

———. *Donum Veritatis*. May 24, 1990, vatican.va.

Congregation for the Doctrine of the Faith. "Some Comments on the Notification of the Congregation for the Doctrine of the Faith regarding Certain Writings of Fr. Marciano Vidal, CSsR." May 15, 2001, vatican.va.

Cooke, Bernard J. "Progressive Approaches to Ministry." In *What's Left? Liberal American Catholics*, edited by Mary Jo Weaver, 135–46. Indiana University Press, 1999.

Coppen, Luke, and Brendan Hodge. "German Catholics Left Church in Record Numbers Last Year." *The Pillar*, June 8, 2023, https://pillarcatholic.com/p/german-catholics-left-church-in-record.

Corecco, E., ed. *La Synodalité: La participation au governement dans l'Église*. Unesco, 1992.

Coriden, James A., ed. "Toward a Declaration of Christian Rights: A Position Paper." In *The Case for Freedom: Human Rights in the Church*, 5–14. Corpus Books, 1969.

———, ed. *We, the People of God . . . a Study of Constitutional Government for the Church*. Our Sunday Visitor, 1967.

Corrin, Jay P. *Catholic Progressives in England after Vatican II*. University of Notre Dame Press, 2013.

Cyril of Jerusalem. *Catechetical Lectures*. Translated by Edwin Hamilton Gifford. In *Nicene and Post-Nicene Fathers*, Second Series, vol. 7, 1–157. Hendrickson, 1994.

Dahl, Nils. *Das Volk Gottes: Eine Untersuchung zum Kirchenbewusstsein des Urchristentums*. 2nd ed. Wissenschaftliche Buchgesellschaft.

Daley, Brian E., SJ. *Christology in Early Christianity: Collected Essays*. Eerdmans, 2025.

———. "Sign and Source of the Church: Mary in the *Ressourcement* and at Vatican II." In *Mary on the Eve of the Second Vatican Council*, edited by John Cavadini and Danielle Peters, 31–54. University of Notre Dame Press, 2017.

Daley, Daniel. *God's Will and Testament: Inheritance in the Gospel of Matthew and Jewish Tradition.* Baylor University Press, 2021.

Daniélou, Jean, SJ. *The Lord of History: An Essay on the Mystery of History.* Translated by Nigel Abercrombie. Cluny, 2022.

———. *Why the Church?* Franciscan Herald, 1974.

Dassmann, Ernst. *Ämter und Dienste in den frühchristlichen Gemeinden.* Verlag Nobert M. Borengässer, 1994.

Davis, Charles. "A Loving Defense of a Church That Never Was." *National Catholic Reporter*, June 26, 1968.

———. *A Question of Conscience.* Harper & Row, 1967.

———. "Theology and Praxis." *Cross Currents* 23 (1973): 154–68.

———. *Theology for Today.* Sheed and Ward, 1962.

De Broucker, Jose, ed. *The Suenens Dossier: The Case for Collegiality.* Fides, 1970.

De Gaál, Emery. "Augustine of Hippo: The Reciprocal Dependence of Faith and World." In *Joseph Ratzinger in Dialogue with Philosophical Traditions: From Plato to Vattimo*, edited by Alejandro Sada, Tracey Rowland, and Rudy Albino de Assunção, 24–30. T&T Clark, 2024.

———. "Mission, Inculturation, and 'Interculturality' in the Thinking of Joseph Ratzinger / Benedict XVI in Relation to Africa." In *Joseph Ratzinger and the Future of African Theology*, edited by Maurice Ashley Agbaw-Ebai and Matthew Levering, 183–213. Pickwick, 2021.

———. *The Theology of Pope Benedict XVI: The Christocentric Shift.* Palgrave Macmillan, 2010.

De La Soujeole, Benoît-Dominique, OP. *Introduction to the Mystery of the Church.* Translated by Michael J. Miller. The Catholic University of America Press, 2014.

De Lubac, Henri, SJ. *Catholicism: Christ and the Common Destiny of Man.* Translated by Lancelot C. Sheppard and Elizabeth Englund, OCD. Ignatius, 1988.

De Lubac, Henri, SJ. *The Church: Paradox and Mystery.* Translated by James R. Dunne and Anne Englund Nash. Ignatius, 2021.

———. *Corpus Mysticum: The Eucharist and the Church in the Middle Ages.* Edited by Laurence Paul Hemming and Susan Frank Parsons. Translated by Gemma Simmonds, CJ, with Richard Price and Christopher Stephens. University of Notre Dame Press, 2007.

———. *The Motherhood of the Church.* Translated by Sergia Englund, OCD. Ignatius, 1982.

———. *Paradoxes of Faith.* Translated by Paule Simon and Sadie Kreilkamp. Ignatius, 1987.

———. *La postérité spirituelle de Joachim de Flore: De Joachim à nos jours.* Edited by Michael Sutton. Cerf, 2014.

———. *At the Service of the Church: Henri de Lubac Reflects on the Circumstances that Occasioned His Writings.* Translated by Anne Elizabeth Englund. Ignatius, 1993.

———. *The Splendor of the Church.* Translated by Michael Mason. Ignatius, 1986.

———. *Vatican Council Notebooks.* 2 vols. Translated by Andrew Stefanelli and Anne Englund Nash. Ignatius, 2015–16.

Deane, David. *The Tyranny of the Banal: On the Renewal of Catholic Moral Theology.* Lexington Books, 2023.

Deaton, Angus. *The Great Escape: Health, Wealth, and the Origins of Inequality.* Princeton University Press, 2013.

DeConick, April D. *Holy Misogyny: Why the Sex and Gender Conflicts in the Early Church Still Matter.* Continuum, 2011.

Delahaye, Karl. *Ecclesia Mater. Chez les pères des trois premiers siècles: Pour un renouvellement de la pastorale d'aujourd'hui.* Cerf, 1964.

Delio, Ilia, OSF. *Making All Things New: Catholicity, Cosmology, Consciousness.* Orbis, 2015.

Demeuse, Eric J. *Unity and Catholicity in Christ: The Ecclesiology of Francisco Suárez, S.J.* Oxford University Press, 2022.

DeVille, Adam A. J. *Everything Hidden Shall Be Revealed: Ridding the Church of Abuses of Sex and Power*. Angelico, 2019.

Dianich, Severino. *Magistero in movimento: Il caso papa Francesco*. EDB, 2016.

Dickson, John. *Bullies and Saints: An Honest Look at the Good and Evil of Christian History*. Zondervan, 2021.

Didymus the Blind. *Commentary on Zechariah*. Translated by Robert C. Hill. The Catholic University of America Press, 2006.

Diriart, Alexandra, SASJ. *Ses frontières sont la charité: L'Église Corps du Christ et* Lumen Gentium. Lethielleux, 2011.

Dodaro, Robert, OSA. "*Sensus Fidelium*: Sense of the Faithful." In *The Faith Once and for All Delivered: Doctrinal Authority in Catholic Theology*, edited by Kevin L. Flannery, SJ, 229–49. Emmaus Academic, 2023.

Duchatelez, Kamiel. "La notion d'économie et ses richesses théologiques." *Nouvelle revue théologique* 92 (1970): 267–92.

Dulles, Avery, SJ. *The Catholicity of the Church*. Oxford University Press, 1985.

———. *A Church to Believe In: Discipleship and the Dynamics of Freedom*. Crossroad, 1987.

———. "Church, Ministry, and Sacraments in Catholic-Evangelical Dialogue." In *Catholics and Evangelicals: Do They Share a Common Future?*, edited by Thomas P. Rausch, 101–21. InterVarsity, 2000.

———. *The Craft of Theology*. Expanded ed. Crossroad, 1995.

———. "The Emerging World Church: A Theological Reflection." *Proceedings of the Catholic Theological Society of America* 39 (1984): 1–12.

———. "The Eucharist as Sacrifice." In *Rediscovering the Eucharist: Ecumenical Conversations*, edited by Roch Kereszty, O.Cist., 175–87. Paulist, 2003.

———. *Magisterium: Teacher and Guardian of the Faith*. Sapientia, 2007.

Dulles, Avery, SJ. *Models of the Church.* Expanded edition. Doubleday, 1987.

———. "Nature, Mission, and Structure of the Church." In *Vatican II: Renewal within Tradition*, edited by Matthew L. Lamb and Matthew Levering, 25–36. Oxford University Press, 2008.

———. *The Reshaping of Catholicism: Current Challenges in the Theology of the Church.* Harper & Row, 1988.

———. "The Theology of Worship: Saint Thomas." In *Rediscovering Aquinas and the Sacraments: Studies in Sacramental Theology*, edited by Matthew Levering and Michael Dauphinais, 1–13. Hillenbrand Books, 2009.

Dupont-Fauville, Denis. *L'Église mère chez Henri de Lubac.* Parole et Silence, 2009.

Dvornik, Francis. *Byzantium and the Roman Primacy.* Translated by Edwin A. Quain, SJSJ. Fordham University Press, 1966.

East, Brad. *The Church: A Guide to the People of God.* Lexham, 2024.

Ebelebe, Charles A., CSSp. "An Inculturated Church in Africa: Lessons and Failings since *Ecclesia in Africa*." In *Faith in Action*, vol. 2, *Pastoral Renewal, Public Health and the Prophetic Mission of the Church in Africa Since the Two African Synods*, edited by Stan Chu Ilo, Justin Clemency Nabushawo, and Ikenna U. Okafor, 27–52. Pickwick, 2020.

Eckholt, Margit, and Johanna Rahner, eds. *Christusrepräsentanz: Zur aktuellen Debatte um die Zulassung von Frauen zum priesterlichen Amt.* Herder, 2021.

Emery, Gilles, OP. "Le sacerdoce spiritual des fidèles chez saint Thomas d'Aquin." *Revue Thomiste* 99 (1999): 211–43.

———. *Trinity, Church, and the Human Person: Thomistic Essays.* Sapientia, 2007.

Emon, Anyer M. "Islamic Natural Law Theories." In Anver M. Emon, Matthew Levering, and David Novak, *Natural Law: A Jewish, Christian, and Islamic Trialogue*, 144–87. Oxford University Press, 2014.

Erasmus, Desiderius. *The Praise of Folly*. Translated by Clarence H. Miller. Yale University Press, 1979.

Erickson, Amy J. *Ephraim Radner, Hosean Wilderness, and the Church in the Post-Christendom West: A Dialogue on the Shape of Waiting*. Brill, 2020.

Esler, P. F. "Family Imagery and Christian Identity in Gal. 5:13–6:10." In *Constructing Early Christian Families: Family as Social Reality and Metaphor*, edited by H. Moxnes, 121–49. Routledge, 1997.

Eusebius. *The History of the Church from Christ to Constantine*. Translated by G. A. Williamson, revised and edited by Andrew Louth. Penguin, 1989.

Evans, G. R. *Bernard of Clairvaux*. Oxford University Press, 2000.

Evdokimov, Paul. *Orthodoxy*. Translated by Olivier Clément. New City, 2011.

The Extraordinary Synod—1985: Message to the People of God. St. Paul Editions, 1986.

Faggioli, Massimo. *Joe Biden and Catholicism in the United States*. Bayard, 2021.

———. *The Liminal Papacy of Pope Francis: Moving toward Global Catholicity*. Orbis Books, 2020.

———. "Will Trumpism Spare Catholicism? Emerging Alignments Are Cause for Concern." *Commonweal*, April 22, 2024.

Fejérdy, Áron. *L'Église de l'Esprit du Christ: La relation ordonnée du Christ et de l'Esprit au mystère ecclesial; Une lecture de Vatican II*. Academic Press Fribourg, 2013.

Fernández, Víctor Manuel. "El 'sensus populi,' Legitimidad de una teología 'desde' el Pueblo." *Teología* 72 (1998): 133–64.

Firestone, Reuven. *Jihād: The Origin of Holy War in Islam*. Oxford University Press, 1999.

First Vatican Council. *Dei Filius*. In *Decrees of the Ecumenical Councils*, vol. 2, *Trent–Vatican II*, edited by Norman P. Tanner, SJ, 804–11. Sheed & Ward, 1990.

Fisher, Anthony. *Unity in the Church: Bishops, Synodality, and Communion*. The Catholic University of America Press, 2023.

Flett, John G. *Apostolicity: The Ecumenical Question in World Christian Perspective*. IVP Academic, 2016.

Flipper, Joseph S. *Between Apocalypse and Eschatology: History and Eternity in Henri de Lubac*. Fortress, 2015.

Flores, Deyanira. "Virgin Mother of Christ: Mary, the Church, the Faithful Soul—Patristic and Medieval Testimonies on This Inseparable Trio." *Marian Studies* 57 (2006): 97–172.

Flynn, Gabriel, and Paul Murray, eds. *Ressourcement: A Movement for Renewal in Twentieth-Century Catholic Theology*. Oxford University Press, 2011.

Fogliacco, Nicholas. "The Family: An African Metaphor for Trinity and Church." In *Inculturating the Church in Africa: Theological and Practical Perspectives*, edited by Cecil McGarry and Patrick Ryan, 120–58. Paulines Publications Africa, 2001.

Folliet, Joseph. *World Catholicism Today*. Translated by Edmond Bonin. Newman, 1961.

Forestier, Luc. "Le pape François et la synodalité: *Evangelii gaudium*, nouvelle étape dans la reception de Vatican II." *Nouvelle revue théologique* 13 (2015): 597–614.

Francis, Michael Kpakala. "The Church in Africa Today: Sacrament of Justice, Peace, and Unity." In *The African Synod: Documents, Reflections, Perspectives*, edited by the Africa Faith and Justice Network under the direction of Maura Browne, SND, 119–30. Orbis Books, 1996.

Francis. *Amoris Laetitia*. Apostolic exhortation, March 19, 2016, vatican.va.

———. *Episcopalis Communio*. Apostolic constitution, September 15, 2028, vatican.va

———. *Evangelii Gaudium*. Apostolic exhortation, November 13, 2013, vatican.va.

———. *Gaudete et Exsultate*. Our Sunday Visitor, 2018.

———. *Laudato Si'*. Encyclical letter, May 24, 2015, vatican.va,

———. *Walking Together: The Way of Synodality*. Orbis Books, 2023.

Franon, Eugène. "The Religious Philosophy of Fr. Tyrrell." In *Defending the Faith: An Anti-Modernist Anthology*, edited and translated by William H. Marshner, 197–210. The Catholic University of America Press, 2017.

Fries, Heinrich, and Karl Rahner, SJ. *Unity of the Churches: An Actual Possibility*. Translated by Ruth C. L. Gritsch and Eric W. Gritsch. Paulist, 1985.

Fritz, Peter Joseph. "Catholicity and Translatability: Renewing Rahner on the World Church." *Theological Studies* 83 (2022): 400–423.

Frost, Carrie Frederick. *Maternal Body: A Theology of Incarnation from the Christian East*. Paulist, 2019.

Gagliardi, Mauro. *Revelation, Hermeneutics, and Doctrinal Development in Joseph Ratzinger*. Emmaus Academic, 2024.

Gaillardetz, Richard R. *By What Authority? Foundations for Understanding Authority in the Church*. 2nd ed. Liturgical, 2018.

———. *Ecclesiology for a Global Church: A People Called and Sent*. 2nd ed. Orbis Books, 2023.

———. "Infallibility and the Ordination of Women." *Louvain Studies* 21 (1996): 3–24.

———. *An Unfinished Council: Vatican II, Pope Francis, and the Renewal of Catholicism*. Liturgical, 2015.

Gaillardetz, Richard R. *While I Breathe, I Hope: A Mystagogy of Dying*. Liturgical, 2024.

Galot, Jean, SJ. "Mère de l'Église." *Nouvelle revue théologique* 86 (1964): 1163–85.

Garrigues, Jean-Miguel. *L'Épouse du Dieu vivant: Marie plenitude trinitaire de l'Église*. Parole et Silence, 2000.

Geffré, Claude, OP. *The Risk of Interpretation: On Being Faithful to the Christian Tradition in a Non-Christian Age*. Translated by David Smith. Paulist, 1987.

Gertrud the Great of Helfta. *The Herald of God's Loving-Kindness: Book Three*. Translated by Alexandra Barratt. Cistercian Publications, 1999.

Giambrone, Anthony, OP. *The Bible and the Priesthood: Priestly Participation in the One Sacrifice for Sins*. Baker Academic, 2022.

Gilles, Anthony E. *People of God: The History of Catholic Christianity*. Franciscan Media, 2000.

Gladd, Benjamin L. *From Adam and Israel to the Church: A Biblical Theology of the People of God*. IVP Academic, 2019.

Goichet, Emil. *Alfred Loisy et ses amis*. Cerf, 2002.

Gomez, Cristina Lledo Gomez. *The Church as Woman and Mother: Historical and Theological Foundations*. Paulist, 2018.

Gorman, Michael J. *Cruciformity: Paul's Narrative Spiritual of the Cross*. Eerdmans, 2001.

Görres, Ida Friederike. *The Church in the Flesh*. Translated by Jennifer S. Bryson. Cluny, 2023.

Goyret, Philip. *Church and Communion: An Introduction to Ecumenical Theology*. 2nd ed. Edited by Joseph Thomas. Translated by Philip Goyret and Joseph Thomas. The Catholic University of America Press, 2022.

Graebe, Brian. *Vessel of Honor: The Virgin Birth and the Ecclesiology of Vatican II*. Emmaus Academic, 2021.

Gregory of Narek. *The Blessing of Blessings: Gregory of Narek's Commentary on the Song of Songs*. Translated by Roberta Ervine. Cistercian Publications, 2007.

Gregory of Nyssa. *Anti-Apollinarian Writings*. Translated by Robin Orton. The Catholic University of America Press, 2015.

Griffith, Sidney H. *The Church in the Shadow of the Mosque: Christians and Muslims in the World of Islam*. Princeton University Press, 2008.

Grillmeier, Aloys. "Chapter III, Article 28." In *Commentary on the Documents of Vatican II*, vol. 1, edited by Herbert Vorgrimler, translated by Lalit Adolphus, Kevin Smyth, and Richard Strachan, 218–26. Herder and Herder, 1967.

Groome, Thomas H. "The Catechesis of Priesthood." In *Priestly Ministry and the People of God: Hopes and Horizons*, edited by Richard R. Gaillardetz, Thomas H. Groome, and Richard Lennan, 168–76. Orbis Books, 2022.

Gútierrez, Gustavo. *A Theology of Liberation*. Orbis Books, 1973.

Haight, Roger D., SJ. "The 'Established' Church as Mission: The Relation of the Church to the Modern World." *Jurist* 39 (1979): 4–39.

Halík, Tomáš. *The Afternoon of Christianity: The Courage to Change*. Translated by Gerald Turner. University of Notre Dame Press, 2024.

Hamer, Jérôme, OP. *The Church Is a Communion*. Translated by Ronald Matthews. Geoffrey Chapman, 1964.

Hamilton, H. F. *The People of God*. 2 vols. Oxford University Press, 1912.

Häring, Bernard, CSsR. *My Hope for the Church: Critical Encouragement for the Twenty-First Century*. Translated by Peter Heinegg. Liguori, 1999.

Harrington, Daniel J., SJ, and James F. Keenan, SJ. *Paul and Virtue Ethics: Building Bridges between New Testament Studies and Moral Theology*. Rowman & Littlefield, 2010.

Hartsfield, Ivan L. *Sanctified Imagination: Christian Holiness in Afro-Pentecostal Tradition*. Pickwick, 2023.

Haslinger, Herbert, ed. *Wege der Kirche in die Zukunft der Menschen: 50 Jahre nach Beginn der Würzburger Synode*. Herder, 2021.

Hauerwas, Stanley. *Matthew*. Brazos, 2006.

Hays, Richard B. *Echoes of Scripture in the Letters of Paul*. Yale University Press, 1989.

Healey, Joseph G. *Building the Church as Family of God: Evaluation of Small Christian Communities in Eastern Africa*. AMECEA Gaba Publications, 2012.

Healey, Joseph G., and Donald Sybertz. *Towards an African Narrative Theology*. Orbis Books, 1996.

Healy, Nicholas M. *Church, World and the Christian Life: Practical-Prophetic Ecclesiology*. Cambridge University Press, 2000.

Healy, Nicholas J., Jr., and Matthew Levering, eds. *Ressourcement after Vatican II: Essays in Honor of Joseph Fessio, SJ*. Ignatius, 2019.

Hebblethwaite, Peter. *The Runaway Church*. 2nd ed. Fount, 1978.

———. *Synod Extraordinary: The Inside Story of the Rome Synod, November/December 1985*. Doubleday, 1986.

Heid, Stefan. *Altar and Church: Principles of Liturgy from Early Christianity*. Translated by Susan Johnson. The Catholic University of America Press, 2023.

Heiler, Friedrich. *Der Katholizismus: Seine Idee und seine Erscheinung*. E. Reinhardt, 1970.

Heim, Maximilian Heinrich. *Joseph Ratzinger: Life in the Church and Living Theology. Fundamentals of Ecclesiology with Reference to* Lumen Gentium. Translated by Michael J. Miller. Ignatius, 2007.

Heinemann, Heribert. "Demokratisierung oder Synodalisierung? Ein Beitrag zur Diskussion." In *Kirche sein: Nachkonziliare Theologie im Dienst der Kirchenreform*, edited by W. Geerlings and Max Seckler, 349–60. Herder, 1994.

Hellerman, Joseph H. *The Ancient Church as Family*. Fortress, 2001.

———. *When the Church Was a Family: Recapturing Jesus' Vision for Authentic Community*. B&H Academic, 2009.

Hillebert, Jordan. *Henri de Lubac and the Drama of Human Existence*. University of Notre Dame Press, 2021.

Hiney, Tom. "The New Agnosticism." *First Things* no. 338 (December 2023): 17–22.

Hinze, Braford. "Transforming Priestly Identity and Ministry." In *Priestly Ministry and the People of God: Hopes and Horizons*, edited by Richard R. Gaillardetz, Thomas H. Groome, and Richard Lennan, 101–8. Orbis Books, 2022.

Hipp, Stephen A. *The One Church of Christ: Understanding Vatican II*. Emmaus Academic, 2018.

Holland, Tom. *Dominion: The Making of the Western Mind*. Little, Brown, 2019.

Horan, Daniel P., OFM. *Catholicity and Emerging Personhood: A Contemporary Theological Anthropology*. Orbis, 2019.

Horn, Gerd-Rainer. *The Spirit of '68: Rebellion in Western Europe and North America, 1956–1976*. Oxford University Press, 2007.

———. *The Spirit of Vatican II: Western European Progressive Catholicism in the Long Sixties*. Oxford University Press, 2015.

———. *Western European Liberation Theology 1924–1959: The First Wave*. Oxford University Press, 2008.

Horowitz, Elliott. *Reckless Rites: Purim and the Legacy of Jewish Violence*. Princeton University Press, 2008.

Hosinski, Thomas E., CSC. *The Image of the Unseen God: Catholicity, Science, and Our Evolving Understanding of God*. Orbis, 2017.

Houtart, François, OSB. *Challenge to Change: The Church Confronts the Future*. Edited by Mary Anne Chouteau. Sheed and Ward, 1964.

Hovorun, Cyril. *Political Orthodoxies: The Unorthodoxies of the Church Coerced*. Fortress, 2018.

Howell, Kenneth J., ed. and trans. *Clement of Rome and the Didache: A New Translation and Theological Commentary*. CHResources, 2012.

Huizenga, Leroy, A. *The New Isaac: Tradition and Intertextuality in the Gospel of Matthew*. Brill, 2009.

Hünermann, Peter. "The Ignored 'Text': On the Hermeneutics of the Second Vatican Council." Translated by Natalie K. Watson. In *Vatican II: A Forgotten Future*, edited by Alberto Melloni and Christoph Theobald, *Concilium* 2005/4, 118–36. SCM, 2005.

———. "On the Specific Theological Character of the Sacrament of Matrimony." In *Authentic Voices, Discerning Hearts: New Resources for the Church on Marriage and Family*, edited by Thomas Knieps-Port le Roi and Aldegonde Brenninkmeijer-Werhahn, 133–50. LIT, 2016.

Hütter, Reinhard. *Aquinas on Transubstantiation: The Real Presence of Christ in the Eucharist*. The Catholic University of America Press, 2019.

———. *John Henry Newman on Truth and Its Counterfeits: A Guide for Our Times*. The Catholic University of America Press, 2020.

———. "Progress, Not Alteration of the Faith: Beyond Antiquarianism and Presentism: John Henry Newman, Vincent of Lérins, and the Criterion of Identity of the Development of Doctrine." *Nova et Vetera* 19 (2021): 333–91.

Hvidt, Niels Christian. *Christian Prophecy: The Post-Biblical Tradition*. Oxford University Press, 2007.

Ilo, Stan Chu. "African Ecclesiologies." In *The Oxford Handbook of Ecclesiology*, edited by Paul Avis, 615–38. Oxford University Press, 2018.

———. "Beginning Afresh with Christ in the Search for Abundant Life in Africa." In *The Church as Salt and Light: Path to an African Ecclesiology of Abundant Life*, edited by Stan Chu Ilo, Joseph Ogbonnaya, and Alex Ojacor, 1–33. Pickwick, 2011.

———. "Conclusion." In *The Church as Salt and Light: Path to an African Ecclesiology of Abundant Life*, edited by Stan Chu Ilo, Joseph Ogbonnaya, and Alex Ojacor, 149–56. Pickwick, 2011.

———. "Depolarizing Catholic Ecclesiology: Mediation between the Theologies of *Communio* and *Concilium* in Uzukwu." In *Under the Palaver Tree: Doing African Ecclesiology in the Spirit of Vatican II—The Contributions of Elochukwu E. Uzukwu*, edited by Stan Chu Ilo and Caroline N. Mbonu, 120–46. Pickwick, 2023.

———. *A Poor and Merciful Church: The Illuminative Ecclesiology of Pope Francis*. Orbis, 2018.

International Theological Commission. *Synodality in the Life and Mission of the Church*. vatican.va.

Irenaeus of Lyons. *Against the Heresies*. Translated by Dominic J. Unger, OFM Cap., with Irenaeus M. Steenberg. Paulist, 2012.

———. *On the Apostolic Preaching*. Translated by John Behr. St. Vladimir's Seminary Press, 1997.

Isasi-Díaz, Ada Maria. *En La Lucha/In the Struggle: Elaborating a Mujerista Theology*. Fortress, 2004.

Ivereigh, Austen. "Foreword: Embracing Synodal Conversion." In *Witnesses of Synodality: Good Practices and Experiences*, edited by Jos Moons, SJ, ix–xiii. Paulist, 2024.

Ivereigh, Austen. *The Great Reformer: Francis and the Making of a Radical Pope*. Henry Holt, 2014.

Jenson, Robert W. *Systematic Theology*. Vol. 2, *The Works of God*. Oxford University Press, 1999.

Jerome. *Exegetical Epistles, Volume 1*. Translated by Thomas P. Scheck. The Catholic University of America Press, 2023.

John Paul II. *Ad Tuendam Fidem*. Apostolic letter, May 18 1998, vatican.va.

———. *Ecclesia in Africa*. Apostolic exhortation, September 14, 1995, vatican.va.

———. *Ecclesia de Eucharistia*. Encyclical letter, April 17, 2003, vatican.va.

———. *Ordinatio Sacerdotalis*. Apostolic letter, May 22, 1994, vatican.va.

Johnson, Ella. *This Is My Body: Eucharistic Theology and Anthropology in the Writings of Gertrude the Great of Helfta*. Liturgical, 2020.

Johnson, Luke Timothy. *The First and Second Letters to Timothy: A New Translation with Introduction and Commentary*. Yale University Press, 2001.

———. *Imitating Christ: The Disputed Character of Christian Discipleship*. Eerdmans, 2024.

Journet, Charles. *The Church of the Word Incarnate: An Essay in Speculative Theology*. Vol. 1, *The Apostolic Hierarchy*. Edited by Matthew K. Minerd. Translated by A. H. C. Downes. Emmaus Academic, 2025.

———. *The Church of the Word Incarnate: An Essay in Speculative Theology*. Vol. 2, *The Internal Structure of the Church*. Translated by Matthew K. Minerd. Emmaus Academic, 2025.

———. *L'Église du Verbe incarné: Essai de théologie speculative*. Vol. 3, *Sa structure interne et son unité catholique (Deuxième partie)*. Editions Saint-Augustin, 2000.

Journet, Charles. "Sancta Mater Ecclesia." In *Dictionnaire de spiritualité*, vol. 4/1, col. 460–68. Beauchesne, 1961.

Julian of Norwich. *Showings*. Translated by Edmund Colledge, OSA, and James Walsh, SJ. Paulist, 1978.

Jürgensmeier, Friedrich. *Der mystische Leib Christi als Grundprinzip der Aszetik*. Schöningh, 1933.

Kaiser, Robert Blair. *Inside the Jesuits: How Pope Francis Is Changing the Church and the World*. Rowman & Littlefield, 2014.

Kamali, Mohammad Hashim. *Shari'ah Law: An Introduction*. Oneworld, 2008.

Kaminsky, Joel S. *Yet I Loved Jacob: Reclaiming the Biblical Concept of Election*. Abingdon, 2007.

Kantorowicz, E. H. *The King's Two Bodies: A Study in Medieval Political Theology*. Princeton University Press, 1957.

Käppeli, Thomas. *Zur Lehre des hl. Thomas von Aquin vom Corpus Christi mysticum*. Bonifatius-Druckerei, 1931.

Kärkkäinen, Veli-Matti. *An Introduction to Ecclesiology*. 2nd ed. IVP Academic, 2021.

Käsemann, Ernst. *Die wandernde Gottesvolk: Eine Untersuchung zum Hebräerbrief*. Vandenhoeck & Ruprecht, 1938.

Kasper, Walter. "The Apostolic Succession: An Ecumenical Problem." In *Leadership in the Church: How Traditional Roles Can Serve the Christian Community Today*, translated by Brian McNeil, 114–43. Crossroad, 2003.

Katongole, Emmanuel. *Born from Lament: The Theology and Politics of Hope in Africa*. Eerdmans, 2017.

———. "The Church of the Future: Pressing Moral Issues from *Ecclesia in Africa*." In *The Church We Want: African Catholics Look to Vatican III*, edited by Agbonkhianmeghe E. Orobator, SJ. Orbis, 2016.

Katongole, Emmanuel. "Of Coffins and Churches: Seven Marks of an Emerging African Ecclesiology." In *The Church We Want: African Catholics Look to Vatican III*, edited by Agbonkhianmeghe E. Orobator, SJ, 190–202. Orbis, 2016.

———. *The Sacrifice of Africa: A Political Theology for Africa.* Eerdmans, 2011.

Katongole, Emmanuel, with Jonathan Wilson-Hartgrove. *Mirror to the Church: Resurrecting Faith after Genocide in Rwanda.* Zondervan, 2009.

Kereszty, Roch, O.Cist. "Synodality, the Magisterium, and the Faith of the People of God." *Communio* 48 (2021): 638–62.

Kerr, Fergus, OP. "Church: Brotherhood and Eschatology." *New Blackfriars* 51, no. 598 (March 1970): 144–54.

King, Karen L. *What Is Gnosticism?* Harvard University Press, 2003.

Kirwan, Jon. *An Avant-garde Theological Generation: The* Nouvelle Théologie *and the French Crisis of Modernity.* Oxford University Press, 2018.

Kirwan, Jon, and Matthew K. Minerd. "Translators' Introduction: A Dialogue Delayed." In *The Thomistic Response to the Nouvelle Théologie: Concerning the Truth of Dogma and the Nature of Theology*, edited and translated by Jon Kirwan and Matthew K. Minerd, 1–85. The Catholic University of America Press, 2023.

Kirwan, Michael, SJ. "'Speaking Well': Euphemistic Theology and the Synodal Way." In *Synodality and the Recovery of Vatican II: A New Way for Catholics*, edited by Stephen J. McKinney, Thomas O'Loughlin, and Beáta Tóth, 135–47. Messenger Publications, 2024.

Knops, Stephan. "Die Würzburger Synode: Krisenindiz—Zeitdiagnose—Zukunftsplan." In *Synodalität in der katholischen Kirche: Die Studie der Internationalen Theologischen Kommission im Diskurs*, edited by Markus Graulich and Johanna Rahner, 136–52. Herder, 2020.

Knorn, Bernhard, SJ. "The Church and the Churches: Ecclesiology and the View of Non-Catholic Christians in the Roman School." In *The Roman School: Nineteenth-Century Jesuit Theology and Its Achievements*, edited by Aaron Pidel, SJ, Matthew Levering, and Justin M. Anderson, 35–77. Brill, 2024.

Kocian, Pierre, OSB. *Marie et l'église: Compénétration des deux mystères*. Parole et Silence, 2018.

Kocik, Thomas M. *Apostolic Succession in an Ecumenical Context*. Alba House, 1996.

Kombo, James Henry Owino. *The Doctrine of God in African Christian Thought*. Brill, 2007.

Komonchak, Joseph A. "*Humani Generis* and *Nouvelle Théologie*." In *Ressourcement: A Movement for Renewal in Twentieth-Century Catholic Theology*, edited by Gabriel Flynn and Paul D. Murray, 138–56. Oxford University Press, 2012.

Koster, Mannes D., OP. *Ekklesiologie im Werden*. Bonifacius-Druckerei, 1940.

Krokus, Christian S. *The Theology of Louis Massignon: Islam, Christ, and the Church*. The Catholic University of America Press, 2017.

Küng, Hans. *Can We Save the Catholic Church?* William Collins, 2013.

———. *The Church*. Translated by Ray and Rosaleen Ockenden. Sheed and Ward, 1967.

———. *The Church—Maintained in Truth: A Theological Meditation*. Translated by Edward Quinn. Seabury, 1980.

———. *Infallible: An Unresolved Enquiry*. New expanded edition. Translated by Eric Mosbacher, Edward Quinn, and John Bowden. Continuum, 1994.

———. "Is the Second Vatican Council Forgotten?" Translated by Natalie K. Watson. In *Vatican II: A Forgotten Future*, edited by Alberto Melloni and Christoph Theobald, *Concilium* 2005/4, 108–17. SCM, 2005.

Küng, Hans. *On Being a Christian*. Doubleday, 1976.

———. *Structures of the Church*. Translated by Salvator Attanasio. Thomas Nelson, 1964.

Küng, Hans, and Walter Kasper, eds. *The Plurality of Ministries*. *Concilium* 74. Herder and Herder, 1972.

Kupczak, Jarosław, OP. *Before* Amoris Laetitia*: The Sources of the Controversy*. Translated by Grzegorz Ignatik. The Catholic University of America Press, 2021.

Kwasniewski, Peter A. *Bound by Truth: Authority, Obedience, Tradition, and the Common Good*. Angelico, 2023.

———. *The Road from Hyperpapalism to Catholicism: Rethinking the Papacy in a Time of Ecclesial Disintegration*. Vol. 1, *Theological Reflections on the Rock of the Church*. Arouca, 2022.

Lacey, Michael J., and Francis Oakley, eds. *The Crisis of Authority in Catholic Modernity*. Oxford University Press, 2011.

Lamb, Matthew L., and Matthew Levering, eds. *The Reception of Vatican II*. Oxford University Press, 2017.

———. *Vatican II: Renewal within Tradition*. Oxford University Press, 2008.

Langland, William. *Piers Plowman: The C Version*. Translated by George Economou. University of Pennsylvania Press, 1996.

Lash, Nicholas. "Theologies at the Service of a Common Tradition." In *Different Theologies, Common Responsibility: Babel or Pentecost?*, edited by Claude Geffré, Gustavo Gutiérrez, and Virgil Elizondo, English edition edited by Marcus Lefébure, *Concilium* 171, 74–83. T&T Clark, 1984.

Laurentin, René. *La Vierge au concile*. Éditions du Seuil, 1965.

Le Guillou, M. J., OP. *Christ and Church: A Theology of the Mystery*. Translated by Charles E. Schaldenbrand. Desclee, 1966.

Leahy, Brendan. *The Marian Profile in the Ecclesiology of Hans Urs von Balthasar*. New City, 2000.

Lee, James K. "Patristic Ecclesiology in the Latin West." In *T&T Clark Handbook of Ecclesiology*, edited by Kimlyn J. Bender and D. Stephen Long. Bloomsbury, 2020.

Legge, Dominic, OP. *The Trinitarian Christology of St Thomas Aquinas*. Oxford University Press, 2017.

Legrand, Hervé. "La sinodalità, dimensione inerente alla vita ecclesiale: Fondamenti ed attualità." *Vivens Homo* 15 (2005): 5–42.

Lehner, Ulrich, L. "The Ecumenical Vision of Beda Mayr, OSB (1742–1794)." In Beda Mayr, OSB, *A Defense of the Catholic Religion: The Necessity, Existence, and Limits of an Infallible Church*, translated by Ulrich L. Lehner, 1–20. The Catholic University of America Press, 2023.

Leithart, Peter J. *Revelation 12–22*. Bloomsbury, 2018.

———. *Traces of the Trinity: Signs of God in Creation and Human Experience*. Brazos, 2015.

Lemna, Keith. "The Synod on Synodality in Light of Pope Francis's Theology of Mission." *Nova et Vetera* 21 (2023): 509–39.

Levenson, Jon D. *The Hebrew Bible, the Old Testament, and Historical Criticism: Jews and Christians in Biblical Studies*. Westminster John Knox, 1993.

———. *The Love of God: Divine Gift, Human Gratitude, and Mutual Faithfulness in Judaism*. Princeton University Press, 2016.

Levering, Matthew. *The Abuse of Conscience: A Century of Catholic Moral Theology*. Eerdmans, 2021.

———. *Aquinas's Eschatological Ethics and the Virtue of Temperance*. University of Notre Dame Press, 2019.

———. *The Betrayal of Charity: The Sins that Sabotage Divine Love*. Baylor University Press, 2011.

———. *Christ and the Catholic Priesthood: Ecclesial Hierarchy and the Pattern of the Trinity*. Hillenbrand Books, 2010.

Levering, Matthew. "The Christian Bible and the Promised Land." In *The Challenge of Catholic-Jewish Theological Dialogue*, edited by Matthew Tapie, Alan Brill, and Matthew Levering, 275–300. The Catholic University of America Press, 2025.

———. "The Church as Temple of the Spirit: Is There Room for Magisterial Error?" *Communio* 50 (2023): 7–36.

———. *Did Jesus Rise from the Dead? Historical and Theological Reflections*. Oxford University Press, 2019.

———. *Engaging the Doctrine of the Holy Spirit: Love and Gift in the Trinity and the Church*. Baker Academic, 2016.

———. *Engaging the Doctrine of Israel: A Christian Israelology in Dialogue with Ongoing Judaism*. Cascade, 2021.

———. *Engaging the Doctrine of Jesus (and Mary): A Traditional, Historical-Critical, and Mariological Christology*. Cascade, 2025.

———. *Engaging the Doctrine of Marriage: Human Marriage as the Sign and Sacrament of the Marriage of God and Creation*. Cascade, 2020.

———. *Engaging the Doctrine of Revelation: The Mediation of the Gospel through Church and Scripture*. Baker Academic, 2014.

———. *An Introduction to Vatican II as an Ongoing Theological Event*. The Catholic University of America Press, 2017.

———. "Natural Law in Bénézet Bujo, Paulinus Odozor, and Stephen L. Brock." In *Continuing the Quest for Morality Truly Christian, Truly African: The Achievement of Paulinus Odozor, C.S.Sp.*, edited by Maurice A. Agbaw-Ebai and Matthew Levering. St. Augustine's Press, forthcoming.

———. *Newman on Doctrinal Corruption*. Word on Fire Academic, 2022.

———. *Reconfiguring Thomistic Christology*. Cambridge University Press, 2023.

———. *Sacrifice and Community: Jewish Offering and Christian Eucharist*. Blackwell, 2005.

Levering, Matthew. "What God qua God Must Do: Providence, Predestination, and the Limits of *Sacra Doctrina*." In *Love Become Incarnate: Essays in Honor of Bruce D. Marshall*, edited by Justus H. Hunter, T. Adam Van Wart, and David L. Whidden III, 193–213. Emmaus Academic, 2023.

———. *Why I Am Roman Catholic*. IVP Academic, 2024.

Levering, Matthew, and Jeffrey L. Morrow, eds. *Catholic Modernism: Tyrrell, Loisy, and the Ongoing Challenge to Dogmatic Christianity*. Emmaus Academic, forthcoming.

Lévy, Bernard-Henri. *The Genius of Judaism*. Translated by Steven B. Kennedy. Random House, 2017.

Lewis, Bernard. *The Political Language of Islam*. University of Chicago Press, 1988.

Liégé, P. A., OP. "The Mystery of the Church." In *The Historical and Mystical Christ*, edited by A. M. Henry, OP, translated by Angeline Bouchard. Fides Publishers Association, 1958.

Lindbeck, George A. *The Church in a Postliberal Age*. Edited by James J. Buckley. Eerdmans, 2003.

Llosa, Alvaro Vargas. *Liberty for Latin America: How to Undo Five Hundred Years of State Oppression*. Farrar, Straus and Giroux, 2005.

———. *Rumbo a la Libertad: Por Qué la Izquierda y el "Neoliberalismo" Fracasan en América Latina*. Planeta, 2005.

Lohfink, Gerhard. *Does God Need the Church? Toward a Theology of the People of God*. Translated by Linda M. Maloney. Liturgical, 1999.

Loisy, Alfred. *The Gospel and the Church*. Translated by Christopher Home. Isbister, 1903.

Lombardi, Josephine. *Marian Approaches to Synodality*. Paulist, 2024.

Long, Steven A. *Analogia Entis: On the Analogy of Being, Metaphysics, and the Act of Faith*. University of Notre Dame Press, 2011.

Luciani, Rafael. *Francis and the Theology of the People*. Orbis Books, 2017.

———. *Synodality: A New Way of Proceeding in the Church*. Translated by Joseph Owens, SJ. Paulist, 2022.

Lusvardi, Anthony R., SJ. *Baptism of Desire and Christian Salvation*. The Catholic University of America Press, 2024.

Luther, Martin. "On the Councils and the Church." Translated by Charles M. Jacobs with revisions by Eric W. Gritsch. In *Luther's Works*, vol. 41, *Church and Ministry III*, edited by Eric W. Gritsch, 9–178. Fortress, 1966.

Lynch, Patrick, SJ. "Servant Ecclesiologies: A Challenge to Rahner's Understanding of Church and World." *Irish Theological Quarterly* 57 (1991): 277–98.

Madrigal, Santiago, SJ. *Karl Rahner y Joseph Ratzinger: Tras las huellas del Concilio*. Sal Terrae, 2006.

Magesa, Laurenti. "The Future of the African Synod." In *The African Synod: Documents, Reflections, Perspectives*, edited by Maura Browne, SND, and the Africa Faith and Justice Network, 163–71. Orbis, 1996.

Maldari, Donald C., SJ. *Christian Ministry in the Divine Milieu: Catholicity, Evolution, and the Reign of God*. Orbis, 2019.

Malloy, Christopher J. "Rahner: The Withering of Faith." In *The Faith Once and for All Delivered: Doctrinal Authority in Catholic Theology*, edited by Kevin L. Flannery, SJ, 31–68. Emmaus Academic, 2023.

Mannion, Gerard, ed. *Pope Francis and the Future of Catholicism:* Evangelii Gaudium *and the Papal Agenda*. Cambridge University Press, 2017.

———. "A Teaching Church That Learns?: Discerning 'Authentic' Teaching in Our Times." In *The Crisis of Authority in Catholic Modernity*, edited by Michael J. Lacey and Francis Oakley, 161–92. Oxford University Press, 2011.

Mansini, Guy, OSB. *The Development of Dogma: A Systematic Account*. The Catholic University of America Press, 2023.

Mansini, Guy, OSB. *Ecclesiology*. The Catholic University of America Press, 2021.

———. "Episcopal Conferences and the Local Renewal of Sacramental Doctrine." In *The Faith Once and for All Delivered: Doctrinal Authority in Catholic Theology*, edited by Kevin L. Flannery, SJ, 283–305. Emmaus Academic, 2023.

Maritain, Jacques. *On the Church of Christ: The Person of the Church and Her Personnel*. Translated by Joseph W. Evans. University of Notre Dame Press, 1973.

Marmion, Columba, OSB. *Christ, the Life of the Soul*. Translated by Alan Bancroft. Zaccheus, 2005.

Marschler, Thomas. "Zeichen der Zeit als neuer *locus theologicus*?" In *Jesus Christus—Alpha und Omega: Für Helmut Hoping*, edited by Jan-Heiner Tück and Magnus Striet, 38–56. Herder, 2021.

Marshall, Bruce D. "The Whole Mystery of Our Salvation: Saint Thomas Aquinas on the Eucharist as Sacrifice." In *Rediscovering Aquinas and the Sacraments: Studies in Sacramental Theology*, edited by Matthew Levering and Michael Dauphinais, 39–64. Hillenbrand Books, 2009.

Martín, Gonzalo Barbed. *Una anciana muy joven: Historia de la Iglesia*. Ediciones Palabra, 2022.

Martin, Jennifer Newsome. "Neo-Thomist and *Ressourcement* Theology." In *The Oxford Handbook of Deification*, edited by Paul L. Gavrilyuk, Andrew Hofer, OP, and Matthew Levering, 480–98. Oxford: Oxford University Press, 2024.

Martin, Ralph. *Will Many Be Saved? What Vatican II Actually Teaches and Its Implications for the New Evangelization*. Eerdmans, 2012.

Martyn, J. Louis. *Galatians: A New Translation with Introduction and Commentary*. Yale University Press, 1997.

Mascall, E. L. *Christ, the Christian and the Church: A Study of the Incarnation and Its Consequences*. Longmans, Green, 1946.

Mascall, E. L. *Corpus Christi: Essays on the Church and the Eucharist*. 2nd ed. Longmans, Green, 1965.

Matera, Frank J. *New Testament Ethics: The Legacies of Jesus and Paul*. Westminster John Knox, 1996.

Maurus, Hrabanus. *On the Formation of Clergy*. Translated by Owen M. Phelan. The Catholic University of America Press, 2023.

Mbuy-Beya, Bernadette. "Women in the Churches in Africa: Possibilities for Presence and Promises." In *The African Synod: Documents, Reflections, Perspectives*, edited by Maura Browne, SND, and the Africa Faith and Justice Network, 175–87. Orbis, 1996.

McBrien, Richard P. *Church: The Continuing Quest*. Newman, 1970.

———. *Do We Need the Church?* Harper & Row, 1969.

———. *The Remaking of the Church: An Agenda for Reform*. Harper & Row, 1973.

McCann, Dennis P. *New Experiment in Democracy: The Challenge for American Catholicism*. Sheed & Ward, 1987.

McCue, James F. "Apostles and Apostolic Succession in the Patristic Era." In *Eucharist and Ministry*, edited by Paul C. Empie and T. Austin Murphy, 138–77. United States Catholic Conference, 1970.

McCullough, Ross. *Freedom and Sin: Evil in a World Created by God*. Eerdmans, 2022.

McGrath, Alister E. *The Nature of Christian Doctrine: Its Origins, Development, and Function*. Oxford University Press, 2024.

McGreevy, John T. *Catholicism: A Global History from the French Revolution to Pope Francis*. Norton, 2022.

McGuckin, John Anthony. *The Path of Christianity: The First Thousand Years*. IVP Academic, 2017.

McGuire, Brian Patrick. *Bernard of Clairvaux: An Inner Life*. Cornell University Press, 2020.

McIntosh, Mark A. *Divine Teaching: An Introduction to Christian Theology*. Blackwell, 2008.

McQueen, Moira. *Walking Together: A Primer on the New Synodality*. Novalis, 2022.

McWhirter, Jocelyn. *The Bridegroom Messiah and the People of God: Marriage in the Fourth Gospel*. Cambridge University Press, 2006.

Meiers, Anna Elisabeth. *Eschatos Adam: Zentrale Aspekte der Christologie bei Joseph Ratzinger/Benedikt XVI*. Friedrich Pustet, 2019.

Menke, Karl-Heinz. "Hans Küngs Definition der Kirche als Synode und das ITC-Dokument 'Synodalität in Leben und Sendung der Kirche.'" In *Synodalität in der katholischen Kirche: Die Studie der Internationalen Theologischen Kommission im Diskurs*, edited by Markus Graulich and Johanna Rahner, 196–219. Herder, 2020.

Mersch, Emile, SJ. *The Whole Christ: The Historical Development of the Doctrine of the Mystical Body in Scripture and Tradition*. Translated by John R. Kelly, SJ. Bruce, 1938.

Merton, Thomas. *The Living Bread*. Farrar, Straus & Giroux, 1956.

Mettepenningen, Jürgen. *Nouvelle Théologie—New Theology: Inheritor of Modernism, Precursor of Vatican II*. Continuum, 2010.

Metz, Johann Baptist. *Theology of the World*. Seabury, 1969.

Michel, Virgil, OSB. *Christian Social Reconstruction: Some Fundamentals of the* Quadragesimo Anno. Bruce, 1937.

Michelet, Thomas, OP. "Deaconesses and Diaconate." Forthcoming in *Nova et Vetera* 23 (2025).

Milbank, John. *The Suspended Middle: Henri de Lubac and the Renewed Split in Modern Catholic Theology*. 2nd ed. Eerdmans, 2014.

Milliner, Matthew J. *Mother of the Lamb: The Story of a Global Icon*. Fortress, 2022.

Miranda, José Porfirio. *Communism in the Bible.* Translated by Robert R. Barr. Orbis, 1982.

Mitterer, Albert. *Geheimnisvoller Leib Christi nach St. Thomas von Aquin und nach Papst Pius XII.* Herold, 1950.

Möhler, Johann Adam. *Symbolism: Exposition of the Doctrinal Differences between Catholics and Protestants as Evidenced by Their Symbolical Writings.* Translated by James Burton Robinson. Crossroad, 1997.

———. *Unity in the Church, or, The Principle of Catholicism: Presented in the Spirit of the Church Fathers of the First Three Centuries.* Translated by Peter C. Erb. The Catholic University of America Press, 1996.

Moloney, Francis J., SDB. *The Gospel of John.* Liturgical, 1998.

Montero, Roman A. *All Things in Common: The Economic Practices of the Early Christians.* Wipf & Stock, 2017.

Morard, Martin. "Les expressions 'corpus mysticum' et 'persona mystica' dnas l'oeuvre de saint Thomas d'Aquin: Références et analyse." *Revue Thomiste* 95 (1995): 653–64.

Morerod, Charles, OP. "The Decree on Ecumenism." In *Vatican II: Renewal within Tradition*, edited by Matthew L. Lamb and Matthew Levering, 311–41. Oxford University Press, 2008.

Morra, Stella. *Dio non si stanca: La Misericordia come forma ecclesiale.* EDB, 2015.

Morrow, Jeffrey L. *Alfred Loisy and Modern Biblical Studies.* The Catholic University of America Press, 2018.

Moss, Candida R., and Joel S. Baden. *Reconceiving Infertility: Biblical Perspectives on Procreation and Childlessness.* Princeton University Press, 2015.

Msafiri, Aidan G. "The Church as Family Model: Strengths and Weaknesses." In *African Theology Today*, edited by Emmanuel Katongole, 85–98. University of Scranton Press, 2002.

Müller, Alois. *Ecclesia-Maria: Die Einheit Marias und der Kirche.* Universitätsverlag, 1951.

Müller, Gerhard Ludwig. "Das trinitarische Grundverständnis der Kirche in der Kirchenkonstitution 'Lumen Gentium.'" *Münchener Theologische Zeitschrift* 45 (1994): 451–65.

Murray, Paul, OP. *Saint Catherine of Siena: Mystic of Fire, Preacher of Freedom*. 2nd ed. Word on Fire, 2020.

Nelson, R. David, and Charles Raith II. *Ecumenism: A Guide for the Perplexed*. Bloomsbury, 2017.

Nepil, John L. *A Bride Adorned: Mary-Church* Perichoresis *in Modern Catholic Theology*. Emmaus Academic, 2023.

Neufeld, Karl Heinz. "Henri de Lubac SJ als Konzilstheologe." *Theologisch-Praktische Quartalschrift* 134 (1986): 149–59.

Newbigin, Lesslie. *The Household of God: Lectures on the Nature of the Church*. SCM, 1953.

Newman, John Henry. *Certain Difficulties Felt by Anglicans in Catholic Teaching*. Vol. 1. Longmans, Green, 1897.

———. *An Essay on the Development of Christian Doctrine* [1845]. Edited by Stanley L. Jaki. Real View Books, 2003.

Nguyen, Theresa Marie Chau, OP. *The Splendor of the Church in Mary: Henri de Lubac, Vatican II, and Marian Ressourcement*. The Catholic University of America Press, 2023.

Nichols, Aidan, OP. *Figuring Out the Church: Her Marks, and Her Masters*. Ignatius, 2013.

———. "Henri de Lubac: Panorama and Proposal." *New Blackfriars* 93 (2012): 3–33.

———. *The Thought of Pope Benedict XVI: An Introduction to the Theology of Joseph Ratzinger*. 2nd ed. Continuum, 2007.

Nicklas, Tobias. "All Must Interpret for All, and All Can Err: A Roman Catholic Perspective." In Stefan Alkier, Christos Karakolis, and Tobias Nicklas, *The Promise of Ecumenical Interpretation: Protestant, Catholic, Orthodox*, translated by Jacob N. Cerone and David M. Moffitt, 33–52. Fortress, 2024.

Nicklas, Tobias. "Together with the Lord on the Way to the Lord." In Stefan Alkier, Christos Karakolis, and Tobias Nicklas, *The Promise of Ecumenical Interpretation: Protestant, Catholic, Orthodox*, translated by Jacob N. Cerone and David M. Moffitt, 188–95. Fortress, 2024.

Nicolas, Jean-Hervé, OP. *Catholic Dogmatic Theology: A Synthesis*. Book 3, *On the Church and the Sacraments*. Translated by Matthew K. Minerd. The Catholic University of America Press, 2024.

Nicolas, M.-J., OP. *Théotokos. Le mystère de Marie*. Desclée, 1965.

Nji, Tegha Afuhwi. "*Africae Munus* in the Light of Prophetic Praxis: A Liberation Theology for Africa? A Critical Engagement with Ratzinger." In *Africae Munus: Ten Years Later*, edited by Maurice A. Agbaw-Ebai and Matthew Levering, 225–61. St. Augustine's Press, 2022.

Nkemngong, James. *Odozor: The Man, the Priest and the Scholar: Interview with Rev. Fr. Paulinus I. Odozor*. Privately printed, 2024.

Noble, Alan. *On Getting Out of Bed: The Burden and Gift of Living*. InterVarsity, 2023.

Noceti, Serena. *Reforming the Church: A Synodal Way of Proceeding*. Translated by Joseph Owens, SJ. Paulist, 2023.

Noonan, John T., Jr. *A Church That Can and Cannot Change: The Development of Catholic Moral Teaching*. University of Notre Dame Press, 2005.

Norris, Frank B. *God's Own People: An Introductory Study of the Church*. Helicon, 1962.

Novak, David. *The Election of Israel: The Idea of the Chosen People*. Cambridge University Press, 1995.

Nyamiti, Charles. *Studies in African Christian Theology*. Vol. 4, *Christ's Ancestral Mediation Through the Church Understood as God's Family: An Essay on African Ecclesiology*. CUEA, 2010.

Nyerere, Julius. *Ujamaa: Essays on Socialism*. Oxford University Press, 1968.

O'Collins, Gerald, SJ. "On Richard P. McBrien's *Do We Need the Church?*" *Heythrop Journal* 10 (1969): 416–19.

O'Gara, Margaret. "Apostolicity in Ecumenical Dialogue." *Mid-Stream* 37 (1998): 175–212.

O'Mahony, T. P. *Why the Catholic Church Needs Vatican III*. Columba, 2010.

O'Neill, Colman, OP. "St. Thomas on the Membership of the Church." *The Thomist* 27 (1963): 88–140.

O'Neill, John F. *Trinitarian Ecclesiology: Charles Journet, the Divine Missions, and the Mystery of the Church*. The Catholic University of America Press, 2024.

Oakley, Francis. *Council Over Pope? Towards a Provisional Ecclesiology*. Herder and Herder, 1969.

———. "History and the Return of the Repressed in Catholic Modernity: The Dilemma Posed by Constance." In *The Crisis of Authority in Catholic Modernity*, edited by Michael J. Lacey and Francis Oakley, 29–56. Oxford University Press, 2011.

Oakley, Francis, and Bruce Russett, eds. *Governance, Accountability, and the Future of the Catholic Church*. Continuum, 2004.

Obiezu, Emeka Xris, OSA. "The Church in Africa and the Search for Integral and Sustainable Development of Africa: Toward a Socio-Economic and Politically Responsive Church." In *The Church as Salt and Light: Path to an African Ecclesiology of Abundant Life*, edited by Stan Chu Ilo, Joseph Ogbonnaya, and Alex Ojacor, 34–64. Pickwick, 2011.

Odozor, Paulinus Ikechukwu, CSSp. "The Church as Family of God in Africa." In *Handbook of African Catholicism*, edited by Stan Chu Ilo, 573–85. Orbis, 2022.

Odozor, Paulinus Ikechukwu, CSSp. *Morality Truly Christian, Truly African: Foundational, Methodological, and Theological Considerations.* University of Notre Dame Press, 2014.

Oeldermann, Johannes. *Die Apostolizität der Kirche im ökumenischen Dialog mit der Orthodoxie: Der Beitrug russicher orthodoxer Theologen zum ökumenischen Gespräch über die apostolische Tradition und die Sukzession in der Kirche.* Bonifatius Verlag, 2000.

Ogbonnaya, Joseph. "The Church in Africa: Salt of the Earth?" In *The Church as Salt and Light: Path to an African Ecclesiology of Abundant Life*, edited by Stan Chu Ilo, Joseph Ogbonnaya, and Alex Ojacor, 65–87. Pickwick, 2011.

———. "Ecclesiological Developments in the Majority World." In *T&T Clark Handbook of Ecclesiology*, edited by Kimlyn J. Bender and D. Stephen Long, 274–89. Bloomsbury, 2020.

Ojacor, Alex. "The Church in Africa and the Search for Abundant Life: Signposts for Renewal and Transformation of God's People in Africa." In *The Church as Salt and Light: Path to an African Ecclesiology of Abundant Life*, edited by Stan Chu Ilo, Joseph Ogbonnaya, and Alex Ojacor, 88–98. Pickwick, 2011.

Okure, Teresa. "Church-Family of God: The Place of God's Reconciliation, Justice, and Peace." In *Reconciliation, Justice, and Peace: The Second African Synod*, edited by Agbonkhianmeghe E. Orobator, SJ, 13–24. Orbis, 2011.

Olson, Edwin E. *And God Created Wholeness: A Spirituality of Catholicity.* Orbis, 2018.

Onaiyekan, John Olorunfemi. "The Church in Africa Today: Reflections on the African Synod." In *The African Synod: Documents, Reflections, Perspectives*, edited by Maura Browne, SND, and the Africa Faith and Justice Network, 211–19. Orbis, 1996.

Onuoha, Martin. *Actio Divina: The Marian Mystery of the Church in Joseph Ratzinger's Theology.* Peter Lang, 2021.

Onwubiko, Oliver Alozie. *The Church in Mission in the Light of Ecclesia in Africa*. Paulines Publications Africa, 2001.

Origen. *Homilies on Isaiah*. Translated by Elizabeth Ann Dively Lauro. The Catholic University of America Press, 2021.

———. *Homilies on Psalms 36–38*. Translated by Michael Heintz. The Catholic University of America Press, 2023.

Orji, Cyril. *Unmasking the African Ghost: Theology, Politics, and the Nightmare of Failed States*. Fortress, 2022.

Ormerod, Neil. *Re-Visioning the Church: An Experiment in Systematic Historical Ecclesiology*. Fortress, 2014.

Orobator, Agbonkhianmeghe, SJ. *The Church as Family of God: African Ecclesiology in Its Social Context*. Paulines Publications Africa, 2000.

———. *From Crisis to Kairos: The Mission of the Church in the Time of HIV/AIDS, Refugees and Poverty*. Paulines Publications Africa, 2005.

———. *Religion and Faith in Africa: Confessions of an Animist*. Orbis, 2018.

Orthodox-Roman Catholic Consultation in the USA. "Apostolicity as God's Gift in the Life of the Church." In *The Quest for Unity: Orthodox and Catholics in Dialogue: Documents of the Joint International Commission and Official Dialogues in the United States 1965–1995*, edited by John Borelli and John H. Erickson, 125–30. St. Vladimir's Seminary Press, 1996.

Otu, Idara, MSP. *Communion Ecclesiology and Social Transformation in African Catholicism: Between Vatican Council II and African Synod II*. Pickwick, 2020.

Ounsworth, Richard, OP. *Joshua Typology in the New Testament*. Mohr Siebeck, 2012.

Parsch, Pius. *We Are Christ's Body*. Translated by Clifford Howell, SJ. Fides, 1962.

Patrick, Anne E., Bernard J. Cooke, and Diana L. Hayes. "Worship in the Spirit: A Renewed Vision of Liturgy and Spirituality." In *What's Left? Liberal American Catholics*, edited by Mary Jo Weaver, 155–75. Indiana University Press, 1999.

Payne, Daniel. "Read Pope Francis' Response to the 'Dubia' Presented to Him by 5 Cardinals." October 2, 2023, www.ncregister.com/cna/pope-francis-response-to-the-dubia.

Peet, John C. *The Politics of the Crucified: The Cross in the Political Theology of Yoder, Boff, and Sobrino*. Pickwick, 2021.

Pellitero, Ramiro. *Ecclesiología*. 2nd ed. EUNSA, 2019.

Perrier, Emmanuel, OP. "Fiducia supplicans face au sens de la foi." https://revuethomiste.fr/contenu-editorial/chroniques/lumieres-et-grains-de-sel/fiducia-supplicans-face-au-sens-de-la-foi, accessed January 6, 2025.

Perrone, Giovanni. *Praelectiones Theologicae*. Vol. 1. Leroux, Jouby, 1854.

Pesch, Otto Hermann. *Thomas von Aquin: Grenze und Größe mittelalterlicher Theologie*. Matthias Grünewald, 1989.

Peter Chrysologus. *Selected Sermons, Volume 3*. Translated by William B. Palardy. The Catholic University of America Press, 2005.

Petráček, Tomáš. *The Bible and the Crisis of Modernism: Catholic Criticism in the Twentieth Century*. Translated by David Livingstone and Addison Hart. University of Notre Dame Press, 2022.

Phan, Peter C. *In Our Own Tongues: Perspectives from Asia on Mission and Inculturation*. Orbis Books, 2003.

———. "World Christianity: Its Implications for History, Religious Studies, and Theology." *Horizons* 39 (2012): 171–88.

Philippe de la Trinité, OCD. *What Is Redemption? How Christ's Suffering Saves Us*. Translated by Anthony Armstrong, OSB. Emmaus Road, 2021.

Philips, Gérard. "The Church in the Modern World." In *The Church and the World*, edited by Johannes B. Metz, *Concilium* 6, 5–22. Paulist, 1965.

———. "Mariologische Perspectieven: Maria en de Kerk." *Mariale Dagen* 12 (1953): 9–78.

Pidel, Aaron, SJ. *Church of the Ever Greater God: The Ecclesiology of Erich Przywara*. University of Notre Dame Press, 2020.

———. "The Church of the 'Few' for the 'Many': Ratzinger's Missiology of Vicarious Representation." In *Joseph Ratzinger and the Healing of the Reformation-Era Divisions*, edited by Emery de Gaál and Matthew Levering, 297–318. Emmaus Academic, 2019.

Pié-Ninot, Salvador. *Eclesiología: La Sacramentalidad de la Comunidad Cristiana*. 3rd ed. Sígueme, 2006.

———. *Hacia el "Primado Sinodal y Diaconal" del Papa Francisco: Documentos Histórico-eclesiológicos del Ministerio Petrino*. BAC, 2021.

———. *La Sinodalidad como el "Caminar Juntos" en la Iglesia*. Centre de Pastoral Litúrgica, 2021.

———. *La Sinodalitat Eclesial: "L'Església té nom de Sínode.* Facultad de Teologia, 1993.

Pinckaers, Servais, OP. "La morale et l'Église Corps du Christ." *Revue Thomiste* 100 (2000): 239–58.

Pitre, Brant. *Jesus the Bridegroom: The Greatest Love Story Ever Told*. Image, 2014.

———. *Jesus and the Last Supper*. Eerdmans, 2015.

Pitre, Brant, Michael P. Barber, and John A. Kincaid. *Paul, a New Covenant Jew: Rethinking Pauline Theology*. Eerdmans, 2019.

Pius X. *Pascendi Dominici Gregis*. Encyclical letter, September 8, 1907, vatican.va.

———. "Syllabus Condemning the Errors of the Modernists *Lamentabili Sane*." 1907, https://www.papalencyclicals.net/pius10/p10lamen.htm.

Pius XII. *Humani Generis*. Translated by N.C.W.C. Pauline Books, 1950.

———. *Mystici Corporis*. Encyclical letter, June 29, 1943, vatican.va.

Plate, Manfred. *Das deutsche Konzil: Die Würzburger Synode. Bericht und Deutung*. Herder, 1975.

Plumpe, J. C. *Mater Ecclesia: An Inquiry into the Concept of the Church as Mother in Early Christianity*. The Catholic University of America Press, 1943.

Prevot, Andrew. "Henri de Lubac (1896–1991) and Contemporary Mystical Theology." In *A Companion to Jesuit Mysticism*, edited by Robert A. Maryks, 279–309. Brill, 2017.

———. *The Mysticism of Ordinary Life: Theology, Philosophy, and Feminism*. Oxford University Press, 2023.

Procopius. *The Secret History*. Translated by G. A. Williamson and Peter Sarris. Penguin, 2007.

Prügl, Thomas. "Synodality and the Conciliar Tradition of the Church: Medieval and Early Modern Experiences of Synodality." *The Thomist* 87 (2023): 191–210.

Przywara, Erich, SJ. *Christentum gemäß Johannes*. Glock und Lutz, 1954.

———. *Katholische Krise*. Edited by Bernard Gertz. Patmos, 1967.

Putz, Oliver. "'I Did Not Change; They Did!': Joseph Ratzinger, Karl Rahner and the Second Vatican Council." *New Wineskins* 2 (2007): 11–31.

Quanbeck, Warran A. "A Contemporary View of Apostolic Succession." In *Lutherans and Catholics in Dialogue*, vol. 4, *Eucharist and Ministry*, edited by Paul C. Empie and T. Austin Murphy, 178–88. U.S.A. National Committee of the Lutheran World Federation, 1970.

Queiruga, Andrés Torres. "Vatican II and Theology." In *Vatican II: A Forgotten Future*, edited by Alberto Melloni and Christoph Theobald, *Concilium* 2005/4, 21–33. SCM, 2005.

Raby, Elyse J. "Beyond 'Women in the Church': Gender and Ecclesiology since Vatican II." In *Vatican II at 60: Re-Energizing the Renewal*, edited by Catherine E. Clifford with Stephen Lampe, 115–34. Orbis Books, 2024.

Radcliffe, Timothy, OP. *Listening Together: Meditations on Synodality*. Liturgical, 2024.

———. *What Is the Point of Being a Christian?* Burns & Oates, 2005.

Radner, Ephraim. *Church*. Cascade, 2017.

———. *A Brutal Unity: The Spiritual Politics of the Christian Church*. Baylor University Press, 2012.

———. *The End of the Church: A Pneumatology of Christian Division in the West*. Eerdmans, 1998.

———. *Mortal Goods: Reimagining Christian Political Duty*. Baker Academic, 2024.

———. *A Profound Ignorance: Modern Pneumatology and Its Anti-Modern Redemption*. Baylor University Press, 2019.

———. *A Time to Keep: Theology, Mortality, and the Shape of a Human Life*. Baylor University Press, 2016.

———. *Time and the Word: Figural Reading of the Christian Scriptures*. Eerdmans, 2016.

Radner, Ephraim, and David Ney, eds. *All Thy Lights Combine: Figural Reading in the Anglican Tradition*. Lexham, 2022.

Rahner, Hugo, SJ. *Mater Ecclesiae: Lobpreis aus dem ersten Jahrtausend christlicher Literatur*. Benzinger, 1944.

———. *Our Lady and the Church*. Translated by Sebastian Bullough, OP. Zaccheus, 2004.

Rahner, Johanna. "Glaubenskrise?—Gotteskrise?—Kirchenkrise? Versuch einer aktuellen Standortbestimmung." In *Begegnungen—Entgegnungen: Beiträge zur modernen Gottesfrage, kontextuellen Theologie und Ökumene: Festgabe für Ulrike Link-Wieczorek zum 60. Geburtstag*, edited by Johanna Rahner and Andrea Strübind, 93–109. Evangelische Verlagsanstalt, 2015.

Rahner, Johanna. "Klerus und Laien: Genese und Transformation eines typisch katholischen Paradigmas." In *Synodalität in der katholischen Kirche: Die Studie der Internationalen Theologischen Kommission im Diskurs*, edited by Markus Graulich and Johanna Rahner, 170–95. Herder, 2020.

Rahner, Johanna, and Thomas Söding, eds. *Kirche und Welt—Ein Notwendiger Dialog. Stimmen katholischer Theologie*. Herder, 2019.

Rahner, Karl, SJ. *The Christian Commitment: Essays in Pastoral Theology*. Translated by Cecily Hastings. Sheed and Ward, 1963.

———. *The Christian of the Future*. Herder and Herder, 1967.

———. "Christianity and Ideology." In *The Church and the World*, edited by Johannes B. Metz, *Concilium* 6, 41–58. Paulist, 1965.

———. "Christianity and the New Earth." *Theology Digest* 15 (1967): 275–82.

———. *The Church after the Council*. Translated by Davis C. Herron and Rodelinde Albrecht. Herder and Herder, 1966.

———. "Church and World." In *Sacramentum Mundi: An Encyclopedia of Theology*, 6 vols., 1:346–57. Herder and Herder, 1968–1970.

———. "Considerations of the Active Role of the Person in the Sacramental Event." In Karl Rahner and Johann Baptist Metz, *Finding God in a World Come of Age*, edited by Roger Haight, SJ, Alfred Pach III, and Amanda Avila Kaminski, 49–80. Fordham University Press, 2024.

———. *Investigations*. Vol. 22, *Humane Society and the Church of Tomorrow*. Translated by Joseph Donceel. Crossroad, 1991.

———. *Meditations on Freedom and the Spirit*. Seabury, 1978.

———. *The Shape of the Church to Come*. Translated by Edward Quinn. Seabury, 1974.

———. *Theological Investigations*. Vol. 11, *Confrontations 1*. Translated by David Bourke. Seabury, 1974.

Rahner, Karl, SJ. *Theological Investigations.* Vol. 14, *Ecclesiology, Questions in the Church, the Church in the World.* Translated by David Bourke. Seabury, 1976.

———. *Theological Investigations.* Vol. 18, *God and Revelation.* Translated by Edward Quinn. Crossroad, 1983.

———. *Theological Investigations.* Vol. 20, *Concern for the Church.* Translated by Edward Quinn. Seabury, 1981.

———. "Towards a Fundamental Theological Interpretation of Vatican II." *Theological Studies* 40 (1979): 716–27.

Ratzinger, Joseph. "Announcements and Prefatory Notes of Explanation." In *Commentary on the Documents of Vatican II*, vol. 1, edited by Herbert Vorgrimler, translated by Lalit Adolphus, Kevin Smyth, and Richard Strachan, 297–305. Herder and Herder, 1967.

———. *Called to Communion: Understanding the Church Today.* Translated by Adrian Walker. Ignatius, 1996.

———. *Church, Ecumenism and Politics: New Essays in Ecclesiology.* Translated by Robert Nowell. Crossroad, 1988.

———. *Das neue Volk Gottes: Entwürfe zur Ekklesiologie.* Patmos, 1969.

———. "The Ecclesiology of Vatican II." *Conference of Cardinal Ratzinger at the Opening of the Pastoral Congress of the Diocese of Aversa (Italy).* September 15, 2001. *L'Osservatore Romano,* weekly edition in English, January 23, 2002.

———. *"In the Beginning . . .": A Catholic Understanding of the Story of Creation and the Fall.* Translated by Boniface Ramsey, OP. Eerdmans, 1995.

———. *Many Religions—One Covenant: Israel, the Church, and the World.* Translated by Graham Harrison. Ignatius, 1999.

———. *The Meaning of Christian Brotherhood.* Ignatius, 1993.

———. *Milestones: Memoirs 1927–1977.* Translated by Erasmo Leiva-Merikakis. Ignatius, 1998.

Ratzinger, Joseph. "On the Position of Mariology and Marian Spirituality in the Totality of Faith and Theology." In *The Church and Women: A Compendium*, edited by H. Moll, 67–81. Ignatius, 1988.

———. *Pilgrim Fellowship of Faith: The Church as Communion.* Translated by Henry Taylor. Ignatius, 2005.

———. *Principles of Catholic Theology: Building Stones for a Fundamental Theology.* Translated by Mary Frances McCarthy. Ignatius, 1987.

———. *Volk und Haus Gottes in Augustins Lehre von der Kirche.* St. Ottilien, 1954.

Ratzinger, Joseph, and Hans Maier. *Demokratie in der Kirche: Möglichen und Grenzen*. Lohn, 2000.

Rausch, Thomas P. *Authority and Leadership in the Church: Past Directions and Future Possibilities*. Glazier, 1989.

Raymond of Capua. *The Life of St. Catherine of Siena*. Translated by George Lamb. TAN, 2003.

Reese, Ephrem, OP. "Congar's Imperfect Critique of 'Hierarchiology'." *Nova et Vetera* 20 (2022): 545–74.

Reese, Thomas, SJ, ed. *The Universal Catechism Reader: Reflections and Responses*. HarperCollins, 1990.

Resnick, Irven M. *Marks of Distinction: Christian Perceptions of Jews in the High Middle Ages*. The Catholic University of America Press, 2022.

Riches, Aaron. "Henri de Lubac and the Second Vatican Council." In *T&T Clark Companion to Henri de Lubac*, edited by Jordan Hillebert, 121–56. Bloomsbury, 2017.

Rikhof, Herwi. "Thomas on the Church: Reflections on a Sermon." In *Aquinas on Doctrine: A Critical Introduction*, edited by Thomas G. Weinandy, OFM Cap., Daniel A. Keating, and John P. Yocum, 199–223. T&T Clark International, 2004.

Rist, John M. *Infallibility, Integrity and Obedience: The Papacy and the Roman Catholic Church, 1848–2023*. James Clarke, 2023.

———. *What Is Truth? From the Academy to the Vatican*. Cambridge University Press, 2008.

Rivella, Mauro, ed. *Partecipazione e corresponsabilità nella Chiesa: I Consigli diocesani e parrochiali*. Àncora, 2000.

Roelvink, Henrik. "The Apostolic Succession in the Porvoo Statement." *One in Christ* 30 (1994): 344–54.

Rolnick, Philip. *The Long Battle for the Human Soul*. Vol. 1 of *A Post-Christendom Faith*. Baylor University Press, 2021.

Root, Michael. "Normal Ecumenism: Ecumenism for the Long Haul." *Pro Ecclesia* 28 (2019): 60–77.

Rosmini, Antonio. *Of the Five Wounds of the Holy Church*. Edited by H. P. Liddon. Rivingtons, 1883.

Ross, Susan A. "The Bride of Christ and the Body Politic: Body and Gender in Pre–Vatican II Marriage Theology." *Journal of Religion* 71 (1991): 345–61.

Rousseau, Jean-Jacques. *Emile, or On Education*. Translated by Allan Bloom. New York: Basic Books, 1979.

Rousselin, Emmanuel. *Nouvel Adam et Serviteur souffrant: La substitution du Christ au pécheur à la lumière de saint Thomas d'Aquin*. Cerf, 2022.

Routhier, Gilles. *Le défi de la communion*. Médiaspaul, 1994.

———. "Marcher ensemble et vivre la synodalité." In *Précis de Théologie Pratique*, edited by Gilles Routhier and M. Viau, 637–49. Lumen Vitae, 2004.

Rowland, Tracey. "Between the Theory and the Praxis of the Synodal Process." *The Thomist* 87 (2023): 233–54.

———. *Beyond Kant and Nietzsche: The Munich Defense of Christian Humanism*. Bloomsbury, 2021.

———. "Joseph Ratzinger on Democracy within the Church." *Communio* 50 (2023): 635–56.

Rowland, Tracey. *Unconformed to the Age: Essays in Catholic Ecclesiology*. Emmaus Academic, 2024.

Ruddy, Christopher. "'For the Many': The Vicarious-Representative Heart of Joseph Ratzinger's Theology." *Theological Studies* 75 (2014): 564–84.

———. "'Smaller but Purer?': Joseph Ratzinger on the 'Little Flock' and Vicarious Representation." *Nova et Vetera* 13 (2015): 713–41.

———. "Synodality and the Second Vatican Council." *The Thomist* 87 (2023): 211–32.

Rush, Ormond. *The Eyes of Faith: The Sense of the Faithful and the Church's Reception of Tradition*. The Catholic University of America Press, 2009.

Russell, Heidi. *The Source of All Love: Catholicity and the Trinity*. Orbis, 2017.

Sabra, George. *Thomas Aquinas' Vision of the Church: Fundamentals of an Ecumenical Ecclesiology*. Matthias Grünewald, 1987.

Sander, Hans-Joachim. "Eine Topologie Gottes in den Zeichen der Zeit." In *Zweites Vatikanisches Konzil: Programmatik—Rezeption—Vision*, edited by Christopher Böttigheimer, 157–79. Herder, 2014.

Sandnes, Karl Olav. *A New Family: Conversion and Ecclesiology in the Early Church with Cross-Cultural Comparisons*. Lang, 1994.

Sarto, Pablo Blanco. *Benedict XVI y el Concilio Vaticano II: De la historia a la hermenéutica*. EUNSA, 2022.

Scannone, Juan Carlos, SJ. *Theology of the People: The Pastoral and Theological Roots of Pope Francis*. Translated by Kris Fankhouser and Carmen Fernandez-Aguinaco. Paulist, 2021.

Schall, James V., SJ. *Liberation Theology in Latin America: With Selected Essays and Documents*. Ignatius, 1982.

———. *On Islam: A Chronological Record, 2002–2018*. Ignatius, 2018.

Schall, James V., SJ. *The Regensburg Lecture.* St. Augustine's Press, 2007.

Scheeben, Matthias Joseph. *The Mysteries of Christianity.* Translated by Cyril Vollert, SJ. 2nd ed. Emmaus Academic, 2023.

Schelkle, Karl Hermann. "Bruder." In *Reallexikon für Antike und Christentum*, vol. 3, edited by T. Klauser, 631–40. Hiersemann, 1954.

Schenk, Richard, OP. "Places and Times: Searching for a Theological *Topica*." *Nova et Vetera* 19 (2021): 163–89.

Schillebeeckx, Edward, OP. *Church: The Human Story of God.* Translated by John Bowden. Crossroad, 1990.

———. *God the Future of Man.* Translated by N. D. Smith. Sheed and Ward, 1968.

Schindler, David L. "Catholic Theology, Gender, and the Future of Western Civilization." *Communio* 20 (1993): 200–39.

Schmaus, Michael. *Katholische Dogmatik.* Vol. 3. Max Hueber, 1958.

Schmemann, Alexander. *For the Life of the World: Sacraments and Orthodoxy.* 3rd ed. St. Vladimir's Seminary Press, 1973.

Schnackenburg, Rudolf. *The Church in the New Testament.* Translated by W. J. O'Hara. Seabury, 1965.

———. *The Epistle to the Ephesians: A Commentary.* Translated by Helen Heron. T&T Clark, 1991.

———. *The Gospel of Matthew.* Translated by Robert R. Barr. Eerdmans, 2002.

Schnackenburg, Rudolph, and Jacques Dupont, OSB. "The Church as the People of God." Translated by Herbert A. Musurillo, SJ. In *The Church and Mankind*, vol. 1 of *Concilium: Theology in the Age of Renewal*, 117–29. Paulist, 1965.

Schockenhoff, Eberhard. "Der Glaubenssinn des Volkes Gottes als ethisches Erkenntniskriterium? Zur Nicht-Rezeption der kirchlichen Sexualmoral durch die Gläubigen." In *Der Spürsinn des Gottesvolkes: Eine Diskussion mit der Internationalen Theologischen Kommission*, edited by Thomas Söding, 305–30. Herder, 2016.

Schreiter, Robert J. *The New Catholicity: Theology between the Global and the Local*. Orbis, 1997.

Schwartz, Regina. *The Curse of Cain: The Violent Legacy of Monotheism*. University of Chicago Press, 1997.

Scott, James M. *Adoption as Sons of God: An Investigation into the Background of HUIOTHESIA*. Mohr, 1992.

Second Vatican Council. *Lumen Gentium*. In *Vatican Council II*, vol. 1, *The Conciliar and Postconciliar Documents*, rev. ed., edited by Austin Flannery, OP, 350–426. Costello, 1996.

———. *Unitatis Redintegratio*. In *Vatican Council II*, vol. 1, *The Conciliar and Post Conciliar Documents*, edited by Austin Flannery, 458–59. Costello, 1996.

Seewald, Peter. *Benedict XVI: A Life*. Vol. 1, *Youth in Nazi Germany to the Second Vatican Council, 1927–1965*. Translated by Dinah Livingstone. Bloomsbury, 2020.

Segundo, Juan Luis. *The Community Called Church*. Orbis Books, 1973.

———. *The Sacraments Today*. Orbis Books, 1974.

Semmelroth, Otto. *Mary, Archetype of the Church*. Translated by Jaroslav Pelikan. Sheed & Ward, 1963.

Shaw, Gordon. *The Cost of Authority: Manipulation and Freedom in the New Testament*. Fortress, 1982.

Sheen, Fulton J. *The Mystical Body of Christ*. Word on Fire, 2023.

Shortall, Sarah. *Soldiers of God in a Secular World: Catholic Theology and Twentieth-Century French Politics*. Harvard University Press, 2021.

Sirilla, Michael G. *The Ideal Bishop: Aquinas's Commentaries on the Pastoral Epistles*. The Catholic University of America Press, 2017.

Sobrino, Jon, SJ. *The True Church and the Poor*. Orbis Books, 1974.

Söhngen, Gottlieb. "Vom Wesen des Christentums." In *Die Einheit in der Theologie*, 288–304. Zink, 1952.

Spadaro, Antonio, SJ, and Diego Fares, eds. *For a Missionary Reform of the Church: The Civiltà Cattolica Seminar*. Translated by Demetrio S. Yocum. Paulist, 2017.

Spadaro, Antonio, SJ, and Marcelo Figueroa. "Evangelical Fundamentalism and Catholic Integralism: A Surprising Ecumenism." *La Civiltà Cattolica* 4010 (July 13, 2017).

Spence, Hartzell. *The Clergy and What They Do*. Franklin Watts, 1961.

Stählin, Wilhelm. *Die Katholizität der Kirche*: Evangelisches Verlagswerk, 1957.

Stark, Thomas Heinrich. "The Historicity of Truth: On the Premises and Foundations of Walter Kasper's Theology." In *The Faith Once and for All Delivered: Doctrinal Authority in Catholic Theology*, edited by Kevin L. Flannery, SJ, 69–100. Emmaus Academic, 2023.

Steven, Luke. *Imitation, Knowledge, and the Task of Christology in Maximus the Confessor*. Cascade, 2020.

Stevenson-Moessner, Jeanne. *The Spirit of Adoption: At Home in God's Family*. Westminster John Knox, 2003.

Stewart, Alistair C. *The Original Bishops: Office and Order in the First Christian Communities*. Baker Academic, 2014.

Suenens, Léon-Joseph. *Coresponsibility in the Church*. Translated by Francis Martin. Herder and Herder, 1968.

Sullivan, Ezra, OP. *Alter Christus: Priestly Holiness on Earth and in Eternity*. Sophia Institute Press, 2022.

Sullivan, John. "Reflections on Engaging with Synodality." In *Synodality and the Recovery of Vatican II: A New Way for Catholics*, edited by Stephen J. McKinney, Thomas O'Loughlin, and Beáta Tóth, 85–96. Messenger Publications, 2024.

"Synodale Kirche." *Internationale Katholische Zeitschrift Communio* 51 (2022).

Tanner, Mary. "The Anglican Position on Apostolic Continuity and Apostolic Succession in the Porvoo Statement." *Louvain Studies* 21 (1996): 114–25.

Tanquerey, Adolphe, SS. *The Spiritual Life: A Treatise on Ascetical and Mystical Theology*. Translated by Herman Branderis, SS. Desclée, 1930.

Theobald, Christoph, SJ. "L'exhortation apostolique *Evangelii Gaudium*: Esquisse d'une interpretation originale du Concile Vatican II." *Revue théologique de Louvain* 46 (2015): 321–40.

———. "The Principle of Pastorality at Vatican II." In *The Legacy of Vatican II*, edited by Massimo Faggioli and Andrea Vicini, SJ, 26–37. Paulist, 2015.

———. "The Theological Options of Vatican II: Seeking an 'Internal' Principle of Interpretation" Translated by Paul Burns. In *Vatican II: A Forgotten Future*, edited by Alberto Melloni and Christoph Theobald, *Concilium* 2005/4, 87–107. SCM, 2005.

Thomas Aquinas. *Commentary on Letter of Saint Paul to the Romans*. Edited by J. Mortensen and E. Alarcón. Translated by F. R. Larcher, OP. The Aquinas Institute for the Study of Sacred Doctrine, 2012.

———. *Commentary on the Letters of Saint Paul to the Corinthians*. Edited by J. Mortensen and E. Alarcón. Translated by F. R. Larcher, OP, B. Mortensen, and D. Keating. The Aquinas Institute for the Study of Sacred Doctrine, 2012.

Thomas Aquinas. *Commentary on the Letters of Saint Paul to the Galatians and Ephesians*. Edited by J. Mortensen and E. Alarcón. Translated by F. R. Larcher, OP, and M. L. Lamb. The Aquinas Institute for the Study of Sacred Doctrine, 2012.

———. *The Sermon-Conferences of St. Thomas Aquinas on the Apostles' Creed*. Edited and translated by Nicholas Ayo, CSC. Notre Dame: University of Notre Dame Press, 1988.

Thompson, Daniel Speed. *The Language of Dissent: Edward Schillebeeckx on the Crisis of Authority in the Catholic Church*. University of Notre Dame Press, 2003.

Thurian, Max. *Mary: Mother of the Lord, Figure of the Church*. Translated by Neville B. Cryer. Mowbray, 1985.

Tillard, Jean-Marie, OP. *The Bishop of Rome*. Michael Glazier, 1983.

———. *L'Église locale: Ecclésiologie de communion et catholicité*. Cerf, 1995.

———. "Theological Pluralism and the Mystery of the Church." In *Different Theologies, Common Responsibility: Babel or Pentecost?*, edited by Claude Geffré, Gustavo Gutiérrez, and Virgil Elizondo, English edition edited by Marcus Lefébure, *Concilium* 171, 62–73. T&T Clark, 1984.

Tillette, Xavier, SJ. "Henri de Lubac: The Legacy of a Theologian." *Communio* 19 (1992): 332–41.

Tilley, Terrence. *Inventing Catholic Tradition*. Orbis, 2000.

Tjørhom, Ola. "Apostolic Continuity and Apostolic Succession in the Porvoo Common Statement: A Challenge to the Nordic Lutheran Churches?" *Louvain Studies* 21 (1996): 126–37.

Torrell, Jean-Pierre, OP. *Jésus le Christ chez saint Thomas d'Aquin*. Cerf, 2008.

———. *A Priestly People: Baptismal Priesthood and Priestly Ministry*. Translated by Peter Heinegg. Paulist, 2013.

Torrell, Jean-Pierre, OP. *Saint Thomas Aquinas*. Vol. 2, *Spiritual Master*. Translated by Robert Royal. The Catholic University of America Press, 2003.

Tracy, David, with Hans Küng and Johann B. Metz, eds. *Toward Vatican III: The Work That Needs to Be Done*. Seabury, 1978.

Tromp, Sebastian, SJ. *De Spiritu Sancto anima Corporis mystici*. 2 vols. 2nd ed. Pontificia Universitas Gregoriana, 1948 and 1952.

Tück, Jan-Heiner. *A Gift of Presence: The Theology and Poetry of the Eucharist in Thomas Aquinas*. Translated by Scott Hefelfinger. The Catholic University of America Press, 2018.

Twomey, Vincent, SVD. *Apostolikos Thronos: Rival Accounts of Roman Primacy in Eusebius and Athanasius*. Emmaus Academic, 2023.

Tyrrell, George. *Medievalism: A Reply to Cardinal Mercier*. Longmans, Green, 1908.

———. *Through Scylla and Charybdis: Or, the Old Theology and the New*. Longmans, Green, 1907.

Ukelina, Bekeh Utietiang. "New Evangelization in Africa: Learning from the Culture of Love in the Early Church." In *The Church as Salt and Light: Path to an African Ecclesiology of Abundant Life*, edited by Stan Chu Ilo, Joseph Ogbonnaya, and Alex Ojacor, 130–48. Pickwick, 2011.

Ukwuije, Bede, CSSp. "Political Theology and Liberation Theology in the Works of Elochukwu Uzukwu." In *Under the Palaver Tree: Doing African Ecclesiology in the Spirit of Vatican II—the Contributions of Elochukwu E. Uzukwu*, edited by Stan Chu Ilo and Caroline N. Mbonu, 179–96. Pickwick, 2023.

Ureta, José Antonio, and Julio Loredo de Izcue. *The Synodal Process Is a Pandora's Box: 100 Questions and Answers*. Translated by José A. Schelini. The Foundation for a Christian Civilization, 2023.

Urfels, Florent. *La Pâque du Messie: Introduction à une théologie eucharistique du judaïsme*. Parole et Silence, 2013.

Uzukwu, Elochukwu E. *A Listening Church: Autonomy and Communion in African Churches*. Orbis Books, 1996.

Vall, Gregory. *Learning Christ: Ignatius of Antioch and the Mystery of Redemption*. The Catholic University of America Press, 2013.

Vanhoozer, Kevin J. *Hearers and Doers: A Pastor's Guide to Making Disciples Through Scripture and Doctrine*. Lexham, 2019.

———. "A Mere Protestant Response." In Matthew Levering, *Was the Reformation a Mistake? Why Catholic Doctrine Is Not Unbiblical*. Zondervan, 2017.

Vanhoozer, Kevin J., and Daniel J. Treier. *Theology and the Mirror of Scripture: A Mere Evangelical Account*. IVP Academic, 2015.

Viana, Antonio. *Organización del Gobierno en la Iglesia: Según el Derecho Canónico Latino*. 3rd ed. EUNSA, 2010.

Vinzent, Markus. *Resetting the Origins of Christianity: A New Theory of Sources and Beginnings*. Cambridge University Press, 2023.

Vitali, Dario. *"Un Popolo in cammino verso Dio": La sinodalità in* Evangelii gaudium. San Paolo, 2018.

———. *Verso la sinodalità*. Qiqajon, 2014.

Voderholzer, Rudolf. *Meet Henri de Lubac*. Translated by Michael J. Miller. Ignatius, 2008.

Voges, Stefan. *Konzil, Dialog und Demokratie: Der Weg zur Würzburger Synode 1965-1971*. Ferdinand Schöningh, 2015.

Von Rad, Gerhard. *Das Gottesvolk im Deuteronomium*. Kohlhammer, 1929.

Von Soden, Hermann. "Adelphos." In *Theologisches Wörterbuch zum neuen Testament*, vol. 1, edited by Gerhard Kittel, 144–46. Kohlhammer, 1964.

Vonier, Anscar, OSB. *A Key to the Doctrine of the Eucharist*. Wipf & Stock, 2002.

———. *The People of God*. Burns, Oates & Washbourne, 1937.

———. *The Spirit and the Bride*. Assumption, 2013.

Waldstein, Edmund, O.Cist. "Bernhard Häring's Moral Theology." In *The Faith Once for All Delivered: Doctrinal Authority in Catholic Theology*, edited by Kevin L. Flannery, SJ, 101–24. Emmaus Academic, 2023.

Walsh, Christopher. "De Lubac's Critique of the Postconciliar Church." *Communio* 19 (1992): 404–32.

———. "Henri de Lubac in Connecticut: Unpublished Conferences on Renewal in the Postconciliar Period." *Communio* 23 (1996): 786–805.

Watson, Natalie K. *Introducing Feminist Ecclesiology*. Sheffield Academic, 1996.

Wells, Jo Bailey. *God's Holy People: A Theme in Biblical Theology*. Sheffield Academic, 2000.

Wheeler-Reed, David. *Regulating Sex in the Roman Empire: Ideology, the Bible, and the Early Christians*. Yale University Press, 2017.

White, Thomas Joseph, OP. *The Incarnate Lord: A Study in Thomistic Christology*. The Catholic University of America Press, 2015.

———. "The Precarity of Wisdom: Modern Dominican Theology, Perspectivalism, and the Tasks of Reconstruction." In *Ressourcement Thomism: Sacred Doctrine, the Sacraments, and the Moral Life*, edited by Reinhard Hütter and Matthew Levering, 92–123. The Catholic University of America Press, 2010.

Williams, Rowan. *Passions of the Soul*. Bloomsbury, 2024.

Winner, Lauren F. *The Dangers of Christian Practice: On Wayward Gifts, Characteristic Damage, and Sin*. Yale University Press, 2018.

Witherington, Ben, III. *Grace in Galatia: A Commentary on Paul's Letter to the Galatians*. Eerdmans, 1998.

Wood, Jacob. *To Stir a Restless Heart: Thomas Aquinas and Henri de Lubac on Nature, Grace, and the Desire for God*. The Catholic University of America Press, 2019.

Wright, N. T. *Paul and the Faithfulness of God*. Book I, Parts I and II. Fortress, 2013.

XVI Ordinary General Assembly of the Synod of Bishops. "For a Synodal Church: Communion, Participation, Mission." https://www.synod.va/content/dam/synod/news/2024-10-26_final-document/ENG---Documento-finale.pdf, accessed on January 22, 2025.

Ye'or, Bat. *Islam and Dhimmitude: Where Civilizations Collide*. Translated by Miriam Kochan and David Littman. Fairleigh Dickinson University Press, 2002.

Young, Frances M. *Brokenness and Blessing: Towards a Biblical Spirituality*. Baker Academic, 2007.

Young, Robin Darling. "An Imagined Unity: Henri de Lubac and the Ironies of Ressourcement." *Commonweal* 15 (2012): 13–18.

———. "A Soldier of the Great War: Henri de Lubac and the Patristic Sources for a Premodern Theology." In *After Vatican II: Trajectories and Hermeneutics*, edited by James L. Heft with John O'Malley, SJ, 134–63. Eerdmans, 2012.

Zizioulas, John D. *Being as Communion: Studies in Personhood and the Church*. St. Vladimir's Seminary Press, 1985.

———. *Eucharist, Bishop, Church: The Unity of the Church in the Divine Eucharist and the Bishop during the First Three Centuries*. Translated by Elizabeth Theokritoff. Holy Cross Orthodox Press, 2001.

———. *The Eucharistic Communion and the World*. Edited by Luke Ben Tallon. T&T Clark International, 2011.

Index